PELICAN BOOKS

FRANCE IN THE 1980s

John Ardagh was born in Malawi, East Africa, in 1928, the son of a colonial civil servant. He was educated at Sherborne School and Worcester College, Oxford, where he took an honours degree in classics and philosophy. He joined *The Times* in 1953, and from 1955 to 1959 was a staff correspondent in Paris and Algeria. It was during this time that he began what has since proved to be a long love–hate relationship with the French – with rather more love than hate. Back in England, he worked for a while in television news, then was for five years a staff writer on the *Observer*, and from 1966 to 1968 was managing editor of *The Good Food Guide*. He had long nursed the idea of writing a book about changes in France that could not easily be summed up in newspaper articles, and this led in 1968 to the publication of his first major study of modern France, *The New French Revolution*, later reprinted and revised as *The New France* in successive Pelican Books editions, 1970–77. His next work was *A Tale of Five Cities: life in provincial Europe today* (1979). Besides writing books, he is a freelance journalist and broadcaster, working frequently for the BBC and French radio, and writing intermittently for such papers as *The Times, New Society, Washington Post* and *Le Point*. He is a passionate believer in the battered old ideal of European unity. His other special interests include the cinema and gastronomy, and he is devoted to almost every aspect of French life. He lives in Kensington, is married to the publisher Jenny Towndrow, and has one grown-up son and two omnipresent Burmese cats.

JOHN ARDAGH

FRANCE IN THE 1980s

PENGUIN BOOKS
IN ASSOCIATION WITH SECKER & WARBURG

Penguin Books Ltd, Harmondsworth, Middlesex, England
Penguin Books, 625 Madison Avenue, New York 10022, U.S.A.
Penguin Books Australia Ltd, Ringwood, Victoria, Australia
Penguin Books Canada Ltd, 2801 John Street, Markham, Ontario, Canada L3R 1B4
Penguin Books (N.Z.) Ltd, 182–190 Wairau Road, Auckland 10, New Zealand

—

First published in Great Britain simultaneously by
Penguin Books and Secker & Warburg 1982
Reprinted 1982

First published in the United States of America by Penguin Books 1983

—

—

Made and printed in Great Britain by
Richard Clay (The Chaucer Press) Ltd,
Bungay, Suffolk
Filmset in Palatino

To my wife
JENNY

and to my son
NICHOLAS

CONTENTS

MAP   10

PREFACE   11

1 INTRODUCTION   13

2 THE ECONOMY, MODERNIZED BUT MENACED   28

Post-war renewal: from Monnet's Plan to Barre's medicines   30
Industry's ambitious leap forward   42
Cars, aircraft, computers: the triumphs and troubles of
    advanced technology   62
Nuclear expansion: Giscard plans boldly, then Mitterrand
    modifies   76
Elitist technocracy: a waning asset?   82
A new look to labour relations   93
The Socialists in power: reflation and nationalization   115

3 REFORM AND RENEWAL IN THE REGIONS   123

The crusade for regional development   124
Brittany's revival: mirage or reality?   131
The New Cathars of Lower Languedoc   143
Grenoble: the legend and its wounds; Toulouse: a symbolic
    white-and-pink ice-cream; Lyon: more Crédit wanted for the
    Lyonnais   153
Factories, finance, transport, telephones – a variable record of
    regional progress   173
Devolution at last: exit the prefect; more powers for mayors and
    regions   187

4 BACK TO NATURE:
   THE FARMING REVOLUTION COMES FULL CIRCLE   206

The Young Farmers' revolt: peasants become businessmen   207
Productivity goes crazy: butter mountains and Bulgarian *foie
    gras*   221
Back to Lower Languedoc: the grapes of wrath   228
Does the nation owe its farmers a living?   233

New flowers in the rural desert: the crusade to save the Lozère   237
The 'dung drop-outs' in search of utopia   248

5 IN THE CITIES: THE QUEST FOR 'QUALITY OF LIFE'   258

Paris, beloved monster, at grips with traffic-jams and
    skyscrapers   259
Solving the housing shortage – at a fancy price   289
Urban environment: the yellow bicycles of La Rochelle   295
Community versus privacy: from new-town 'blues' to
    new-town 'Reds'   300
Culture in the provinces: from Malraux's 'Maisons' to the new
    operatic snobberies   323
Ecology in fashion: Giscard did his bit, then was struck by
    anti-nuclear blast   336

6 DAILY AND PRIVATE LIFE:
   TOWARDS A MORE OPEN SOCIETY?   347

Feminism wins a battle – but not at the price of femininity   347
Abortion and birth-control reform: better late than never   360
Families, friendship, formality: the myth of French inhospitality 368
Sharing the post-war affluence: some citizens have more
    'égalité' than others   376
Leisure and consumer modes: 'le weekend' in a rural dream-nest   386
In the shadow of the hypermarkets: what future for the little
    shops?   396
The vogue for 'la nouvelle cuisine': gastronomic decadence or
    renewal?   409
The holiday mania: happiness is a straw-hut 'village' with 'le
    Club' in Greece   423
The Welfare State: a costly new craze for health   443
Catholics: the Church declines, but religion revives   452
Foreigners: Germans are now welcome, Algerians less so   462

7 A MUDDLED NEW DEAL FOR YOUTH   472

Reform in the classroom: does more equality spell decline?   472
Universities: the sour fruits of autonomy   493
Grandes Ecoles: bastions of privilege   510
La Jeunesse: reticence, not rebellion   514

8 ARTS AND INTELLECTUALS:
   A CREATIVE DECLINE?   527

The Left Bank philosophers: trendiness and tyranny   528
Have Barthes and Robbe-Grillet killed the French novel?   540
Theatre: the director-as-superstar eliminates the playwright   548

Cinema: from the trumpets of the *nouvelle vague* to the
    flute-notes of a new realism   556
Television: an end at last to the blight of State monopoly?   578
The Press, free but fragile   596
Music: a joyous renaissance   603

9 CONCLUSION   617

The new France under Socialism   617
Towards a more trustful society?   638

ACKNOWLEDGEMENTS   656

BIBLIOGRAPHY   659

INDEX   663

PREFACE

I researched and wrote the first draft of this book during the last two years of President Giscard d'Estaing's rule, in 1979–81. Then I was overtaken by events. And in the latter part of 1981 I revised the book, to take account of the new and different France that is emerging under President François Mitterrand and his Socialist Government. So the book gives, I hope, a fairly clear picture of the Socialists' first months in power, of their plans for reform, and of the prospects that may lie ahead for this new Socialist-led France. But the reader must realize that the body of the book was written before the elections that brought the Left to power. And I trust that he or she will therefore forgive the various inconsistencies.

Not that this is primarily a book about politics. It is not about Mitterrand, nor Giscard, nor de Gaulle. It is a study of French society in transition since the war. I have dealt briefly with politics – in the first and last chapters – only so as to supply the reader with the necessary background for following the book's main themes, which are economic, social and cultural. This is not because I think politics unimportant, but because this ground has been fully covered by other Anglo-American observers of France, more expert in politics than I am. I have drawn on some material from my previous book (*The New French Revolution*; in paperback, *The New France*), but essentially this is a fresh look at the France of the 1980s.

I first lived in Paris from 1955 to 1959 as a correspondent of *The Times*, and I have returned to France regularly ever since, often staying there for several months each year. During this past quarter-century I have seen the style and mood of the nation change radically, and more than once. Like other francophiles, I have developed a sharp love–hate relationship with this stimulating and exasperating race: but love has triumphed over hate, and I feel as emotionally committed to France as to my own country, and as much at home with French as with British people. I say this in order to explain the spirit in which this book has been written. I have been severely critical of many things in France, but much in the way that a progress-minded Frenchman might himself be critical. The book tries to look at France from within, more from a French than an English point of view; and it takes for granted all that is great and unique and lovable about French civilization. As the French say, *qui aime bien, châtie bien*.

Paris is not France, and my own speciality has always been to explore the French provinces. I flatter myself that I now know almost every corner of France, and I have hundreds of French friends all across the country. In order to research this book, and its predecessor, I travelled throughout the regions, talking to literally thousands of people: technocrats and schoolgirls, peasants and factory workers, grocers and theatre-directors. Everywhere, even in Paris, I met with courtesy, readiness to help, and the highest degree of Gallic communicativeness: France may be a complex country, hard to understand and sometimes trying to live in, but she is ideal terrain for the note-taker. And if you go out to meet the French on their own terms, rather than patronizing them in English, they can be as charming as any people on earth. What is more, I wish to kill the myth held by foreigners that the French are inhospitable. I myself have been invited to lunch or dinner in several hundred different French homes: I say this not to boast, but to set the record straight.

My list of acknowledgements is on page 656.

Chapter 1

INTRODUCTION

The French have already been through one revolution, of a sort, since the war. Now, with the coming to power of the Left, they are possibly embarked on a second, of an entirely different nature. A new era has begun.

The first revolution was economic and psychological, and it took place roughly between the early 1950s and the mid-1970s. During that time, France went through a spectacular renewal. A stagnant economy turned into one of the world's most dynamic and successful, as material modernization moved along at a hectic pace and an agriculture-based society became mainly an urban and industrial one. Prosperity soared, bringing with it changes in life-styles, and throwing up some strange conflicts between rooted French habits and new modes. The French themselves were changing, or so it seemed. After the decades of sloth, many of them grew fired with a new energy, a zealous new faith in the cure-all of economic growth and technical progress. Long accused of living with their eyes fixed on the past, they now suddenly opened them to the fact of living in the modern world – and it both thrilled and scared them.

Then in the 1970s the mood began to change again. The novelty of modernism wore off, as the French adjusted to it. The post-1973 energy crisis brought the shocked realization that steady expansion was not after all such a trusty creed. Above all, the French grew aware that material progress had in itself by no means cured all the basic ills of their rigid society, still beset with barriers and inequalities, still saddled with a number of outdated structures of which the most blatant was the over-centralized and too pervasive machine of the State. Insecure in the new 1970s world of self-doubt, the French also began turning back to their roots and their traditions. Nostalgia was in vogue, so was ecology. And it was in this mood that in May and June 1981 they elected a Socialist President and then voted his party into an absolute majority in the National Assembly, after twenty-three years of Right-of-Centre rule.

Today the Socialists are striving, according to their own lights, to back up the earlier economic revolution with the overdue reform and modernization of society and of the nation's structures. This sounds fine, in many ways: but they intend to go a good deal farther than a high percentage of Frenchmen would wish. Their aim is to make a 'sharp break with capitalism' and to create an irreversible shift in the balance of society and the economy: as Mitterrand has said, 'A great historic undertaking lies before us.' So this change of government in France is much more radical than, say, what the Americans, British or West Germans have been used to since the war, with their more frequent alternations of power. Yet it remains to be seen how far the changes will really go in practice. French history has often shown – witness the Revolution and its aftermath – that this conservative and traditionalist nation has ways of absorbing change and bending it to its will, so that the final *status quo* is not always so different from the previous one.

The roots of the earlier post-war renewal were psychological, and to trace them we must look back to the war itself and even earlier: to the shock of the 1940 defeat and the Occupation, and to the upturn in the birth-rate which began modestly just before the war. France in the 1930s was an extreme example of the general Western malaise of the time: industrial production was declining, and the mood of the nation was sullen, protectionist and defeatist, with many of the classic symptoms of decadence. The population too was gently falling. Nowadays, when the Third World's population explosion is a major global problem, it may seem odd to regard a low birth-rate as a national calamity. But although for a poor country a high birth-rate is a menace, for a developed nation like France the opposite is true, as most experts agree; and France is still under-populated in relation to her neighbours and to her own geography. As early as 1800 she began to fall behind her European rivals in her rate of growth, due to social and political factors such as the Napoleonic laws of equal inheritance. In 1800 France was the most populous country in Western Europe, with 28.3 million against Britain's 16 million and 22 million in what is now Germany; by 1910 France had risen to only 41.5 million, overtaken both by Britain (45.4 million) and Germany (63 million). Then came the ravages of the Great War, when France suffered worse than Germany or Britain. After 1918 the decline continued: by 1935 the birth-rate had fallen to 87 per cent, e.g. seven births to eight deaths. In 1940 Germany was able to put nearly twice as many men of military age into the field as France – and the results were all too evident.

In the 1930s French politicians grew seriously worried at the decline. In 1932 a first attempt was made to remedy it, with the institution of family allowances, and by the outbreak of war these were just beginning to show results: from 1935 to 1939 the birth-rate crept up from 87 to 93 per cent, though it was still below par. Then the Pétain Government, what-ever its other faults, at least promoted a strong pro-family policy, with continued allowances, so that denatality under the Occupation was not as great as might have been expected. After the Liberation the child allowances were extended and are now among the highest in Europe, often accounting for over 30 per cent of a worker's income. They were certainly a major cause of the demographic boom of the post-war years, but not the only one. It must be attributed also to more spontaneous psychological factors, to what the demographer Alfred Sauvy has called 'a collective conscience', a survival instinct forced into action by the shock of wartime defeat. According to Sauvy and others, this rising birth-rate then in turn improved the nation's morale, thus contributing to the new dynamism of the post-war era. In 1945–6 the rate spurted suddenly from 93 to 126 per cent and then stayed at more or less that level until the 1950s: in most European countries it fell back in the 1950s after an early post-war spurt, but in France it held steady for longer. The annual net increase of births over deaths stood at between 250,000 and 350,000 right up until 1974, and thanks to this and to immigration (including 800,000 settlers from Algeria in 1962–3), the population increased from 41 million in 1946 to 53 million in 1977. This together with the rural exodus provided a growing pool of labour which contributed crucially to industry's ability to expand so fast in the years up to 1973. '*Le bébé-boom*' also brought with it a new cult of youth, and a new faith in youth as a symbol of national rejuvenation, in a land hitherto addicted to patriarchal values and the prerogatives of age. It is true that more recently the birth-rate has fallen again, quite sharply, and this has caused some alarm. But the fall has been less dramatic than in many other countries, such as West Germany: France still has one of the highest levels of natality in Europe, with births exceeding deaths by an average 200,000 a year.

The second fundamental factor behind the French post-war re-covery was the effect of the defeat of 1940 and the Occupation. These humiliations, coming after the decadence of the 1930s, provided the French with a much-needed traumatic shock: it opened their eyes to the root causes of their decline, and stimulated a few of the more forceful ones to prepare action to stop it happening again. The British were spared this kind of salutary shock: maybe that is one reason why we failed to develop the same post-war energy, and zest for hard work, as the French, Germans and others.

Even the Vichy regime, though odious in many respects, contained one or two incidental elements which helped to pave the way for later recovery. I have mentioned the family allowances: in agriculture, too, and in regional development, Vichy's corporatist policies may have helped to generate a new sense of local self-dependence. But much more important than Vichy itself was the fact that the war gave the French a breathing-space in which to rethink the future. Under the enforced paralysis and inactivity of the Occupation, they had time to ponder, plan and regroup, while the British were far too busy fighting. Many of France's post-war achievements and reforms can be traced back in inspiration to those years. On the land, young peasants of the Christian farming movement began to form little groups that later took the offensive to modernize agriculture; in the Church, priests and laymen were preparing the way for a new social activism that was to transform the spirit of Catholicism in France. Even Sartrian existentialism had its roots in the Occupation. Elsewhere, little groups of *Résistants* and Free French were plotting how to renovate the nation's economy and structures: the most important of these groups was formed around Jean Monnet in Washington, and out of it grew the 'Plan' which was to play such a vital role in the post-war revival.

After 1945, industry and the civil service steadily began to discover a belief in expansion and progress that was absent before the war. The innovating technocrat came to the fore, in place of the conserving bureaucrat. At first this new ethos was confined to a few pioneers in key posts, like Monnet and his team, and to local élites that sprang up sporadically around the country, like the Young Farmers. The rest of the nation stayed with its eyes on the past, protecting its positions *acquises*. Gradually however, during the 1950s and 1960s, the new spirit spread more widely to infect public opinion as a whole. And this was the big difference from pre-war France. Previously, the French had lived by a set of values based on stability, the golden ideal: now they moved to new values of growth and reform. Ordinary people came to believe in progress and accept the need for change – even if, when change actually presented itself, many of them might still fight hard to defend their vested privileges!

It is often assumed abroad that the French recovery was due essentially to de Gaulle and his decade of political stability, 1958–69. But I doubt if this is really so. Though his regime achieved a good deal, it also hindered much or simply continued a process already in motion. In nearly every sector the transformations were under way by the time he returned to power in 1958, though overshadowed by the crises of colonial wars and by weak, shifting governments. The Plan had laid the first foundations of industrial recovery, and then a strong and stable civil service helped to provide continuity of politics despite fluctuating Ministries. And it was the Fourth Republic, not the Fifth, that prepared French opinion for the EEC and signed the Treaty of Rome, which has done so much to spur French industry forward and open French eyes to a wider international outlook. This is not to say that de Gaulle's own record was negative. In the first years after his return, he was able to restore French self-confidence and foreign confidence in France. And in many instances, as we shall see, his strong Government did succeed in applying vital and difficult reforms, where its weak predecessors had failed. But there was much else that it did not do, or did badly. And as many of the initial post-war changes took some years to reach fruition, the Gaullists often managed to steal the credit for them, unfairly.

The 1960s under de Gaulle were modernization's heyday, when France visibly put on a new coat of paint. For better or worse, picturesque squalor gave way to a new glitter, sometimes garish, sometimes elegantly French. Quiet old streets filled up with Renaults and Citroëns; in the Seine valley with its ruined abbeys and castles, new factories emerged; rows of much-needed apartment blocks appeared on the outskirts of every town. In Paris, the grey house façades along the boulevards were scoured clean, while skyscrapers began to alter the city's familiar skyline, and odd novelties such as '*le drugstore*' made their début. All this led some to fear that France was losing her soul, selling out to an ill-digested Americanization. But most people welcomed this ritzy new world of affluence and technology. After all, the French have always been devoted materialists in their way, and after some initial reticence they threw themselves into the consumer society as eagerly as any people in Europe. It was the urge to make money and enjoy the fruits of it that lent a potent motivation to their post-war work mania: like the Germans, they rebuilt and modernized their country through a mixture of technical flair, material ambition and sheer sustained hard work at all levels, from manager to shop-floor worker and farmer.

It has been a mighty saga, this post-war modernization of a country that in some ways has been making a leap straight from the early nineteenth to the late twentieth century. The French, who do not do things by halves, have moved in one swoop from the little corner shop to the largest hypermarkets in Europe. In many firms, modern business efficiency has become a cult, as young executives adopt an American ethos and enthuse about *le marketing*. And some other changes go far deeper than this. Under the momentum of economic advance, society has shifted its equilibrium. Agriculture's share of the active population has fallen since the war from 35 to 9 per cent; farms have modernized, the old-style peasant is dying out. This mass immigration from the country to the towns, coupled with the high birth-rate, caused France in the post-war period to undergo the kind of rapid urbanization that Britain knew in the past century. Many cities have tripled in size. The provinces, derided thirty years ago as 'the French desert', have shared at least as much as Paris in the upswing of affluence and industry, so that towns such as Rennes or Tours, quiet backwaters till the 1950s, have become vibrant with new activity.

However, these and other changes have been far from smooth. They have created many tensions, as small archaic firms are pushed out of business or as people struggle to adjust to new surroundings. The French have not adapted at all easily to the new strains and demands of city life – partly this is the fault of their own mistrustful and unneighbourly temperament. But their new prosperity has also been most unevenly shared, and this has been less their own fault. De Gaulle's and later Governments did, it is true, carry through a number of reforms, to help poorer people, or to try to bring the fusty old formal structures of French public life into line with the new conditions and aspirations. But these reforms were not enough: often they were blocked by vested interests. And so the frustrations built up. These found their sharpest expression in the May '68 uprising, which was sparked off by a few Leftist students, then joined more widely by millions of French of all sorts. May '68 had complex causes, but above all it was a protest against the failure of economic change to be matched by social and structural change: it was the cry of a new-rich society discovering that expansion in itself was not enough. It was an attempt not to put the clock back, but to shift the direction of progress. The well-to-do bourgeois students were in revolt against a stifling education system that had not geared itself to the new modern world. Then hordes of others – workers, *cadres*, professional people – gave vent to their own frustrations at the hierarchy, bureaucracy and entrenched privilege that dominated public and working life. In itself, the May revolt soon fizzled out. It led to some university reforms, and to a round of wage rises: but it did not alter the political *status quo*. Yet its wider influence lingered on. In working life, in education, even in families, it dealt a permanent blow to the patterns of obedience to authoritarian rule, hitherto so marked in France. It brought a new insistence on personal freedom, and it ushered in the ideal of '*la participation*' (which the individualistic French so often preach, but rarely find it easy to apply in practice). As in other countries with their 1968 rumblings, the revolt heralded the ecology trends of the 1970s. It was also a forerunner of the final victory of the Left in 1981.

In the meantime, however, the majority of French were still afraid to risk the adventure of a Left-wing Government that might open the door to the Communists. So for some years they continued to keep the

Centre-Right in power. Yet many of them still wanted change, of a kind. Valéry Giscard d'Estaing, who became President in 1974, was a member of the technocratic Establishment, but also a man who seemed to understand and share these yearnings of the French for some new deal. He came to power with a promising blueprint for what he called an 'advanced liberal society', to meet the new needs of the age and fulfil some of the hopes of '68. True to his word, he made a good start with a few hardy social reforms such as the legalization of abortion. But then he faltered. In part he was the victim of circumstance: his reformism was overtaken by the more urgent priority of having to shore up an economy now in crisis. But, more to the point, this weak and enigmatic character seemed to lose interest in trying to change French society, or he ceased to believe that he could do so. His increasingly secretive and monarchic style of rule began to alienate even many of his own supporters.

By the end of 1980, much the same Right-of-Centre regime had been in power for twenty-two years and it was growing stale and cynical. Many Frenchmen, of all persuasions, were well aware of the harmfulness of this lack of the alternation of power that is normal and healthy in a democracy. Yet the Left, riven by its own Socialist/Communist conflicts, did not seem to offer an effective option. Its string of electoral defeats disheartene1 those millions of voters who believed that only a Leftward change of regime could provide real social progress. Yet other millions of Frenchmen feared terrible consequences if the Communists were to take a share in power. So France was polarized into two blocs, more so than in the 1960s when the umbrella of de Gaulle's prestigious paternalism had provided a degree of national consensus. People grew disillusioned with all politicians and parties: yet they knew that the road to a better future could not bypass politics. It was quite a dilemma.

This sullen public mood was exacerbated by the post-1973 economic slow-down, which has coloured daily life in France as elsewhere. Giscard's Government did react vigorously to the crisis, so that the French economy held up better than might have been expected. Yet France was vulnerable, and by early 1981 unemployment had reached 1.6 million. So the French, after their exhilarating boom years, were now caught up in the general economic and spiritual malaise of the West since the mid-1970s. More than in many countries, the crisis seems to have hit hard at the French psyche – for the very reason that expansion had hitherto been so specially potent a creed. Maybe a god has failed? The French had become so used to a steady 5 or 6 per cent annual growth that a drop to 1 or 2 per cent now seemed a calamity. You could even argue that they have been reacting like spoiled children, deprived of some luxury toy, for in fact real incomes continued to rise in 1973–9, if at a slower rate; only a minority of jobless people were suffering real hardship. So *la crise* – the word ever on all lips – has so far been less material than psychological: a fear of worse to come. In the boom years, the French had come to expect an unending vista of ever larger cars, smarter flats, more lavish holidays. Now they are forced to reckon that this kind of happiness can be fragile. The technocrats' ardent gospel of growth has begun to ring hollow in their ears.

These diverse influences – from May '68 via the political impasse to the economic threat – had by 1981 led the people of France into a strange phase, quiescent but not entirely negative. Beneath a rather grey public surface there were curious undercurrents, as people groped in very disparate ways towards new outlets for their ideals and desires. In a word, they were shunning formal public life and turning back to private satisfactions both hedonistic and spiritual, to a renewal of links with the traditional past, and to a search for new kinds of community on a very local, small-scale and practical level. Oddly, this entire trend seemed to be simultaneously a defence against the economic crisis *and* a reaction against the too-rapid material change which had preceded it. It also symptomized the general weariness with politics. Ideologies were now out of fashion, as were institutions of all sorts. Various bodies saw their following or their prestige decline, alike the Left-wing unions and the Church, the universities and the organs of State. Instead, the French were engaged in '*le repli sur soi*', a trend endlessly discussed by sociologists – that is, a withdrawal into privacy, into greater dependence on personal resources, on small circles of family or friends, or very local forms of community. To take but one example: the churches were still emptying, yet more people were turning to little informal groups of private prayer. At the same time, this nation of ex-peasants was nostalgically seeking some renewal of contact with its rural roots and with nature. It was turning its back on vast technocratic projects, the 'gigantism' in vogue in de Gaulle's and Pompidou's day, and was seeking out 'quality of life'.

It all added up to quite a striking change of mood. These new tendencies began to emerge even before the 1973 energy crisis, and they seemed to mark a desire of the French to regain their balance and rediscover their identity, after the era of hectic modernization. But it did not mean they were rejecting modernism and the consumer society – they wanted to have their cake and eat it, to find ways of reconciling their new affluence with their old traditions and enjoy the best of both. One leading social analyst, Professor René Rémond, suggested to me in 1980: 'The pendulum has been swinging back. In the 1950s the French moved from the values of stability to those of growth and change. Now they are shifting back to stability. So we see the persistence of traditional values. But I do not regard this as reactionary.'

It is entirely possible to see the victory of Mitterrand over Giscard in May 1981 as the logical outcome of this new trend and not as a swing away from it. In veering to the Left, the French were voting for change and progress, yes, but not for the kind of modernistic progress they had known in the preceding decades. In a television interview on June 30th, the astute young sociologist Bernard Cathelat said of the two main candidates: 'On the one side was a man who represented the technocrat, the manager, the serious modern thinker . . . On the other, a man who personified more the politician, the traditional father-figure . . . On one side were the themes of technological progress, economic competition, the opening out of France to the world. On the other, themes of decentralization, egalitarianism, a more human concern with quality of life – paradoxically, a model of society perhaps inspiring more security, despite the transformation that it represented.' And Cathelat went on to suggest: 'Progress is changing its moral significance. I think we have now come to the end of a thirty-year cycle when the idea of progress was identified with economic expansion, technology, internationalism . . . In these elections, it is likely that many people voted for another concept – a progress based more on a prudent return to the repository of past experience; related more to private quality of life than to distant adventures; linked to notions of ecology, mutualism, self-help. Perhaps the key lesson of this election is that our definition of "Progress" must be revised.' A paradox indeed. Cathelat may well be right that a part at least of Mitterrand's electors were conservatives by temperament, above all seeking security and tradition: yet they have voted for a programme that will involve quite a shake-up. Of course there were many other reasons too why people voted for the Socialists. Many, the habitual Left-wing electorate, were seeking more social equality. And a decisive number of middle-class Centre voters switched to Mitterrand simply because they wanted a change, after all these years. They were fed up with Giscard. So they opted for the only change that was finally available: Socialism, with all its risks.

Whatever these contradictions, the victories of Mitterrand and his Socialists straightway created a cheerfully relaxed and even euphoric mood in France in the summer of 1981, shared even by many who had not voted for the Left but felt vaguely relieved that the long political stalemate had ended. Rationally they were anxious; yet they could not help joining in the excitement of a new era. The alternation of power, routine in many countries, was a startling novelty for France: yet it passed off entirely peacefully, despite the controversial reforms ahead, and the French felt proud that their democratic institutions, when put to the test, were working so smoothly. The Socialists and the French nation now entered on a honeymoon period which Mitterrand himself called 'a state of grace': his aim, he said, was national reconciliation, with no crude acts of revenge against the outgoing regime.

François Mitterrand, aged sixty-four, now at last had the supreme power for which he had fought and waited so long – and it was a massive power, with the National Assembly, the unions and most big town councils all on his side. He wanted to press ahead fast with his reform programme, yet he also wanted to reassure. His first act was to appoint a very moderate Government, led by the Centre-Right rather than the Left of his party. As Prime Minister he chose Pierre Mauroy, mayor of Lille, a large, affable, warm-hearted man with social-democrat views and a rare talent for gently cajoling people into sensible compromises. The Foreign Minister, Claude Cheysson, the Economy Minister, Jacques Delors, and the Minister for the Plan, Michel Rocard, were also all of them well known as moderates and realists. In fact, about the only doctrinaire Left-wing Socialist in a senior Cabinet post was Jean-Pierre Chevènement, in charge of science and technology. Mitterrand also took the controversial step of inviting four Communists into his Government: but they were given relatively minor posts, and were there only on sufferance. Mitterrand brought them in as part of his strategy of winning the quiescence and support of the Communist Party (PCF) and its powerful trade union. In parliamentary terms he did not need the Communists, for his own party had an absolute majority. So this was not a coalition Government: it was a Socialist Government, with the Communists in guest roles. In the May and June elections the PCF vote, normally 20 per cent, had slumped to 15 or 16 per cent, and for many middle of the road Frenchmen this greatly diminished the scare of having a Left-wing Government. The Socialists were now fully in command. One liberal observer said: 'The Left has taken power in the best possible conditions. The change had to happen sooner or later, and it's now happened in the safest way for democracy – with a full mandate for the PS and the PCF as mere followers-on.'

The new Government's extensive programme of reforms will be looked at more closely during the course of this book. The measures fall into two broad categories. First, there are those which are specifically Socialist in character and have the purpose either of reducing social inequalities or of weakening the role of capitalism in the economy. Secondly, a number of other reforms are intended to update and liberalize the structures of French public life. These latter measures, not in themselves Left-wing, could equally have been enacted by an intelligent Right-of-Centre Government: in fact, some of them mark a bid to carry through properly certain changes (for example, in local government, labour relations and the media) that were vaguely essayed by previous regimes.

In the first category, the biggest and most controversial venture is the nationalization of most private banks and of several major industrial groups. Together with this goes a whole series of measures to narrow the inequalities of wealth and make life easier for workers: a wealth tax, the raising of basic wages, a thirty-five-hour working week by 1985, earlier retirement, a fifth week of paid holidays, subsidized holidays for the poor and a reflation policy aimed at reducing unemployment. In the second category, the guiding principle behind many of the reforms is devolution in local affairs and a cutting back of the power of the State, in this most centralized nation. This is in line with the Socialists' thinking that citizens should have more freedom to manage their own affairs. An overhaul of local government includes a major cutback in the powers of the State-appointed 'prefects' and the granting of more autonomy to the regions and other local units. In its French context, this is a bold step: the Socialists in fact regard it as the centrepiece of their entire reform programme. They aim also to free radio and television – at last – from direct State control, and to allow more decentralization in cultural affairs, and maybe in education. Finally, plans are going ahead for liberal improvements in France's often-criticized police and judiciary systems: one of the new Government's first acts was to abolish the death penalty.

These social, cultural and administrative changes have been welcomed by the broad majority of public opinion. Those concerning the media and local government are especially popular. But about the economic reforms there is rather more dissension. Will the nationalizations really do anything to help the economy? Some critics point to a basic contradiction here in the Government's strategy, since it is aiming to reinforce State control over finance and industry with one hand, while relaxing it in local and cultural affairs with the other – albeit that the motivations in the two cases are very different. The debate here is hotly engaged, and we shall return to it.

Can the great Socialist adventure succeed? Can it really provide the answer to France's modern needs, and meet the aspirations of the majority of the French people (clearly, it cannot hope to please them all)? This of course is the major question-mark over the future of France today. But I will add three others, which in some degree relate to it.

The first is whether France can now become a more open society, not only more egalitarian in terms of money and opportunity, but also less stratified, less mistrustful, less encumbered by tenacious vested interests, less in thrall to the power of the State. For some years a number of France's ablest and most reform-minded social analysts[1] have argued that France is still too much a 'blocked society', not really as open, mobile and democratic as the United States or even Britain. According to this theory, which I largely share, the economic whirlwind since the 1950s has rendered out of date the age-old social and administrative structures of France, and only slowly and painfully have these been adapting to meet the new conditions. The French may have changed their life-styles, but their basic character-traits, built round individualism, social mistrust and desire for formalism and routine, have inevitably been slower to change, and so has the legal and official framework deriving from the French character. French society has always practised a certain tolerance and respect for individual liberty: but in order to uphold these very virtues it has made itself into a segmented rather than a flexible society. It is a system that served France not too badly in the old days, helping to ensure a certain stability. But modern conditions require a different, more adaptable framework.

In private and family life, and in purely social relations, France has certainly evolved a good deal in the past two decades. Here the French, if belatedly, have been following the British, Americans and others along the path towards greater freedom and informality. Women have achieved a striking new emancipation. Sexual permissiveness has developed remarkably during the 1970s. Within the family, paternal authority now weighs less heavily and parent/child relations are more frank and equal. In daily life, the pompous use of titles is waning, and home entertaining has become much more relaxed and casual. Even in schools, since 1968 the old disciplinarian spirit has yielded to a more easy and human rapport between teachers and pupils. There are many, especially among the old guard, who regret these various changes and fear they are symptoms of a decline of moral values. But most people see them as positive. However, if we turn to official and working life, we see the 'blocked society' still in action. Social mobility may have been increasing a little: yet, in very many careers, promotion may still depend on having the right contacts and diplomas, and if you fail to acquire these in youth then your chances of advance may be blocked for ever. The basic system is still profoundly élitist.

The structures of the State, too, have been slow to evolve. Till now, France has still laboured under the Napoleonic and Jacobin heritage of an

1 Notably Michel Crozier: for his influential books, see Bibliography, p. 659.

excessive centralization. A strong bureaucracy, sometimes dynamic and effective, sometimes slow and top-heavy, has spread its tentacles into every corner of life. Admittedly, strong technocratic government has carried many advantages for France, especially in the economy where long-term central planning has been a motor of progress. But State technocracy, that guiding light of the post-war era, is today seen as a mixed blessing. Many people feel that its nanny-knows-best approach tends to discourage local initiative or drive it into sullen opposition. Governments in the '60s and '70s were fully aware of these dilemmas. They at least paid lip-service to the need to decentralize, and after 1968 they even carried through one or two reforms in this direction, notably in the universities and town councils. But, however sincere its intentions, the Government always ran up against that scourge, the mistrustful and contentious French temperament. Give the French autonomy, and often they will abuse it by splitting into warring factions. This happened notably with the 1969 university reforms, which consequently did not work out too well. So the influential Jacobin lobby continued to argue that the French do still need a strong centralized State, to hold them together. But others retorted that this is a vicious circle: whatever the risks inherent in devolution, it is a lesson that has to be learned the hard way, chaos and all, if society is to become more fully responsible and democratic.

The French have had a long love–hate relationship with the State. They resent it, yet cling to its apron-strings and expect it endlessly to provide. People grouse non-stop against State supervision, yet fail to circumvent it by making use of the scope they do have for improving their own lot. Thus local citizens will sign angry declarations demanding Government funds for some new venture, say a crèche or a youth club: it will seldom occur to them, as in Britain, to group together, raise the money, then run the scheme themselves. Happily, there have at last been some signs of change here in recent years: at a very local level, people are finally showing more readiness to form *ad hoc* associations for this kind of self-help. Today, the Socialist Government plans to build on this. Its devolutionary measures will reduce the role of nanny and oblige people to do more to look after themselves. It is a bold and necessary step. But its success will require more than official reforms, however well-intentioned. These can only be a first stage. There will also have to be a change in French attitudes, and a new kind of civic spirit.

The second question-mark over the future is whether the French can hold on to their new prosperity and complete the modernization of their economy. Much of course will depend on the future of the Western economy as a whole, with which that of France is now so closely bound up. But much will depend, too, on the French themselves, and here there are some reasons for doubt. Will the French be prepared to continue their hard-work drive? As in West Germany, there are signs today that many younger people are deserting the work ethic and opting for a different ethos. Industry, with its technological flair and new commercial verve, has so far weathered the West's economic crisis quite well – but how will it now fare under Socialism? Inequalities of income in France have hitherto been among the highest in any advanced country, so the Socialists' plans for wealth redistribution are not unreasonable: but their programme is an expensive one to carry through when times are hard. Their economic policies, though generous, have yet to prove their realism. And if they fail, the poor will suffer along with the rich.

The final question is very different but equally fundamental: in modernizing, has France been losing her soul, the essential qualities of her unique civilization? French and foreigner alike are aware that much of what is best and best-loved about France, more maybe than in most countries, is intimately bound up with a certain traditional civilized way of life and thought – in the arts and philosophy, in food and fashion, and much else. And today? Some of the signs of change may at first seem ominous, above all in the world of Parisian creative culture. The *Ville Lumière* is no longer the world's art capital; her theatres are full of foreign plays and revivals, her literature has lost its human universality, her intellectual brilliance has grown oddly arid and esoteric. Why? It may in part be an aspect of the general creative malaise in the West today, sharpest in France by contrast with her past glory. Or is it that the French have become so absorbed in urgent economic matters, be it in boom years or lean ones, that they have pushed into second place their creative involvement in literature and painting? At all events, our old image of the French, fecund and original in the arts and philosophy, but financially weak and politically unstable, has needed to be revised in the past decades.

Like any newly modernized country, France inevitably has been losing some of her picturesqueness beloved of tourists – as tower blocks replace romantic alleyways, or as peasant wives don jeans and put their folk-costumes into mothballs. But does this mean that France has really been losing its essential Frenchness? A decade ago it seemed this might be so. Few outward changes in the France of the 1960s were more startling than the massive incursions into ordinary speech of the new hybrid language known as *franglais*, as *le drink* and *le planning* became common coinage and boutiques with such names as *Le Smart Shop* appeared on the boulevards. In central Paris the old *bistrot* began to yield ground to the hamburger bar and *le fast-food*. The French, so it seemed, were losing some of their old originality and becoming oddly imitative, especially of their sworn rivals, the Anglo-Saxons. Their national pride cried out against the process but seemed unable to stop it.

Today, the dangers of the sillier kind of Americanization seem to have receded. The *franglais* craze is well past its prime. The French are proving that they are able to digest foreign influences and even lend them an authentic national flavour: *un drugstore*, for example, is now something typically Parisian, quite unlike a drugstore. The French have also proved themselves able to innovate original new formulae in their own style and then export them: witness the world-wide success of that inimitably French invention, the Club Méditerranée. In short, the French have not lost their old flair. Moreover, in the nick of time they have now become alert to the dangers being caused to their countryside and urban heritage by hasty modern development. After the erection of so many skyscrapers and other eyesores, the accent since the mid-'70s has turned to nature conservation, to the careful restoring of old buildings and city centres. The results often show a true Gallic sense of style.

François Mitterrand himself, passionate lover of nature, of French history and nineteenth-century literature, seems to personify the very strong trend in recent years towards a renewal of links with the past, with tradition. Local folklore and handicrafts are being revived; history books are best-sellers; *cuisine*, in decline in the 1960s, is now again a passion. So the wheel has come full circle in two decades, since the French were first smitten with the craze for modernism. Of course this new vogue for nostalgia might spell decadence if carried too far; yet for a nation to lose touch with its own traditions, especially a nation such as France, could be equally damaging. Today, foreign influences are by no means excluded; but the accent is all on the local, the regional, the truly French. So 'Frenchness' after all is triumphantly reasserting itself. Could this herald a new era of inspired creativity for the French genius? Or is it the ominous sign of a new parochial insularity?

Such, in brief, are some of the problems and opportunities facing the French in the 1980s. In the following chapters they will be examined more closely.

Chapter 2

THE ECONOMY,
MODERNIZED BUT MENACED

France's post-war 'economic miracle' today appears either solid or fragile, depending on which way you look at it. Like most other Western nations, France faces all the uncertainties of a new economic age; like them, she is at grips with mounting oil bills, high inflation and unemployment. That she has managed so far to cope fairly well is a tribute to the astonishing transformations of the past thirty years, which have turned this former agriculture-based society into the free world's fourth industrial power, in many ways highly modern, and far ahead of Britain. A nation formerly known for its exports of perfumes, fine wines and *haute couture* is now in the forefront of advanced technology in telecommunications, aeronautics and much else; and since 1979 France has even drawn level with Japan as one of the world's four leading exporters, behind only the United States and West Germany.

The British have viewed all this with a mixture of envy and grudging admiration. How have those damned French managed it? Is it due to that oft-quoted mystery panacea, central State planning? Or, as many people believe, is it much more the result of some deeper renewal of national ambition and the will to work hard, allied to the dynamism of a new breed of entrepreneurs for whom State bureaucracy is less a help than a hindrance? How is it that so much of French industry and business (though by no means all) has altered its outlook so radically, from the old protectionism to an aggressive new concern with high productivity and free world competition?

France's recovery in the 1950s and 1960s came as a surprise to many people abroad, for in the early post-war years it had been camouflaged by recurrent financial crises and political upheavals. It was not until the early 1960s that we really became aware of a change in France more profound than the change of regime under de Gaulle. Industrial production, having regained its pre-war peak by 1951, then more than *tripled* in 1952–73 and was growing twice as fast as in Britain. Of course, France was starting from a much lower level than Britain, and this belated industrialization partly explains the high growth rate. But France acquired a momentum that enabled her by 1967 to overtake Britain both in output and in standard of living, and since then she has pulled clearly ahead. More recently, like other Western nation, she has run into economic crisis. But in fat years or lean ones it has been the same story: the resolute ambitious nationalism of the Fifth Republic's Right-of-Centre Governments has continually provided the economy with its potent spur. *La gloire française,* under Giscard at least, was no longer so much military or even cultural, as industrial and commercial.

It is true that only compared with Britain do the statistics of France's progress look so spectacular. The other five EEC founder members have almost equalled her own expansion rate since the late 1950s. And Germany's economy remains stronger than hers. But the French so-called 'miracle', in its French context, has been the more remarkable of the two, for it has been achieved in the face of France's fundamental ailments. Some of these have now come a long way towards being cured, notably in industry. But many structural weaknesses, rooted in old French traditions, have proved slower to remedy. Lack of vigour in the banking world, an out-of-date fiscal system, clumsy distribution networks, poor liaison between pure and applied research – these are some of the burdens that the economy has had to carry with it and that Raymond Barre in particular tried to tackle in 1976–81, with varying results. He knew well that France can less and less afford the luxury of these and other inbuilt flaws, now that her economy is no longer sheltered behind its frontiers but open to the full force of global competition; and especially this is so in today's tough climate, for a nation with no oil resources of its own. But the French enjoy a challenge. Again and again, through the crises of the past twenty-five years, industry has responded with remarkable resilience – evidence of how far it has progressed since the early post-war years.

Today, the Socialist Government is embarked on a new economic strategy that differs in many respects from Barre's. In place of his monetarist rigour, it has begun to reflate and to boost public spending: a Keynesian solution seldom in fashion in the West today. The Government's most urgent practical priority is to limit unemployment, now above 2 million. But it is also stepping up the already powerful role of the State in the economy, by nationalizing a number of leading industrial groups and almost all private banks – and here it is clearly inspired by doctrinal anti-capitalist motives. Many experts doubt whether these moves will really help the French economy. Under Socialism, will industry be able to retain its remarkable post-war dynamism? It is a question to be explored at the end of this chapter.

POST-WAR RENEWAL:
FROM MONNET'S PLAN TO BARRE'S MEDICINES

In the eighteenth century France was the strongest and richest power in the world. But soon after 1800 she began to fall back, and failed to keep pace with the rapid industrialization of Britain and Germany. In the late nineteenth and early twentieth centuries she spent huge sums on her colonial empire, but neglected development back home. During the inter-war years, this was a pleasant and cheap country for the foreigner to visit, but not such a happy place for the French to live in, especially the poorer ones, and in the 1930s, industrial output was actually in decline. Then came the Second World War, which brought less loss of life than the first but more serious physical damage. By 1945, France's railways were shattered and their rolling-stock depleted; her ports, her northern towns and many of her factories were devastated.

And yet, as in the case of Germany, the very scale of this destruction was a blessing in disguise: it brought a chance to make a new start on modern lines. The British, who had the misfortune never to be defeated, lacked the same impetus.

The opportunities might have been muffed, had not a number of Frenchmen emerged from the war with a new determination. Some had used the enforced inactivity of the war years to think seriously about the future and to explore new ideas and techniques: that is how the Plan was born. Then, many of the older deadbeat generation came out of the war publicly discredited by their part in the Vichy regime or the Occupation. This enabled new, younger men to push them aside and to fill some of the key posts of industry and the public service. Civil servants, or some at least, began to move from a static to a more dynamic concept of their role: whereas before the war they had been the faceless executives of a smooth, unchanging routine, now they came to see themselves as animators, reformers, apostles of economic progress; and a few industrialists followed suit. This discarding of the economic pessimism of the 1930s was, of course, fairly general in the West after the war; in France it stood out most sharply, just because of the gravity of the earlier decline. And economists broadly agree on this view of the French revival, though sometimes with bewilderment. One American, Professor Charles P. Kindleberger, after examining and discounting a number of purely economic explanations of the French recovery, declared it to be 'due to the restaffing of the economy with new men and to new attitudes'.[1]

In 1946 Jean Monnet launched his First Plan, under the slogan

1 *France: Change and Tradition*, Gollancz, 1964.

'modernization or downfall'. This was a long-sighted austerity plan that gave the immediate housing crisis a much lower priority than the rebuilding of basic industries such as steel, coal and electricity. Then in 1947 Marshall Aid began to arrive in Europe, and in France this provided the investment funding needed for the success of the First Plan. Meanwhile, the traditional French flair for technology and engineering was given a new lease of life, as experts received the funds and encouragement to design and build new cars, aircraft, railway engines and much else. And throughout the post-war decades the high industrial growth rate was helped along by another very important factor, too: this was the mass exodus from the farms, which gave factories a steady supply of new recruits, with a peasant's readiness to work hard.

Yet the 1950s were not easy years. Parallel with the patient rebuilding of key industries went a succession of financial crises due to the archaic structure of much of the rest of the economy. For the euphoric resurgence of new men and new ideas was confined at first to a few pioneers: the rest of the nation, *la vieille France*, stayed attached to its old ways, resisting change, and in 1953 one expert described the new industries as 'merely an isolated enclave of modernism inside old France'. The clash between the two structures produced imbalance and was one cause of the alarming inflation rate (averaging 29 per cent a year in 1947–53): it was like giving a sick man too strong a medicine or putting too powerful an engine in a rickety car. The balance of payments grew steadily worse. Fourth Republic Governments patched over the budgetary cracks, but were too weak and short-lived to apply basic remedies. Yet, to their credit, they did pursue two basic lines of policy that were to safeguard the future: they allowed the Plan to continue its work; and in the mid-'50s they took the courageous decision to go into the EEC despite the opposition of most private industry.

De Gaulle in 1959 inherited a situation where industrial output was rising rapidly yet France's finances were in a fearful state. The franc was trailing along as almost the weakest currency in Western Europe. And with the first of the EEC tariff cuts due to be made in January 1959, it seemed that France might have to suffer the ignominy of being the only member to invoke the escape clauses which could protect her from the shock of competition. Such a prospect was intolerable for de Gaulle, who instructed his finance experts to prepare drastic remedies. The franc was devalued by 17.5 per cent (to the level it was to hold for the next ten years) so the EEC tariff cuts could be respected; as a boost for French morale, the decimal point was shifted and a New Franc born, equalling one hundred old ones; and, most daring of all for this land of protectionism, trade liberalization with other OECD countries was pushed to the unprecedented level of 90 per cent. These reforms were the greatest economic achievement of de Gaulle's eleven-year regime, and the results were immediate. Gold and other reserves, down to almost nil by 1958, began to climb again and went on doing so, on and off, for the next ten years. In thus ripping open the cocoon round her economy, France had indeed taken a risk: but she was now far better prepared to face the test of EEC competition.

The Gaullist decade was one of rapid growth, often reaching 5 or 6 per cent a year. But inflation had been merely curbed, not cured, and this led the Government into occasional stop-go policies including an austerity programme introduced in 1963–4 by de Gaulle's young finance minister, a certain Valéry Giscard d'Estaing. By 1968 the economy was again in very good shape, with its built-in weaknesses seemingly under control; and one sign of its strength and resilience was the relative ease with which it recovered from the May '68 crisis and its after-effects. Production made up for lost ground so rapidly after the strikes that the final growth rate for 1968 was 4 per cent, less than average but creditable in the circumstances. During the Pompidou years, with Giscard back at the Finance Ministry, the economy again bounded ahead, and soon exports were rising by some 10 per cent a year and annual growth was at around the highest level in Europe. So this was the rosy picture when the oil crisis hit the West at the end of 1973, shortly before Pompidou's death. Before we examine how France has reacted to the sterner times since then, let us look briefly at some of the factors behind the post-war recovery: the role of the State and of its Plan, and the influence of the EEC on French industry.

The State plays a stronger and more interventionist part in the French economy than is the case in most Western democracies. Whether this *dirigiste* system is beneficial is a matter of constant debate. But its tradition is not a new one. The oldest French nationalization, that of the tobacco industry, dates from Louis XIV; it was in his reign too, and later under Bonaparte, that the first ventures in centralized economic planning were made. Then in the nineteenth century the mines, the railways, the banks and heavy industry, though remaining in private hands, were all built up with the help of public capital. So when large-scale formal nationalization came, in the '30s and '40s, it did not mark such a turning-point as in Britain. The Popular Front Government made a start before the war; it took over most armament factories, the railways and to an extent the Bank of France, and it set up State aeronautical firms. The immediate post-war Governments then made a more sweeping movement – a task eased by capitalism's taint of Nazi collaboration: they swiftly nationalized the Renault car firm (its owners had helped the Germans) as well as Air France, the coal-mines, electricity and gas, and the larger insurance companies and clearing banks. Much of this was done in an anti-capitalist spirit, with de Gaulle's backing.

Today, as we shall see later in this chapter, the Socialists are embarked on a further wave of nationalizations. But it is the first since 1946. Hitherto, only some 15 per cent of manufacturing industry has been in State hands, a lower figure than in Britain today. After the initial post-war fling, later French Governments never carried out nationalization for its own sake, as Labour has done in Britain: the few moves in this direction in the 1960s and 1970s were dictated either by pragmatism or by what was seen as defence of French sovereignty. Thus the State has built up its own oil concerns, but essentially with the aim of reducing French dependence on the Seven Sisters. And when in 1978 the State took majority holdings in the big steel firms, it did so not with Tony Benn's motives but because it saw no other option: the private owners were bankrupt and patently incompetent.

Yet in other respects the State influence over the whole of private industry and business has always been strong, and this is the essence of French *dirigisme*, which operates through a mix of bureaucratic regulations and high-level personal contacts, together with the State's dominant control of the finance markets. The State owns most of the larger credit bodies, so that firms depend on it for much of their financing of loans. Since the war not only the three biggest banks, but also the main insurance companies and credit institutions such as the powerful Caisse des Dépôts, have all been in State hands. In addition, many firms rely heavily on State purchases. And the Ministry of Finance has much formal power: a firm must seek its authorization over a far wider range of matters than in Britain. Under this system, the State has acted as a bossy but protective nanny to private companies.

This *dirigisme* has often been criticized, especially in recent years. One critic was Raymond Barre, an economic liberal, and he sought to reduce State control. Today, with a Socialist regime, *dirigisme* is back in favour; yet even the Socialists are divided about it. Under modern conditions, is *dirigisme* a source of strength or weakness for the economy? – this debate is a complex and crucial one, and we shall return to it. In a word, the common view today in 'liberal' circles is that too much State control often puts a damper on private firms' initiative and may thus be a waning asset now that France has so open an economy: yet, by this same view, *dirigisme* in the earlier post-war decades was mainly a source of strength, at a time when private industry was backward and needed a strong lead. There seems little doubt that dynamic State leadership has done much for economic development since the war, in a nation with a tradition of the State as entrepreneur and initiator of bold schemes, especially regional ones, of a kind that in Britain tend to be undertaken more locally or haphazardly, if at all. Often the State will take the lead by setting up some development body associating public, private and local interests, and thus it has pioneered such ventures as the big new tourist resorts on the Languedoc coast, the new 'scientific park' near Cannes, and the huge oil and steel industrial complex at Fos, near Marseille. The State has also coordinated the work of public and private firms to endow France (under Giscard) with Europe's most ambitious nuclear programme, and with ultra-modern industries in sectors such as aerospace and telecommunications. And private firms usually go along with State plans. The system enables the Government to set long-term goals, then see that all work together to carry them out, and to this end it has one most effective weapon – the élitist technocratic network of the Grandes Ecoles, very special to France (see pp. 82–92).

It was in this *étatiste* context that the Commissariat-Général du Plan was able to play so effective a role in rebuilding France's post-war economy. And today France still owes an incalculable debt to the man who inspired and founded it, the late and great Jean Monnet. This warm idealist and international visionary was not himself a typical technocrat at all: his family were brandy distillers in Cognac, and his first knowledge of the world was gained in the humble role of overseas salesman for the Monnet cognac firm. Later he worked for the United Nations. He came to know the United States well and to admire its efficiency; and during the war he and a group of friends began to plot how to pull France up towards American levels – by novel, non-American methods. In 1945 he met de Gaulle in Washington and won him over to the idea of the Plan. A year later the first five-year plan was approved, and Monnet became Commissioner-General, a post he held till 1952. Never a conformist, Monnet broke at once with many of the taboos and formalities of French administration. Unlikely groups of people, Communist union leaders and old-style financiers, were shoved together at short notice without form or ceremony. Instead of long, formal memoranda, there were often little notes scribbled by Monnet on slips of pink or yellow paper while walking in the woods near his quiet home west of Versailles. Rather than long, elaborate business lunches, there were working meals of un-French simplicity in the Plan's headquarters, an elegant little private house on the Left Bank. Life there was in some ways more monastic than bureaucratic, with working sessions taking little account of office hours or weekends. According to some accounts, there was even a faint air of revivalism about the inter-industry meetings of those early years, where the planners communicated their faith.

This helps to explain why a certain mystique grew up around the Plan, both in France and abroad. Many otherwise unexplained achievements were credited to it by public opinion; there's been an element of faith-healing about it. Many economists, in fact, are dubious about just how valuable it has been in strictly *economic* terms. Some argue that much of the French recovery would have happened anyway, and they point to Germany's even greater progress with no planning. Yet few of them disagree about the value of the Plan's psychological influence on industry. It tore some of the barriers of secrecy from private firms, helped to create a new climate of productivity and competition, and induced different categories of people to think and work together as in France they had rarely done before.

The two main facts about the Plan are, first, that it has always been 'voluntary' and 'indicative' rather than formally binding; and secondly, that although it is a Government department, it is simply a forum for drawing up blueprints and exchanging ideas, without the executive powers of a Ministry. It has sought to guide the economy in a certain expansionist direction, and Governments have tended to use its forecasts and advice as the basis of their policy, at least until recently; but neither they nor private firms have been under a formal obligation to do so. The Plan has been effective simply because both parties, State and private industry, have usually agreed to collaborate with it. Its full-time secretariat has never been more than forty strong, a brains trust of clever, mainly youngish men, drawn from the civil service, universities and industry.

In its heyday, the Plan's basic task was to set targets for growth, in different sectors, over five-year periods. First its staff would discuss with the Government the best expansion rate to aim at, both overall and within each industry. Then the Plan would convene its 25 'modernization commissions', to apportion the details of growth within each sector. These commissions were Monnet's great innovation, a sharp break with French practice: the heads of private firms large and small, some union leaders, and civil servants, would sit round the same table over a period of months, thrashing out in detail how to achieve their targets, say, in textiles, pig-breeding or aluminium. The sum of their reports would then go to Parliament for approval. And this process is still carried out today, in a more modest and less influential way. The whole system is flexible and strictly empirical, in defiance of earlier French tradition. It is what the French call *une économie concertée*, a working compromise between economic liberalism and *dirigisme*. One foreign observer has commented: 'The roles have been reversed from the nineteenth century when the British were the pragmatists and the French were doctrinaire.'

The Plan's major success in its earlier years was in winning the support of the heads of smaller private companies, so often individualistic and suspicious of the State. Gradually it managed to instil in many of them a new awareness of the need to invest, to increase productivity, to explore export markets, to group together for shared research or sales. All this helped to prepare firms for the Common Market. While the first two Plans concentrated on industry, the Third (1958–61) and Fourth (1962–5) then widened the range to include welfare, housing and social development. Sections of the Plan are now regionalized, and each little town is proud to have its own mini-plan as a segment of the national one. In fact the Plan, long accepted by Government and big business, has now merged into the landscape of daily economic life. At the same time the national importance of the Plan, as a motor of the economy, declined during the 1960s and 1970s and this for a number of reasons. First, political stability under de Gaulle and his successors not only made the Plan less necessary as a factor of continuity: it also caused it to be identified with the Government as it never was under the quick-changing Prime Ministers of the Fourth Republic. De Gaulle tended to exploit the Plan, either as a scapegoat for unpopular measures, or as window-dressing; and anti-Gaullists, whether business or unions, grew less ready to cooperate with it. So the basis of Monnet's sacred non-party *rendez-vous* was undermined. Secondly, French industry by the 1970s was relatively so strong that it no longer needed the old kind of molly-coddling; and France's economy was now so open to the world that it was less amenable to purely domestic planning. The Plan, you could say, had served its purpose and was thus the victim of its own success. Thirdly, forecasting and the fixing of growth targets grew less feasible in the uncertain climate after 1973. Yet the Plan continued to work, in a more discreet way: it no longer had much influence on private industry, but the Government still made use of it as a think tank for specific problems. The Plan, you could say, had become less a particular organization than an element in the national way of thinking: each Ministry, each State agency, each private firm, was now doing its own planning, inspired in one way or another by the original Monnet ethos. This at least was the situation by 1981. Today, the Socialists are restoring the Plan to a more central role, as we shall see.

When the Treaty of Rome was signed, in March 1957, it was thanks to the Plan in no small measure that several industries were already modernized and in a state to stand up to the new outside competition.

One of the largest, steel, had already learned to face the German challenge under that valuable dress-rehearsal for the Common Market, the European Coal and Steel Community, founded in 1951. The French employers' federation, the Patronat, had strongly opposed the creation of the ECSC, and were later surprised to find that French steel *was* able to compete. This helped to modify the Patronat's later hostility to the EEC preparations. Their fears about the EEC were understandable, seeing how backward and cloistered so much of French industry still was in the mid-'50s, at least compared with Germany's. However, the Treaty of Rome was successfully pushed through Parliament, more for political than economic reasons, by a handful of politicians on the Left and Centre led by the far-sighted Robert Schuman. Meanwhile, the Patronat was also being coaxed along by a few enlightened leaders within its own ranks, who realized at an early stage just how much France might benefit in the long run. So, when the treaty was finally signed, the Patronat faced up to reality and many individual firms set about adapting to the new circumstances, after the long decades of protectionism. They sent sales teams abroad, often for the first time; they encouraged staff to learn German or Italian; they put in new equipment, or varied their product to suit new markets. And, again to their surprise, they found that their fears of the German juggernaut had been exaggerated. An official at the Plan told me: 'What we like best about the Common Market is that it helped shock our industry into modernizing.' As in 1940–44 – and this time *before* defeat and without bloodshed! – the German menace had again proved a catalyst.

French trade with the rest of the Six began to increase rapidly, as the tariff barriers came down by 10 per cent a year. In the brief period 1958–62 France trebled her sales to the rest of the Six, a record exceeded only by Italy, and today over 50 per cent of all French exports go to EEC countries, twice the proportion in 1958. The sectors that have done best are those that were already well organized, such as cars and luxury goods. For example, in 1958 France exported a mere 11,000 cars to Germany and 2,000 to Italy: for 1977 the respective figures were 292,000 and 271,000! At the same time, by the process of give-and-take, some other French industries have been cut right down by the new competition, for example by refrigerators from Italy or office furniture from Germany. But the overall balance is positive; and although it has often been said that France expected, by joining the EEC, to lose out on industrial exports but make up on her agriculture, in fact her industry has done equally well. Today many Frenchmen, inevitably, share Europe's general scepticism about the workings of the EEC in practice, its clumsy bureaucracy, its endless political horse-trading; but almost

every executive believes that it has done a valuable job for French
industry, and it is rare to meet any businessman who in the British sense
is an anti-marketeer (see also p. 466). The EEC has helped firms not only
by creating wider sales markets, but also in some cases by facilitating
cross-frontier expansions or tie-ups: for example, the unusual but not
unique case of a mechanical firm in Lyon whose owner told me: 'A few
years ago I met the head of a similar firm in Hamburg and we decided to
work together. His firm used to be stronger on exports, but our production was better. Now, by pooling our research and marketing, and
standardizing our products, we've both of us pushed up our sales
everywhere.'

The hard years for the West since the first oil crisis of 1973 have again
shown up both the resilience of the new modernized industries and the
dangers of old weaknesses still unsolved. For a nation with no oil of her
own, obliged to import 75 per cent of her energy needs, France has not
fared too badly: her response to the world economic slow-down has
been about average, not as buoyant as Germany's, better on the whole
that Britain's or Italy's. In a word, the franc has held up better than
expected; growth has slowed, but less so than in many countries; inflation is again a scourge; and unemployment has become a serious problem for the first time since the war.

When the crisis first began to bite at the end of 1973, France had a
dying President, Georges Pompidou, who took no action. By the time
Giscard came to power, in May 1974, the signs of recession were ominous: so he and his Prime Minister, Jacques Chirac, quickly took their first
austerity steps, and for the next two years they tackled the crisis with a
breathless succession of stop-go measures that inevitably brought erratic
results. The first squeeze provoked a sharp fall in investment and tens of
thousands of bankruptcies, and helped to send unemployment soaring
towards the million mark. Growth was −2 per cent in 1975, the first
minus figure since the war: but by skilful reflation in the nick of time this
was then followed by 5 per cent growth in 1976. Similarly, a highly
dynamic exports policy helped to convert a 14,000-million-franc deficit in
1974 into a 5,000-million-franc surplus the next year, despite rising oil
bills. But the 'go' measures simply aggravated inflation which by 1976
was running at 11 per cent, twice the German or American figure – and it
was little consolation to France that by now this was a world problem
rather than a French domestic one, and that she was not quite the worst
sufferer. As unemployment rose, the Government sought to pacify the
Left by allowing wage increases to outpace inflation, thus creating a
familiar spiral. The franc grew weaker, and Giscard was forced to aban-

don his ill-judged re-entry into the EEC's Mark-dominated currency 'snake'.

It was thus a delicate situation that Raymond Barre inherited as Prime Minister in August 1976 (after Chirac had resigned, for reasons unconnected with the economy). Barre was an unusual man for the job; not a career politician but an academic, yet with wide experience of public affairs and a reputation for canny pragmatism – 'He is France's best economist,' Giscard proudly told the nation. Avuncular in manner yet tough and stubborn, Barre had his own precise ideas on what should be done, and he at once told the French they were living above their means and this must stop. He set in motion two major lines of policy: (a) an immediate austerity programme to combat the crisis; (b) a longer-term structural overhaul of the economy, with the aim of making it as modern and competitive as Germany's. Each policy made good sense in itself: but in their effects they sometimes clashed.

The austerity programme began with higher taxation and a temporary freeze on wages and prices, then continued in classic vein with a series of strict monetary and credit controls, cuts in public spending, and measures to induce wage restraint. The basic aim was to hold the franc steady and contain inflation, even at the cost of further unemployment. At the same time, Barre the 'liberal' economist embarked on a wider strategy. France, he argued, would always be vulnerable to crises such as the present one, so long as unresolved structural weaknesses persisted. French industry, in order to face a growing intensity of world competition, must be freed from excessive Government intervention and made to stand on its own adult feet: the law of the survival of the fittest must operate, whatever the cost. So the time had come, he said, to modify the *dirigisme* which had marked France since the war.

True to his word, in 1978 he lifted industrial price controls in every sector except oil and pharmaceuticals: henceforth, it would no longer be the role of the Ministry of Finance to fix the prices that industry could charge in each range of goods. In 1979, this new freedom was extended to services and commerce too. It was a major break with French tradition, bringing France in line with 'liberal' countries such as Germany, with the aim of introducing a greater spirit of competition and responsibility. Of course it carried the danger of price rises, fuelling inflation – and there was a howl of 'we-told-you-so' from Barre's critics when a *baguette* of bread, that sacred commodity, rose overnight by an average of 22 per cent. But bread was just the kind of product which had hitherto been underpriced, by State bureaucrats anxious to keep the retail index down – and its quality had suffered accordingly. In general, industry did not abuse its new freedom, and by 1981 there was little evidence that the lifting of controls had in itself added to inflation. In fact, as intended, Barre's measures helped many firms to rationalize their production, thus giving a boost to flagging investment.

In other sectors of the economy, Barre embarked on policies not so different from those which the Thatcher Government was later to apply in Britain. In the public services, he intensified the policy of *la vérité des prix* which had begun under Pompidou: State concerns such as railways and electricity were told they must expect less in the way of subsidies and were allowed to raise their charges nearer to the true market level. In its aid to private industry, too, the Government began to follow a similar line. Barre made it clear that public funds would become less available for shoring up 'lame duck' firms, whatever the cost in jobs. And, to prove his word, in 1978 he insisted on lay-offs of more than 20,000 men in the stricken steel industries of Lorraine and the Nord, though he did soften the blow with high indemnities. His philosophy was ruthlessly clear: industries must become efficient and pay their way, or perish. The State would put its emphasis on helping the expansion of those modern high technology industries, such as electronics, where France was well placed in world markets: this was the way of the future. But in other, older sectors there would have to be contractions: in textiles, for example, where France was inevitably undercut by emergent Third World countries; or in steel and shipbuilding, where France's creaky old firms could not easily compete in conditions of world recession. As in the first post-war years, the message was: modernization or downfall.

This could well be seen as a wise policy for the longer term. But it was a costly and painful one to apply in a time of recession; and its immediate effect was to push up the unemployment total, which had been only 500,000 when Giscard took power but by early 1981 was above the one-and-a-half-million mark. The unions made angry noises, but they failed to provoke large-scale strikes: Barre, luckily for him, was able to count on the relative weakness of French unions, and on the reluctance of workers to put their jobs at risk through confrontation.

The major failure of the Barre austerity programme was that it did not reduce inflation as planned: in 1980 this was running at 13 per cent, above the Western average and the worst level in France for over twenty years. However, Barre did manage to hold the franc steady, thus enabling France to keep her place in the new and improved version of the 'snake', the European Monetary System set up in 1979. This was useful to industry. The growth rate, too, despite Barre's squeeze, was still running at slightly above the now modest Western average: even in gloomy 1980, GNP grew by 1.5 per cent. And the Government's vigorous exports policy helped the trade balance to swing back into a handsome surplus after 1976. But this advance was then wiped out by the round of hefty oil price increases in 1979, which pushed France's oil imports bill up to 120 billion francs for 1980 (in 1973 it had been a mere 15 billion). The sizeable trade deficit of 58 billion francs for 1980 showed how vulnerable the French economy remains to the energy crisis.

As his supporters were quick to point out, it was bad luck on Barre that these price rises came just at the time when his austerity plan seemed to be bearing some fruit. In 1979–80 he came under growing pressure to reflate, alike from the Gaullists and from the Left who accused him of sacrificing jobs to his precious stability of the franc. But Barre, backed by Giscard, stuck stubbornly to the view that it was wiser to hold back growth now so as to be better placed to relaunch it later. In public, he dealt sarcastically with his critics, smugly claiming that he knew what he was doing and no other policy would work. Once, when asked about the plight of the unemployed, he replied à *la* Marie Antoinette, 'Let them start their own businesses.' It was his rough and complacent manner, as much as the austerity plan itself, which fuelled his unpopularity. Early in 1981, France's economists were still arguing about whether his policies were right or disastrously wrong. Some felt that he had not been tough enough. But, whatever his overall impact on the economy, there is no doubt that he helped spur forward the modernization of French industry.

The Socialists have now come to power with a very different philosophy from Barre's and a commitment to some radical reforms. But they have also been at pains to project a reassuring image: economic realities will be faced, and the effort of modernization will not be relaxed. As well as reform, there will be some continuity. The senior Ministers put in charge of this field are moderates and non-Marxists – notably, Jacques Delors, Minister of the Economy, a pragmatist who served brilliantly on the staff of the Gaullist premier, Chaban-Delmas. Delors is in favour of retaining Barre's price liberalization. And he, Mauroy and others are pledged to continue the promotion of high technology and the restructuring of industry. At the same time the Socialists are reflating in an effort to reduce the dole queues. And their programme of nationalizations – of several big industrial groups and all private banks – seems to herald a certain return to the classic *dirigisme* that Barre was modifying. Will these and other changes prove a step forward, or back, in economic terms? Will the Socialists' generous but expensive social measures prove compatible with the need to keep French industry competitive on world markets? These are big questions today. The Patronat is worried, for France's sake as well as its own. And if we look at the brave record of French industry since the war, we may see why.

INDUSTRY'S AMBITIOUS LEAP FORWARD

One vital element in the post-war success of industry has been the decline of the old-style family firm and the rise of a new dynamic breed of manager. These new men are often American-trained, often very talented too; they make a cult of hard work, they are obsessed with productivity and new technology, and they have excitedly discovered le marketing, which the French used to ignore so much that they have no word for it and needs must borrow ours. These managers are of different kinds: the main distinction is between the salaried élitist products of the Grandes Ecoles and the self-made whizz-kids who have built up their own firms. Both have made a big contribution. Both are successors to an older style of family management, usually authoritarian, wary of expansion and innovation, that used to be the dominant feature of French industry. Many such family firms still survive, but their numbers and influence have been declining. Many an owner, worried by modern competition, has retired to a chairman's desk and handed over the reins of daily management to a skilled executive. In some cases, conscious today of the need for profit and investment, he has put his shares on the market rather than go on running his firm as a private money-bag. Nepotism, hitherto rife, has now waned: many patrons used to regard the family firm as a way of giving sinecures to doltish cousins or nephews, but today they realize that this spells disaster.

Today there are several distinct styles of management in France, so it is hard to generalize. The new salaried top executives have brought a new spirit and approach to many older firms. Many of the younger ones have been to the United States on long business courses – to the Harvard school, for instance – or have been learning modern methods at new American-influenced business schools in France, such as the famous INSEAD (Institut National des Sciences Economiques et de l'Administration) at Fontainebleau. Such men have been trying, often intelligently and with success, to marry French habits and psychology to the best of American methods. Several major firms have allowed themselves to be reorganized by American management consultants. And so, through these and other factors, American notions of group responsibility and decision-taking have permeated a number of firms, and modern marketing techniques have finally become all the rage. Not that these changes are always a total success: the French have a tendency to fall in love intellectually with new ideas and then not bother too much with their application; in some firms, new American jargon and gadgetry barely conceal the persistence of old French habits of rigid hierarchy and routine; and the French, though improving, are still backward at financial management and cost-accountancy by Anglo-American standards. But in their ardent concern for exporting, for plant modernization and rational use of men and resources, they have moved far ahead of the British – and hitherto they have been much helped by the relatively low level of restrictions imposed by the unions.

For a number of complex reasons, industry enjoys far higher prestige than in Britain as a career open to the talents; and so it attracts a higher calibre of graduate recruit, which in turn lifts its prestige yet further. In large firms, especially the State-owned ones, a number of the top staff are *polytechniciens* or other Grande Ecole *alumni*. As we shall see later in this chapter, it would be wrong to subscribe to the myth that these men are all brilliant and dynamic: but today there is an equally misleading myth that as managers they tend to be duds. Many members of this élite are highly effective: for example, Roger Fauroux, an *énarque* (as the ENA alumni are called: see pp. 84–5) and Inspecteur des Finances who moved across into private industry after some years in State service, and recently as managing-director of St-Gobain has been the driving force behind the expansion of this hugely successful French multinational (taken over by the State early in 1982). His personal contacts with his former civil service colleagues have been not without value to his firm, in this land of *étatisme*.

In a very different style, the 'new wave' of French management also includes a heterogeneous group of more-or-less self-made men who, without any élite training, have built up small firms to achieve dazzling results. Some have inherited tiny family concerns and expanded them into empires; others have come in from outside, or even started from the shop-floor. And the French 'miracle' owes much to these *fonceurs* (whizz-kids) who have dynamically disproved the usual rule that in France you get nowhere without the right connections and diplomas. Such men include Jean Mantelet, founder of the Moulinex electrical firm; Paul Ricard, the king of *pastis*; or Laurent Boix-Vives, who built up Rossignol into the world's leading producer of skis. This kind of free-enterprise maverick is as vital a French phenomenon as the Grande Ecole smoothie. And both species, at their best, have in common today an openness to new ideas and new markets, a readiness to take risks, a new willingness to speak and learn English (see p. 467) or other languages, a self-confidence, a faith in the future of French industry (now tempered a little, it is true), and a mania for work – 'I work a twelve- to thirteen-hour day, including Saturdays, and that's what keeps me healthy. On Sundays I go hunting,' said one typical member of the new wave, owner of an electronics firm. One incentive has been high financial rewards. Average salaries in 1980 ranged from 250,000 francs for heads of small firms to 600,000 francs for heads of large ones. According to one survey, only American bosses have higher net incomes – but this is now likely to change under Socialism, owing to higher taxation.

These are the men who, with active State support, engineered industry's Great Leap Forward during the boom years. In order to face the new world competition they had to grapple with one of its biggest weaknesses: the small size of the average firm and the shortage of really big ones. Back in 1964, a much-quoted article in *Fortune* made the point that of the world's 64 largest firms, 49 were American, 5 German, 4 British and *none* French. Today, France still has too many very small old-fashioned firms, though the crisis is helping gradually to weed out the weaker ones. But in the modern sectors of industry, there has been a steady process of mergers, diversification, regrouping, and the setting up of joint subsidiaries – all much encouraged by the Government. Examples include the merger of St-Gobain (glass) and Pont-à-Mousson (engineering); and Peugeot's merger with Citroën followed by its take-over of Chrysler (Europe). Today, no less than nine French firms figure among the world's 100 largest: in order of size of turnover, they are Peugeot-Citroën, the Compagnie Française des Pétroles, Renault, Elf-Aquitaine (oil), the Compagnie Générale d'Electricité, St-Gobain-Pont-à-Mousson, Péchiney-Ugine-Kuhlmann (aluminium and chemicals), Rhône-Poulenc (chemicals and pharmaceutics) and Thomson-Brandt (electrical).

The better firms have invested intelligently in new equipment, they have pushed productivity up close to American levels and have given technical innovation its head. As a result, while some sectors of industry remain backward, in others France has moved into the forefront of advanced technology, able to export massively both her product and her techniques. Giscard's Ministers were delighted to cite the roll-call of achievements. France leads the world in fast-breeder nuclear reactors and is second only to the US in off-shore oil technology; Michelin developed the radial tyre, while other firms are out in front with new gas tankers, high-speed trains and aluminium processes; France's vast armaments industry has annual exports worth 20 billion francs, thanks to Dassault's aircraft, Matra's missiles and much else; in telecommunications, microelectronics, biotechnologies, aerospace, automobiles, France is the pace-setter of Western Europe. Today the Socialist regime is scaling down the export of armaments, for moral reasons: but it aims to go ahead with the rest of the high-technology policy.

One result of this policy in the 1970s was a huge growth in exports of manufactured goods. This was a novel departure for France, which in 1957 along with Italy had the highest tariff barriers of the Six, backed by a history of protectionism dating from the fifteenth century. But soon after the war a new outlook began to emerge as teams of young industrialists, prompted by the Plan, went on study tours of America and came back convinced of the need to sell abroad. Renault then led the car industry into the export field. Even today the trend is by no means general – two-thirds of all exports come from the 400 largest firms – but the creation of the EEC has stimulated many smaller companies to look outside their frontiers for the first time. France has been spurred also by the decline of her former protected colonial markets in Africa, and especially since 1973 by the need to offset the growing new oil import bills. Her exports as a share of GNP have risen since 1957 from 13 to 25 per cent, and she is now level with Japan as third equal among the world's exporters.

This is a fine *tour de force* – but can French industry sustain it, in face of the so-called 'American challenge'? One of the big problems facing European firms in the past twenty years has been how to compete in a world increasingly dominated by the giant US-based multinationals such as IBM, with their superior resources for research and development. In the EEC's earlier years, some people believed that the answer could be to create 'European' firms of American size through cross-frontier mergers; and Governments encouraged this. But it did not happen: differing national habits, differing fiscal and legal systems, proved too dissuasive. In the 1960s the only successful inter-EEC merger of any size was between two photographic firms, Agfa of Germany and Gevaert of Belgium, while most companies found it more useful to form links with American expertise than to cooperate with each other. However, the more recent success of the Airbus Industrie consortium (see p. 72), French-led, is now setting what may be a new trend. And there has been another remarkable development in recent years: Europe has been forging its *own* multinationals, not through inter-EEC mergers but by the spontaneous world-wide expansion of some big national firms. Thus the St-Gobain group today has factories in fourteen countries, mostly in the EEC but also in North and South America. So France is taking a lead in Europe's riposte to American hegemony.

French firms in fact are now taking a leaf out of America's book and are beginning to invest abroad on a large scale, as they rarely did in the old days. This outward movement has now reached the same level as that of new foreign investment inside France, and is by no means confined to nearby EEC countries: across the globe, from Singapore to São Paolo and even South Carolina, you find new French-owned factories. The reasons? – as one *patron* put it, 'Labour costs are far lower than in France. Third World countries are eager to industrialize, and if we don't step in first our competitors will, and they'll take our markets.' Today Renault and Peugeot-Citroën have factories in Latin America, Africa and Eastern Europe; Bidermann, the big textile firm, is producing in Taiwan, Hong Kong and even in China; Thomson-Brandt builds TV sets in Spain and Singapore; BSN, a leading French food firm, is making yoghourt in Brazil; and so on. What is more, after decades-of heavy American investment in Europe, a few French firms are now repaying the United States in their own coinage by investing *there*! The sectors include textiles, glass, telephone equipment and motor tyres: Michelin, a rare example of an old-style French family firm that is brilliantly managed, has expanded so fast that it is now one of the world's leading tyre producers and has set up several factories in South Carolina. The reasons are the same: the desire to penetrate the American market, and the fact that even American labour costs are often below French ones, owing to the high French social security charges on employers. In the interests of French economic *grandeur*, Giscard's Government discreetly supported this new global colonization; and Mitterrand is now doing so too, despite worried noises from the unions that it takes potential new jobs from France. The Patronat claims this is not so, that investment abroad has a multiplier effect which helps industry back home too.

The Government also encourages foreign investment in France – under certain conditions. The birth of the EEC brought a rush of American firms looking for footholds inside the new Community; and in the '60s and '70s France proved a favourite venue for the American or other investor, attracted by her seeming political stability, her hard-working labour force, and so on. Of her industrial assets, 17 per cent are now foreign owned, a figure only a little below that for Britain (20 per cent). Americans take the lion's share (IBM, Caterpillar, Ford, Motorola are among the many firms with plant in France), followed by the Dutch and Belgians, then the Germans, while the British lately have made a speciality of buying up luxury hotels such as the Plaza Athénée (Paris) and the Carlton (Cannes). Today, to the surprise of many observers, the Socialists' arrival in power has not deterred the continued flow of foreign industrial investment.

For a while in the 1960s the whole issue became explosive, as national pride was involved. While Americans seemed to see France as the most desirable growth area in Europe, de Gaulle was not too happy about this dubious compliment. He saw threats to national independence. And on many occasions he and then Pompidou vetoed applications by American and other companies: Fiat was prevented from trying to take over Citroën. Under Giscard, the doctrinaire hostility eased and policy became more pragmatic, and today it is remaining so under Mitterrand. While the creation of a new factory is almost always welcomed, proposed foreign acquisitions of existing French firms are looked at more carefully; but they have usually been allowed, even encouraged, if they seem likely to stimulate exports, or provide new jobs especially in development areas, or bring new technology to a sector where France is short on expertise. Even so, what officials call 'a French solution' is preferred whenever possible: if an ailing French firm needs to be saved by a takeover, a foreign bid for it may be rejected if the Government can find a French buyer even at a lower price. In this context the 'Ducellier affair' caused some stir in 1979. Bendix (US) wanted to sell to Joseph Lucas (UK) its majority share in the auto-components firm, Ducellier. Eager for France to build up its own strength in this sector the Government encouraged Ferodo, a French company, to make a bid for Bendix' share of Ducellier, and threatened to veto Lucas. Lucas took the matter to court, and finally a compromise was reached whereby it and Ferodo would share Ducellier. The affair showed that the Government, while ready to be flexible, was not prepared for any sell-out of what it saw as French national interests.

Today the broad strategy, under Mitterrand as under Giscard, is that the Government does not want any one industrial branch to pass too largely under foreign control. This applies especially to 'sensitive' sectors such as computers; also food-processing, where France is trying hard to build up a national industry that is still relatively weak despite the importance of her agriculture (see p. 227). So, after a few American take-overs of French fruit-canning, biscuit and animal-feed concerns, there was something of a clamp-down and firms such as Britain's United Biscuits saw their projects vetoed. When the famous Château Margaux vineyard came on the market, the Government ensured its sale to a French grocery chain, at a price below the offers made by German and US firms: the reason given was that the Margaux label was part of the national heritage! *A fortiori* the State sees to it that France keeps virtually total control in 'strategic' sectors such as armaments and aviation. As for computers, that key modern industry, the Government was for some years in a dilemma, for it saw that American firms were so far ahead in technology that it had little choice but to invite their participation. In 1964, amid national humiliation, de Gaulle even allowed France's leading computer firm, Machines Bull, to be sold to General Electric (US). But France's own computer industry has since pulled itself up, and today is even forming joint ventures with American firms on an equal basis.

This is the policy today, in many sectors; French industry ought now to be strong enough to invite high-technology foreign investors no longer as 'colonizers' but as equal partners. One Minister said, typically, 'We are no longer a second-rate nation, for whom any link with the Americans is an act of subordination.'

The equality is not always achieved, however, for the state of scientific research is still very uneven in France, leading to much dependence on imported know-how. It is true that in recent years a few key firms have made brilliant progress with their own research – Rhône-Poulenc (chemicals), Dassault (aircraft), Thomson and CIT-Alcatel (electronics), and some others – and this lies behind the current French breakthrough in some advanced technologies. But although the State too has spent a fair amount on research (much of it for military purposes), relatively few other private firms are doing nearly enough to keep them abreast of their world rivals. Roger Fauroux of St-Gobain told me: 'Our research budget is adequate for our daily needs, but not for making a leap forward into new technology. So, for our move into semi-conductors, we've had to form a joint venture with an American firm, buying their techniques.' The French 'balance of patents', as it is called, is severely adverse: for example, France sells only one patent to the US for every four she buys in return. In 1960 that proud French achievement, the Caravelle, lost the chance of a large sales order from China as its pressurization system was an American patent, in those days forbidden for sale to Peking.

Historically, France has a fine record of scientific invention, but her problem has been a failure to marry the three separate threads of pure academic research, practical innovation, and industrial application. While Pasteur and then the Curies were at work in their laboratories, French innovators were among the leading world pioneers in photography, cinematography, some aspects of electricity and aeronautics. But industry and pure science inhabited – and still inhabit – two separate worlds; and one reason why French industry fell behind that of Britain and Germany in the nineteenth century was the negligence of French firms in applying the inventions of the time, many of them French. Until recently, public opinion tended to regard discovery as its own reward, an attitude summed up by a remark I once heard a Frenchman make to an American: 'No, we don't have pasteurized milk in France, but we do *have* Pasteur!'

Times have since changed: today many firms are all too eager to apply the latest research, while their engineers and other scientists can produce brilliant results when given the right backing. Hence the recent impressive French achievements in nuclear and solar power, telecommunications, aerospace, and so on, helped by a State budget for research which for 1980 reached 14,463 million francs. But the effort is concentrated on major projects in a few key modern sectors: in the more humdrum world of consumer goods, food-processing or pharmaceuticals, France lags. And as advanced research grows more specialized and hence more expensive, most firms face a shortage of equipment, while not nearly enough is being done for European coordination. France's research spending (1.8 per cent of GNP) has till now been below the level of its main rivals, Germany and Japan (both 2.2 per cent).

Above all, France hitherto has not solved the problem – partly political – of the gulf between industry and the academic milieux. The State gives sizeable funds to the universities and to the Centre National pour la Recherche Scientifique, the largest body of its kind in the world. But the 'pure' scientists in these ivory towers are nearly all on the Left, suspicious and ignorant of private industry and its needs, unwilling to defile themselves by helping to shore up capitalism. 'If you ask them why they do their research', scoffed one *patron*, 'they'll say it's "for the glory of humanity" or "a worthy end in itself". To bother with its application is "dishonourable".' One example: Giscard's Government urged the National Agronomic Research Institute to sign contracts with food-processing firms, for mutual benefit: but when the institute's director tried to do so, he was met with a four-month protest strike by his research staff! The result of this whole situation has been that many firms, denied the benefits of France's own pure research and unable to afford much of their own, have been forced to seek help abroad. Giscard's Government grew anxious and began to restructure the CNRS, with the aim of gearing it more closely to industrial needs.

Today the Socialist regime is stepping up the research effort, which it sees as a vital factor in its plans for using big national development projects to promote economic growth. The State's civil budget for research has been raised by 30 per cent, to reach a handsome 2.5 per cent of GNP; and all research is now coordinated by a powerful Ministry led by a senior Socialist, Jean-Pierre Chevènement. What is more, the current nationalization of twelve major groups may possibly help to narrow the damaging gulf between industry and academia. The effect of these take-overs will be to increase from 26 to 53 per cent the proportion of all research that is done by or for companies in State rather than private hands. The Left-wingers in the CNRS and the universities will thus find far more scope for collaborating with the public sector – and under a Government of which they can now approve. They will have less cause to equate industry with hated capitalism; and this may make them readier to angle their research towards practical ends.

Giscard's Minister of Industry, André Giraud, an energetic and persuasive figure, had a modest success with his own pet solution. He believed in sponsoring innovation and homespun invention as much as advanced research. He told me in 1979: 'So much technical progress, in the past, came from ingenious innovation by individuals – look how the car was invented, or the ball-point pen. This remains valid, even in an age of costly technology. So I'm urging small firms to try out novelties – a typewriter for the disabled, for instance. The French are an inventive people, and I'm sure we have a money-spinner here.' Some people dismissed Giraud's ideas as cranky; but a number of firms responded fruitfully. The Socialists are now continuing the encouragement.

Indeed, not all of France's new industrial dynamism has come from the large firms. A number of smaller ones too, often run by the kind of self-made whizz-kid I described earlier, have shown a flair for exploiting new technologies and expanding into world markets, usually in specializing fields. One case often cited and which I have mentioned earlier is that of Rossignol, which in 1956 was no more than a family-run artisan workshop turning out a few pairs of skis in a small town near Grenoble. A new manager was brought in, Laurent Boix-Vives, and he has steadily built up the firm to become the world's largest ski producer, with factories in five countries including the US, a staff of 3,600, and 22 per cent of the world market. He was helped by the rapid growth of skiing as a sport; but also, in face of strong Austrian competition, he showed drive and imagination in developing new techniques and sales outlets. At Castres, near Toulouse, Pierre Fabre was the owner of a simple chemist's shop who in 1961 patented a medicine today used for treating blood deficiencies: he founded a laboratory for it which is now one of France's largest pharmaceutical firms, with an annual turnover of more than 300 million francs and exports going to seventy countries. All this, from scratch in twenty years.

Needless to say, few smaller firms have shown quite the enterprise of these and other star cases. France entered the EEC bearing the albatross of a myriad tiny manufacturing concerns: some 600,000 of them employed less than twenty people. Some goods, that in Germany or Japan were made in factories, were in France still produced on a cottage-industry basis – a system that might ensure high craftsmanship in some fields, but in marketing and other techniques was often so inefficient as to be uneconomic. In the past twenty years many thousands of these firms have been pushed out of business, or have sold out or merged of their own accord, and the process has been intensified under the post-1973 crisis. Today about 15,000 firms close each year; and the proportion of workers in companies with less than 200 has fallen since the mid-'60s from two-thirds to just over one-third. Slowly therefore, and often with hardship for individuals, the necessary adaptation is being made; but it is still far from complete.

Fortunately, as in farming, the world of small industry has thrown up a few leaders who have been urging upon it the need to adapt. One powerful figure in post-war France has been Léon Gingembre, an eloquent needle-manufacturer from Normandy who founded the federation of Petites et Moyennes Entreprises (PME) and was for many years its president and evangelist. Until the late '50s he and his colleagues were allies of the reactionary grocer-demagogue Pierre Poujade, and like him they preached that the State and society had a duty to subsidize helpless little businesses. But then Gingembre, like the Patronat, saw the light: he gave up his hostility to the EEC, accepted the inevitable, and threw his immense influence into persuading his million members in industry and commerce to modernize and regroup, or perish. 'If a small firm is to have any *right* to survive,' he now said, 'it must be able to compete.' And so the PME set up services to help its members to export or make use of modern technology. Following this lead, a number of small firms began to group together. In Normandy, for example, seven makers of agricultural tools formed a joint supplies and sales service, and were thus able to break into foreign markets; in Marseille eight coppersmiths set up a joint research service which led to a contract from the Atomic Energy Commission. Slowly there was a change of heart in the traditional France of tiny self-centred firms, hitherto suspicious alike of each other and of progress. And the Government went ahead with its policy of encouraging mergers.

Some industries – cutlery and watchmaking are good examples – are only now awaking from medievalism. The little town of Thiers in Auvergne calls itself 'the French Sheffield': but until recently it had no modern factories, and even today its side-streets are lined with hundreds of little cutlery workshops, producing thousands of different models. Many of them cling sentimentally to Thiers' long traditions of cutlery, established in the thirteenth century; and some of the dark and dingy *ateliers* I visited seemed to be still in that century. I met old men who had spent their working lives lying on their bellies on wooden planks, polishing knives: a few suffered from chronic rheumatism because electricity was not introduced till the 1960s and before then the polishing-wheels were turned by water from a stream below. But though conditions have now improved, the old artisan work is steadily dying out in face of foreign competition: Thiers, in order to survive, has finally shifted its emphasis to new factories which today account for 90 per cent of its cutlery output. The irony is that the new mass-produced knives are

not of the same quality as those produced by the old artisan methods: but
they bring far more profit.

The watch industry too has managed to adapt in the nick of time.
Until ten years ago, some 200 separate firms made watch parts and 200
others put them together, while only seven did the combined operation.
Some 3,000 brands of watches were then sold by 11,000 independent
watch-shops, which controlled all repairs and dictated the markets. But
as cheaper or better-made watches flooded in from abroad, the industry
was faced with extinction: so the Government applied a heavy hand for it
to modernize, with some success. Today, half the small firms have closed
and the industry is dominated by three main groups, using the new
technology of quartz watches; the cartel of the little shops has been
circumvented by the mass selling of watches in supermarkets and tobac-
conists. Thanks to all this, French annual watch production has risen
since 1967 from 9 million to 14 million. Such is the drama of small
industry's difficult adaptation to a new and harsher world, where only
the fittest will survive.

Giscard had his sights set on a long-term plan for France, as a nation
whose wealth and world influence would reside in her technological
advance and industrial modernism. This was not quite the same as de
Gaulle's vision in the 1960s, when economic prowess was geared more
towards showy and costly prestige symbols. Under Giscard, there were
no sequels to Concorde, nor to that ill-fated flagship of Gallic grandeur,
the 63,000-ton liner *France*. Launched at St-Nazaire in 1962, this noble
vessel did well for a few years on the North Atlantic routes: but then she
fell foul of the energy crisis, and after piling up heavy losses was taken
out of service after only twelve years. She was sold to the Saudis who
sold her to the Norwegians who today are using her for Caribbean
cruises. Many a patriotic tear was shed, but the charges of Gaullist
prestige-hunting were not easy to defend.

Giscard's priorities were more severely practical. He felt that French
industry, *all* of it, must be ruthlessly streamlined to face the new and
uncertain conditions of tough world competition, for only thus could
France be strong. And he sought to achieve this by mixing old-style
French *dirigisme* with a new dosage of German-style liberalism, and
firstly by the removal of price-controls. In fact, the Patronat itself had for
years been demanding an end to these controls – 'We're grown up now,
and we no longer need the Government to treat us like infants,' said one
of its leaders in 1976.

This is how the controls used to work. If an electrical firm, say,
wanted to increase the price of some model, it had to get together with its

competitors and prepare a joint dossier showing how production costs and other factors had affected business. It took this to the Ministry of Finance which then weighed the economic and social implications. After much haggling, the decision on a new price – to be applied by all firms – was taken by the bureaucrats. The system obviously distorted competition, and often made it harder for a firm to balance its books or plan its production: it is argued today that the steel industry might not have got into such a plight had it been able to raise its prices as it wished at the right time. In practice the controls were not always applied as rigidly as might appear on paper, and many astute firms found ways round them, but the system was resented. Roger Fauroux of St-Gobain told me: 'We had to bargain all the time – and we didn't always win, often for absurd and arbitrary reasons. It was time-consuming and demoralizing. We felt *administrés.*' Worse, the system tended to encourage *ententes*, notably among smaller firms who would share out the market between them since they could not compete on prices – the opposite of economic efficiency.

Barre's lifting of controls in 1978 had generally beneficial results. Firms reacted responsibly and did not raise their prices unduly, while the new freedom enabled many of them to rationalize their production and thus increase investment. Some smaller companies, unused to doing their own pricing, did take a little time to adjust and learn the ropes· but the reform on the whole brought an added spirit of competition, forcing firms to stand on their own feet while also allowing them more scope. The Patronat welcomed it. However, in freeing prices the Government had by no means abandoned its wider role of guiding industry, which it could still exercise through its control of the banks and credit bodies, its regional incentives, the network of high-level personal links, and so on. *Dirigisme*, under Barre, was very far from dead. And most industrialists, as in Japan, were glad to be able to continue looking to the State for some help and leadership, provided it did not interfere too closely. Roger Fauroux was at pains to draw a distinction for me between what he saw as 'good' and 'bad' *dirigisme*: 'The day-to-day bureaucratic control of our every detailed move is certainly counter-productive, and we are glad that Barre has reduced this: the freeing of prices has been an important step. But longer-range policy *dirigisme* – the setting of targets, the restructuring of industry – remains very useful to us, and to other firms. For example, St-Gobain has now moved into the electronics and computer field, via a joint venture with an American company, and for this we have taken guidance and financial help from the Government, whose experience of world technological trends is greater than ours in a sector that is new to us. I personally am not ashamed to accept this kind of State

advice.' And so, under Barre's new-style semi-*dirigisme*, Patronat and
Government were on easier terms than at any time since the war. As we
shall see, it is far from certain how far the Socialists will now undo Barre's
work and return to a more classic *dirigisme*.

In 1976–81 the Giscard–Barre recipe for industrial success was
crystal clear. Giscard said, 'We must move towards a specialized
economy . . . in the sectors of high technology. We must gradually give
up the production of mass goods at low prices: that is not our speciality.'
So his Government deployed loans, tax incentives and other forms of aid
to boost the advanced modern industries, while older less competitive
ones were restructured or left to wither away. A senior economist at the
Elysée told me, 'The hallmark of French exports, in the new technologies
just as in our traditional wines or perfumes, must be high quality and
sophistication – it's no use trying to compete with T-shirts made in
Malaya. Yes, maybe in the short term this restructuring will lead to
unemployment: but to shore up outdated industries in order to save jobs
would in the long term be suicidal. Competitivity *must* be the first
priority.'

This long-term cure was not easy to apply in a time of recession,
when the unions were clamouring for immediate measures to limit
redundancies: it was like trying to perform a surgical operation on a
patient also suffering from pneumonia. Indeed in the period before the
1978 elections the Government did not always have the courage of its
economic convictions: many times public funds were used to bale out
dying firms. But after the elections Barre showed rather more vigour,
though in his efforts at restructuring he still had to tread a delicate
balance. His strategy was threefold: (a) lame ducks judged to be incur-
able were left to their own devices – in theory at least, though a few were
still kept going with State aid, in politically sensitive areas such as
Brittany; (b) firms in crisis, but deemed to be salvageable if radically
overhauled, were given public money for doing so: this happened in
shipbuilding; (c) when a whole area suffered from the decline of a basic
industry, as in the Lorraine steel belt, the Government tried not so much
to shore up that industry as to bring in new modern firms to take its
place. For this purpose a Special Industrial Reconversion Fund was set
up in 1978, and had some success in the Lorraine and Nord steel areas, as
well as in the Nantes/St-Nazaire shipbuilding zone and elsewhere.

The fate of the once-mighty textile empire of Marcel Boussac was a
clear indication of how the new world climate had affected French
industry, and of how lame ducks were treated by Barre. Boussac himself,
by now over ninety, used to personify the old-style French family *patron*:
he grew so rich from textiles that his racing stables were second only to

the Aga Khan's, and he owned seven *châteaux* where in aristocratic style he entertained princes and top politicians. But then he began to fight a losing battle against Third World competition, and he failed to adapt. Amid stories of gross mismanagement and family wrangles, his firm by 1978 was losing 10 million francs a month – so he looked around for a saviour. But the Government refused point blank to underwrite his survival plan. André Giraud, Minister of Industry, even insulted the tottering tycoon publicly in Parliament: 'We have no intention of throwing public money at a group that has not the slightest notion of basic accounting methods.' So Boussac was obliged to sell out cheaply to another big textile group, Agache Willot, which had a line in cheap consumer goods. Whereas Boussac's prestigious cloth used to be styled into *haute couture* dresses by Dior and St-Laurent, under Willot the firm now began to turn out synthetic nappies and plastic bags – an ironic end to a proud name.

Of all lame duck sagas, the most bizarre was that of Manufrance, which in 1976–80 emerged repeatedly into the headlines like a serialized black comedy. Known affectionately as *'la vieille dame'*, Manufrance was a fusty old firm in the depressed industrial city of St-Etienne, and its activities were an odd hotch-potch: it made shot-guns, bicycles and sewing-machines, it ran a large mail-order business and a chain of general stores across France, and it published a highly profitable hunting magazine, *Le Chasseur français*, with monthly sales of 500,000. In the old days the firm had been one of the glories of French industry and commerce, but it then failed disastrously to move with the times. Its management, smug and incompetent, saw no reason to invest in new equipment, so rooted were they in the myth of the old lady's invincibility: yet their guns and bicycles were being undercut by modern rivals, their mail-orders dwindled with the loss of France's colonies, their shops were outflanked by the bold new hypermarkets. By 1976 the firm was losing 40 million francs a year and bankruptcy loomed. This was old-style French industry at its worst, and on my own visit in 1979 I was appalled – semi-derelict nineteenth-century workshops, obsolete machinery unchanged for years; worse than anything I'd seen even in Britain.

Manufrance might soon have died a natural death were it not for one curious complication. By a legacy from a former shareholder, 22 per cent of its stock belonged to St-Etienne town council (the only such case in France), and in the 1977 local elections a Communist-led coalition won the *mairie* on a platform of rescuing the city's prestigious status-symbol and the 4,000 jobs involved. There followed an arcane three-year struggle, with all sides playing the most devious parts – the Communist mayor and his CGT[2] allies, the Government, the management, the bankruptcy receiver, even the Swiss banks. One rescue plan followed another, only to be torn up and discarded, as new managing directors – there were seven in five years – came and went with equal speed. They cast around for some industrial group ready to take over the stricken lady, but none was prepared for such a risky venture, least of all with the Communists breathing down their necks. Then in 1979 the firm went into liquidation and a holding company was formed to manage its production and its assets; and to back this the Communists found a Left-wing insurance company plus, surprisingly, a Swiss finance group. But State aid was urgently needed too – and the Government was in a dilemma. Here surely was a prime case of a lame duck deserving to die, in an outmoded industrial sector with little potential: yet, in sensitive St-Etienne, Giscard did not want to provoke a Left-wing backlash. Eighty per cent of the firm's workforce was CGT, and already they had several times occupied the factory and threatened its management with violence. So Paris dithered. Before the 1978 elections, in a bid to outflank the mayor, it prudently put in 8 million francs of aid. Then after the election victory it cut off further aid. But later Giscard changed tack again. He decided that the best course was not to be seen to kill, while not striving officiously to keep alive. That is, he tried so to manoeuvre that the death of Manufrance would appear to be at least as much the Communists' responsibility as that of the State. So he promised new aid, but only on condition that other partners backed an effective rescue plan – and this by now was looking less and less feasible.

By October 1980 the game was finally up. The holding company too went into liquidation and the bankruptcy tribunal closed the firm down. Annual losses were now running at 120 million francs, and successive lay-offs had reduced staff to 1,875. Plans went ahead for carving up the corpse by selling off the lucrative *Chasseur français* (which any publisher would be delighted to run), and also the shops and mail-order business (which if reorganized might be made profitable). But what of the gun and cycle factory which only the Communists claimed had any viable future? Here the *mairie* and CGT quickly stepped in, occupied the plant, and declared they would keep it going as a workers' cooperative – a scheme to which the Government sceptically gave its blessing. In fact, only 600 workers were by now involved in production (the rest were on the commercial side), and since 1973 far larger factories had closed with far less fuss. So you could say that *l'affaire* Manufrance was a political storm in a teacup, whipped up by the Communist bid to save the firm, by the

2 Confédération Générale du Travail, the big Communist-led union; see p. 109.

dear old lady's sentimental value to the Stéphanois, and by the fact that
unemployment was already far above the average in this city of decaying
nineteenth-century industries. There are two morals to be drawn from
the affair. First, in today's harsh world a firm that delays its modernization too long is doomed. But, secondly, Barre's policy of being ruthless
with such firms was still tempered now and again with political ruthlessness, or so the Elysée insisted, whatever Barre may have wished. Had it
not been for the local Communist offensive, Manufrance would probably
have died in 1977 and much money and useless effort would have been
spared.

This affair was small beer, however, compared with the high drama
that came to a climax in January 1979 in the Lorraine steel town of
Longwy – France's most serious labour unrest since 1968. For some years
the French steel industry had been a lame duck of diplodocus size, and
thus was worse hit than those in many countries by the world steel
recession of the late 1970s. So Barre applied his medicine. In this case,
there was no question of killing the industry completely, for steel was
seen as a strategic national asset, and to rely solely on imports was
unthinkable. Instead, Barre obliged the private steel firms to contract
drastically and to retrench.

France's traditional steel industry is concentrated in northern Lorraine close to old iron-ore deposits, also in the Nord around Valencien-
nes, with pockets elsewhere. Under the impetus of Jean Monnet the
industry was modernized in the early post-war years, and for a while it
stood up well: output doubled from 1950 to 1966, to reach over 19 million
tons a year. The family firms gradually merged to form two major
groups, Sacilor and Usinor. But – a familiar story – as the years went by
they failed to invest adequately in new equipment, for keeping up with
the rising productivity of rival countries. Partly this was their own fault,
but it was due equally – as State officials today admit – to the price-
control system which severely curbed their profits. Lorraine, its own
iron-mines wearing thin, also found itself ill-placed geographically for
receiving imported ore: so the policy began of building new steel mills on
the coast. Usinor's plant at Dunkerque did well, receiving Mauretanian
ore by ship right on its doorstep. A larger steel complex was then built at
Fos, near Marseille: but by the time this was ready it was engulfed by the
world recession, and Fos has never lived up to its hopes.

By the mid-'70s, despite some investment in new plant, French
overall productivity was 30 per cent below Germany's and less than
half that of Japan. There was serious overmanning, so in 1977 the
Government sanctioned cuts of over 10 per cent in the 150,000-strong

work-force: Lorraine, with 80,000 steelworkers, bore the brunt. But it soon became clear that this remedy was not drastic enough, as the steel firms piled up losses of over 4 billion francs for 1977 and their debts began to exceed their annual turnover. The Government and the firms had long made the mistake of supposing that the crisis was merely due to circumstances, whereas in France's case it really went deeper, it was structural. So late in 1978 Barre swung into action. He agreed to bale out the two steel giants with what amounted to provisional semi-nationalization, alien to his philosophy, but the only pragmatic solution. The State took over the firms' debts by acquiring 67 per cent of their shares, at a cost of 11 billion francs, thus giving it a virtual monopoly. Barre dismissed the firms' bosses and replaced them with trusted State technocrats. And he agreed on an urgent plan for 22,000 lay-offs (16,000 of them in Lorraine), including the closure of several mills. The moment of truth had arrived.

The Lorrains were aghast. This land of Verdun, this homeland of Joan of Arc, has long been a citadel of French patriotism, strengthened by its enforced annexation to Germany in 1871–1918; and now Lorrains felt that France was betraying them. Not that their economic crisis is new: along with the Nord, this is one of the two main regions of France where the post-war problem has been one of reconverting an archaic industrial tissue, rather than enticing new factories to rural zones as in the West (see pp. 127–9). For some years the State and local bodies had strained their sinews to work the miracle of diversification – and with some success in the coal-belt towards the Saar, and in the Vosges. Hundreds of small firms moved in there, attracted by Lorraine's central position in the EEC and by its skilled and hard-working labour force; and by 1978 the old declining industries (coal, textiles, steel) accounted for only one-third of productive jobs, against two-thirds a decade previously. Go to a little town such as Creutzwald, near the Saar, and you will find eight new factories built since 1966 – seven of them German – making plastics, TV sets, etc. This reconversion has been due as much as anything to the dynamic policy of the Coal Board, anxious to find new jobs for its laid-off miners. But go further west, to the sad valleys between Thionville and Longwy where steel for centuries has been a way of life, and the picture was, and is, very different. Here industrial decay hits you in the face as sharply as on Tyneside or Clydeside. Rail tracks to closed factories are lost in weeds. Grimy canals, once busy with barges, stagnate in disuse. Derelict mineshafts crown the hills, above valleys where the steel-furnaces belch their black, pink and orange fumes over the ugly terraced houses. In ghost towns, many shops are closed and shuttered – so unlike the New France. The steel towns, oddly, have names like Hayange, Uckange, Gandrange – but these are angels with dirty faces.

However, the Lorrains are tough, resourceful, stoical, and they do not take adversity lying down. Barre's redressment plan was a sane one, economically: but he presented it tactlessly, in his usual take-it-or-leave-it manner. He gave little indication that replacement jobs would be provided, or that compensation would be other than the usual dole allowances. At first the Lorrains were stunned with disbelief: then they began to react. The leading local paper, *Le Républicain lorrain*, by no means an organ of the Left, mounted a campaign to rally the region to demand a better deal from Paris, and soon it had 50,000 people marching through the streets of Metz. Its deputy editor, Charles Bourdier, later gave me his own emotional account: 'Our motives were purely economic and human, not political-regionalist as they might have been in Brittany or Languedoc. By November 1978 we became aware that the people in the steel towns felt utterly abandoned. Reports were coming in to us of suicides, nervous breakdowns, mounting delinquency, a rising collective anguish. The unions warned us that they could no longer control their rank-and-file and that sabotage was imminent. I felt that the normal democratic framework was breaking down, leaving a void: the local steel bosses had abdicated, the prefect no longer carried credibility, the Church meant nothing, the politicians were preaching to thin air, and the CGT was so narrowly political that its members were deserting it in thousands. We saw a real danger of uncontrolled explosions – five kids in a factory could suddenly smash the place up. Or Longwy would set up its own République Populaire in the French romantic revolutionary tradition. And then the riot police would move in . . .'

It all but happened. Longwy, an ugly town of 80,000 people in a narrow valley beside the Luxemburg frontier, was the centre worst menaced by the Barre plan. This one-industry town had already suffered from earlier cuts, and now its remaining steel workforce of 12,700 was due to be halved. Disaster loomed. Then in January the reaction began. Autonomous groups of young workers held their factory managers prisoner, attacked a police station, halted trains, occupied Government offices and threw the files out of the window. At first the union leaders seemed powerless, but finally the CGT managed to take control of the revolt and prevent it getting out of hand. Elsewhere in Lorraine the CGT had been losing support: but Longwy was, and is, a Communist bastion, and so for the next few weeks the CGT and the Party virtually ran the town. Their aim was to score a victory over Paris and force Barre to climb down, but without the odium of provoking violence. They set up a pirate radio station in the *mairie*, calling on all the workers of France to show solidarity in their fight. And atop a high slag-heap they put a giant neon sign that blinked out their message through the night:

'*SOS emploi*'. The same slogan was scrawled on walls throughout the steel belt.

By now the Elysée was growing scared that Longwy might indeed spark off a new May '68 in France. So Giscard began to make conciliatory noises. In mid-February he announced that he understood the 'despair and fury' of men who had worked for decades in the same plant. He also put pressure on Barre, not to modify the cutbacks but to find ways of alleviating their impact. So the Government intensified its efforts to find new replacement firms to move into the steel region. In a time of economic crisis this was not easy, but it was possible – and Barre had clearly been imprudent in his timing: he should have delayed the announcement of the steel closures until some agreement had been reached on alternative investment. But the Government had underestimated the likely extent of the steelworkers' enraged reactions.

The *deus ex machina* was Ford Motor Company, which it so happened was then thinking of setting up a large new assembly plant somewhere in Europe, with 8,000 jobs. At the Elysée Giscard ceremoniously received Henry Ford, who expressed active interest in Longwy! Soon Ford's high-powered prospectors were buzzing around the doomed steel town. As Giscard hoped, this potent new threat to their home market quickly struck panic into the hearts of France's own car firms, so the Government was able to twist their arms. *Dirigisme* thundered into action: 'If you don't agree *now* to invest in Lorraine, we'll sign up with Ford', was the message spelt out clearly to Renault and Peugeot-Citroën. And it worked. To this day, it is not clear whether the Government was bluffing: was it really ready to let the Americans in? Or was it using Ford as a weapon of blackmail? Given the official policy – as described earlier – of preferring 'French solutions' in key industries such as automobiles, it is probable that Giscard was almost as keen as the French car firms to keep Ford out if possible. At all events, that is what happened. Ford dropped out of the picture, and within weeks Renault, Peugeot-Citroën and a few smaller concerns (in electronics etc.) had agreed to invest in new plant providing 6,000 or so jobs by 1983, in Longwy and some other steel towns. This meant an abrupt addition to their own forward investment plans, involving economic risk, and they took the step reluctantly. But they had little choice. The episode provides a striking example of what many people may see as the positive side of *dirigisme*: the ability of a strong French State to dictate its law to industry, when needs be. Admittedly, Renault is State-owned: but in theory at least it is master of its own investment policies.

The workers were encouraged, but still far from pacified. They saw that the new jobs would not be arriving until at least two or three years after their own lay-offs, and that the new investment would still leave a shortfall of 10,000 or so jobs in Lorraine alone. So, under further pressure, the Government agreed on a series of indemnities that were far more generous than anything originally planned. Early retirement, with pensions of up to 90 per cent of wages, was granted to 12,000 workers aged fifty or more, in Lorraine and the Nord; a further 4,000 were offered retraining schemes, with guarantees of finding new jobs in other sectors; and 6,500 staff, mostly young ones, took advantage of lump sums of 50,000 francs each as golden handshakes. All this was worked out voluntarily, with no enforced sackings, at an eventual cost to the State of 7 billion francs. But the social objective was achieved: Longwy soon returned to outward calm. However an undercurrent of unease remained. Some workers feared, with reason, that the automobile jobs might prove equally vulnerable. Many of them resented the 'indignity' of having to turn to ordinary car production after the 'nobility' of the steel trade with its specialized skills. 'There's a psychological trauma,' one union leader told me in Longwy; 'steel has existed here for so long that it's hard for people to adapt to any other work. They can still hardly understand why their world has come crashing around their ears.' By the end of 1979 a ghostly quiet had settled over the town, as older laid-off workers took to cultivating their gardens – literally – and younger ones hung listlessly around the bars and cafés, wondering whether to retrain or move off to another region. Indeed, through all the long years of French steel crises this has been one of the problems: the lack of mobility of labour in France (see p. 176). Peasants will leave the land and move to far-off cities, but industrial workers expect new jobs to be brought to *them*; and Lorrains more than most are attached to their homeland. In the early 1970s about 2,000 of them did agree to move to the new steelworks at Fos, but they saw this more as an exile than a move to the sunny paradise of Provence. And in the big crisis of 1978–9, the unions firmly opposed any further mass exodus from the grey skies and northerly climate of beloved Lorraine. It did not make Barre's task any easier.

However, all sides finally emerged from the crisis with the feeling that they had won something. The workers got the compensation and security they needed. The Government had bought industrial peace, at a price, and was now able to enforce on the steel firms the rationalization that it considered essential. Official economists, after doing their sums, were claiming that the heavy budgetary cost of the pay-offs could be amortized within three or four years, in terms of the firms' improved viability. And the firms had won the aid they needed for this change, albeit at the short-term price of their freedom. Several uneconomic blast furnaces were quickly closed, and the Lorraine workforce, 84,000 in

1974, was being pared down to 41,000. As a result, productivity rose by some 30 per cent in 1979–80, moving close to German and Belgian levels and well ahead of British and Italian ones.

A victory of sorts, it seems. Sacilor began to lose money less heavily, while Usinor even showed a modest profit for the first half of 1980. But, alas for the Barre rescue plan, world market conditions worsened, and in November 1980 the EEC countries felt obliged to limit voluntarily their steel production for a period of at least eight months. Rapidly it became clear that only an upturn in the world economy would enable the French steel firms to draw full benefit from Barre's draconian measures. Viability might still be some way off. Yet Barre in the circumstances had clearly taken the best course open to him, and he seemed to have vindicated his basic philosophy: that between killing off a lame industry and shoring it up wastefully there can be a third and more positive solution. At a price, he had won a battle in his crusade to cure the weaknesses of France's older industries.

Today the steel industry is presenting the new Socialist Government with one of its first major policy tests. Barre's lay-offs have clearly not been enough, and a further 30,000 jobs may now have to be lost in steel for the firms to become viable. Yet the Socialists – for political and doctrinal reasons – are likely to be more lenient with lame ducks than was Barre. They may prefer to put public money into shoring up the steel industry, rather than risk a fresh crisis on their hands in Lorraine. So a tussle may well develop within the Government, between the economic 'realists' such as Delors, who might wish to follow a Barre-type line, and those on the Left who will want jobs to be saved at any price. In any event, the two big steel groups have now been fully nationalized, a logical end to a process already begun. And few tears have been shed. But the State is also taking over some far more successful big firms, in such advanced sectors as electronics and aeronautics. Here the advantages of public ownership are less evident. So let us now look briefly at some of the most brilliant of France's post-war industrial ventures.

CARS, AIRCRAFT, COMPUTERS: THE TRIUMPHS AND TROUBLES OF ADVANCED TECHNOLOGY

The automobile has been *the* success-story of post-war French industry, and today French cars are everywhere: the tough Peugeot 504 on the dirt-roads of Africa, the sleek Citroën CX outside rich men's homes from Munich to Melbourne, the compact little Renault 5 in the streets of New York where it is marketed as 'Le Car'. How has it all been achieved? – through a mixture of dynamic salesmanship, bold investment (State-encouraged), concern for quality, and a flair for technical innovation. Ever since the pioneering days of Panhard and Louis Renault in the 1890s, the car industry has held a place of honour in this land of creative engineers; and today the emphasis is still on daring new ideas of design, comfort and fuel economy.

After the war the shattered industry rebuilt itself, and already by the late 1950s it was strongly placed as the world's fourth car-producer and France's chief exporter. Since then its growth has been second only to Japan's and its output is now nearly three times that of Britain. One motivating factor has been the French public's mania for cars (see p. 442), which helps to keep the home market buoyant. The French have built a popular mystique around the national makes: the robustness of Peugeots, the bizarre ingenuity of Citroëns, the dexterity and economy of Renaults – these have become legendary. After the war France concentrated first on small cheap cars such as the Renault 4 CV and the tin-can Citroën 2 CV, but then she moved also into larger, elegant saloon models such as the big whale-like Citroëns. However, her *forte* today is still her range of smaller family cars, and her speciality is the relatively low petrol consumption of even the larger vehicles. This helps to keep her exports high, in an oil-anxious age. It is one reason why – so far – her car industry has weathered the post-1973 crisis better than most of its foreign competitors.

Current annual production of over three million cars comes from just two giant groups: the nationalized Renault, and the private Peugeot-Citroën (which since 1978 includes the former Chrysler Europe). These are the two largest automobile groups in Europe, and among the six largest in the world. Concentration is thus more advanced than in any other French industrial sector: the firms, and the Government, believe this to be necessary in order to stand up to the American and Japanese titans. France sells abroad just over half her output, and annual exports exceed imports by some 1.8 million vehicles to 670,000; Britain's equation is almost the reverse!

Louis Renault founded his firm in 1899. He was a young self-taught mechanic who in the manner of Ford or Nuffield built the firm over the next forty years into one of Europe's leading car companies. In 1944 he was charged with Nazi collaboration; the State confiscated his empire and, this being the era of nationalizations, decided to hold on to it. Some inspired technocrats were put in to run it on commercial lines, and straightway they made it into a torch-bearer for all French industry. Its central factory at Billancourt, in the Paris suburbs, was the first in Europe to use automation, in 1946. And soon there poured off its assembly lines a remarkable new baby car, the *'Quatre Chevaux'* (i.e. 4 h.p.), which had been planned secretly during the war by Renault technicians. The 4 C V was a symbol of the social philosophy which was then to guide the Régie Renault, notably under its former chairman, Pierre Dreyfus (today Minister of Industry). This technocrat–humanist regarded the car as a social instrument to which every family had a right, a novel idea in the France of those austere early years. So he concentrated on the mass turnout of small and cheap cars, the models gradually growing in size only as French living standards rose. Thus in 1956 the 4 C V began to give place to the slightly larger Dauphine, one of the most brilliant small cars of its day; and this in turn gave place to the larger R 10. Today Renault has a complete range, up to the 2,664 c.c. R 30: but its most popular model today is the trim and sturdy little R 5, ideal for coping with rising petrol prices and kerbside parking, which in 1980 was capturing 15 per cent of the French domestic market.

Another feature of the Dreyfus philosophy, rare in those days, was that a firm owes its workers more than just good wages. With discreet State backing, Renault after the war led the field in welfare and labour relations, often to the annoyance of more staid private firms. Not only does the Régie spend an unusual amount of money on housing, education and other schemes for its workers, but in 1954 it pioneered a new kind of labour charter, the Convention Collective. This committed the firm to regular annual wage increases, in return for a commitment by the unions not to strike except as a last resort. The charter was later adopted by many other industries. For years it worked well at Renault: yet it did not prevent the May '68 uprising, when it came, from being fiercer and lasting longer than in most other French firms, and this was followed by other strikes in 1971 and 1975. Maybe one explanation is that *les métallos de chez Renault*, well paid and politically sophisticated, are critical of the firm's paternalism. Materially privileged, they are more open than most French workers to new ideas of self-management (see pp. 104–5).

Renault has been through many ups and down over the years and not always has it shown a profit. It had a bad patch in the mid-'60s, after over-extending its model range. But today it seems to have fully recovered its earlier dynamism, stimulated by the challenge of harder world conditions. Its lorry division (Saviem/Berliet) is not doing too well: but today the Régie has an intelligent policy of diversification, to guard against the day when the world car and lorry markets may slump for good and all, and so it now also makes machine tools, farm machinery, bicycles, marine engines and much else. Renault has often been cited as a rare example in the West of a nationalized firm that is commercially successful, and inevitably this raises the question of what are its real relations with the State. The latter appoints its chairman, and expects to be kept informed of its long-term policies. But it gives the Régie no privileged loans, and does not interfere in its routine management which is that of any private firm. Seeing that Renault is operating in a field of intense world competition, this is the only sane solution. It cannot be treated like domestic monopolies such as the Post Office or State railways, under the scrutiny of bureaucrats. In a land where industry habitually submits to some Government guidance, Renault does so very little more than any private firm.

Citroën, Renault's old rival, could hardly be more different. From 1934 until its take-over by Peugeot in 1974–6, Citroën was controlled by the Michelin tyre company which had bought it when its founder, André Citroën, went bankrupt. The Michelin family empire remains the most arrogant and fanatically secretive in French industry, and Citroën took its colouring from them. It treated unions with a chilly disdain. Even a new executive recruit was first screened to make sure he had no Left-wing views. Modern methods too were frowned on: Citroën would scorn publicity, take little trouble with exports and handle many domestic clients with cavalier contempt. American doctrines of planned obsolescence were equally disregarded: Citroën believed in making cars that, like the 2 CV, could be kept in production for twenty years or more. And such was the firm's mechanical genius that it was able to get away with these methods, and in the early 1960s it made the best progress of any French car firm.

Now that Michelin has sold control of Citroën to Peugeot, the approach has been changing. No longer does Citroën neglect advertising and exports. But its Normandy testing-ground for new models is still guarded by ten-foot walls and patrols of vicious dogs, and maybe wisely: the firm's dedicated team of designers work two decades ahead of production, and it depends on its reputation for unrivalled advance in design. Those cars with their weird shapes are solidly reliable: the internals are designed first, then the body is planned round them. Born in 1948, the famous old 2 CV may look like an old tin can, but it is comfortable and resilient, does 50 miles to the gallon, and has been called 'the world's most intelligent car'. Its newer and less inelegant sister version, the Dyane, is still selling well. The big frog-nosed DS and ID, and the newer CX, are noted for their road-holding, comfort and hydro-pneumatic suspension which makes them flop gently when they stop, like tired elephants. They have been the official ministerial car in many countries, including France. De Gaulle had a fleet at the Elysée, and twice he owed his life to their excellent wheels and brakes: once, in a night storm, when a tree fell across his path, and then when he was shot at by the OAS and his chauffeur had to make a quick get-away on bullet-punctured tyres.

Peugeot, with its main factory at Sochaux in the Jura, is a family firm controlled by a wealthy and clannish Protestant dynasty: several members of its board are Peugeots. If less so than at Michelin, the accent here too is on aloofness, pride and discretion: the head office in Paris with its black glass façade does not even have the company's name outside it. Peugeot does all it can to discourage unions and expects total fidelity from its staff, in the old paternalist style. It conducts its affairs with a Protestant thoroughness and prudence; and its cars, like their makers, are sober and reliable, with qualities that might seem more German than French. Their reputation for toughness has been proven by frequent victories in Safari rallies.

In the earlier post-war years the car industry's task was simply to meet the needs of a hungry domestic market which in 1945 had only a million cars on the roads. But then Renault began to pioneer exports. Foreseeing the way the world car market was likely to move in the free-trade '60s, it did not want France to be left out of the new competition. So in 1957 it attacked the US market, with unexpected initial success: the Americans had never seen a car so small or cute as the Dauphine before, and they bought 200,000 in three years, often as playthings for wife or kids. But Detroit hit back with its own small cars, the 'compacts'. Then the mighty Volkswagen arrived on the American scene, and Renault retreated in defeat, eclipsed by a swarm of Beetles.

By the mid-'60s the French had come to realize that having four separate rival firms was an extravagance (the fourth was Simca, controlled by Chrysler since 1963). They must group together, with each other or with outside partners. First Dreyfus proposed non-aggression pacts in turn to Volkswagen, Fiat and Ford, but was quietly snubbed: 'We'll lick you because we're stronger,' said Henry Ford II. Then in 1966 Renault startled the car world by announcing an association with Peugeot, for some joint production. This soon helped to revive the Régie's flagging fortunes – but it left Citroën looking very isolated: for all its technical prowess, the weaknesses of its haughty management policy were telling, and by the late '60s its sales were dropping badly. Citroën saw that in the new age of battle between giants it might have to modify its splendidly quirky behaviour, and so it reached for *ententes* with more orthodox firms. When in 1968 Agnelli of Fiat offered to buy 45 per cent of its assets for a new Fiat-Citroën holding company in France, the Michelin family said yes; but de Gaulle said no. He knew the deal would soon lead to Citroën being swallowed up by its more dynamic Italian partner. A compromise was allowed, with Fiat taking 15 per cent: but neither side found this very helpful, and Fiat withdrew in 1973. It was another failure for the ideal of inter-EEC mergers preached by the federalists.

So Citroën, now losing money faster than ever, turned to an obvious saviour: Peugeot, with its spectacular record of expansion. This time the Michelin family sank their pride in a big way: in two stages in 1974–6 they sold 90 per cent of their interest in Citroën to Peugeot, which secured a massive State loan for the purpose. Peugeot/Citroën, each with some 19 per cent of the French home market, were now ahead of Renault (35 per cent). The latter's technical tie-up with Peugeot continued, but was phased down. The Peugeot/Citroën merger has since worked out well, and Citroën's fortunes have revived now that its innovative genius is backed by Peugeot's sound management. 'Our success has been due to the marriage of two very different firms,' a Peugeot chief told me in 1979; 'we allow each to keep its own image, personality and sales network, while behind the scenes we integrate production and spare parts.'

Peugeot, with its added size and confidence, now set its sights on the top world league. In a move characteristic of the way French industry works, it bought over an élite civil servant as its new Chief Executive: Jean-Paul Parayre, handsome, fortyish, a *polytechnicien* with a senior job in the Ministry of Industry. This ambitious technocrat, so it seemed, would give Peugeot's family management the extra thrust and world vision that it needed. And it so happened that the ailing Chrysler was then looking for a buyer for its European factories, in France (Simca), Britain and Spain. In August 1978, in a *coup* that filled all the headlines, Parayre bought these up for $230 million plus some $200 millions worth of stock, thus making Peugeot the largest car group in Europe and the fourth in the world. 'This decisive step,' he declared, 'will give us the size required to face up to our biggest rivals. The brutal expansion of Japanese car companies, and the American industry's switchover to more internationally acceptable models, means competition on a global scale.' Also, it pleased French national pride that Simca after fifteen years had been bought back from the Americans! But, alas for Parayre, Peugeot has since been finding it none too easy to digest its Chrysler catch, today renamed Talbot. The UK factories, long plagued by strikes and low productivity, proved a very dubious acquisition, and in fact at the end of 1980 Peugeot decided to close the plant at Linwood, near Glasgow – to the fury of the Scots. In face of growing world recession, Peugeot also had to pare down its Talbot operation inside France. It was soon clear that Parayre had not made such a clever *coup* after all.

However, this has not prevented Peugeot-Citroën from forging ahead with their own cars on world markets. Renault and Peugeot-Citroën today have both developed into big multinationals with world-wide activities. And in an age when recession may at any moment cripple all but the most efficient firms, both are following similar global strategies: the streamlining of production through joint ventures where possible; the relentless search for new markets; vigorous investment abroad. In France itself, these firms have each built new factories in the past decades: Renault in Le Mans, Normandy, the Nord; Peugeot in Mulhouse; Citroën in Rennes, Lorraine, the Ardennes; and so on. They have also embarked on joint ventures in France: thus in the Lille area Renault operates a gearbox factory with Peugeot, and an engine plant with Peugeot and Volvo, so that the rival cars – the Renault 20 and the Peugeot 505 – actually have the same engine!

Abroad, Renault and Peugeot have both recently started joint ventures with Fiat in Italy, while Citroën and Peugeot own factories in South America and South Africa. Peugeot-Citroën's investment policy is especially bold. Citroën in 1976 signed a contract with the Rumanian Government for a new factory there, now turning out a special model: the plant is operated by a joint subsidiary, owned 30 per cent by Citroën and 70 per cent by the Rumanian State: a notable example of a joint venture with a Communist country. Peugeot's main foreign operation has been in Nigeria, where in 1973 in face of strong competition it won a contract with the Lagos Government for the building of a jointly owned factory at Kaduna for the assembly of its 304, 404 and 504 models. To ship out the components, Peugeot set up a veritable airlift, with several large planes leaving France each day. Nigeria has recently overtaken West Germany to become Peugeot's leading export market. An executive summed up to me the group's foreign expansion policy: 'We are pragmatic, we seize our chances where we can – we want to get in first and not leave the market to others. It is now becoming harder to set up our *own* companies abroad, in the Third World for instance, for those countries now want to develop their own car industries: so the answer lies in joint ventures with them, as in Nigeria and Rumania. In the longer term we may find ourselves competed against by the plant we have thus helped to build, but we have no other choice: if *we* didn't go ahead with these ventures our rivals would do so, and we'd lose out even more.'

Renault's *forte* is exports: 57 per cent of its product is sold abroad. One reason for this success is that it has built up its own world-wide sales force, with 10,000 dealers. Also it has assembly plants in twenty-six countries across five continents, accounting for over a third of its output. And now, like Peugeot-Citroën, it is turning more and more to joint ventures, too, with big expansions for example in Mexico, Turkey and

Portugal. Above all, like some other large French companies, it is joining in the lucrative new French sport of invading the United States. After its setbacks in the 1960s, Renault renewed its export campaign there recently and has had some success with the R 5 ('Le Car'), helped by the new American preference for small cars. But, like other European car firms, it has found itself hampered by American anti-pollution regulations, and by the dollar's fluctuations. So the answer is clear: wheel in your Trojan horse and, as in the Third World, build or assemble *inside* the American citadel. This Renault is now doing, on a joint venture basis. In 1979–80 it took a 46 per cent stake in American Motors, the fourth largest US car maker, and from 1982 in A M's factories the two firms will jointly produce a new Renault model conceived for the American market. Meanwhile, Peugeot-Citroën has followed up its purchase of Chrysler Europe with another big deal with Chrysler: the American firm is to help the French group to sell its cars in the United States, and later it will assist with their manufacture there too. Lafayette must be smiling in his grave. De Gaulle too.

Renault and Peugeot-Citroën are today locked in a fierce but fertile rivalry, both at home and abroad. After Peugeot's leap forward in 1978, Renault hit back so strongly that it soon caught up again. In 1980 its share of domestic sales was 40.5 per cent, against the Peugeot group's 37, the rest being imports. In the first crisis years of 1974–5 France's car industry took a heavy jolt as in other countries, but it soon bounced back with almost the same resilience as in Germany and Japan – and far more than in Britain, Italy or the US – and in 1975–8 annual output rose from 2,544,000 to 3,113,000. Then 1979 was a record year, in terms of numbers of cars sold. But in 1980–81 France was hit by the shock-waves of the new recession spreading from the United States, and this time, while Renault stood up well, Peugeot-Citroën faltered. In 1980 the group's sales fell by 20 per cent, some factories were put on short-timing, and a trading loss was registered of over 2 billion francs, Peugeot's first annual loss since the war. The group had overreached itself, partly due to Parayre's miscalculations. It was a sad and sudden decline, after Peugeot's years of steady expansion, and it proved once again how mercurial are the motor industry's fortunes in today's world.

So the French car industry is braced for hard times ahead. But, unlike steel, textiles and some other sectors, it now faces problems that are largely external and world-wide and no longer due to its own weaknesses. It has made mistakes since the war but on the whole has modernized brilliantly, learning that the only way to stand up to General Motors is to imitate it. The industry has a number of assets. One is the completeness of its model range, especially in the lower and middle brackets, with intelligent family cars such as the Renault 18, the Peugeot 305 and the new Citroën Visa, all well suited to the new motoring climate. Even a larger French model such as the tank-like Renault 16 (I myself have owned two, since 1973) is far more nimble and *nerveuse* (responsive) than its average British or even German counterpart. Above all, since 1973 French backroom experts have been applying their traditional flair to the great problem of the day, that of fuel economy – and with some success. They have introduced diesel models that are almost as pleasant to drive as normal ones. And through improvements to engines and body aerodynamics they have brought down petrol consumption by an average 10 per cent since 1973, with a further similar cut expected by 1985: France here is equalling the great American fuel-saving efforts. So, while the trade unions cry woe, the manufacturers retain a guarded optimism for the future. A Peugeot chief said: 'The untapped potential in the Third World is so vast that the danger of saturation in the West is not such a problem.' And Gilles Guérithault, editor of the leading motor magazine *L'Auto-Journal*, told me in 1980: 'For thirty years now in this business I've been hearing prophecies of instant doom, and I'll believe it when I see it. People now will want smaller and cheaper cars – but more and more of them will still want cars. And the French have the flair to adapt quickly to any new demand.' We shall see.

France's aviation industry has shown equal flair and brilliance since the war. Its one big commercial failure, Concorde, was less its own fault than that of Anglo-French governmental bungling. Today the industry is much the most successful in Europe, pace-setter in the Airbus consortium and leading producer and exporter of helicopters and military aircraft too.

National pride is heavily involved, especially as the French have been pioneers of aviation since the days of Blériot, the first man to fly across the Channel, in 1909. In the first part of the century France's aircraft industry led the world: but by 1945, after working half-heartedly for the Germans, it was nearly derelict. Its main firm, Sud-Est Aviation of Toulouse, was reduced to making refrigerators, and for the next few years French factories looking for employment had to fall back on producing British or American models under licence. But the renaissance in the next decade was spectacular. Sud-Est was one of several aircraft firms that had been nationalized in 1936;[3] and in 1946 the Government put at its head a gifted young technocrat, Georges Héreil. He rapidly

3 Its name was changed to Sud-Aviation in 1957, after a merger, and then in 1970 to Aérospatiale (or S N I A S, acronym of its full title) after more mergers with other firms. Today Aérospatiale is still entirely State owned.

rebuilt the firm's workshops and began to plot how to restore France's position. With over 90 per cent of world construction in American hands, the problem was to find a weak point, an aircraft no one else had yet made. The answer, it seemed, was a fast, medium-range twin-jet: so in 1952 the Government gave Héreil the go-ahead and the funds for the Caravelle. This was the full measure of the French triumph: to have succeeded in creating the Caravelle at a time when the British and American industries with their wartime experience were still far ahead in expertise.

Héreil took a gamble that few private firms then would have dared. Believing that the Americans would not bring a similar jet into service before the early '60s, he insisted that the Caravelle be ready by 1959. This meant taking the unusual risk of investing 400 million francs in an initial batch of forty before any airline, even Air France, had placed orders. For three years a team of engineers and designers worked round the clock, in Toulouse, capital of the aviation industry. The operation was almost wholly French, save for the Rolls Royce engines. Air France had the first Caravelles in service by 1959, as planned: they were an immediate success, and other airlines such as Alitalia and S A S began to buy in some numbers. The Caravelle's speed (500 m.p.h.), its silence, comfort, and resistance to fatigue, put it ahead of other aircraft in its class. On a trial flight to Rome, it was blessed by the Pope.

A total of 286 Caravelles were sold to thirty-four airlines before production ceased in 1972: it was by far the most successful European plane of its day. But Héreil largely failed in his ambition of breaking into the American market: he persuaded United Airlines to buy a score, but other US airlines fought shy, partly because Boeing was preparing something even better – the 727, which soon far outstripped Caravelle's world sales. So the latter's dent in the US-dominated world market, though impressive by European standards, remained modest. Aérospatiale also made the mistake – not since repeated with Airbus – of failing to follow up Caravelle with a generation of related models. Instead, the firm fell victim to an Anglo-French governmental miscalculation that the world long-distance market was about to turn supersonic and Europe must not miss out. Soon, Aérospatiale and the British Aircraft Corporation were jointly at work on the greatest winged white elephant of all time. Enough ink has been spilt on this sorry Concorde affair, and I shall add only a few brief comments. First, Héreil's successors had argued against the project from the start, but they were shouted down by prestige-hungry Governments. Second, Concorde should either have been killed in the bud, or built rapidly: no doubt it could never have paid its way, but it was the delays caused by endless Whitehall shilly-shallying that hugely added to its final deficit. Thirdly, though misconceived commercially, in terms of technology the aircraft was another triumph for French aviation; and visitors to Toulouse were always impressed by the enthusiasm and dedication of the men at work on the prototypes. They were let down by the politicians and sales experts. In the end, the 'captive' Air France and British Airways were the *only* airlines that bought the fourteen Concordes built for sale, and five of these were given to them as presents in 1979 after no other takers had emerged. It would have seemed an unrelieved tragedy, were not Airbus by then doing so well.

·   The long political wrangles and delay over Concorde did not prove that such joint projects are impossible; simply that they need to be tackled differently. No one European country on its own can today make a major civil aircraft for the world market: but the technical and practical cooperation must involve the minimum of Government interference. This is the lesson that Airbus has learned from Concorde. And the six-nation Airbus Industrie, set up in 1970, is a consortium of aircraft firms, with Governments' roles limited to providing financial backing and overall blessing. This is working well. Aérospatiale and its German, British, Dutch and Spanish partners each make elements of the Airbus A 300, which is then assembled at Toulouse (the Belgians have now joined in too for the new smaller model, the A 310). Aérospatiale and Deutsche Airbus GmbH are *ex aequo* the major partners, each with some 33 per cent involvement: but in practice the French are the dominant force in the whole operation, for Germany's post-war aircraft industry is younger, smaller and less experienced.

Airbus A 300 is a wide-bodied subsonic 250-seater, ideal for medium-range routes and a far more realistic project than Concorde. The first models went into service in 1974, with Air France. But world sales at first were sluggish – only one plane was sold in 1976! – for Airbus could not have been born at a less happy moment, in the wake of the first energy crisis. But then the world market picked up, and when America's Eastern Airlines ordered thirty-two the breakthrough began. By 1981, some thirty-three airlines the world over had bought or ordered a total of well over four hundred models of the A 300 and the slimmer 200-seat A 310 (due to be ready in 1982): orders were coming in so fast that production could not keep up with demand. Airbus had cornered a third of the world market in aircraft of its kind: its sales were running second only to Boeing's, having far outstripped those of its two other American rivals, Lockheed TriStar and the DC–10. The mood in Toulouse was triumphant. A French official at Airbus Industrie told me: 'Europe has proved at last that it *can* cooperate effectively, to avert the danger of an

American monopoly. And we are preparing a family of other models for the future: we shall not repeat our mistake with Caravelle, which never had a valid successor.' To cover its production costs, Airbus needs to sell eight hundred. This figure is still a long way off, but the consortium is confident that it can be reached, since the world demand for medium-range aircraft is estimated at nearly three thousand for the decade ahead.

Aérospatiale has also been stepping up its output of helicopters (see p. 98), both military and civil, of which it is the world's third largest producer after Bell and Sikorsky. It exports to ninety-four countries, and has made a big dent in the American civil market. The firm makes a sizeable profit on its helicopters, as it does on its large output of missiles. But losses on Concorde have been so great that Aérospatiale was in the red eight years running in the 1970s and is only now starting to show a profit again. This State-owned company is run on commercial lines: but in practice, partly because of the nature of its product, much of it military, it is more closely supervised than Renault. This State backing brings some advantages, allowing it to take risks that a private firm might not dare; equally, it can lead Aérospatiale into dubious politically inspired adventures that a private firm might avoid.

France's other major aircraft producer, Dassault-Breguet, is one of the two or three most brilliantly successful firms in France. Much has been due to its founder and principal owner, the legendary Marcel Dassault, now aged ninety, an aircraft fanatic who began designing planes himself in 1918 and is now reputedly the richest man in France. Though now retired, he is still an inspirational force behind his company, which exports 80 per cent of its product. Its speciality is military aircraft, notably the famous Mystères and Mirages, which have been sold in large numbers around the world: Dassault sold 1,400 Mirage III multi-role fighters, over a thousand of them for export to twenty-two countries including such dear friends as Libya, Israel and South Africa. In the civil field, Dassault has also done well with its small executive jet, the Falcon: five hundred have been sold, many of them to American tycoons. Today, the company is embarked on the biggest gamble in its history. At a cost of 6,000 million francs it has developed the prototype of a highly sophisticated twinjet Mach 2.5 strike aircraft, the Mirage 4000 – but before the placing of a single order. The French Air Force said it could not afford so expensive a plane, so for once there are no State funds. But Dassault is banking on being able to sell it to richer countries than France, notably in the Arab world: the Saudis have been showing an interest. Even so, the risk involved is enormous. Under Giscard, the State took a 20 per cent interest in Dassault, and this has now been increased to 51 per cent by the Socialists. They will control more strictly its military sales to 'aggressive' or Right-wing regimes; but otherwise they are unlikely to change its style of operation. They will try at least to help it to retain its old flair, a virtuoso pace-setter in France's strategy of high-technology exports.

France's aircraft industry today has a productivity more than twice as high as Britain's: it employs only 105,000 people, against 219,000 in Britain, yet its sales are 15 per cent higher. Several factors underlie the industry's post-war success. Not only does the Government help it in various ways, notably with funds for investment in prototypes (the Mirage 4000 is a rare exception): it also has promoted the most intensive system of air education in the West. The aeronautical Grandes Ecoles have expanded fast and enjoy high prestige. Private aero-clubs flourish too: there are 23,000 licensed pilots in France. Since Blériot's day the French have been an air-minded people; and the idealistic pilot Saint-Exupéry, who died on air service in 1944, has always been one of the most popular authors among French young. So the success of Aéro-spatiale and Dassault stems from this background of national enthusiasm and scientific progress.

In other advanced modern industries – computers, micro-electronics, telecommunications, space-satellites etc. – the French have had to face a choice between trying to go it alone, taking the lead in European joint ventures or, where this is not feasible, accepting a degree of dependence on American know-how. In computers, back in the 1960s the Government reluctantly came to accept that French or even European independence was just not possible: American techniques were too far ahead. So a dual policy was launched. On the one hand, American investment was encouraged: the Bull takeover was permitted, and IBM was allowed to build up its strength in France. At the same time, the French tried to develop their own national computer programme, with the creation in 1967 of the State-backed Compagnie Internationale pour l'Informatique (CII). But this soon found itself unable to compete with the American giants, so in 1973 a European venture was launched, with a tie-up between CII, Siemens and Philips. But this too failed. So the Government sank its pride and turned to the only practicable alternative: CII formed a combine with the American-controlled Honeywell-Bull (Honeywell having by now taken over General Electric's interests in Bull). This was soon working well. Though relying heavily on American technology, the semi-autonomous French group CII-Honeywell-Bull had majority French ownership and by 1981 was operating on about the same scale as its big American partner. In integrated and micro-circuits, too, some leading French firms such as Thomson-CSF, St-Gobain and

Matra all launched into joint ventures with US companies, thus gaining access to the latest American technology without too heavy a sacrifice of national independence. For years the French had been obsessed by the fear that they were falling behind in the race towards the new technologies: but now they have been catching up, in these key sectors of electronics, by associating with American companies or borrowing their techniques. Today, most of these big electronics firms are being nationalized. Whether they will fully retain their dynamism remains to be seen. But the Socialists claim that they are anxious to maintain the national emphasis on advanced electronics; and the policy of joint ventures with the Americans will probably continue too.

In telecommunications, the French have been much more successful in developing their own advanced industries single-handed. The ordinary French telephone service (see p. 183) has finally been improved out of all recognition in the past decade, thanks to a massive input of State funds; and within this context a number of private firms have been encouraged to pioneer some of the world's most sophisticated modern techniques in videophones, digital switching systems and remote data processing. These do well on the export market. Another achievement is in space satellites, where the French are leading an ambitious joint European project. It was de Gaulle in 1960 who initiated France's own space programme: the results were meagre, and he was accused of useless and costly prestige-hunting. But the venture has since borne some fruit. Today ten nations are involved in the European Space Agency's programme for the Ariane space rockets, under French technical management. The first launch, in French Guyana in 1979, was a success. Since then, there have been a few delays and setbacks, and the American space shuttle's triumph has devalued Ariane a little. But the project still goes ahead, with another successful launch in 1981. Ariane models have been ordered by Intelsat, the international agency, and this is expected to enable French industry to pick up a share of the lucrative new world market for satellites. 'Our space programme is more than a matter of prestige, it is also big business,' one French scientist told me eagerly; 'France is now the world's third power in space. We've smashed the American-Soviet monopoly.' The money thus earned – as from cars and aircraft – will hopefully go some of the way towards paying for France's energy imports. These, like Ariane, have gone rocketing upwards.

NUCLEAR EXPANSION:
GISCARD PLANS BOLDLY THEN MITTERRAND MODIFIES

France is endowed with relatively few natural energy resources of her own – hydro-electricity, some gas, coal-mines now wearing very thin – that is about all. So during the heady years of industrial growth she had to turn more and more to imports for her supplies: oil imports rose rapidly from 26.9 million tons in 1960 to 116.3 million in 1973; but this did not seem to matter too much as oil was cheap. Then the oil price explosion hit France harder than most of her peers, for she has to import nearly 75 per cent of her energy needs, against an EEC average of 55 per cent. Her oil bill for 1980 was 120 billion francs.

For a nation always so concerned with its independence, the post-1973 situation was alarming politically as well as economically. And France has reacted to the energy challenge more determinedly than almost any other industrial power. Today she is pursuing a four-point strategy: vigorous conservation measures; increased imports of cheap coal; a search for new forms of energy, notably biomass and solar; and nuclear growth. Under Giscard, France's nuclear programme was the most advanced and ambitious in the world, and ecological protests were not allowed to deflect it. After a slow start in the nuclear field, the oil crisis shocked France into action: while in 1973 nuclear power provided only 1 per cent of her energy, by 1981 nearly 30 per cent of her electricity was nuclear-generated, and Giscard's aim was to increase this to 70 per cent by 1990. Today the Socialists are cutting back on Giscard's programme, but less radically than had been expected. France is still going for nuclear growth.

Of France's own natural energy resources, the coal-mines were nationalized just after the war and then modernized so well that productivity for a while was the highest in Europe. Output was pushed up to 60 million tons a year. But all the principal mines – in the Lille area, Lorraine and the southern Massif Central – are today nearing exhaustion and many have closed completely. French coal, mostly poor in quality and hard to extract, now works out 60 per cent more expensive than imported coal: so domestic production is down to some 21 million tons a year, while 30 millions are imported, from all over the world. But this does not mean that France is ceasing to rely on coal: far from it. Not only are imports increasing, but the Coal Board and the State-backed oil companies are being encouraged to buy up foreign mines – in Australia, South Africa, America – so as to ensure some national control over supplies. A typical French policy. Thus Total has acquired a 50 per cent share in a mine in Wyoming. And industries at home are being urged, where possible, to switch from oil to coal or gas as their main fuel.

Electricity was also nationalized in 1946. And immediately Electricité de France set about planning to exploit every drop of power from a country rich in hydro-electric possibilities, the *houille blanche* ('white coal') as it is called. In the post-war years the EDF built or sponsored more than thirty new dams, mainly in mountain areas and along the Rhône – and very impressive some of them are too. In 1966 EDF also pioneered the world's first tidal power dam, across the Rance estuary in Brittany: but this, though technically interesting, has not proved very profitable and has not led to any sequels. Today, France's hydro-electric potential is almost fully harnessed.

The third main domestic source of raw energy is natural gas. There was great excitement in France after 1951 when the largest deposit yet found on the west European mainland outside Holland was struck at Lacq, north of the Pyrenees near Pau. Today, some 230 acres in this valley are covered with a network of brightly coloured pipes and cylinders, while at night the security flares from the wells blaze out for miles like a city on fire; to make use of the gas and its sulphur by-product, several big industries have settled in the area, making aluminium, fertilizers and so on. The Lacq deposits provide the equivalent of some 7 million tons of coal a year, or nearly a third of France's gas consumption: the rest is imported, mainly from Algeria, Holland and the Soviet Union. But France's own reserves will begin to run dry after about 1985, and scientists expect no major new discoveries. By A D 2000 there may be no more natural gas in France – another argument for the nuclear policy.

Yet whatever the extent of nuclear growth, for many years to come there will probably still be heavy dependence on oil. Even more than in most countries, oil has long been a complex political issue in France, and is seen as affecting sovereignty. Since the 1920s France has been trying to gain more control over the inevitable imports by securing for her own oil industry a degree of independence from the Seven Sisters – and with some success. As a result of mergers, by 1976 the Government had managed to create one mammoth State-controlled company, Elf-Aquitaine, which has been seeking to do for France's oil industry what Mattei for a while did for Italy's. It has made oil-prospecting deals with Middle East countries, thus breaking the American and Anglo-Dutch monopolies there. And thanks to Elf-Aquitaine and the leading private oil firm, the Compagnie Française des Pétroles, about half of French importing and refining is now controlled by French companies – just as the Government had planned. The motives are more political than economic, for France gains little in the way of foreign currency savings.

Until about 1971 the French obtained about 40 per cent of their oil from the Algerian Sahara, where they had joyfully discovered it themselves in colonial days. But Algeria then nationalized remaining French assets and today meets only 3 per cent of French oil needs: the bulk now comes from Iraq and Saudi Arabia. Meanwhile French companies are actively engaged in the ongoing search for oil around the world's oceans, while in offshore technology France has built up an expertise second only to America's. This gives a boost to exports, and to prestige, but does little to solve the vaster problem of oil imports. So the French since 1975 have also been drilling in their own waters, notably off western Brittany. But little has yet emerged save gaseous bubbles, and few scientists think it likely that France can expect any North-Sea-style bonanza.

Therefore Giscard's Government stepped up not only its nuclear effort but also its energy-saving campaign, with a wide range of measures mixing persuasion and compulsion. The public response has been fairly good. A new State agency coordinates the struggle, offering grants to factories for installing fuel-saving devices. Also it is now illegal to heat homes or offices above 19°C even on the coldest day; double-glazing and other forms of insulation, though not yet obligatory, are strongly encouraged; speed limits have been tightened both for cars (see p. 442) and lorries; and the auto industry, as we have seen, is playing its part by trying to devise less fuel-greedy vehicles. It is claimed that these and other measures are so far producing economies equal to 16 million tons of oil a year, and the aim is to increase this figure steadily without jeopardizing either industrial output or living standards. Already oil imports have been reduced since 1973 from 116 to 106 million tons a year.

Another new State agency now coordinates the search for new forms of energy – geothermal, biomass and above all solar. No one expects quick miracle results, given the present state of technology: by 1985 these 'new' energies will still be supplying less than 3 per cent of France's overall needs. But by A D 2000 this figure could be 10 per cent or more, and French research is working for the day when technology may allow a much more important breakthrough in the future. Officially, the French believe strongly in solar energy: with a budget in 1979 of 276 million francs, France's solar programme is second only to that of the United States. The main effort is in the Pyrénées-Orientales (capital, Perpignan), France's sunniest department where Europe's first experimental solar furnace has been active since 1970, at Odeillo: sixty-three big mirrors reflect the sun onto a tower-shaped boiler, backed by a gigantic concave prism of more mirrors. This spectacular apparatus is used for industrial tests on such things as ultra-refractory materials, and has even produced a little electricity just to show that the sun *can* do so.

Now a much larger 95-million-franc power plant, Themis, is being built near by: it will have a 280-foot tower, mirrors spread over fifty acres, and an output of three megawatts. This equals a bare 2 per cent of the department's electricity needs, but Themis is not intended as more than an experimental prototype.

Small solar power stations might before long prove useful in remote Third World areas, where there is plenty of sun but ordinary electric power is costly because of transport: in Europe, however, it will be many years before electricity from solar sources can be made economic. So a debate is going on over the choice of priorities. Some critics argue that the Government is wrong to devote 60 per cent of its solar budget to costly experiments with electricity, where prospects are so uncertain, and that it should do more to promote the much simpler direct use of the sun's heat for domestic purposes. But here too there are problems of viability. In the Pyrenees and elsewhere, a few private houses today use solar panels for central heating, with official subsidies; but, as in other parts of the world, the basic drawbacks have not yet been solved. Not only do the panels make the house façades look ugly, but no effective means of energy storage for central heating has yet been found. So, even in a sunny area, solar panels can in Europe provide only about 40 per cent of a home's year-round needs, and it takes thirty years to amortize the installation costs even though the fuel is free. In France, as in America, scientists are busily trying to find ways of storing the energy through the sunless winter (when the heating is most needed) so as to make the system economic. In the meantime, the only viable domestic use for solar energy lies with water-heaters. It is relatively easy to install a device on a roof that harnesses sunlight to provide hot water for a house, a block of flats, or any public building. France has far fewer of these heaters than Japan or Israel, where sunlight levels are higher, but at last she is making progress: in 1979–80 there was a tripling of the number of homes thus equipped, from 20,000 to 60,000. At present a solar water-heater retails at about twice the price of an ordinary electric one. On average it takes eight years to amortize this difference in terms of saving on fuel bills, and the Government has been trying – with only slow results – to educate the public into seeing this as a useful economy.

Some other new forms of energy offer immediate prospects, too, and one is geothermal. In many parts of France there are underground hot springs, and over 10,000 homes are now equipped for heating from these: the plan is to increase this figure to 500,000 by 1990. France is also starting to exploit her biomass resources: the tapping of solar energy accumulated in trees and other plant life, which some experts believe might be able to yield the equivalent of 25 million tons of oil a year by

AD 2000. And, as in Brazil and some other countries, industrial alcohol is now being introduced experimentally as a part-substitute for petrol in cars. Clearly, these various new schemes offer no early panacea for the energy problems of France or any other nation. But, with the future both of oil supplies and of nuclear safety in doubt, it is certainly right to encourage scientists to work on long-term research into alternative sources of energy. France here is in the lead in Europe.

France has been leading Europe too in nuclear development – amid controversy, and today amid agonizing reappraisal. For many years she has belonged to the military club of atomic Powers (she exploded her first bomb in 1960), but only in the 1970s were the brakes lifted on applying this expertise for making electricity on any scale. De Gaulle pursued a nationalist go-it-alone policy, spurning American technology and relying on home-produced natural uranium gas-cooled reactors. This hardly proved viable, despite the prowess of France's own scientists. But then in 1969 Pompidou made an historic about-turn, switching to the American light-water system based on enriched uranium: he saw it as the only sane economic choice, albeit at the price of some dependence on foreign technology. So a French firm, Framatome, began to build pressurized water reactors under licence from Westinghouse.

When the energy crisis came, the Government was thus in a position to speed up the nuclear programme very fast. By 1980 France was completing new power stations at the rate of some 6,000 megawatts a year; she had twenty reactors in service and another twenty under construction; and every two years she was building as much nuclear plant as Britain had done in the past thirty. France has been helped also by having large uranium deposits of her own, now yielding nearly 2,000 tons a year. Above all, without relying on American technology, the French have become the world's pioneers of the next generation of reactors, the fast-breeders: Superphénix, the 1,200 MW fast-breeder now being completed near Lyon, is due to come onstream in 1983 (it is not affected by the Socialist cut-back), and it places France in the forefront of nuclear technology. 'If Superphénix is successful,' said one American expert, 'the French will have taken a six-year lead on us, and may be able to dominate world markets for nuclear power in the 1990s.' Nuclear know-how has become a major French export.

Under Giscard, the nuclear programme of course came under attack from ecologists (see pp. 343–6) and other pressure-groups; but they made much less impact than in many other countries, while the general public debate on nuclear hazards was less urgent than, say, in the United States or West Germany. Determined not to be driven from its chosen course, the Government was helped by the opinion polls which showed two Frenchmen in three as favouring nuclear power; the main political parties all favoured it too, including the Communists, though the Socialists were becoming more reticent. So, whereas in some countries nuclear programmes have been slowed right down by anti-nuclear lobbies backed by public opinion, France under Giscard went steaming ahead. Sit-ins or other protests would sometimes delay work on a new project, but no site was abandoned under such pressures. And when in 1979 the famous accident occurred at Three Mile Island, Pennsylvania, French officials quickly pointed out that though French reactors were of the same basic type, their design was different and a similar accident thus far less likely. The public, in its mass, accepted this. So Giscard calmly ordered a speed-up of nuclear construction, an action which would have been politically unthinkable at that moment in almost any other industrial country. The Government's view, reiterated constantly, was that France had simply no alternative to nuclear power, if national independence and living standards were to be maintained. And the majority of Frenchmen acquiesced in this, pushing to the back of their minds whatever doubts they might feel about the risks.

Since May 1981 the new Socialist Government has been patently in a dilemma over how far to modify Giscard's programme. The party, which contains quite a strong anti-nuclear element in its rank-and-file, put into its election manifesto a pledge to cancel all future nuclear projects. But Mitterrand himself was evasive about this during his presidential campaign. And after the elections it rapidly became clear that the new Socialist rulers, faced with harsh economic realities, were having second thoughts about the wisdom of too drastic a cutback. Most of the Ministers in charge of the economy and industry are relatively pro-nuclear. They are well aware that a halt to nuclear expansion would not only hugely increase the oil bill; it would also put at risk up to 150,000 jobs in France's big nuclear industry, just at a time when the Government is giving priority to the fight against unemployment. Mitterrand seems to have accepted this viewpoint. So in the summer of 1981 the new Government decreed less of a slowdown than had been expected. It halted work on only five new nuclear sites, instead of the expected fourteen, and it allowed others to go ahead. This mightily displeased the ecologists (see p. 346). Indeed official nuclear policy is today causing more controversy than ever it did under Giscard, for the Left is deeply divided on the issue. The Communists are strongly pro-nuclear, and their union, the CGT, has even demonstrated against the cutbacks: on the other hand, the big pro-Socialist union, the CFDT (Confédération Française Démocratique du Travail), is equally angry that the cutbacks have not gone further. It is a paradoxical situation, with the Government under fire from opposing factions within its own ranks and obviously unable to please both at once.

The new Government presented its overall energy policy in October 1981. Its revised target is that annual nuclear output should reach 57 million tons of oil equivalent by 1990, compared with the figure of 73 million set under Giscard. But the Government is still expecting nuclear power to meet 28 per cent of French energy needs by 1990, only slightly less than the Giscard target of 30 per cent. These figures may seem contradictory. The explanation is that the new Government thinks that its predecessor seriously overestimated future energy needs and was thus misled into too ambitious a nuclear programme. All forecasts have now been scaled down. So the nuclear cutback, though in itself over 20 per cent, is a bare 7 per cent in relative terms. Work is today going ahead on six new power stations. At the same time, the Government is intensifying measures for energy conservation. It will even re-open a few local coal-mines (a move of doubtful economic value). And above all it is speeding up the development of 'new' energies, notably biomass and solar, with the aim that these will gradually make up for the slackening of the nuclear effort. The aim is that by 1990 only 32 per cent of France's energy needs will be met by oil, as against some 50 per cent today. And so France is harnessing all her scientific expertise, her ingenuity, her State planning apparatus, for the great battle for energy survival. 'We may not have oil, but we do have ideas,' said one official.

Under Giscard, the nuclear programme was often cited as a prime example of French *dirigisme* at its most effective: a strong central Government takes a bold decision, follows it up with careful planning, then applies it resolutely. It is France's famous technocrats who plan and execute these State schemes, nuclear or other, and since the war France's style of economic management has been basically technocratic. But this, like nuclear power itself, is a subject of controversy.

ELITIST TECHNOCRACY: A WANING ASSET?

France's post-war economic triumphs have been achieved in a land where – hitherto, at least – the trade unions have been weak and divided, where inequalities of income have been among the highest in Western Europe (see pp. 383–6), and where the levers of power have been mostly in the hands of a small self-perpetuating technocratic élite. It is possible to argue – provocatively – that in strict *economic* terms this situation has so far been more beneficial than harmful: it has encouraged personal effort and group discipline, while union weakness has kept the labour force fairly docile. But the counter-argument – and it has come not solely from the Left – is that not only are the inequalities unjust and potentially explosive, but that already the rigidities of the power structure have been creating some *in*efficiencies. So what price technocracy? Is it compatible with true democracy, and is it even the most effective way of running an economy? Has France's 'miracle' been achieved because of, or despite, her very special élitist system? And how far will the Socialists now, in practice, modify that system? The debate is loud and long in France, and it lies at the heart of the modern French dilemma.

The concept of technocracy has always been stronger in France than in Britain, and under the Fifth Republic the power of those known loosely as 'the technocrats' has increased. It took a step forward under de Gaulle, who despised the old-style career politicians and put civil servants with a technocratic outlook into many key Ministerial posts: Pierre Sudreau, Edgard Pisani, Olivier Guichard and others. Pompidou and Giscard continued the process. Under Giscard, the technocrats were everywhere, in State agencies and Ministers' cabinets, supposed apostles of practical modern efficiency and rational planning. Today, Mitterrand may be seeking to dilute the system a little, but even he still relies on it heavily.

In the heady period of post-war renewal, many technocrats were bound by a common idealistic faith in technical progress as a key to human happiness. If asked to name the archetype, many Frenchmen might mention the late Louis Armand, a *polytechnicien* engineer who reorganized France's railways after the war, led the Government's search for mineral wealth in the Sahara in the 1950s, pioneered Euratom, produced with Jacques Rueff in 1960 the key report on structural reform and then rounded off a fabulous career by heading the Channel Tunnel study group (which the British sabotaged). Armand, who died in 1971, was typical of idealistic technocrats, a man of vision as well as action: it is hard to conceive of a mere engineer in Britain enjoying the same status as public sage and Grand Old Man. But Armand's kind of inspired ethos has today waned. Many technocrats have abused their power, and the public no longer regards them with such awe and admiration; often they are seen as remote, impersonal figures, cut off from real human needs, arrogantly imposing their decisions in the belief that they with their special expertise are bound to know best. The revulsion against them was one element in the Socialists' 1981 victory. For Giscard is an arch-technocrat, while Mitterrand is not a technocrat.

Giscard's years in power intensified the old debate about that uniquely French élitist system whereby public life, both political and economic, has long been dominated by the upper stratum of the civil service known as *les Grands Corps de l'Etat*, recruited mainly from two all-powerful colleges. Is the system a key factor behind France's envied economic dynamism? Or, as many people now believe, has it become an obstacle to the growth of a more open society and therefore to real progress? Unlike his predecessors, de Gaulle the soldier and Pompidou the former *lycée* teacher, Giscard was a supreme product of this system. He wears *all three* of its proudest badges, 'X', ENA, IF – that is, he is one of the very few men in France to have passed through *both* the Ecole Polytechnique *and* its younger rival, the Ecole Nationale d'Administration, *and* then to have joined the Inspection des Finances, most influential and exclusive of the Grands Corps. Many of his chief aides at the Elysée, and some of his senior Ministers since 1974 (Chirac, Poniatowski, François-Poncet, though not Barre), were fellow-*énarques* (the nickname for ENA old boys), pragmatists different in outlook and background from the old-timers of the Fourth Republic. So Giscard's regime was seen in France as an apotheosis of the gradual takeover of political power since 1958 by the new civil service mandarins and technocrats with their tight old-boy networks.

Not that the system itself is new: some Grands Corps date back long before Napoleon. The corps' mechanism is highly complex and subtle, and there is nothing like them in Britain. They consist of a dozen or so State collegiate bodies that operate parallel to the Ministries: each has a specific technical role – for instance, the Inspection des Finances audits State accounts – but their more significant function, by tradition, is to keep State and industry supplied with a pool of top-level talent, mobile and polyvalent. This is immensely useful. The corps are in two camps, in constant rivalry: 'technical' ones (such as the Corps des Mines), led by engineers recruited essentially from the mighty Polytechnique (see pp. 511–12), a Napoleonic creation; and 'administrative' ones (such as the IF) whose members today are drawn mainly from ENA, the postgraduate civil service college set up in 1946.

Each school and corps has its active old-boy loyalties, especially strong among *les X*, as *polytechniciens* are nicknamed. A few other leading Grandes Ecoles too have influential networks, such as the Ecole des Hautes Etudes Commerciales (HEC). All this may bear some relation to the days when the British Cabinet and Whitehall were dominated by Etonians, Wykehamists and Balliol men; but whereas in Britain these old-school-tie networks are today weakening and becoming largely social, in France they have become stronger than ever and more specifically professional. Moreover, the prestige of the great Ecoles and the grander Corps, and the golden careers they offer, may explain why so much of France's finest young talent is tempted to join them. Conversely, such fields as broadcasting or journalism, the universities or merchant banks, offer lower prestige and few outlets than in Britain, so that the kind of brilliant graduate who might aim for the BBC or the City is more likely in France to go into public service or industry, not only into the *cabinets ministériels* but into a wide range of State agencies and industries and even private firms that recruit their leaders from the Grands Corps. All this may carry various advantages for the economy, as compared with Britain where high-level technical and administrative education has a far lower status. And so, as the British look a little enviously at France's post-war economic progress, it might be right to attribute some of it to the élitist system. Yet the system is always under criticism in France. Polemical books have appeared recently with such titles as *La Mafia polytechnicienne* or *L'Enarchie, ou les mandarins de la société bourgeoise* – usually written by ex-alumni, stricken with conscience at their own presence in this privileged upper-crust world, cut off from the people, rigidly defending vested interests.

Let us look first at the ENA stream, which has been steadily gaining fround over *les X* as the early post-war *énarques*, now in their fifties, secure more and more of the top posts. The school, a few metres from St-Germain-des-Prés, recruits mainly from the more prestigious Paris *lycées*, via 'Sciences-Po'. During their twenty-nine months with ENA, students spend part of their time on practical attachment to embassies abroad, to *mairies* or (hitherto) prefectures,[4] and the rest acquiring the techniques and correct attitudes of the upper civil service. The final exam then classifies them in order of merit, enabling the top ones to choose – in order – the thirty or so places offered each year by the Grands Corps. The rest of the annual output of about a hundred must settle for ordinary jobs in Ministries or other public bodies; but even this, such is the prestige of ENA, ensures them a safe if less glorious career for life.

Of the five corps served by ENA, traditionally the most sought-after by those high on the list is the Inspection des Finances, followed in order by Conseil d'Etat, Cour des Comptes, Corps Préfectoral (till now, at least) and lastly Corps Diplomatique. This may seem odd: why should the prospect of becoming an ambassador or prefect have had less appeal than joining one of the other corps whose work seems relatively dull and anonymous? – the Cour des Comptes, like IF, has the job of verifying public accounts, while the Conseil d'Etat advises on legal disputes between State and citizen. But there is more to it than this. The Quai d'Orsay, like the Foreign Office, has seen its appeal decline in an age

4 Now that prefects and prefectures have been down-graded and rechristened by the Socialist Government (see p. 200), they will probably have less appeal for ambitious young *énarques*.

when the exciting diplomatic work is done by jet-setting Kissingers, and ambassadors are 'mere post-boxes'. The prefectoral corps, it is true, raised its prestige in the '60s and '70s. But even this has not been able to compete, in the eyes of ambitious young *énarques*, with the advantages of those three corps that offer unrivalled freedom and scope, and have often been the best springboards for a political career, whether of Right or Left: Chaban-Delmas and Michel Rocard are both *inspecteurs des Finances*, while Chirac is a member of the Cour des Comptes, and Michel Debré is a *conseiller d'Etat*, as is Jacques Attali, Mitterrand's chief economic adviser at the Elysée.

Consider the Conseil d'Etat: with its elegant premises in the Palais Royal, it is almost a political club, and to join it is a little like becoming a Prize Fellow of All Souls, with the significant difference that one is *far* closer to the seats of power. The young *conseiller* is expected to work there for his first four years after ENA, but with a bit of initiative he can in practice combine this with more exciting work too. He may, to quote a specific case, spend his morning at the Conseil on some typical routine work – adjudicating on whether parents of children born in adultery can claim family allowances – and his afternoon at the Quai, advising the Minister on East–West strategy. The pay, too, is no disincentive: a twenty-six-year-old told me that his annual salary from the Conseil was 120,000 francs, and on top of this he was picking up 50,000 francs from various public jobs. After his four years his path might be open – depending on his personal contacts – to a regular post of some power in a Minister's *cabinet*, with a basic salary of some 140,000 francs at thirty-two.

Once a member of a corps, you remain so for life and are salaried by it. So, if your political or business career comes unstuck for a while, you can always make a tactical retreat to safe obscurity, and from there plot some bold new venture, without money worries in the meantime. Many less ambitious souls do in fact prefer to work inside their corps all their lives, not attempting the rat-race. So the system can be accused of offering easy sinecures to a pampered few, but it does also provide a flexibility that, arguably, enables a brilliant and energetic man to make a full and diverse use of his talents in the State's service – and most abler men do work very hard. As an ordinary Ministry bureaucrat, you are strait-jacketed by the hierarchy; as a *corpsard*, you can take endless productive sabbaticals. And this reservoir of top talent is valuable to the State.

It is the *inspecteurs des Finances* who have most successfully exploited this system. Their corps is attached to the Ministry of the Economy, and its junior members spend their time – as under the Monarchy – touring

France to check that State funds are not being misspent. But the more senior ones have manoeuvred their way into every corner of real power. The President of Electricité de France is an *inspecteur*; so is F.-X. Ortoli, former President of the EEC Commission; and in industry so is Roger Fauroux of St-Gobain. One interesting case is that of Claude Pierre-Brossolette, who was head of Giscard's staff at the Elysée and then moved across to be president of Crédit Lyonnais, one of the leading State-owned banks. By unwritten custom, every Minister is expected to have in his *cabinet* at least one *inspecteur*, chosen by the corps and acting almost as a spy for *les Finances*. The Inspection is a real mafia, maintaining its hold over public life not only through intellectual superiority but also by fostering a calculated mystique: 'Do not allow the politicians you serve to understand you too well,' the secretary-general of the corps recently advised a batch of new members; 'preserve the mystery of your economic intuition and they will respect you the more.'

The *inspecteurs* are often resented by the *polytechniciens* in the rival camp whose fiefs – such as French Railways – they have been invading. *Les X* form a much larger mafia than the *énarques*, with a stronger solidarity: they are also much more conservative, and their qualities are less evident. After a two-year general technical course at their famous military college (formerly beside the Panthéon, now in the southern suburbs), they mostly go on to more specialized post-graduate *écoles d'application* of which the most superior are the Ecole des Mines and the Ecole des Ponts et Chaussées (a few 'X', such as Giscard, opt instead for ENA). The old boys of each of these colleges constitute a corps, of haughty exclusivity. They are less closely involved in the political scene than the various ENA corps, but they do play a part: men of the Corps des Mines held key posts under Giscard both at the Elysée and the Quai. And whereas the engineers from the other Grandes Ecoles (such as Centrale) remain in technical jobs, *les X* will often become senior administrators (or even ministers, such as Giraud). In ministries such as Transport or Industry, and in the big State bodies running electricity, oil supplies, postal services and so on, they have a near monopoly of power. Rivalries are intense even between different clans of the mafia, notably *les Mines* et *les Ponts*, each with its own fiefs; in some administrations where both clans are present, they fight 'frontier battles' with all the savage pettiness of a demarcation dispute between British unions. But they will always drop the feud and close ranks in face of their common adversary, the non-'X'. Any 'X' will usually try to fill a vacancy on his staff with another 'X', and will prefer to do business with another 'X' or help out another 'X', whether he knows him or not. It can cause intense bitterness, among those who do not belong.

This virtual closed shop has some negative aspects: it can lead to conservatism as often as to dynamism. Many 'X' develop a *rentier* spirit: protected by their status which ensures them a cushy job for life, they feel little concern for new ideas and methods: for example, blame for the former inadequacies of the French telephone system was often laid at the door of the 'X' who run it. The drama of the *polytechniciens* is that, trained as engineers and not executives, they find themselves in a competitive world of modern management for which they are seldom suited. It is true that a new wind has been blowing in recent years: a number of younger 'X' and others have been on graduate courses in the United States to places such as the Harvard Business School, and have come back with new ideas. But they are still a minority.

Meanwhile a growing number of 'X' (such as Jean-Paul Parayre, the head of Peugeot-Citroën) have been buying themselves out of State service and moving into private industry or commerce, where they can command vast salaries. And some *énarques* are doing the same. So the old tradition of devotion to public service, on which the Grands Corps were founded, is today mixed with stronger motives of personal self-interest, and this is sometimes criticized. Many firms welcome these élitist recruits with open arms, less, very often, for their actual abilities than for their precious contacts. If you have an 'X' or *énarque* on your staff, he may be able to ring up just the right pal in the ministry that is blocking the crucial permit you need. Once the French branch of Sony was in dispute with the Ministry of Finance on some vital issue and found itself getting nowhere – until Sony in Tokyo astutely appointed an 'X' as its director for France: he quietly settled the problem with another 'X' in the Minister's cabinet. It happens all the time.

So these networks, and other lesser ones, have created an intricate mesh of close personal links between public and private sector: banks, ministries, industrial firms and so on. This has some advantages in a France notorious for its rigid compartmentalization: a few men at the top, speaking the same language, have been able to short-circuit the bureaucratic *lenteurs* of contact between administrations, and get things moving. The Plan, as we have seen, benefited hugely from these links. They can even bestride political barriers too – useful in polarized France. Though the Communists are outside the system, the Socialists have always been part of it; and in the 1970s Rocard was able to use his friendship with fellow *inspecteurs* at the Elysée to mediate behind the scenes in some crises with the unions.

And yet, though the élites are a means of bypassing some of the blockages in French society, they in turn create others. One critic of the system, J. C. Thoenig, writes in his book *L'Ere des technocrates*:[5] 'The existence of groups so enclosed, with practices so monopolistic, may be one of the principal obstacles to the adaptation of the administration to modern management.' His criticisms are directed mainly against the technical corps, where these faults tend to be more evident than in the ENA corps. How far is he right?

It is not easy to draw up a balance-sheet. One of the virtues of the system is that it allows youngish men with modern ideas to reach positions of influence, without having to wait for dead men's shoes; and this creates a good mix of innovation and experience. Another virtue is integrity. The State, by paying its senior servants highly and treating them well, has over the centuries built up a body of men who – with far fewer exceptions than in other Latin countries! – are honest and unbribable. They are largely free, too, from party political pressures, even if in turn they may influence or enter politics. And most of them, for all their rivalries and intrigues, do retain a sense of vocation and public service. Yet time and again in France one is struck by the contrast between the energy and inspiration of some individuals and the rigidity of the system enclosing them: it is as if the two are related, and initiative thrives on the challenge caused by the rigidities.

There are three main aspects to this rigidity:

– A degree of competition between the corps may be healthy, but some, especially the technical ones, carry it too far: like medieval barons, they spend much of their energies on conducting sallies into each others' territories, trying to extend their influence or protect their vested interests. This leads to failures of cooperation, or even to attempts to sabotage each others' projects, and does not always make for economic efficiency.

– A more serious problem is the gulf that exists, in any public body, between the élite stream and the rest. Promotion on merit from the middle ranks is rare: if by ill chance you failed to acquire the right diplomas from some Grande Ecole in your youth, you have little means of moving far up the hierarchy, however able you may prove yourself. The closed shops prevent it. This is especially true in the technical bodies, also in the Ministry of the Economy where by custom the key posts are reserved for *inspecteurs*, and if you join an ordinary department you tend to stay there for life. Inevitably this leads to frustration, apathy and lack of initiative in the middle ranks where so much of the regular work is done; able people, if they are barred from the élite, have little

5 Editions d'Organisation, Paris, 1973.

incentive to enter public service. Fortunately, however, there are recent signs of a break in this ice-pack. First, since the 1970s ENA has begun to accept late entrant lower-rank civil servants in their thirties who have shown ability in their work and are now given a second chance to enter the élite stream. So the élite is widening its gates a little to a more humble kind of recruit; but it still remains an élite. Secondly, the rigid barriers in the State service are no longer mirrored so much in private industry: here it is easier than twenty years ago for an ambitious technician or junior cadre to move up the hierarchy without the right diplomas, and conversely a man will no longer get a top job just because of his élite diplomas; he must also prove his worth.

· – A third barrier is that between the public service and other professions: people rarely move from one to the other. The university world is a proud ghetto and its professors would rarely deign, or be invited, to take up public duties. Raymond Barre, who for son.e years has alternated between university and civil service duties, is a rare exception. Similarly, a brilliant businessman or industrialist would rarely be co-opted into State service as often happens in the United States or even Britain. He would just not be accepted without the right pedigree. It is true that a reverse process happens often enough, especially under the Fifth Republic: State technocrats become managers of private firms. But *les corps* will not allow the process to be two-way. It is partly a matter of pedigree but also of family custom, in a country where the bourgeoisie has its own internal barriers: some leading families are traditionally producers of civil servants, others of academics, while others own factories – and that is the way it stays. Many Frenchmen today think that this lack of cross-fertilization has become a drawback.

Simon Nora, a distinguished *inspecteur des Finances*, told me: 'Our élite system was a great asset until a decade or so ago – that is, in the post-war years when our politics were unstable and France was fast modernizing and industrializing. The technocrats then were a dedicated *clergé*, the secular priests of progress, pulling France forward with autocratic zeal. But that phase is over. Today France is largely modernized and what is needed is something else, the emergence of a more open and egalitarian society where ordinary people can participate more. The system is now an obstacle to that.'

Of course, on paper, Polytechnique and ENA are perfectly democratic: anyone can go there, the entry and passing-out exams are impartial, and there is no nepotism at this stage; that comes later, inside the corps system. But in practice the intake is overwhelmingly bourgeois and – in the case of ENA – Parisian to boot. This is partly a matter of social convention, partly of teaching: only a few fashionable Paris *lycées* are properly geared to provide the specialized teaching that the ultra-competitive entry exams demand. Undoubtedly ENA has succeeded superbly in the role given to it: to turn out, within a certain conformist mould, a certain kind of able administrator. The average *énarque* (a term with a ring of Grecian wisdom) is markedly more confident, articulate and enthusiastic than his British counterpart. But he goes straight into a privileged desk job and rarely has contact with 'the people'. There is a growing feeling today that he should at least start in the ranks in some way. Polytechnique's intake is a little more varied and provincial than ENA's and even includes a few children of workers and peasants: but from the moment he or she enters, the 'X' is every bit as secluded as the *énarque*. Thus the system may be a factor behind the French citizen's regular sense of grievance against the State, and the alienation hitherto felt by the working class.

This is not new. Read Balzac, and you will find the same criticisms of *les* X as are made of *énarques* today. And since the war the system has changed little: the creation of ENA has simply strengthened the grip of *its* Grands Corps. One recent trend has been the growth of a new inner mafia, made up of those of the élite who are also old boys of the Harvard Business School or the Massachusetts Institute of Technology. These super-mandarins have played a positive and crucial role in the recent modernization of French management. But they are using their new prestige to carve out new vested interests.

Visit ENA or Polytechnique today, and you will find plenty of students ferociously critical of the system they are entering. Yet they stand to gain too much from it to be prepared, except in a few quixotic cases, to try to transform it by calling its bluff. In 1972 a whole 'year' of *énarques* decided bravely, on passing out, to boycott the three grander corps in favour of mere ministries or prefectures. But their gesture has had no sequel. It seems that effective reform of the system can come only through *either* basic changes in higher education – such as integration of ENA and the Grandes Ecoles into the university structure – *or* through a new Government staffing policy for the upper administration. Many radicals strongly advocate both these courses: but either would provoke fierce resistance. Giscard, though aware of its drawbacks, was not only a legatee of the system but at heart a believer in it; and he was not ready to do more than make small adjustments.

So what of the Socialists? Many of them in the past have been outspokenly critical of the system: yet they have now come to power with no overall plan for reforming it. And they too have an interest in preserving it. A number of senior Ministers are among its products – Rocard, Cheysson, Fabius, Chevènement, etc. – while today the *cabinets ministériels* are every bit as full of young Socialist *énarques* as they were of Rightish ones until 1981. *Plus ça change* ... The Socialists will certainly need to depend on the authority and stability of the existing structure, especially if they are to succeed in their delicate task of extending the role of the State in the economy. They will need every talented *corpsard* they can find.[6] Nevertheless, there *are* now some prospects that the system may be modified in *ad hoc* ways. Mitterrand is less a believer in financial technocracy than Giscard; and under his reign the lawyers of the Conseil d'Etat and the academics of the Ecole Normale Supérieure may rise in influence, while the star of the mighty Inspection des Finances may wane a little. More important, the decentralization of local government will not only slash the power of the prefectoral corps; it will also probably reduce the influence of the big Paris-based technical corps such as the Ponts et Chaussées. Instead of working for a centralized structure, many of their members will now come under the aegis of the new regional and local authorities, and this could well dilute the strength of their mafia. The new Government also has plans to continue the process, begun tentatively under Giscard, of widening the social intake into ENA and the other Grandes Ecoles and of reducing the gulf between the Grands Corps and the rest of the civil service. So 'the system' may become a little more flexible: but it will certainly not be dismantled.

Probably this is just as well. I suggest that, on balance, the virtues of the system still outweigh its defects, at least in economic terms. It still throws up enough talented and forceful leaders to justify itself. But the weightiest charge against it today is not its inefficiencies but its injustices: it perpetuates the role of the State as nanny. And this could lead to trouble, for the mood of the French has been changing and people are now less ready to leave their destinies in the hands of technocrats who claim to know best. The Socialists are well aware of this: indeed, they know it was one of the factors that brought them to power. And their overall plan for French society today is to allow citizens to take more control of their own day-to-day affairs. But the aloof world of the Grandes Ecoles will still fight hard to defend its influence and its privileges. It is a world that so far has proved less sensitive to the new national mood than has the milieu of *patrons* and managers in private industry. Indeed, the past few years have seen some strange stirrings in French labour relations.

6 For the readiness of senior civil servants to switch to serving their new Left-wing masters, see pp. 628–9.

A NEW LOOK TO LABOUR RELATIONS

'Today, a firm will not in the long run make a profit unless it can set up real team-work and democracy among its staff. This worthy humanist aim is also sound economics.' These brave words I heard from the head of a big factory near Marseille, who for some years has been seeking to apply this philosophy. It is not exactly the language one might expect to hear from French management, often regarded as among the most authoritarian in Europe. Indeed, such ideas are still far from typical: but they have been gaining ground, and are a portent of the post-1968 climate in France. Ever since the trauma of May '68, French labour relations have emerged from their former rigidity and are now in a complex and exciting phase of fluidity and experiment: while the world of the Grands Corps has remained static, the parallel world of the Patronat has been subtly evolving, as many firms – through enlightened self-interest or other motives – seek to come to terms with their workers' new aspirations for job-enrichment and 'participation'. This campaign of discreet neo-paternalism has been waged in the teeth of the main Left-wing unions, for this is not West Germany where the two sides snugly cooperate in *Mitbestimmung*. In France, these unions remain deeply suspicious of the Patronat and doctrinally hostile to 'collaboration with capitalism'. So management has been manoeuvring to outflank them, while also busily exploiting the notorious rivalries and internal frailties of French unions. Today, with the coming to power of a new Government far more closely allied to the unions, the balance of power may well shift and the unions may recover some of the initiative they had lost to the Patronat. So labour relations seem set to enter an even more complex phase. Yet already it is clear that the victory of the Left has not in itself cured the unions' innate weaknesses.

A foreign visitor to Paris in recent years, seeing the boulevards filled so often with demonstrating workers and their angry banners, might conclude that the unions are powerful and poised on the brink of insurrection. He would be wrong. These protest marches have been little more than a ritual, a way of showing the flag and making up for the unions' inability (through lack of funds and grass-roots support) to carry out more effective action such as long strikes. Against an EEC average of 43 per cent, only 23 per cent of the French workforce is unionized, and this figure has been falling. Why is it so low? One reason may be that the individualistic Frenchman is not a club-joiner; another, that workers have been wearied by the incessant bickerings between the unions, which in France are divided on lines of politics and ideology, rather than by craft or trade as in Britain. The biggest union, Confédération Générale du Travail, with about 1.2 million members (it claims many more) is virtually controlled by the Communist Party. Its main rival, Confédération Française Démocratique du Travail (about 900,000), has Socialist sympathies; like the CGT it is 'revolutionary', that is, pledged to the overthrow of capitalism, and includes many *gauchiste* elements though its leadership recently has become more pragmatic. Third comes Force Ouvrière, a 'reformist' union prepared to cooperate with management: its moderate stance has paid off and its numbers (almost 900,000) have been rising. There are also some smaller bodies, such as the white-collar Confédération Générale des Cadres (350,000).

The political divisions on the Left in France have been mirrored in the conflicts between CGT and CFDT, and between both and FO, making effective joint union action often very difficult. This may help to explain why since 1968 the French strike level in industry has been low: in 1977, the number of man-hours lost through strikes was 175 per thousand workers, compared with 398 in the US, 405 in the UK, 835 in Italy. For many years now, instead of long strikes the unions have tended to organize one-day general stoppages, which make them appear strong and militant but achieve little; they are a safety-valve for discontent. So the unions' bark is worse than their bite. They brandish revolutionary slogans, they angrily denounce the Patronat: but in day-to-day shop-floor relations they tend to be fairly amenable, more so than in Britain. This is not only the result of weakness: many shop-stewards are realistic men who accept the need for disciplined work and higher productivity. Nor has French industry been plagued by the endless demarcation disputes and the workers' closed shops that in Britain result from the power and intransigence of the rival craft chapels within firms. And the French economy, relative to ours, is the beneficiary.

This strange mixture of union dogmatism and docility is probably one of the reasons why France had lagged behind many other Western countries in developing modern labour relations. Even today, the German style of co-management at board level is rejected in France by unions and employers alike, in the private sector, while even the rank and file shows little keenness for it. What ordinary workers seem to want is more share in day-to-day decision-making at shop-floor level, and this is where the progress is now coming. The first timid reforms date from just after the war, when de Gaulle set up obligatory *comités d'entreprise* (works councils) in firms with a staff of over fifty. These are still in force today. Each council is chosen by the staff from candidates generally put forward by the unions, and has monthly meetings with management. The council supervises welfare and social activities, and is also supposed to act as a forum where managers can keep staff informed of their policies and even seek their advice. But this latter function has never worked too well. The unions have tended to look on the councils as irrelevant to their main objectives, while many managements too have been uncooperative, complaining that the staff delegates lack the right background and knowledge for worthwhile economic consultation – 'All the *comités* do is arrange the Christmas parties,' is a jibe one often hears. Firms also have what are called *délégués du personnel*, whose job it is to channel grievances about working conditions to the management: these generally work better than the *comités*, perhaps because their role is more down to earth. De Gaulle in the 1960s made it clear that he saw these two minor institutions as merely the embryo of a grander utopia of 'participation'; and in 1967, as a step towards it, he decreed a law obliging all firms with a staff of over fifty to distribute to them a small portion of their profits in the form of shares. The Patronat was not exactly thrilled; and the unions too were lukewarm, most of them regarding profit-sharing as *'une tarte à la crème'*, a capitalist lure to weaken the workers' solidarity. But the scheme has since gone quietly ahead, and by 1974 was providing employees with an average extra 3 per cent of their salary. The Socialists today have plans to strengthen the role of the *comités d'entreprise*, as we shall see.

The recent new mood in labour relations was born of the May '68 uprising: this ushered in the new ideals of 'participation', of which profit-sharing is only one small aspect. The revolt was sparked off by students, but millions of workers soon joined in without waiting for their unions' orders. They occupied their factories, hoisting red flags on the roof and in many cases locking up their bosses in their offices. Nine million took part in the strike, the largest in Europe since the war. Motives were very mixed (see pp. 494–5 and pp. 618–19). Some aspirations were the usual material ones; but the strike was also the explosion of years of frustration: an outburst against employers' aloofness and secretiveness, against the repetitiveness of much modern factory work, against the rigid and bureaucratic chains of command, the fear of delegating authority and the lack of group discussion, which characterized French industry at all levels. In some firms, the *cadres* were the ones who led the revolt against a system of which they, like the workers, were victims. This was novel in modern France: rarely before in this stratified society had two social classes, *cadres* and workers, taken action together. Finally the union leaders gained control of the movement and pressed for the immediate aim of higher pay: so the Government and Patronat were able to bring the strikes to an end by offering large all-round wage increases and promising a fairer deal in labour relations. But what kind of deal? This seemed to demand a change of heart, more than of texts. De Gaulle talked a lot about 'participation' in the months after May, and vaguely proposed the ideal of some kind of management/labour partnership which he had nursed over the years and saw as France's historic answer to the old dilemma between capitalism and communism. But little was to come of this in practice. The unions had other objectives, and May '68 did bring them one important gain. A law passed later that year at last accorded them the kind of legal status inside a firm that had long been usual in Britain and many other countries. Shop stewards now had the right to do union work in the firm's time, to have their own offices inside factories and to do canvassing or other such work on the premises. The unions saw this as the ending of a serious anomaly and the major achievement of the strikes. They also emerged from May '68 with their own prestige enhanced, due to their 'responsible' behaviour during the revolt, and this brought them – for a while – an increase in membership and influence.

The wider legacy of May '68 lay in its effect on work relations inside firms. Of course this varied immensely, making it hard to generalize. When the red flags were hauled down, the pattern of command outwardly returned much as before, though with sporadic signs of improvement. In some cases, contacts across the hierarchic barriers became easier and less formal, and white- and blue-collar workers emerged with a clearer sympathy for each others' problems. 'I had no idea before May,' an engineer told me in Toulouse, 'of the bitterness of the workers' sense of isolation from the executive life of the factory.' In other cases the barriers went up again much as before, and in some older family firms there was even a hardening of positions, a last-ditch attempt to hold on to authority. But a majority of employers did accept that some change, at least of style, was now necessary. The wiser among them did not fail to note that the strike had been bitterest and lasted longest in the autocratic old-style firms like Citroën, whereas those with a more enlightened labour policy had much less trouble. Many firms now began to take personnel relations more seriously: their personnel manager, previously an ignored junior executive, now became a man with a big desk and a large staff, equal in status to the sales director. In some cases, the workers in turn were now liberated from a certain class inhibition, and began to come forward to talk informally to their bosses about their work. All in all, May '68 brought in a new questioning of the old assumptions about authority, and it sounded the death-knell of a certain rigidly autocratic French style of command, both in factories and offices. Things have never been quite the same since.

The post-May-'68 mood soon began to influence the thinking and policies of the Conseil National du Patronat Français, the federation of almost all French employers both large and small. This body had hitherto been stuffily old-fashioned. Though it had shown in the case of EEC entry that it was in fact capable of adjustment to change, until the early 1970s it remained an incarnation of the more stolid aspects of French management. Its huge, gloomy headquarters near the Etoile, with their heavy marble pillars and elderly uniformed *huissiers*, seemed an accurate reflection of the CNPF's bureaucracy and narrowness of outlook, which showed especially in its authoritarian attitude to labour relations. However, a liberal pressure-group within its ranks, the Centre des Jeunes Patrons, had since the 1950s been propagating a new philosophy: that a *patron* has a moral duty to his workers, he must associate them with his policies, and he should regard profit as a means for the wealth of all, not just of his family or shareholders. The CJP's inspiration, as with many of the more dynamic forces of the France of that period, was rooted in radical new-style Catholicism (see pp. 453–4). It had some influence, though the Patronat formally rejected its doctrines and in 1965 even expelled the CJP leaders from its own board. But May '68 then gave the CNPF quite a jolt: so it began to look more sympathetically at some of the CJP's ideas and at last to take labour questions seriously.

Soon a new liberal-minded figure of some charisma came to the fore in the Patronat, and in 1973 was elected its President: François Ceyrac. Few other men have had more influence on French affairs in the past decade. Ceyrac, burly, tall and craggy-faced, is an expert on labour matters who knows how to talk diplomatically with the unions; and gradually he has been able to persuade most of his senior colleagues of the need for a change of strategy.[7] Inevitably, a number of firms today remain in the old reactionary mould, wielding the heavy stick with their staff or insensitive to their views. But among the rest a broad consensus has been taking shape: that it is in employers' own long-term interests to meet the workers' new aspirations, for this can often increase productivity and may avert future unrest. So a number of themes are today in vogue with the Patronat, unimaginable before 1968: job enrichment, flexible hours and other steps to make working life pleasanter; more group work and fewer tedious production-belts; and the right of workers to take part in daily shop-floor decisions (but *not* in the formulation of company policy: co-management is still taboo). The Patronat today is embarked on a policy of 'social marketing', by projecting a new more benevolent image, by challenging the unions on their own ground for the right to defend workers' interests, and by competing with them actively for the loyalty of staff. And the unions have been hitting back,

7 Ceyrac retired in 1982, replaced by Yvon Gattaz.

especially since May 1981. 'Like a girl with two suitors, the employee stands to benefit from this competition,' said one *patron*.

In the vanguard of this movement, a handful of like-minded factory owners and managers have been pioneering new methods with a missionary zeal. The most striking success has been achieved, oddly enough, in a State-owned firm – at Aérospatiale's big helicopter factory at Marignane, near Marseille, the largest in Europe. Here the inspirational force has come from the plant manager, Fernand Carayon, one of the most impressive men I have met in modern France. Bald-headed, sixtyish, Carayon has a Grande Ecole background but is not the usual aloof technocrat: he is a man with the common touch, and has always been a bit of a maverick. He talks fast and excitedly in a sharp Midi accent. Besides the remarks I quoted at the start of the sub-chapter, this quirky idealist and new-style paternalist will come out with others such as, 'The head of a firm today must be a committed social activist, as much as any union leader,' or, 'A *patron* who is not accepted by his staff as deserving that title is no true *patron*.'

In 1967 Carayon was called in to rescue the Marignane plant, then in serious trouble. He found it filthy, disorganized and plagued by strikes: the CGT had two-thirds of the vote at works elections. He had the reputation of being tough, but also of knowing how to win workers' trust. He had the added asset of being a local man, from Aix-en-Provence. First he toured the factory repeatedly, talking to staff at all levels. 'Let's install industrial democracy together,' he said. 'What's that?' they asked. 'I don't know yet but let's work it out,' he said tactfully. So he involved every employee, in every department and workshop, in a rethink of the factory's reorganization. The CGT opposed his entire venture, but he won the backing of the two moderate unions, Force Ouvrière and the Confédération Générale des Cadres; and his radical innovations in work methods, springing from his own philosophy, soon proved popular. As a result, in the next ten years these two unions' share of the works vote rose from 25 to 65 per cent while that of the CGT fell by the same amount – and since 1968 there has not been a single strike. Yet the level of union membership, 60 per cent, is over twice the French average. A group of young workers told me: 'We belong to FO, not by ideology, but because in this factory it's the only effective union for promoting our interests. It's succeeded in working out a real entente with management, for our mutual benefit.' The CGT remains stubbornly hostile, on principle – and loses out.

Carayon's central innovation has been to divide the factory with its 6,500 staff into semi-autonomous groups, each responsible for a wide range of the assembly process – a little like the job-enrichment ventures at Volvo and Fiat. The role of the leader of each group is to 'animate' his team, to keep them informed, encouraged and, where necessary, disciplined. 'This firm used to be centralized and rigidly hierarchic, in the old French tradition,' says Carayon. 'My view is that a hierarchy is like a set of shelves in a room: the higher it goes the less useful it is. I set about to restore the human scale, which for me means efficiency.' He has also done away with punch-card clocking-in and as in many French firms today he has established flexible working hours. Within the range of 6.30 a.m. to 6.30 p.m. an employee can arrange his 41½-hour working week largely to suit himself. He keeps his own tally of hours worked by feeding a card into a computer: this remains a secret between him and the computer and is seldom checked on. The system is rarely abused – 'because we trust our staff and they know it'. In each workshop there is a rest-room, with telephone and soft-drink and food dispensers, and a worker is free to slip off there for a few minutes without seeking permission – most unusual in a French factory. Carayon claims: 'If a worker can take a break and relax now and again, in his own rhythm, he works better.' Junior staff are also allowed to learn several trades, transferring from one workshop to another: one added means of job-enrichment.

In the new workshop making the light Ecureuil (Squirrel) helicopter, Carayon has gone a stage further. Each helicopter is assembled almost *in toto* by a team of two or three workers who agree to a certain output of work per week and can then do it entirely in their own time, knocking off for the weekend when they have finished, often on a Thursday. (Would any British factory union permit such a scheme?) The workers are artisans, specially trained for this group activity which Carayon sees as 'a return, in a sense, to the ideal of the individual craftsman. By doing away with dull mechanical gestures, it adds to a worker's motivation.' Of course, the assembly of sophisticated units such as helicopters is especially suited to this kind of team-work: it would not be so easy in an ordinary mass-production conveyor-belt factory, nor in a heavy steel plant. But here it succeeds so well that Carayon is thinking of allowing staff to do some of the light assembly work in their own homes. And productivity gains have been considerable. The Ecureuil is now being built five times as fast as its less complex predecessor, the Alouette. And since 1967 the factory's total production has soared: it now exports to ninety-four countries.

Carayon is a benign paternalist, though he hates being called that. He told me that he is scornful of Yugoslav-style worker-management, which he thinks is rarely efficient. 'Policy decisions must remain entirely with the company. Egalitarianism is a false concept, it leads to mediocrity and laziness. Managers are a necessary élite, but the manager also has a moral duty to see that his workers are happy. He must be able to decentralize authority, so that decisions can be taken faster, and closer to those affected by them.' Aérospatiale's top management in Paris had its qualms at first about Carayon's methods, so radical by French standards; but it has gone along with them, seeing that they bring results. In fact his system is now being applied in most of the group's other factories, including the Airbus assembly plant at Toulouse. And in 1979 Force Ouvrière and the CGC finally won majority control of the group's central works committee, dislodging the long-entrenched CGT: for Carayon, a further vindication of his strategy.

One or two other big firms have begun to essay cautiously the new work methods, which of course are not unique to France. At Peugeot's modern engine plant near Lille, production-belts are replaced by small autonomous teams each assembling an entire car engine: but this system, like the older one at Volvo in Sweden, has run into technical difficulties. Renault has had better results in an engine factory near Paris. However, most of the pioneering in work relations has come in smaller private firms, under the lead of some idealistic *patron.* One of the first to innovate was Jean Ballerin, chairman of the Faiveley electronics firm, with a total staff of seven hundred at factories in Touraine and the Paris area. Since the early 1960s Ballerin has divided all the personnel, both manufacturing and clerical, into groups of ten or twelve people: each holds a monthly meeting where internal work matters are thrashed out and decisions taken democratically. One executive told me: 'Our aim has been to demystify management. A junior worker used to feel that his boss had all the answers and the know-how: but now the staff find they too are capable of helping to work out solutions. The head of each group has the role of adviser or animator. But of course the company keeps control of basic policy matters.' The system seems to work. One sign is that union branches in the firm have disappeared since 1970 through lack of support. My own impression was of a cheerful, relaxed, hard-working firm. Working hours are flexible, and as at Marignane, each employee keeps his or her own tally of hours worked per week – 'If anyone cheats or slacks, it's the group that sanctions him.'

Another notable pioneer is Georges Chavanne, chairman of the engineering firm Leroy-Somer, with factories at Angoulême. Here too the staff work in groups and share in decision-making. Chavanne's ideal is that 'no factory should be so large that the manager cannot shake hands with each employee every day': his desirable maximum is a hundred and fifty, though in practice some of his units are larger. Over at Auxerre, after 1968 the chairman of the Guilliet machine-tool firm, Jean-Albert Mary, embarked on a more radical course, inviting his eight

hundred workers to vote to endorse his own appointment and that of
other senior staff. Workers also took part in decisions on what the firm
should produce and what new equipment it should buy. This led to some
problems, but on the whole it worked smoothly and the firm expanded
steadily. However, Mary's style of paternalism was less tactful than
Carayon's. 'Mes bougres,'[8] he would say loftily of his staff, 'I do their
thinking for them,' and he sought to impose a set model on them. He also
made it clear he was out to smash the CGT. This union's influence fell for
a time, but then it hit back: Mary, increasingly contested by his staff,
suffered a nervous breakdown and resigned, and the whole experiment
collapsed. The episode proved the fragility of these schemes, nearly
always dependent upon one star leader.

The most spectacular venture of all, and one that attracted much
publicity, took place in the 1970s in the unlikely setting of a famous Paris
luxury hotel, the Plaza-Athénée. It was due to an original and charismatic figure, Paul Bougenaux, in this case, not a do-gooder from the boss
class but a man who had come up from the lowest ranks of the hotel's
own staff, thus lending this movement rather more of a grass-roots
flavour than the others. He began in the hotel thirty years ago as a
washer-up behind the bar, then rose to be head porter as well as hotel
shop-steward for Force Ouvrière. Because of his exceptional human
qualities, in 1969 he was made manager, and the man who appointed
him was none other than Sir Charles Forte, whose Trust House Forte
group had just bought the hotel. The Plaza-Athénée was in a bad way,
losing money; and when Bougenaux proposed the remedy of a staff
participation system dear to his heart, the capitalistic Sir Charles –
surprisingly? – agreed to let him try it out. Bougenaux regrouped the
staff into small semi-autonomous units and was thus able to inspire them
with his own humanist ideals. There were monthly meetings, where the
most junior bell-boy could put his views on how the hotel should be run
– 'You can't imagine,' Bougenaux told me, 'how much this changed the
hotel's atmosphere. The staff began to look happy and enjoy their work.
No more punch-cards. And breakages fell by half, for each group now
had to balance its budget and was aware how much these things cost.'
He gave me an example of the shared decision-taking: 'When the hotel's
silver was to be replaced, at vast expense, we collected ten samples
and each member of staff was invited to give his or her choice. Most
of us opted for the same elegant set, save one young commis-
waiter who didn't like it. "Look at the milk-pot," he said, "the handle's

8 'Bugger' – as in English, sometimes used colloquially as a term of affection,
without sexual overtones.

too heavy. Every waiter will be spilling the milk each morning." None of us had noticed it. So that commis saved us a costly mistake.'

Bougenaux was able to improve morale, and hence quality of work, to such an extent that he rebuilt the hotel's fortunes. By 1974 it was showing a steady profit again. He introduced a generous staff profit-sharing scheme, well above the legal minimum, and he increased the lower-range wages so that chambermaids were earning 6,000 francs a month, more than twice the average for large hotels. Bougenaux was soon a national figure, touring France to lecture on his methods; and Giscard awarded him the Légion d'Honneur. Informal and quizzical in manner, totally without 'side', Bougenaux is a pragmatic idealist some-what in the mould of Edouard Leclerc or Gilbert Trigano (see pp. 397–400 and pp. 426–37). Although as manager he kept a firm hand on the hotel, his style was less paternalistic, and closer to worker co-management, than that of Carayon or Ballerin. After all, he is a unionist, who came up the hard way. But in the end he got the chop: in July 1979 Sir Charles suddenly dismissed him, and set the headlines flaring. Was the Italian–Scottish tycoon jealous that Bougenaux was getting more pub-licity than he did? Was he afraid that the thirst for *participation* would infect the rest of his world-wide empire? Or were there other factors? Anyway, Bougenaux today is running hotels outside France: at *le Plaza* his scheme is still more or less in force, but it is not the same without him.

This little band of reformers – Carayon, Chavanne and a few others – are all friends, and they keep in close touch. They are still no more than a vanguard: but slowly their ideas have been catching on more widely. While a dozen or so star cases such as Carayon's attract the limelight, it is reckoned that about a hundred other firms too have been modestly but successfully carrying out their own schemes of one kind or another: often, especially in a small firm, the boss deliberately avoids publicity for fear of stirring up CGT reprisals. Of course there are plenty of sceptics who doubt whether the movement can ever get really far. Look, they say, at its intrinsic limitations. In nearly every case, success appears to depend on some convinced and persuasive leader; if he goes, then the scheme usually founders, and such men are not easy to replace. In nine cases out of ten, too, the impetus has come from management, rather than from rank-and-file pressure as happens more often abroad, for example in Sweden and America. All this is true. And yet, if manage-ment does apply its scheme tactfully and cogently, the staff nearly always end up welcoming it, whatever the CGT militants may do. This says something about the national character. Despite May '68, the French still respond to the lead of benevolent de-Gaulle-style paternalism; in a working context, they are still relatively weak at collective initiatives (save those of protest).

In the 1960s the Patronat's council, the CNPF, were at first suspicious of the early innovations by Ballerin and others. But after 1968 the mood began to change, and when Ceyrac became President of the Council in 1973 he discreetly threw his weight behind the new trend: he and Carayon are personal friends. Today it is official Patronat doctrine to put the accent on job-enrichment and on what is called 'worker self-expression on the shop-floor'. Of course there are still plenty of old-style stick-in-the-mud *patrons*, but they are becoming fewer. In the larger firms, at least, most managers are today intelligent enough to swim with the new tide, with a variety of motives, often inseparably mixed. Some may feel a genuine concern for their staff's well-being; others have a main eye for profit, if increased worker motivation can be seen to raise productivity and reduce grievances, thus undercutting union influence. At all events, several birds can cleverly be killed with one stone. So *ad hoc* changes are today under way on a broad front, if seldom as radically as at Marignane. The number of firms that allow flexible working hours, a mere dozen in 1971, reached 8,000 by 1976 and today is 20,000. More and more companies are prepared to train their manual workers in several skills, so that they can rotate between workshops, thus reducing monotony. And a growing minority of employers permit some staff to work at home where practicable (this especially suits housewives): Majorette, a toy firm at Lyon, sends its vans daily round the near-by housing estates to collect the miniature cars that women assemble in their living-rooms. Finally, a few companies in agreement with their staff have rearranged the standard forty-hour week on a four-day basis: instead of the usual five eight-hour stints they work four ten-hour stints. This can suit both sides. The staff have the pleasure of a regular three-day weekend, while the employer cuts down on energy and other overheads by being able to switch off from Thursday night to Monday morning.

While employees tend to welcome these various measures, the two 'revolutionary' unions have been understandably wary of what they see as a Patronat campaign to limit their power and reduce their appeal. But they have not been at all sure how to reply. Their reactions have varied, depending on local factors and personalities. In some firms, CGT militants at first opposed innovations such as flexible hours and even tried to sabotage them; later, seeing the damage this did to the union's popularity, they backed down. The CGT dislikes management-inspired autonomous work-groups: in some cases, as at Marignane, it has taken a hard line against them, but in others it has felt it wiser to go along with them rather than risk losing support among workers. At the Berliet lorry plant in Lyon, when management began to introduce a scheme of this kind, the CGT adopted the tactic of cooperating to the point of trying to take control of the new work-groups and run them in its own way – at which point the employers in turn got scared and dropped the project! But this was a rare case. Generally, the more open-minded CFDT has been less opposed than the CGT to the Patronat's innovations: one CFDT national leader, Michel Rolant, told me: 'If the Patronat's new ethos can encourage the more archaic and autocratic employers to evolve – and there are still lots of these – then this is in the workers' interests and we are not hostile. But,' he added, 'we do insist on the unions being involved too, on the shop-floor. We don't want *patrons* to create a direct day-to-day dialogue with workers as individuals, pushing us on to the sidelines.' Yet this is just what has been happening. Today, under the Socialist regime, the Carayon-type innovations can be expected to continue, for they are patently popular with staff. But the unions are now expected to play more part in them.

The Patronat's aim is to keep basic control of the innovations, or at least to prevent them from developing to the point where workers share in company policy-making. Curiously, the two big unions also show little interest in this kind of reform, at least in private firms. So – just as in Britain – well-meaning official moves in this direction have hitherto not got far. When Giscard came to power he revived de Gaulle's grand design for *participation*. Promising that reforms towards worker co-management would be a major element in his quest for an 'advanced liberal society', he appointed Pierre Sudreau, a liberal-minded ex-Minister, to draw up proposals. The Sudreau commission's report, in 1975, recommended various steps to improve working conditions, suggesting notably that larger firms should be invited on a voluntary basis to set up 'supervisory councils' including worker delegates. This proposal was not as radical as the German *Mitbestimmung* reforms that were voted about the same time: but it drew hostile reactions from both Patronat and unions. So the Government prevaricated. However, the Sudreau Report was not entirely in vain. Many of its ideas influenced individual *patrons*, and it certainly helped to shape the Patronat's new philosophy. Some of its lesser proposals even found their way on to the statute books. Thus one recent law obliges a firm to present its staff with a regular balance-sheet on all personnel and welfare matters; other laws improve the regulations governing safety, hygiene, noise levels and the like. But the central proposition, on worker delegates, was only marginally applied. True, a new legal framework was provided whereby, in firms with more than 2,000 employees, a few senior staff appointees could sit on supervisory councils, but only if both sides wished it. This was adopted in some firms, but it rarely added up to much. One quite liberal-minded *patron* gave me a typical comment: 'These councils have little value, as the real policy decisions have been taken in advance at board meetings. I'm all in favour of shop-floor *participation*, but not at management level.'

The Socialists then came to power with vague ideals of co-management. A new labour law in the spring of 1982 is expected to introduce a form of *Mitbestimmung* into all State-owned firms: so, at St-Gobain, Rhône-Poulenc, Aérospatiale and elsewhere, staff delegates will now sit on management boards (Carayon may not be too pleased). Mauroy has said that the now greatly enlarged public sector should become 'a privileged area of social innovation'. Here the Socialists have taken account of the views of the unions, which are ready enough to help co-manage public companies, especially under a Left-wing regime, but remain unwilling to become 'accomplices' in capitalist firms. So in the private sector there will be no *Mitbestimmung*, at policy level. However, the new labour law will oblige *patrons* to grant the unions far more say over working conditions, shop-floor routines and welfare matters. The unions will thus be well placed to counter-attack against the Patronat – and many *patrons* are worried. As for rank-and-file workers, they still show little enthusiasm for sharing in top decision-making: what they want – and are now slowly getting – is a fuller say in routine decisions affecting their daily working lives.

Some workers have been tempted by another solution, that of forming their own industrial cooperatives. The worker cooperative movement in France dates from the nineteenth century and today is more alive than in Britain, but less so than in Italy or Germany, while France has nothing to compare with the celebrated Mondragon venture in Spain. Some 35,000 French workers own and run a total of over 500 little firms, grouped in a national federation. But there are few people, even Left-wing idealists, who reckon that this kind of enterprise has much of a future, even under a Socialist Government. The agonies of the notorious Lip crusade have shown how great are the perils. In 1973 the Swiss-owned Lip watchmaking factory at Besançon went bankrupt and closed. The 1,000 employees refused to accept this. In the manner of the Triumph workers at Meriden, near Coventry, they took over the factory and proceeded to keep it in production themselves. There followed a series of legal wrangles, with the owners suing them for theft of property. *'Les héros de Lip'* stuck to their guns, won some appeals and were cheered on by the Left-wing Press as the vanguard of a new kind of industrial revolution. But gradually they were worn down by the sheer economics of trying to produce and sell watches under these homespun

conditions, in a fiercely competitive market. Sales fell, and the cooperative workforce dwindled to 250. Finally, in 1980, Besançon's Socialist ·
town council and other local well-wishers came to their aid, providing
new premises and new financial backing, and a modest new start was
made. But in the present economic climate, and especially with cheap
foreign watches pouring into France, it is doubtful whether Lip can do
more than – shall we say? – tick over. It has not proved the new
trend-setter that some fondly hoped.

The relentless rise in unemployment, as in other countries, has been
casting a frightening shadow over the labour scene. It is at the root of
many of the tensions between unions and Patronat, for the French
especially dread high unemployment, just as the Germans dread inflation. In Pompidou's day the jobless total began to nose above 500,000,
and 1 million was at that time regarded as the ceiling of political accepta-
bility. But what has now happened? By December 1981 the figure had
passed 2 million[9] and was still climbing: there was much anxiety, and
some hardship, but no popular explosion, for most workers were too
scared of losing their jobs altogether to risk lengthy strikes. Giscard's
Ministers were repeatedly at pains to point out that there are special
demographic reasons why the figure is so high, in a tolerably prosperous
economy: the booming birth-rate of the 1950s and 1960s has recently
been flooding the market with young job-seekers, while the very low
birth-rate of the 1914–18 period means that relatively few older men have
been retiring. Ministers stressed that this unfortunate coincidence of
factors will have worked itself through by about 1985. Maybe so: but it
can be little consolation to those now waiting in the job queues.

Giscard's Government tried applying various palliatives to the
unemployment crisis. It sought to attract new industries into areas in
need of reconversion, as in Lorraine. It poured billions of francs into new
job-creation schemes for young people, with moderate results. And it
deployed costly, complex and controversial systems of unemployment
benefit. Until 1979 these benefits were most unfairly shared out, for they
depended on the recipient's seniority and the level of his social security
contributions. An employee made redundant 'for economic reasons'
was entitled for the first year to an indemnity equal to 90 per cent of his
salary, provided he had paid sufficient contributions. This seemed
generous. But in practice only about 20,000 people a year proved eligible

9 According to OECD figures, France in September 1981 was above the Western
average, with 7.8 per cent of the active population unemployed. Other percentages were: UK 10.9, Italy 8.3, USA 7.2, West Germany 5.4, Japan 2.2.

for the full 90 per cent, and most of these were *cadres*, not workers. They had little incentive to look for another job quickly; and so the familiar complaints grew that high benefits were breeding laziness, that it paid to live on State charity, and that many people were earning more on the dole than others in jobs. Worse, the system was such that those with low social security gradings, or out of work for reasons other than redundancy, got a bare subsistence allocation, if that: almost half the unemployed got nothing at all, including notably those seeking a job for the first time, who by definition had not yet joined social security. Yet half of those out of work were, and still are, under twenty-five. All this caused a growing outcry. Finally in July 1979, after lengthy talks with the unions and Patronat, the Government introduced a new system, even more complex but socially far less unjust, as is generally agreed. Everyone is now covered, including school leavers and women seeking jobs for the first time. The 90 per cent scale is replaced by a lower regressive one of 75 to 60 per cent of former pay, but more widely allocated; and an exception is made for low-paid workers who are guaranteed 90 per cent of the legal minimum wage (see p. 384). So the dole now at least staves off starvation: previously, many jobless had to rely on family charity. In 1979 the new system was costing 27 billion francs, of which the State paid 7 billion and the rest came from employers' and workers' contributions. The Socialists are now improving the benefits further, notably for the lower-paid.

The new Government is today making the fight against unemployment its urgent priority. But it knows full well that the jobs crisis is not due solely to the recession, it is also structural; and clearly the French, like others, will have to learn to live with a high level of unemployment for some years to come. France in theory is prosperous enough to be able to cope with this and to guarantee those out of work a tolerable living. But if their hardship is to be reduced, public attitudes too will have to evolve, so as to remove the stigma often attached to being unemployed, in a nation that traditionally sets a high moral value on work. A parallel solution is to share the burden more evenly, by shortening the working week so that more jobs are available. As in some other EEC countries, the unions have been pressing for this: they want a reduction from a 40- to a 35-hour week, without any drop in wages. In 1979–80, tripartite negotiations on this never got anywhere, for the Patronat was hostile, predictably. But now the Socialist Government is firmly backing the unions and has set the target of a 35-hour week by 1985. It has even warned the Patronat that, if it still says 'no', it will impose the scheme by legislation. So far, the Patronat is now being more conciliatory, and in July 1981 it agreed to the initial step of reducing the

basic working week from 40 to 39 hours without loss of pay. But many
patrons are acutely worried about the extra costs involved, in a time of low
profits. And some business experts are predicting that, far from creating
new jobs, a shorter week for the same pay could well have the reverse
effect: many firms may feel obliged to reduce their staff.

Rising unemployment has led also to union/Patronat tensions over
the crucial issue of job security and redundancies. Here the hub of the
problem is that many employers allege that they are disinclined to take
on new permanent staff because it is so hard to obtain official permission
to make lay-offs. In fact they often exaggerate this difficulty. True, a set
of rules has long protected the French employee against arbitrary dismissal, while a *patron* wishing to make redundancies must first apply to the
Ministry of Labour and then go through a series of complicated procedures. This takes time, often up to six months: but if the economic case
for the lay-offs is reasonable, permission is rarely withheld. The red tape
may be more tedious than in many countries, but the redundancies are
ultimately no less achievable: some 300,000 were made in 1978, and
St-Gobain for example was able to reduce its workforce by 10,000 in
1974–9. However, the complexity of the Ministry's rituals seems to have
scared many firms, mainly the smaller and less resourceful ones. In the
later 1970s they grew ever more hesitant to recruit, fearing that a further
decline in the market would leave them high and dry with surplus staff.
As a result, over 100,000 jobs were simply not filled, notably in local
trades. A small builder in Biarritz told me in 1978: 'I have a staff of seven,
and I'm turning work away all the time. I could do with twice the
number, but I'm afraid. Also, if my workforce goes above ten, I'm
saddled with a much more complex and costly system of social security,
etc.: that's the law.' Thus many firms adopted the approach that small is
prudent, and it hardly helped employment.

The Government grew worried. It did not want to relax the rules
governing lay-offs, so it came up with another solution: urged on by the
Patronat, in 1979 it produced a new law making it very much easier for
firms to take on temporary staff, at all grades. Short-term contracts of up
to one year could now be offered, and hordes of employers large and
small soon rushed to take advantage of this, since it could save many a
tussle over lay-offs. In many firms, over half the new recruits are now
engaged on this basis; Peugeot is not hiring initially on any other terms.
At the end of a year, however, a firm must either part with the employee
or grant him a permanent contract. The law may have done something to
slow down the rise in unemployment. But it ran into strong criticism,
from the unions and the Left as well as other critics who shared the view
that it was far from just. It has been creating a climate of unease and

insecurity among this growing body of short-term recruits, most of them young. They are not covered by staff insurance schemes, collective wage agreements or the like, so the law drives a discriminatory wedge between them and the permanent staff. Also, the law enables an employer to do his own weeding-out: at the year's end, he can retain the good recruits and get rid of the duds, or indeed the Leftist trouble-makers. The unions were furious at a law which they regarded, perhaps a little too readily, as one more aspect of the Patronat's 'persecution' of them. One CFDT leader said to me in 1980, 'The Government has again yielded to Patronat pressure. By trying to split the workers into different categories, all very mobile and transient, the Patronat aims to make it harder for us to influence and organize them.' The unions made verbal protests at the new law, tried to rally their members on strike against it, but failed: it was one more portent of their weakness. How unlike Britain, where the all-powerful unions would surely get any such measure killed in the bud. However, times are now changing in France. The new Government, so closely allied to the unions, has promised to modify Giscard's law: short-term contracts will not be banned, but they will be controlled more strictly. And now the Patronat in turn is groaning again. It has warned that this new Socialist policy, like the shorter working week, may prove counter-productive in terms of employment.

The big French unions are so different from each other, in their make-up, their tactics and ideology, that they rarely manage to unite for effective joint action. This adds to their weakness. Rivalries between them have always been intense, both at local and national level. The main leaders – the CFDT's Edmond Maire, a shy, reflective idealist, and the CGT's Georges Séguy,[10] a true Communist prole, jovial but tough – contrive a façade of comradely unity when they do meet in public, which is seldom, but when apart they repeatedly denounce each other's policies. And there are few signs that the new governmental alliance of the Left has greatly altered this pattern.

The CGT's policies tend to reflect the twists and turns of Communist Party strategy. In the days of the *Programme Commun* it was at pains, like the PCF, to appear liberal-minded; then after 1977 it swung back to a more aggressive stance, and became less ready than the other unions to sign national agreements with Government or Patronat. In past decades the CGT had won some success by pressing harder than the other unions for immediate practical gains such as higher wages and better conditions – hence its relatively large body of members, many of them non-Communist. Today it seeks to preserve this wide appeal, for

10 To be replaced in June 1982 by Henri Krasucki, a true Stalinist.

example by retaining a few 'token' Socialists and Catholics on its governing body: but the real power, at every level, is firmly in the hands of PCF
loyalists. Broadly, they are of two kinds. Many shop-stewards are
idealistic Communists of the old school, warm-hearted believers in
human brotherhood, men of honour in their way who bargain toughly
but keep their word – 'You know where you are with them,' said one
patron. But the upper ranks of the union have more recently been penetrated by a younger breed of zealots, some of them ex-*gauchistes* from
May '68, steely apparatchiks whose approach is more ruthless and cynical. Thanks to their influence, and that of the Party, the CGT's language
today is virulent and nationalistic. It favours protectionism: 'To preserve
jobs in the textile industry,' say CGT leaders, 'France should close her
frontiers to cheap Third World imports' – so much for the brotherhood of
man. And if a firm goes bankrupt, the CGT retorts: 'We reject the whole
capitalist concept of profitability. Society's first duty is to keep factories
running, for the benefit of those whose jobs depend on them.'

Despite its revolutionary talk, the CGT also remains anxious to
preserve its 'responsible' image, disapproving of wildcat strikes and
parading as the champion of order. Many shop-stewards, though not all,
are still ready in practice to reach sensible shop-floor compromises with
employers, in order to keep factories going and thus preserve jobs. So
you could say the union's bark remains worse than its bite. However,
that bark has significantly changed its tone in recent years. After about
1977, obedient to Party policy the CGT put its stress at least as much on
political action as on true union objectives. With slogans and posters it
carried *la lutte politique* on to every factory floor, systematically opposing
every Government measure, and harnessing workers' discontent in the
cause of the PCF's power struggle against its enemies, Socialist and
Giscardian alike. It would use pretexts such as unemployment to try to
stir up strikes and stoppages with blatant political motives. And this did
not always go down too well with the rank-and-file. Indeed, it was a
major reason for the CGT's fall in membership by an estimated 30 per
cent in 1978–80. The union claims 2.3 million members; but according to
inside sources only some 1.2 million have paid their dues.

Since the 1981 elections the CGT not surprisingly has returned to a
milder stance, for it can hardly launch right away into attacking a Left-
wing Government. However, its leaders have made it clear that the
union will remain as vigilant as ever 'in defence of workers' interests'
and that it is not bound by any political agreement between the ruling
parties of the Left. In fact, the CGT remains as much as ever an arm of
the PCF. So, if the latter wished at any time to bring pressure on its
Socialist partners, it could easily use the weapon of CGT-led strikes or

other protests (see p. 634). Meanwhile, CGT/CFDT relations have out-wardly improved a little, but beneath the surface the rivalry is as sharp as ever. The CFDT still criticizes its rival for being too pro-Soviet (it backed martial law in Poland, in December 1981) and for prejudicing workers' true interests by dragging politics into union matters.

The CFDT itself is a union with a curious history. Liberal–Catholic by origin, it was more or less moderate until May '68 when many of its militants became smitten with the new *gauchiste* virus. So for the next few years the CFDT showed itself far more radical than the CGT, far readier to combine traditional union thinking with new notions such as *autogestion*. Today it has settled down a little, but it is still a lively and diversified body, with a mix of elements from far Left to moderate, and it tries to run itself democratically from the base up, while the CGT remains centralist in true Soviet style. The CFDT's leader, Edmond Maire, is one of the most influential and far-sighted public figures in France today. Gentle and pensive in manner, he is far removed from the familiar trade-union demagogue; a man of personal vision – 'the Jean-Jacques Rousseau of French unionism', he's been called – who is trying to hew a new path somewhere between Marxism and social democracy. In Maire's ideal society, workers would run their own factories and ecology would reign triumphant. But he is also a pragmatist. And when the Right was in power he came to the view that it was no use waiting idly for utopia: a union must meanwhile accept the realities of an imperfect system and bargain to improve the workers' lot within it. So in 1978–81 he embarked on a strategy of trying to create a real dialogue with the Government and even to influence it with his own thinking. This was very different from CGT tactics; it was also strongly contested by extreme Left elements within the CFDT itself. Maire knew that he was treading a delicate balance, for his own union as much as the CGT is doctrinally opposed to 'collaboration with capitalism' on the German model. But Maire claimed that he was bargaining, not collaborating; and his policy did bring some concrete results – notably the improved system of unemployment benefits, which was partly his work.

Today, while careful to retain its non-political identity, the CFDT is having some influence in the shaping of Socialist reformism. The union has failed, to its regret, to persuade France's new rulers to abandon nuclear power: but many of the Government's new social and labour proposals are based quite closely on CFDT thinking. Maire himself is an old friend of several Ministers. And it is a sign of the times that the CFDT's senior economic expert, Hubert Prévot, an *énarque*, has now moved into Jean Monnet's old seat as head of the Plan.

The third big union, Force Ouvrière, has long pursued a policy

closer to the German style (witness Marignane). But FO's main strength
is in the public services, not in industry. Since the 1978 elections, only
FO has seen its numbers rise. The level of union membership in France,
already low, has fallen since that date from some 25 to 23 per cent of all
employees: in manufacturing industry it is a bare 19 per cent. Moreover,
most curiously, the coming to power of the Left in 1981 did not immediately produce any surge of new union recruits, as happened after May
'68 and after the Popular Front's victory in 1936. While CGT numbers
have plummeted since 1978, even the CFDT has found it hard to hold its
membership. And in many firms unions have had trouble in fielding
their full quotas of candidates for the works elections. So why are the
unions facing this erosion of support? One can point to a few circumstan-
tial causes: the increase in temporary jobs, the successes of the Patronat's
blandishments, the lay-offs and shut-downs in traditional labour-
intensive industries – steel, shipbuilding, textiles – which have always
been union bastions. But there are deeper psychological factors too,
relating to the general French mood since the later 1970s. As I stress often
in this book, the French have been questioning or rejecting formal
institutions, and the unions are among the victims. After the Left's
electoral defeat in March 1978, the consequent disillusion with the
parties of the Left spilled over into a disenchantment with their union
allies too, and notably with the politicking of the CGT. In one electronics
firm, a skilled worker told me: 'The CGT has set about politicizing the
comité d'entreprise and *délégué du personnel* meetings, so that bodies
intended to deal with welfare matters have become the scenes of stormy
political battles – for the CFDT and others are obliged to hit back. Instead
of discussing, say, some practical problem of safety or hygiene, we waste
hours debating Marxism or the sins of Ronald Reagan. We're furious at
the way these shop-steward politicos use the works council as a forum
for their own crusades' – a common complaint. Under the new regime
this climate may now change, at least to the profit of the non-Communist
unions. But as yet there are few signs of it.

    The unions likewise have for some years found it hard to rouse the
workers out on strike. The rank-and-file may well be discontented; but,
as always when times are tough, they are reluctant to jeopardize their
jobs by downing tools. Also the weak French unions do not have the
funds to support lengthy strikes. It is true that the casual visitor to France
may get a very different impression: there are constant little strikes in the
public services – the Paris Métro stops for a day, postal workers stage a
go-slow, traffic controllers halt all air flights, or bags of refuse lie uncol-
lected on the pavements. For the tourist all this is both tedious and very
noticeable. But – with some exceptions – these tend to be mere token

protests lasting a day or two. And they have found little echo in manufacturing industry.

In the Giscard period a further explanation of the low strike record was that the Government, at least until 1980, allowed real wages to go on rising slightly faster than inflation. France has no formal incomes policy, but most industries are governed by collective wage agreements whereby employers commit themselves to price-indexed wage increases. And this continued to operate even under the Barre austerity plan. So there has been less emphasis than in Britain on wage restraint, and consequently not the same round of strikes caused by leap-frogging wage demands. In 1980 the Government did finally begin to insist on a tightening of belts, and for the first time it pressured firms into keeping their wage increases slightly below the inflation rate. There were angry cries from unions and workers, yet still no wave of strikes.

There is however one aggressive new tactic which the unions have been using in place of strikes, and that is the factory sit-in, a riposte to the wave of bankruptcies in smaller firms since about 1974. When a factory threatens to close, or to make sizeable lay-offs, the unions will often organize a sit-in, lasting several months in some cases. The red flag is hauled up, and sometimes the owner or manager is briefly kidnapped or shut up in his office. By 1975 these factory occupations had become routine, and in 1979 there were reckoned to be about a hundred and eighty in progress at any one time, mostly in very small firms. Though the *putsch* at Lip had helped set the trend, in very few other cases have workers made similar attempts to form an industrial cooperative if the plant has closed. Nor are their aims primarily ideological, despite the bold banners and slogans – '*Les ouvriers au pouvoir*!' Essentially the sit-in is a bargaining tactic, to persuade the employer to think again or the Government to step in and find a buyer who will save the firm. In just a few cases this has brought results, or at least it has led to a compromise whereby the factory stays alive. It does not happen often, but often enough for unions to feel that their strategy is justified.

In a sense, these sit-ins can be seen as one more token of union weakness and lack of following, for it requires only a handful of activists to 'occupy' a factory, whereas marshalling the whole staff for a proper strike is far more difficult. At all events, the Patronat has regarded the sit-ins as little more than irritating pin-pricks. In the 1978–81 period, the Patronat would readily exploit every union frailty, and was far readier than a few years back to deal toughly with trouble-makers. In the spring of 1980, at St-Nazaire, there was a lightning strike and sit-in at the American-owned Eaton gear-box plant: the manager was locked in his office for a few hours and punched in the face. Three days later he announced his intention of sacking seven 'undesirables', including the CGT and CFDT shop-stewards. This was first refused by the local labour inspector, then accepted by the Ministry in Paris, and the men departed. In 'red' St-Nazaire, a traditional stronghold of union militancy, management action of this kind would not long ago have provoked riots and massive strikes. This time there was merely a small protest march through the town and a short token strike at Eaton by sixty unionists.

Elsewhere, a few employers even began to use the weapon of suing unions for losses caused by strikes or sit-ins. The first test case came at a lorry factory in Lorraine in 1979. When the CGT called a strike, the firm took the precaution of asking those workers opposed to it to sign their names saying so: some 250 signed, out of 1,400. The strike went ahead, paralysing the factory; but when it was over the company hauled the CGT before a tribunal which ordered the union to reimburse 350,000 francs to the 250 non-strikers in compensation for lost wages. Then in 1980 the Alsthom-Atlantique engineering group started a more ambitious court case, suing all three main unions for 6 million francs in loss of earnings as a result of a two-month strike. The unions denounced these 'provocations' by the Patronat as 'scandalous', just as they claimed that innovations such as short-term contracts, group work and work done at home, were all directed at reducing their own membership and influence. They may have had some reason to feel paranoid: but they also had themselves to blame.

Today, now that they have a Government of their own colour, the union militants can be expected to take new heart and hit back more vigorously at the Patronat. As one *patron* put it to me, 'Under Giscard, the Patronat was the Government's wife and the unions its concubine: now the roles are reversed' – an odd concept, when you come to think of it. However, a Government led by reasonable men like Mitterrand, Mauroy and Delors will be at great pains to avert sterile confrontation between unions and employers. Its aim will be to build up a new kind of partnership between the two sides, based on mutual trust, under a system where workers will have more rights than before but without management feeling that its authority is undermined. Can this be achieved? Besides introducing a degree of co-management into public firms, the Government wants to ensure that employees in private firms are at least fairly consulted by their bosses. This will be done by strengthening the *comités d'entreprise* – not by changing their formal structure but by going back to their original 1946 charter and seeing that it is now properly applied, as has seldom yet been the case. Managers, while retaining the ultimate rights of decision-making, will be obliged to keep their staff fully informed of company policy and to consult them in advance about major new plans.

This is a very modest step towards *autogestion*. It could work out, so long as both sides show good faith. As the *comités* are made up largely of union delegates, we can expect to see the unions now becoming more assertive inside firms; and this worries many *patrons*, especially the old guard, who fear that a Left-wing regime in France could now be the cue for endless shop-floor contestation and a sapping of their own authority. Possibly this will happen, in a few of the more authoritarian old-style firms such as Michelin, where union activists have been roughly treated in the past and may now attempt a kind of revenge. But, elsewhere, the *patrons'* fears may prove exaggerated. For one thing, the average French worker is unlikely to become a union devotee overnight, just because the Left has come to power: union membership is more likely to remain at a low level. The signs are that the CGT has continued to lose support since the elections. And today most expert observers foresee a further steady decline in its archaic style of union militancy, and the rise of new and more constructive styles of staff/employer collaboration. After all, except in a special crisis situation such as that at Longwy in 1979, the mass of French employees today are less interested in classic confrontation led by union firebrands: what they seek, rather, is job enrichment, participation, better conditions – all the undoubtedly popular innovations preached by Carayon and others. And the issue now is whether unions and *patrons* can work together to provide this new deal. An old-style management that turns its back on this kind of progress will find a restive staff taking sides with the unions against it. But an enlightened management, by winning over its staff, will also be able to win over the unions, or some of them. After all, there need be no gulf between the two sides. At the Plaza-Athénée, Bougenaux before he became manager was the hotel shop-steward of the pro-Socialist Force Ouvrière. This may have been an exceptional case: but the task of France's new rulers today is to discover and encourage more men like Bougenaux. Then we shall see whether hotel milk-pots can, after all, contain the germ of some new democratic utopia for the poor bloody wage-earner.

THE SOCIALISTS IN POWER: REFLATION AND NATIONALIZATION

The Right-of-Centre Governments of de Gaulle, Pompidou and Giscard did pretty well with the economy in the period 1958–81. They made some mistakes, and they certainly failed to cure all the structural weaknesses. But they provided a climate where industry was able to surge

ahead, helped by a mix of State guidance and dynamic private enterprise. Even under Giscard's mandate, which happened to coincide with
the tough post-1973 years of world recession, productivity in France
continued to rise by over 4 per cent a year, faster than in any other big
industrial country except Japan. Raymond Barre failed in his bid to
reduce inflation: but he held the franc steady, and he gave a potent spur
to the further modernization of industry. By encouraging the big high-
technology firms, by modifying State control, and other measures, he
left French industry better placed for facing the growing competition of
world markets.

Now the Socialists have arrived, and are in the process of giving the
economy a different slant and of rewriting some of its ground-rules.
They are motivated, you could say, by generous ideals of sharing out
wealth more fairly, of giving workers more say in the running of firms,
and of healing the wounds of unemployment. But just how realistic is
their economic strategy? To some observers, it seems an uneasy blend of
sound business sense and outdated semi-Marxist dogmatism. By again
reinforcing the *dirigiste* role of the State, may they not encourage the old
bogey of bureaucracy and thus dampen business enterprise? And if,
abandoning Barre's rigour, they try to save jobs by a costly shoring-up of
lame-duck firms, may they not weaken France's competitivity? These
are some of the fears widely voiced today.

There are three main planks in the Socialists' economic programme:
redistribution of wealth; reflation; and nationalizations. On the first
point, the new Government rapidly took action in June 1981. It raised the
minimum wage and welfare benefits, slapped special interim taxes on
the rich, and then introduced a new annual wealth tax (see p. 386), with
plans for a more complete fiscal reform to follow in 1982. These measures
will not in themselves do much to help the economy. But in terms of
social justice they seem reasonable, for inequalities of wealth have long
been more flagrant in France than in almost any other Western country.

The second point, reflation, is more important and more controversial. In a bid to reduce unemployment – which by autumn 1981 was 1.85
million and still climbing – the Government has embarked on a
Keynesian policy of massive public spending and easier credit. This cuts
right against the current wisdom in the West, where most nations are
fighting the recession with some degree or other of monetarist austerity,
as Barre had done. But the Socialists, partly for doctrinal reasons, do not
go along with this solution. Mitterrand immediately created 54,000 new
jobs in public services, with a promise of 125,000 more to come in the next
year or so. He allowed various Ministries to increase their budgets; he
pumped new money into job training schemes; and he cut interest rates

so as to help industrial investment. The inevitable result has been a huge rise in the State budget deficit, which is expected to be about 100 billion francs for 1982 (in 1980 it was 24 billion): this will partly be met by loans and by increased taxation, to fall heavily on the upper-income groups. By early 1982 this policy had as yet achieved little in terms of employment.

Thirdly, the programme of nationalizations, described by one French paper as 'the biggest change in the French economy since 1944'. Here the Government decided to act fast. First in the autumn it completed the take-over of the two big steel firms, Sacilor and Usinor. Next it negotiated the acquisition of majority holdings in the Dassault aircraft company and the dynamic Matra group, which is strong in armaments and electronics. Then in the winter of 1981–2, in face of dogged opposition from the Right, it laboriously pushed through Parliament a Bill that nationalizes thirty-six private banks (see below) and five leading French multinationals: the Compagnie Générale d'Electricité (industrial electronics), Pechiney-Ugine-Kuhlmann (aluminium, chemicals), St-Gobain-Pont-à-Mousson (glass, electronics), Rhône-Poulenc (chemicals) and Thomson-Brandt (electronics, electrical goods). The foreign subsidiaries of these groups are not affected. Three other French groups which are partly foreign-owned will be taken over a little later, after negotiations with the parties concerned: CII-Honeywell-Bull (electronics; US interest), ITT France (telephones; US interest) and Roussel-Uclaf (chemicals, West German majority holding).

This is not a random list, as can be seen. The take-overs will bring a number of advanced or 'strategic' sectors under full or substantial public ownership. The State will now control almost the whole of the aeronautics industry (it already has Aérospatiale); the major part of the armaments and steel industries; and very sizeable chunks of the electronics and chemical industries, which till now have been entirely in private hands. It is quite a drastic step, for a nation within the capitalist world. Indeed, senior Socialist Ministers have been divided on the wisdom of these nationalizations. Mauroy himself is not very keen on them, nor is Delors, nor Rocard, nor the Industry Minister, Pierre Dreyfus (who was himself so brilliant a chairman of the State-owned Régie Renault in 1955–75, and must know the problems involved better than anyone!). Some of these 'moderates' are believed to have urged Mitterrand to reduce the list or delay the timetable. But they were overruled, under pressure from the President's team of economic advisers in the Elysée, most of them doctrinaire Left-wingers. Nationalization has long been part of Socialist dogma, and it was in the party's election programme. So Mitterrand is committed to it – and what is more, he believes in it. One of his aides told me in July 1981: 'He feels it necessary to strike an irreversible blow at the power base of capitalism, if an effective new order is to be created in France. The alternative – controlling the big private groups' profits more tightly – would not be adequate.'

Defenders of the Government's programme point out, fairly enough, that nationalized industries have always worked rather well in France, far better than in most countries. Renault is a shining example; so is the oil giant, Elf-Aquitaine; and so, apart from the Concorde bungle, is Aérospatiale. Public ownership lies deep in the French tradition; and the Socialists claim today they are merely extending a process developed under the Popular Front and then in 1944–6 under de Gaulle (see p. 32). Moreover, the Government has pledged that the new nationalized groups will have exactly the same freedom from day-to-day State interference as Renault has always enjoyed. Like Renault, they will be run on commercial lines like a private firm. and they will be encouraged to go ahead fully with their high-technology policies, and their export drives. They will be, it is suggested, 'a whole new series of Renaults', and it is hoped that, like Renault, they will act as pace-setters for their private competitors. Critics who complain that the buying up of these firms will weigh heavily on the State exchequer and on the taxpayer (it will cost an estimated 41 billion francs), the Government replies that compensation will be spread gently over fifteen years. *Tant pis* for the shareholders.

Whatever the Government's reassurances, there are many Frenchmen who see this nationalization programme as a rash and gratuitous act. What possible benefit can it bring the economy? It is not even being done under pressure of popular opinion, which is largely indifferent: it is being done to satisfy a dogma. In strict economic terms, is it wise to tamper with firms that are doing very well, expanding and making profits, like St-Gobain and Dassault? Admittedly, a British-style policy of State take-overs of dying ducks like Leyland is probably a good deal stupider, or certainly more costly. But to nationalize a healthy and dynamic firm is hardly likely to improve its performance, even in France. Renault was taken over in 1944 under entirely different circumstances: it was confiscated, as its owners had collaborated with the Nazis. Then the Régie Renault profited from the spur of competition from French and foreign car firms in a tough open market. But, today, the new nationalizations are so extensive in sectors such as electronics that they risk leading to virtual State monopolies: this could reduce real competition and hence, very possibly, efficiency. To this the Government's answer is that, no, these high-technology sectors are today so internationalized that French firms will be forced to remain just as competitive. Well, maybe – provided there is no new protectionism. But the major case against the nationalizations is that they will give an excessive new boost to the power of the State, in a land where arguably the State is already too pervasive. The total percentage of the economy in public hands, already 35 per cent, will now rise to 50 per cent. As for the State's overall share of industrial production, this is likely to rise from its present 15 per cent to some 35 per cent. This could lead to the spread of unwieldy bureaucracy. And it hardly seems in line with the Socialists' ideals of decentralization in other fields.

The same arguments could apply to the take-over of private banks and credit bodies, now going rapidly ahead. This will create a State near-monopoly in a sector where already, it is felt, the dominance of the State has been a handicap to business. French banking, 70 per cent in State hands ever since the war, has long been notable more for monolithism than dynamism. Of the world's ten largest banks, no less than four are French – the three State-owned giants (Banque Nationale de Paris, Crédit Lyonnais, Société Générale) and the mutualist Crédit Agricole, the largest of all. These and the smaller private banks – Paribas, Suez, Rothschild, etc. – have expanded greatly since the mid-'60s, opening new branches at home and abroad and attracting new customers: the cheque-book, hitherto a bourgeois rarity, has finally become as common a daily tool as in Britain or America, and in fact it is illegal not to allow a customer to pay by cheque (conversely, the signing of a dud cheque carries stiff penalties). But by Anglo-American standards these banks, especially the State ones, are stuffy and cautious, reluctant to indulge in risk financing, and this can inhibit industrial ventures. The State's control of the major banks and savings bodies has served to restrict private finance and impede the growth of the Bourse!: one among several reasons why the Bourse is so much feebler than its London counterpart, the Stock Exchange. Indeed the weakness of the capital market has long been one of the biggest problems of the French economy, for it has caused shortages of finance for industrial investment.

This did not fit in at all with Raymond Barre's vision of a dynamic free-enterprise economy, so in 1978–80 he took steps to strengthen the Bourse, and with some success. He also sought to invigorate French banking, with incentives to promote competition and lighten bureaucracy. By 1981 this was bearing some fruit. But in a land where so much banking is State-run the inherent paradox is this: the State at least in theory encourages its three banks to operate like private ones and does not interfere in their daily running; but this in turn enables them to resist State attempts at reform of their internal workings, while the banks still remain dependent on the State for their overall policies. This stalemate leads to a lack of flexibility, harmful to the investment needs of modern industry, especially when the Bourse remains weak in face of the State's finance apparatus. *Etatisme* is thus trapped in its own devices, as the 'liberal' Barre was well aware. and now the new Socialist measures are likely to make these matters worse, or so it is widely feared. The mutualist banks are to remain free, also the foreign banks operating in France and a handful of tiny local banks. But the main private banks, handling 16 per cent of French credit, are coming under public ownership. It is the first time that any industrial country in the free world has nationalized the totality of its credit system. Real competition will be further reduced. and the results may not be healthy.

After Mitterrand's election, the business world at first reacted with alarm. There was panic selling on the Bourse, where the share index dropped by 30 per cent. The franc came under heavy pressure, and Delors was able to keep it within the European Monetary System only by raising interest rates to a record 20 per cent, and then in October by making a discreet devaluation. In the autumn the panic subsided a little and the Bourse gradually picked up by some 7 per cent. The Patronat, too, began to adjust to the new realities. At first, after the Socialist victory, some old-guard *patrons* had threatened a virtual state of war against the new regime, and this led union leaders to protest that the Patronat was planning to 'sabotage the economy wilfully' by refusing to invest or take on new staff. But then Mauroy and Ceyrac, those two veteran conciliators, had a long and fairly amiable talk; and after this the majority of *patrons* settled into accepting the necessity of some form of wary cooperation with France's new rulers. 'Make no mistake,' said one liberal *patron*, 'this Government for us is much more a threat than an ally. But destructive tactics against it would only harm us, too. We have no choice but to go along with the new regime and try to curb its excesses.'

By early 1982 the reflationary policy was jogging along without spectacular effects. The economy had not come crashing, as prophets of doom on the Right had predicted: but nor had there been any sudden triumphal recovery, as some naïve Socialists had hoped. Inflation had been pushed up to 14 per cent, but this was less than had been feared. Reflation had also stimulated production a little, so that the Government's target of 3.3 per cent growth for 1982 was not being dismissed as too absurd by outside experts such as OECD. But unemployment remained obstinately high: by the end of 1981 it had passed the 2 million mark and showed no sign of falling. Mauroy and Delors were engaged on a massive campaign for new jobs, including special incentives for firms that were ready to introduce early retirement schemes or a shorter working week, thus creating more employment for the young. But the Patronat remained wary. Most *patrons* claimed that higher taxation, higher social charges and other new measures were squeezing their profits and thus making it impossible to invest or take on extra staff: the year's most alarming statistic was that fixed capital investment by private industry had fallen by as much as 11.5 per cent in 1981. Today, for its policies to succeed, the Government badly needs the active support of private firms, which still make up two-thirds of French industry. But the Patronat, worried by the recession and scared of Socialism, is still reluctant to take the risk of new investment.

The brightest aspect of the present situation is the presence of Delors himself. In his first eight months in office, he has handled the economy with skill and moderation, and has emerged as a figure of real authority. He appears to have convinced Mitterrand of the need to avoid excessive radicalism, and he has won the confidence of the Patronat, who see him as their best ally in the Government. The business world is glad that he has largely retained Barre's price de-control, and that he and Dreyfus are both keen on the high-technology policy. The decision to save the essentials of Giscard's nuclear programme is also seen as a welcome sign of pragmatism. But, if the economy worsens, will Delors be able to retain his grip? Coupled with the expensive new social measures (higher basic wages, longer holidays, shorter working hours and so on), reflation is pushing up firms' costs, and this could reduce their competitivity and lead to a fall in exports and more bankruptcies (there were 20,000 in 1981). Far from limiting unemployment, reflation could increase it. At this point the Government would be faced with two choices. Either it could make a U-turn to some modified Barre-like austerity, thus sacrificing its principles and possibly its popularity. Or else it could plunge further into reflation, and seek its salvation in a protectionist closing of frontiers (as the big unions and some dogmatic Socialists are already urging). Whereupon, Delors might either resign in disgust, or be pushed out in favour of some harder-line Socialist. Not a happy prospect. But as one economist has said, 'The Socialists will find it just as difficult as Barre did to fight simultaneously against inflation and unemployment, and they may well have no better luck.'

This may prove an unduly pessimistic scenario. But, whatever happens, there is another likely trend that worries many liberal observers: the strengthening of classic French *dirigisme*. The Socialists believe in this, in economic affairs, just as they believe in its opposite, devolution, in regional, civic and social affairs: it is an odd paradox in their thinking. After its years of decline, the role of the Plan is now to be reinforced. This could in some ways be valuable, especially as the new Minister in charge of the Plan is the enlightened Michel Rocard: but a return to too much Monnet-style planning could prove unsuited to France's contemporary needs, now that her economy is so wide open to world market forces. One of Raymond Barre's great achievements was to have lightened a *dirigisme* that had become a burden. As he saw it, tight State control over a firm's every move was no longer an asset: industry today needed more freedom and self-reliance, and the capital markets needed more scope, if they were to compete effectively with the mammoth private enterprises of America, Germany and Japan. On the other hand, Barre fully agreed that the State must retain an active role in long-range policy guidance. So his aim was to achieve a balance between this 'constructive' *dirigisme* and a new liberalism over company policies. But under the Socialists, with their different philosophy, the danger today is that 'negative' *dirigisme* may reassert itself, for old-style bureaucratic *étatisme* is still strongly entrenched in the civil service. Not only is the State taking direct control of many firms, but the Government is now likely to be more interfering in the running of private ones, and one Patronat leader told me he felt this could carry dangers: 'Hitherto firms have been fairly free to follow realistic policies according to the needs of the market. But now, with political motives, or under union pressure, the Government may intervene to push us into actions that are just not good business.' It is a clash of philosophies. Possibly the Patronat is squealing before it is hurt: but the Socialists have yet to prove that they can combine economic pragmatism with their own cherished principles.

The Socialists have come to power with many generous and valuable ideas for changing French society. But, alas, France like other Western nations is in the middle of a difficult economic period, and will only survive through efficiency, rigour and hard-headed realism. This is not an easy time for carrying through the kind of programme that the Socialists envisage. If it misfires, then the results of thirty-five years of dogged modernization will be jeopardized. And the whole nation will be the poorer, workers as well as *patrons*.

Chapter 3

REFORM AND RENEWAL
IN THE REGIONS

In this most centralized of nations, today the regions are getting a new deal at last. Mitterrand is granting them a measure of self-government, and is even abolishing the prefects who have long ruled them so tightly in the name of the State. Politically, it is quite a revolution. But it must also be seen as the belated sequel to earlier revolutions, economic and cultural, that since the war have altered the balance between Paris and the provinces. As in some other countries, regional awareness has been growing. The trend is stronger in some regions, those with a true historical identity, than in others, and it takes many forms. Some people are reviving local languages and folk-cultures; others have been pressing for more autonomy, while tiny separatist groups, not at all typical, have even resorted to violence in Corsica and Brittany. But the amazing post-war revitalization of the provinces has its deepest roots in France's economic renewal, which since the 1950s has brought a surge of new activity to sleepy towns that for too long had been eclipsed by Paris. The 'real' France has asserted itself, and finally the State has had to take note.

Until about thirty years ago, the French provinces were second to none in Europe for lethargy and bourgeois narrowness. Dijon, Poitiers, Reims and a score of other towns, with their soaring cathedrals, their graceful old streets and their calm reflection of history – how delightful they were to visit, and how tedious to inhabit. In no other country was the contrast more striking between the dazzling capital and the rest, '*le désert français*' as it was sometimes called. Nowhere was 'provincial' quite such a term of contempt as in Paris: even the Larousse dictionary defined it as 'gauche, undistinguished'. French literature is rich in examples of Parisian writers' love-hatred of their home towns, from Flaubert's Rouen to Mauriac's Bordeaux; for the deadness of the provinces has gone hand in hand with strong local attachments, and many a Parisian would proudly proclaim, '*Moi, je suis bourguignon*', or Gascon, or Auvergnat, but never dream of going back to make a career there. Paris over the centuries sucked the blood out of her provinces, appropriating their intellectual life, their talent and initiative, their powers of decision on the smallest matters.

This picture has been changing since the war. The rural exodus, the new industry, wealth and mobility have given a new liveliness and self-awareness to many towns and their regions. And this time Paris has not been able to hog all the new progress and prosperity as she did in the last century. In fact, this city has become so frenetic that many smart Parisians are dropping their old scorn and beginning to move to the provinces. The cultural revival of many towns has been striking: new theatres, concerts, art galleries, research centres, help to make life more exciting, and the influx of new populations has created a more open and varied society.

Regional development has become a French obsession, a pillar of Government policy as much under Mitterrand as it was under de Gaulle or Giscard. And this is irreversible. If some regions – such as Lorraine – are today victims of recession, this gives the policy all the more impetus. But we have to distinguish clearly between economic or cultural decentralization, and political devolution. Of the latter, there was little sign under the Right-of-Centre Governments of the 1958–81 period. They eagerly poured money into aiding the provinces, but they kept control of how most of it was spent; and despite a few tentative reforms they gave up little effective sovereignty. The regional assemblies set up in 1972 had no direct mandate and few powers of decision. Politicians would preach the need for more decentralization, but French traditions have always proved a stubborn obstacle, and the central power of the State has long been a source of discontent. Today, the Socialists are carrying out what seems to be a real devolution, at all levels of local government including the region. It may prove a big step forward. Many people believe that France sorely needs a proper regional framework, and that without it her larger towns such as Bordeaux or Lyon cannot fulfil their potential as regional capitals in the manner, say, of Stuttgart, Barcelona or Turin. It is a complex issue, to be analysed in this chapter.

THE CRUSADE
FOR REGIONAL DEVELOPMENT

The origins of this centralization go back to the Capetian monarchs, who welded one nation out of the diverse peoples living in what is now France. In more modern times, the great centralizer was Napoleon. He carved up the old provinces, which under the *ancien régime* had enjoyed a certain autonomy, and he replaced them with ninety arbitrary 'departments', mostly named after rivers. Brittany, for example, no longer had any legal existence: Rennes, its chief town, became the capital of Ille-et-Vilaine. In charge of each department Napoleon placed a prefect, a strong ruler answerable to Paris, and this is still the system today.

Through the nineteenth century the political dominance of Paris encouraged other forms of centralization too. When the railways were built, for
political and strategic reasons their network was traced radially round
Paris with a few good cross-country lines, so that even as late as 1938 it
was quicker to go from Toulouse to Lyon via Paris (683 miles) than direct
(340 miles). When heavy industry grew up, some of it settled near the
coal and iron-ore mines of the north-east or the upper Loire, but much of
it went to Paris, to be near the sources of finance and the key Ministries.
Yet at this time new techniques and transport systems were, in other
countries, encouraging *de*centralization.

The big banks gradually became centred in Paris, while the snobberies of the literary salons joined with the hold of the Sorbonne over the
State university network to deprive the provinces of much of their
intellectual resources. And the masses arrived too, hungry for work. The
great Parisian building programmes of Baron Haussmann in the 1860s
saw little counterpart in the provinces, and this helped to draw to the
capital hundreds of thousands of destitute peasants. The statistics are
astonishing. From 1851 to 1931 the population of greater Paris went up
by 4.4 million, that of the Nord and of the Lyon–St-Etienne area by 1.8
million, while that of the rest of France dropped by 1.2 million. Paris'
share of France's population rose in this period from 5 to 15 per cent, and
by the 1931 census many lesser provincial towns were smaller than they
had been in 1800. In Britain, London saw a similar growth, but it was
shared by many other towns too. No wonder that France, even today,
has fewer large towns than Germany, Britain or Italy.

By 1939 the greater part of the wealth of France was concentrated in
Paris or in the country *châteaux* of Parisians; and workers' salaries in Paris
were 40 per cent higher than in the provinces. All this time France had
been investing eagerly in countries like Morocco and Senegal, where the
legacy of this inter-war colonial growth still catches the eye. But she
neglected her own provinces, notably the south and west, and this
wasted resources. The notion grew up of 'two Frances', divided by a
diagonal line from Caen to Marseilles. To the east, Paris and 85 per cent
of the industry, the big modern farms and Parisians' rich Riviera playgrounds; to the west, a territory more thinly populated than Spain
(except in Brittany), with poor farms and towns without industry. Only
since the war has this imbalance caught public attention.

Even before 1945, the pendulum had begun to swing back. The
pre-war strategic decentralization of a few car and aircraft factories may
have played a small role. Then came those familiar blessings in disguise,
Vichy and the Occupation. A number of dynamic personalities withdrew
from Paris to the 'free' Vichy zone where the southern provinces, cut off

from the capital, were forced to act and think for themselves. Lack of transport crippled national sales of Paris newspapers, and gave the provincial Press a chance to build up a strength it has since held.

After 1945 a consistent movement gathered pace, due to Government action and various spontaneous factors. The sudden up-swing in the birth-rate was not confined to Paris, and curiously it gave a psychological boost to stagnating towns. The rural exodus, now faster than ever, was still directed mainly towards Paris but by no means exclusively: since the war Greater Paris has grown from six to ten million, but many other towns have trebled in size and Grenoble has quadrupled. In an overpopulated world, concerned about pollution and quality of life, this may seem a dubious achievement; indeed, the 1970s saw a popular reaction against France's precipitous urbanization. But after the war France had no choice but to urbanize if she was to become modern; and in many ways she is still underpopulated for her size and resources. Paris is still the only town to have passed its optimum size: its congestion, high costs, and commuting problems have led to an under-current of neurosis and have begun to drive some people away. Engineers, professors and executives begin to see that life in some other towns, in the warm south or near the sea or mountains, may be more human and pleasant, even if less intellectually stimulating. Among younger middle-class people a new and astonishing anti-Parisian snobbism has even begun to replace the old anti-provincial snobbism. Today, *more* such people move to new jobs in the provinces than follow the classic route of Julien Sorel, to seek fame and fortune in the capital, and it is almost *more* chic to say that you live and work in Annecy or Avignon than in Montparnasse – a strange reversal.

The 1975 census results confirmed that for the first time in centuries the net migration is away from Paris. The net flow into the Paris region fell from 700,000 in 1954–62 to 377,000 in the next census period, 1962–8, and 87,000 in 1968–75. A closer breakdown shows that this last figure would be *minus* if foreign immigrants to Paris were excluded. In fact, some 20,000 Parisians are moving away each year, very often back to their native province, to work or to retire, and this is greater than the traffic in the other direction. It marks a profound historical change, and concerns workers as well as the middle classes.

Very few of the emigrants regret the move. The rhythm of life is calmer than in Paris, the children can have more fun, often there are good theatres and concerts and gradually you can create a new social circle. It is true that one or two big towns, such as Marseille, are now in danger of catching the Parisian disease of hectic activity and congestion. But most towns offer a happy and harmonious balance between new-style animation and old-style *douceur de vivre*. A man can find a villa with a garden only ten minutes' drive from his office; he has time to linger over a *pastis* with friends in a café; he can fit in a game of tennis or a swim on a summer evening after work, as the Parisian can rarely do. The growth of car ownership, of faster trains and air services, all have helped to make a life away from Paris seem less like exile to a cultured family used to its stimulus. With a working week in Nantes or Grenoble, then sometimes a weekend in the capital, a cake can be had and eaten. This important new mobility has influenced staid provincial towns. Some of the keenest new local pride and dynamism comes from young citizens who have moved in from elsewhere, who are ready to put down new roots but still want to keep in touch with the rest of France: a change from the outlook of the old Breton whose pride was never to have ventured onto 'foreign' soil east of Rennes. Towns have been coaxed out of their ancient slumber, made more aware of each other and the world. This is common experience in many countries, but in the context of past French neglect it is especially significant.

These spontaneous changes would probably have occurred any-way, as France modernized. But they have been further stimulated by Government action. *'Aménagement du territoire'* as the French call it (regional development in the widest sense) was almost unheard of before the war, but soon became a major priority of Monnet and his planners. In 1947 Jean-François Gravier, a young geographer attached to the Plan, published his famous book, *Paris et le désert français*, which brilliantly analysed the economic problems. He showed how the neglect of the west wasted the country's resources, while the concentration on Paris and other key areas led to high costs. France, he said, could not become a modern nation unless this was remedied. These warnings deeply impressed official milieux, and many of his proposals soon became accepted State policy. The Government began to encourage local 'expansion committees', and in 1950 it created the first series of subsidies and tax concessions for firms willing to shift their factories from Paris or open new ones in the less developed areas. Later it imposed rules to restrict the creation or enlargement of factories in the Paris area.

These steps met with a few successes – for example, a big new Citroën factory at Rennes – but the incentives were generally not strong enough. Most firms preferred to move their factories out to somewhere near the capital, such as Rouen or Orléans, rather than to the west. So when the Gaullists came to power they intensified the *aménagement* policy. In the areas where it was hardest to attract private industry, the Government set a lead with its own bold schemes, such as atomic and space centres in Brittany, tourist and irrigation projects in Languedoc. In order to facilitate large-scale planning, the ninety departments were grouped into twenty-two new economic regions, some corresponding to the old provinces: the department kept its existing functions, but the region had a new coordinating super-prefect.

Above all, in 1963 a new Government agency was created, the Délégation à l'Aménagement du Territoire et à l'Action Régionale (DATAR). This is a highly original French conception, and on the whole it has worked well. With its compact team of dedicated young technocrats, it acts as a kind of ginger-group, stirring Ministries and other bodies into action, and it has a dual role: to stimulate new economic ventures where they are most needed, and to lay the ground for these by urging improvements in infrastructure and environment. In most countries, including Britain, these two functions are much less closely integrated. DATAR has evolved a doctrine of making the most harmonious use of national space, by siting activities where they best fit natural resources and human needs. It has a weaponry of incentives, with grants of up to 25 per cent for the Massif Central, Languedoc and Corsica, as well as parts of the Pyrenees, Brittany, Lorraine and the Nord; the rest of the west is at 17 per cent. In addition to these carrots, it sometimes uses the stick. Its record has been variable (see p. 173), but at least it has helped to check much of the eastward drift of industry, and it points to the fact that in 1968–75 the growth of the west in terms of numbers of new jobs was four times the French average. But it has done less well in the rural south-west and Massif Central, and since about 1975 it has been forced into a much more defensive strategy: its most urgent priority has become the reconversion of older industrial areas worst hit by the crisis, notably the steel and textile zones of Lorraine and the Nord. This distracts DATAR's attention from areas still struggling to industrialize. A Breton leader complained in 1979: 'DATAR, first conceived as the high-fashion dressmaker of a new French industry, has become simply the patcher-up of its old clothes.'

Despite this different new climate, the French official zest for regional planning remains buoyant. *Aménagement du territoire* has been elevated into a science and a philosophy, the subject of endless speeches, books and congresses. As recently as November 1979, with a fanfare of trumpets Giscard launched the most elaborate of post-war regional schemes, a ten-year Plan for the Greater South-West (Aquitaine, Midi-Pyrénées, Languedoc-Roussillon). One aim was to help these three regions to prepare for the new competition with Spain when she joins the EEC. Most of the ideas and the funding come from Paris, but Giscard was careful not to dictate the plan to these sensitive regions: local *notables* were scrupulously consulted in its preparation. Launched in a pre-election period, the project clearly had its vote-catching aspect. Yet this does not preclude the sincerity of its field-workers today, as they lyricize over schemes for solar energy in the Pyrenees or food factories in fertile Béarn.

Regional policies have seen many failures and delays, yet the enthusiasm they generate still has an authentic basis. France today still presents her planners with some of the exciting challenge of a virgin land. It is one of the few parts of Western Europe where there is still the space, and the resources, for ambitious ventures; and as one talks with the planners, one gets just a glimpse of the vision that inspired the developers of the New World. Whereas in Britain it is a question of patiently rebuilding old eyesores like Glasgow and Merseyside, in France few industrial areas present this kind of derelict mess. Corbusier-style ideas can have their fling: linear cities on virgin plains, factories in the depths of unknown valleys, tunnels under high mountains. Since the war, this freedom of space has favoured the harmonious siting of new factories (where landscapes are spoilt, it is more often the fault of tourism or housing), and France is lucky to be making her real industrial revolution in an age of mobility and clean fuel.

Since the 1950s the enthusiasm of the planners has percolated, in some places, to more local bodies, chambers of commerce, municipal and departmental councils. Their preoccupations have been shifting, from the details of their own budgets to a sense of participation in wider schemes. It is an uneven process and there is plenty of obstruction, or political bickering and horse-trading, especially in places where the Communists share local power. But in many other cases, the focus of heated local argument is now less on questions of political doctrine and more on practical economic or social matters. In Toulouse, I happened to attend an animated debate of regional councillors. Twenty or so years earlier, they might have been discussing, say, the Church schools issue, or conscription in Algeria, or Mendès-France's 'wicked' attack on the privileges of home distillers. This time their debate was on how to expand Toulouse airport, and whether the motorway to Bordeaux could be completed in two years or three.

Regional planning of course suffers from the usual French chasm between theory and achievement. Splendid blueprints may fall foul of bureaucratic inertia, ministerial rivalries, or lack of funds. Ask any Frenchman what he has done, and excitedly he will tell you all he is about to do – and yet, if only one of his projects sees the light, it is better than having no ideas or eagerness at all. Many executives and *notables*, even at local level, are mesmerized by geographical obsessions that sound weird to English ears. Towns are pieces on an enormous chessboard, and the mere drawing of lines across a map yields some strange reality of its own. Towns are seen in relation to each other, like little groups of magnets, and translated into English terms a local French dignitary or official might talk like this: '*Swindon, bien que dans l'orbite londonienne, peut profiter d'une certaine vocation bristolienne, et tout en s'inspirant du rayonnement intellectuel oxfordien, elle se situe bien pour remplir un grand destin au carrefour des grandes axes de demain – de l'agglomération birminghamoise jusqu'à South-ampton aux portes de l'Amérique, et de l'hinterland*' – current franglais – '*galloise jusqu à Harwich, plaque-tournante de l'avenir scandinavienne.*' Every-thing is seen in terms of '*les grandes axes de demain*'. Does the mayor of Swindon talk like that?

Parallel to its industrial policies, the Government for many years has sought to stimulate the cultural and intellectual life of provincial cities, so as to counter the appeal of Paris. In the 1960s big new arts centres (Maisons de la Culture) were built or projected in some towns, not always with the happiest results (see p. 325). Provincial universities were encouraged to expand faster than those of Paris, and in 1969 were granted a measure of autonomy, though this too has not been the greatest success (see p. 496). More recently, several Grandes Ecoles and national research bodies have been transferred from Paris. In 1965 the Government designated eight of the largest towns as *métropoles d'équilibre* (Lyon, Marseille, Toulouse, Bordeaux, Nantes, Lille, Stras-bourg, Nancy/Metz), with the aim of helping them to expand rapidly and acquire some of the same amenities and metropolitan flavour as Paris. This could be seen as little more than a typical French conceptual gesture – can a town's destiny be decided by parading a new formula? In fact, the towns did expand fast anyway, and this soon brought a new danger in its turn: some of them, notably Toulouse, were attracting too much of the activity of their region and thus creating their own 'desert' around them. So from 1973 the eight *métropoles* were left to find their own equilibrium; and, in line with the new emphasis on local 'quality of life', a plan was launched for encouraging middle-sized towns (see p. 300).

This shift coincided with the industrial slow-down, which has intensified economic competition between the regions, now that new jobs are so few. Even the most dazzling boom cities of the '60s, led by Grenoble and Caen, are feeling the pinch of unemployment, and every town, every region, is lobbying more frantically for a larger share of the dwindling supply of new industry. Some regions, such as Languedoc, have long complained – with a certain perversity – that Paris at once 'colonizes' and neglects them. Some big towns, such as Lyon, have long felt they could manage their affairs better, were not the main centres of decision still in Paris. But these feelings may change, as the Socialist Government's devolution plans take effect. We shall now look at two of the most assertive regions, and three of the most interesting cities, as they were on the eve of the great reforms of 1981.

BRITTANY'S REVIVAL: MIRAGE OR REALITY?

'The French have destroyed us. In the past, they killed off our small industries so that our people had to emigrate. They gave us an inferiority complex. They tried to suppress our language and culture. For me, France is a foreign country.' Those fiery words were spoken to me by a gentle scholar, Per Denez, professor of Celtic languages at Rennes. Not all other Bretons would put it so strongly, nor feel it so difficult to be both Breton *and* French. Yet there is a wide undercurrent of grievance, today made up of three strands: an urge to reassert the neglected Breton *persona*; a desire for more autonomy; and a fear that Brittany, out on its lonely peninsula, is the eternal economic victim.

In reality, the province has come a long way towards prosperity since about 1960, thanks to a Government assistance that the Bretons do not always credit, and also to their own efforts (a people as dreamy and passionate as the Irish, as whimsical as the Welsh, yet as tough and hard-working as the Scots). But the local industries are still too few and too vulnerable, and the post-1973 crisis has hit harder than in most regions. Unemployment has risen sharply, the new prosperity looks fragile, and Bretons have reason to be worried.

I write as an Irishman, who feels more at home in Brittany than in any other part of France. This is France's Celtic fringe, a wild mysterious poetic land not unlike Wales or Ireland, where the desolate central moorlands slope down to fertile coastal plains, and Atlantic rollers break on rocky headlands. In many villages, the strange stone calvaries and ossuaries, with their ornate carvings, are witness to a very special religious past, linked to the terrors of death at sea. Brittany was not annexed to France until 1532, later than most provinces; and its people retain more sense of a separate identity than others in mainland France, while the visitor may find this region more 'un-French' in character than any other save perhaps Alsace.

When Bretons put on their costumes for summer festivals, it may be with an eye for the tourist trade, yet their concern for their traditions is real, and in some respects under revival. Young poets, writing in Breton, link modern political themes to the ancient legends of Merlin or Tristan and Isolde. When Breton teenagers hold a 'hop' in a village hall, nowadays they use the stately slow-swaying Breton dance forms, as well as traditional Breton music which somehow is transmuted into Breton 'pop'. This awareness of a Breton identity has increased greatly in the past ten or fifteen years, and has reawoken a sense of past wrongs. An executive in his forties told me, 'We have been oppressed for a century. As a boy, I was punished whenever I spoke Breton at school.' He reminded me that in 1947 a Socialist Minister of Education, Marcel Nagelen, had decreed: 'The task of teachers in the Breton-speaking areas is identical with that of French teachers in Algeria: assimilate the population at any price.' And look what then happened in Algeria.

Times have changed, and today the Breton language is more freely permitted. But it remains illegal in France to advocate secession, and this has had the effect of driving underground a small hard-core of nationalist extremists, who feel that violence is their best weapon. The Front de Libération de la Bretagne first became active in 1966. It has carried out sporadic bomb attacks in Brittany on police and public buildings, on nuclear stations and State TV transmitters, and in 1978 even on the Palace of Versailles; and scores of its members including priests have been arrested and some sentenced to prison. However, this terrorism is only very indirectly connected with the much wider economic disquiet and cultural renewal. The average Breton may feel a sneaking sympathy for the tiny groups of FLB activists, but he deplores their violence, nor does he really support their ideals of separatism. Most Bretons accept that total independence in this modern age would not make good economic sense for a relatively poor land of two-and-a-half million people. True nationalism is a much weaker force than in Scotland. But what Bretons do want is a better economic deal and a fuller say in running their own affairs.

Strangely enough, a moderate widely based political movement for internal autonomy (as opposed to secession) has never got going. It has always been pre-empted by extremists. Before and during the war, Breton separatists were on the far Right: they collaborated with the Nazis, who wooed them with cynical promises, and this gave the ideal of autonomy a bad name. Today, the FLB is not only violent but anarcho-Leftist. Parallel to it, there has grown up since the mid-'60s a legitimate non-violent autonomist party, the Union Démocratique Bretonne, which has won a few seats on local councils notably in Brest. But it is rather too closely allied to the Communists for most Breton tastes, and some people describe it as 'Stalinist'. Its appeal is bound to remain limited.

So why is there not a more widely representative movement, akin to the Scottish Nationalist Party, or the Plaid Cymru in Wales? Well, not only is the preaching of secession still illegal, but only in the past few years has the Government tacitly sanctioned parties advocating federalism: there are clauses in the Constitution that could, in theory, be invoked against even this. Also, as the Plaid and the SNP have often found to their cost, in a general election voters tend to think in terms of the government they want in London or Paris, and to feel that a vote for a regional or smaller party is a vote wasted. These are potent factors. And yet, today, there is little doubt that if Bretons really wanted to create a united autonomist party, they could get away with it; and if this sent deputies to parliament, it could seriously embarrass the State. It is partly the Bretons' own fault – this militant but not always realistic people – if they have failed to rally behind a constructive movement that could put pressure on Paris by peaceful means. 'Maybe we're too Celtic,' said one intellectual; 'we're incapable of organizing politically, we can only throw bombs.'

Under Giscard, most Bretons felt that political progress was blocked. As we shall see later in this chapter, the regional assembly set up in 1972 was not able to be much more than a rubber-stamp body, subservient to the prefect: it was not directly elected, its budget was minimal, it could take few decisions. So what was the answer? The view of most Breton leaders and intellectuals was that, for the immediate future, they must channel their campaign into economic and cultural action. Xavier Grall, a passionate nationalist writer, told me soon before his death in 1981: 'Our only course is to build up our culture, as the spiritual basis for a new political thrust when the time comes. Many people have done this under oppression – for instance, the Irish under the British, the Slovenes under the Austrians.' And Per Denez, no Leftist, added: 'I've entirely lost faith in Giscard's reformism, he's betrayed his promises on devolution. Our combat now is a total one, political, economic, cultural.'

This cultural renewal is fairly recent. It was fuelled by May '68 and its ideals of do-your-own-thing, and has since taken diverse forms. First, the groups of intellectuals, seeking through arts and literature to counter-balance the inevitable decline in day-to-day folk styles as the peasantry disappears: while the *coiffes* die out in the villages, the poetry clubs grow in the towns. New novels written in Breton are fetching bigger sales, maybe up to 4,000; literary reviews have been started; one or two theatre groups act plays in Breton. Perhaps one should remain a little sceptical, for in quality this movement does not begin to compare with the pre-1922 Irish writers, and the new activity may only have a limited impact. It suffers from the usual Gallic – and Celtic – tendency to split into factions. For instance, there is rivalry between the Breton-speakers (*bretonnants*) and the rest: Xavier Grall, most ardent of Bretons, felt a sense of shame that he was brought up in a French culture and was incapable of writing his poetry in Breton. And Brittany's two writers most famous in France as a whole, Per-Jakez Hélias and Jean-Edern Hallier, are regarded with some scorn by the Breton zealots. Hélias' saga of his own Breton peasant family, *Le Cheval d'orgeuil* (1975), sold 1.2 million copies in France, but he is that horror, a pro-French Republican. Hallier, who lives in Paris, wins some respect for his passionate espousal of what he calls *'celtitude'* (the specificity of Celtic culture), but his megalomaniac pirouettes in Paris salons (see pp. 536–7) cause a smirk down west.

Despite these reservations, there seems to me something strong and pure and noble about the new Breton culture at its truest. In a remote village of the interior there lives the majestic and mysterious Glenmor, a burly bearded poet-singer with the looks and presence of Solzhenitsyn. He can magnetize an audience with his thunderous voice and the stern rhythms of his own songs . . . *'Deiz ha deiz, hir ha berr, o youc'hal . . .'* It is enough to set any Celt's pulse racing, from Quimper to Connemara, from Lorient to Llangollen.

A popular figure such as Glenmor has links with the much wider revival of *bretonnisme* among a whole youth generation. The 1970s saw a craze for the *'fest-noz'*, the local fête or dance where musical groups play Breton instruments such as the *bombarde* (a kind of oboe) or bagpipes. The movement began spontaneously, but rapidly became commercialized, as true Breton folk-song merged into a more hybrid new Breton pop, even Breton rock. Bretonism became fashionable, and even created an export industry, a mini-Nashville. Alain Stivell, a folk-singer in a less serious vein than Glenmor, became a cult hero, selling millions of records not only in Brittany. Today the *fest-noz* and music craze is past its peak, but young people continue to show a new interest in their Celtic roots, and youth clubs have success with classes of Breton wrestling (similar to Cornish) and lectures on Breton history (which is not taught in State schools). The pan-Celtic annual folk festival at Lorient draws big crowds, while Breton folk groups are now paying more regular visits to festivals in the other Celtic lands: this is a rediscovery of an ancient tradition, for, ever since the French annexation, Bretons have tended to lose contact with other Celtic cultures. Even today, it is surprising how few Bretons have visited Wales or Ireland; however, town-twinnings are now growing, Quimper with Limerick and so on.

It is the language revival, above all, that attracts an eager minority of young people. This is a complex issue. Breton used to be the main everyday language, but Paris then applied its assimilation policy, first winning over the bourgeoisie to French, then trying to stamp out Breton among the peasantry. From the late nineteenth century, State teachers would punish pupils who spoke Breton in school, teasing them mercilessly or making them stand in class with a stone or clog tied round the neck. Per Denez says that his mother-in-law, as a child, was once locked up for the night in the school's basement. This kind of policy was quite effective, for it terrorized many ordinary Bretons who looked on the local teacher as 'superior' and it inculcated a sense of inferiority: young men joining Army units on military service found themselves insulted and despised if they spoke Breton or could not manage proper French. And so, almost to this day, poorer-class parents who spoke Breton between themselves would actually try to prevent their own children from learning it: they wanted to protect them from what they felt would be a handicap! One hears countless stories of this. I met a youngish man, son of Breton-speaking small-town shopkeepers who had taught him only French. When as a teenager he started going to Breton soirées and *fest-noz*, he literally wept with joy to discover his heritage for the first time. He then went away to college and learned Breton on his own. When he came home, his father was furious and hit him in the face: '*Fiston*, after all we've tried to do for you, why inflict this on us?'

These attitudes are now changing, and Paris has recently relented its campaign. Yet the legacy of the long war of attrition is that Breton in this century has steadily been dying out as a daily language, and the postwar rural exodus has even hastened the process, as the once isolated peasant class has moved to new jobs in the cities. Today, in nearly all areas, Breton is spoken only among people who know each other well, in families or between pals in cafés, and is no longer a *lingua franca*. Figures are hard to come by, as the State refuses any census on the subject; but estimates are that in 1930 about 1.2 million (half the population) spoke Breton fluently, while today the total is at most 600,000, of which about half use it as their first language at home. The figure is still falling as the older peasants die.

At the same time a revival, numerically still modest, has come from an entirely different quarter: the intellectuals and the very young. Since the 1960s, the Government has moved towards tolerating Breton and other regional languages in France; and Giscard formalized this in a 'cultural charter for Brittany' proclaimed at Ploërmel in April 1977, where he pledged support for the Breton 'cultural personality'. Many Bretons saw this as mere vote-catching, or as a sop to placate their anger at his refusal to increase the powers of the regional assemblies. But the new policy has brought some gains. For some years now Breton has been allowed as an option in the *baccalauréat*, and it can be taught for up to three hours a week in State *lycées*. About 2,000 *lycéens* a year take this option, and the figure might be much higher were there more teachers. In 1979 a youth actually took the risk of writing all his *bac* exam papers in Breton (except for the French language paper): the State examiners were not amused, but after consulting Giscard's charter, they conceded. It caused quite a sensation. How times have changed.

In 1977 the pioneers of the new language campaign opened a chain of private nursery schools where only Breton is spoken. One of Rennes' two universities offers a higher diploma in Breton, organized by Per Denez: but the Ministry still refuses to grant this the status of *licence* (B A). Denez is a leader of the Celtic International and has given all his life to the cause of his language. He told me he was sceptical of Paris' softer line: 'Since Ploërmel, there's a new approach – but what does it mean? The Ministry is obliged to offer extra school hours for Breton, but its officials here deliberately fail to recruit the necessary staff. If anyone shows a keenness for teaching Breton, he's likely to be posted to another part of France.[1] There's a discreet sabotage going on. As I see it, Paris' hope is that Breton as a daily language will die out of its own accord with the older generation, and be confined to a harmless minority of twenty thousand or so intellectuals and students.' It could be added that the regional stations of the State-controlled TV and radio, staffed from Paris, did little to follow the spirit of the Ploërmel charter. Under Giscard, TV provided about twenty-five minutes a week in Breton, radio a little more – but only about a tenth as much as the BBC's fourteen hours a week of programmes in Welsh for Wales. Under the Socialists, with their programme of decentralization of TV and radio, matters are now likely to improve.

Everywhere I heard complaints of lack of teachers for school classes in Breton. Many parents, too, are even today reluctant to urge their children to learn it, and the initiative usually comes from the kids themselves, once they reach the age of about fourteen and become aware of what it is to be Breton. Then they are often very eager. But are their numbers enough to compensate for the decline among the old? Many cultural leaders are pessimistic about the future of Breton, and they realize the difficulties of keeping a regional tongue alive in an age when the pressures are all to learn 'useful' major languages, notably English. Look at the fate of Irish, and Gaelic. But this raises the whole question: does a nation, or an autonomous people, need its own language? After all, nationalism is far more potent in Scotland, where hardly anyone

1 See p. 492 on educational centralization.

speaks Gaelic, than in Wales with its hordes of Welsh speakers; Ireland after independence made efforts to promote Irish as its official language, but found it more practical to go back to English. To this Per Denez replied: 'But the Irish case proves my point. Once a people is free, it can do what it likes without complexes. But a people struggling for survival needs a language as a weapon and a focus of identity. That is my crusade.' A brave but uphill task.

Meanwhile, local economic leaders are embarked on a parallel crusade: to create new exports, new trade links with the world, and thus 'liberate' Brittany from economic over-dependence on Paris. The province lacks an industrial tradition, and finds it hard to attract new investors so far from Paris. Its fishing is in crisis, its great naval ports of Brest and Lorient have seen their role decline. Agriculture, it is true, has modernized greatly, but this in turn adds to unemployment as a surplus population steadily migrates from the farms (see Chapter 4). Moreover, Brittany lies at the western extreme of a France whose focus since 1960 has shifted eastwards towards the EEC centres of gravity: so, if their main trade and other economic links remain via Paris, Bretons are bound to feel deprived. Is there another solution? Most Breton leaders believe that one answer is to take their trade destiny in their own hands and turn its focus seawards again and towards their British and Irish neighbours; that is, to resume the old trading and maritime role that Brittany held before the bear-hug of Napoleonic centralism. Claude Champaud, president of the region's economic and social committee, told me: 'Brittany knew three golden ages: in Druidic times, under the Roman conquest, and in the post-Renaissance era. In these periods, this was a great trading centre, our textiles, tin-mines and agriculture all flourished. But these were times when Britain and Spain were flourishing too: we *need* these lands for our trade. We are weak when France forgets the sea and pursues a "Lotharingian" policy. Today, with or without Paris, we must get back to the old ways.' In fact, D A T A R goes along with this idea, and for the whole Atlantic coast has launched the strategy of *'Eurocéan'*: 'The under-developed west,' said one planner, 'must no longer be thought of as on the EEC's periphery, but as a forward zone, Europe's gateway to the West, its watery frontier with the Americas.' For all the fanciful rhetoric, the idea is not absurd.

Some dynamic Bretons are already putting this into practice. The key figure on the economic scene is the amazing Alexis Gourvennec, peasant, shipping tycoon, ruthless riot-leader, pan-Celtic visionary, a man who has done more than any other in this century to rescue his native Brittany from poverty and forge new trade links. He grew up as a small farmer in the Morlaix district of north Finistère. In 1961, aged twenty-four, he won national fame when he led his fellow-peasants in riots against exploitation by the middlemen, then pressured the Government into radically changing its farm policies, and went on to build up a large and powerful cooperative of vegetable producers (see pp. 210, 225). His toughness and militancy are typically Breton: his economic foresight is more unusual. He soon realized that farming progress alone could not solve local problems, so in the mid-1960s he set up a North Finistère expansion committee that lobbied intensively in Paris, and in 1968 was instrumental in persuading the Government to allocate massive new funds for Brittany, including 6 million francs towards building a deep-water port at Roscoff, north of Morlaix. In fighting for this port he was gambling on Britain's entry into the EEC and the new trade that would follow: the existing means of transporting Breton vegetables across the Channel were circuitous and slow, as there was no other non-tidal port on the north coast west of St-Malo. A direct ferry to Plymouth was the answer – but who was to run it? Gourvennec approached several shipping firms who all turned the project down as unlikely to be viable ('Roscoff? – where's that? Sorry, we never do trade with the Russians,' scoffed a London broker). So the farmers' cooperative decided to launch its own company (today called Brittany Ferries), to the scorn of other firms such as Townsend Thoresen who expected them to flop – '*Vous n'êtes pas des armateurs mais des amateurs.*' But by hiring the right technical skills the farmers succeeded. In 1973, when the port was ready, they opened the now successful daily ferry service to Plymouth, which has done a lot to develop trade and tourism between '*la petite et la Grande Bretagne*'. The cooperative exports some 50,000 tons a year of its own potatoes and 20,000 tons of cauliflowers: in addition, there is a growing two-way traffic in meat, fish, eggs, heavy freight of all sorts, and 200,000 tourists. The cooperative owns 53 per cent of the shares of Brittany ferries, and other local interests the rest. It is believed to be the only example in Europe of farmers starting their own shipping line, and taking the lead in regional economic expansion.

Later BF opened an even more successful service from St-Malo in eastern Brittany to Portsmouth, and then a Roscoff–Cork line. But this expansion has not been without controversy. Gourvennec can deal ruthlessly with those rash enough to thwart him, and he has his own 'commando force' of local workers and fellow-farmers. When in 1975 the German TT Line had the impudence to open a Southampton–St-Malo ferry to rival the one BF was planning, the Right-wing Gourvennec formed alliance with the CGT-led dockers and seamen at St-Malo, and sent busloads of his commandoes to prevent the TT's *Mary Poppins* from docking. She slunk back to Hamburg. Gourvennec, and the CGT, alleged that TT were using a flag-of-convenience boat with underpaid Filipino crews and this was unfair competition which they had the right to stop. Even so, many people including Breton leaders felt that this time Godfather Gourvennec had gone too far: was this the EEC spirit of free enterprise? Bonn, furious, lodged protests. But Paris took no action: Giscard would rather have powerful Gourvennec as friend than foe, in sensitive Brittany. Often a mere phone call to some Ministry, threatening 'trouble', was enough to make the Government give Gourvennec what he wanted. Though proudly Breton, he is no separatist, his aims are purely economic, and so Paris found him useful. As with the language issue, the Giscard Government was often at pains to placate Bretons where possible, in an effort to defuse political and economic grievances.

Gourvennec has several times used these strong-arm methods. When there was a sit-in strike at the Crédit Agricole bank in Quimper, he sent in his heavies to evict the strikers. They left quietly. 'Fascist,' murmur some people. 'Yes, I admit we sometimes behave illegally,' Gourvennec told me, 'but we have no option. Everyone has to use pressure: workers go on strike, so we farmers use what means we can. Pious speeches get you nowhere. But we never injure people.' He is a stocky peasant turned jet-hopping tycoon, and cultivates the style *jeune patron dynamique*, restless, open-shirted. But though rich he lives modestly in his farmhouse near Morlaix, and prides himself on his earthiness and rejection of high-life graces: at a banquet for Brittany Ferries in a top Paris restaurant, he brushed aside the Mumms and Margauxs and told the waiter, '*Donne-moi un bon coup de rouge, mon vieux.*' He is also an idealist, with a Celtic gift of the gab. He told me that like most Bretons he had warmly welcomed the entry of Britain and Ireland into the EEC, and was a little disappointed with the results, but hoped for better times. 'Our ferries are part of a strategy of putting Brittany on the centre of the map. The main EEC north–south axes are too far east, along the Rhine and Rhône. We want a great new trade route, from Spain up the west coast of France, cutting across Brittany to Roscoff, to link with the motorway from Plymouth to Glasgow – *le grande axe de demain*! We shall escape Paris at last. In modern times the Celtic lands have ignored each other too long: we must return to the close links of our ancestors.' In fact, this new highway is more likely to go to St-Malo, via Nantes and Rennes. This will still satisfy BF's interests, but not those of Finistère, nor of Plymouth. The project is far behind schedule, due partly to bickerings between Rennes and Nantes, two bitterly rival cities which are respective capitals of the regions involved, Brittany and Pays de la Loire.

'Regionalism is all very well,' said a haughty Jacobin in the *préfecture* in Rennes, in 1980, 'but French regions often fail to cooperate with each other. They still need the State to look after them.'

Tenacious, assertive, but not always level-headed, Bretons have tended for decades to blame their economic woes on Paris' 'neglect'. But from about 1960, the charge ceased to be nearly as justified as once it had been. De Gaulle loved the Bretons, who had provided so many of the Free French in the war; and after his return to power the Government proclaimed for Brittany an 'electronics and nuclear vocation'. It built a major space-communications centre at Lannion; it persuaded electronics firms to set up plant in Brest, Rennes and other towns; and it began to provide Brittany with its own sources of energy, through the Rance tidal dam and a new nuclear centre in Finistère, one of France's first. The Bretons were not satisfied. In response to serious agitation and violence in 1968–9, a worried Government than launched a much more extensive aid programme, and until the later '70s it poured more money into Brittany than any other region. The telephone system was fully automated ahead of most provinces; new research centres were set up, and Grandes Ecoles transferred from Paris; work started on a network of new trunk roads, today nearing completion; and funds were given for a giant new dry-dock at Brest, able to repair 500,000-ton tankers. In 1975 State companies began the search for off-shore oil, west of Finistère – and Breton hopes rose romantically that Brest might become a second Aberdeen and all would be solved! So far, no oil has been found, but in 1981 the search was still going on. On a more immediately practical level, DATAR for some years has been offering handsome grants to woo investors to Brittany, especially to the west, an area where the level of industrial employment is only half the French average. It is not an easy task, but some private firms have responded, and until the world's economy faltered in the mid-'70s new industry was creating 5,000 extra jobs a year. All in all, it cannot be said that the Fifth Republic has neglected Brittany economically, whatever the motives.

Thanks to these efforts and local ones too, Brittany has come a long way in the past twenty years – as is apparent in the spruce new buildings on every side. Except in parts of the wild interior, this does not *look* a depressed area. Industry may still be inadequate, but agriculture has made spectacular progress (see p. 212 and p. 225): this used to be a region mainly of subsistence farming, but now it is one of the major food-exporting zones of the EEC, and is also beginning to exploit its potential for food-processing. The growth of tourism too has brought new wealth, especially to the coastal areas, where neat new hotels and holiday villas dot the meadows and woodlands beside the rocky coves and sandy beaches. Here at Quiberon, on the south coast, Monsieur Hulot took his momentous holiday.

New prosperity of course is unevenly spread. It is most evident in tourist spots, in the richer farming areas, and in the eastern part of the province nearest Paris. Here Rennes, the capital, provides a good study case in how larger French provincial towns have changed and blossomed since the war. From 1953 to 1977 it was lucky to have one of the most enlightened and go-ahead mayors in France, Henri Fréville, a local university history professor, originally MRP, then pro-Giscard *centriste*. When he took office, this dignified town of old grey buildings was sleepy and far from rich. It had long been a centre of army, law and learning, but it had no industry to provide jobs for the young emigrants who were arriving fast from the over-populated farmlands. Fréville's first and biggest *coup* was to persuade Citroën that Rennes was just the place for the big new provincial factory they wanted to build. Today this has 8,000 workers. Some other new industries followed, the university and scientific milieux expanded, and Rennes steadily won a new confidence. Its population has grown since the war from 95,000 to 250,000. For the newcomers, Fréville built housing estates of above-average quality and made efforts to endow them with better social and leisure amenities than were usual in the new French suburbs of the 1950s and '60s (see p. 301).

Thanks to his policies and to many spontaneous factors, Rennes has grown far more lively. An older inhabitant told me: 'It used to be dead after seven at night: now some cafés are still full after midnight. Though it's sad in a way, the Breton *coiffes* are gone from the streets and the girls wear Paris dresses. In the '50s the shops were seedy, their window-dressing unchanged since 1910: now there are smart boutiques everywhere.' Fréville took the initiative for the building of a large Maison de la Culture, one of the few still successful in France. Its theatre director told me: 'Rennes has acquired an entirely new spirit in the thirty years I've known it. The staid older Rennais have been submerged by the new ones, the students, the technicians from Paris, the peasants arriving with the open outlook of *émigrés*. It used to be said, "Nothing ever catches on here except fire" (there was a big fire in 1720), but now there's a curiosity and desire for the new. You can see it in the Breton revival, also in the growth of ciné-clubs, or our own success with playwrights like Beckett' (see p. 324). The Rennais' desire for the new was finally Fréville's undoing. This energetic idealist proved just how much a good mayor can do for a town, even in centralized France, and without being a mere stooge of Paris – as a *centriste*, he strongly opposed de Gaulle in the '60s. But he was also criticized for being an autocratic paternalist, and when he retired in 1977 his regime was blown away by the wind of change that swept the Left to power in so many big French towns in the local elections of that year. The new mayor is a young Socialist, of a very different stamp, ruling in uneasy coalition with the Communists (see p. 317).

Brest, the region's second city, also fell to the Left. Throughout Brittany, rising unemployment and factory closures helped to fuel the Leftward swing of 1977 and made Bretons aware of how precarious their new prosperity still is. How ironic it is, too, that just when Brittany at last seemed in sight of curing its economic backwardness, the post-1973 crisis risks cancelling out much of the progress made. In Rennes itself the jobless total is still fairly modest, but in the towns of the west such as Brest and Lorient it has risen to over 10 per cent, well above the national average. Here scores of small firms have closed. What is more, the important deep-sea fishing industries of Lorient and Concarneau have been badly affected by foreign competition, rising costs, falling prices, Atlantic over-fishing, the new 200-mile limit and Britain's controversial restrictions on EEC fishing rights in her waters. At Lorient, where a number of trawlers were lying idle, I was greeted with anti-British anger: 'We've created *Europe verte*, of a sort,' said a skipper, 'but not yet *Europe bleue.*'

Brittany's manufacturing industry is proving vulnerable to the crisis because so much of it is recent, the results of the past twenty years' efforts. In hard times, a major company will usually close or run down first its newest units, and this has been happening: big lay-offs at some of the new branch factories making telephones and other electronic equipment. A Breton economist said: 'The investment involved is so light that any of these installations could be closed tomorrow, at the whim of some board in Paris or abroad. In fact, our lack of an industrial tradition is a more serious handicap than our geographical isolation. There's not the executive experience here, the talent emigrated years ago: you find Bretons managing firms in Lyon or Grenoble, not here.' This is true, and it makes it all the harder to attract new investment. Not nearly enough new jobs are being created to keep pace with a continuing rural exodus of some 10,000 a year. Traditionally these people have made for Paris, but its appeal is now waning: in a recent survey, young Bretons were asked whether they would leave the region if they were certain of getting a better-paid job elsewhere, and 77 per cent said, 'No, we'd rather stay.' This is a new trend, and the 1976 census figures show that for the first time in this century more Bretons are returning than emigrating. True, most of these are retired people; but younger ones, wooed back by official incitements of job prospects, are liable to end up resentful.

'We have clear proof,' Claude Champaud told me in 1979, 'that the Government is again deserting Brittany and shifting its priorities else-where.' Many others share this anxiety. And even a State planner at the *préfecture* in Rennes admitted to me, 'Yes, Brittany used to be *the* privileged region, but now it has to share more of the aid with others, Lorraine and the south-west for instance, because of their problems. It just has to accept this.' But Bretons, when aroused, do not accept easily. In 1972, workers at the Joint Français electrical plant at St-Brieuc staged one of the longest and angriest strikes of the decade in France, in protest at being paid 30 per cent below Paris levels. More recently, Bretons on the north-west coast were understandably furious at the Government's inefficiency and lack of foresight in handling the *Amoco Cadiz* oil-spill disaster of 1978; and in 1980 the villagers of Plogoff, in south Finistère, staged the most resolute demonstrations yet seen in France against a proposed nuclear site (see pp. 340–46 for both incidents).

In 1981, the Socialist Government's first measures for devolution in France were cautiously welcomed by most Bretons. Their regional assembly would now have more power, and the hated influence of Paris would recede. But the real Breton autonomists were still far from satis-fied. They began to demand a special statute for Brittany, as Mitterrand was now offering to Corsica. Bretons today feel that the devolution now under way is a step forward, but that the battle must still go on – to achieve even more self-rule, to avert economic decline and to assert a cultural separateness. And so the *pobl Vreizh*, the Breton people, con-tinues to explore its psyche to the tune of *bombardes* and the bardic challenge of Glenmor. Is this a passing fashion, common to the reasser-tion of local identity in many parts of Europe? Or is it a deeper and more durable revival, and if so, where will it lead? It is the question that Yeats and his friends posed seventy years ago: can the gleam of a new Celtic Twilight herald a Celtic dawn?

THE NEW CATHARS OF
LOWER LANGUEDOC

Languedoc, sluggish and recalcitrant, is the one mainland province where anti-Paris feelings are even stronger than in Brittany. Like Brit-tany, it has a keen sense of its separate historical identity, it is trying to keep alive its ancient language, and is in the throes of a political-cultural revival, with separatist fringe. But there are differences. This is not the misty north but the Midi, a land of cypress and cicada where old men play *boules* in dusty village squares and under the dazzling sun the pace of life is easy. While Bretons are go-getting and alert for progress,

Languedociens are slow and unenterprising, with no local Gourven-necs. So the State decided to take the lead and impose its own develop-ment schemes on an area not very ready to help itself. The results have been – shall we say? – controversial.

The term 'Languedoc' is ambiguous. Until Napoleon's day, the noble province of the 'tongue of *oc*'[2] stretched far to the west beyond Toulouse, its historic capital. But today's modern economic 'region' of Languedoc-Roussillon is a hotch-potch: shorn of the whole Toulouse area, it consists of the eastern or 'lower' Languedoc along the coast, plus Roussillon (French Catalonia) to the south and bits of Provence and the Massif Central to the north. It is a good example of how the 1964 regional carve-up ignored many of the old provincial boundaries. To complicate matters further, the recent locally based regionalist movement claims sway over the much wider area known vaguely as 'Occitania', covering most of southern France. But the heartland of the new Occitan zealots is the Bas (lower) Languedoc, from Carcassonne to Nîmes. In the twelfth and thirteenth centuries this was also the heartland of the Cathar here-tics, and though the religious element is long buried, the region still simmers with the Cathar spirit of dissidence, especially prevalent amongst its vinegrowers. This coastal plain, backed by dry stony hills, produces 40 per cent of all France's wine and most of her cheaper table wine (see Chapter 4).

The vine has been described as 'Bas Languedoc's sole wealth, and its tragedy'. In the mid-nineteenth century factories flourished on this coast, and one of the first railway lines in France ran from Montpellier to the port of Sète. But the vine killed this brief age of industry. When French wine consumption rose rapidly in the later nineteenth century, the Languedociens found they could produce plenty and cheaply on their sunny slopes, and it was much less trouble than building factories. Today the vineyards roll for miles on every side, and life is easy when the grape grows fat on the red earth and needs little attention. Vines and climate have united to produce a lethargic, conservative temperament, excitable and refractory only when local interests seem menaced – that is, when the wine market is threatened or when Paris tries to introduce economic change. And this Paris has done. This fertile plain with its thick population, lying strategically on the main route into Spain, seemed to the Government ideal for development, and in the 1950s and early '60s it chose Bas Languedoc for two of its major post-war schemes: the canal, the biggest irrigation network in Europe; and the largest State-

2 So named, historically, because 'yes' in the Occitan language is '*oc*', not '*oui*' as in standard northern French.

sponsored tourist project in history. It was a technocrat's dream, *carte blanche* to make bold new strokes across the map. But involving the local population has had its problems.

The monoculture of cheap wine was economically harmful, yet it could not easily be diversified without water for other crops. So in the 1950s the State set up a company that dug a wide master canal in the east from the Rhône to Montpellier, and later built dams in the west in the hills behind Béziers. A network of little canals began to transect some vine areas. The company then found two or three pioneers who uprooted their vines and demonstrated that the same acreage of apple or pear orchards could earn six times as much, if irrigated. Other growers were invited to follow suit. And how did they react? They formed 'committees of defence against the canal', they rioted in the streets, they behaved, in short, like Victorian farmers who feared those new-fangled trains would run over their cows. Very few vines were uprooted. The canal ran into debt through lack of clients, and the company had to sanction what at first it had regarded as intolerable: use of the canal to irrigate vines. It is true that today vines account for only 12 per cent of the 100,000 acres actively using the canal's water, which serves mainly the non-vinegrowing plain south of Nîmes. Here yields of fruit, asparagus and tomatoes have risen sharply. But this has led in turn to new problems owing to EEC fruit surpluses, and – irony – some new apple orchards have been recently uprooted. On a purely technical level the canal is a huge success, and the company has made money by exporting its advanced techniques to many countries. But to Bas Languedoc, heralded by the planners twenty years ago as 'a new California', it has not brought as much new prosperity as was hoped. If this is due partly to the European fruit problem, it is also the fault of the stubborn vine-growers. They could find other marketable crops – rice, soya, vegetables – that with help from the canal could earn them a better living than their often unsaleable wines. But they will not take the risk of replanting.

The Government has also been trying to entice new factories to a region with little tradition of modern industry. This has proved all too easy in the north-east corner, beyond Nîmes, along the great axis of the Rhône valley. Elsewhere, new factories of any size are still few and far between, with the exception of an IBM plant at Montpellier now employing 2,500. However, the State's major effort for the region has been the tourist project, started in 1963, and this has been much more of a success than the canal.

From the Rhône delta to the Pyrenees lay a hundred and twenty miles of open sandy beaches, backed by stagnant lagoons. This coast had never been exploited, for the mosquito reigned supreme, and bathers were few. Yet the Riviera and Costa Brava were nearing saturation as Europe's tourist hordes grew yearly. So the Government decided to build a chain of eight big modernistic resorts, with a double objective: to give a needed boost to the region's economy; and to help France's tourist balance by providing an overspill for the Riviera, and hopefully deflecting some visitors both French and foreign from moving on to Spain. First, a chemical *Blitzkrieg* destroyed the mosquitoes, the lagoons were dredged and purified, the whole coast was zoned in a massive blueprint. In the key areas marked out for the resorts, land prices were pegged so as to avoid a gold-rush speculation that might have ruined the scheme at an early stage. This policy succeeded. An inter-ministerial Mission based in Paris and Montpellier was set up to master-mind the whole project, while locally constituted Sociétés d'Economie Mixte, associating chambers of commerce and other bodies, were charged with providing the infrastructure and services for each resort. This work continues today, for the project is not yet completed. As the land becomes ready for building, the SEMs sell or lease much of it to private developers, who construct the hotels, holiday flats, marinas and so on, and then run them on a profit basis. But they have to adhere to the master-plan, originally prepared by Georges Candilis, a disciple of Le Corbusier. This is capitalism, but controlled. Between the resorts are wide spaces where nature supposedly is protected. 'Our aim,' said a planner, 'has been to avoid the ugly anarchic development that has spoiled Florida, the Costa del Sol, parts of the Côte d'Azur, and so many other places.'

The results may not suit all tastes, but they are not a failure. A new road network has been built and three million cypresses and other trees planted, to act as windbreaks on this flat coast. After some delays, the whole project is now about two-thirds finished and finally, maybe by 1990, will have provided 280,000 new tourist beds, half as many as on the whole Côte d'Azur. Some resorts are still in an early stage, others are nearly completed and very busy in summer: the number of visitors to the coast rose from 500,000 in 1965 to 1,682,000 in 1976. By 1977 the State had spent some 700 million francs on the project, and private developers – including Dutch, German, Swiss, British and Japanese – a further 3,000 million. One major criticism, however, is that the Government has failed to ensure as much lower-cost 'popular' accommodation as it had promised. The initial aim was to prevent the new resorts from falling mainly into the luxury bracket: family holiday organizations were encouraged to buy land for camps and modest villas, while the anti-speculation measures were intended to keep down rents and other costs and make this feasible. But this policy soon ran into conflict with sterner realities. The Mission, having invested so heavily, came under pressure from its financial backers, the State and private banks, to amortize costs rapidly, and it soon found that up-market holiday flats and hotels brought higher and quicker returns than 'social' tourism. The private flats and villas by the beaches have been selling fast to well-heeled Parisians, Germans and others: but there are very few cheaper flats, while the functional mass holiday camps have been pushed into less favoured sites. 'For Paris, this is a commercial victory but a moral defeat,' said a local sceptic in 1980. It is in fact a typical example of how, under de Gaulle or Giscard, the genuine social ideals of the planners were often thwarted by the capitalist 'system'. Possibly this will now change under Socialism. At all events, the new resorts have more in common than was intended with the rich new development round Cannes, even if most of them *look* very different from a traditional seaside town.

Deliberately, the resorts vary in style, from pastiche fishing-port to the Brasilia-on-Sea of La Grande Motte. Each has its own architect (Candilis himself is no longer involved). Perhaps the most attractive is Port Camargue, to the east, where a vast harbour has been created out of marshland, in such a way that the town seems to be built on water, like Venice: there is a maze of little peninsulae dotted with villas, where the owner can moor his boat by his front door. Cap d'Agde, near Béziers, is like an operetta stage-set of an old Mediterranean fishing-village, with pretty buildings in pastel shades: phoney, but pleasing. Some of the resorts further south, however, are much uglier and are doing less well. An exception is Port-Barcarès, near Perpignan, where a Japanese supermarket consortium has built a vast hotel and has also taken over the *Lydia*, a converted Greek passenger-boat now parked high and dry on the beach and used as smart casino and restaurant. Near by, a British firm has developed a £6.5 million nudist resort, Aphrodite, with 550 bungalows. Nearly all its clients are French and German, with very few British. ('Surprising,' said one wag, 'seeing it's the British who can least afford to buy clothes.') Naturism is now a major growth industry on this coast, and even the most puritanical of town councils have succumbed to the lure of its lucre and have ceased trying to ban it. The new nudist holiday-town at Cap d'Agde, Europe's largest, has casinos, super-markets, night-clubs, the lot, and accommodation for 20,000 bodies who may sometimes resemble the young Brigitte Bardot but more often an ageing Hamburg *Hausfrau*.

La Grande Motte, near Montpellier, is the most sophisticated and highly publicized of the resorts: a space-age vision with motor-yachts and beach-parasols added. Coloured sun-blinds cover the honeycomb façades of the famous ten-storey ziggurat pyramids of holiday flats, row upon row of them. Some of the new ones are in the weirdest shapes and colours: one resembles a giant fairground wheel, painted purple. Not everyone might choose to spend a holiday in these surrealistic pop-art surroundings, however jolly the colours and lavish the amenities (fine boutiques and restaurants). Yet La Grande Motte is now always full in high summer, it can take 40,000 tourists at a time, and its marina for 1,800 yachts is as busy as almost any on the Riviera. Folly or masterpiece? – the resort will in any event survive as a monument to the heady modernism of the de Gaulle and Pompidou eras. Today its 'gigantism' is officially out of favour, and newer tourist projects such as that on the Aquitaine coast are much more discreet. Yet the Languedoc-Roussillon resorts, in their own way, have much to commend them. They could have been far worse. They are well spaced out on this long coast, and the Government has indeed fulfilled its aims of resisting pressure from speculators for building a 'wall of concrete' along the stretches in between, *à la* Costa del Sol.

The project has created 20,000 new full-time jobs and many seasonal ones. It has certainly helped the region, and for this reason local mayors and other *notables* tend to cooperate tacitly with the work of the Mission and the developers. But in public they often tirade against it as 'Parisian neo-colonialism': in fact there is a widespread local grouse that the project has brought less money to the region than to outside interests, the Paris banks, the international promoters and so on. Inevitably this is true. Sixty per cent of the resorts' new shops, hotels and other ventures have been created by entrepreneurs from elsewhere. And the tourists themselves, who crowd the roads and nearby villages in summer, have led to a mild wave of xenophobia among a local people who – although so many migrations have passed their way in history – seem to share little of the Mediterranean tradition of welcome to visitors. '*Touriste=con*', I saw daubed on some walls.

So, rather than remain 'colonized', why do people not take more initiative to help themselves? They are an odd lot these Languedociens. Tribal memories run so deep that Paris' brutal suppression here of the Cathar (Albigensian) heresy in the thirteenth century is still a live issue, and still the root of local hostility. The Cathars' doctrine of pious asceticism may itself be long extinct – the Midi is far from ascetic! – yet politically and psychologically their spirit of heresy remains amazingly present. There has even been a recent revival of interest: new books on the Cathars are local best-sellers,[3] and summer-school and university seminars on the subject are often held in this region. To this day, people have

3 Not to mention Emmanuel Le Roy Ladurie's international best-seller, *Montaillou*.

not forgiven Simon de Montfort and Louis VIII for the massacres at Béziers and Montségur and the events that followed, the wiping out of the troubadour civilization, the annexation to the Crown by fire and sword. And by a strange telescoping of history all this is mixed up in local minds with modern discontents, notably those of the vinegrowers, so that Giscard and de Montfort have been lumped together as responsible for what Emmanuel Maffre-Baugé, vitriolic ringleader of the growers, denounced to me as 'Paris' seven centuries of heartless colonization of this Occitan nation'. To the east, in the Protestant area from Nîmes to the Cevennes, historical resentment of Paris' crushing of the eighteenth-century camisard revolt is almost equally alive. All in all, it makes for a region that is not only anti-Paris but always cussedly eager to march out of step with the nation. Witness *'les cathares du rugby'*: because the French national game is fifteen-a-side, a number of thirteen-a-side rugby teams have sprung up in the Carcassonne area.

One more paradox is that this conservative and individualistic people has in recent years voted firmly for the Left, less from Left-wing conviction than because the Government has been Centre-Right. Now that France has voted the Left to power, Languedoc may well swing Right! As it is, even in the 1978–81 National Assembly, of the twelve deputies of the Gard, Hérault and Aude, six were Communist, five Socialist. All major towns are now run by Left coalitions, with Communist mayors at Nîmes, Alès, Sète and Béziers, Socialist ones at Montpellier, Narbonne and Carcassonne. Many leading Socialists are demagogic bourgeois figures of the old SFIO school (Section Française de l'Internationale Ouvrière), and much of their support is from the Poujadist-minded vinegrowers.

As many observers noted to me, this through-the-looking-glass world of local politics has a markedly Italian flavour: it is a *commedia dell'arte* of role-playing and wheeler-dealing where ideology counts for less than human contact. The real hatreds are directed against unseen Paris or newcomers to the area, notably Parisians: but between *les gars du pays*, even political foes, there exists a conspiratorial mateyness. In some towns, notably Sète and Nîmes, I found a cosy Peppone/Don Camillo relationship between Communist mayor and Rightist president of the chamber of commerce – *'On se tutoie*, especially when we're angry.' Even the Socialist/Communist conflict has been less sharp than in most parts of France.

The complex of being 'colonized' has some basis, for in Gaullist or Giscardian days the State was often tactless. Technocrats from Paris would impose their schemes without consulting adequately (see p. 342), or try to claim all the credit without letting local people feel that they too had played a part: like an impatient father who never lets his dullard son win at draughts. In 1977 the head of DATAR announced via the Press that he was 'convoking' all local deputies to Paris: not having been asked directly, they were furious at his gaffe and refused to go. This kind of situation would raise the hackles even of the more reasonable local leaders. A Socialist professor at Montpellier said in 1980: 'Yes, the State has done a lot for this region, but in the wrong way. It treats us as it once treated Algeria. Indeed we *are* an underdeveloped land, like South Italy or the Mahgreb, we have no native industrial class, we lack the talent or experience to solve our own problems and stand up to the pressures from Paris. And this creates an inferiority complex which paralyses our power of action – a familiar vicious circle. Here at least the Marxist analysis is perfectly valid.'

Local leaders make speeches clamouring for more industry, but in practice they do little to help attract it; and some officials from Paris suspect that at heart they oppose an industrialization that could bring in younger men with new ideas and disturb local habits. This fear of change is seen especially among the vinegrowers. It is true that two farming brothers on the coast at Cap d'Agde changed their vineyards not into orchards but into a tourist site which then became part of the new nudist city – and the brothers have made a fortune. But this is an exceptional case of local enterprise. Many growers are peasants, others are middle-class townees living in their decaying family mansions – 'They are waiting for some golden age to return,' said one critic; 'the vine round here is considered *un métier noble*, not mucky like pig-breeding, and people find it hard to adapt to new realities.' They spend some of their time agitating against cheap Italian imports, or the threat of Spanish imports, and they rally round their flag-bearer, the flamboyant Emmanuel Maffre-Baugé, who epitomizes the spirit of these '*cathares de la vigne*', as they have been called.

Maffre-Baugé is a burly, jovial man in his fifties who has a farm in the Hérault valley. He is from the local landed gentry and used to be a Rightish Catholic. But fury at Government wine policies drove him to join the Socialists; and then in 1979 he startled his friends by agreeing to stand on the Communist list for the European elections. His reason: only the PCF was really protecting the growers by opposing Spain's EEC entry. He was elected, and now cuts an incongruous figure as the Red Cathar of Strasbourg; at heart, he is the least Communist of men. Pouring me glass after glass of his very drinkable *vin du pays*, he said: 'I'm a Left-wing Christian, disgusted by the way we're victimized by Paris finance groups. We're ignored culturally too – who in Paris knows of the wonderful Occitan poets? I feel deeply Occitan, my blood is the juice of these grapes: but I'm French too, I'm no separatist. For my beloved homeland, with its exquisite troubadour civilization, I want a French federal solution where we can take our own decisions at last.' Warming to his rhetoric, he went on in his tangy Midi accent: 'If I want my cat to pee in this corner rather than that, I have to ask bloody Paris first. We waste half our time on endless journeys there, yet if we didn't go, our voice would never be heard. We love our mother France, even though she's become more like a cruel stepmother. There's been a profound reawakening here in the past ten years, and people are asking: what the hell are we doing in this centralized French *galère*? We don't want to leave it, but we do want a fair deal.'

This new regionalist trend is even more confused and disparate than in Brittany, and is charged with emotionalism. On the one hand, a tiny band of romantics have been plotting a new Occitan 'nation': their leader has even nominated a provisional 'government', has marked out his frontiers and assembled historical maps to assert the reality of 'Occitania'. But the trouble with this crazy dream is that Occitania was never a nation, it was simply the medieval name for all the diverse lands speaking the 'oc' tongue, and it covered a vast area up to Lyon and Bordeaux and into Spain and north-west Italy. A Languedocien may like the concept, but if you ask a Lyonnais or Bordelais if he feels Occitan, he might reply, 'What's that?'

Two rather more serious movements, with a more genuine if still limited following in the Languedoc, are Lutte Occitane and the newer Volem Viure Al Pais ('we want to live in this land'). The former has a few supporters among Leftist intellectuals, notably in Montpellier; VVAP appeals more widely, mainly to young ecologists and to the vinegrowers with whose grievances it identifies. The leaders, Robert Lafont and Yves Rouquette, are both teachers: Lafont is a federalist, Rouquette has separatist leanings. Neither movement lets off bombs like the Breton FLB, or does anything more violent than daub walls with the 'OC' slogan and sometimes incite the farmers to riot. But though culturally active, these movements have a political influence that is near to zero, and they seem to be past their peak. They are disregarded by most local political leaders of the Left, who are more concerned with the new Government's plans for stronger powers for the regional assemblies. Of course Languedoc wants more autonomy; but most people accept that, politically, Occitania is a nonsense compared with the reality of near by Catalonia, or indeed of Brittany.

Culturally, however, matters are different. The Occitan cultural revival of the past ten years is in some ways more flourishing and strongly based than that of Brittany. Perhaps one reason is that this colourful Mediterranean culture was always richer than that of the Bretons, and being Latin it was less in contradiction with that of Paris, therefore suffered less from assimilation. Today, university centres of Occitan studies in Toulouse and Montpellier are making serious efforts to rediscover the cultural heritage. Occitan, close cousin to Provençal, is still spoken in some rural areas, and the vogue among urban teenagers for learning it is stronger than in the case of Breton: several thousand a year take it as an option in the *bac*. Some new poets and novelists are writing in Occitan, though few are of much distinction. Occitan pop singers such as Marty draw ready audiences; and so *à la mode* is the trend that supermarkets have even launched publicity slogans in Occitan. More seriously, Occitan theatre and folklore groups of some quality have sprung up, notably the *Ballets Occitans* based in Toulouse, while the Occitan summer university at Nîmes draws the faithful by thousands from all over southern France, to dance the *crozada*, to hear lectures on the Camisards, or to explore the ballads of the troubadours. Some town councils, not to be outdone, have been flying the red-and-gold flag of Languedoc over their *mairies* – the gesture is cultural, not political – and have made their street-signs bilingual, both in French and Occitan. In Montpellier, the Rue des Anciens Combattants now bears the added name, oddly, of Carriera de la Vaca (Street of the Cow).

Lower Languedoc has come quite a long way, in economic terms, in the past twenty years. The tourist project, the canal, the new factories such as IBM have all made their impact, even if not as much as was hoped. The vinegrowers may have refused to uproot, but they are cooperating in improving the quality of their wines. Above all, the local economy was given a boost in the early 1960s by the arrival of well over 100,000 repatriates from Algeria: some 25,000 settled in Montpellier alone. They are an enterprising breed, these *pieds noirs*[4] as they are called, and they took over many dying farms and businesses and made them buzz. Sometimes they were resented, but on the whole they have assimilated well, in this southern climate not so different from the one they left behind. The absorption by France of over 800,000 *pieds noirs*, mostly in the Midi, was one of the great achievements of the '60s, and was possible in that era of fast economic expansion. It would not have been nearly so easy today.

However, despite the progress, lower Languedoc remains sullen and refractory, and the impact of the post-1973 world slow-down has not helped. In relations with Paris, hitherto there has been a psychological

4 When the first French settlers arrived in Algeria, the barefoot Muslims called them after their black shoes – and the nickname has stuck.

vicious circle, which can be summed up as follows. Under Giscard, a State official, exasperated, said to me: 'The only way to get anything done round here is for us to take the initiative and present the local *notables* with a *fait accompli*. If we leave it to them, all they do is quarrel and prevaricate. They're a hopeless lot.' And a *notable*, equally exasperated, said, 'We know that Paris despises us, but that doesn't help. They should try to win our support and encourage our own ideas, not merely criticize and treat us like kids. The economy may have improved since 1960, but the power balance is just the same.' So how can it change? Already under Giscard there were signs that Paris was beginning to show more tact, for in preparing the new Plan for the South-West in 1978–9 the Government was more careful than before to consult and involve local bodies. But Paris still kept the last word. Now the Socialists, with their devolution plans, aim to smash the vicious circle once for all. Languedoc will be left to take its own decisions on a wide range of matters. But will the Languedociens be able and ready to rise to the challenge, and develop a greater sense of economic initiative? Old attitudes die hard. After all these centuries, the region has grown used to feeling that Paris has castrated it and thus there is nothing more constructive it can do than scream. At Montségur and Béziers, the martyrs' blood is not yet dry.

GRENOBLE: THE LEGEND AND ITS WOUNDS;
TOULOUSE; A SYMBOLIC WHITE-AND-PINK ICE-CREAM;
LYON; MORE CREDIT WANTED FOR THE LYONNAIS

There are some parts of France where local initiative has blossomed abundantly and the State has not felt the need to coax new industry or decree new schemes. This is true of some big cities of the east, and of none more than Grenoble. This 'little Los Angeles in the Alps' became a legend in France in the 1960s, a paragon first of industrial and scientific boom, then of municipal enterprise and the innovative search for a new open society. While Languedoc looked back at the Cathars, Grenoble was plotting the millennium; and reporters, sociologists and other pilgrims came here to behold France's future and see if it worked. The saying was: what Grenoble does today, France does tomorrow.

A nuclear scientist took me up to the old fortress on the cliffs above the city. We watched, as the sun set over the jagged Vercors massif, and the ranks of new skyscrapers below us glimmered from pink to grey. There it sprawled in its flat valley within a ski's leap of the high Alps, this showpiece of a nation's hoped-for destiny. 'We're from Paris,' said my friend, 'but it's not like moving to the provinces, it's living in the France of the future.' That was in the 1960s. Today, the ecstasy is less apparent: *Grenoble, le mythe blessé* (see pp. 161 and 313) was the title of a book published in 1979. Is it merely that some other towns have been catching up with Grenoble, encroaching on its pioneering role? Or, more negatively, that its bold blueprint of social and technological progress has not in practice been working out so well, in the morose climate of the late 1970s? Maybe a bit of both. Yet it is still a very exciting city, the most municipally adventurous, the most intellectually sophisticated, the least provincial, in the provinces.

In the 1820s Stendhal wrote of his native town, 'What could I add if I were God?' He was referring to the landscape: Grenoble was little more than a village. Some things have not changed since his day: the Alpine freshness in the air, the close backdrop of snow-peak or steep forest behind every street. But man has added plenty else, without waiting for God. The valley of the Isère beneath its toothy rocks teems with some of the most advanced industries and science centres in Europe. The population, 80,000 in 1945, reached 400,000 (with suburbs) by 1975. Eight people in ten are immigrants to the town, a high proportion of them students or *cadres*, and they come from many lands. This unusual degree of mobility gives local life a slightly American style. There is some arrogance and rootlessness, but also more informality than you find in most older cities. 'You can wear ski-clothes in a smart restaurant,' I was told, 'and no one minds or notices, as they might in Lyon.'

Long before the war Grenoble was already a pace-setter, in some cases by accident. It created the first funicular in France, the first *syndicat d'initiative*, the first scheme of family allowances, the first hydroelectricity, even the first stirrings of the French Revolution. Since the war it has become a natural magnet for the pioneer. For example, in 1960 the first French family-planning clinic opened here, semi-illegally. And in 1965 it was the first big French town to stage a municipal 'revolution', by electing a young mayor from among the new immigrant technocrats, rather than from the local elderly bourgeois *notables*, as has been the French tradition.

What has made Grenoble so special? It has certainly not been due to Government policy. One answer lies in those surrounding mountains. The town's industrial strength originates from the near-by discovery of hydro-electricity in the last century; and today it is the skiing and the scenery, above all, that attract the young élites from Paris, for no other big French town is so near the mountains. The rest has been a snowball effect: the more factories and intellectuals came, the more others tended to follow. The university (now split into three) has the highest percentages in France both of non-local and of non-French students;

and professors, too, tend to make Grenoble their number one choice for a career outside Paris.

This was no more than a quiet burg noted for its glove-making when, in the 1860s, some French engineers experimented with a new idea of drawing electric power from the near-by waterfalls. Factories large and small then settled near this new source of power: some were little paper mills which you can still see today in the steep clefts of the Chartreuse massif. And Grenoble has never looked back. Its population doubled from 1872 to 1926, at a time when most of France was static. By the 1950s the largest firms were Merlin-Gerin (electro-metallurgy) and Neyrpic (turbines and hydraulic research), both European leaders in their fields. The university was also expanding fast especially in science, and it was this which prompted the Government in 1956 to choose Grenoble as the site for France's principal nuclear research laboratories, today with a staff of 2,000. Then in the 1960s industry took a new direction. Some of the older mechanical firms, based on hydro-electricity, passed their prime. But more advanced industries readily arrived to work with Grenoble's pool of research scientists: Péchiney opened electro-chemical research laboratories with a staff of 2,000, while American investors have included Hewlett-Packard (mini-computers) and Caterpillar (tractors). Becton, Dickinson, a US paramedical firm, not only set up a new plant but also put its European head office in Grenoble, confident that this was a good centre for attracting high-level international staff. Grenoble has thus proved the best example in France of the 'multiplier effect' – investment breeding further investment. Whereas in some places – such as Brittany – new industry has been implanted as an alien growth, here it animates its environment and is animated by it.

For example, Grenoble took the lead in France in promoting liaison between universities and local industry. In the US or Britain this is not uncommon, but French professors with their ivory-tower traditions have tended to scorn practical work, and hence the lag today in applied research (see p. 49). Grenoble even ninety years ago had begun to promote a new outlook, when pioneering industries first settled in this remote academic town, and in 1892 the world's first university course in industrial electricity was held here. Since the last war, firms have commissioned the institutes and science faculties for special research jobs, while academic specialists make use of the firms' laboratories and experience. This cooperation has encouraged new investment: for example, the invention of a new power magnet by Grenoble's world-famous physicist, the late Professor Néel, led to the creation of two factories specializing in this. One scientist commented: 'The human contacts are easier here than in most towns, and this helps the liaison. I'm sure the skiing has a lot to do with it. It's easier to iron out your problems with some industrialist or top civil servant when you're up in a funicular with him.'

Eventually, the economic and scientific 'revolution' made its impact on civic life. The new high-powered immigrants became steadily more numerous, and socially more assertive, than the original nucleus of local lawyers, doctors and others who normally rule the roost in a French town of this kind. And this led to Grenoble's second and even more fascinating 'revolution', the municipal one. Through the boom years of 1950–65 the *mairie* had remained in the hands of the old guard of Grenoble-born *notables*, in turn Socialist or Gaullist by label but conservative by temperament. And the newcomers were not yet sufficiently organized or civically aware to dislodge them. Almost nothing was done for town-planning. The city spread its tentacles along the valleys, and rents and land prices shot up unchecked. I remember seeing a new ring of peripheral skyscrapers in southern Grenoble in 1959, and coming back six years later to find that other rings had grown beyond them, like the rings of a tree. It reminded me of posters in Texas, 'Don't park your car in this lot: there'll be a new building in an hour.' All very exciting for boom-worshippers, but inconvenient for people living in a city that had vastly outstripped its public services.

Then in 1964 a certain Hubert Dubedout of the Nuclear Centre found that his water supply kept failing in his fourth-floor flat. Thousands of others were in similar plight, for the mother-city of hydro-electricity was served by a water system unchanged since 1883. Dubedout launched a campaign to get the mayor to do something, and succeeded. Encouraged by this, he and some friends from the scientific élite formed a non-party group to contest the 1965 local elections. Allying with the Socialists, they succeeded to everyone's surprise in defeating the Gaullist-led ruling coalition. The egg-head immigrants had found their force at last: nearly all voted for Dubedout. He and his energetic team then revitalized the *mairie* and worked to get Grenoble ready for the 1968 Winter Olympics. Besides preparing a huge new ice-rink this involved a complete overhaul for the town. A new airport and motorways had to be built, a new railway-station and post-office, and an Olympic village to house 4,000. Three-quarters of the total cost of 1,000 million francs was borne by the State; the town had to find most of the rest, and some of the burden fell on rate-payers. But Grenoble acquired in two years a permanent modern infrastructure that otherwise would have been spread over twenty. It did not all go smoothly. In one case, the mayor of an adjacent commune refused to let a new road to the Olympic village pass over his territory because – typical of France – he feared it would bring new housing, and he did not want his village to change.

Twice re-elected, Dubedout today is still mayor. He is an ex-naval officer and engineer from Pau, now in his late fifties, slim, good-looking, urbane, disdainful in manner; a man a world apart from the traditional mayor of a big French town. When I first met him, at a pompous lunch in the *préfecture* for elderly notables from near-by villages, he winked at me in front of the prefect as if to say, 'I feel as much an outsider here as you.' His 1965 victory was greeted by some observers in Paris as a national portent, a breakthrough into local politics by the kind of non-partisan pragmatist who normally steers well clear of the world of municipal intrigue: 'With men like Dubedout, public life is no longer the same,' wrote *Le Monde* excitedly. In a sense the paper was right, for some lesser towns have since thrown up their own Dubedouts, if not of the same calibre. But Dubedout himself, under pressure, has been forced in the past fifteen years to become more of a party political animal than he intended. He soon found it impossible to retain a non-party stance in this highly politicized town. His sympathies were already radical-progressive, and he helped Mendès-France when the latter chose a Grenoble constituency for his brief come-back in 1967–8. Later Dubedout joined the Socialist Party, and is now a deputy, as big-town mayors tend to feel they need to be. Faced with the local Right, he has been obliged since 1971 to rely on Communist electoral support, grudgingly given; and since 1977, like nearly all other Socialist mayors, he has ruled in coalition with the PCF. It is not easy, for the dislike is mutual. In addition, he is harassed regularly by campus *gauchistes* and by the bourgeois Right, each accusing him of being the creature of the other. All in all, his re-election has never been smooth.

Such are the inevitable tribulations in France of the pragmatic idealist turned politician. Nevertheless, Dubedout has doggedly gone ahead with a remarkable series of civic innovations, helped by an equally dedicated group of Socialist councillors, nearly all of them non-Grenoblois like himself. His superb new 37-million-franc *mairie*, all fountains and modern art, glass and marble, is no mere showpiece but the headquarters of a campaign to create a new style of local administration. He has been trying to break down some of the usual French social and bureaucratic barriers, and to associate citizens more actively with day-to-day government, rather than merely 'administer' them in the French manner. The pattern of success has been uneven, and we shall look at it more closely in later chapters (see pp. 308–13 and 317). He has tried to encourage neighbourhood associations to play a more positive role. He was the first French mayor to persuade suburban communes to join with the big city in a voluntary association for some planning and management, a scheme that has since been widely copied elsewhere. He has started a Bologna-style restoration of parts of the old town, and has tried to reduce private traffic by improving public transport. He has poured money into all kinds of new cultural activities, crowned by a Maison de la Culture that is the largest and most active in France, but costly. Above all, he has built a utopian 'new town' in the suburbs, with the controversial aim – only partly successful – of forging a new kind of integration of social classes, putting special emphasis on helping Algerians and other poorer families. This may be revealing of Dubedout's own spiritual odyssey of the past fifteen years. A close friend of his said to me: 'He came to power with a naval and scientific background, a cool believer in efficiency. But gradually he's moved towards a real concern for individual suffering and under-privilege. Probably it's through the regular contact he's had with his poorer constituents. Beneath that disdainful mask, he's a humanist, more than a technocrat-politician.'

Dubedout's very qualities and idealism seem to have added to his difficulties in this town of factions. At first he tried to achieve a broad popular consensus for his policies, but this ran into trouble – one aspect of *le mythe blessé* – and soon he was under pressure from three sides. The Communists have always been against him. Today within the town council itself, where they hold 17 of the 43 seats, they ostensibly cooperate with him. But the tensions are the same as in other Left-ruled towns; and out in the field, in the day-to-day life of suburb and *quartier*, PCF activists are continually sniping at the mayor's authority, or trying to wrest control of projects (see p. 321). This is predictable. Possibly more serious is the fact that a liberal element of the bourgeoisie, who initially were attracted by Dubedout and his new approach, have since deserted him. They could not stomach his becoming a Socialist deputy nor especially – what irony – his post-1977 alliance with the Communists. Moreover, many older Grenoblois see Dubedout as the symbol of the seizure of power by the newcomers, and they resent being 'dispossessed' of their town.

So Dubedout fell victim to the French polarization of the 1970s, and this was seen also in his changing relations with Paris: the third pressure on him. De Gaulle in the late '60s admired Dubedout and his reformism, and so did Chaban-Delmas during his 'new society' premiership in 1969–72: so the local prefect in those days was fairly cooperative. But, despite Giscard's proclaimed liberalism and wooing of the Socialists, more recent administrations in practice took a harder line with Left-wing towns. Grenoble was no longer in favour. This was partly a gut-reaction to the challenge of the Left: 'Paris today sees me as an enemy,' Dubedout told me in 1979; 'yes, of course it's a pity in a way that civic affairs are at the mercy of national politics. But in France one hasn't much option.' Under the new regime, Dubedout will now find Paris more helpful again, and the local Communists may become less obstructive too.

Under Giscard, there were economic pinpricks too. Barre's national austerity measures included new orders to prefects, and to local Ministry of Finance officials, to put curbs on municipal spending: civic dossiers requiring State financial participation were now more rigorously scrutinized and often rejected (see p. 189). This added to the new tensions between Dubedout and the prefect. It also forced him to cut back on a number of welfare and cultural projects that were an essential part of his new deal, another reason why the legend was wounded.[5] However, the new Socialist reforms, abolishing the *tutelle* of Paris over local finances, will certainly help Dubedout, even if, in these austerity times, he will probably find it necessary to keep a tight control over his own budget. And even a legend needs money to stay buoyant.

Inevitably, the legendary days of Grenoble's industrial expansion are over too. True, the post-1973 economic crisis hit Grenoble later than most towns: unemployment (5 per cent) remains below the national average, and most of the big newer firms are still doing quite well. But a number of smaller ones have closed, notably in textiles, machinery and building. And new investment has of course grown scarce. Even before 1973 there was talk of Grenoble nearing 'saturation', both industrial and demographic, in its confined plain where three valleys meet. In a sense its boom was always something of a freak, given its geographical position, 350 miles from Paris and off the main trade routes: Lyon, sixty miles away, the regional capital, may lack Grenoble's zest but is better situated. Today, greater Grenoble's population increase has slowed right down. In itself this is probably no bad thing: but can the town retain its unusual pioneering spirit, when its heady expansion has lost its momentum and its mystique?

Another legend now nursing its wounds is that of the local university/industry links. Only the nuclear research centre has managed to intensify its work with local firms. Elsewhere, the liaison has fallen off since the 1960s, and one reason is that technology is now so much more specialized, and French communications so much improved, that a firm will often find it more convenient to commission a research job elsewhere. 'It's just as easy,' said one manager, 'to ring up Toulouse, or even

5 In this context, *'mythe'* is better translated 'legend' than 'myth'. 'Legendary' means true and amazing: 'mythical' tends to mean false, or at least unprovable.

Tokyo, and hire exactly the expertise we need. Links with universities are as close as ever, but no longer so local.' Another reason, paradoxically, has been the physical growth of Grenoble's university. In the old days, this was a serene little world of human scale, where liaison with firms was based on personal contacts built up by a few key professors such as Louis Néel: today, the vast cohorts of teachers are more anonymous, more harassed by their own administrative concerns, also more Left-wing and therefore more wary of serving the *patronat*.

Since the late 1960s the university has not only been split into three but has been transposed *en bloc* with its 32,000 students to a spacious new campus in the suburbs. This is fine in itself, but it has drawn the university world more than ever into a ghetto (see p. 508), and this in turn has changed the town's atmosphere, in many ways for the worse. When the main university centres were downtown, the streets and cafés were thronged with students, noisy, untidy, but lively. Today, a majority of them live out in their campus hostels, they disappear at weekends to the ski-slopes or their families, and a visitor to central Grenoble might hardly believe that this is a famous university city. Sad, in a way. The few spots in town where students still gather, such as the Maison de la Culture, are widely scattered. In fact, Dubedout's method of coping with the city's mushroom growth has been to encourage polycentrism, with several new shopping and leisure centres, and suburbs linked by wide avenues. This is a victory for decongestion, and it eases traffic; but it has meant that, except in the tourist season, the attractive old part of the town is nearly deserted at night, and Grenoble lacks the evening animation of a less well re-planned city, such as Toulouse or Montpellier. The 'mini-Los Angeles' allusion is not so far-fetched. But perhaps you can't have it both ways.

So where does Grenoble go next? It is hard to go on staying out in front as a record-breaker, as any star athlete knows. Socially speaking, some waning of the pioneering spirit has been inevitable, as many new Grenoblois put down their roots, cultivate their gardens, and behave more like ordinary French citizens and less like bivouackers in a scientific gold-rush town. Before long, they will even become 'old' Grenoblois. And yet, Grenoble is not a failure, despite the hazards of the 1970s. One token of its success is that a number of other towns have caught something of its spirit, whether industrial, municipal or social, so that its contrast with them is now less striking: the new social informality, in the 1960s so novel here for France, has imperceptibly become more general. Yet Grenoble remains special, in many ways. There is an intensity here in public and working life, probably enhanced by the bracing climate, also by the sense of being isolated amid mountains, a separate society with no important hinterland save Alpine villages. People work harder than in most towns outside Paris, and are more open to new ideas. And even though many of the newcomers are now settling down, the level of mobility remains well above the French average: many of the ambitious young cadres, in the factories and research centres, belong to a new French breed who will always move on to a better job elsewhere, while others take their place. So the Californian phenomenon continues, with new human energy responding to environment.

If Grenoble's economic legend has waned, it is because that kind of heady expansion is no longer possible, no longer in vogue, no longer seen as a model for the future. But Grenoble has not lost the industrial gains it has made. It is still a favourite venue. 'We're delighted,' said an official at the *mairie* in 1979, 'that the national telecommunications centre (CNET) has just rejected the demands of DATAR to create a big new unit in Brittany, and is coming here instead, with five hundred boffins. It helps to restore *une certaine idée de Grenoble.'*

The municipal legend is still real. There is still more experiment, debate, civic effervescence here than in any other big town, and Dubedout has not failed despite the obstacles. He and his team of Socialists in the *Mairie* are still manically active, aware of their mission – 'I wish they'd learn how to slow down,' said one of their colleagues, 'they're too much the prisoners of this utopian vision of Grenoble. They'll wear us all out, and themselves.' Indeed, Dubedout when I re-met him in 1979 seemed much more tired and tense than ten years previously. Tired, but by no means finished. Pierre Frappat, a local teacher, the author of this sympathetic but critical study of his home town, *Grenoble, le mythe blessé,* told me that when it was published in 1979 some silly Paris reporter rang him up excitedly, 'Are you the author of *Grenoble, le mythe assassiné?'* No, said Frappat, he had chosen his adjective with care. And wounds can heal, in that mountain air – so long as it is not first the myth of 'the New France' that is assassinated by the decline of the West.

Toulouse[6] is the one other big French city to have grown and changed as radically since the war as Grenoble, but in a different way. They present an interesting contrast. While Grenoble's industrial boom was largely spontaneous, Toulouse was pushed into it by a concerted State policy, helped by a huge local farm exodus. In Grenoble, the municipal dynamism has come from the new immigrant élites led by Dubedout; Toulouse

6 For a much fuller analysis of modern Toulouse, see my book *A Tale of Five Cities*, Secker & Warburg, London, and Harper & Row, New York, 1979.

too has its newcomer élites, but the *mairie* has remained in the hands of the 'native' Toulousains, with a succession of uninspired mayors. Their style of government has not always proved equal to tackling the problems caused by rapid urban growth.

The dilemmas of lower Languedoc are reflected here, in upper Languedoc, in the different context of a big town recently industrialized. Toulousains take an exceptional pride in their ancient and lovely city of mellow rose-pink brick; they have their own anti-Paris tradition, and also by nature they are somewhat lazy, and were long suspicious of modern industry. Yet the Government from the early 1950s has used Toulouse as the foremost pilot-zone of its campaign to promote new activities in the remoter or less developed provinces. The result is a fascinating example of the paradoxes inherent in the conflict, in Gaullist and Giscardian days, between State regional policies and local aspirations. Was this Government dynamism versus local inertia? – or local tradition fighting to assert itself against Parisian centralism? – or both at once?

Fifty years ago this was a sleepy market town, and in 1939 its population was only 180,000: today, with suburbs, it is well over half a million. Not only has the city drained much of the surplus farming folk from the smallholdings of the backward hinterland, it has also taken in 30,000 *pieds noirs*, to add to the 25,000 Spanish refugees from the Civil War, few of whom have yet gone back to Spain. New executives, scientists and others have flocked in from Paris and other parts of Europe, lacing the city's old parochialism with a new cosmopolitan air. It seems to have crossed that mysterious threshold where a medium-sized town takes on the atmosphere and life-styles of a metropolis: the suburbs grow larger than the main part of the city, townsfolk become commuters, Paris-style quick-lunch bars and night-spots proliferate, and you can no longer reach the open country in a pleasant walk from the centre. Today this is a dusty, strident, lorry-filled town, with oases of old-world quiet. Driving in on the main road from Paris, you must first crawl for miles past warehouses, hypermarkets, discount emporia selling utility furniture, and high-rise blocks of equally utility flats. Then in the ancient city centre the ambience changes. Even in November, the café-terraces are filled with sunbathers enjoying their two-hour lunch-break (still common in the Midi), while groups of old men lazily play *boules*. The evenings are magical in the narrow streets and little squares of the old town, where the rose-pink façades of the medieval churches and palaces glow under discreet floodlighting. In the unkempt little cafés of the Place du Capitole, students are singing or arguing politics, while well past midnight the big *brasseries* and so-called 'drugstores' are full and some boutiques still open. The suburbs at night are silent and dreary, but this very Latin city has the Latin sense of *agora*, enticing all to the nightly parade of its animated centre. Toulouse is an irritating but fiercely impressive place, a volatile polyglot melting-pot, very different from its sedate bourgeois rival, Bordeaux.

The post-war State planners found that its spontaneous economic development was hampered, not only by local lack of enterprise, but by sheer geography. It is out on the rim of the EEC, not even on the sea like Bordeaux, nor on a major river route. It is in a cul-de-sac: its nearest neighbour, Spain, lies across the high Pyrenees. Toulouse often regards its vocation as to be 'the gateway to Spain' and to open up new French markets there; this may now become feasible, as the new democratic Spain prepares to join the EEC, but it still requires a better tunnel under the Pyrenees.

Why should new industry have wanted to settle in a town so badly placed? To counter this problem, the Fourth Republic planners decided to make a special effort, using as a starting-point the existing armament and aircraft factories that had been set up here around the time of the Great War so as to be as far from the Germans as possible. In the 1920s the city's aerial vocation had taken another stride when Mermoz, Saint-Exupéry and others pioneered flights to Africa, using southerly Toulouse as their base. Then, after 1945, the Government developed it as the capital of the French aircraft industry (see pp. 70–73), first with the Caravelle, then with ill-starred Concorde, now with the successful Airbus.

The pioneers were aware also of a need to diversify, to avoid too much reliance on older heavy industries (such as armaments) whose transport costs would suffer from the city's position. Aeronautics seemed to link naturally with electronics, so in the mid-'60s Paris decided to make Toulouse the key centre in its drive to expand this industry. It implanted the French firm, CII, and enticed investment by two American ones including Motorola (see p. 421). A complementary step was the decision to make the city France's leading centre for scientific research and higher studies in electronics, aeronautics and space. The two main aeronautic Grandes Ecoles were moved here from Paris, also the National Centre for Space Studies, and scores of other scientific colleges and institutions have been set up. The science faculty (now a separate university) has been expanded, and Toulouse today has more students (48,000) than any other town outside Paris. The aim has been to sidestep geographic isolation by making this *'la capitale de la matière grise'*, where advanced industries and research centres can help each other. As in Grenoble, the interaction has not been ideal but a start has been made.

And the new grey matter comes to sunny Toulouse quite willingly. Cohorts of modern-minded élites have migrated here from other parts of France, and Europe. Yet this new wave has barely been assimilated by the old Toulouse society, nor has it taken charge and pushed it onto the sidelines as in Grenoble. The 'real' Toulousains, born and bred here, have looked on the State-directed modernization of their city with some suspicion, as you might expect in Languedoc. And so today there are two Toulouses: two societies, two mentalities and ways of life, that co-exist uneasily and have only recently begun to mix.

You can notice this contrast, visually. Fly over the city, as it sprawls astride the Garonne on its wide plain, and it looks like some giant vanilla-and-strawberry ice-cream: the old city of pink brick is ringed by a white circle of new flats, factories, colleges and laboratories, a gleaming superstructure grafted onto the old core. Here the two rival élites confront each other: on the one side, the energetic scientists, pilots, professors and managers, together with the resourceful *pieds noirs* and other immigrant entrepreneurs; on the other, the 'real Toulouse' as it sees itself, a traditional bourgeoisie of doctors, lawyers and landowners. They live secluded within their graceful pink palaces in the old city, easy-going and meridional, historically disdainful of profit, patriotically involved in the living past of a city that once ruled all Languedoc. They have never forgiven Napoleon for stripping Toulouse of its powers and reducing it to the status of mere capital of the poor Haute-Garonne department, on a par with tiny Foix (population 11,000), capital of Ariège. And it is not considered adequate compensation that since 1964 Toulouse has been partially resurrected, as capital of the highly artificial new 'region' of Midi-Pyrenées. *L'anti-Paris*, this city is still called.

These rivalries have been a hindrance in local affairs, as in many French towns. Until very recently at least, you had only to get stuck in one of the endless traffic-jams, or look at the derelict state of some historic quarters, to realize that all was not well with local government. Since 1904 *'la ville rose'* had been a Socialist and Radical stronghold, and until 1971 the *mairie* was in the hands of a fiercely anti-Gaullist, anti-Paris, left-of-Centre coalition. The mayor, Louis Bazergue, a petit-bourgeois lawyer, became a by-word in France for a certain kind of old-style Socialist potentate of the Midi, on bad terms with his prefect. He applied his Socialist principles by amassing a private fortune through astute property deals, and it is said that one of his officials had two rooms in the *mairie*, one empty and tidy for receiving civic visitors, one at the back full of papers where he did paid work on the side for a building firm. The *préfecture* was not always as alert as it should have been to check such abuses.

Bazergue's merit was to recognize that Toulouse must modernize and develop, as the mayor before him until 1958 had failed to do. In lesser matters where he had the funds to be his own master, Bazergue was able to achieve a good deal: for example, improving the city's pavements, street lighting and drainage, previously a disgrace. But where he needed the State's cooperation he ran into trouble – and no French town has adequate finance for its own large-scale projects, without State help. Yet Bazergue was an autocrat who insisted on operating on his own terms, without proper consultation. Hence mayor and prefect tended to obstruct each other's schemes, and public services lagged far behind the city's rapid growth. When the Government set up a town-planning unit for the area, Bazergue refused to collaborate, saying it was an intrusion on his own preserve. Yet his own town-planning consisted too often of prestige projects embarked on with inadequate feasibility studies. The largest of these was for a new super-suburb to house 100,000 people, the notorious Le Mirail. Bazergue won Government backing and work began: but after 1965 Paris began to cut funds, and under the cross-fire of ministerial vetoes and local bungling, the project fell far behind schedule. The prefect claimed it was too grandiose; Bazergue alleged the Minister of Construction was exacting revenge for some local political defeat. Conflicts of this kind were common. 'The Gaullists victimize me,' Bazergue told me; 'Bordeaux under Chaban gets far more aid than we do.' There was some truth in this. But the fault was on both sides.

Toulouse finally fell to the Right in the 1971 elections. The new mayor, Pierre Baudis, proved a very different figure, a quiet man in his sixties, courteous, prudent, excellent at baby-kissing. What is more, he was a Giscardian, so relations with the *préfecture* improved considerably. Funds were no longer withheld arbitrarily; projects were discussed amicably, and disagreements were now kept to a practical level and not inflamed emotionally into issues of pride. An example concerns two disused Army barracks near the centre of town. Bazergue had been trying for years to secure these useful sites, but the Army's price was excessive. Baudis in 1976 lobbied his friend Prime Minister Barre, who prevailed upon the Army to drop its price by a third. At the next elections, Baudis was able to present this as a great victory (possibly Barre had acted deliberately so as to help him retain his marginal seat). And yet, though Baudis' diplomacy may have brought results, he is hardly a dynamic mayor. He has not shown much imagination, nor innovated, beyond easing the traffic-jams by building new ring-roads. From being aggressively opposed to Paris, Toulouse merely changed into a town readier to acquiesce in the State's scheme of things. By chance, or more probably for reasons of local character, it has not had the kind of strong mayor who in some other big towns has been able to achieve so much.

Classic French centralism has applied to business as well as government. Most of the big local firms have their headquarters in Paris or abroad, and almost all banks in Toulouse are run from Paris. This is one reason why locally owned industry has tended to be so lethargic and backward. While Aérospatiale was preparing Concorde, thousands of tiny local firms were still in a nineteenth-century cottage-industry stage, and most had fewer than ten employees. These firms – in textiles, building or food-processing – have been dying out fast as the new big ones grow, so even in the 1960s the employment situation was not improving very fast. However, from the late '60s there were signs that 'old Toulouse' was waking at last from its ancient slumber to embrace the industrial age. Surprisingly, the town began to throw up its own new generation of entrepreneurs, for whom 'expansion' and 'productivity' were no longer dirty words. The owner of one moribund textiles firm handed over to his sons who brought in a new outlook, attacked the export market, and increased turnover twelvefold in four years. A local doctor patented a drug, and from this built up a pharmaceuticals firm that took over laboratories in other parts of France and began exporting as far afield as Argentina and Japan. Another young man set up a workshop making trendy leather trousers and jackets, and within two years had a hundred and thirty employees and was selling briskly to Germany. The culmination came in 1971 when this new generation won control of the Chamber of Commerce. The sitting president, an old fogey worthy of the local folklore museum, was ousted by a Toulousain whizz-kid in his forties, manager of an oxygen firm, who set about preaching expansion. He secured the funds for a modern business centre which has now been built at the airport, and he persuaded the airlines to create new international flights. 'Toulouse,' he told me, 'is at last becoming industry-minded in its own right, instead of letting Paris call the tune.' The message has sunk home. If you can't beat Parisian neo-colonialism, join it.

Ironically, this change of spirit was promptly followed by 1973 and the ensuing economic crisis which – as in Brittany – risks cancelling out some of Toulouse's splendid progress. Just when the local firms were making their belated transformation, newer and larger ones implanted from outside began to suffer from world recession. Aérospatiale's factory went through a bad phase in the period of the run-down of Concorde, but has since recovered thanks to Airbus (see p. 72); however, in the late '70s several of the new electronics and computer firms were laying off staff, and unemployment became a serious problem in Toulouse for the first time since the war. The city today is marking time, a little anxiously. It is still in the process of coming to terms with its sudden growth from old market town to scientific and industrial metropolis. The radical changes of the past twenty years have finally brought a new and more open spirit, new links with the world, a decline of the old wary insularity. But the new industry is fragile. And Toulouse, like other big French towns, has been irked till now by the *tutelle* of Paris, which has hampered it from becoming a fully adult metropolis. But now, under the new reforms, it will be the capital of a region with a certain autonomy, and this may make a change.

The constraints imposed by Paris have been felt even in Lyon, France's second city, a conurbation of over 1.2 million. If you take an early morning Airbus flight from Lyon to Paris, you may well travel with three hundred or so indentikit executives, all in the same neat suits, all clutching the same black briefcases. And on the evening flights they all come back, their briefcases hopefully full of those vital dossiers and protocols secured in Government offices. Once I went to interview a Lyon city councillor. 'Transfer me no more calls,' he told his secretary – 'unless of course it's the Ministry of Finance in Paris.' I smiled. He smiled too: 'Sorry, that's France for you.'

This dignified old mercantile city at the confluence of Rhône and Saône has been trying hard in recent years to loosen the hold of centralism and create for itself a proper international role, equal to that of its peers, say, Turin or Düsseldorf. It has made some progress, but it has not been easy. Lyonnais may be less flamboyantly anti-Paris than Toulousains, for their temperament is different, more stolid and phlegmatic; but they are irked, just the same. Lying on Western Europe's best north–south trade route, Lyon was for centuries a leading European centre of banking and commerce, and its silk industries were famous. Its Bourse dates from the fifteenth century, before that of Paris. Then, with the first industrial revolution, many of France's leading engineering and chemical firms were born here, such as Rhône-Poulenc and Péchiney. But the later nineteenth century was also the period of concentration of decision-making in Paris: most larger firms felt obliged to move their head offices there, including the great bank that bears the city's name, the Crédit Lyonnais. Lyon's banking prowess waned sharply, and the city lapsed into a straight-jacketed provincialism. This trend continued even in the early post-war years: Lyon's modern industry was expanding fast, yet the decisions affecting it were increasingly taken elsewhere, as a result of State financial pressures and national-level mergers.

However, since the 1960s Lyon has been trying to reassert itself. Though it could not alter its organic links with the capital, at least this hitherto rather stuffy town has become more outward-looking, and has given itself a modern face-lift. Much was due to Louis Pradel, the *centriste* mayor from 1958 to 1976, one of the most enterprising in post-war France. He may not have possessed the social ideals of a Dubedout, but he was a modernist in the 1960s sense, and he believed that if Lyon was to bid for a true international role, then it must first be given the right infrastructure. This he achieved, with State aid, and the results today are impressive. New motorways circle the outer suburbs. The new international airport has direct flights to seventy-one world cities. The comfortable *métro*, opened in 1978, has provided the provincial Lyonnais with some hint of living in a metropolis. Parts of the old town have been restored, and the Renaissance façades along the *quais* of the two rivers have been repainted in their original pastel shades, pink and yellow, making Lyon look less grey. Above all, and most controversially, on a 55-acre site known as La Part Dieu, Pradel built an enormous office complex, with a 500-foot skyscraper and other high-rise blocks of glass and steel. La Part Dieu contains a public library with over a million volumes, a bizarrely-shaped 2,000-seat concert hall, and what is claimed to be the largest shopping centre in Europe. Unfortunately, the post-1973 recession has since prevented the venture from being any great commercial success, and some of the new offices are today standing empty. What is more, many older Lyonnais object to this 'Manhattanization' of the city skyline. But there it stands, for better or for worse, Lyon's little challenge to the future.

Lyon has been changing socially too. Despite its central position and entrepreneurial traditions, this for centuries has been a remarkably enclosed society. Its élite of bankers, merchants and manufacturers has been famous for industriousness, bourgeois conformism and outward puritanism (in most matters save, maybe, love of *cuisine*). They never showed much interest in the outside world, nor made strangers feel welcome. A British doctor who runs a cancer research agency in Lyon told me: 'When I and my foreign colleagues arrived in 1966, a leading local hostess thought it her duty to invite us to dinner, to meet local doctors. She put our group at one table, and the Lyonnais at another! I never saw any of them again for years. And Parisians told me they felt just as foreign here as we did. But this has since been changing. Masses of Parisians and others have arrived to live here, and Lyon has perforce become a more mixed and open society, more aware of the world. I now dine quite informally *chez* Lyonnais friends.' Economic expansion has drawn more than 10,000 *cadres* and their families from Paris and elsewhere, and census figures show that from 1962 to 1975 the proportion of inhabitants native to Lyon fell from 66 to 48 per cent.

Sheer commercial growth, and the improvement in road and air links, have made Lyon steadily more cosmopolitan and Europe-minded. It was Pradel who secured for Lyon the WHO-backed International Cancer Research Agency, in the face of competition from Geneva and Grenoble. Since then, the number of branches of foreign banks has risen to twelve, and of consulates-general (as opposed to mere honorary consulships) to thirteen. Habitat and Marks & Spencer have stores here; a young Briton has opened two 'pubs', the Merry-go-Round and the Red Cow. Culturally, too, Lyon has become much more lively, and in some respects has up-staged Paris: France's leading theatre manager Roger Planchon (see p. 324), and leading restaurateur Paul Bocuse (see p. 412) both have their bases here. This sober town has even distinguished itself in recent years by becoming a notorious centre of organized crime and prostitution – a sure sign that it is entering the big-city league at last.

Yet such 'progress' cannot alone fulfil Lyon's dream of becoming liberated as a true metropolis. It must also attract what is called 'an apparatus of decision-making'. A young councillor explained to me: 'Pradel modernized the town. *He* made the bride beautiful: *our* job now is to get her married – to the world. She can't go on living with her Paris parents.' For some years these parents have themselves been aware of the drawbacks of centralism, and even under Giscard they proclaimed their desire to build up Lyon as 'an international centre of service industries, a counterweight to Paris'. In DATAR hearts, this was sincere. But in practice there have always been ministerial interests and traditions pulling in the opposite direction. Even today, under the Socialists, many Lyonnais remain sceptical.

For decades, the Lyonnais groused at Paris but did little. Then, in the 1970s, a few senior bankers and businessmen began putting pressure on the Government to help them reactivate the city's historic role as a centre of banking and finance. Paris did show some response, and a few modest results emerged. The big State-owned banks such as Crédit Lyonnais have now greatly increased their ceilings on transactions that can be decided locally, and the Banque Nationale de Paris has physically transferred from Paris its department dealing with the Rhône-Alpes region, so that most of its decisions affecting the area can now be taken in Lyon; previously, 96 per cent of them were referred to Paris for approval. Also the Banque de France has set up a special directorate in Lyon (its first outside Paris), with sizeable powers of funding. But sceptics point out that these and similar measures are mere geographical transfers, not real devolution: the central control of these banks remains in Paris. A more authentic attempt to provide Lyon with its own independent financial base was the creation in 1978 of a new autonomous body, Siparex, with an initial capital of 100 million francs and the role of raising local finance for local medium-sized firms. After a slow start, this is working quite well. The local banking scene has become livelier: each year, more private banks open branches in Lyon, and fifty-six are now represented. Local industrialists see all this as a modest first step towards reducing financial dependence on Paris.

DATAR in its turn has been trying to persuade French companies, especially those who manufacture in the Lyon area, to transfer all or part of their head office activities from Paris. This is not easy, for most firms prefer to keep their HQs near to the vital Ministries; and executives and their wives, who often are willing to swop Paris for the sun of the Midi or the Alpine snows, are less easily enticed by the workaday image of Lyon. So DATAR saw it as quite a *coup* when the giant Rhône-Poulenc, a Lyon firm by origin, in 1977 transferred the head office of its fertilizer division to Lyon (where most of its Research and Development plant is situated), followed in 1980 by its textiles division. Some other big firms, including Péchiney and Framatome, have made similar moves.

But powerful economic pressures are still pushing in the opposite direction too. Berliet, the Lyon lorry manufacturer, always prided itself on being one of the very few big French firms to keep its head office at its provincial plant: but with the takeover of Berliet by Renault/Saviem, this office in 1978 was moved to Renault's own HQ in Paris. It was a blow to Lyon's pride, and to its coffers: Berliet represented some 12 per cent of local banks' turnover. The director of Siparex told me: 'As you can see, it's a race against time, this campaign to decentralize, when modern mergers are driving the other way.' Lyon's bid to become 'a capital of decision-making' has been hampered too by the post-1973 slow-down, which has caused a number of firms both French and international to delay plans to put head offices there.

This may prove temporary. The real long-term issues are political. Rhône-Alpes may not be an 'authentic' region like Brittany, yet it too has been keen for more regional autonomy, and this it will now get. However, many Lyonnais believe that the city will never achieve its metropolitan ambitions unless the State also decentralizes its own civil service. All the Ministries, and especially the all-powerful Finances, still keep their decision-taking staff in Paris and have only low-grade offices in towns such as Lyon: and so it is to Paris that businessmen must go cap-in-hand once or twice a week. In 1981 the two cities became linked by a new high-speed express train, cutting the former four-hour journey to under three hours, and making it quicker to go by rail than air between city centres. This is being officially trumpeted as another step in Lyon's modern progress: but many Lyonnais fear that in terms of decentralization it might prove counter-productive, bringing the city even closer to the orbit of Paris. Maître André Soulié, liveliest of Lyon town councillors, told me in 1979: 'The Government is two faced. In trying to build up this city as a capital of service industries, it may be sincere – but will the policy work, if it lacks the courage to break the Jacobin habits of its own civil servants? Today we are warning Paris bluntly, "If you continue to pretend that physical decentralization is real devolution, when it's not, you'll have a revolt on your hands, in this and other towns."' Today, the Socialists have heeded that warning, at least in part. It is not yet certain that even they will now decentralize the decision-taking powers of the Ministries themselves, for here Jacobin vested interests are indeed deeply rooted. But, at least, Lyon and its region will now have more power of their own, and thus will become less dependent on those Ministries. So Lyon might now have a chance of moving into a higher European league. Strasbourg and Nice in their very different ways are international cities; but, outside Paris, Lyon alone can aspire to a major European economic role. Until now, compared with a town of the same importance, such as Stuttgart, Turin or even Manchester, it has seemed to be lacking in confidence or control of its destiny. But now, when the phone rings from the Ministry, will the *mairie* at last cease to tremble?

France's five other major cities are Marseille, Bordeaux, Nantes, Lille and Strasbourg. Gaston Defferre, suave bourgeois Socialist of the old school, has been mayor of Marseille since 1953,[7] and he runs the city as if it were his private property (he even owns two of its leading newspapers). Despite constant battles with the former State administration, he has done quite a lot for town-planning: a new *métro*; a tunnel under the Vieux Port to help cure traffic-jams that are still among the worst in Europe; the rebuilding of much of the town centre. This brash, torrid city of a million people is strongly proletarian, strongly Levantine, as famous for its *mafia*-style gangsterism as for its *bouillabaisse*. It is still the first seaport of the Mediterranean, but like many other big ports its golden days seem to be over, and it has not attracted nearly enough new industry to make up for the decline in its shipping and ship-repairing roles. After the collapse in 1978 of its biggest repair firm, Terrin, local unemployment climbed to 9.6 per cent, twice the national average. And Marseille has not yet managed to benefit as it might have done from the new Fos complex (see p. 57), which it has treated as rival rather than

7 Today he is Minister of the Interior: see p. 200.

associate. Perhaps its fortunes will revive when the Rhine–Rhône canal is built.

Bordeaux is a lesser port, with an equally celebrated mayor, Jacques Chaban-Delmas, leading Gaullist. Until about 1958 this had the reputation of being the least active of France's larger towns. Its narrow-spirited mercantile ruling class, straight out of the pages of Mauriac, still clung to the illusion of Bordeaux as a great seaport. They rebuilt the damaged harbour after the war, only to find that half its cranes were soon idle: the port suffered from the loss of France's colonies and a decline in the shipping trade for coal and wood, and the area had little industry save for its wines. But after de Gaulle's return to power, Chaban-Delmas' hour came. Using his new prestige as President of the National Assembly, he persuaded the cautious burghers to accept a change of course. More important, he was able to secure the right funds and decisions from Ministries, especially when he later became Prime Minister; in fact, no other big French town has benefited so blatantly from this kind of favouritism. Firms dependent on State contracts were induced to set up new factories, including Dassault and Thomson-CSF (electronics); in 1971 Ford Motors located its first plant in France here, and by this date Bordeaux had become a true industrial town for the first time in its life. Chaban revived its cultural life too, with a prestigious annual international arts festival; he was instrumental in the building of new ring motorways and commercial centres; and he saw to it that the new university campus is one of the most impressive in France. Most important, he took the initiative for a big new deep-water port for tankers and container ships, opened in 1976 at Le Verdon on the tip of the Médoc peninsula. This is claimed to be the leading roll-on-roll-off container port on Europe's Atlantic coast, and its south-westerly position in the EEC is seen as its crucial asset. The port's director told me, 'We are relatively so near the Americas and Africa that we can cut three or four days off the return Atlantic voyage to, say, Le Havre or Rotterdam, and this could save a big ship a million francs.' He added with the usual French modesty, 'We shall transform the geographical economy of western Europe.' This has hardly happened: but at least Chaban has transformed Bordeaux.

Nantes, further north, is a lesser counterpart of Bordeaux: another graceful city and port with a conservative tradition, which in the post-war decades expanded rapidly and acquired a new vitality. Recently it has been hit by the decline in shipbuilding, though less seriously so than its neighbour, St-Nazaire. Lille, metropolis of the Nord, is also at grips with reconversion of older industries, in this case textiles within the conurbation and coal and steel in nearby areas. Under its Socialist mayor, Pierre Mauroy, now Prime Minister, Lille is a well-ordered town, much more lively than its sombre exterior might suggest. Finally, the proud city of Strasbourg has benefited industrially from its strategic position on the Rhine, but at the same time feels the pressure of German competition. It thrives on tourism, and on the boost to its commerce given by its growing role as European parliamentary capital. These then are some of France's main cities – but how do they fit into the general scheme of things? We shall now look in a little more detail at the successes and failures of regional development, in terms of industry, services and communications.

FACTORIES, FINANCE, TRANSPORT, TELEPHONES – A VARIABLE RECORD OF REGIONAL PROGRESS

On DATAR's fifteenth birthday in 1978, its director proclaimed with pride, 'During this time we have changed the economic map of France.' How far is it true? As may appear from the survey I have given of a few key towns and regions, DATAR's overall success has been uneven. Probably its greatest achievement is that the growth of industry in the Paris region has been slowed right down and finally put into reverse. The statistics are revealing. From 1954 to 1962 the total of industrial jobs in this region was still rising at about the same rate as in the provinces – no great feat for decentralization. But in 1962–73 the Paris region had a net loss of 77,000 industrial jobs (about 5 per cent), while the rest of France gained 670,000, a rise of 15 per cent. This was quite a victory for the persistent efforts of DATAR, backed by increasing restrictions on the extension of plant in greater Paris. Big firms such as Renault have thus devoted all their rapid expansion to the provinces, and in some cases (notably Citroën) have transferred factories from Paris. But since about 1974 the growth in the provinces has of course slowed sharply. And even in the boom years, the new industry did not always go to the areas which needed it most.

The broad geographical pattern of development, over the past twenty years, is complex but clear. The towns that are fairly near Paris but outside its region – Caen, Rouen, Reims, Orléans and others – have all done especially well in attracting new industry, and so has much of the south-east, as we have seen in Lyon and Grenoble. But these are not DATAR priority zones, far from it. The already highly industrial regions of Nord and Lorraine are well placed at the heart of the EEC, but have had to face the problem of reconverting their older declining industries, coal, steel and textiles. With DATAR's help, they have had some success, but have proved vulnerable to recent crisis; and the same applies to some other older industrial pockets, such as the shipyards around Marseille, and the St-Etienne basin. In the still under-industrialized west, the campaign to entice new firms has borne fruit in certain places, notably on the coast at Bordeaux and Nantes, and to some extent in inland towns such as Pau, Toulouse and Rennes. But in many of the less populated parts of eastern, central and south-west France, there has been far too little new employment to cater for the steady exodus from the farms.

In fact, latest census figures show that the old notion of a France split down the middle – rich industrial east, poor rural west – is giving place to a new and more complex pattern. In demographic terms, the rough outline is that population and activity are tending to shift to the coast, leaving a declining hinterland: the principal zone of ageing and falling population, and of economic depression, is no longer the west as such, but a broad swathe of territory cutting across France from north-east to south-west: it starts in the Ardennes and Lorraine, takes in the upper Marne area, narrows to skirt northern Burgundy, then broadens out to include most of the sprawling Massif Central (Clermont-Ferrand itself excepted) and ends up in the Pyrenees. Twenty-four departments today have more deaths than births, and most of them lie in this zone. It is a decline that worries the planners, haunted by the ghosts of *le désert français*. So in 1975, with a loud roll of drums, the Government launched a long-term development programme for the big middle sector of this zone, the Massif Central (it happened to be the homeland of Giscard himself, and of his then Prime Minister, Jacques Chirac – coincidence?). In an effort to check the population drift, the programme includes special funding for forestry, communications and new small-scale industries (see pp. 239–40).

In striving for 'a more harmonious distribution of economic activity across France', the Government has proclaimed two main concerns. One is purely economic. The costs of creating new factories and the accompanying infrastructure are up to 50 per cent higher in an area such as greater Paris than in the less developed regions. Imbalance is thus a waste of national resources. Gravier pointed this out in 1947; and despite the progress made, it is still a factor today. The second concern is human. Young provincials are no longer so willing to migrate across France to Paris or other big cities. Most of them want to find work in their own region, and very often in smaller towns.

Yet, despite the cash incentives, it is not always so easy to persuade the industrial Mohammed to come to the popular mountain. By the early 1960s, most firms wishing to move from Paris had done so, and since then most new industry in the provinces has been new creations rather than transfers. Some firms have hesitated to take the plunge for fear they could not persuade enough of their executives and senior technicians to follow them. It is true, as I described earlier, that this is not the problem that it used to be, and Parisian *cadres* have now become readier to move to the provinces; but of course they are choosy about where they go. They may be enticed by the sunny south, but will think twice about settling, say, in gloomy St-Etienne or the grey-skied Ardennes. Often it is the wives who are cautious about moving to a new town without friends and without a well-known *lycée* or university for the children (significantly, it is university towns such as Caen and Grenoble that have expanded fastest).

The companies themselves tend to prefer to locate new plant within fairly easy reach of Paris. So – with a few obvious exceptions – it is the towns within a 150-mile radius of the capital that have most easily attracted new industry. If a firm is prepared to set up a factory further afield, it may face a dilemma. In order to have access to a local pool of skilled labour, used to hard industrial work, it may opt for an area that already has this kind of tradition, for example, the towns of Lorraine or the Alès coal basin (Gard) with their declining older industries. But it may not find it so easy to attract the *cadres*. On the other hand, if it goes to the more rural west or south-west, the *cadres* may come more willingly, but the firm may feel that the local ex-peasant population will not provide the kind of qualified labour it needs.

In order to combat these problems, DATAR has a complex system of incentives. Subsidies for new factory installations are nil in the case of a wide orbit around Paris and most of the south-east, but range up to 25 per cent for the more remote or depressed areas, and cover up to 60 per cent of costs in the case of transfers of plant *from* Paris. There are also various tax exemptions and other forms of aid. Since 1963, over 5,000 operations have benefited in some form from these incentives, but they are rarely decisive when it comes to choosing a location. Firms find them an attractive bonus, but other factors usually weigh more heavily in the final resort, such as communications, transport costs and labour. Usually DATAR is left to apply the carrot as best it can, but sometimes the Cabinet will step in at a higher level and use the stick, that is, threats or other pressures. This is not difficult, in a land where the State controls most finance and where many firms depend on State contracts. It is reported that in order to get one big electronics firm to set up plant in Brittany, Paris threatened to suspend its contracts. And we have seen how the State in 1979 persuaded car firms to go to Lorraine (see p. 60). But these are infrequent examples. The general policy of the Barre Government was to be 'liberal' with private firms.

Within this context DATAR has had a fair measure of success. It claims that since 1963 almost half the new industrial jobs in France have been created in its 'priority zones', which cover about half the territory but include less than a third of the population; and even *Le Monde* has referred to 'a regional policy that has begun to bear fruit'. But in the last few years of economic crisis the fragility of these achievements has become apparent, as we have seen in Brittany. The crisis has forced DATAR to switch its top priorities, from industrializing the west to the more urgent task of trying to stem the rise of unemployment in older industrial areas: in 1978 it launched a special 3,000-million-franc reconversion fund, with the aim of creating new jobs notably in the steel and textile districts of Lorraine and the Nord and the shipyard zones in and around Marseille and St-Nazaire. This has had some success, mainly in Lorraine. And in France there is not much alternative to this kind of policy. In America, when an industry declines or big factories close, the workers move off elsewhere. But in France this mobility, though traditional among peasants and now becoming common with *cadres*, has not yet spread to industrial workers. As in parts of Britain, they expect – rightly or wrongly – that the new jobs must come to them. We have seen this in Lorraine (see p. 61). And at Decazeville in the Aveyron, when the local coal-mines had to be run down and the miners were offered resettlement in State mines elsewhere, they refused: to press home their point that new industry must come to them, eight hundred miners stayed at the bottom of a pit for several weeks over Christmas.

The Government has to perform the balancing act of trying to fulfil rival demands in many places at once, both east and west, without enough new investment available. What is more, for many years some cities of the former regime alleged that its campaign to develop the west was in reality a bit two-faced – for a quite different reason. Since the late '50s the growth of the EEC and of German competition made it imperative to build up French industry where it was already strong, in the east: so heavy industrial firms in Alsace and the Rhône valley were allowed to expand at full tilt, and the new steel and petro-chemical complexes at Fos and Dunkerque were encouraged. The Government claimed that there was no incompatibility between the two policies and both were needed. However, today it becomes increasingly hard to find the resources for both. The three major infrastructure projects for the 1980s are the Rhine–Rhône canal, the Paris–Lyon high-speed express, and the Channel Tunnel; all are in the east, and all are likely to draw new trade and industry there. This may be necessary, for France to compete with her main EEC rivals. But the people of the south-west, and the Bretons, are entitled to wonder whether in practice they are getting the priority that is promised them. To build up a balanced France and also a strongly competitive France: these two rival imperatives are not always so easily compatible. The Socialists have inherited this dilemma.

Having halted the industrial growth of Paris, the Government in the 1970s turned its attention to what is called 'tertiary decentralization' – the transfer to the provinces of the headquarters of certain State bodies and private firms. As we have seen in Lyon, this is a complex issue. One aim of the policy is the classic DATAR one of creating more jobs in the regions, in this case white-collar ones: Paris still has 40 per cent of all French office jobs, for 20 per cent of the population. But another aim, supposedly, is to decentralize certain aspects of economic decision-making: this is much harder to achieve, and is fraught with equivocations.

In 1974 DATAR set up the Association Bureaux Provinces – similar to the former Location of Offices Bureau in Britain – which has been wooing firms of all kinds to establish their offices away from Paris. The State has modestly set a lead, by evacuating lock-stock-and-barrel to the provinces a few national services, which do not thereby cease to be centralized units but at least cease to clutter up Paris. Thus the Quai d'Orsay has transplanted to Nantes its department dealing with French citizens resident abroad, while the Société Générale, one of the big State-owned banks, has moved its securities service, involving 1,200 people, also to Nantes. Other big banks have moved some central departments to Bayeux and Orléans. But only a few Ministries or other bodies are prepared to make this kind of transfer, and often the opposition comes from their own middle-level staff. In 1972, Pompidou proudly announced that the State meteorological office was to be shifted *in toto* from Paris to Toulouse. There followed years of bureaucratic wrangles, and obstructions by staff unions, and in 1980 the first stage of the move was still at least two years away.

It has proved even harder to persuade private firms to shift their head offices; and one main reason, of course, is their desire to stay near the key ministries and sources of finance, which in turn will not move – a vicious circle. In the mid-'70s the Government began to use its full armoury of publicity to promote Lyon, Nice and Strasbourg as centres for office headquarters, not only national but international. This has borne a few modest results, in Lyon as we have seen, also in the Nice area where the Government has created a 'park' for scientific research and advanced service industries on a splendid open 6,000-acre site at Valbonne, near Antibes. Here Air France has transferred its world-wide reservations service, and two or three American-owned companies have set up their European head offices. But many other firms, though much solicited by D A T A R, have refused to make the move, and Valbonne Park's expansion is behind expectations. A firm's staff may jump at the idea of living on the Côte d'Azur, but management often thinks it more prudent to stay in Paris.

This attitude is unlikely to change, until the system of financing has become more decentralized. At least a start was made under Giscard. The least conservative of the big State banks, the Banque Nationale de Paris, took quite a momentous step – in its French context – when in 1975 it began transferring its regional management offices from Paris to the actual regions. Hitherto, if a client, say, in Marseille wanted a loan, the decision would be referred to the bank's south-eastern regional office, located *in Paris*! But now, in some of the larger cities, BNP has built centres for dealing with these matters more locally. This kind of physically decentralized decision-taking has long been the norm in many countries, and France is now slowly following suit. But the BNP and the other big banks are still under central management; and in France there are few regional banks of any size. Aware of the drawbacks, the Government in 1979 appointed Jacques Mayoux, a top civil servant well known as a trouble-shooter, to chair a commission making proposals for an overall reform of the banking system. His main suggestion was that the big State banks should be virtually carved up: they should either create truly autonomous divisions in the provinces, or set up holding companies there with some regional shareholding. The Paris banking world reacted by digging its heels in, to prepare for a long battle in defence of its privileges.

In 1978 Giscard promised he would speed up the transfer to the provinces of certain public departments. No doubt he was sincere: but the civil service mandarins in Paris have always wanted to retain the ultimate control, wherever the new offices may be located, and it requires courage and a strong will to go against this long Jacobin tradition. The Ministry of Finance still shows little desire even to decentralize internally, that is, to grant more powers of decision to its regional offices. And until this happens, private firms will have little incentive to follow suit. The issue is a political one, and it remains to be seen whether the Socialists will now have the strength to impose their ideals of devolution on their own civil service.

The development in France of a modern transport and communications network is a less controversial matter, where the State is not victim of the same inhibitions. Here the progress in the past ten or fifteen years has been remarkable, and has done much for regional development.

After a slow start, the Government has finally endowed France with one of the best transport systems in Europe: major new bridges, canals and tunnels have been built or are under preparation; rail and internal air services are excellent; the motorway programme, after years of delay, has moved ahead fast in the '70s despite the energy crisis. Even that old sick joke, the French telephone service, is being cured at last of its notorious backlogs.

French railways, nationalized in 1937, ended the war with four-fifths of their engines and coaches destroyed, and much of their rolling-stock, track and stations also out of action. But this, as with some other industries, proved a blessing in disguise. Louis Armand, France's greatest post-war technocrat, in 1946 became president of the Société Nationale des Chemins de Fer Français, and he set about rapid and vigorous modernization. He closed down 6,000 miles of uneconomic branch lines, and he gave generous budgets to research technicians to prepare new locomotive designs; as a result, France today not only exports electric and diesel engines in some numbers, but her trains have several times broken world speed records. They are reputed as among the most swift and efficient anywhere, also the most comfortable: the new French-built 'Corail' carriages are rather like the first-class sections of an airliner, with their adjustable tables enabling meals to be served to a passenger where he sits. Punctuality of trains is helped by a system of reduction of bonuses for drivers late without cause, and the high record of punctuality is one reason for the very low accident rate. It is also noticeable that, in a very cold winter spell, SNCF trains go on running smoothly while British Rail suffers chaotic delays.

Only 26 per cent of the total track is electric, but this carries more than 75 per cent of all traffic, for it includes most main and suburban lines. Fast 'Turbotrains' – using gas turbine engines, a bit like an aeroplane's – are now in service on some major inter-city lines, for example Lyon–Strasbourg, Lyon–Bordeaux and Bordeaux–Toulouse. Inter-city connections have thus vastly improved from those pre-war days when it was quicker to go from Toulouse to Lyon via Paris than direct; but they are not yet fully adequate, compared with the major lines radiating from Paris where famous trains – the 'Mistral' to Marseille, the 'Capitole' to Toulouse and others – cruise at 90 m.p.h. or more.

Today, the SNCF is at work on its greatest venture (Channel Tunnel apart), the building of a new railway from Paris to Lyon for the 'Train à Grande Vitesse', a sleek orange-and-white 'bullet train' that will be a rival to the high-speed 'Shinkansen' from Tokyo to Osaka. The TGV entered into service on the first section of this line in 1981, and is due to be running the whole course by the end of 1983, when it will cruise at up to 185 m.p.h. and link France's two main cities in two hours. Later it will be extended to St-Etienne and Marseille. The big loser will be Air Inter, the State-owned domestic air line, which is expecting a drop of 80 per cent in the traffic on its busiest route, Paris–Lyon.

However, Air Inter may recoup its losses with other routes, for internal air services have been expanding rapidly after a slow post-war start. Through the 1950s they were held back by narrow-sighted objections from the SNCF, whose interests have never been lightly cast aside by the Government because of the heavy post-war investment. But finally the Government realized that the lack of air flights was harming its industrial policy for the regions, even discouraging foreign investors: one firm at least chose Savoy for its plant simply because it was near an airport with links to Paris, at Geneva. So from about 1960 Air Inter was allowed to expand fast. Some private air lines have followed suit, and today France claims to have the most elaborate domestic air network in Europe. Toulouse, for example, is now linked to Paris by eight flights a day each way, and its annual passenger traffic grew from 40,000 in 1954 to a million in 1979.

As in the case of railways, the initial tendency was to follow the French centralized tradition and to radiate all flights from Paris. Lyon, Toulouse and Bordeaux had no links with each other until 1965. But since then DATAR has made attempts to encourage inter-city flights, and flights between those cities and the outside world, in the interests of the regions' economy. This policy has had quite a success. Limoges, for example, started direct flights to Lyon two years *sooner* than to Paris, and today also has daily flights to the little town of Aurillac, 100 miles to the south-east, while an even tinier Massif Central town, Mende (population 11,000), has daily links to Clermont-Ferrand and Montpellier – by eight-seater Islander! Compared with the rich and huge United States, France's map of scheduled flights may still look sketchy, but compared with Britain it is highly developed. And DATAR has been helped not only by Air Inter but also by one or two enterprising new private regional airlines, notably Touraine Air Transport, created at Tours in 1968 and now running some fifty regular services. Despite French centralism, the regions now have their own air links with the world: for instance, you can fly direct from Marseille to Moscow, from Lyon to Bangkok, from Grenoble to Düsseldorf, and to London all year round from a whole range of places such as Colmar and Poitiers.

The motorway network has always been a sore subject of debate in this car-mad country. As with air services, there was a very slow start. In 1967 France still had only 490 miles of motorway, less than Britain or even tiny Holland, and far less than Italy or Germany; not till 1970 was the central Paris–Lyon–Marseille *autoroute* laboriously completed. One reason for France's lag was that this spread-out country enjoys the legacy of about the best network in Europe of traditional main and secondary roads: they run dead straight across plains, or are splendidly engineered in hilly areas, and are a delight compared with most roads in Britain. So motorways seemed less of an urgent need than in more densely populated lands. But with the growth of traffic and cities, this steadily became less valid. Another factor in the delay was that public works of this kind are by tradition carried out by the State, which would neither spend much money itself on motorways nor allow private firms to build them. But finally the Government realized that the growing bottlenecks on some older roads were holding up industrial traffic, even keeping foreign tourists away. And in 1969 a free-enterprise-minded Minister of Equipment, Albin Chalandon, persuaded Pompidou to let private operators step in, with private capital. Soon these were at work on several new *autoroutes*.

This changed the whole picture. France rapidly overtook Britain and has now almost caught up with Italy in total mileage. Despite the energy crisis, in 1975–6 she was opening new stretches of motorway at the fastest rate in Europe, 350 miles a year, and by 1980 her overall network was over 3,200 miles. Motorways today radiate from Paris to Dunkerque, Strasbourg, Nice, Perpignan, Poitiers, Caen and so on, linking at several points with other countries' networks. Thus some of the worst of the old bottlenecks have been cured. No longer is Béziers, on the old main road into Spain, a congested mass of infuriatedly hooting tourists every summer. Some inter-regional motorways have also been built, but with a lower priority, as you might expect. Not until late 1979 was Toulouse joined to the national network, via Narbonne; and the much-needed Toulouse–Bordeaux *autoroute*, finally linking Atlantic to Mediterranean, will not be finished till 1982, years behind schedule. Similarly, the final section of the Lyon–Geneva motorway was completed only in 1981.

Some other notorious congestion-spots are still awaiting bypasses, as the British visitor may find to his cost. He arrives at Calais, but before he can reach the 140-mile stretch of motorway to Paris at Lilliers, he must first negotiate forty-five miles of narrow, congested road through a succession of ugly little towns around St-Omer. It is not the happiest introduction to *la belle France*. In many places, this is still the trouble: you can drive for scores of miles at maximum speed along an *autoroute* or dual-carriageway, then get stuck for an hour in the suburbs of some town. In populated districts, one problem is that the sacred French rights of land ownership make expropriation for sliproads a slow and costly business, lasting up to four years.

Motorists feel aggrieved that France, along with Italy, is one of the very few European countries to exact tolls on motorways, except on short sections near main cities. The tolls are quite high, averaging 13 to 20 francs per 100 kilometres. As a result, many private cars and lorries choose to go on clogging up the old roads, thus lessening the usefulness of the new investment: it is reckoned that motorway traffic might rise by 30 per cent if there were no tolls. The Government argues that France's traditional road network is so costly to keep in repair that it could not pay for the motorways too, nor subsidize those run by private firms, without an exorbitant rise in other motoring taxes. But the motoring and transport organizations argue that the tolls are too high, seeing that the cost of petrol (about 4 francs a litre in 1981) is also above the EEC average. At least the motorways are elegantly landscaped, and not disfigured by publicity hoardings as in Italy. They even – a typically imaginative French touch – carry attractive brown pictorial signs every few miles, informing you that on your right is some fine medieval abbey, on your left some famous vineyard or factory, and so on. Perhaps it makes the tolls more bearable.

In 1979, with the energy crisis worsening, the Government began to cut back the motorway programme. Some major projects already in hand are not being affected, notably Poitiers–Bordeaux (the final section of the Paris–Bilbao route) and Nancy–Dijon (the final section of a direct route from the Ruhr and Lorraine to the Midi). But some other projects (Bayonne–Toulouse, Le Mans–Rennes, etc.) have been postponed; or rather, the emphasis is now being switched from new motorways to the widening of existing main roads into fast dual carriageways, with urban ringways. This costs much less, and no tolls are exacted on these expressways. It seems a sensible compromise. At the same time, by aiding the SNCF to modify its tariffs, the Government has been trying to encourage more passengers and freight to go by train. Whereas in 1969–73 the SNCF had closed a further 4,400 miles to passenger services, there were no more closures at all in the first five years of the energy crisis. And yet despite these and other oil conservation measures, the individualistic French are still using their cars as much as ever.[8]

The motorways, the Paris–Lyon TGV, the big new international airports of the '70s at Satolas (Lyon) and Roissy (north-east Paris) – these have been elements in a general State policy of modern infrastructure. In de Gaulle's day, a splendid 100-million-franc road tunnel was built under Mont Blanc, linking Savoy with north-west Italy, and a single-vault suspension bridge was thrown across the lower Seine at Tancar-

8 For energy conservation, see p. 78; for French motoring habits, see p. 442.

ville, followed later by another across the Loire estuary. In those days, grandiosity was in favour, and some schemes were conceived as much with an eye to prestige as economic advantage. Today, cost-effectiveness is weighed more carefully. Yet the French still show a readiness to plan imaginatively, and on a large scale where needed. It seems no coincidence that in the '60s and early '70s most of the initiative and ideas for a Channel Tunnel came from the French side, although Britain, being an island, stood to gain most from a project that in her feebleness she then shelved in 1975. The new scheme, put forward jointly in 1979–80 by British and French Railways, has now been approved. But it is far more modest, simply for a single-track rail. If the French had got their way, they would have built something far more useful both for the motorist and for heavy haulage. Now they are going ahead with an almost equally ambitious project for another new EEC link: the building of a wide 145-mile canal from the Rhine at Mulhouse to the Saône (and hence to the Rhône). It will take ten years to build, at a cost of at least 7,000 million francs, and will finally provide Europe with its first complete Mediterranean-to-North-Sea waterway for heavy barges. It should help the Lyon area to trade with Germany, and give the port of Marseille a better chance to compete with Rotterdam for the commerce of the Ruhr. There are some who argue that the vast sums could have been better spent on other forms of transport; and the Lorrains, already in enough trouble, are distinctly sore at being by-passed. But the canal could be a real asset for Europe.

The change that has come over the French telephone service in the past few years is truly amazing. France today is ahead of the rest of Europe in pioneering the practical application of videophones, home viewdata systems and other electronic marvels. Yet, simultaneously, the Post Office is still struggling to meet the demands of millions of homes for their first ordinary telephone, after its decades of fearful neglect. Only very recently has the French telephone ceased to be a sick joke, a national shame. In 1970, France still had only one-fifth as many lines per capita as Sweden and fewer than Greece, and the saying went, 'Half the nation is waiting for a phone to be installed and the other half for a dialling tone.' Trunk lines were so few that during the day you might spend ages fruitlessly dialling a number in some other part of France. The dismal queues waiting to make trunk calls in many a post office were a disgrace for a nation calling itself modern; and many new factories and offices in the provinces had to survive for months with only one or two lines. This wasted thousands of business man-hours a day, and in some cases dissuaded firms from moving their plant to the regions. Finally the

Government woke up to the dangers of all this, and from about 1970 began to sanction massive investment by the Ministry of Posts and Telecommunications.

The past failures were not due to lack of technological flair – France has always been in the forefront here – but to poor organization and, above all, under-investment. Post-war governments showed a curious tendency to regard the telephone as a private bourgeois luxury rather than a business and social necessity: the early 'Plans' ignored it. However, in the 1970s an active consumer group rallied public opinion and put pressure on the Government. The Secretary of State in 1976–80, Norbert Ségard, was a talented thruster with a reputation for getting things done. He managed to stir up his bureaucratic ministry, and he was also allotted the funds: the telephone investment budget rose from 2,500 million francs in 1969 to 24,500 million for 1979.

The statistics are impressive. The number of lines has increased since 1970 from 4.2 million to over 17 million and is planned to reach 28 million by 1985. In 1970 France had fewer than half as many lines per capita as Britain or West Germany: today she is only 10 to 15 per cent behind and hopes to catch up by 1984. Over 99 per cent of the network is now automatic, and internationally so: a remote Breton farmer – provided he is lucky enough to secure a telephone – can dial Tokyo or São Paulo, whereas ten years ago not only would he have had to ask the village operator and then wait hours, but the local exchange would shut down completely outside office hours, lunch-time included.

The French still gripe about the service, but cannot fail to notice the improvements. The number of trunk lines has quadrupled since 1970, and generally one can now get through first time. And the Ministère des Postes, Téléphones et Télécommunications are finally catching up with the practice in most civilized countries by building pavement kiosks. Until recently, to make a call you had to go inside a post office (when it was open), or use a noisy café, or late at night try the police station in an emergency. It was very tiresome. But today there are some 60,000 street kiosks. They break down or are vandalized no more frequently than in Britain.

The queues in post offices are now much shorter, but the overall situation is still far from perfect. New telephones are being installed at the rate of nearly 2 million a year, but demand grows almost as fast and the waiting list is still over a million. The average time that a private applicant must wait for an installation has been cut since 1975 from sixteen to eight months – bravo! – but this is still absurdly long. The problem is that demand has been rising much faster than forecast. While 87 per cent of French homes now have a refrigerator, only 50 per cent have a phone, and the days are past when the average working-class family thought such a luxury outside its grasp. They now expect it, but cannot go out and buy one in the High Street, like a car or TV set. So the PTT's hopeful target for 1985 is to increase the percentage of homes with telephones to 90 and cut the average wait to two weeks. The French mass public has suddenly discovered the telephone, as if it were some latest invention like the mini-computer, and magazines are full of sociological articles with such titles as, 'Has the Telephone Changed the Human Relations of the French?'

Another deficiency of the service is that it is one of the world's more expensive. Calls cost much more than in the United States, and a new subscriber has to pay 400 francs for the privilege of being connected, even if he is merely inheriting an existing instrument in the flat to which he is moving and no technical work is required. This sum, like all subscribers' dues, is regarded as government tax. And the built-in attitude of the PTT's staff is that subscribers are *administrés*. If there appears to be a mistake on your bill, and you query it, your chances of gaining satisfaction are no better than one in five.

In the view of many of the PTT's critics, the high costs and other persistent shortcomings are in part a legacy of bad management. The service is run on an outdated civil service basis, clumsy in its bureaucracy and still saddled with much antiquated routine equipment. Yet – a familiar French irony – the research sections of the PTT are staffed by brilliantly inventive engineers in the vanguard of progress. Soon after the war, France pioneered the world's first experiment with long-distance automatic dialling, and today she is one of the four or five world leaders in the development of remote data processing. While millions wait for a phone in their living-room, the PTT has now excitedly set up a videophone link (a kind of closed-circuit cable TV, available for business talks) between Paris and Abidjan. And in 1978 it opened a data transmission network, for use by business firms, based on the Transpac packet-switching system, pioneered by French industry. Moreover, France today leads Europe in experiments with new 'view-data' systems for the general public. In the Paris suburb of Vélizy, 2,500 subscribers are now taking part in one such pilot project, which uses the telephone to link an adapted TV set to the big central computer databanks, and turns the home screen into an instant newspaper, encyclopaedia, mail order service, booking office and so on. In the Ille-et-Vilaine department of Brittany, a similar kind of experiment scheduled for 1982 will use the TV screen to provide all subscribers with an electronic telephone directory. If this goes well, it is planned that by 1992 all France will be using this system and there will be no more cumbersome paper directories.

Some people remain sceptical about how far these expensive schemes will go, or how useful they will really prove to be. A leader of the consumer pressure group told me, 'These brilliant engineers are far more keen on spectacular prestigious pilot schemes than on serving the public.' But at least recent Ministers have tried to induce the PTT staff to become more consumer-conscious. Aware of the bad image of the service, Ségard launched massive publicity campaigns – 'We make the old folks less lonely', etc. Much has in fact been done to improve the service, but the progress has been more impressive in quantity than quality. Further modernization requires a basic administrative shake-up, and this has been blocked by the unions at the PTT, through fear of change and redundancies. Plans were put forward under Giscard for separating the telephone and postal services and putting the former on a full commercial basis. But the unions vetoed the scheme. So the consumer remains at the mercy of a State service that allows him little redress. More telephones means more *administrés*, a bonanza for the bureaucrats.

It is noticeable too that while telephones have improved at least in numbers, the postal service – formerly France's pride – has been getting steadily worse. Like A. A. Milne's bears. Until a few years ago the PTT could boast that a letter posted anywhere in France would arrive at its destination the next day. Today even for first-class mail this is true only in three cases out of four, while second-class letters often take weeks. Thefts of parcels by postal workers have become much more frequent, and in ten years the number of registered packets that simply vanish has increased four-fold. In 1979 M. Ségard admitted publicly, 'The post in France is in a grave state of crisis,' and promised a shake-up. But it is not easy to cure a malaise that is common to the postal services in other countries too, including Britain and the United States, and has much the same causes. Strikes are frequent, morale is low. A senior official told me: 'Postal work used to have quite high prestige – remember Tati's jolly village postman in *Jour de Fête*? But the growth of telex and modern telephone systems have pushed the post into a backwater. Only the dullards who can't find other work will take on sorting or delivery jobs. And in France a State service cannot hire foreigners, so we can't take on bright immigrants as in Germany or Britain. We're left with a lot of dolts who are lazy, incompetent grousers, with little sense of public service.' The telephone service has improved through getting more money: the postal service is failing through human factors. At the lower levels, public servants in France are losing their traditional sense of public responsibility; it is a malaise today felt throughout the State administration.

DEVOLUTION AT LAST: EXIT THE PREFECT;
MORE POWER FOR MAYORS AND REGIONS

The prefect in his blue-and-gold uniform, political servant of the Ministry of the Interior, is he really the ideal figure to be in charge of local government in a modern democracy? To this the new Socialist Government has answered an emphatic 'no'. Under the wide-ranging reforms being introduced in 1982–3, the prefect is stripped of much of his executive power and is rechristened 'commissioner of the Republic'. Much of his control over local affairs passes into the hands of elected bodies in the communes, departments and regions. This devolution stops some way short of creating a federal system, on the West German or American pattern. But it is certainly the most radical attempt yet made to dismantle France's highly centralized structure and to strengthen local democracy.

The Socialists regard this as much the most important of their innovations for reshaping French society, more so than the nationalization of key industries or the redistribution of wealth. Mauroy has called it *'la grande affaire'* of Mitterrand's seven-year mandate. The reform is certain to run into varied opposition from vested interests, and it may well fail to work out smoothly in practice. But, according to the opinion surveys, it does seem to correspond roughly to what most French people want, alike on the Left and the Right.

Before we examine the new Socialist blueprint, we should explore in some detail the complex and devious system that it will replace. In terms of efficiency, no less than of democracy, it is hard to draw up a fair evaluation of this system, which itself has repeatedly been revamped by piecemeal reforms over the past twenty years. There are many civil servants in other countries who have long admired the authority of the prefectoral structure and have envied the power it has given the State to initiate projects in the regions, as well as the stability it has provided in times of unrest. On the other hand, there are many who realize that the prefect has not been fully master in his own domain: both he and the mayors have frequently been victims of the same heavy State machine, whereby rival Ministries have spread their tentacles through the provinces, jealously guarding their separate local fiefdoms, liaising inadequately, causing delays and muddles. The prefect has had only partial control over this unwieldy bureaucracy, which has often sapped the spirit of civic initiative. In practice, local government has also been based on an uneasy balance of power between prefect and mayor (plus other leading *notables*), for the locally elected mayor, too, has always been a figure of influence, especially in a big town. In this tacit diarchy of autocrats, it is the ordinary citizen's voice that has tended to get left unheard in day-to-day affairs, and this the Socialists now hope to remedy.

Already in the 1960s there were growing pressures for reform, based on the feelings that State control should be reduced *both* at the local level of towns and villages *and* at a wider regional one. This led to the 1971–2 reforms under Pompidou, which did give the communes a shade more financial autonomy and set up, timidly, new regional assemblies. But the latter had very limited powers and no direct franchise. Giscard near the end of his mandate then put forward a reform that, if enacted, would have given a new freedom to the communes. But, under Jacobin pressures within his own ranks, he baulked at true regional devolution. This, he said, would cause the State to fly apart. And yet, many leading Frenchmen, and not only Socialists, have long held that France cannot become a modern open society without more democratic autonomy at regional level: France cannot stand aside from a trend that has been gaining ground in neighbouring countries such as Spain and Italy. Today this voice has been heard. A key component in the Socialist reform is the setting up of directly elected regional assemblies, each inheriting a fair measure of power from the prefect. So will the State now fly apart? We shall see.

Local government has a three-tier structure. At the bottom level, the whole of France is divided into 36,383 communes, most of them villages, some big towns such as Lyon or Marseille. Unlike the departments created artificially in 1790, the communes are deep-rooted historical entities, usually with a strong local pride. Each has its mayor and council, elected every six years. Mayors play a far stronger role than in Britain, and a majority of them retain office for decades, local father figures. Yet the mayor is also the servant of the State in the commune, and till now has been responsible to the prefect for ensuring that the regulations from Paris are carried out. The middle tier is that of the ninety-six departments, each with a council (*conseil général*), which is directly elected but hitherto has been seldom effective. At the top are the twenty-two regions, created in 1964, each grouping a handful of departments. The Socialist reforms will retain these same three tiers, but will grant to each of them a good deal more autonomy.

Under the outgoing system, in force until 1982, each department had its prefect, and each region its super-prefect who was also the prefect of the department where the region's capital was situated: thus in his *préfecture* in Bordeaux the regional prefect of Aquitaine was also prefect of the Gironde. The regional prefect's role was essentially to coordinate economic planning, while the departmental prefect was more a political governor. As conceived by Napoleon, his first task was to maintain law and order, and by 1981 he still controlled most of the police and was expected to keep the Government informed on local opinion and political developments. He would even act as a kind of electoral agent for the Government, and might give advice or information to *majorité* candidates or urge local *notables* to stand for election. But this aspect of his work was on the wane in post-war years, as increasingly he became caught up in economic duties. Besides coordinating the ever more complex activities of the multiple Ministerial services within his borders, he had to supervise the *conseil général* and the communes. Often his working relations even with anti-Government mayors were perfectly sound; but each possessed a tacit veto on the other's projects, and quite often would use it.

At first sight the system might seem heavily weighted against the commune's freedom of action. The prefect had the right to suspend a mayor or councillor from office (and occasionally would do so), or to prohibit a council from acting on a matter outside its clearly defined competence. Many major matters – health and welfare, low-cost housing, school education – which in Britain or Germany are in varying degrees managed by the local authority (albeit with backing from the State) in France have always been controlled primarily by the State (albeit with some civic participation): the balance has been different. Thus, in a French town, State officials have done jobs that in other countries are carried out by municipal staff. This goes some way to explain why local authority budgets in France have hitherto equalled only 15 per cent of the total State budget, compared with 50 per cent in Britain and 80 per cent in Germany. And this relative lack of autonomy has had another aspect too. The revenue that a town could raise from local taxes was so limited, by law, that even in matters where it had some freedom – roads, transport, culture, sport, etc. – in practice it had to rely on financial partnership with the State, which through loans or subsidies provided about 70 per cent of the finance for local investment projects. There were norms here: for main roads and major new buildings the State paid about half the cost; for drainage or a sports ground, 20 per cent, and so on. And to obtain one franc the commune had first to secure State approval of the project as a whole. It could in some cases go ahead on its own, if it wished: but seldom would it feel it had the money to forego the luxury of State aid. So it was at the mercy of Ministerial delays, or arbitrary last-minute cuts by the Ministry of Finance. Or its projects might be vetoed. This might sometimes be sheer vindictiveness, if the commune had *mal voté*; but more often the factors were bureaucratic caution or parsimony, or sheer muddle and inertia. Urban renewal schemes could wait five years or more for the go-ahead: Rouen once had to wait thirteen for permission to rebuild a main square.

Until 1971 a commune had to present its annual budget in full detail to the prefect for his prior approval. This oppressive aspect of *la tutelle* was then modified: communal accounts were henceforth scrutinized in advance only where State money was involved or if some irregularity was suspected. Yet in other respects the State's formal powers of control remained enormous. If a mayor wanted to alter the status of a municipal employee, or erect a public monument, or even change a street-name, the relevant Ministry could intervene (the Socialist mayor of Rennes told me in 1979, 'We wanted to change some of our staff to another category which involved paying them a mere fifteen francs a month extra. For this I had to have a long talk with the Prefect who said, "This is too much for me, I'm passing it on to my Minister." Yes, I've learned what *la tutelle* means!'). Many communes ended up resentful, and sometimes in turn would block State projects for their area. In theory the State might have the legal power to override this, but in practice it tended to be cautious for obvious political reasons and preferred the carrot to the stick. In fact, one of the roles of the prefect was to mediate between mayors and ministerial bureaucrats. For the prefect, after all, was a kind of diplomat. He had a luxurious flat in his majestic *préfecture* where he would entertain lavishly; he presided in uniform at major ceremonies; and if he died in office he was buried with full military honours. Like a diplomat, he was moved from post to post every few years, partly for promotion but also to prevent him from becoming too involved with his 'subjects'. If he was under fifty or so, he was almost certainly an *énarque*,[9] as were most of the abler members of his staff. Some prefects might share the limitations of the technocrat: but the better ones have been men of culture, common sense and personal presence, skilled at conciliation and persuasion in a local world of endless wheeler-dealing.

This may help to explain why, in daily practice, there was so high a degree of complicity and inter-dependence, in the complex milieu of local government prior to the 1982 reforms. Despite the strong formal powers of the State and the weakness of local finances, mayors and other *notables* were in turn able to exert quite an influence on Paris, in diverse ways. For one thing, mayor and prefect, though rivals, needed each other. A mayor of the Left such as Dubedout might complain about his prefect, yet he knew how to reach a *modus vivendi* with him, and vice versa. A good prefect and a go-ahead mayor often shared common aims, whether of economic expansion or 'quality of life', and they were obliged

9 For the nature of *énarques* and technocrats, see pp. 82–92.

to collaborate on projects; they also had a joint interest in preserving peace and order and avoiding disruptions that might discredit them both.

Above all, the tradition in France – unlike that in Britain – has long been for an ambitious politician to try to build a strong local power base, often by seeking election as mayor of a big town; or, put the other way, it is often the mayors of big towns who have found it easiest to climb high in national politics. For, whatever the limits hitherto on a town's autonomy, within that town the mayor is a big boss, *un patron*, and the new Socialist reforms are unlikely to alter this. Chaban-Delmas in Bordeaux, Lecanuet in Rouen, Defferre in Marseille, Mauroy in Lille, are among the many recent examples of big-town mayors with a national role. And a successful mayor usually stays in office for many years, often decades, thus becoming a focus of local loyalty, whereas the prefect and his senior staff were always on the move. What is more, the French have a curious tradition called *le cumul des mandats*, whereby the more offices you hold simultaneously, the more power you can wield: thus a prominent figure who is a mayor, and probably a deputy or senator too, has found himself enticed into also playing a leading role in the departmental council and/or regional assembly. He might join national commissions too. Many of these men have always carried terrific clout in Paris. And so, for all these reasons, a prefect or Ministry official would be careful how he handled a strong local *notable* who could easily go above his head, to a Minister or even to the Elysée (see p. 245). This was mainly true, of course, of pro-Government *notables*. But, even in opposition, a Defferre or a Mauroy carried clout too. After all, a prudent civil servant knew that he might one day have a change of masters. As indeed he now has.

A clever and influential *notable* was often able to play off one Government service against another and thus manipulate them, for the State, that centralizing monster, was also in practice a hydra whose diverse heads were frequently in conflict or at cross-purposes; both at national and local level there were fierce and long-standing rivalries between certain Ministries and agencies, and liaison was far from perfect despite the prefect's efforts. In fact, rival State officials would often prefer to deal with a mayor or other *notable* than with each other, and this again increased the *de facto* influence of the latter and the need the State had of them. The sociologist Michel Crozier has observed:[10] 'Despite the hostility and complaints that he causes, an agent of the Ponts et Chaussées communicates better with the local *notables* than with his departmental director of the Ministry of Equipment . . . Between civil servant

10 *On ne change pas la Société par décret*, Grasset, Paris, 1979, p. 119.

and *notable* there develops a complicity based on common experience, complementary interests and identical standards.' So it was small wonder that the freemasonry of French *notables*, loudly though they might complain against the formal State tutelage, were in practice often opposed to any proposed reform that threatened their vested interests through an alteration of the structures.

This convoluted system was workable, it had its strengths, and many pundits have argued that it was democratic. Professor Vincent Wright, after presenting an analysis fairly similar to the one I have given, has concluded:[11] 'The existence of 37,000 mayors may be inefficient to the protagonists of economic rationalism, but it is a source of immense strength for local democracy.' On the other hand Crozier, whose analysis of the pre-1982 system was also quite similar, reached a very different conclusion:[12] 'This honeycomb network of power and decision-making confines *notables* and civil servants within an enclosed circuit; it prevents the citizen from intruding into public affairs, it creates and perpetuates the game of favours and privileges, the conservatism of the élites, the rigid separations between rival bodies.' Crozier has long argued that only a radical shake-up, creating new élites, can destroy this harmful closed shop. His view and that of other critics – myself included – has been that the pre-1982 system was lacking both in democracy and efficiency. The multiple power cliques were obstacles to progress and prevented the citizen from sharing in decision-making, except via elections. The practice of *le cumul des mandats* has concentrated too much power in too few hands and has given the busy potentate too little time to concentrate properly on any one of his duties. Also, as Crozier pointed out, the system has actually incited a mayor to behave like an autocrat in his town:[13] 'An astute mayor knows that it is not a wise policy to invite the citizens to participate. The mayor owes his power to the fact that he alone has the ear of the State administration. In order to keep his power, he must remain as the indispensable intermediary, and this requires aloofness, secrecy and citizen non-participation. Our present system is in fact a government at two levels: universal suffrage designates a small number of *notables*, who then organize among themselves a relatively hermetic style of decision-making.' Possibly Crozier put it too strongly; but rare are the Dubedouts who have attempted a different style. We shall assess later whether the new Socialist reforms are likely to improve the situation.

11 *Provincial Pressures in a Jacobin State*, 1979. I am indebted to Professor Wright for a number of facts and ideas in this chapter.
12 op. cit., p. 125.
13 op. cit., pp. 132–3.

By 1981 some of the structures of local government had become archaic. They were devised for the old rural France and had not been adequately updated for modern urban needs. This applied above all to the departmental *conseil général*. This enfeebled version of an English county council was directly elected and had its own modest budget for some services such as secondary roads, public assistance, rural drainage. But it met only twice a year, its budget and agenda were prepared by the prefect and in practice it usually did what he told it. It might have had more prestige were it not elected on a 'rotten borough' basis, weighted in favour of rural areas rather than towns. For example, until 1972, in the Haute Garonne, Toulouse, with two-thirds of the department's population, elected only four of its thirty-nine councillors. Under the 1972 reforms, four hundred new urban cantons were created in France (each canton elects one councillor), and this did somewhat improve things: Toulouse now had eight *élus*. But the imbalance was still considerable, and this lack of representativeness made the *conseil général* a bit of a joke. Its members were usually elderly. Constitutionally it had the power to be more effective than it was, but it lacked the energy. So people tended to forget about it. Yet it was the only body with a direct mandate between the level of Parliament and that of the communes, and this was a lack.

The communes too have had their out-of-date aspects, some of which – though not all – may now be improved by the new reforms. First, the complex issue of local finances. In recent years most towns have become heavily in debt. It is true that the State, after 1966, allowed the communes some new forms of tax-raising, but it also imposed V A T on their spending, thus taking away with one hand as much as it gave with the other. And in the austerity years of the late '70s it became more niggardly with its own contributions to their budgets. This left the communes in a dilemma. Their own local revenue came mainly from rates and a company tax on salaries. Since 1970 the State also allowed them to raise their own loans for financing certain public works, and this proved useful: Marseille in 1972 secured a 120-million-franc loan from private banks to help pay for its new *métro*. But loans meant debts. With rising costs, most towns ran increasingly into the red, and by 1980 the communes' global debt was put at 100 billion francs. In order to try to limit this, most towns felt obliged to put up rates faster than the level of inflation: in 1975 they rose on average 22.5 per cent, while inflation was 10 per cent. And in some cases this sparked off a ratepayers' revolt. All this will seem familiar to British or American ears. Equally familiar is the problem that rocketing costs in city centres were driving businesses and residents into the suburbs, so that the central commune would find its revenue falling. Mayors grew alarmed. Some aspects of the situation were their own fault: often they had embarked on over-ambitious projects which the ratepayers were not pleased to pay for. But the real issue was that French towns were under-financed. For their routine equipment and running costs, the State neither doled them out enough money nor permitted them to levy enough themselves.

Another trouble with France's communes has been their size: most are too small, while the larger ones have hitherto been too monolithic in their government. In a village, everyone knows the mayor; but in a town the size of Lyon or Bordeaux, the citizen has tended to feel remote from the work of the town hall. The tradition of mayoral autocracy has reinforced this, and only recently have a few towns such as Grenoble begun to establish ward associations and district branches of the *mairie* (see p. 317). The ward structure is less developed than in Britain. And the most serious flaw in the pre-1982 situation derived from the electoral system, which in most larger towns produced councils that were grossly unrepresentative. The Gaullists in the early 1960s invented a single-list system for all towns of over 30,000 people, whereby any party or coalition won all the seats, or none. It was the antithesis of proportional representation. The Gaullists did this cynically, in the days when they were strong, knowing that it would help them and their allies to take control of most cities. Later it rebounded against them, for the last municipal elections, in March 1977, happened to come at a time when the Left was united and in the ascendant, so the system helped Left-wing coalitions to take total control of 159 of the 221 towns in this category. But the main factor was that, whoever won, there was simply no formal opposition at all on a council. In Bordeaux, there was not a single Left-wing councillor to gainsay Chaban; in Lille, Mauroy's Socialist/Communist coalition had a total monopoly; and so on. This hardly stimulated democracy and free discussion. What is more, it meant that when there was a change of power, the new team would arrive at the *mairie* without any experience of the council's affairs: when the Left won Rennes in 1977 after twenty-four years of rule by the *centriste* Henry Fréville, the new thirty-three-year-old Socialist mayor and his colleagues had the noblest of intentions, but made mistakes through sheer ignorance. For the 1977 elections Giscard did modify the system for the four largest communes, Paris, Lyon, Marseille, Toulouse, which were divided into electoral wards and did thus admit opposition members to their councils. This was a step forward, but Giscard baulked at extending it to other towns for the 1983 elections. Happily, the Socialists are now committed to a return to a normal multi-party system in all towns, based on proportional representation.

However, the Socialists seem less likely to tackle another weakness in the communes' structure: the fact that most of them are far too small. This flaw cannot be blamed on the State: it is largely the communes' own fault, for since the war they have proved reluctant to regroup rationally. There are two types of problem here: (a) the spread of conurbations has engulfed small surrounding communes which still cling defiantly to their independence, sometimes obstructing the growth of an urban area's joint services; (b) many rural communes, now depopulated, no longer make sense as administrative entities. The map of France's communes has barely altered since the last century. There are still 36,383 of them, more units of local government than in all the rest of the EEC. Over 11,000 have less than two hundred inhabitants; one has three people, and most of its statutory council of nine live elsewhere! The smaller communes generally lack the finances and the know-how to provide the social facilities that are nowadays expected: yet to persuade them to merge, as a modern economy requires, has not proved easy. Not only do mayors and councillors want to avoid losing office, but the citizen too is emotionally attached to his commune. The village *mairie*, the mayor with his sash conducting a wedding or opening a fête, this is something very real, especially in a society where the rediscovery of rural traditions is today *à la mode*.

So, for electoral reasons, all Governments have always proceeded warily over mergers. Very rarely have these been enforced. The Government has tried exhortation, and financial inducements, notably since 1971 when a new law allowed sizeable loans and tax advantages to communes agreeing to merge. But the response has been feeble. Since 1959 only about 1,200 communes, less than 3 per cent of the total, have disappeared through mergers. Small communes fear that to be swallowed up by a larger one would mean the loss of 'human scale' (as they put it) and maybe higher taxation. When a village near Lille was invited by the prefect to integrate either with Lille or Roubaix, the mayor retorted, 'We are like Poland in 1939, trapped between Germany and Russia!' All over France you could almost hear the bells of all the little Clochemerles tolling their sympathy for his *esprit de clocher*. It may seem curious that this elephantine State would not deal with the flea tickling its ear: but when there are 36,383 fleas you have to be careful, and the communes' jealous exercise of their legal rights has been one price they have exacted from the State for its intrusions in other respects.

The Giscard Government largely stopped trying to produce total mergers. But it continued with a more realistic policy, begun in the 1960s, of encouraging communes urban or rural to group themselves into 'syndicates' or 'districts', for joint planning or the running of some common services such as water, sewage, public transport, with some

· pooled financing. This has worked fairly well, and over half of all communes now belong to some such association. But it has not really solved the problems of coordination in the big conurbations. Here, the Gaullists in 1967 tried the radical measure of actually imposing a new structure, the *communauté urbaine*, on four big centres: Bordeaux, Lille, Lyon, Strasbourg. This is a little like the new English metropolitan county. Central and suburban communes each keep their own identity and mayor, with some responsibilities, but they also unite to form a joint council with its own budget, in charge of town-planning and many services. This has been working fairly smoothly, despite inevitable frictions between Left- and Right-wing suburbs, and it has since been copied voluntarily by five smaller conurbations including Brest and Le Mans. The drawback is that the duplication of some staff and services at the two levels is expensive and top-heavy.

Owing to local rivalries, some urban areas refused for many years to create even a 'district', despite the inconveniences. A star case was Toulouse in the 1960s under Louis Bazergue (see p. 164). This commune is lucky to cover a wide area with plenty of vacant land, and this at first led Bazergue to believe that he could develop the town without reference to its neighbours. But soon the suburban communes were expanding much faster than the city itself, notably Colomiers, near the aircraft factories, under its ambitious Socialist mayor, André Raymond. He attracted scores of new firms, which vastly increased his town's revenue from local taxes. This infuriated Bazergue, who refused even to be on speaking terms with his fellow-Socialist. He retaliated, too, by refusing to help the burgeoning suburbs to meet their growing needs in public utilities, where the city itself was already fairly well organized. Grudgingly it sold them water, but would not extend its bus routes outside its town boundaries. The peripheral communes tried to group together for some utilities, but this was barely practicable. Clearly some kind of syndicate was needed for the conurbation, and this the prefect suggested, but Bazergue at first refused. Then he took fright that the Government might impose on him a *communauté urbaine* – horrors! Feeling cornered and isolated, with the 1971 elections approaching, he suddenly changed his tack to one of charming cooperation and accepted the prefect's proposal for a joint planning committee, which set to work. Amazingly it was the first time that Bazergue and his local fellow-mayors, most of them also Socialist, had ever sat round a table together: 'At last he shakes hands and says "bonjour,"' Raymond told me. After Bazergue's fall from power in 1971, matters further improved, and the conurbation now has a syndicate which runs a number of joint services rationally: no longer do you have to change buses at the city boundaries, as if crossing a national frontier. Temperamental Toulouse may be an extreme case, but the episode underlines the strength of communal pride in France. The commune is a living reality, not to be tampered with lightly. Probably there is no harm in allowing it, however small, to retain a certain identity, including the folklore of the mayor with his sash: but ways must be found of combining this with efficient and coordinated management. This is the thinking behind the new Socialist plans – as we shall see – but it may not be easy to achieve.

Amid the welter of piecemeal reforms of local government under de Gaulle, Pompidou and Giscard, it was possible to pick out three main strands: (a) the State, under one set of pressures, reduced its tutelage over the communes; (b) under a different set, it made gestures towards regionalism; (c) it simply sought to streamline its own administration. It was this last aspect that guided the twin Gaullist reforms of 1964. First, in the name of efficiency, the departmental services of most Ministries were regrouped under the umbrella of the prefect. This was only partially effective, for many local services managed to hold on to a kind of autonomy. Moreover, though hailed as a feat of decentralization, the measure was no more than an administrative reshuffle.

The second and more important 1964 reform was based on a realization that the department had become too small a unit for modern economic planning. So the departments were grouped into regions solely for this purpose; in other respects they kept their old functions. The departments (except in the Paris area) are all much the same size, though their population varies from over 2 million to under 100,000. Their size was conceived in Napoleon's day so that an official in his capital could travel by stage-coach to any part of his domain and back 'between sunrise and sundown'; but the motor car has killed all that. What is more, it was clear by the 1960s that big new projects such as the Languedoc canal cut across departmental boundaries and caused problems of official liaison; and in an era devoted to eager expansion, economic decisions needed a wider sweep. So the regional *préfectures* were created, marking an increase in national power for the prefectoral corps. To 'advise' the prefect, a new locally designated consultative body of worthies was also set up in each region, but these proved totally ineffectual.

By the late 1960s the public feeling was growing that the regions needed more than prefects and France needed a properly democratic regional structure. This was one of the many motifs of the 1968 explosion, as we have seen in Brittany. De Gaulle, who understood these aspirations, put forward a project in 1969 that might really have meant something, but it was defeated for reasons largely unconnected with its own merits or defects, and he resigned. Then after a decent interval Pompidou revived it in a different form in 1972. By now, regionalism was fashionable all over Europe, and Paris reluctantly felt it had to do something. So it set up two new indirectly chosen bodies in each region. One was purely consultative, an economic and social council of local delegates from chambers of commerce, etc. The other had a shade more substance, being made up of the deputies and senators representing the region in Paris, plus certain *conseillers généraux* and town councillors. This regional assembly had a small budget of its own, derived from local taxes, to a ceiling of 37.5 francs a year *per capita*, and from this it could finance some local projects on its own initiative. The regional prefect was also supposed to consult it on all planning matters.

The reform did mark a small step forward. At least the 'region' was finally legalized as a political institution. But as the assemblies' powers were limited to the use of their minuscule budgets, the prefects in practice kept the authority, and they would always look to Paris. Within each region it was the prefect who had the staff and facilities for drawing up detailed projects, and he tended to present them as a *fait accompli* to the assembly, which lacked the resources and usually also the know-how for this kind of work. It is true that in one or two regions a Socialist-led assembly under a strong leader did manage to stand up to the prefect: the Provence assembly, chaired by Gaston Defferre, once rejected the prefect's annual proposals and voted its own. So it could be done, but only within a limited range of action. And above all, the assembly did not have the moral authority of a direct popular mandate. It was merely a college of existing dignitaries, most of them elderly and cautious by temperament, and more tired and overworked than ever through this added *cumul* of their *mandats*. The assemblies have had little local impact.

In 1972 the Government stressed that its reform was intended to be '*évolutive*', a first step towards possibly more radical measures later. Then Giscard, at the time of his election in 1974, indicated that he was ready to move on to the next crucial phase: direct regional elections. But in 1975 came separatist flare-ups in Brittany, Languedoc, Alsace and notably in Corsica where secessionists killed two policemen. Even in Corsica, France's number one problem, supporters of outright independence have never been more than about 2 per cent of the population. But the Jacobin-minded Gaullists were able to exploit the troubles as evidence that any more devolution could lead to a break-up of the State. And Giscard back-tracked, apparently under Gaullist pressure. Either through political expediency, or else from a real change of heart, or both,

Giscard soon swung against regionalism, and in December 1975 he declared publicly that France was not a nation the size of the United States and could not expect a federal structure. His Government had two main fears. First, that devolution would encourage secessionist trends in certain regions. Second, and perhaps more pertinent, that directly elected Left-dominated assemblies in some regions would increase the influence of the Opposition. Eight assemblies had Socialist presidents. The Government was also worried by the regional experiment in Italy since 1970, where Emilia and Tuscany elected Communist-led assemblies and thereby helped the rise of the PCI. Giscard himself told me in 1979, when I visited him at the Elysée: 'The French are so contentious that regional devolution would immediately create local fiefdoms opposed to the State. France is like that. So we cannot yet take the risk. It is better to give more autonomy first to existing smaller entities, the commune and the department, and this is what we are now doing. As for the aspirations of the Bretons and others, they can be fulfilled by economic and cultural measures, by helping to keep local languages alive, and so on.' He could not have been more explicit.

Giscard may have been hesitant about the regions, but he saw clearly that local government needed some change, and he was sincere in his desire to strengthen democracy at the more local level. So a complex reform Bill was drawn up in consultation with France's *notables*, and in 1979–80 it began its tortuous way through Parliament. Giscard saw this project as a major change. 'It is not a mere administrative measure,' he said, 'but a reform of the State itself and of its relations with citizens. The State is going to hand over to the local authorities a large part of its prerogatives.' In practice, the State's annual subsidy to a commune would no longer be allotted per item but handed over in a lump sum for the council to use much as it pleased. This in theory at least would greatly reduce the prefect's tutelage over its finances. Then, in a later phase, the State would transfer a number of its responsibilities to the department or commune, in such matters as low-cost housing, welfare and school buildings. Though imperfect, this reform could have proved quite radical, within its limits. But for a whole variety of reasons it ran into strong opposition from *notables*, civil servants and others; and Parliament delayed its passage for so long that by the 1981 elections it was still far from the statute book. Once again, as in so many other spheres, French vested interests had frustrated Giscard's plans.

And now a new era begins. The Socialists, once in power, gave high priority to a master-plan which they had long pondered while in opposition and for which they have apparent Communist support. It is a much more far-reaching reform than Giscard's, and is central to their philosophy of creating a more equal and participatory society, and – as Mauroy put it in June 1981 – of 'giving the State back to its citizens'. The Socialists see devolution as a reform that could win the broad consensus of the nation, being neither of Right or Left: unlike many of their economic measures, it carries with it no particular Socialist or Marxist dogma. The man charged with carrying the plan through is the veteran Gaston Defferre, now seventy-one, who has been given the significant title of Minister of the Interior and of Decentralization (that, in a traditional French context, sounds like a contradiction in terms!). Defferre and Mauroy have both long been mayors of big cities and presidents of their regional assemblies, so they know well at first hand what it is to be irked by State tutelage. Both are ardent regionalists. Mitterrand, though less of a regionalist, has backed them. He said, on taking office: 'France needed a strong central power to come into being. Now it needs strong local powers to avoid falling apart. An anachronistic State structure carries the seeds of revolt. People today . . . need to find their identity. In the end, they'll blow up the walls that restrict them rather than suffocate.' So, in his view, *lack* of devolution is the danger that could cause the State to fly apart.

Acting with deliberate haste (which the Right denounced as 'scandalous'), the Government presented its outline law to the National Assembly in July 1981. This will be followed by more detailed laws, so that the reforms will come into force gradually during 1982–3. If all goes as planned, this is what the new system will be. In 1982 the prefects will probably be renamed 'commissioners of the Republic' and will cease to have any *a priori* control of local authorities' budgets or decisions. These commissioners will keep their blue-and-gold uniforms and some ceremonial duties and will still live in their grand prefectures, to be renamed 'departmental halls': but their main task will be limited to coordinating the State services within their area. And a number of matters hitherto controlled by the State will be transferred to the local authorities (communes, departments, regions) which will 'administer themselves freely' with a minimum of State supervision. The exact share-out of responsibilities is still being decided. But probably the regions will look after economic planning and cultural affairs, while the departments will deal with some infrastructure and welfare matters, and towns will be in charge of their own planning, environment, housing and services. The State will still keep control of large national projects such as nuclear stations.

Certainly the department's *conseil général* will be strengthened, and all local bodies will have more power to raise their own finances. The money they get from the State will come in a lump sum, to be spent as they please (in this, as in some other matters, the Socialists' blueprint is quite close to that prepared by Giscard in 1979, though they are reluctant to admit it!). As for the commissioners, they will still have the right to intervene *a posteriori* if they suspect a council of some irregularity, and the matter will then go to public enquiry. Their political role, as watch-dogs of the Ministry of the Interior, will end. But they will still be in charge of the police, and of law and order, and will retain certain reserve powers in the event of a national emergency.

These reforms may not prove easy to apply in practice. They are bound to provoke much opposition, just as Giscard's did. They may be popular with the public as a whole, but there are powerful vested interests which will stand to suffer from such a shake-up in the *status quo*. The mandarins in the Paris Ministries, the big State technical agencies such as the Ponts et Chaussées and their technocrats in the field, not least the prefectoral corps itself, all these and others will rightly see the new devolution as a threat to their established fiefdoms. They have not been able to block the reforms' passage through parliament: but they might try to seek ways of obstructing their application. It would not be the first time in France that a reform has met this reaction from bureaucrats.

Even the mayors and other *notables*, though seemingly the ones who will benefit from the new system, are proving in some cases wary of it. For they will no longer be able to use the prefect as scapegoat. For example, the new law proposes transferring from prefect to mayor the task of granting building permits. Hitherto if a mayor wanted some permit refused, he could often discreetly persuade the prefect's staff to make the decision, and they took the blame. Now, it will be for him to do so – 'and it's highly invidious,' said one, 'to refuse an elector a permit'. In all kinds of matters, mayors realize that in face of their electors they will now lose their precious State alibi for their own failures or unpopular decisions. So some of them are none too happy about the extra powers offered them by a reform that threatens to upset their settled habits. This attitude may prove a handicap to the new system.

Some liberal observers, too, are not so sure that the cause of grass-roots democracy will really be served by the transfer of added power to the mayors and other *notables*. Will not the reform make the average mayor into even more of an autocrat than he is already? The Socialists are aware of this problem, and they have their answers. First, they are planning to restrict at last the *cumul des mandats*: probably no one will be able to hold more than two elected posts, and mayors may not be allowed to be members of the regional assemblies. This will limit empire-building, and it may throw up a new breed of younger *notables*. Also, the eclipse of the prefects should probably strike a blow at the 'enclosed circuit' of decision-making denounced by Crozier (see above, p. 192) and force mayors to share with their citizens a more open style of administration. They will lose their privileged links with Paris, or so it is hoped.

The success of the new system will depend above all on money – on whether the Government is ready to allow local authorities the extra financing commensurate with their new responsibilities. The Giscard project was tight-fisted on this score, and this was the main complaint against it. Today, Mauroy is suggesting that local councils' direct share of all French tax revenue should go up from its present level of 18 per cent to 25 or even 30 per cent. Local bodies would presumably have the right to levy new taxes, while continuing to receive State allocations. But a change of this kind would need the approval of the Ministry of Finance, that mighty State within a State, always parsimonious, always reluctant to give up any jot of control of the nation's purse-strings. Tough political bargaining probably lies ahead.

A key aspect of the new reform is that the region will at last come into its own. The first direct elections to the regional assemblies will probably be held in March 1983. These bodies, it is hoped, will now cease to be mere ciphers: they will have larger budgets than before and a degree of autonomy in matters such as economic planning and culture. The assembly's president will take over executive power from the prefect. This is still a long way from a federal system; but it is welcomed as a step forward by regionalists, who have long argued that the department alone is too small and artificial a unit to provide the framework for a devolutionary structure. The department, after all, is no more than the result of arbitrary strokes on the map by the Revolution's technocrats in the 1790s, while the regions – or most of them – have their roots far deeper in the ancient soil of France. Proof: when a man from Avignon says '*Je suis du Vaucluse*' he is stating a legal fact, but when he says '*Je suis provençal*' he is making an emotive statement, and the same could be said of an Auvergnat speaking of the Haute-Loire, or a Norman speaking of the Eure, and so on. Moreover, in face of the German *Länder*, or the new Italian regions, or Catalonia, or Scotland, or the Yugoslav republics, the French department is too tiny to make much sense in a regional structure (that, for the Jacobins, is precisely its charm!).

The Jacobins are still powerful and vocal in France, especially in the Gaullist party, and now they are shrieking with alarm that France will fly into fragments. 'There are several ways to kill a nation, and regionalization is one of them,' says Michel Debré, Jacobin-in-chief. But how real is this danger? One Jacobin argument has always been that give separatists an inch and they will take a mile. But, even in Brittany and Corsica, separatists represent only marginal factions; these regions would never secede. In July 1981 the Government promised Corsica a special statute, with more autonomy than the other regions, and as a result terrorism there has died right down. The general view today is that a degree of regionalism in France, far from stirring up dreams of secession, will effectively isolate or defuse separatism. However, there does exist another danger, inherent in any regional system. This is that some regions are bound to elect assemblies hostile to the Government of the day in Paris – either today under the Left, or tomorrow maybe under the Right. And, given the contentious French temperament, this could well lead to worse conflicts than in many countries. But the Socialists are prepared to face this risk, and to trust that the practice of autonomy will lead to the getting of wisdom. After all, the French do also have a talent for compromise. And the Communist Party's leading expert on regionalism, Felix Damette, told me in July 1981: 'We think it entirely healthy for French democracy that some regions should remain in Right-wing hands.' Moscow papers, please copy.

A more valid argument against the new system is that to have three separate tiers of local government could prove cumbersome and expensive, with the danger of wasteful rivalry and overlap between the regional assembly and the departmental *conseils généraux*. This is a real risk, and can be reduced only if the responsibilities of the different tiers are very clearly defined. Critics of the reform are also producing the old argument that greater financial autonomy may increase the disparities between richer and poorer regions and make the role of DATAR harder; or that rival assemblies might hold up inter-regional schemes by failing to cooperate, as has been prefigured in the case of the Nantes–Rennes highway. Aware of these risks, the Government is determined that the national Plan should keep a strong coordinating role, with powers to redistribute resources fairly between the regions. Finally, some regionalists would have liked to see the Socialists take the opportunity of regrouping the regions on a different pattern. It is often argued that the present twenty-two regions are too numerous and too small, in a European context, and that the boundaries of some were stupidly drawn in 1964. Whereas some regions, such as Alsace or Burgundy, correspond to real historical and cultural entities, a few others are hybrids: Midi-Pyrénées for example has been carved out of parts of Languedoc and other old provinces, while Normandy is two separate little regions. An intelligent regrouping could strengthen the sense of regional identity. But the Government feels that such changes would lead to endless squabbling, and that on this score it is better to leave well alone.

In any event, the Socialists are showing plenty of boldness in their overall reform of local government. The Left, after waiting twenty-three years to win power nationally, is straightway preparing to give some of it up, and that seems quite a brave step. So will the Socialists really have the courage of their convictions? Will they carry out fairly the measures they are planning, or will they in practice be tempted to retain rather more State control than the new law envisages? ('All parties,' said one Gaullist, cynically, 'are regionalist in opposition, and Jacobin when in power.') This remains to be seen. The reform is a big leap into the unknown, and it may well not work perfectly. Its critics, especially on the Right, point to a number of hazards. First, may not the new system increase the conservative *esprit de clocher* of many a commune? As we have seen in Languedoc, much of the post-war initiative for progress has come from the often-derided State technocrats. And Jacobins have long argued that more local autonomy might lead to anything but more progress. Despite a certain rejuvenation *à la grenobloise* among the ranks of *notables*, the mayor of many a small town is still an elderly lawyer or doctor, with political nous but few economic ideas, and many communes still refuse to share in a wider project unless they feel certain to benefit. It is not certain that mayors will use their new power either to invest imaginatively or to develop local democracy – or so it could be argued.

Linked with this is the argument that local life may now become over-politicized. Where a party gains control of a council, it will now be able to do much as it likes, and its politically motivated decisions will no longer be balanced by the arbitration of the prefect. Many local taxpayers might come to regret this. Notably, the reform could help the Communists to tighten their grip over their fiefs. Since 1977, the PCF controls the *mairie* in 72 of France's 221 larger towns, including St-Etienne, Reims and Le Havre. It is true that these councils have been careful to preserve correct relations with the State, and in its demagogic way their record of civic administration is sound, even socially go-ahead. But whereas the Socialists are openly democratic, the PCF has been trying to build up a state-within-the-State, wherever it can. Increased autonomy for their communes could encourage virtual Communist enclaves, and this might carry risks for the nation, alike under a Socialist-led Government or under a future Right-wing one. Or such is the fear sometimes voiced.

The counter-argument to these various anxieties is one that for years has lain at the heart of the French dilemma and is a constant theme of this book. So long as the State-as-nanny remains in charge, this simply shrivels local initiative or drives it into opposition. The vicious circle has to be broken; and with all its risks some devolution has to be tried – even if it leads to a transition period of conflict and muddle – if France is to evolve towards a properly participatory democracy. This is roughly the thinking behind the Socialists' project. Michel Crozier, no Socialist but an ardent devolutionist, sees plenty of hope in the new reform, provided, he says, that the region is not paralysed by the department. If the *cumul des mandats* is properly restricted, then, he thinks, regional elections could throw up a new and dynamic generation of younger local leaders – a whole fleet of new Dubedouts – who hitherto have been excluded from the 'system' or have excluded themselves though distaste for the 'hermetic complicity between *notables* and the State'. This, argues Crozier, would break the sterile hold of the older potentates whether of Left or Right, and bring much needed new blood and new democratic openness into a France that he still sees as *'la société bloquée'*. He recognizes the risk of 'politicizing the provinces', but thinks the risk has to be taken. Some people think his views too utopian; but they have plenty of support. And the French people, in their mass, are ready to go along with the Socialists' devolutionary adventure: an opinion poll in July 1981 showed 73 per cent in favour of it.

In January 1982 the National Assembly gave its approval to the law conferring a special status upon Corsica. The island will now have its own directly elected parliament, with greater powers than those due to be given to the mainland regional assemblies: it will be able to table laws about Corsica's relationship with Paris, and the Government will have to seek this parliament's approval before initiating projects on the island. This is likely to satisfy all but the tiniest handful of Corsican nationalists. At the same time, the principal decentralization Bill for the mainland regions worked its way through the two Houses of Parliament in Paris between October 1981 and January 1982. It suffered some amendments, but survived more or less intact and finally became law. It was to begin entering into force in the spring of 1982, and will be followed up by other, more detailed laws defining the exact new share-out of responsibilities between the State and the various levels of local government. The first regional elections will be in March 1983. So Toulouse will then become more of a true regional capital than it has ever been since the thirteenth century. An elected regional assembly will be holding sway there in the Capitole, as the ancient city glows red in the sunset. For the victims of Simon de Montfort, after seven centuries, that will be some revenge.

Chapter 4

BACK TO NATURE:
THE FARMING REVOLUTION
COMES FULL CIRCLE

In a speech in 1977, President Giscard d'Estaing described agriculture as France's *'pétrole vert'* (green oil), a supreme national asset. The parallel was perhaps a little fanciful, but there is no doubting the potential of a country that has much the largest cultivable area, and the biggest output, of any EEC member. The only trouble is that food does not gush out of the earth like oil: it involves the daily toil of millions. And French farming today, despite its spectacular post-war progress, still faces the dilemma of how to reconcile the nation's economic requirements with the human demands of the family farm.

In the decades after the war, French farming went through what even cautious scholars described as a 'revolution'. In no other aspect of French life has change been so dramatic, or the conflict between old and new so sharp. After 1945, farm mechanization soon began to make economic nonsense of France's vast peasant community and the great exodus began, to new jobs in the towns. Nearly six million people have now moved off the land, and agriculture's share of France's active population has dropped from 35 per cent in 1939 to 9 per cent in 1981. The movement continues, but is now slowing down, and the figure is expected to level off at 5 or 6 per cent in about 1990.

Even more important has been the change in attitudes. Farmers used to be a social class apart, afraid of progress. But after the war a strange thing happened: a new generation of modern-minded young farmers, with a totally different outlook from their parents, began to arise not from the rich estates of the northern plains but from the poorer smallholdings of the south, west and centre. They promoted a new creed, entirely novel in this milieu, a creed of technical advance, producer groups and marketing cooperatives. And it is thanks largely to their efforts that productivity per head has grown six-fold since the war. Whereas in industry this kind of impetus came above all from State technocrats, on the land much of it was due to the farmers themselves.

Not all French farming has been affected; the old-style peasant, sozzled, semi-illiterate, living little better than his animals, does still exist in some areas. But he is a dying species. Traditional peasant society, once such a strong and picturesque feature of France, is passing away, and the new-style farmer is more like a small businessman; often he has a handsome car and a modernized home, and his children are scarcely different from town children. Thus the old class of *les paysans*[1] is steadily becoming integrated into society.

However, the uneasy 1970s have brought farmers up against a new range of complex economic problems. The E E C's Common Agricultural Policy has helped French farming as a whole, but its price-support system unfairly benefits the richer more than the poor farms, and its free market has exposed the less efficient to new competition. In an age of European surpluses, increased productivity is no longer always the best answer. And rocketing land prices have led many young farmers into heavy debts. All this is happening at a time when the French, after their rapid post-war urbanization, are now looking again to their rural roots. Cities and factories no longer offer a steady supply of new jobs; many young people dream of a simple country life. So the pendulum has begun to swing back. To increase the farming population again would not be economically realistic; but the whole question is now posed of how to make the best use of France's vast rural heritage. Farm leaders insist on retaining the smallish family farm as the basic unit, and are against too much extension of large-scale industrial farming. But they are ready to help the countryside and villages to blossom with new activities, based on tourism, leisure, crafts, modern-style cottage industries. So, as France moves towards the so-called post-industrial era, town and country will move closer together.

THE YOUNG FARMERS' REVOLT:
PEASANTS BECOME BUSINESSMEN

France thirty years ago had 'two agricultures', as was often said: one, the big arable and cattle farms of the Paris basin and the north-east plains, as rich and up to date as almost any in Europe; two, the far smaller holdings of most of the rest of the country. Even in fertile areas, subsistence farming was often of a level unthinkable in, say, Holland or England, while stark poverty was common in the Massif Central and other upland areas. The pattern has since shifted considerably, as many small farmers – helped by the rural exodus – have managed to enlarge their acreage and win a new prosperity. But farming is still immensely diverse, by region and by produce, and this makes it hard to generalize. A market gardener of the fertile north Breton plain faces very different problems from a

---

1 The word *'paysan'* denotes the whole social class of people who earn their living from the land, as farmers or labourers. It is a less archaic and pejorative term than 'peasant'. 'Countryman' might be a fairer translation.

struggling sheep-breeder in the central highlands, while the prosperous sugar-beet growers of Picardy are in a world apart from the agitated producers of cheap Languedoc wine.

Briefly, the story of the post-war 'revolution' is as follows. Before the war, all but the few large estates lay sunk in lethargy and a kind of fatalism. *Paysantisme* was a way of life, a doctrine that nothing could or should disturb 'the eternal order of the fields'. The laws of equal inheritance, dating from Napoleon and earlier, were a major cause of the absurdly small size of farms. And then the notorious 1892 reforms of Jules Méline, Minister of Agriculture, pushed up high tariff walls round France to protect the farmers – but this simply caused stagnation. Curiously, it was in that weird interregnum, the Vichy period, that the stalemate began to be broken. Vichy, with its 'corporatist' views, set up local farmers' syndicates, and although these were swept away at the Liberation, they may have helped to sow the seeds of the practical peasant collaboration and unity that were lacking in France hitherto and have developed, in a different way, since the war.

In 1946, the First Plan set about trying to coax the small farms out of their archaism. It made farm machinery its top priority outside industry, and with striking results: the number of tractors rose from 35,000 to 230,000 by 1954, and productivity rose rapidly too. The much needed rural exodus was also gathering pace. But dangers soon arose: France's industrial growth and its attendant inflation hit the farmer badly, for food prices did not keep pace. The 1950s were marked by continual rural protests and disturbances, led by Right-wing demagogues of the old school. The weak Fourth Republic governments gave them the kind of aid they wanted, but the small farmers found to their surprise that this helped mainly the big, well-organized farms. Discontent went on, reaching a peak of violence in 1957, with the burning of crops, and tractors barring the main roads. All this, and the wild-mouthed demagogues, gave French townsfolk as well as foreigners a picture of the farmer as a comic and ignorant anarchist, always complaining, his head firmly in the sand. Yet his plight was genuine, if partly his own fault. It was time for a new outlook, and new leadership.

And it came, in the late '50s, from an unexpected source. Like so many of the progressive influences in early post-war France, it was rooted in militant Leftish Catholicism: nearly all the new young radical leaders came from the Jeunesse Agricole Chrétienne. This youth movement had been founded by the priesthood in 1929 to combat rural atheism. But during the war the JAC took on a more secular tone. Among the very young sons of small farmers, mostly still in their teens, there occurred one of those strange psychological changes that seem to have marked the destiny of France at that time. The danger and responsibility of their wartime activities, often in the Resistance, gave them an early maturity and seriousness. Many began to ponder on how they could avoid a life of certain hardship and poverty, short of leaving the soil which was their home. Some, deported to Germany, saw there the examples of small farms that *could* be run on modern lines. But how could it be done in France?

By 1945 the initiative in the JAC was out of the hands of the priests, and the accent was on learning economics, self-help and sharing of labour – new and amazing in the peasant world. One aim was to give members something of the general culture they had missed through leaving school so young, often at twelve. The JAC organized amateur drama, singing contests and sports. More important, local groups set about studying modern accountancy and new farming techniques. But the Jacists soon found that to apply these new ideas in practice was not so easy. In this patriarchal society, on most farms the way was blocked by fathers who would have nothing of the new methods. Many Jacists saw little hope but to wait maybe ten or twenty years for fathers to retire. But the JAC was well organized nationally, and it became clear that the next step must be to carry the campaign into national farming politics.

This was especially the view of Michel Debatisse, who took over the JAC leadership in 1951. Debatisse, today thirty years later still the most influential farmer in France, was typical of the JAC of those days. He was born in 1929 near Thiers in Auvergne, where his parents had a thirty-five acre hill farm. The few dairy cows, poultry and vegetables barely gave them a living, though at least this was one of the 25 per cent of farms that then had running water. Michel left school at thirteen. He was a squat, badly dressed youth, but his rough-cut face had – and has – a fierce strength, and he quickly developed wider ambitions. He began to write articles for the JAC paper in Paris, and by 1950 was editing it. Soon he and his friends reached the age when people normally leave the JAC, yet their campaign had hardly begun; where could they carry it next? The main union, the Fédération Nationale des Syndicats des Exploitants Agricoles (FNSEA), was in the hands of the older and richer farmers of the north: but it had a moribund junior section, the Centre National des Jeunes Agriculteurs (CNJA), and in 1957 the Debatisse faction managed to take over its key posts, and began to use it as a militant pressure-group. As one step towards breaking down the peasants' isolation, meetings were held jointly with industrial workers' unions – most unusual in France. Debatisse toured the country, stirring up support, while other CNJA leaders were dispatched to glean new ideas or techniques from Kansas, Denmark or the Ukraine.

The CNJA also began to form links with the Plan, and with the young technocrats who came to power with de Gaulle in 1958. They found a similarity of language and interest, and Debatisse was elected the youngest-ever member of the Economic and Social Council. The breakthrough was beginning. The CNJA proposed to a sympathetic Government that its policy be switched to investment and structural reform: they wanted drastic measures to persuade older farmers to retire, to take land from unproductive hands and give it to new tenant farmers working in groups. Michel Debré, the reform-minded Prime Minister, had an ear for these ideas: he drew up a *loi d'orientation* partly inspired by them, and in 1960 managed to push it through Parliament. For the first time a French Government was turning its back on the heritage of Méline.

But this law was no more than an outline of principle, and the Government proved slow in applying the decrees to put it into force. In the very special farming region of western Brittany, the Young Farmers' rising irritation suddenly reached flashpoint in May 1961, when a seasonal glut knocked the bottom out of the potato and vegetable markets. At Pont-l'Abbé, farmers set fire to ballot-boxes in local elections and filled the streets with tons of potatoes sprayed with petrol. Then at Morlaix, 4,000 young farmers invaded the streets with their tractors at dawn on June 8th, and seized the sub-prefecture in protest. This was the epoch of putsches in Algiers, and the newspapers excitedly drew the parallel. But these farmers were not terrorists: they were relatively prosperous vegetable growers, in the rich coastal plain between Morlaix and Roscoff. When their leaders, Alexis Gourvennec and Marcel Léon, were arrested by the police, sympathy riots spread throughout the west, down to the Pyrenees. It was the largest and most effective farmers' demonstration in post-war France, and it marked a decisive turning-point.

For the first time farmers were demonstrating *for* progress, not against it. For the first time the riots were led and organized by the new leaders, not the old demagogues. '*L'Agriculture de Papa est morte'* read the triumphant banners. Gourvennec (see p. 138), an ex-Jacist, was only twenty-four; an arrogant, eloquent young man who today is a near-millionaire and a legend in France. He and his fellow Bretons were protesting at the marketing system, and not for the first time: the previous year, in a less violent version of their famous 'artichoke wars', they had sent lorry-loads of artichokes straight to Paris to sell on the streets, after the Breton middlemen had refused them a fair price. The growers were furicus that the Government had continually urged them to produce more, yet had done nothing to reform the archaic marketing system, so that prices always collapsed in a good season. Gourvennec and his local farmers were well organized and far from poor; their problems were different from those of a region like Debatisse's. But both shared the same dynamism and reforming zeal, whether the reforms most needed were of markets or of land.

Paris responded quickly after the Morlaix affair. Gourvennec had friends in the Ministry, and it is alleged that some of them had secretly advised him to stage the riot in order to get things moving! In August de Gaulle appointed an ex-prefect, Edgard Pisani, as Minister of Agriculture, and in the next five years he proved the most forceful and far-sighted figure to have filled that usually unwanted post in this century. He at once drew up a *loi complémentaire* of decrees to activate the 1960 law, and got them approved. This Pisani Law, as it is called, set up a new pension fund to encourage old farmers to retire; an agency for buying and redistributing land; stricter rules against absentee landlords; and measures to encourage farmers to form groups both for marketing and for shared production. The law has ever since remained the basis of Government policy for the modernizing of agriculture and in the 1960s it was steadily applied, with varying success, as we shall see.

The young farmers consolidated their political victory in Paris; soon they had strongly infiltrated the FNSEA itself, of which Debatisse was president from 1971 to 1979. Inevitably, time and power have changed these ardent radicals into cautious middle-aged pragmatists, and it could be argued that today they are too corporatist in their defence of the family farm against large-scale industrial farming. But at least their 'revolution' has brought the major part of French peasant farming into line with modern realities.

The past twenty years have seen tremendous modernization and structural change. Some of it has been spontaneous: the steady exodus to the towns has enabled those who remain to buy up or rent the land vacated, and the average size of farms has thus risen since 1955 from thirty-five to seventy acres. This and other factors – the consumer boom of the 1960s, EEC subsidies, improved marketing and production techniques – have helped most farmers to increase steadily their standard of living, though it has levelled off in the past few difficult years. Progress has also varied by region – much faster in Brittany than in many parts of the centre and south-west – and disparities are still great between the big rich farms, the new middle-sized ones and the really poor ones. Many problems are still to be solved, but nearly everywhere a new spirit has emerged. Sometimes the outward contrasts are striking. In a Breton farm kitchen, a big colour TV set stands beside the ancient open fireplace;

near Avignon, one son in a farmer's family hoes potatoes while his brother goes to work at the near-by nuclear factory; in the chalky uplands of the Aveyron, an old man vacantly minds the cows while his daughter does the accounts by micro-processor. Home comforts have steadily improved; and for good or ill the peasant's life is becoming 'urbanized', as it has long been in Britain.

On the north-west Brittany plain, in 1979 I called on Jean-Pierre Le Verge, aged thirty-three, a local CNJA leader, in his comfortable modern farmhouse. 'We grew up in utter poverty,' he said, pouring me *un scotch*. 'My father had only twenty-seven acres, eleven cows, some cauliflowers – and six children. I remember as a teenager not being able to afford a five-franc ticket for the local fête. In 1960 we still had no running water, no heating save a wood stove, no TV or even radio, no car, just an old horse-cart. I left school at fourteen. But ten years ago my brothers and I persuaded my father to retire and to let us modernize the farm. We worked at it night and day, we felt like real revolutionaries. Now we have a big modern piggery with three hundred and twenty sows for breeding, and we've enlarged the farm to sixty acres. My net income is about 140,000 francs a year, but as we've invested 400,000 francs in improvements there's a lot of loan to pay back. We have a new Peugeot 504, a colour TV, hi-fi, more gadgets than we need. The first holiday of my life was in 1975, but now my wife and I go to the Côte d'Azur. Yes, we see ourselves as having totally integrated into society, we live like town people – but we work much longer hours, maybe sixty-five a week.'

An exceptional success story, but by no means unique. In 1979 I also visited a maize farmer south of Clermont-Ferrand, Jean-Marie Crochet, whom I had not seen for fifteen years. I found that he and his brother had doubled the size of their farm, to three hundred acres. The rough barn where I had formerly spent the night was now a suite of new bedrooms, and the house had been modernized lavishly, with tiled floors and sun-terrace. M. Crochet and his wife have two cars (one an Opel 2100), and he travels as far afield as Brazil for his cooperative. One daughter is studying science at Clermont university. 'When I was a boy,' he said, 'our social life was with the other peasants in the village. But the village is now half derelict, and my own children make their friends in the near-by towns. Our life has become far more mobile, our horizons far wider. But some of the old local warmth is lost.' The Crochet brothers run their sizeable farm on their own, with no paid staff save local students hired for harvesting. It is the same story in many country areas. Farm labourers have become far fewer; those that remain earn a decent basic wage, and many have had technical training. And the peasant farmers on their small mechanized farms are now integrated into the local business community – 'Apart from a few sad anachronistic cases, they're often the smartest people around,' said a girl in one small town. A farmer near Rennes told me: 'This used to be considered a decadent profession, but now we have prestige. I no longer envy town-dwellers.'

Until a few years ago it was usually the girls who left the farms first, for the towns. More than the actual discomfort, they hated the isolation, the drudgery and sense of inferiority, and they rarely wanted to marry a farmer. A town girl would never think of doing so. But today the trend is two-way: some girls are still leaving the land, yet at the same time *over a third* of young farmers now marry the daughters of non-farmers! In this ecological-minded age, many town girls now have a yen for country life, and they see that no longer is it so bleak nor does it make them social outcasts. Also, young *paysans* and non-*paysans* today come into contact far more frequently, at dances and so on. 'We have left our ghetto,' says Michel Debatisse.

In the towns, class divisions remain fairly rigid in France (see p. 379); but in villages and rural areas, class structures have altered far more. In the very old days, the village was ruled by an élite of local *notables* – the *châtelain*, the *curé*, the schoolteacher, the lawyer – who acted as intermediaries between the peasants and the rest of society. But since the war these *notables* have been drifting away or losing influence: *châtelains* today often have jobs in Paris, while the calibre of local teachers has declined and so has the role of the *curé*. And the peasants, more forceful and educated than before, have taken affairs into their own hands to produce their own élites. Many more of them than in the old days are mayors or even *conseillers généraux*. In an area near Nantes with a feudal tradition, a small farmer with strong Left-wing views, Bernard Lambert, spoke to me with bitterness of the pre-war days when his father was a share-cropper (a system now virtually abolished): 'He would always lift his cap to the *châtelain* and call him "*Monsieur notre maître*". Once, when he won a radio in a raffle, the landlord confiscated it because we were in debt. But our relations with the gentry have changed a lot. Some of them are quite human nowadays – you should meet my neighbour, the Comte de Cossé-Brissac!' To prove his point, this militant Marxist lifted the phone: '*Ecoute, mon vieux, je t'envoie un journaliste anglais – d'accord?*' Amazed by the *tutoiement*, I took my leave of the Lamberts in their drab cottage, and drove under cover of truce through the social barricades to the baronial hall where the young gentleman-farmer count gave me *un scotch* on a Louis XV sofa: '*Oui, c'est un brave type, Bernard – un peu excité, un peu farfelu, mais il est bien.*' This may be an extreme example: in some parts of France there is still suspicion between rich farmers and small ones. But steadily the barriers are coming down, both between the rural classes and between *paysan* and *citadin*. As the farmers become urbanized, so also the townsfolk penetrate into the country, buying up old houses for weekend or summer visits, or for retirement (see p. 394).

Modernization of farming would have been far more difficult, had not the Debatisse generation succeeded in making some inroads into the French farmer's deep-rooted individualism. There has been a big psychological change. Farmers have been learning to group together, especially for joint marketing. The new generation has also put a stress on education: farmers' sons now stay on at school to take technical diplomas, or they go on to get a degree in agronomy before returning to run the family farm. Hundreds of new agricultural colleges and evening institutes have been opened by the Government, under pressure from the younger farmers who often also form their own technical study groups. A young farmer's wife in the Aveyron told me of her patient efforts to get a group of ill-educated wives to study modern techniques of farm accountancy, a task traditionally left to women on small farms.

In putting the accent on technical expertise and the sharing of effort and equipment, the post-war generation realized that it might be an essential way of saving the family farm. Mechanization has spread steadily, with tractors now numbering 1,420,000. It is true that at first the tractors were often badly used, especially by older farmers who would buy one proudly as a status symbol without having large enough fields or the right know-how. A man accustomed to an instinctive *rapport* with oxen or horses was often unable to run a machine. But the younger farmers have generally managed more intelligently. In Normandy, a CNJA leader with a three-hundred-acre cattle and wheat farm told me: 'We formed a group of twenty-two farmers, and bought a silage machine, harvesting equipment and several tractors in common. We share all costs. In this area, it's quite an accepted way of working now, except among the older farmers.'

This kind of group farming is new since the war, and it cuts across the peasant's traditional individualistic suspicion of his neighbour. Or rather, in a sense it goes back to a pre-nineteenth-century tradition of mutual aid, later eroded by the Napoleonic and Mélinian reforms. First in the 1950s many groups were formed privately, then the Pisani decrees granted financial aid and a legal structure to groups jointly owning equipment or sharing it out. There are now more than 5,000 of these. Besides helping to pay for sophisticated machinery, the system brings other advantages. Now that salaried labourers are scarce, it can provide a pooling of labour for many jobs, and the chance of a rota for milking and minding livestock which enables the farmer to take a weekend off or even a holiday. The groups also facilitate specialization of produce, useful in the EEC context. Above all, they enable units to be larger and more viable without removing their family farm basis or the individual's responsibility.

In the Aveyron, a heartland of the JAC movement, a bold experiment has taken place that carries the sharing a stage further. Here at Espalion, in the lovely valley of the Lot, a farmer called Belières grouped a score of small farms into a *banque du travail*: each man-hour is set a price, according to the type of work, and if a farmer spends a morning helping a neighbour, or lends equipment, he is credited in the labour bank's accounts, usually kept by one of the wives. At the end of the season, gains and losses are paid off, like a game of poker. It is a way of securing group work without anyone feeling cheated, and its success at Espalion has led to the creation of other work banks in France, especially in regions of small farms. Some chambers of agriculture have set up teams of auxiliary farm workers, who can be hired by a farmer to replace him in case of illness or absence.

Group farming does not always work smoothly. Some groups have failed and split up, either because the older members failed to cooperate; or because the women kicked against the need for joint accounting; or because the principle of shared decisions was too much for the peasant spirit. The same problem can occur in the case of a different kind of State-backed group, the GAEC (Groupement Agricole d'Exploitation en Commun), which facilitates the enlargement of farms by enabling the land itself to be jointly owned. There are some 6,000 GAECs, and generally they succeed when the owners belong to the same family, as in the Le Verge and Crochet cases quoted above. But GAECs between neighbours are much more rare, and often they fail. 'I tried to form one,' said a Breton farmer, 'but we found we didn't really trust each other, especially the wives.' Individualism dies hard.

Peasant conservatism has also been a hindrance to solving the problem of soil parcellization. Fly over many parts of France and you will see a crazy quilt of thin strips; quite a modest farmer may have twenty or thirty tiny fields, not next to each other but scattered over miles. This is partly the result of the equal inheritance laws, as farms were split up between sons and then the parcels changed hands. And it has not made it easier to operate, say, a combine-harvester.

The official remedy is the controversial policy of *remembrement* (regrouping): by subsidizing up to 80 per cent of the legal and field costs, the Government tries to entice farmers to make rational swaps, and since 1945 more than 27 million acres have been *remembrés*. The results have been variable, far better in the go-ahead north than in the sluggish south. In many small-farm districts, the older peasants have resisted *remembrement*, through fear of getting a worse deal, or through emotional attachment to their own bits of soil. A farmer may finally accept the idea in theory; but when the work starts, he will be struck with sentimental horror, and refuse to give up the field where his father taught him to plough or the apple-tree his grandmother planted. In the Aveyron, the commune of Privezac provided a *cause célèbre*. In 1963 it had voted 90 per cent for *remembrement*, so surveyors arrived and drew up a plan. Then there were protests. The village split into two camps, but *across* the traditional rural lines of Reds against Whites, teachers against priests. In the pro-*remembrement* camp, the young Catholic Jacists were led by the Socialist mayor, an ex-teacher; against them were the older farmers, led by the deputy mayor, a Catholic ex-officer. When bulldozers arrived to tear down hedges and start the regrouping, the old guard charged them on tractors and tore up the surveyors' markers. The police then made some arrests, and the work did finally go ahead.

Regrouping is not imposed on a commune unless over half the farmers are in favour. But in the Aveyron today only twenty communes have yet been *remembrées* out of three hundred and seven, and in near-by Lozère the figure is three out of a hundred and eighty: here I met a goat-breeder with eighty-five acres split into fifty far-flung parcels. Recent cut-backs in State funds, as much as lack of local cooperation, have led to a slow-down in the whole process, in this as in other regions. However, *remembrement* is less useful in these hilly livestock-breeding areas than in the crop-growing districts further north where much more of it has been done. Here the land is now much easier to work with machinery, and many farmers say that without the regrouping they could never have achieved a decent living.

In some cases the conflicts have been aggravated by the officials, who reshuffle the land without tact. The job needs psychologists as much as surveyors. More serious than this, *remembrement* has been blamed for doing ecological damage. Frequently hedges, trees and embankments have been torn down in order to get the exchange right to the exact square metre; this has destroyed shelter for animals and in some areas, notably coastal Brittany, it has led to soil erosion where fields face prevailing winds. After an outcry from many farmers and ecologists, the surveyors are now being more careful, and some replanting has begun. In theory at least, there need be no incompatibility between a reasonable *remembrement* and protection of the environment.

The balance in the farming world has shifted considerably in the past twenty years. Though he still grumbles, the average small farmer is now at least passably well off. But on the margin of his society there still exists a kind of 'Fourth World' of real poverty. Essentially this is a social problem. Only a score of miles from Gourvennec's smiling coastal plains, you can find grim upland hamlets where the soil is stony and no one is left save a few old people. Parts of central France are in the same predicament. Here people eke out a living from useless polyculture, that inevitable curse of so much poor-soil farming: a patch of vines for the family's own vinegary wine, a cow or two and some mangy chickens, cabbages struggling to grow on a chalky hillside. Meat is a once-a-week luxury; children, if there are any, are kept from school to help with the chores, and sleep in haylofts. The working day is sixteen hours, and a family's income may be less than 10,000 francs a year. Yet the farmer is afraid of getting loans for home improvements, for this kind of peasant fears debts. This milieu will either depopulate totally, or else it can evolve only through a change of generations. In a poorer part of Brittany in 1964 I met an old farmer who, rather than spend money on mending the broken gates and gaps in his hedges, made his wife and children stand guard in turns all day, to stop the cattle from straying. Fifteen years later, he had died, and his son had done the mending.

Most farmers today have wider horizons than this, and are at grips with modern economic problems of European dimension. Their worries are market prices, overheads and the cost of land. Paradoxically, while the rural exodus has freed many millions of acres, the young farmer finds it ever harder to obtain good land at reasonable cost, and this complex issue is at the heart of farm politics today in the 1980s.

Rural emigration has had a varying effect. In some areas already thinly populated the exodus has now reached or even gone beyond its safe limits, and there are dangers of a virtual desert. But in other regions, for example Brittany and Poitou-Charante, there are still too many people on the farms for all to gain a decent living, and the drift continues. In these areas the total number of farms has dropped by at least half since the war, and farmers expect it to fall by a further 20 to 40 per cent over the next two decades and then stabilize at what they see as the right size for the family farm. This would give a national figure of about 6 per cent employed in farming, against 9 per cent today (in Britain it is 2.7). Of course, it is still mainly the young who leave. On over a third of French farms there is no successor in the family, and 57 per cent of *chefs d'exploitation* are aged fifty or more, while only 8.2 per cent are under thirty-five. This high age level worries many farm leaders. But in fact there is no longer any shortage of young applicants for farms. All they lack, very often, is the cash.

Attitudes are changing among the young. The new ecological ethos of the 1970s, the improvements in the farmer's life-style, and above all the rise in urban unemployment, these and other factors have made many sons of farmers less keen to leave the land, and have even prompted some emigrants to return. In Brittany in the 1960s I met a couple *all ten* of whose children had left the farm, but this would be unthinkable today. On average, where two sons out of three might once have left, now it is one out of three. Above all, it is no longer so regularly the brightest who depart, leaving the dullards behind. Some clever sons too prefer nowadays to forego the city rat-race. But the irony is that, just when this change of heart is occurring, rocketing land prices are making it hard for the young to find the land they need for a viable unit. It is the law of supply and demand. The spread of industry and housing estates, the building of motorways, the huge growth since the early 1960s in the number of secondary residences and homes for retirement, all this has pushed up land prices in many areas. And the inevitable cycle of specula-tion has set in, as many older farmers prefer to cling on to their land as an investment. In the Aveyron I was told, 'Young people used to leave by choice: now more often it's when they have no other choice.'

In a nation with so strong a rural tradition, *la terre* can still rouse powerful emotions, and the laws and customs of land tenure are com-plex. Before the war feudalism was still common, and while some farmers clung proudly to their own ancestral acres, others were *métayers* (share-croppers), paying their landlords a tithe. A reform in 1946 replaced the *métayage* system with a tenancy statute which gave greater security from eviction and replaced the tithe with an annual rent. This is in force today; but despite its obvious benefits to the farmer, it has created its own problems. Firstly, although a system of tribunals keeps the rents at modest levels, this in turn gives the landlord little incentive to keep the farm buildings in repair or make improvements. And it can bind the tenant in a new way, as a recently arrived young couple in Auvergne told me: 'This place was a ruin when we came, and the landlord wouldn't spend a franc. We sank all our capital of 75,000 francs into basic modernization – but it's the landlord's property, so we can hardly afford to leave.'

A second problem is that, as in the case of some urban housing rent acts which aim to protect the tenant (e.g. in Britain), the tenancy statute has proved counter-productive: because tenants can appeal against high rents and cannot easily be evicted, many owners prefer not to lease out their land. Rather they will try to sell it, or else hang on to it as an investment, but without farming it properly themselves. Good rented land is thus scarce on the market. About half of all French agricultural land is rented rather than owned by the farmer, but if the young farmers had their way the figure would be higher. When they want to start a farm, or extend an existing one to viable size, often they find they have no choice but to buy the land, with costly mortgages. The Crédit Agricole, the world's largest farm bank, has done a great job in funding the modernization of French farming, but the loans that it offers so readily to farmers have drawn them into piling up huge debts. To rent would be cheaper. Of course to buy the land does increase the farmer's permanent estate, but at the price of his living standards. 'When I'm dead then I'll be rich,' some of them say. This would be less of a problem if good land were not so expensive. It is still cheaper on average in France than in most other EEC countries; but prices have risen much faster than inflation, more than doubling in real money terms in 1960 to 1977. By 1979, land was costing some 9,000 to 14,000 francs an acre in average cultivable areas, and a young farmer might need about a million francs capital to buy an adequate-sized sixty-acre property.

Back in 1961, the Pisani Law had made two innovations with the aim of helping younger, modern-minded farmers to obtain land. Both have played a useful but limited role. One was a fund – which has since become EEC policy – to encourage old farmers to retire. This has been used by some 450,000 families, but its pensions are modest, varying from 1,500 to 8,000 francs a year. More important, Pisani set up Sociétés d'Aménagement Foncier et d'Etablissement Rural (SAFERs): regional agencies with powers to buy up land as it comes on the market, to make improvements and then resell it to the most deserving, probably a young farmer wanting to use modern techniques. The SAFERs also have some rights of pre-emption, at fixed prices, and so in some cases have been able to curb speculation. They were greeted at first as the heaviest blow ever struck in France at the sacred rights of property, but in practice the scheme has worked slowly and patchily, more effective in some regions than others. It has been impeded by the usual French legal delays, maybe up to five years per transaction, and it suffers from limited funds. Since 1962 the SAFERs have handled the buying and selling of some three million acres and have helped about eighty thousand farmers to acquire land, but 90 per cent of these cases have been extensions of existing farms. Today the new generation of under-thirty-fives is indignant that nearly all the land coming on to the market – via SAFERs or not – goes on enlargements rather than helping the young to find their first farm. In pre-war days, sons would each tamely receive their own portion on a father's retirement, under the equal inheritance laws; these still exist, but modern conditions have rendered them obsolete in practice, and a second son wanting to stay on the land will need his own farm. But here is the dilemma. With overheads rising so fast, small farmers find that the minimum viable size of a farm is steadily rising too: if fifty acres was valid ten years ago, today it might need to be seventy-five. So, how is enough land to be found *both* for extending farms to the necessary size *and* for helping the young to settle? In all but the poorest areas, this is today a major issue.

The Aveyron, with its small-to-medium-sized livestock and potato farms, is an area that typifies many of these problems. Here Raymond Lacombe, a former local JAC leader now just turned fifty, has fifty-five acres where he raises dairy cows and pigs. On my visit in 1979, I found that materially his life had improved a good deal since I first met him in 1964: the old muddy track to his farm is now a metalled road, he and his wife each run a Peugeot, they have modernized their farmhouse, and whereas Lacombe left school at fourteen, his eldest girl is at university. But, like other local farmers, Lacombe complains that since about 1974 it has been a struggle to keep income abreast of inflation. 'Costs rise so fast that a farm this size is no longer viable the way it used to be. And it's hard to find new land I could afford, even though the number of farmers is still falling' – the population of the commune, 717 in 1911, had dropped to 426 by 1962 and is now 346. When I asked whether he regretted not having himself left the land as a young man, he laughed, 'No, I love this place. If I had my time again, I'd still stay, but with fewer illusions.' Were either of his schoolboy sons ready to join him on the farm and take over one day? – 'It's not at all sure. One boy wants to leave; the other wants to train as an agronomic engineer, and he might stay. But he prefers machines to animals, that's his trouble.'

Lacombe, like many farmers, wants the Government to control land prices and index them to inflation. Another remedy demanded by the small farmers' leaders is that it should take action against 'unserious' part-time farmers and others who hoard their land unproductively. One farmer in five has another, full-time job; usually these are people living near towns who now work in an office or factory but use their old smallholding for their family needs, with maybe a patch of vines, a few cows and vegetables. Other *cumulards* are townee speculators who buy up land and then do little with it. Full-time farmers are indignant at these 'dog-in-the-manger amateurs', and have been demanding laws to discourage them by giving 'real' farmers a special status and privileges. Some farmers want all French land to be zoned, with rules that cultivable areas must be professionally farmed. Their grievances are understandable, but their views and their approach too often smack of corporatism.

Under pressure from the farmers' unions, Giscard's Government in 1979–80 pushed through Parliament a new *loi cadre* for agriculture. It was aimed especially at helping young farmers, by new measures to make the renting of land easier, to restrict excessive land price rises, to strengthen the S A F E Rs and retirement schemes, and to discourage part-time farming and the unproductive use of land. In 1981 the Socialist Government then took this law a stage further. One of its first steps on coming to power was to increase grants for young farmers: it also announced a plan for setting up local land offices to check speculation. The farmers welcomed these various measures, which could well be of value to them, in an era when agricultural issues have been rendered so complex by Common Market regulations and the opening of French frontiers to wider competition.

PRODUCTIVITY GOES CRAZY:
BUTTER MOUNTAINS
AND BULGARIAN *FOIE GRAS*

The E E C's controversial Common Agricultural Policy, introduced in the 1960s, has altered the entire focus of French farming – 'If we have a grievance today, we go lobbying in Brussels as much as Paris,' say the farmers. Originally they had set high hopes on the C A P; they saw that France was starting with the lowest wholesale prices of the Community and the largest production, thus it seemed inevitable that the gradual alignment of prices and dropping of internal trade barriers would benefit French farmers more than others. Had not France agreed to the E E C partly because she felt that her gains in agriculture would compensate for Germany's probable gains in industry?

On balance, the results have certainly been positive for French farmers. The C A P's high level of fixed prices in most sectors has helped them to earn a better living, and this goes some way to explain the relative calm of the farming scene (Midi vinegrowers excepted) since 1967. From 1963 to 1977, the E E C's share of French agricultural exports rose from 38 to 66 per cent, within a protected market where prices are at nearly twice average world levels. However, farmers are much less starry-eyed about the C A P than fifteen years ago. One of its disappointments, as they see it, is that France's partners have greatly increased their own production since the mid-'60s, and thus have not provided nearly so large a ready market as was hoped, for France's own vast output. Also many smaller French farmers are finding it hard to keep up with their more modern and efficient competitors in Holland and Denmark, notably in the pigmeat and dairy sectors where the E E C is self-sufficient. Increased productivity is thus not always the panacea that it seemed in the early post-war years. Above all, small farmers are all too aware that the C A P unfairly helps the rich more than them.

The economic basis of the CAP is highly complex. Briefly summarized, it consists of a Community levy on agricultural imports into member countries from outside the EEC, redistributed to farmers in the form of price supports and export subsidies (the supports cover, essentially, sugar, beef and pigmeat, dairy products, most cereals, table wines, some fruit and vegetables). This protectionist system aims to encourage EEC self-sufficiency, and helps mostly those countries that are net food exporters, that is, it helps mainly the French (and Irish and Dutch) farmers, even if not quite as hoped. But it has proved expensive for national budgets, since the price supports and other subsidies have been allowed far to exceed the size of the levy, thus leading to heavy annual deficits. This is because the EEC, yielding to pressure from various farmers' lobbies, originally fixed the prices for most products around the level of the highest then obtaining and not the average. For instance, if wheat was cheapest in France and dearest in Germany, it was the German rather than the French price that was chosen for the CAP. This has simply encouraged farmers to overproduce in many sectors, knowing that their surpluses will be bought up anyway, and then sometimes dumped on world markets. The 'butter mountains' of the '70s, with the cheap sale of surplus butter to Russia, caused a scandal; and by 1979 the CAP was eating up about 75 per cent of the EEC's £8,750 million budget. Political horse-trading, too, has falsified the price policies. For instance, the EEC now has a wheat surplus thanks largely to the massive output of the big north French farms; yet the wheat farms of Bavaria and some other parts of Germany remain mostly small and ill-organized, and their owners have pressured Bonn into insisting on high wheat prices. And Paris, for reasons of high policy, has yielded to Bonn's wishes in return for favours elsewhere. Inevitably this has discouraged farmers from shifting more of their production from wheat to meat, where the EEC is still a net importer.

As the CAP's subsidies are paid on quantity of produce, inevitably the system benefits most the big rich farmers who need it least. The large farms of northern France with their high productivity have done handsomely, while less efficient smallholders gain relatively little. It is the same in other EEC countries, and clearly the CAP's unified price system is unfairly suited to a Europe where farming is so diversified. Only about a tenth of the CAP's funds are devoted to what is called 'guidance', that is, to grants for improving structures and reconverting uneconomic farms; nearly all the rest goes on supports.

The cost of these price supports falls heavily on the EEC taxpayer, and the British in particular are aggrieved, understandably. But British opinion is wrong to suppose, as it usually does, that 'it's all the fault of the French', or that the CAP is simply a conspiracy to bolster up inefficient French peasants. The truth is more complex. Poor peasants benefit less than rich farmers – *including* British ones! And German farmers' lobbies have been as much to blame as French ones for the insistence on high prices. In the late '70s the Germans also benefited more than the French from the CAP's 'compensatory' mechanism, set up to prevent the undercutting of the unified market by those countries (including France) whose currency was declining against the Deutschmark.

It is important to stress that the French farming world, or most of it, is not blind to the injustices of the CAP; it is aware of the need to reduce the surpluses, and is even ready to make a few sacrifices. By 1981 it was prepared to consider proposals (strongly supported by the new Socialist Government) for putting a ceiling on the amount of subsidy that any one farmer could receive for a given produce. But the farmers' unions are totally opposed to any dismantling of the basic CAP system of a free, unified and protected market. Michel Debatisse told me, 'The CAP itself is not negotiable; but, within it, all is negotiable.' Above all, the farmers do not want the price supports to be replaced – as has been suggested – by a system of subsidies for the individual on the criterion of his needs. This is a matter of pride, even with the poorer farmers who suffer from the present system. 'We do not want to become *des assistés*, dependent on State and EEC charity,' several of them told me. And the farmers' unions are still powerful and united enough to be able to defend what they see as their vital interests.

Livestock-breeders in particular find that the CAP and its open market have brought them new problems by adding to competition. In pig production, the EEC roughly balances its needs; but within the EEC, France is a net importer – mainly from Holland and Germany – to the level of about 20 per cent of her consumption. This is because only a few pig-breeders, the big ones, can easily compete on equal terms with the Dutch, Danes and Germans, whose piggeries are on average more modern and cost effective. 'We should have invested far more in new equipment years ago,' said one farmer in Brittany, where more than half of French pigs are bred; 'so now, if we want to increase sales, we have to export outside the Community. But that's not easy as world prices are lower. The best answer could be to develop pigmeat food-processing here: most of our pork leaves Brittany unprocessed, in carcass.' Breton breeders find themselves handicapped by having to pay higher prices for feedstuff than their EEC rivals, and a major reason is that the port of Rotterdam has secured a near-monopoly of the crucial Thai tapioca trade – such is the kind of bizarre detail around which the EEC farming world today revolves!

Sheep-breeders too have been menaced by the new competition, notably by Britain's imports into the EEC of cheap New Zealand lamb. French breeders, generally smaller and less efficient than their rivals, even managed in 1979–80 to pressure the Government into maintaining restrictions on the entry of these imports into France, in defiance of EEC rules. Finally the French climbed down: but this 'lamb war', while it lasted, caused quite a stir. France's cattle-breeders, on the other hand, have been better able to hold their own in the EEC, and some of the big cattle and dairy farms are among the best in Europe. But here the problem is that the smallish farmer is more readily inclined to devote himself to milk and dairy production, where he is protected by generous EEC price guarantees, than to launch into the more uncertain business of rearing cattle for slaughter, where markets fluctuate. Thus the EEC's dairy surpluses pile up, while it still has to import some beef and veal. France, land of the *biftek* and Europe's heaviest meat consumer after Belgium, shares the shortage. The Government for years has been trying to persuade farmers to step up beef production, at the expense both of dairy goods and of wheat, but not with great success. Some farmers are put off by the corruption and muddle still common in the meat markets; others, when it comes to a choice between meat and wheat, feel a distaste for the servitude and hazards of cattle-rearing. A young farmer in Normandy, with a sizeable cattle *and* wheat farm, told me: 'Whatever Paris may want, *I'm* stepping up the accent here on wheat – it pays far better. The meat market tends to collapse, and guaranteed prices are low. Wheat needs less investment and is given better loans; if you rear a calf, you have to wait three years to get your money back, and there's often the risk of disease. But the corn harvests are nearly always good. Above all, cattle demand constant attention with never a weekend off, and hired cowmen are hard to find. Farmers won't accept this any more, they want leisure like people in town.'

In order to compete in the new Europe, France has been obliged to modernize her internal marketing system, and this has been one of the main changes of the past twenty years. The former chaos of French marketing was legendary. Produce might change hands several times on its way from farmer to housewife, or travel hundreds of miles from its country farm to the Paris markets, only to be sent back for sale near its point of origin. The isolated peasant was powerless in the hands of unscrupulous middlemen, who saw to it that the consumer paid up to five or six times what the producer had been given.

However, since the 1960s the Government has sponsored the building of modern marketing centres which have helped to reduce the abuses. And the farmer himself has become much more businesslike. He has begun to take marketing into his own hands, and by forming sales groups is now able to combat the *Diktat* of the middlemen. Hundreds of State-assisted farmers' marketing groups, Sociétés d'Intérêt Collectif Agricole, have had good results in preventing prices from tumbling in a crisis, in sectors where CAP pricing is flexible. In the Aveyron, Raymond Lacombe told me: 'We started a meat SICA here in 1962. It saves us a lot of time and trouble. We don't have to go to the market individually, a SICA lorry collects our livestock and sells it for us, sometimes as far afield as Italy. And the dealers don't cheat us so much any more, as the SICA is beginning to know the markets as well as they do. But it took some years to persuade the older farmers to take part in the SICA.' Slowly, French cattle farmers have been learning to defend themselves against what one called 'the mafia of corrupt little dealers and butchers'. They have been helped by the setting up of a national chain of slaughterhouses which offer the farmer a fair scale of prices.

SICAs have been specially effective in fruit and vegetable sectors, which are highly vulnerable to seasonal price fluctuations and are not covered by CAP price guarantees. In north Finistère, soon after the 1961 'artichoke war', Alexis Gourvennec (see pp. 138 and 210) set up a SICA that today is the most famous and powerful in France. With 4,000 members, it has a near monopoly in an area producing 70 per cent of French artichokes and cauliflowers, and has succeeded in imposing fair prices on the middlemen. If prices threaten to drop too low, then the SICA withholds produce, and has done this several times. So never again, since 1961, does the Breton grower earn a handful of centimes for a kilo of artichokes sold in Paris shops at twenty times the price. In their ultra-modern auction centre at the SICA headquarters in St-Pol-de-Léon, linked by telex to the rest of Europe, the farmers can regulate their prices, using a stop-the-clock Dutch auction system. In periods of glut, they divert part of their produce for their own canning and deep-freezing plant. This is an exceptional success story, but then Gourvennec is an unusual leader and the men of his area are unusually dynamic and disciplined. Down in the Midi, on the fertile plains around Nîmes and Avignon, the problems of seasonal gluts of apples, cherries and peaches have not yet been solved so fully. Output has soared, and in high season the wholesale price of a kilo of peaches may drop to a few centimes. The farmers have sometimes resorted to riots, or to the more elegant practice of offering free peaches and pamphlets to passing tourists.

The French centripetal tradition has meant that, at least until recently, far too great a share of national produce has transited via Paris.

So the Government in the 1960s built a dozen or so provincial *marché-gares*, big modern markets beside railways on the outskirts of cities. They are linked by telex and are able to help direct produce to where it is needed and reduce price fluctuations. They have certainly led to quicker and more open transactions, and have reduced dependence on Paris. Then in 1969 the gigantic Paris central market of Les Halles was transferred almost *in toto* to a big new *marché-gare* in the suburbs, at Rungis, near Orly airport. For a century Les Halles had physically handled much of the food for the Paris region; it was a huge blood-sucking spiders' nest of middlemen where vested privilege and muddle went hand in hand. It was also colourful, and many a nostalgic tear was shed at its transfer. But a victory has been won for the decongestion of central Paris (see p. 274) – and for better marketing; the middlemen have not found it so easy to reconstruct their mafia in their sleek new premises. However, the vast improvement of marketing in France since the '60s has been due less to the *marché-gares* than to the rapid growth of the farmers' cooperatives, doing their deals directly by telex with the supermarket chains and wholesalers.

Farmers' cooperatives began in France eighty years ago. In the past decade they have expanded tenfold, notably on the food-processing and marketing side, galvanized by the challenge of what they tend to see as their natural enemy: American capitalism! France has for long had a weak and fragmented processing industry, and in the 1960s a few American multinationals sought to exploit this vacuum and establish useful footholds within the EEC. Libby's set up a tomato canning plant near Nîmes, and put local growers under contract; Ralston-Purina, feedstuff producer, opened a large chicken slaughterhouse near Rennes, and invited contracts from local poultry breeders. Many French farm leaders, especially the Leftist ones, reacted angrily to what they saw as 'neo-colonialism', likely to reduce the farmer to a 'peon', deprived of responsibility, dependent on the policy whim of his foreign-based sponsor. This issue of 'vertical integration', as it is called, created angry headlines. The Government then stepped in, and tacitly promised the farmers that it would limit this kind of American investment, provided they made efforts to develop their own processing. The gambit worked. Libby's *has* reduced its production, while in the same area a farmers' cooperative, Conserveries Gard, has opened its own peach- and pear-canning factory, today one of the largest and best of its kind in Europe – much bigger, in fact, than the local Libby's plant. In many other parts of France too, the farmers have been able to steal this kind of march on the capitalists: as in Britain, they now make sure that by means of cooperatives they retain their share of the processing industry. The Government has helped, by vetoing some foreign ventures in this sensitive sector, and 'vertical integration' is no longer an issue. In fact, in some cases cooperatives are now perfectly ready to collaborate with industrialists, provided it is on an equal basis. Since 1977, a new sweetcorn canning factory near Pau has been operated happily in fifty-fifty partnership by Green Giant and a local cooperative. The farmers supply the corn, and Green Giant the canning know-how.

The processing industry has been late to develop, in this nation of fastidious eaters who prefer the taste of fresh food. French values of farm-fresh quality, so closely related to the genius of French country cooking, are at the opposite end of the scale from industrial values of packaged efficiency. Fine, but it can lead to odd anomalies. Ironically, a nation with a peach glut nearly every summer still imports tinned peaches for its out-of-season needs, after destroying tons of rotting, surplus peaches in August. However, the picture is now changing. The food-processing industry is expanding fast, it employs 565,000 people, and some big firms are now in the multinational league, such as BSN-Gervais Danone (baby-foods, dairy products, cakes, drinks). And many farm cooperatives are joining the movement. One makes and sells a leading brand of yoghourt, Yoplait, while in 1977 the huge Landerneau cooperative in Brittany opened a factory that freezes 25,000 tons a year of locally grown vegetables. Much of this is for export: but even the French housewife is now thawing towards frozen foods (see p. 411).

Many farmers now recognize that, in the present EEC context, one of the surest ways for them to be able to increase their sales is to develop the local processing of their goods: Breton vegetables and pigmeat are prime examples. They recognize, too, that a long-term necessity for French agriculture is to increase exports of all sorts – both of fresh food and processed – world-wide, for there is only limited scope for new outlets within the EEC. If France is to exploit to the full her precious *pétrole vert*, it must come through exports – but to where? and of what?

Curiously, until about 1968 this mighty farming nation had a net trade deficit in food and drinks; traditionally, exports were limited mainly to quality wines and spirits, a few cheeses, and suchlike. But the trade balance cannot live on Moët and Martell alone, nor on quaint bicycling onion-sellers. The EEC and the productivity boom have changed the old pattern, and today France is a heavy net exporter of cereals, sugar and dairy products as well as wines. In these sectors she has a global surplus of 35 per cent, balanced by a deficit in all else, notably processed goods, meat, fruit and vegetables. This leaves her today with an average overall trade surplus of 8 per cent in food and drinks, and the Government's aim is to push this to 20 per cent. But to find new outlets is not easy, and it is wishful thinking to suppose, as a Breton farmer told me, that 'the EEC butter and milk-powder mountains would be levelled overnight, if we had a proper export policy'. Efforts are indeed being made to induce the Japanese, Arabs and others to buy more French butter, while the FNSEA has been exhorting farmers to 'adapt produce to the needs of foreign markets'. But this is a long-term process. One faster remedy is probably for France to try to reduce the deficit in those sectors where she imports but could produce more: for example, by stepping up canning, and, believe it or not, the making of *foie gras*. The nation that invented this delicacy today imports a third of its needs, mostly from Bulgaria and Israel where costs are much lower. Some of it is flown in fresh to the Bordeaux region, heartland of good *foie gras*, where that delicious 'local speciality' on your plate may well have come straight from some *kibbutz* or Communist goose collective. Newcastle's coal imports were never as succulent. At least, efforts are now being made to induce French farmers and their families to spend more time on the tedious – and repugnant? – daily chore of force-feeding the poor geese.

Agriculture is so uncertain and vulnerable a profession, so much at the mercy of unpredictable changes in the weather and in world markets, that farmers are still a little scared of the new challenges of a more open market, in Europe and the world. Their new prosperity seems to them precarious. Hence their panic reactions, in the late 1970s, to the proposed entry of Spain into the EEC. Fruit and vegetable growers fear that Spain, with its lower costs and warmer spring weather, will be able to undercut them and steal their European markets. And those most afraid of all are the producers of France's cheap table wines.

BACK TO LOWER LANGUEDOC:
THE GRAPES OF WRATH

'Midi vinegrowers riot again: anger over surpluses and foreign imports' – that has been a common headline since the war. Few other French farmers are so stubborn and unruly as the vast tribe of producers of cheaper wines, and only under protest are they now adapting at last to modern conditions. But first let it be clear that France has two wine industries – rich and poor – with entirely separate problems. One, the minority industry of more expensive wines, led by Burgundy, Bordeaux, Champagne. This élitist little world is highly efficient, and certainly it does not riot. Its sales both in France and abroad have been rising happily, and it rarely causes the Government any headaches. True, the Bordeaux fraud scandals of 1974 provoked a stir and gave a temporary setback to clarets, but this was soon overcome. Fine wines still find ready buyers, even in these hard times, although some of the secondary vintages – Beaujolais and Sancerre for example – are in danger of being overpriced.

The second and much larger group are the producers of table wines, which rarely get exported but make up over two-thirds of total French output. These growers number hundreds of thousands, about half of them in Languedoc (see p. 144); many are smallholders, producing inferior plonk on a few ill-organized acres. Repeatedly since the war they have panicked, at the threat of falling prices in a bumper year. More recently, since the coming of the CAP, they have had to face also the flood of cheap Italian imports, and now the threat of even cheaper Spanish ones. Their lobby is politically powerful, and sometimes violent, and governments have generally pandered to it.

Paris has made various kinds of attempts to solve, or at least palliate, the chronic overproduction of unsaleable wine. Under the Fourth Republic it spent millions of francs a year on buying up and destroying surpluses. Then in 1953, as we have seen earlier, it tried a more constructive policy: it offered subsidies for uprooting poor vines and replacing them with other crops. This met with only a moderate response: in the next few years no more than 5 per cent of all vineyards were uprooted. The policy was discontinued in the early 1960s, and instead the Government began to encourage the replacing of poor vines with 'noble' ones, more likely to find a market. This is still the plan today. For, with rising prosperity, the French public has increasingly demanded better table wines, and so have foreign buyers.

This vulnerable sector of agriculture is more closely supervised by the Government than any other; wines and vines alike are scrupulously inspected and graded. The highest grade of wine is *appellation d'origine contrôlée* (production in an average year, about 11 million hectolitres), then come *vins délimités de qualité supérieure* (2.5 million hl), then a new category, *vins de pays* (6 million hl), then the *vins ordinaires* (37 million hl). Many farmers have responded to the call for quality, so that without any lowering of standards many thousands of acres of vines are upgraded each year to the intermediary VDQS and *vin de pays* categories – and very drinkable they are too – or to AOC. Production varies so much per year that statistics can be misleading: however, from 1970 to 1978 AOC wines' share of total output rose from 15.4 to 21.6 per cent.

Yet there is still over-production of cheaper wines in a bumper year. After the creation of the CAP, at first it was hoped that a solution could be for France to find massive new export outlets in the EEC. Indeed, in the 1960s French wine exports to her partners doubled for AOC and quintupled for the lower grades. This was due partly to the raising of

quotas, partly maybe to psychological factors. The Germans, Dutch and
Belgians have been drinking far more imported table wines (and, as the
French complain bitterly, the British too might be very ready to help
drink up their surpluses, were it not for the outrageously high UK excise
duties on wines!). But French farmers soon found, to their alarm, that
their Italian rivals benefited more than they did from the new open
market. Italian wines, more cheaply produced, less carefully graded and
often more robust than French ones, began to flood the French domestic
market too. Under EEC rules, the Government could not legally stop
these imports, nor prevent the big French firms such as Nicolas from
fortifying France's own wines with the stronger Italian ones: some
Mezzogiorno wines are 14° or 15°, against an average 10° in the Midi. By
1972, Italian imports were 8 million hectolitres a year.

This coincided with a series of big French harvests in the early 1970s.
The growers were left with vast unsold stocks, and although the
Government as usual bought these up for distillation, the growers considered the price guarantees too low to allow them a living. So in the
summer of 1975 came the inevitable explosion. As so often before in this
century, the Languedoc wine lobby used violence as its weapon: this
time, in order to get Paris to impose restrictions on Italian imports. They
disrupted the tourist trade by blacking out signposts; they blockaded the
port of Sète, entry point for much Italian wine. The Chirac Government,
scared of social unrest in a period of mounting economic crisis, yielded to
their demands by flouting EEC rules: it put import duties of 12 to 16 per
cent on Italian wines. Rome was furious, and so was Brussels. The EEC
even began the painful process of arraigning France before its Court of
Justice, but it failed to come up with any remedies for the real cause of the
crisis – European overproduction. The European wine lake was left to
expand beside the butter and fruit mountains.

Nor did the duties reduce imports enough to satisfy the growers.
Early in 1976 there was more and worse violence: riots and rallies
throughout the Midi, in which a farmer and a policeman were killed near
Narbonne; attacks on lorries and depots of importers of Italian wines,
with hundreds of thousands of hectolitres destroyed. In many areas,
angry farmers and riot police were in a state of near war. Finally in April a
scared Government made more concessions to the growers; among
other measures, it promised new loans and tax concessions to the poorer
ones; it coaxed an extra subsidy out of the EEC to help distil surpluses;
and it set up a new 'Office du Vin' to help regulate prices and improve
marketing. Once again, the Midi found that violence can pay.

The crisis seems to have had a relatively happy ending, for by the
close of 1976 the EEC Commission had managed to reconcile the rival

Paris and Rome governments into seeking joint solutions to their common problems of over-production. The Italian Government – hitherto very lax in nearly every aspect of its wine policy – agreed to join with France in banning all planting of new vineyards, and in granting new subsidies for uprooting of poor vines, helped by CAP funds. This has borne rapid results: the EEC's total vine acreage was reduced by 2 per cent in the next three years. France dropped her imports tax, and in 1977 a new CAP scheme came into force that, after a bumper harvest, gives subsidies to the farmer for the long-term storage of his wine, guarantees sales at minimum prices, and helps pay for distillation of surpluses.

The 1977 and 1978 harvests were modest (under 60 million hectolitres in France), so they did not put the scheme to the test. But 1979 broke all records: French vines 'pissed' (as farmers say) 83.5 million hectolitres. Yet the Midi growers, though anxious, were not up in arms that winter as might normally have been expected. They had already been placated, by their share of a total CAP subsidy of 220 million francs under the new scheme. This is only 2 per cent of the CAP's overall 'guidance' budget, yet it does seem a costly way of buying peace. The real problem of over-production has been expensively patched over, but not yet solved, and a better solution is essential, before Spain joins the EEC. One highly relevant factor is that the French public, under the influence maybe of anti-alcohol campaigns, continues to drink less and less cheap plonk (see p. 451). Consumption of AOC wines holds steady, but sales of *ordinaires* have been slipping by about 1 per cent a year for some time, and in 1979 they slumped by 5 per cent. This makes it all the more urgent to step up the campaign for removing the worst vines and improving the quality of the cheapest wines. But, down in the Languedoc, this runs up against various problems both economic and emotional, as we have seen.

Here most hillside vines can produce tolerable wines, but on the plains are wide acres where the terrain just does not permit improvement of quality. Efforts to persuade the growers to uproot have generally fallen foul of two factors. First, the average farmer is fanatically opposed to saying good-bye to the crop that his ancestors have grown lazily in this sunny land since Roman days. Next, the few pioneers who did agree to uproot and plant orchards soon found they had an equally unsaleable glut on their hands – not an encouragement. So the official stress is on replanting with better vines, and this has met with a good response: 30 per cent of vineyards have been thus upgraded since 1962. But the bizarre economics are such that farmers find this may not increase their income. Under French rules, the lower classified grades (VDQS and *vins de pays*) are limited to outputs of 20 to 30 hectolitres an acre, whereas for unclassified *vins courants* there are no limits and yields can in some years exceed 60 hectolitres an acre. Yet price differentials are rarely more than 25 per cent for the producer, who thus retains some incentive to go on producing a lot of poor, unmarketable plonk, knowing that the State and the EEC will partially bale him out. Either way, with a little goodish wine or a lot of baddish wine, a small farmer with thirty or so acres finds it hard to make a living.

Thus the poorer growers are in an economic trap not entirely of their making. Yet they could do far more to help themselves. Their marketing and promotion still tend to be archaic and inefficient: if these improved, they could push up the price of the better local v DQs (such as Corbières) which are undervalued by today's standards. A Corbières, selling in a shop for 7 francs, is often just as good as a Beaujolais or Bordeaux at three times the price. But the Languedoc, through its own fault, has not yet managed to pull free of its old image as producer of the working man's *gros rouge*. Its classified wines are much better than their reputation.

Slowly, however, the age-old crisis surrounding France's cheaper wines has been sorting itself out in the past decade, as vineyards improve, as farmers learn new methods and group into cooperatives. But now comes a new threat, from Spain. Emmanuel Maffre-Baugé, ringleader of the Languedoc growers, told me in his usual fruity style: 'Without special rules to protect us, Spain's entry into the EEC will wipe out a large part of the Midi vineyards. And the unrest here would then be more than all the police in France could control.' Growers know that Spain, in the EEC, would be even better placed than Italy to undercut their markets. Like Italy, it has lower labour and other costs than France, and far laxer quality controls too. One Midi economist said, 'Spain could wholesale its table wines here at 70 centimes a litre, against our 1.20 francs. Most Spanish *ordinaires*, too, are more robust and drinkable than ours, and yields are far below potential: with improved techniques, Spain could double its output and the EEC wine lake would be an ocean.' The growers at first opposed Spanish entry outright. Now, finding that cause lost, they are lobbying Paris to impose special conditions and restrictions, and this will certainly be done. But the Government could also use their plight as leverage to demand from them some *quid pro quo*. Many officials in Paris believe that limits should be imposed on *vin courant* yields per hectare throughout the EEC: this, they argue, is the only long-term answer to surpluses. But in the Midi it could provoke a fearful backlash from the Poujadist growers, many of whom see it as their inalienable right to produce as much as they wish and be paid for it. Politically, such a solution may not be possible at least until the older generation is dead.

DOES THE NATION
OWE ITS FARMERS A LIVING?

Agriculture – vinegrowers apart – is no longer the stormy political issue that it used to be in France, when it made and unmade governments under the Third and Fourth Republics. Steadily it has slipped towards the sidelines of national life, overtaken by other problems such as education and unemployment. The farmers stayed strangely silent during the student and worker troubles of 1968; and their reactions to the economic crises of the '70s, which on occasion have reduced their real income, have been much less violent than they might have been in the old days.

To an extent this calm is evidence of the progress made, almost imperceptibly, towards completing the basic transformation. Modernization has gone steadily ahead. And though many small farmers remain in poverty, their numbers are dwindling into an ever smaller and thus less influential minority; to put it callously, they have become a social rather than a political problem. Another reason for the calm is that, for the past fifteen years, the Government has pursued policies of appeasement, through domestic measures and strong support for the CAP. For example, in 1974 fuel and other costs rose dramatically, yet farmers were not able to counter inflation with immediate wage demands, as workers did, and their real incomes fell by 10 per cent: so the Government pumped in emergency subsidies and tax concessions totalling an extra 2,700 million francs, including an ingenious 'aide à la vache', a direct grant of 160 francs per cow to compensate for a sharp fall in meat and dairy prices. Maybe Debatisse's close friendship with Jacques Chirac, then Prime Minister, counted for something! More special aid followed the severe drought of 1976, and there was more again in 1981 and 1982. All in all since 1973, with annual ups and downs, farmers' incomes have been enabled to keep pace with inflation.

In the pre-1981 era, farm leaders believed that a policy of tacit but critical cooperation with the Government was the best way to ensure that it came regularly to their aid. The post-war Young Farmers' movement completed its seizure of union power in the 1960s, and Michel Debatisse remained president of the FNSEA until 1979. He was briefly a Euro-MP, then served for eighteen months as Giscard's Secretary of State for the food-processing industries, where he proved as much at ease in the Elysée as with his fellow-peasants of the Auvergne. Though today out of power, he remains an influential figure, and his moderate-progressive views are accepted FNSEA doctrine. He and his friends have won their battle to save the family farm as the basis of agriculture. But the passage of time has inevitably made them less radical, and anxious to conserve the gains won for the small farmer.

This is not to say that all small farmers support Debatisse's compromises. MODEF, a Communist-backed movement, has quite a wide following among the poorer and older ones, and it opposes the CAP. But it lacks the leadership to be effective, and can make few constructive proposals since its *de facto* support for the private farm runs counter to Communist philosophy. A Leftist movement with a more sincere and coherent policy, but fewer members, is that of the Paysans Travailleurs, who want guaranteed minimum earnings for small farmers and limits on the incomes of rich ones. They are strong in Brittany, where they have clashed with the mighty Alexis Gourvennec. Besides presiding over his vegetable SICA, he has moved into pig-breeding which he finds far more profitable, and he now has the largest pig-farm in France, yielding 30,000 piglets a year. The thousands of small, less efficient Breton pig-breeders took fright that his capitalist approach would put them out of business, and in 1976 a commando of Paysans Travailleurs raided and damaged his new piggery. He scoffed to me: 'These silly Leftists have their heads in the sand. Farming is no longer a peasant way of life, it's a capitalist industry that must follow the law of the strongest. There are still 5,000 too many farms in Finistère to be viable, and they must die.'

This is the central issue today. Does the community owe its farmers a living? Or is farming a competitive industry like any other, where non-viable units must go out of business? Can overall food-production be made fully efficient, without sacrificing the small producer? Gourvennec here is in a tiny minority: Debatisse and nearly all other farm leaders, while not going all the way with the Leftists, are adamant that the small farm must be kept alive for *social* reasons, and that capitalist expansion must therefore be contained. A touch of corporatism, maybe.

Any farmer bold enough to step out of this line may earn enemies. Down in the Aveyron, south of Rodez, the four young Grimal brothers have developed intensive lamb-rearing on a scale remarkable for France. In 1971 they took over their father's 100-acre farm and have increased its turnover 150-fold: they rear 30,000 lambs a year, the biggest output of any farm in the south-west, as well as producing ewes' milk for the cheeses made at near-by Roquefort. They live in four newly built chalets, Scandinavian style, spaced out on a wide neat lawn. In this elegant modern setting, unusual for rural Aveyron, I met the dynamo behind the venture, eldest brother Raymond, thirty-four, who talked in the manic, thrusting style of Jacques Chirac, his idol. 'I believe in self-help and capitalism,' he said, pouring me whisky from a magnum-sized bottle. 'I was the bright one of the family, so father sent me to take a law degree at

Clermont-Ferrand; he wanted me to "succeed", that is, go to Paris. But I love my homeland, I wanted to come back. This horrified my father, but finally he let us run the farm and expand it. We built modern covered sheepfolds, we bought two hundred acres near Albi for growing feed-stuff. We work furiously hard, but now we have all the foreign holidays and home luxuries you could wish – yet in 1970 this was a poor farm without even running water.'

Grimal's views and methods are very different from those of the Aveyron farming establishment, smallish farmers of the Debatisse generation such as Lacombe (see p. 220) who are far more union-minded. 'The meat market,' said Grimal, 'is still a bit of a mafia, where dealers cheat producers. But we Grimals are now big enough to stand up to them and negotiate good prices. So I prefer not to join Lacombe's SICA, which destroys the small producers' incentive by giving too much pro-tection. Frankly I despise Lacombe and his friends, and their corporat-ism. Yes, I admit that they, Debatisse, and others did do a lot after the war to drag farming up from their parents' level: but now they've become too conservative, they won't take risks, all they do is band together and lobby the Government, which weakly panders to them. Farming here is far too small-scale, it can't or won't get beyond a certain level of intensive efficiency. Local people are jealous of us, they complain we behave not like farmers but industrialists; yet we *are* local farmers, merely showing what can be done with initiative and modern methods.' Local breeders fear they could be put out of business by the double competition from Grimal *and* cheap British and New Zealand imports. 'But it's their own fault,' says Grimal: 'if they intensified as we have done, they could compete and find new markets.'

Grimal's arrogant *sauve-qui-peut* individualism offends the coopera-tive ethos defended by most farm leaders. Debatisse summarized his own philosophy to me: 'Of course there is much to learn from Grimal's dynamism, but if too many farmers behaved like him, it would be dangerous. His success in fact proves that the family farm is the most efficient unit, and others must be coaxed towards the same efficiency. But if the average farm is to be competitive, farmers must group together, for marketing and so on. A *sauve-qui-peut* approach would kill off all except a few strong ones, and we'd have a fearful human problem on our hands.' Debatisse went on to suggest that the post-1973 economic crisis has even increased the need for the family farm: 'Industry is no longer creating new jobs, mass urban unemployment is here to stay, a lot of thinking is going on about how best to share this out among the nation – and so it now seems less useful than ten years ago to bring the farm population right down to less than 6 per cent. At the same time, more young people are rejecting the urban rat-race, they want to stay on the land or return to it. So it becomes more important for the nation that the family farm should be strengthened and provide new opportunities, even if this costs money.' It is a view I heard often from country people, sometimes put more crudely: 'Better to subsidize people to stay on the land, than have to pay them to hang around in cities on the dole.'

There may be much sense in Debatisse's approach, but is it not also an alibi for the farmers' corporatism? They may have 'left the ghetto' in economic and psychological terms, they no longer feel inferior, they are more or less integrated into society; but professionally they are still a guild, like lawyers or architects who will not let outsiders take up practice. They often try to prevent non-farmers from taking up farming. And although the FNSEA claims to favour 'inter-professionalism', in practice farmers are wary of joint ventures that might allow industrialists, wholesalers or others any strong foothold in *their* world. All this was well understood by Pierre Mehaignerie, Minister of Agriculture in 1977–81, and probably the best man in that job since Pisani. A gentleman-farmer from eastern Brittany, tall and urbane, with an American wife, he had a detached and sceptical manner unusual in a politician, and in 1979 he gave me a balanced view: 'Yes, farmers *are* still a bit corporatist. For example, they tried to prevent the consumer protection bodies from being involved in the new farm law, which was narrow of them. Yet this corporatism used to be much worse: it's on the wane. Yes, of course I admire people like Grimal, and to have more farms like his would add to national efficiency – but it could also be socially dangerous if it sent others bankrupt. My policy is to help the medium-sized farm of sixty or eighty acres to be fully viable, as it can be in a good area.'

It is true that Mehaignerie made some demagogic concessions to the farmers: his *loi cadre*, enacted in 1890, was weighted heavily in favour of the family farm and against industrial farming (he knew the power of the FNSEA lobby). Yet he also showed courage in trying to urge farmers to collaborate more closely with other professions, to accept more open competition, to think more in terms of the consumer's needs.

The Socialists then came to power with farm policies in practice not so different from Mehaignerie's, though the style was new. The first Minister, Edith Cresson (see p. 349), was a lady with outspoken views and a forceful personality. Finding the FNSEA leaders too closely linked with the previous regime, she began to encourage their Left-wing rivals, the MODEF and the Paysans Travailleurs; and this annoyed Debatisse and his friends, who had now lost their privileged links with the Government. However, despite this switch in alliances, Cresson's actual programme for helping younger and smaller farmers was not far removed from the Debatisse ideology. She raised installation grants for young farmers and took other steps to make it easier for them to stay on the land. 'We must stop the rural exodus: better have more peasants than more unemployed,' she said, echoing the words of her political adversary, Debatisse.

Above all, the Socialist Government proposed to its EEC partners an overhaul of the CAP on the lines of a scheme drawn up by Edgard Pisani himself (now a Socialist). Under this scheme, ceilings would be placed on the subsidies that any one farmer could receive for a given produce. In Socialist eyes, this had two merits. First, it would give the bigger farmers less incentive to over-produce, thus, hopefully, reducing the famous surpluses. Secondly, by striking at the worst of the CAP's injustices, it would help to narrow the gap between rich and poor farmers. By the autumn of 1981 these ideas were being viewed sympathetically in many EEC capitals. No longer could the paranoid British claim that France was blocking all reform of the CAP.

France could learn much from Holland, where industry and agriculture collaborate easily, and where the average farm is relatively small yet highly modern and efficient. French farming has already come a long way in this direction since the war. As the last of the older generation retire, as more young farmers emerge with a new outlook, it may become easier in the next decade to reconcile the ideal of the family farm with the desire of France to maximize her 'green oil' potential. Production will become more intensive in the fertile regions – at least two-thirds of French farmland – where farmers will work mainly in cooperatives. But this leaves unsolved the problem of the poorer upland areas, where the soil is thin or stony and the slopes are steep. Should farmers still be encouraged – and subsidized – to eke out a living here? Or would it be more sensible to turn these areas over to forestry and tourism, to make them into nature reserves? The debate has become a topical one. It ties in with a changing French attitude to the countryside, as a new generation confusedly seeks a return to nature.

NEW FLOWERS IN THE RURAL DESERT: THE CRUSADE TO SAVE THE LOZÈRE

A few miles from the farms of Grimal and Lacombe, on a hilltop just outside Rodez, a small modern factory stands as the symbol of a new stirring in the heart of *la France profonde*, the desire of a new urban generation to return to its rural roots. Here the factory owner, Michel Poux, machine operator, has finally realized his childhood dream. He has quit the Paris he hated and come back to his homeland.

His parents were small farmers who found it hard to make a living in the Aveyron uplands near Rodez. In 1948 when he was seven they moved to Paris, where he had a technical education and got a good factory job. 'But from my early teens,' he told me, 'my *idée fixe* was to return to live here, *dans mon pays*. I loathed Paris with its traffic-jams and lack of greenery. I would come on holiday to my grandparents and only here amid these gentle hills did I feel alive.' But he soon found there was too little industry in the Rodez area to suit his skills; he tried in vain, repeatedly, to get a job. Finally, after marrying a local girl, he took his courage in his hands, built a house outside Rodez on a mortgage, and started a tiny workshop on the ground floor, producing machinery parts. He was encouraged by his former boss in Paris who promised sub-contracting. Against the odds, Poux succeeded: he now has a staff of sixteen, and has just built a proper factory. 'Transport is a problem, here in the Massif Central, but with our light precision products we don't need much heavy freight. Yes, at first I earned much less than in Paris – but after eight years back here, I still have this happy feeling of being all the time on holiday. And I'm not the only case. My brother and his wife had a prosperous small business in Paris, but they've moved back here at half the income. They couldn't stand any more commuting – *métro, boulot, dodo.*'

For the Aveyron, this is a revolution. Its population had been falling steadily from 415,000 in 1886 to 278,000 at the 1975 census, and is just beginning to level off. There are still more Aveyronnais in Paris than back home. It was normal for the bright ones to emigrate, men like Roger Cazes who arrived penniless and illiterate in Paris in the 1920s and later became the famous owner of the Left Bank literary brasserie, Chez Lipp. (Like Maugham's verger, where would he have got if only he'd been literate? – maybe running an obscure café in the Aveyron!) But Aveyronnais are not only enterprising, they also retain a loyalty to their *pays* that is remarkable even by French standards, and though they may have left, they do not forget. One Paris industrialist, obliged to transfer his factory, chose Rodez because that was where he came from. Generally it is hard to entice new factories to this remote area; but whenever new jobs do exist, Aveyronnais exiles will eagerly flock back for them. I met a number of people who had left Paris for lower-grade jobs at lesser wages. And many other parts of rural France can tell similar stories. The message is clear: in a country where regional attachments remain far stronger than in most parts of England, the post-war growth of big cities and big factories is now producing a reaction. A generation of *déracinés* ex-peasants begin to crave a return to their origins, not of course to the farms where land is so scarce, but at least to smaller factories or offices in small towns near the beloved *terroir*.

The numbers involved in this new French urban exodus are not yet more than a few tens of thousand. But they betoken a fundamental shift in French attitudes to rural areas. Paradoxically, there are two opposing currents of migration which involve a kind of race against time. On the one hand, some of the wilder parts of France are still depopulating, as there is not enough work for the young people. On the other hand, little groups of pioneers of various kinds are moving into these areas to try to create new forms of employment – can they do so, in time to prevent the areas becoming a desert?

The Aveyron is relatively successful. But there are many lonelier parts of the Massif Central, and of Savoy, the Jura and so on, where the population has fallen below the minimum needed for making a social life possible and maintaining services. If the farms depopulate, then the village schools and shops close, and the churches and post offices too. It is especially hard on poorer elderly people without cars. The young no longer leave so gladly; they would stay if they could, but often they have no option. The old remain, and they die off. Go into many areas untouched as yet by tourism or the vogue for *résidences secondaires*, and you find these sad, derelict villages.

The problem has now finally caught the attention both of public opinion and of the State. And luckily it happens to coincide – perhaps in the nick of time – with the new ecological yen for country life. In a few areas, notably the Cévennes, educated Parisians sickened by the city rat-race have arrived to try their hand at breeding goats or weaving rugs, living almost like gypsies (see pp. 248–57). But this movement, though picturesque and ideologically fascinating, is no more than marginal. An economically more practical bid to revive the dying areas has come from little groups of entrepreneurs who, with official encouragement, are trying to set up small factories or artisan industries, in villages and little towns. Some are returning natives like Michel Poux. Others are newcomers, often executives tired of the big-city grind who come to the Massif Central with a sense of mission, as to Africa. For example, a young engineer from Toulouse has hopefully opened an electronics workshop with a staff of twelve in a village of the upper Lot valley. The aim is to make a rural economy less dependent on farming, and enable more of those who wish to live in the countryside to do so.

The Giscard Government supported the trend, with a variety of motives besides the obvious social ones. It felt that, quite apart from farming, the remote rural areas had an economic potential for France that could be exploited through improvements to forestry, tourism, artisan work and so on. And there were electoral considerations too: after all, Giscard's roots were in the Massif Central, and so were Chirac's, who was Prime Minister when in 1975 the long-term development programme was launched for that vast and sprawling plateau. It was allotted special funds of about 700 million francs a year. The Socialists have since broadly continued the programme, which has four main aims:

– To promote small industries and traditional handicrafts, especially those using local materials. This has had some success.

– To develop forestry and ancillary wood industries, in a *massif* that contains 15 per cent of the EEC's forest area, but whose resources are ill-organized and under-used. Progress here is slow.

– To improve communications, through faster railway links and new trunk roads. This is being done. In the more urban parts of France, as in Britain, a village often fights to *prevent* a new motorway; but in these remoter areas, the communes vie with each other in lobbying Paris for the privilege of a new trunk road, hopefully a remedy for isolation and decline.

– To promote tourism, notably the deceptively simple back-to-nature holidays now in vogue with French sophisticates.

Here the Club Méditerranée has set a lead with its up-market holiday 'village' devoted to horse-riding, at Pompadour (Corrèze) where Madame de P. lived. The horses are especially *gentils* (see p. 427). Elsewhere, old farmsteads are being fitted out as holiday homes; or you can hire a horse and carriage and jog for days down forest paths, like gypsies – very chic. Many farmers find that it adds usefully to their income to convert an old cottage or stable (with the help of State grants) as a *gîte rural* for summer rental or paying-guests. City dwellers come eagerly to these country lodgings, and lasting friendships are sometimes formed with the farmers; it is one more aspect of the narrowing of the old gulf between *paysan* and *citadin*. There are also one or two places where the tourist can take courses in local handicrafts – basket-making, iron-forging, or distaff wool-spinning 'as granny did it' – and there is even a farm where for 400 francs you can spend twelve days learning how to milk cows, clean their sheds, make hay and practise local recipes. Ideal for the weary tycoon. And clever farmers: they actually get *paid* by their extra summer labour!

The tourist season is short in these uplands, and when the visitors are gone the farmers face long months of relative isolation. They have cars, but distances can be great along tortuous hill-roads, sometimes blocked by snow. And the decline of the old village life has forced farming families to look for other entertainments. The French rural world has not yet fully emerged from a bleak period of mutation between two cultures, the old folk culture, rapidly vanishing, and a new modern one that cannot easily penetrate to remote villages except in the form of television. In the old days there was great poverty, but also a warmth and tradition that helped make it bearable. In Breton moorland farmsteads young people drew round the fire on winter evenings to hear grannies reciting Celtic legends. In the Massif Central, and other parts, there were *veillées* in winter, where neighbours would gather in one farm to weave baskets or shred maize, and make it the excuse for a party. And the harvests! In Auvergne a farmer told me: 'When I was a boy, at harvest-time, the seasonal labourers would come up by hundreds from Clermont-Ferrand and every night in the village hall there'd be noisy parties and dances. Today the job's done by two men with a combine-harvester, and the labourers work in the new Clermont factories. There's hardly any social life in this little village now. In the evenings we watch colour TV, or visit friends who live miles away.'

Social and other activity is being regrouped in the country towns or the big villages of 1,500 or so inhabitants, and a family within range of one of these has a leisure life increasingly urban in style, as in Britain. Raymond Lacombe told me: 'We are only three miles from Baraqueville, with two thousand people, and it's become a very lively little place. It has tennis, judo, a dance club, a big disco that my teenagers adore – and festivals in summer, admittedly put on for the tourist trade. Our local village school is closing, and our younger boy gets picked up by school bus and taken to Baraqueville.' But Lacombe is relatively privileged. There are many upland farms and hamlets where the nearest lively *bourg* is up to thirty miles away; and the local primary school, if it is still open will have one single class spanning the whole age-range. The school bus system is greatly improved, and it is rare now for any child to have to walk several miles to school as in the old days. But rural education inevitably cannot compete in quality with that of the towns, and the farmer remains aware of this handicap.

The really isolated spots tend also to be those where the soil is poorest and the farmer finds it hardest to earn a living. Is there any future for agriculture in these areas? And even if there is, what about the problem of human isolation? Is not the solution an American-type one, where the families regroup in or near the small towns, and the farmer commutes by car to his fields? To study this problem at its most dramatic we must leave the Aveyron, which is relatively populated. We must go next door to the lonely and lovely Lozère, the most appealing, the most quirkish, the most extraordinary of any French department I know.

Lozère, the size of Norfolk, has only one set of traffic-lights. This broke down recently and for a year was not repaired, for the traffic hardly requires it. Sheep are far commoner here than people. But the air is pure, the light is clear in this high rolling wonderland, which is luxuriantly green in summer, scenically not unlike the Scottish Highlands and with some of the same problems. Geologically the northern half of Lozère belongs to the granite plateaux of Auvergne, where stony pasture-lands alternate with sweeping forests of pine and beech. South, across the upper Lot valley, the landscape is different but even more dramatic. Here the arid limestone plateaux of the *causses* are intersected by the famous Tarn gorges, while eastward lie the forested heights and narrow fertile valleys of the Cévennes. The Cévenol peasants in these valleys are still in majority Protestant, still aware of forming a kind of enclave, still bitter at the memory of the eighteenth-century wars against the *camisards*, even though their relations with Catholics today are perfectly friendly.

Partly as a result of its historic isolation before the days of train or car, Lozère today retains a stronger sense of identity and local patriotism than virtually any other French department – more than Aveyron. This is the kind of feeling normally reserved for a region, not an artificial department (see p. 202): who feels romantically patriotic about, say, the Eure-et-Loir? But Lozériens have their own mountain realm – 'It's a kind of land-locked non-violent Corsica,' commented one newcomer; 'not autonomist, that would be nonsense, but defiantly aware of its own separateness.' By an administrative absurdity, Lozère belongs today to the Languedoc-Roussillon 'region'; but Montpellier is a world away across the Cévennes, and Lozère in practice forms a kind of no-man's-land between Languedoc and Auvergne.

Did I say *no*-man? Well, there are a few of the species left, and intriguing they are too. The locals are sturdy mountain stock, as you would expect. Like Jeannine Braget, formidable Joan of Arc of the Lozère handicrafts revival (see p. 246), who bears on her broad middle-aged peasant shoulders the weight of 'my mission to save my land'. Or like two twin brothers, both Catholic priests, one fairly shabby, the other spectacularly so, who combine spiritual and archaeological jobs with the profitable side-line of running a little factory making hospital furniture. 'If there are *prêtres-ouvriers*,' said one twin, 'then why not *prêtres-patrons* too?' And the natives have been joined today by an equally colourful assortment of newcomers – lute-repairers, silk-screen printers, religious prophets, *fils-à-papa* fleeing the shame of their wealth. Lozère attracts the original in spirit.

It is the least populated of any French department, with a density of fourteen people per square kilometre, against thirty-two in Aveyron. The population, 140,000 in 1900, dropped to 74,800 in 1975 and 72,000 today, and is still gently falling. This drama, coupled with the area's unspoiled beauty and peasant character, has made Lozère something of a cult in France today. Sociologists, reporters, State technocrats, do-gooders of various kinds, have come to visit or to stay. Lozère is a problem child, almost a lost tribe, scrutinized and subsidized as though it were somewhere up the Amazon or in the depths of New Guinea. The State has poured in money, through the EEC's mountain aid fund as well as national measures, and has allowed priority treatment. An isolated farmer can get a telephone within two weeks; in Paris, you wait months.

As a result of all this new interest, some parts of Lozère appear prosperous, even animated. Mende, the tiny capital (population 11,000), is quite a sophisticated place, with smart hotels and boutiques. In summer, the tourists arrive in their hundreds of thousands, and the moors and forests are specked with the blue-and-orange tents of *les campings*. But the season is only June to September. Through the long harsh winter, and even in summer away from the tourist routes, the tragi-comedy of Lozère wears a different mask.

This simple kind of tourism, over so short a season, cannot itself provide the new jobs needed to check the population drift; nor can it produce the extra resources needed to balance an economy so heavily dependent on State charity. Farming is slowly modernizing, as best it can in this terrain; but this merely adds to the exodus. So what is the answer? For a start, new industry; but here there is a vicious circle. Some 80 per cent of school-leavers are obliged to go off and seek work in cities elsewhere; nowadays most of them would rather stay, but there are not the jobs. Yet few firms will settle in the area, as they think it lacks skilled labour. One can see their point, for usually it *is* the brighter or more skilled young people who leave, because there are not the skilled jobs . . .

Various idealists have made attempts to break this classic vicious circle. In the mid-'70s an inspired local couple, Hubert and Nicole Pougnet, Christians of the missionary kind, tried to set a new pattern. In St-Chély-d'Apcher and two other townlets of northern Lozère they created five little workshops run on cooperative lines, with help from DATAR. The worker/co-owners were mostly young women, making micro-electronic parts for telephone exchanges, etc. Many were farmers' daughters with local technical diplomas, delighted at last to find jobs locally. And as the material was light, Lozère's remoteness did not cause serious transport problems. 'We are doing God's work here,' Mme Pougnet told me: 'God guides us to improve people's material and social lives as well as their souls.' It was all rather touching. But God had made an error of judgement, for the Pougnets had so little business ability that their venture foundered. However, it has since been revived by a

Parisian entrepreneur and now modestly flourishes with ninety workers. The Pougnets had at least provided the initial inspiration.

Also in St-Chély, another Christian idealist, Frère Gibelin of the Order of the Sacred Heart, is headmaster of a large ramshackle Catholic technical school, dedicatedly training local youth to be skilled workers. 'Our only hope of enabling them to stay,' he said, 'is to give guarantees to firms that we can train staff for them.' He spoke passionately of his sense of mission to 'save' his native Lozère. St-Chély is also the site of Lozère's one sizeable firm, a steel plant of the giant Creusot-Loire group, with four hundred workers. It was set up in this unlikely spot by some fluke in 1917, and has since been repeatedly in difficulty owing to the poor rail links. Creusot-Loire, it is said, would dearly like to close it, but have been pressured not to do so by the Government, fearing the harm this would do to Lozère's image! Clearly if the area has any industrial future, it is not with heavy steel plant but with small light units of the Pougnets' kind. Three or four have arrived recently, in electronics, furniture, perfumes. At least it is a beginning.

The man in charge of wooing new industry is Jean Laquerbe, director of Lozère's expansion committee, a young executive who had tired of managing mammoth hotel developments on the Languedoc coast, and in a back-to-nature spirit moved here with his winsome wife who has set up a rural physiotherapy clinic. He told me: 'People in Lozère are not rich but they're happy, it has the lowest crime and suicide rates in France. I get letters from highly-paid *cadres* in Paris who are longing to come here, even at half the salary. But to the financiers we need, Lozère is still *Ultima Thule*.' Laquerbe is a droll, outspoken character who views with amused scepticism the impact of industry on bucolic Lozère: 'People here are strange. They don't believe in success, and if someone starts a venture their reaction is, "He's sure to come a cropper". They're wary of industry, at least the older ones, and it makes my job harder.' It was a view I heard from others too, including Frère Gibelin and DATAR officials. Older Lozériens, maybe living in Paris, want to come back and retire peacefully and are sentimentally opposed to seeing their homeland change. On occasions they have used their influence to thwart industrial projects. Their conservationism is understandable, but does not help the younger generation. 'It's awful,' said Gibelin, 'that these old fogeys see this place through such rose-tinted glasses. How am I to find jobs for my students?'

This is one of several local conflicts over what Lozère's future should be. Another concerns forestry, where there is a big untapped potential that could create new jobs and revenue; but not everyone agrees on just what to do. Lozère has 500,000 acres of forest, mainly pine, oak, beech and chestnut, including 90,000 acres planted since the war. Some forest land belongs to the State, some to the big private estates; but most of it is parcelled out between small owners, 18,000 of them! Moreover, much of the land is hilly, not flat as in the Landes or in Sweden, and this does not make large-scale tree-felling any easier. Yet there is much that could be done. The Government has been trying to teach the small owners to tend their trees properly, and to persuade them to regroup rationally, as with farm *remembrement*. But this arouses the usual resistance. Once again, individualism and modern economic efficiency are in conflict.

One aim of the Massif Central programme is to double timber output by 1990; at present France, despite her big forests, is a net importer both of wood and paper. And of the wood that Lozère does produce, not nearly enough is processed locally. Curiously, in the whole of the forested Massif Central there is not a single wood-pulp factory or paper mill. Various projects have always come to nothing, and Lozère's own output of wood for pulping has to be sent to a factory in Provence that dictates its price. It is a waste of a local resource. Not all Lozère's wood is of very high quality, but much of it is good enough for constructional timber, even furniture, and the Government has been trying to persuade the scores of little sawmills and wood firms to rationalize, expand, and thus provide new jobs. It is not easy, for the foresters, mill-owners and manufacturers are for some reason barely on speaking terms.

There has been some progress with the creation of new firms making use of local wood, but also some odd failures. One plan for a wood-pulp factory was torpedoed by the local population, who feared pollution. Then in 1977, at Langogne in eastern Lozère, an ambitious project for a factory to make constructional timber met a most sinister fate. It was a Paris firm, with backing from the State and the big banks. But the local sawmill owners, an influential pressure-group, saw the factory as a dangerous rival. They went to the prefect and threatened they would not supply it with wood. This was just before the elections. Paris promptly withdrew its support for the project, which collapsed through lack of finance. 'It was a great pity,' a forestry official confided to me; 'the factory could have stimulated local industry and obliged the sawmills to improve their quality – that's why they were hostile!' It appears that the principal supporter of the mill-owners was Jacques Blanc, the local deputy and secretary-general of Giscard's own Parti Républicain. It was he who pulled the right strings at the Elysée – a classic example of how a strong local *notable* can override a prefect (see p. 191).

Despite these hazards, there are many who believe that Lozère's longer-term future lies much more with forestry than agriculture. Only a few fertile valleys are really suited to modern farming. Elsewhere, on the vast plateaux, the family farm will always have to struggle; and while living standards have risen, so have expectations, and the peasants rightly will no longer submit to their old poverty. But what are they prepared to do about it? I met a couple from Paris who were breeding goats on an eighty-five-acre upland farm: 'We work every day till ten p.m., then collapse exhausted into bed. We have no time, or money, for holidays or treats. *We* have chosen this venture, for our own reasons; but many peasants around us are just as badly off, and *they* did not choose this life, they inherited it. We see little future for farming here, the land is too poor.' Others I met shared this pessimism. Many of them feel that the plateaux should be reforested, and tourist amenities and national parks developed. But the farmers do not want to be driven out. They want to stay in their homes, and somehow be given the means to get richer.

They have some powerful local support. The pillars of the Lozère rural world are François and Jeannine Braget, a most sympathetic couple, enterprising, generous-hearted, both in their fifties, both from local farming families – 'They *are* the Lozère', I was told. He runs the S A F E R office in Mende, she, as we have seen earlier, is the driving force behind the rural handicrafts cooperative. Over a rustic supper *chez eux*, François said: 'Even if it's costly in terms of upkeep of roads and so on, it is essential to preserve the human tissue of hamlets and farmsteads that has existed here for millennia. Your solution, of regrouping the families in the big villages, might work in a wheat-growing area but not one of livestock, where the farmer must be near his pastures. Yes, I know that the wealthy United States has miles of emptiness, but those are virgin lands of conquest, not of an ancient tradition of habitation. So the answer is to increase the size of farms and productivity, and the nation must help pay. If the human tissue went, the Administration would go too, there'd be no more need for Mende, or the prefect, or the bishop.'

One solution preached by the Bragets is pluri-activity. That is why Jeannine set up her cooperative, in 1958. She urges farming families to practise traditional home handicrafts in the winter, thus adding to their income. These crafts were in danger of dying out, but trained artisans have been hired to help the farmers re-learn them, using local materials. They make straw-seated chairs, baskets, wooden lampshades, iron candlesticks and ornaments, pottery, rugs and so on – mostly in the heavy local style, but authentic. The 180 members' produce is then sold mainly in the cooperative's shops in Mende and Paris. The scheme is on a modest scale, and has run into heavy competition nationally, as this kind of revival is now so much in vogue. But Mme Braget perseveres. 'We want to help people to stay in their *pays*, not on charity but through their own work of which they can be proud. It makes the winters more bearable, and it's a renewal of a valid medieval tradition. So long as they have the basic comforts, country people are happier than factory workers. They work long hours, but they're free!'

One exemplary member of the cooperative is the Meynardier family, pious Cévenol Protestants with a fifty-acre dairy farm in a valley south of Florac. Stern biblical texts adorn the walls of their simple living-room, a contrast to the kitschy Virgins of many a Catholic home. The parents have three unmarried sons of seventeen to twenty-three who wanted to stay on the land, so they saw that the only chance was to expand the farm and also diversify. One son is a trained carpenter, another a locksmith. And by French peasant standards what the family have done is remarkable. In winter they make lampshades and various metal ornaments, using sophisticated machines. In summer, they have a licence from the Cévennes National Park to pick wild bilberries, which they make into tarts and crêpes and then go and sell to the tourists who motor to the summit of Mont Aigoual, the local panorama point. Also they have elegantly converted an outhouse into two *gîtes*, booked out with visitors all summer. One Parisian middle-class family come every year and are now their close friends. The Meynardiers are far from rich, but they exude a serenity and confidence. They admitted however that their spirit of enterprise is the exception: the ten other farming families in the commune are much poorer, and less happy, and all the land except in the narrow valley bottom will probably soon be abandoned.

The State has stepped in, and the ubiquitous officials of the National Park are at least trying to administer the growing decultivation of the Cévennes uplands, through wildlife conservation, tree-planting and so on. The Cévenols react with suspicion. By long Protestant tradition they are anti-Paris, and in the Giscard period they jested ruefully about the strange coincidence that the Cévennes has one village called Barre, another called Le Pompidou, while across the Lot valley is one called Chirac! 'You see, we're trapped!' Joking apart, most Government officials do share the view of the peasants and the Bragets that upland Lozère and other such areas must not become a desert. This is national farm policy too, as Debatisse told me: 'If there are no inhabitants left in these lovely tourist areas, they will become a jungle, and we must prevent that.' The debate, then, is over the form and the degree of the inhabitation. The conservationists fear that the State, for purely economic reasons, is putting too much stress on forestry; both Mme Braget and the new young ecology-minded settlers have declared, 'We don't want Lozère to become one vast wood-pulp factory.' Well, if it ever does, it won't be for some decades, at the present rate.

Probably Lozère and other such areas will in practice move towards a compromise solution, where the isolated farmers will become also 'guardians of nature', paid for part-time warden-type duties. To me, the Bragets' ideal of a network of little farmsteads all over France seems in the long term unrealistic. On the other hand, France is not destined to share the vast silences of Wyoming. The oil sheikhs permitting, it ought to be possible for the farmer to move just a little nearer to the friendly lights and cosy comforts of the *bourg*, while retaining the mobility to look after a large farm. And if more little industries and services take the initiative to settle in Lozère, then Mende and other towns will be able to boom and expand. Lozère's population will increase again, but regrouped. More people will be able to enjoy living in the countryside, without having to face the hardships of isolation. This practical human compromise would not seem beyond French ingenuity.

THE 'DUNG DROP-OUTS'
IN SEARCH OF UTOPIA

It is a saga that stirs the imagination, a bit like Arnold's scholar gipsy: the tens of thousands of middle-class students and young urban intellectuals who since 1968 have made their bid for a new rural utopia. They have given up their studies, or their jobs in teaching or other professions, to opt for a 'purer' life of stark simplicity, scratching a living from hill-farming on a few stony acres, or from handicrafts, or both. Many have failed and gone back home. But some have stayed and adapted, and new ones have arrived. Today in the Cévennes alone there are some 3,000 of these *'installés'* (settlers) as they prefer to be known, or *'marginaux'* (drop-outs), as their critics call them.

'Les margi-bouseurs' (*bouse* is cow-dung) is one scornful term for them in Latin Quarter circles. But this scorn for the 'dung drop-outs' is often a kind of jealousy; for every student or ex-student who makes this radical break, there are ten others who vaguely dream of doing so, if only they dared. The trend says a lot about the mood today of a certain French generation. It has also been doing a little to help revive areas such as Lozère, even if it has led inevitably to culture-clashes between *installés* and natives. And some settlers, who came to invent a new autarkic way of life, have found that the adventure has not led them quite where they expected.

Witness the strange case of Ginette Lespine, 'hippy'-turned-*notable*. In 1972 she and a few other Leftist students bought a derelict farmhouse and a patch of land on a steep slope of the Vallée Française, in the heart of the Cévennes. Here they set up a commune (in the Anglo-Saxon sense of the term: the French word is *communauté*). The aim was to live in pure and isolated self-sufficiency, rejecting all society. The ten or so members shared everything, work, property, each other, while shocked rumours spread among the Protestant peasantry of the free-love life-style of these long-haired '*zipis*' (French for hippies). For a while, this idealistic commune seemed to be succeeding. But gradually quarrels developed within the group – over work, money, relationships – aggravated by their isolation. The rural idyll went sour, as they found it impossible to make even a subsistence living on this stony hillside, especially as they knew nothing about farming. The group split up, most members drifted back to the cities. But four of them decided to stick it out; they divided the property, and today they live as two separate couples. Ginette and her mate, Gérard Dutronc, have decided that if they want to stay and survive, they have no choice but to adapt to local ways. They have cut their hair shorter, they dress less outlandishly. On their few cultivable acres they have goats, rabbits, beehives; they sell cheese and honey, do some weaving in winter and plan to grow soft fruit for market on the disused stony terraces. They are still very poor, but they get by. Ginette, who arrived with a *licence* in psychology, has now obtained a diploma in farming, which makes it much easier to obtain State grants for improving the farm. Already they have won a subsidy for this.

They came as rebels against society, hating the State and all its works; now they have come to terms with it, a necessary compromise, they feel. Gradually too they have grown sympathetically involved with the Cévenols, and are now dedicated to helping the area. Their idealism has changed course. They are dynamic and resourceful, and Gérard has taken the lead in forming a young farmers' cooperative. Above all, Ginette in 1977 was invited by the local mayor, a Socialist doctor, to join his electoral list. Some local eyebrows were raised: after all, not so long ago . . . She hesitated, then agreed – and was elected. Today she is a pillar of local society, municipal councillor in charge of public relations, editing the village news bulletin. It is a far cry from the ideals which first brought her to this lonely valley, and the transformation has not been easy.

To the Cévennes and elsewhere, the settlers have come with a variety of motives. The first major influx was in 1968–71, made up largely of young people disillusioned by the failure of May '68 to change French society as a whole. So they set out to build their own mini-utopias, or else they went hopefully in quest of a traditional rural society untainted by the wicked city. Few had much money so they gravitated to depopulating areas such as the Cévennes where land and dwellings were cheap. Some also found a spiritual affinity in the Cévennes, 'a land of historic resistance to Paris', said one. These early pioneers were strongly influenced by the communes and counter-culture movements in America, but the situation they faced in France was different. America still has vast virgin spaces, as well as a long tradition of pioneer settler communities. In France, wherever they went the newcomers came up against the ancient tissue of peasant society, often suspicious of them, as well as a pervasive public administration. They have not had the same freedom of manoeuvre as their American counterparts.

Many at first tried living in communes: it was fashionable in the first liberated flush of the post-'68 period. But most of these soon broke up, for the reasons I have cited. This style of group-living is not in the French temperament or tradition, and Gallic individualism rapidly baulked at the sharing out of property or daily chores, let alone shared intimacy. Of the original commune members who have stayed in the Cévennes, nearly all are now living normally as couples, like Ginette and Gérard. Most communes found they had little to hold them together save a vague desire to break with convention, and the recruitment was often casual, via ads in Left-wing papers: 'Autarky! – girl and three blokes in Cévennes hamlet seek girls to share in farming and maybe much else...' Very few communes today survive, save those with a disciplined religious basis (see p. 458); and it may be significant that in 1979 the one commune I could find in the Cévennes was not French but a group of mainly British actors! – the remarkable Roy Hart Theatre community, near Anduze in the Gard.

The early arrivals soon found, too, that hill-farming was not the easy idyll they have imagined. They had no training, and often little aptitude, for the daily drudgery of milking goats or digging the hard soil. In many cases their funds ran out, and as soon as the cold winds blew they called off the adventure. Only a minority stayed through the first winter. But since then other waves of *installés* have arrived, less dilettante in their approach. In the mid-'70s came the ecologists and artisans, with thought-out ideas on how to make a living in the country; and more recently, the rise in graduate unemployment has prompted a new migration from the cities. Today there are some 10,000 settlers in the rural areas, including 3,000 in the Cévennes and another 3,000 or so in the foothills of the Alps and Pyrenees. Those who have been there some years are tending to integrate into local society and do not expect to leave, while the newer arrivals are much less 'hippy' than the first post-'68 wave, more practical about making ends meet, readier to accept help from public authorities. In fact, as sociologists have noted[2] the

---

2 Notably Danièle Léger and Bertrand Hervieu, to whom I am indebted, as I am to their book *Le Retour à la nature*, Le Seuil, 1979.

movement has undergone a sea-change over the decade. The early utopian vision, of a 'return to the desert' to create a counter-society, has steadily given ground to the different ideal of rediscovering an existing rural society and helping it to survive, or else to the simple personal desire to live and work in the country, with no special sense of mission. This last category is today probably the majority. Hippy drop-outs do still exist, but they are relatively few.

No case is quite like another, so it is hard to generalize, and I had best give a few examples. Some *installés* have changed their trade completely, like the two ex-*lycée* teachers now happily working as masons, or the former TV producer now a cabinet-maker. Others have managed to bring their trade with them. I met one ex-teacher and his wife, a trained nurse, who had left Paris in disgust after '68. He now minds the goats and works as odd-job-man; she is still a State nurse, and tours the villages in her Citroën 2 CV, giving injections. 'I think it's largely because I've been able to go on with my job that we're so happy in this new life,' she said; 'many settler experiments fail because the wife hates it, you get divorces and separations. But I'd rather be a nurse here than in Paris. Our parents were horrified at first by our move and were sure it would fail; but now they're beginning to accept it, even though we still tease them by turning up in our *margi-bouseur* gear at their bourgeois parties.' Another case is that of a young *polytechnicien* of the proud Ponts et Chaussées corps. Bored with élitist careerism, he went off to open a restaurant in the upper Lot valley. He put all his money in it, but he failed, so he took a job as a labourer in a nearby quarry. As an 'X' engineer he was so much more talented at quarrying than anyone else around that with a loan from a friend he was able to buy up the quarry – and now makes more money from it than ever he could have done from his restaurant.

In a hamlet high on the *causse* south of Mende, I met two contrasting extremes of *installé*, living within a few yards of each other. Jacques and Anne-Marie Chauvière, a delightful couple in their twenties, are silk-screen printers who grew bored with working for design and advertising firms in Paris, wanted to start up on their own but found costs far too high in the capital. So they came to Lozère which they knew already through holidays, found a disused schoolhouse for which they pay 350 francs rent a month, and here they now have a thriving little silk-screen printing and design studio, with mainly local clients. 'We've simply transferred our profession to the countryside,' said Jacques; 'we want to help this area, and we're far happier than in Paris.' They are dedicated, and hard-working. They spoke scornfully of their neighbours, Philippe and Jacqueline, in their thirties, authentic drop-outs from well-to-do bourgeois families in northern France – 'Our only motivation,' said Jacqueline, 'is sheer unbridled laziness.' This second couple bought a derelict cottage for 9,000 francs and partially converted it, though it is still somewhat squalid, with no bathroom. Philippe is a failed writer who earns a few francs from odd-jobs when the mood stirs him; Jacqueline dabbles in arts and crafts, but admits that she hates to stick at anything for long. Basically they survive on a regular allowance from their shocked but indulgent parents, like many such *fils-à-papa* drop-outs today. This ultra-bohemian couple I found gentle, relaxed, amusing, seemingly happy, and very friendly. They have a son aged five, and a loose kind of marriage which involves a *ménage-à-trois* with another hippy, with whom Jacqueline goes off for weeks at a time. When I asked the warm-hearted Jeannine Braget what she thought of these 'parasites' in her Lozère, she said, 'I am fond of that family. It's good that some people should do nothing: laziness has its own moral value. In Lozère there's room for all types.'

One type is the idealistic do-gooder. Patrick Lescure, bearded young ecologist and ex-art-student, son of a rich Dijon industrialist, came to Lozère fleeing the 'shame' of his privileged background. He has spent part of his inheritance on renovating a village near Mende, but he hates to talk about his family wealth. He lives simply, married to a local girl, and devotes his energies to the local craft movement and to supporting ecological causes such as Larzac (see pp. 342–3).

Bernard and Françoise Martin are applying their idealism to helping local farmers. Theirs is another classic story. As young *lycée* teachers in Paris, much influenced by '68, they grew to hate the city; and today they are happily struggling to make a living with goats, horses and beehives, on a small farm high on the stony plateaux of northern Lozère. So well have they adapted to local society that the Lozère Young Farmers' Association (CNJA) has elected Bernard its President: another drop-out turned *notable*. He told me: 'I always had a yen for farming. We thought of Australia, but were warned that a French couple wouldn't be welcome there. We came here on a visit and fell in love with the freedom and space of Lozère, but it was hard to find land – here in the north at least, the locals are suspicious of long-haired city types, and they wouldn't sell. But finally we rented a few acres. We've made a real effort to integrate, and it's worked. We were unwed when we arrived, but then we got married so as not to upset local feelings – this isn't the *Rive Gauche*. I helped the local farmers in some disputes with the authorities, over snow-clearance and so on, and they were grateful; that's why they elected me, I think. Most of our friends now are Lozériens, and we have little left in common with our old academic pals in Paris, who know nothing of practical life. Life, I admit, is tough. We work an eighty-hour week, we have no running water, no heating in the bedroom, and the track up to this farm is often blocked by snow for weeks on end in winter. But it's worth it. We'd never go back to Paris.'

I thought him a strange, impressive, D. H. Lawrence-like man, fired by some inner drive, it seemed, as if trying to prove something to himself; finding a fulfilment in the martyrdom of sharing the drudgery of the poorest of upland peasants. Others however have come to rural life in a more happy-go-lucky spirit. Alain and Marie-Antoinette Boutet are also ex-teachers in their mid-thirties, from Orléans. With their small son, their dog Marcel Proust and their Land Rover, they live in a spacious converted farmhouse, isolated up on an empty plateau of the Cévennes, with rolling vistas on every side. Here they earn an *ad hoc* living from looking after horses, doing odd-jobs such as carpentry in near-by villages, acting as a hostel for tourist ramblers in summer and weaving blankets for Mme Braget's cooperative in winter. 'At first we tried goats,' said Alain, 'but it was too much like hard work. Our needs are simple, we don't need much money. I'm not a great worker – and here I have this feeling of being on holiday all the year. We're free! We came here ten years ago worried about Vietnam, but now our worry is the price of hay. I'm motivated by no ideology, not even that of "helping Lozère". We're here because we like it, that's all. The capitalist system is doomed and dying – but at least France is a country where it's still possible to opt for this kind of anarchic rural freedom. So I say, *merci Monsieur le Gouvernement*!' A succinct summary of the philosophy of many *installés* today. And like virtually all the thirty or so *installés* I met in Lozère, I found the Boutets a notably sympathetic, gentle, tolerant and welcoming couple, so different from what they might have been in Paris. Clearly the neo-rural experience is good for the soul.

The reactions of the natives to the settler invasion have varied considerably. At first it all came as a cultural shock to these good peasants who had lived in isolation for so long. They were horrified at the communes, at the idea of group-sex and drug-addicts defiling their virtuous valleys; a few mayors even held up the supply of electricity and water to the newcomers. Some of the early settlers also made clumsy attempts to 'civilize' the locals by putting on avant-garde theatre shows ('we played Mayakovsky in the farms') or by trying to convert them to organic farming. This was not welcomed. But the initial culture-conflicts have now subsided, the communes have gone, and in 1979 most of the settlers I met told me the same story: 'Like all mountain folk, the Cévenols may be suspicious of outsiders, but they also respect hard work. Once they see that we are here to *work*, they accept us.' Especially this is true of the farming *installés*, who share the same practical daily problems as the natives.

Some ambivalence remains, however. As the Hervieu have pointed out,[3] the Cévenols see the settlers both as a threat and an opportunity. 'They're so ready to help, so enterprising, they've given this village a new lease of life, thanks to their children the local school won't be closed down' – that is one reaction. But another may be, *'Our* kids have had to leave home to find work, and here are these newcomers taking over the land. With their degrees, they could have good jobs in town – why come here begging for subsidies?' What puzzles and often angers the Cévenols is that the settlers have come rejecting those same urban values which they, the peasants, have been taught to respect as their goal in life. To win a good diploma, to find a salaried job, to improve your social status, your speech, your dress, to acquire consumer gadgets, to become more like townsfolk, this has been the trend of the peasantry since the war. And now, young townsfolk arrive turning all this on its head. While country people ape town values, people from the city are beginning to ape what they suppose to be country values! For the peasant, it is very bewildering, and has led to misunderstandings. The most sensitive *installés* are aware of the dilemma and try to be tactful. Alain Boutet said: 'When our neighbour told us how thrilled she was that her son had just passed his *bac*, we said yes, yes, how lovely, and avoided giving our views on the absurdity of the whole *bac* rat-race that we've rejected.'

Despite this culture gap, some established settlers by now regard themselves as true Cévenols or Lozériens by adoption. More than one is a mayor, others run clubs for old people, welfare centres and so on. But many other *installés* prefer to stick within their own little colonies, especially where they congregate thickest: in one village, over half the population are settlers. Olivier Liénard, formerly in advertising in Normandy, now does leatherwork and runs an association of thirty similar artisan-settlers, with a handicrafts shop in Florac (full of tourists in summer) and commercial outlets in Paris and Nîmes. Nearly all his friends, he said, are other *installés*. Some Lozériens are resentful of this degree of systematic neo-colonization, as they see it. But very many settlers are much more isolated than this, as much from each other as from the locals. One or two attempts by would-be leaders to unite the newcomers in formal committees, for economic development of the area, have failed through lack of interest. After all, a drop-out by definition is

3 op. cit.; also their article in *Autrement: avec nos sabots*, 1978, p. 66.

often a solitary, self-sufficient type, rejecting collective life; and that is why he left the city. It also struck me that these *installés* have much less contact with each other than Anglo-Saxons would in a similar situation. Alain Boutet said, 'My wife and I prefer our own company, we listen to music and have hardly any social life. We see less and less of other settlers, and when we meet there's little to say – what do I have in common with a goat-breeder, or a potter?'

Lastly, one of the most significant aspects of the settlers' saga is the compromises they have found themselves making, willingly or less so. 'For our first two years,' said a farming couple near Florac, 'we tried to live like noble savages, washing our clothes and ourselves in mountain streams, doing without electricity. It was hell! Finally we decided that you might as well live with your epoch, and after a hard day in the fields you jolly well need a hot shower. Nor did it seem fair to inflict our own purism on our children. So today we have much the same domestic equipment as we'd have in town.' Some settlers as a matter of principle tried at first to live in self-sufficiency, rejecting all dependence on a market economy or on public utilities such as gas or water from the mains. But they soon found this just did not work. Though hesitant to admit it, in a sense they were cutting off their noses to spite their faces: they wanted a certain rural experience, but by rejecting 'the system', they were refusing also the aid that alone might make that experience feasible. Those who stayed in the Cévennes came reluctantly to accept that, for their farming to be viable, they would need the help of State-backed bodies such as the SAFER (see p. 219), and this involved commitments. The subsidies did not come without strings, and to get land and support from the SAFER they had to take a training course in farming. Many have done so. And they have found that the SAFER in fact is glad to help settlers who give evidence of being 'serious'. François Braget, director of the Lozère SAFER, told me: 'These newcomers can be a real asset. They can help us to recultivate areas that were turning to waste, and to save a land that for decades has been dying. They can give new heart to our own youngsters, too, and encourage them to stay. And by acting as "guardians of nature" they can help us beat back the desert.'

The State has taken the Cévennes in hand in recent years, and in the National Park zone its officials are everywhere, with intelligent new policies for land restoration and farming innovations. The settlers have much to gain from collaborating and seeking their aid. What is more, they come from the same kind of social and cultural backgrounds as these State officials, many of them also idealistic and radical in their way. Both groups have more in common with each other than either has with the Cévenol natives: they speak the same language. Most settlers accept this compromise with the State, which has ceased to be a burning issue. But they remain aware of the irony: they came here to avoid the State and have ended up its accomplices – is this necessary pragmatism, or a betrayal of ideals? One *installé* told the Hervieus:[4] 'We fled as far as possible into the desert, into the heart of the forest, and what do we find here but the State?'

· A few extremists have managed to defy this scheme of things, even recently. In 1978 a group of six penniless drop-outs arrived in the wild uplands east of Florac and proceeded to squat in a deserted farmhouse. They lived as a commune, with little but a few goats. The owner protested, and the police evicted them. So they moved to another abandoned farm near by, and when this owner too started to prosecute, the squatters were able to evoke an old law, rarely applied, that declares it illegal to own cultivable land without either using it or renting it out. Despite various attempts at eviction, the courts have upheld this law, and the squatters are still there, though the police are not too pleased. In fact, in the early post-'68 period, the first Cévennes settlers were repeatedly subjected to inquiries by the police, seeking out *'militants gauchistes'* hiding in the countryside. This harassment has now largely ended. But the police are still suspicious of drop-outs who come to the Cévennes with no visible means of support and an anarcho-Leftist air.

The leading *notables* of Lozère today are divided on whether the *installés* can really be much use to the area's future. Some, such as Jacques Blanc, think they can be no more than a marginal and transitory phenomenon, and that Lozère's destiny rests with its own people. Others feel differently, including M. Brajet, and also Dr Monod, the mayor who brought Ginette Lespine on to his council at St-Croix-Vallée-Française: 'The population of the Cévennes has been falling steadily, so new blood is essential. After all their brave battles across the centuries, the Cévenols in recent years had been growing defeatist, they felt their homeland was doomed, they were giving up the struggle, selling off their land and houses cheaply. But this mood is now changing, partly thanks to the settlers, who've shown that success *is* possible here.' But ironically this revival is now making it harder for new *installés* to arrive. The peasants have now grown wise to the potential value of their properties, and land and house prices have been rocketing: a semi-ruined farmstead bought in 1972 for 8,000 francs would today fetch ten times that sum. Competition has been growing, too, from the prosperous searchers after *résidences secondaires*, who are also invading the valleys. As Jeannine Braget told me, 'Today, people fight for a place in

4 op. cit., p. 219.

the countryside ' But the new would-be settlers, few with much money, are likely to be the losers, and their numbers may well drop in the years ahead. It would be sad if this courageous and creative venture were to fade and fail. But in some form or another the new vogue for the countryside will continue. Lozère will still be *à la mode.* So what will its future be? Vast camping-site, and park for chic holiday homes? 'Indian reservation' for protected peasantry? Wood-pulp factory? Or will there still be room for Ginette Lespine and the other scholar gypsies?

Chapter 5

IN THE CITIES:
THE QUEST FOR 'QUALITY OF LIFE'

The vogue for the countryside is one aspect of the much wider new French concern for 'quality of life' which equally embraces the cities. In the post-war decades of heady growth and modernization, the main urban emphasis went – rightly – on solving France's terrible housing shortage, legacy of many years of neglect. New high-rise estates were thrown up all over the place, often with little regard for aesthetics or amenities; but at least the French *were* rehoused, and quantitatively the shortage was largely cured by about 1970. But the sober 1970s then brought a shift in priorities, as a now affluent society began to react against the negative aspects of too rapid urbanization. The French demanded that their new individual prosperity be matched by better public amenities and by steps to make city life more tolerable. Phrases like 'protecting the environment' became as much in vogue as in Britain or the United States. Giscard, when he came to power, quickly associated himself with this new public mood, and launched policies accordingly. He said: 'For the nation that we are today, city-dwellers uprooted from our rural origins, to be modern must mean to live amid greenery and be able to stroll on foot. Our town-planning must fulfil the citizen's desire to return to the warm human contacts of the old rural or small-town way of life.'

In the past few years many town councils have switched their emphasis from large-scale building projects to ecological schemes: for example, La Rochelle's famous system of free communal bicycles. This environmentalist trend is taking many forms today and – unusual for France – is as often due to local or private initiative as to State measures. Throughout the country there are new open-air or heated public swimming-pools, well-equipped leisure and sports centres, advisory clinics, handsome new homes for old people, renovated castles, new museums, and campaigns against noise and litter. In short, the French, like the Germans and others, have belatedly been turning to the kind of welfare and leisure amenities that we in Britain take such pride in having pioneered so many years ago. And with their eagerness, sense of style, and larger budgets, they have been overtaking us in many fields. Every

Clochemerle in France today wants its own *piscine municipale chauffée* as a status symbol.

This is the latest phase in a post-war urban revolution that steadily has been moulding the French into new life-styles and new social attitudes. Many millions have moved from the farms or from slum districts to new dormitory towns, where a traditional French way of life is painfully adapting itself to the very different needs and patterns of modern suburbia. Many people react by a scared retreat into privacy, others by trying to form new clubs and associations – for sport, culture, welfare and so on – that seem to owe more to the Anglo-Saxon than the usual French model. Slowly a new style of local community life is emerging in France, more informal, less institutionalized than in the past; but frequently it falls victim to political rivalries, especially in places where the Communists are on the offensive. Cultural life too has seen a tremendous revival in the provinces since the 1950s, and today it is taking many impromptu and innovative forms – a street festival here, a music group there – in reaction to excessive official spoon-feeding. But culture, too, can become politicized.

This chapter will look in detail at these and other topics, as well as at the new ecology movements – the anti-nuclear campaign, the struggles over pollution and nature conservation. It will look at the Giscard regime's own record in matters of the environment, and at the new Socialist Government's plans. First, we shall see whether the changes in Paris since the war have spoiled or rescued that sublime city.

PARIS, BELOVED MONSTER,
AT GRIPS WITH TRAFFIC-JAMS
AND SKYSCRAPERS

Anyone arriving in Paris from London is at once aware of the difference in tempo. Parisians drive more aggressively, they are always hurrying from one appointment to another, often they are snappy down the telephone or too busy to stop and help a stranger. The brighter side of this medal is a zestful nervous vitality that can be stimulating, and somehow harmonizes with the urban landscape of gaily lit streets, crowded terrace-cafés and smart shop-windows. But Parisians' curse is that their city is too physically congested. The Ville de Paris (the city proper, 'within the gates') has twice the population density of the equivalent area of central London; and apart from the boulevards, most streets are narrow and canyon-like. This congestion leads to tensions in daily living which the Parisians' second curse – their own restless, intolerant, self-willed temperament – is peculiarly ill-suited to coping with. It is a vicious circle.

No wonder that Parisians' feelings have grown so fiercely ambivalent towards a city that has always inspired deep loyalties and whose personal spell, even today, is not lightly broken. 'Paris, what a monster!' people say, almost lovingly. And so the two Parises coexist: the tiring modern town of practical daily life, and the secret personality of a city whose insidious beauty and vitality still survive and even renew themselves. For these reasons, many foreign francophiles like myself find Paris a fascinating and exciting city to visit for a month or two, but we do not want to live there as so many expatriates chose to do before the war. And even Parisians are in growing numbers moving to the provinces.

When I first lived in Paris, in the mid-'50s, the mood was much *more* strained than it is today, but in a different way. Parisians then were still scarred by the trauma of the Occupation, they lived with the shame of colonial wars and repeated political crises, and they had to face a fearful housing shortage, archaic public transport and the gloomy presence of blackened façades even along main streets. Since then, two decades of prosperity and stability have restored Parisians' self-confidence; they are less sullen, and certainly happier. But prosperity has brought new problems: just as it has turned dull provincial towns into lively ones, so it has made Paris, lively already, into too much of a good thing, too hectic.

The city in fact is still paying the price of nearly a century of neglect of town-planning, up until the early '60s. The *Ville Lumière* that the tourist sees is today bright with new paint and scoured façades, but it hides other realities: the congested older commercial districts, the scarcity of green parks and the ugly sprawl of the pre-war suburbs. As the population of greater Paris swelled rapidly after the war, its new suburbs were not provided adequately with services, and the problems grew. But then, just as the conurbation seemed to be on the verge of seizing up like an engine without oil, the situation at last began to be tackled seriously. The Gaullist master-planners of the '60s set to work on the whole shape of the city, colouring their maps with grandiose designs for garden cities and urban freeways. The French do not do things by halves: after years of total disregard, the future of Paris has become a public obsession, the subject of scores of books and reports. And up through the waste land of the old slums and suburbs the shoots have appeared of a new, daring and impressive city.

Whereas virtually nothing of any value was built between 1900 and 1960, the past twenty years have seen bold changes. The housing shortage has been largely solved, and the public transport system has been modernized so vigorously that in the view of some experts[1] it is now the

1 For instance, Britain's *Architectural Review*: see its September 1979 issue, devoted entirely to Paris.

best of any large city in the world. Paris, far more than London, has finally proved its capacity to carry out ambitious modernistic projects: for example, the futuristic 'Beaubourg' arts centre – alias the Georges Pompidou Cultural Centre (see p. 276) – not to everyone's taste aesthetically but a huge popular success. It is true that some other new building has been less well judged, and there are many who feel that the sudden skyscraper boom of the early '70s has spoilt the city's famous skyline. But this high-rise craze is now over, and the accent today is on much-needed improvements to Paris' 'quality of life' – more parks, traffic-free streets, rehabilitation of slum districts and so on. This at least is the stated policy of the controversial Jacques Chirac, who in 1977 became the city's first mayor for 106 years. Paris in modernizing has lost some of its old charm, perhaps inevitably. But it is still an immensely vital city, ever changing, and today it is involved in a struggle to tame its own excesses; to bring back more serenity of living to streets that suffer from hyper-tense activity.

One of the problems of town-planning is that the organic links have never been adequate between inner Paris and its suburbs; the two are entirely distinct, administratively and even physically, separated by the wide sweep of the Boulevard Périphérique (ring motorway) and the vacant zones beside it. Within this ring, and within the old city gates, lies the single commune of the Ville de Paris with its twenty *arrondissements*; its population, though still dense, has been falling steadily, from 2.9 million in 1911 to 2.1 million today. Outside, the hundreds of suburban communes have mostly been growing rapidly, so that the population of the whole conurbation has risen since the war from 5 million to 9½ million, and today more than three Parisians in four are *banlieusards*. There is no overall coordinating body in the manner of the Greater London Council, nothing other than the Ile-de-France Region which until now has had the same limitations as other French regions – and the communes jealously hug their autonomy.

Before looking in detail at the Ville de Paris, let us deal first with the conurbation. Baron Haussmann's rational replanning of central Paris in the 1860s was never extended to the new industrial suburbs that after 1870 grew up higgledy-piggledy outside the gates. Aubervilliers, Les Lilas, Issy-les-Moulineaux – lovely names for ghastly places – these and scores of other townlets arose while Paris was sucking the blood from the rest of France, and they became, as the planning expert Peter Hall put it, 'a vast, ill-conceived, hastily constructed emergency camp to house the labour force of Paris, presenting almost the limit of urban degeneration'.[2]

2 *The World Cities*, Weidenfeld & Nicolson, 1966.

Renoir's pastoral canvas of the Seine at Argenteuil, painted in the 1870s, was soon blotted out beyond recognition.

After 1918 this kind of growth slowed down. But, with land prices so low, a different type of excrescence now appeared in the suburbs, the individual *pavillon*. The Parisian *petit bourgeois* found that he could afford to realize a dream that he shares with the Englishman: a suburban cottage with a garden. But instead of the English ribbon-development of that period, there was anarchy. Some 80,000 little red-roofed *pavillons* spread their ungainly rash of assorted shapes across the outer suburbs, and were among the few new buildings in greater Paris between the wars. Then after 1945 the population again rose rapidly, and new blocks of flats were flung up piecemeal to cope with it. Over 2 million dwellings have been built in greater Paris since the war, to house or rehouse well over half the population. But only since the 1960s has much attempt been made to plan the new suburbs coherently; at first, stray blocks of flats were planted anywhere, usually in vacant gaps where land was cheap; nor was much effort made to provide these sad new dormitories with proper equipment such as hospitals, playing-fields, even schools. Suburban public transport was appalling too, and when the housing crisis was at its worst, in the 1950s, the difficulty of finding a flat near one's work often made matters worse. A worker might have to get up at 5 a.m. to make a two-hour train journey via central Paris to his factory on the far side of town, arriving back home at 8 p.m.

As in so many cases in the France of that period, it was de Gaulle's Government that finally took action, after the Fourth Republic's *laisser-faire*. In 1961 de Gaulle set up a new planning office for the Paris region, under Paul Delouvrier, an assertive technocrat and former delegate-general in Algeria. Greater Paris' population was growing at over 130,000 a year, and Delouvrier believed that so high was France's birth-rate, and so vast the rural exodus, that this trend would inevitably continue, despite the policies of shifting industry to other regions. He foresaw (wrongly, as it today appears) that the Paris region would grow spontaneously to 12 million by 1985 and 14 or possibly 16 million by A D 2000. And his solution was to draw up a grandiose master-plan, to enable the growth to take place coherently, not chaotically as hitherto.

His *Schéma Directeur* (directive outline) of 1963 is still the basis of today's planning, even though it has since been modified to meet changing conditions. The essence of its thinking was that Paris would be asphyxiated unless it were made polycentric. The British post-war solution of 'new towns', previously rejected in the 1950s as not being in the French tradition, was now espoused on a titanic scale, as the *Schéma* decreed five new cities, each with a population due to rise eventually to about 400,000: Cergy-Pontoise to the north-west, Marne-la-Vallée to the east, Melun-Sénart and Evry to the south-east, St-Quentin-en-Yvelines to the south-west. These towns are fifteen to twenty-five miles from the city centre, essentially part of the conurbation and much closer than their equivalents around London, such as Stevenage. It was planned that each town, at the same time as its new housing, would receive also a proper range of amenities so as to make it more than a mere dormitory – shops and schools, leisure and welfare centres, even light industries and offices to reduce the amount of commuting. Building began soon after 1970, and today the towns are more or less successfully taking shape, though on a more modest scale than first planned (see pp. 303–5).

The *Schéma* also decreed new road and transport networks, the decentralization of various activities from the city centre, and a zoning of the suburbs that might make it possible gradually to absorb and renovate the existing ugly mess. The *Schéma* was quickly accused, especially by the Left, as being far too grandiose and technocratic, 'a pipe-dream of polytechnicians'. Such opposition was mostly just political, but there were also more practical objections, over the wisdom of creating new towns on such a scale, and over the *Schéma*'s neglect of a proper green-belt policy like London's. Whatever the force of these and other arguments, the *Schéma* did at least show boldness and imagination. Something was being done at last; without some plan of this kind, Paris would soon have become as monstrously unmanageable as any mushrooming Third World megalopolis.

The French economic boom of the '60s made it possible to release extra funds for renovating the old suburbs, so that outer Paris could at last receive the community services essential for making life tolerable. For example, whereas no new hospitals at all were built in greater Paris in 1934–60, ten were completed in the 1960s. New theatres, colleges, swimming-pools and libraries at last began to enliven *la triste banlieue*, which hitherto had been desperately short of such facilities save in a few privileged bourgeois reserves such as St-Cloud and Versailles. Nanterre, largely working class, received a new theatre and a large new university (to become famous in 1968), and then in the 1970s several leading *grandes écoles* – including Polytechnique and HEC – moved from their cramped quarters in central Paris to spacious new parkland premises south-west of the city.

Perhaps the most successful result of the new planning has been in transport. Six major motorways today radiate from Paris to other parts of France, and all of them link directly with the Boulevard Périphérique, completed in 1970. In today's world it has become fashionable to decry the urban motorway, yet there is no doubt that traffic in greater Paris would rapidly have become stifled without this new network, far more impressive and effective than anything in the London area. The Périphérique diverts all through traffic from the Ville de Paris, while the new tunnels under the Bois de Boulogne enable the motorist to whizz out from the Arc de Triomphe to Versailles in twenty minutes (save at peak hours). In fact, the Périphérique has now become saturated at rush hours, and a much-needed second ring motorway is being built about five miles further out, linking such places as Versailles, Orly and St-Denis. New express Métro lines (see p. 285) go far into the suburbs, and suburban bus services have been improved though they are still far from adequate. Finally, in 1974 the most ambitious of the *Schéma's* transport schemes was inaugurated: the new Charles de Gaulle international airport at Roissy, north-east of Paris, today sharing traffic with the older Orly airport, to the south. Roissy's space-age tubular travelators may confirm Jacques Tati's worst nightmares, but passengers tend to be pleased with this system of rapid access to aircraft, with no long walks. The only snag is that the two airports are so far apart that changing planes from one to the other can involve tedious delays and even missed connections.

The putting into practice of the *Schéma Directeur* has been on balance successful, even though it has been slowed down by the usual hazards of budgetary cuts, bureaucratic and legal delays, human and political opposition. When the 'regions' were created in 1964, Delouvrier became super-prefect of what today is called the Ile-de-France Region, comprising eight departments and an area of 5,000 square miles, much of it rural. Despite his powers of coordination, he soon fell foul of the inevitable inter-ministerial rivalries, often sharper in the Paris area than further afield; for instance, work on the big project at La Défense was held up for years by the failure of the Ponts et Chaussées department to widen the Pont de Neuilly. The prefect even found that the Ministers of Finance and Construction were tending to violate the *Schéma* behind his back; anxious to shore up public funds with help from private finance, they sanctioned hundreds of speculative schemes that broke the strict zoning rules of the master-plan, and he was furious. Above all, Delouvrier ran into opposition from the region's communes, many of them in Left-wing hands and none too ready to comply with the State. Mayors on the Right as well as the Left tended to complain, with some justification, that the authors of the *Schéma* had failed to consult them adequately. Even more than in the provinces, it was the State officials who did the planning and took the decisions: 'How on earth,' said one technocrat, 'can you expect the mayor of some piffling suburb to grasp our real problems? His arguments would simply have held things up.' This tended to be

Delouvrier's own attitude, and his arrogance so annoyed a number of small-town Gaullist mayors that in 1969 Pompidou found it expedient to replace him. After this the 1972 reforms further altered the picture, for the region now had its own assembly and this proved a little more effective than most in France at making use of its limited powers and not letting the prefect dictate all the decisions. Now, under the reforms of the Socialist Government, this region like others is due to receive a greater autonomy with a stronger democratic basis. This may possibly make for better coordination of planning between the 1,278 communes in this vast conurbation.

Since the mid-1970s another major new factor has appeared, which has eased the burden of the town-planners. The region's annual population growth has begun to slow right down, from about 125,000 to a mere 50,000 in 1979. This has been due partly to the decline in the national birth-rate and the recent curbs on foreign immigration, also to the new tendency of Parisians to depart for the provinces. Delouvrier's forecast of a minimum 14 million population by AD 2000 has now been revised to 11 million. This means there is much less urgency to press ahead fast with big projects like the 'new towns'. And this happens to have coincided both with State spending cuts due to the economic crisis, and with the shift in public opinion away from 'gigantism' and towards ecology. So since 1978 the *Schéma Directeur* has been under modification, and this time the decisions are not dictated by the planners but debated carefully by the assembly in consultation with the mayors. Times have changed.

The principal revision is that the target size for each of the five new towns has been reduced from 400,000 to a more realistic figure of 200,000. Most of them now have 20,000 to 30,000 new inhabitants, and are growing by about 6,000 a year. Other changes in the *Schéma* mark an attempt to preserve forests and farming land on the fringe of the conurbation, and to cease indulging the motor car. At last, there is an embryonic green-belt policy. Building of the outer ring motorway (A 86) is going ahead, but its proposed western section has run into strong opposition from Gaullist politicians who do not want it to cut through the forests near Versailles, and officialdom is much more sensitive to this kind of cause than it would have been in the 1960s. Plans for a third ring motorway, ten miles further out, have been postponed indefinitely.

So the race against time, to save the *Ville Lumière* from the twilight of asphyxia, looks as if it is being won after all. The original *Schéma* laid much of the essential new infrastructure; the revised version aims to safeguard the human scale. The vast Paris suburbs today present a bewildering variety of urban styles that is hardly describable. Old villages have been engulfed by new high-rise estates, yet keep something of their village character. The California-style garden cities around Versailles, with their swimming-pools and sun-terraces, contrast with the dour 1950s tenements of the 'Red' eastern suburbs such as Aubervilliers. New flyovers swoop above the jumble of pre-war *pavillons* or grimy factories surviving from the last century. Except in the precincts of the 'new towns', it is mostly higgledy-piggledy and rarely beautiful, but it is vibrant with renewal. The vacant lots and seedy shacks of earlier years are gradually being replaced by ritzy hypermarkets, municipal swimming-pools, avant-garde theatres, clinics, kindergartens, or imposing new *mairies* or *préfectures* of glass and steel.

For the Ville de Paris itself, the issues since the war have been different: when archaic mess lies cheek-by-jowl with historic beauty, how do you modernize the one without spoiling the other? Can a brash up-to-date business metropolis co-exist with romantic *'vieux Paris'*? Baron Haussmann, prefect of the Seine department in 1853–70, modernized Paris in his own manner, driving his broad boulevards through the congested bowels of the old city. To some, he was a vandal; but the commoner verdict was that he turned Paris into the most graceful and well-planned capital in Europe. Without the boulevards, today she could not breathe. But from Haussmann's day until de Gaulle's almost nothing more was done, and one reason lay with the city's feeble local government. From 1871 for more than a century the municipal council had even less autonomy than the smallest village commune; it was allowed no mayor, and was ruled directly by the departmental prefect, for the State was haunted by memories of 1789, 1848 and 1871, and was keen to grant as little power as possible to the 'dangerous' Paris populace. With no mayor to lead them, the generally conservative councillors left the Government to take the main initiatives for planning. Yet they were also peeved at their dependence and did not lack powers of veto; and it was the consequent stalemate between council and State, persisting through the Third and Fourth Republics, that led to the almost total absence of effective new planning. Governments in their turn were too weak or short-lived to challenge the city fathers with controversial projects. Thus an essential measure to decongest the centre by removing the huge food markets (Les Halles), first mooted in the 1920s, was repeatedly blocked by the council right up until the 1960s. Yet in the post-war years business activity and motor traffic in Paris were growing fast, and the failure to deal with the ensuing problems was one factor that led the EEC to prefer the more manageable city of Brussels as its headquarters. Paris, as someone put it, 'muffed her chance to become Europe's capital'.

De Gaulle's return in 1958 brought at last a more forceful Government approach. And the council, itself with a Gaullist majority, acquiesced in the new plans; de Gaulle stood no nonsense! So the next few years saw serious attempts to bring Paris in line with modern needs without spoiling her beauty. Les Halles *were* finally removed, to the suburbs. The blackened façades of public and private buildings were scoured clean. New expressways and much needed new office complexes were projected, while a start was also made on restoring historic areas such as the Marais. The aim was to keep a sane balance between aesthetic and practical priorities, in a city with so much worth preserving but also so much to rebuild. Paris – as mayor Chirac has said more recently – cannot become a museum-piece like Venice; like any modern metropolis, she needs new roads and buildings, but these must be made to blend with the old. This has been the guiding policy of the planners, and in the 1960s it seemed to be working quite well; despite a few aesthetic blunders such as the Montparnasse tower, there was much less ugly piecemeal rebuilding of central office areas than in London. It was only in the early 1970s that things began to go wrong, as Pompidou's regime showed itself less concerned with aesthetics than de Gaulle's, and more lenient towards the high-rise developers in the interests of boosting Paris as a world business capital. Parisians became alarmed at the threat of 'Manhattan-on-Seine', as the Mother of the Muses steadily became the Mother of Mammon.

No one voiced more alarm than Giscard himself, who in 1974 straightway clamped down on the *laisser-faire* policy of 'gigantism' and vetoed new skyscrapers. He also decided to end the anomaly of Paris having no mayor. Was this a genuine liberal move? Or was it, as his critics on the Left were quick to allege, that with slum clearance and rocketing rents the city was rapidly losing its working class, so there was now much less danger of a replay of 1871? (May '68, after all, was no more than a middle-class student frolic, and for many years now the citizens had elected a clear Right-wing majority to the council.) Anyway, Giscard felt that his friend and ally Michel d'Ornano was well placed to become mayor; and it was ironic that the man who actually won the post, in March 1977, was none other than his arch-rival, Jacques Chirac. The ensuing tensions between Elysée and Hotel de Ville caused some difficulties with planning. And yet, whatever their personal frictions, Giscard and Chirac did seem to share much the same vision of where Paris should now move – towards 'quality of life' rather than towers of concrete. Chirac is today undisputed boss of Paris, and the Government – Mitterrand's as much as Giscard's – plays a far less assertive role in planning than before 1977. But before we look in detail at this new situation, and at the curious record in office of bulldozer Chirac, we must examine how Paris has changed physically in the past two decades.

Will any modern skyscraper always be out of place in a city of such classic harmony? Or, if carefully sited and well designed, could it even enhance the city's beauty? It was not until the late 1960s that this controversy broke out, for central Paris had for long avoided the high-rise fever gripping other big world cities. Until that time the only large-scale project of the kind was taking shape well outside the city limits, at La Défense, two miles west of the Arc de Triomphe; within the charmed circle of historic Paris, the few post-war buildings of any note tended to be elegant in themselves and in tune with their surroundings. This was so of the Y-shaped UNESCO headquarters opened in 1958 behind the Ecole Militaire, and of the circular Maison de la Radio beside the river in Auteuil. True, there were some less attractive exceptions, such as the barrack-like science faculty block that now brashly faces the romantic old *quais* of the Ile St-Louis, but at least it is not very tall. In a city where you cannot so much as cut down a tree without permission, there have always been formal rules about the height of new buildings – varying from 20 metres or so in central areas to 37 in outer *arrondissements* – and these were usually abided by, especially when the vigilant André Malraux was de Gaulle's Minister of Culture. His conservation committees had a decisive say in zones of historic value. When the Ministry of Agriculture wanted to build itself a nine-storey block in the Faubourg St-Germain, it was obliged to reduce the plan to five storeys, the same height as the rest of that graceful old quarter.

But then matters changed, under business pressures. Modern office and commercial space was growing desperately short in booming Paris, and developers complained that land prices and other costs were such that they could not make ends meet without building high. The Government gave way. In 1968–70 central Paris acquired its first real skyscraper, and it was a monstrosity, a broad 209-metre tower rising up from the heart of Montparnasse, flanked by two vast rectangular blocks, equally monolithic, each 250 metres long and 60 high. The ensemble contains offices, flats and shops. Most Parisians were outraged, for not only are the buildings ugly in themselves, but the tower is out of scale with the Left Bank skyline and dwarfs nearby monuments such as the Invalides: 'The charm of the view from my office,' joked one executive on the forty-eighth floor, 'is that this is the one building in Paris from which you can't see the tower.' How was the scheme ever sanctioned? Malraux is said to have approved of it personally, an odd lapse of taste.

Other projects soon followed, with buildings less tall but far more numerous. Work started on a planned cluster of *fifty-eight* towers near the Porte d'Italie, each over 80 metres high, to contain shops and offices, and flats for 60,000 people. At least this was out near the periphery, well away from the more beautiful parts of the city. But another project was right on the river, barely a mile downstream from the Eiffel Tower, where a series of 85-metre blocks went up along the Left Bank in what had been a slummy district. At least they are well spaced, set on multiple levels amid small gardens; they are grouped in some harmony with each other, and in terms of urban renewal they have greatly improved the area. But they too have been turning Paris into one more high-rise city. In the early '70s it was the same story in some other districts. Necessary and overdue urban renewal – in the tawdry outer *arrondissements* – suddenly became high-rise smallpox. Paris soon had over sixty new buildings qualifying as 'skyscrapers', and its familiar skyline was changing fast.

In the Pompidou era there were two kinds of debate: the practical and social, and the aesthetic. On the practical side, everyone agreed that slum clearance and renewal were urgent priorities, but the Government's critics argued that the high-rise solution was inhuman and would add to the city's already severe congestion. And the Left in particular strongly contested the arguments of Pompidou and his financial allies that high-rise office blocks were essential for Paris to develop her role as a leading world business capital. The aesthetic debate was even sharper. Many Parisians, especially older ones, objected to modern buildings in any form and wanted the city to stay unchanged. This view had no great influence. A more widely held opinion was that a big city, even Paris, *can* be enhanced by a few really high buildings, even if they are not so beautiful in themselves. The Eiffel Tower caused fury in its time, but today few lovers of *vieux Paris* would want it pulled down; and even the wedding-cake pomposity of Sacré-Coeur has come to seem acceptable because of its gleaming hill-top position. Of course, a skyscraper does pose more delicate aesthetic problems than a church or a slim spike of steel, and there are many modern architects who see Paris' vocation as that of a feminine city of slender towers and spires, not of square blocks. So, if skyscrapers are to be aesthetically permissible, all depends on their design and siting. The lone Montparnasse tower was a disastrous aberration, by any criterion. But in most other cases – as at Italie and La Défense – the planners did at least attempt to group the new buildings in some kind of harmonious balance with each other, rather than let them sprout piecemeal here and there, as in much of London outside the Barbican. The skyscrapers have also been kept away (again, Montparnasse excepted) from the beautiful heart of the city. But outside this inner perimeter they continued to sprout fast, changing the city's skyline.

There were many protests, but in such matters public opinion usually has less impact in France than in Britain. Finally, however, even Pompidou's entourage grew worried about the 'Manhattanization' of Paris, and in 1972 the prefect was ordered to limit the spread of high-rise buildings. Then Giscard came to power, with views that happened to coincide with the ecological shift in public feeling. He at once called a halt to the half-completed Italie scheme, cancelling a plan for a 180-metre tower there. And when Chirac took over *de facto* control of city planning, he continued this policy. Today, the official rules on heights of buildings are again respected, with only rare exceptions. Chirac's director of town-planning, Pierre-Yves Ligen, told me in 1979: 'The developers themselves have now turned against towers, because they know people want neither to work or live in them. I know a developer who does in fact have a permit from the old days to build a tower at Italie, but he's given up his plan to do so, as he doesn't think he'd sell the flats there.' So what is the legacy of the skyscraper boom? Has it ruined Paris irretrievably, or was it checked in time? That is a matter of opinion. Survey the city from any high central point, and you will see clusters here and there towards the periphery, but no downtown high-rise phalanx recalling Chicago or São Paolo. In my view, Paris has not been spoilt, any more than it was by the Eiffel Tower.

Over to the west you will see much the most dramatic cluster, at La Défense. This is in the suburbs, but is best considered in the context of the Ville de Paris, of which it is an integral extension in commercial terms. It has been variously described as 'an aesthetic outrage', 'an air-conditioned nightmare', and 'the most ambitious and exciting new urban project in Europe'. The *Herald Tribune* asked whether its bold and 'surprisingly beautiful' modern architecture was 'un-French or super-French'.

Amazingly, La Défense was conceived under the Fourth Republic. It was to be an office overspill for the cramped Champs-Elysées area and, more, a major new focus for the city's business life – thus accentuating the historic tendency of Paris, as of London, to shift its centre of gravity steadily westward. A 1,700-acre site was chosen astride the tip of the famous axis that runs from the Louvre up the Champs-Elysées to Neuilly. Here, just beyond Neuilly, the three communes concerned were persuaded to collaborate with a State development body, and first the existing mess of shacks, tenements and seedy workshops was gradually cleared. Today, the main high-rise project is nearing completion. About twenty-five skyscrapers of all shapes and sizes, some over forty floors high, rise up around a wide traffic-free piazza; here many big firms such as Esso and IBM have offices, 40,000 people work here by day and 20,000 live in tower blocks. A mammoth shopping-centre, said to be the largest in Europe, opened in March 1981. Underground there are acres of car-parks and a grandiose station of the new express Métro (RER). No cars enter La Défense at ground level: there are ring-roads, while a new motorway is now being tunnelled through the bowels, to carry the heavy through-traffic into the north-west outer suburbs.

Marvel of modernism, or soulless folly? Verdicts on La Défense vary. Many of the towers are dull and squat, but some of the taller ones are strikingly original, their façades made entirely of opaque reflecting glass, steely blue or golden brown, gleaming in the sunset. These buildings prove once again that contemporary French architects are generally more successful when being really modern in glass and steel than when following more traditional styles. Of course, if this ensemble had been set in central Paris, it would have clashed horribly with the classic townscape; but here as an entity on its own it has many merits. And its planners have made efforts to enliven the big central piazza with colour and movement. It is a veritable outdoor modern art-gallery: a huge scarlet stabile by Calder, a fresco by Atila, gaudy grotesques by Miró that look like figures from a carnival float, and a multi-coloured ornamental pool by Agam where fountains rise and fall in tune to music. The piazza also has a souk, a flea-market, outdoor cafés and art exhibitions, concerts on summer evenings, the lot; self-consciously contrived if you like, but not dull. Some blocks of flats are in ziggurat form with bold stripes of red, blue, green and orange; others, by the idiosyncratic Emile Aillaud, are a series of round or petal-shaped towers with random circular windows, their walls 'camouflaged' with stylized cloud-patterns in white, sky-blue and violet. Many modern-minded critics rave over La Défense's lively originality. But from Paris' point of view, the main aesthetic objection to it has been that its towers uncomfortably block the horizon of the great urban vista stretching up from the Louvre. For this reason, Giscard in 1974 cancelled a much-contested plan for giant twin 'mirror towers' that were to form a glinting kinetic backdrop to the Arc de Triomphe, at the far end of La Défense. An alternative is now under discussion: conservationists will again beat their breasts, yet there seems no reason why an attractive modern building should not provide a fitting crown to this majestic thoroughfare.

And commercially is La Défense a success? Initially, a number of big firms leapt at the chance to move out from the congested central business areas, and the first towers were rapidly rented. Then came long delays, with rising costs causing lack of finance, and then the economic crisis put a dramatic halt to the Paris office boom of the early '70s, so that by 1976 many of the completed towers were standing half empty. The project seemed threatened. The Government could not even persuade its own Ministries to make the move; despite pressure on them, Education and Finance refused to transfer departments to La Défense as their staff felt it was too far away. Finally, late in 1978, the Government urgently allocated new funds to improve services, while the Paris office market began to improve spontaneously, and La Défense was in business again. A year later, the only office block with much space unlet was the celebrated Tour Manhattan with its façade of gleaming glass;[3] it belongs to the Emir of Kuwait and he has been choosy about his tenants, refusing to let to any firm trading with Israel! But other firms in other towers include Fiat, Mobil Oil, Crédit Lyonnais and a host of other big names, attracted by rents averaging 600 francs a square metre, half the level of central Paris. The First National City Bank and Elf-Aquitaine are now building their own towers. Yet, ironically, by 1981 the Government had still failed to induce a single Ministry to take the plunge.

Like the Languedoc resorts, La Défense will stand as a memorial to an era of grandiosity that is now ended, for the foreseeable future. It has its faults, but remains a striking example of the French ability to plan imaginatively on a bold scale. And in business terms, La Défense has enabled Paris to expand as a world economic capital without high-rise redevelopment of the older office areas on the Right Bank. Since the 1950s there have in theory been strict restrictions on all new office building in these central areas, where much commercial activity is far too cramped, especially around the Bourse. But the policy has been haphazardly applied. For many years little offices were creeping, often clandestinely, into older residential blocks quite unsuited for them, especially in bourgeois districts such as the sixteenth *arrondissement*. The Government was torn between contradictory needs: to limit congestion, but to allow economic growth. In Pompidou's day, the latter briefly won the upper hand; his aim was to build up the international role of Paris, and British developers in particular moved into the office market on a big scale. But this boom collapsed with the economic crisis, and by 1975 about a million square metres of office space were standing empty in the Paris area. So the problem for a while solved itself. However, under Giscard the rules were again tightened: under latest State regulations, if a landlord pulls down a block of flats he can put offices in the new one only if it includes the same residential space as before, and this is usually not possible, for there are also strict rules limiting density. This policy

3 It was the front-cover illustration of the 1977 edition of my Pelican book *The New France*, predecessor of this present book.

annoys Chirac, whose municipal revenue comes quite largely from taxes on businesses. He has said, 'Contrary to general belief, there are now too *few* offices in Paris. The Government proclaims a policy, which I share, of strengthening the city's world role by attracting international firms to set up headquarters here. Yet the building of offices inside the city is now virtually banned. It's the fault of D A T A R and its policy of transferring services to the regions.'

Chirac also voices concern at the steady decline in the city's population, from 2.8 to 2.1 million since 1954. It is still falling by 40,000 a year. If Paris were less crowded, this would by now be a serious problem, as in some other big Western cities where the residents have deserted the downtown areas. But Chirac must admit that much of Paris is still too congested; people are packed as densely as on Manhattan and twice as densely as in London. Paris like other Latin towns has a tradition of in-city living, which makes for lively animation but has proved ill suited to the growth of traffic and modern commerce. The noise of the high-pitched French car-engines reverberates in the narrow streets between their seven- or eight-storey buildings, especially claustrophobic in the workaday districts that the tourist seldom sees; by comparison most of an equivalent poorer part of London such as Wandsworth or Holloway seems a haven of space and calm. Green parks cover only 7 per cent of the Ville de Paris, less than half the figure for London or New York, and the only parks of any size are at either extremity, Boulogne and Vincennes.

Slum clearance has done something to alleviate the discomforts, after a slow start. By the mid-'60s only about 25 per cent of the real slums had been cleared, and in many poorer quarters you could still find stinking alleys with crumbling façades and dank courts, where large families lived huddled without running water: the 'other Paris' from the chic of the Faubourg St-Honoré. Just as wartime destruction helped France's railways to become more modern than British ones, so Paris planners sometimes envied London's East End for the Blitz! But today most of the really bad slums have either been pulled down or rehabilitated, often through improvements made by the occupiers or landlords. Between the 1968 and 1975 censuses the percentage of homes without indoor flushing lavatories fell from 45 to 26.2 per cent – but that is still a shockingly high figure for a prosperous nation.

Various renewal schemes are gradually easing the congestion. But land costs are so high that most of the new housing is middle class; the slum-dwellers have been moved out to the new suburbs, and for years the Left has complained that Paris is steadily becoming a 'bourgeois ghetto'. But today it is not only the workers who leave: housing is now at such a premium that thousands of young middle-class families too are obliged each year to seek homes in the suburbs, and the city's population is ageing. This is the exodus that worries Chirac. He has launched new programmes for lower-cost housing, and also for helping small factories and artisan firms to survive and expand; and he denounces the Government's 'anti-Paris' policies which he alleges make his task harder. Of course his motives may be mixed, and it is easy to point out that the council needs local industry for its revenue, also that too drastic a decline in population would reduce the political influence of Paris. But at least Chirac *has* succeeded in speeding up the building of subsidized 'social' housing. He has also launched a number of operations for rehabilitation of run-down areas; as elsewhere in Europe, this today is more in vogue than wholesale demolition.

The major renovation scheme in central Paris – Les Halles – has caused more controversy and confusion than any other urban planning project in post-war France. For many years a main cause of congestion in the city had been the concentration there of the nation's central food and wine markets. The latter, the Halle aux Vins, was finally removed in the early 1960s. Under the Fourth Republic the authorities had repeatedly failed in their efforts to winkle the wine-traders out of their ancient stronghold near the Jardin des Plantes: their political lobby was too strong. Then de Gaulle simply banished them by decree to a site in the outskirts, and in their place he sanctioned a much-needed but ugly new university block. It was a Gaullist victory for rational planning, if not for aesthetics.

The central food market, Les Halles, in an ancient and teeming district near the Louvre, took longer to shift. Zola called it 'the belly of Paris', and every morning it blocked whole square miles with its lorries. Whereas London's little Covent Garden was merely a market for samples, Les Halles physically handled one-fifth of the nation's fruit, vegetables and meat. But the middlemen resisted change; they made fat profits out of the organized chaos, and they had a powerful lobby. It took years of pressure before the transfer of Les Halles was finally agreed, in 1963. The meat market was shifted to the north-east outskirts, and in 1969 the fruit and vegetable sections were moved to a spacious modern *marché-gare* at Rungis, near Orly (see p. 226). Today, tourists can no longer jostle with *les forts des Halles* in their blood-stained aprons, as they drink their onion soup at the Pied de Cochon after a theatre or nightclub. Picturesqueness has suffered a blow, but central Paris breathes more easily.

The future of the prime 86-acre site thus vacated was then the subject of a scarcely credible eleven-year wrangle, arising from the widely varying interests of the general public, big business and State prestige. Thousands of architects were consulted, scores of plans were eagerly adopted then bitterly discarded, as the State, the city council and the public fought it out, amid endless outcry and indecision. On one point all were agreed: part of the zone would become a small park, for there was none other in this grimy quarter. But there consensus ended, and the battle-lines were set between ecologists and commercial interests. The latter won the first round, when Pompidou and the city council decided on a world trade centre, with a huge hotel and offices – very much in keeping with his capitalist-imperialist policy for Paris. It was also agreed that below ground level would be a big shopping complex, and below that a vast station for the new express Métro. Pompidou's plans provoked hostility, and defenders of *vieux Paris* were especially shocked when they saw that the demolition of Les Halles involved the tearing down of Victor Baltard's famous wrought-iron market pavilions. Proposals were canvassed for incorporating some of these graceful nineteenth-century structures into the new project, but Pompidou said no. Once again, public opinion proved its weakness in France.

Work began on the Métro station, and a huge hole was carved out. Then Pompidou was followed by Giscard, with a different vision: he listened to the views of local action groups and promptly cancelled the project for a big trade centre, which he agreed was inhuman and out of scale with the area. At last it seemed that ordinary Parisians were influencing the planners. There followed a further long delay while new plans were prepared, and meanwhile the gaping 'Hole of Les Halles' became a stock Paris joke, the largest urban hole in Europe, it was said. Finally in 1976 Giscard approved the sketches for a new and more classic design, with no business complex but a sizeable formal garden a little like the Tuileries; the pendulum had swung right back. The only aspects retained from the earlier plan were the underground station and shopping arcades, by now being built. But the city council was not happy with Giscard's ideas, and when Chirac became mayor there was yet another period of uncertainty and dissension. Ultimately in 1978 Giscard agreed that the State would wash its hands of Les Halles; Chirac took effective charge and promised a definitive solution.

The ungainly hole was finally embellished when the Métro station was opened, followed in 1979 by the shopping centre, known as the Forum. This is a most curious structure. It consists of a large sunken courtyard lined with arcades of glass and aluminium, which allow the daylight to filter into the three labyrinthine tiers of shops, all below surface level. Its admirers call it 'a crater of light' or 'an inverted glass pyramid'. The Forum's 40,000 square metres of selling space contain some of the top names in Paris fashion – boutiques of Cardin, Yves St-Laurent, Ted Lapidus – as well as two hundred other shops, various restaurants, ten theatres and cinemas both avant-garde and commercial, and a FNAC bookshop (see p. 406) as large as any in Paris. The Forum's critics say it is too élitist and already outmoded; on the other hand, you could say that it has brought a welcome touch of class to a humdrum area, and it is proving a commercial success. The FNAC has up to 100,000 clients on a Saturday.

In March 1980, exactly eleven years after the closure of Les Halles, Chirac proudly unveiled his final plan for the vacant ground beside the Forum. It turned out to be something of a compromise. There will be a formal garden with trees, bordered by a fantasy arrangement of steel-and-glass awnings and pavilions; also some office space. There may also be a large aquarium below ground level, together with a small cultural centre. The overall scheme will at least bring more space and more scope for leisure to the commercial maelstrom of central Paris, and it will not weigh too heavily on the city budget – important, if there is to be little business return on the investment. This at least is Chirac's argument. His project is due to be completed by 1984.

Four blocks to the east of Les Halles, there stands the most amazing and famous building in post-war France, the new Georges Pompidou cultural centre, usually known by its nickname 'Beaubourg'. This giant 'cultural Disneyland' of glass and steel and coloured pipes is architecturally far more provocative than anything at Les Halles; yet the Government brought it into being relatively smoothly. One explanation may be that Pompidou, apostle of high finance, was also a contemporary art enthusiast. In 1969 he proclaimed his desire to endow France with a modern cultural complex of the first world rank, both a museum and a place of creativity, where all the arts would rub shoulders. The site adopted was the Plateau Beaubourg, a piece of waste land in a then seedy area. Out of 681 entries, a selection committee chose a design by the Anglo-Italian architectural team of Richard Rogers and Renzo Piano. Their ultra-modernism was not quite what Pompidou had envisaged, but he acquiesced. Many Paris councillors and high officials were aghast, and they tried to block building permits: but the Government pushed the scheme through despite every kind of obstacle. Giscard, when he succeeded Pompidou, did not hide the fact that he was one of the sceptics. But by then it was too late to turn back. The centre was finally opened in 1977, having cost 1,000 million francs.

Its critics called it 'an arty oil-refinery'. Swathed in scaffolding and piping, Beaubourg deliberately wears an unfinished look, and its architects call it 'an inside turned outside': that is, all the service apparatus which is normally hidden away in a building is here proudly displayed, outside, in gaudy colours. The water mains are green, the electricity cables yellow, and the air-conditioning ducts are blue, just as on architects' charts. The main escalator too is on the outside, set in a glass tube that rises diagonally up the six-storey façade, thus providing panoramic views over Paris, and over the interior of the building whose walls are also of clear glass. Inside is Europe's largest modern art museum, a 400,000-volume library, auditoria, vast spaces for special exhibitions, and below ground level a music research centre run by Pierre Boulez (see pp. 606 and 614 on the centre's cultural activities).

Beaubourg at first caused a furore – as the Eiffel Tower had once done, another skeletal structure just as modernistic in its day. But gradually Parisians are coming to accept it, just as they now accept the Eiffel Tower. Its success with visitors is twice as great as expected: an average of 22,000 come each day, more than to the Eiffel Tower and the Louvre combined, more than to any other building in France. Many are attracted out of sheer curiosity, but an increasing majority come to use the cultural facilities, especially the young. As a centre for housing the arts, it might well have been just as effective with a less extravagant exterior, and indeed there are plenty who are drawn to make use of it *despite*, rather than because of, its bizarre appearance. But very many young people and intellectuals are fascinated by its see-through, let-it-all-hang-out quality, and by the snook it cocks at conventional palace-like museums. In fact, the main objections today are less to the building itself than to its siting. 'It would have been fine on the edge of Paris,' said one critic, 'but here it clashes disastrously with the much older buildings all around. It is a threat to the elegance of the Marais, just next door.' Others find this contrast exciting.

The project is one more token of the continuing French readiness to innovate imaginatively on an ambitious scale. Equally remarkable, the often chauvinistic French in this case resisted the temptation to make Beaubourg simply a showcase of national talents. Not only were the architects foreign, but the engineering and steelwork contracts went to British and German firms, a Swede was appointed to run the museum, and many of the new art works bought for it were American. Pompidou wanted an international flavour, and he got it, despite xenophobic murmurings from some quarters. Beaubourg today is a focus of world interest; it is also, as intended, a centre of local animation. It has revitalized a moribund district and has provoked an astonishing activity all around it. On fine days, the broad paved piazza in front of the building fills up spontaneously with fire-eaters, musicians, conjurers, clowns, Hyde-Park-style orators, all attracting the visitors with their medieval sideshows. It is a renewal of the Paris street tradition of *Les Enfants du Paradis*. And the little traffic-free streets between Beaubourg, Les Halles and Châtelet have blossomed with new art-galleries and antique shops, restaurants and *café-théâtres*. The area has become a *de facto* overspill for the now saturated and over-commercialized St-Germain-des-Prés area, and in a rather more attractive style, for much of the zone is now a pedestrian precinct. Chirac has a plan to extend this zone westward, creating a vast walkway stretching through the new Les Halles park as far as the Palais Royal. This could be valuable, for Paris still has too few traffic-free streets for a city of its size.

Today Chirac's overall policy for the city marks a continuation of the brightening-up and restoration schemes begun under de Gaulle. In the 1950s, this capital of European gaiety and chic gave an overriding impression of greyness and lack of paint. It was sometimes picturesque, as in parts of Montmartre and the Latin Quarter, but more often just depressing. Then, with rising prosperity, a number of shops and cafés began of their own accord to brighten their fronts with chromium or marble and fresh paint. But this glittering transformation was superficial, for the façades of upper floors were still black and peeling. Then in 1958 de Gaulle's new Minister of Construction, Pierre Sudreau, issued a warning that the decay was not merely unaesthetic, it was also eating at the fabric of the city. But he found it hard to act, for ground rents of most older buildings were still pegged so low that landlords had a valid excuse for not making improvements (see p. 289). So a law was passed allowing phased rent increases so long as part of the money was spent on cleaning housefronts and courtyards and other basic repairs. At the same time a forgotten law of 1852 was cunningly revived, which had made the *ravalement* ('scraping') of façades compulsory every ten years. This was effective, to many people's surprise, and within a few years the façades in most central areas were scoured pale. Meanwhile Malraux's Ministry of Culture set about cleaning public buildings and monuments; the Louvre, the Opéra, even Notre Dame, were restored to their original sandstone hues without damage to their fabric. This brightening up of the city was outwardly one of the most striking of changes in France under de Gaulle; it made Parisians feel more cheerful, and it did something to revive the badly tarnished image of 'Gay Paree'.

Malraux embarked also on the restoration of some neglected historic districts of Paris, notably the Marais. In the seventeenth century this was the most fashionable district of the city, but by the 1960s much of it was a slum; hundreds of its elegant old buildings had been carved up internally into tenements or workshops. Malraux initiated a law obliging landlords to share in the work and cost of restoration and was thus able to rescue an entire central zone. Today, thanks to his efforts combined with those of the city council and a few rich private owners, many of the loveliest old residences of the Marais are again in beautiful condition. Similar work was done in some other parts of Paris. But Malraux and de Gaulle failed entirely to tackle one of the city's most serious deficiencies, its lack of greenery – and this Chirac is now modestly starting to do. In addition to the fifteen-acre garden at Les Halles, larger parks are in planning or preparation stage near the periphery, notably at La Villette, the Quai de Bercy and the Quai André Citroën. The majestic esplanade in front of the Invalides, in recent years little more than a vast car-park, has now been grassed over; and Chirac has plans for closing to traffic the maze of useless minor roads that transect the Bois de Boulogne, leaving only one or two throughways and the partly concealed motorway. Habitués of the Bois – romantic lovers, nannies with children, prostitutes and the rest – will at last find some respite from the noise and the fumes.

So what is the overall verdict on Jacques Chirac's first years in office? Has Paris in practice benefited from having a mayor again, and so ambitious and controversial a one? Chirac is so often seen as a ruthless Right-wing demagogue that his apparent emphasis on humanism and ecology may seem surprising; and of course there are plenty of sceptics. This is not the place to discuss his inner motives nor his national strategy, of which being a successful mayor of Paris forms only a part. But there is no doubt that he has made an impact on the city. He does not regard his new post as merely honorific, but devotes a large slice of his famous energy and dynamism to the practical daily tasks of government, working long hours late at night in his sumptuous office in the Hôtel de Ville. If there is a baby to be kissed, Chirac smothers him or her with kisses. If there is an old folks' home to be opened, or a charity concert to be held, or a foreign potentate to be fêted, Chirac is toweringly there, with his large handshake and his thrusting rhetorical optimism; 'le Maire-Soleil', he's been called. And what has he actually *done*, besides the town-planning measures already quoted? He has allowed free travel on buses and Métro for the city's 80,000 unemployed. He has arranged free outings and holidays for the aged, given them free telephones, and used the city budget to top up their State pensions by 30 per cent. He has seen to it that the public flower-beds are more colourful, and the pavements swept cleaner, than ever before. He has ordained that 'Paris must be *en fête* every day of the year', that 'poetry must reanimate its streets' and its culture become less élitist, more populist, and to this end he has set up two hundred new local workshops for the citizens' 'artistic self-expression' and has resuscitated a number of traditional festivals long lapsed, such as the fair on the Pont Neuf in June with its folk-dancing, handicrafts and circus stunts. He has doubled the budget for leisure and arts and has launched two prestige projects with a popular flavour: the building of a big new sports complex by the Quai de Bercy, and the refurbishing of the city-owned Théâtre du Châtelet as a national centre of light opera.

As far as it goes, Parisians tend to be pleased with this campaign of sweetness and light, even if many are wary of Chirac's motives. 'The results are mainly cosmetic,' one Left-wing critic told me; 'he needed to prove rapidly that Paris would be changed by having a mayor, so he's launched this showy policy of flowers, fêtes and so on. But on a more serious level he's done little to fulfil his promises of creating new industry and better housing.' And a Giscardian councillor said, 'In a period of austerity, he's more than doubled the budget for civic receptions. He invites Brezhnev and other top-rank visitors to the town hall – it's pure vote-catching, and it'll rebound against him.' In political circles, the main criticism is of Chirac's expectedly autocratic style of rule. Of the city council's 109 members, 40 are on the Left, 53 are Gaullist and 14 Giscardian, but Chirac has managed to win some 7 of the latter over to his cause. This leaves him with a majority of docile supporters and enables him to bulldoze decisions through the council. Its members complain that they are consulted no more than under the old system, the only difference being that their boss is no longer a State prefect but a mayor in rivalry with the State. 'All French big-city mayors are kings, and Chirac more than any,' is a frequent comment. He has put his own loyalists into the key positions on sub-committees and other municipal bodies, and these tend to deliberate in secret – 'Just like the Communists,' said a frustrated Giscardian. Under the new Paris statute drawn up before Chirac was elected, the city is divided into eighteen wards each with its own committee responsible for minor local matters: a worthy attempt at decentralization. But of a committee's members, only one third are the city councillors elected by that ward; the other two-thirds are nominees of the town hall and of the mayor. This enables Chirac effectively to control every single ward committee, including the seven which electorally have Left-wing majorities. The opposition's sense of impotence in municipal affairs is thus increased: the ward committees, like the council itself, are little more than rubber-stamp bodies, and Chirac makes scant effort to consult the Left although it represents 40 per cent of electors.

In its relations with the State, Paris is now juridically in the same position as any other French town (see pp. 187–205). Its new 1977 statute did not increase its financial autonomy; the only change was that by now having a mayor, and so strong a mayor, it at last gained the moral and political power to stand up to the State. In practice, the situation in 1977–81 was dictated by the equivocal relations between Giscard and Chirac, rivals within the Government coalition, and since May 1981 it has been dictated by the hostility between Chirac and the Elysée. But this is nothing new in a big French town. When the Mayor provokes the President politically, the State machine tends to retaliate by exerting its financial controls more tightly, and there is constant argument over who should pay for what. Yet no one today disputes that it was high time this great city had its own mayor: the pre-1977 system, whereby Paris was run as a virtual Government department or sub-ministry, was clearly an absurd and degrading anomaly. The new statute at least allows a more coherent policy, with Paris taking its own planning decisions. But, alas it also demonstrates most forcibly that the French local government system allows a mayor too much autocratic power, and a man like Chirac in the nation's capital is going to exploit this for all it is worth. Nor will the Socialists' new municipal reforms, with their reduction of State tutelage, make things any better. Chirac in his paternalistic way has certainly done a lot for Paris: many of his cultural and environmental measures mark a step forward. But it is a mockery of democracy that this *Maire-Soleil* should be able to upstage Louis XIV in regal insolence.

I have left till last the crucial issue of transport in Paris. Here Chirac has relatively little jurisdiction, for although the city council is responsible for the building and upkeep of roads, it is the police who deal with traffic and street-parking, while public transport is run by a semi-autonomous body responsible primarily to the State.

It is the steady growth of car traffic that as much as anything has impeded the efforts of post-war planners to deal with congestion. Fewer people may live in the city than in the old days, but far more of them own cars, or bring them in from the suburbs. And the Parisian regards the daily use of his car as an inalienable human right. Individualist to the last, he insists on taking it into town in the imprudent hope that he, unlike the next man, will somehow beat the jams and find a parking space. He pleads as alibi the scarcity of taxis or – until recently – the archaism of public transport. So the authorities have faced the same dilemma as in other world cities: in order to keep the traffic moving, is the answer to pander to the motorist by endlessly building new freeways, tunnels and car-parks? Or is it to clamp down on the private car and provide alternatives? For many years the policy in Paris was the former: but now, with the energy crisis, at least an effort has been made to entice the citizen away from his beloved *bagnole*, with better public transport. In the past decade this has improved beyond recognition.

Various measures in the '50s and '60s enabled the authorities just about to keep abreast of an annual 10 per cent increase in the volume of traffic. Underpasses were built, some streets were widened and the one-way system was made the most extensive in Europe; even major avenues like the Boulevards St-Germain and Sébastopol are *sens unique*. Then in the later '60s a more expensive programme was put under way. Notably, tunnels were carved under the Louvre and the Place de la Concorde for a west-to-east expressway right across the city beside the Seine. This was completed in record time, and at most periods of the day it is now possible to cross central Paris at some speed, say from Boulogne to the Gare de Lyon. Exitways from the city were also improved, linking with the Boulevard Périphérique and the national motorways through elaborate networks of tunnels and flyovers – far more impressive than anything in London. But the Right Bank expressway goes only in one direction, and when plans were announced for complementing it with an east-to-west freeway along the Left Bank, there was an outcry at the threat this posed to the Notre Dame area with its famous and lovely *quais*. So Giscard, in the most striking of all his conservationist *coups*, banned the project outright as soon as he took power. Chirac among many others believes today that he was wrong, even on ecological grounds: a plan exists whereby this road could be roofed over, opposite Notre Dame, and the *quais* would be fully protected, indeed improved. But Giscard would not budge, and in matters affecting public monuments the State has the formal powers to trump the Paris council. So that part of the Left Bank is still a bottleneck area.

Traffic moves on average as fast in Paris as in London, but more unevenly. The motorist's progress tends to be either very fast or minimal. You can sweep majestically along the Right Bank, then get stuck for half an hour in the honeycomb of tiny streets towards the Bourse or the Gare de l'Est, caught in a cortège of horn-blowing Gallic frustration. This is the legacy of Haussmann: a few broad roads that mask a maze of narrow ones, often obstructed by cars parked illegally. Parking in fact is a worse problem in Paris than traffic. Far more cars are now owned than there are kerbside or garage spaces for them, and many people have no option but to keep them outside the city limits. The parking nightmare reached its height in the early 1970s, and has since been eased by a number of measures, notably the massive building of underground public car-parks which now have room for 60,000 vehicles. This has done a little to lessen the agony of evening parking in entertainment or residential districts, where the narrow streets between high blocks were simply not made for the motor age. To drive to a dinner party in Passy, or a bistrot or cinema in the Latin Quarter, is not quite the hell that it was ten years ago; but it may still involve twenty or thirty minutes of circling around frustratingly for a space, a vivid reminder that Paris still has twice the density of London.

Parking meters have also been belatedly introduced, and have simplified short-term daytime parking in business areas. For many years the only authorized system of kerbside parking in these zones was that of the adjustable disc placed inside the windscreen, but this was not very effective. Yet four times in the 1960s the city fathers rejected police proposals for parking meters. They judged these too inaesthetic for lovely Paris, and also they thought Parisians would never tolerate such an assault on their 'right' to free parking. By 1970 Paris was the only major world city without meters, but finally the police got their way and the first of these machines made a cautious debut on some central streets – only to be met with a wave of sabotage. Paper-clips, chewing-gum and false coins were shoved into them; some were sawn off in the night. This was partly the work of angry motorists, partly hooliganism; a girl of nine caught choking meters with paper-clips cheerfully admitted, 'All my friends do it.' But the wave subsided, and today there are 40,000 meters and Parisians have come to accept them. They are monitored by girls in blue uniforms called *'pervenches'* (periwinkles) who assign tickets for 50-franc fines for overstaying one's time and 120 francs or more for 'obstructive' parking. The trouble is that 90 per cent of motorists then fail to pay these fines, judging they will probably get away with it as there is inadequate machinery for following them up. It makes nonsense of the whole system, loses the State some 1,000 million francs a year, and could be seen as one more sign that officialdom is still too lenient with the city motorist. However, in 1980 the Government began drafting 'the ultimate deterrent': a new law allowing the removal of driving licences from anyone caught not paying his fine.

Fewer people might use their cars, were it not for the great Paris taxi racket. In theory, licensed taxis are as plentiful as in London or New York; in practice they are far more scarce, especially at times when needed most. They tend to vanish from noon to 2 p.m., and from 6 to 8 p.m. The explanation is that taxi-drivers operate a closed shop, and they exploit the situation by taking leisurely meals at conventional times – 'In New York or London,' wrote Art Buchwald, 'taxis drive their clients to their destination; in Paris, you accompany the *chauffeur* towards his garage or his restaurant.' The drivers' argument is that traffic at peak hours is so slow that they cannot clock up enough cash on the meter to make it worth trading at those times, so they stay at home. And they stubbornly refuse to allow an increase in the number of taxis. Their lobby got this number pegged at 13,000 in 1937, and since then it has risen by only 1,300. Whenever the authorities propose a massive issue of new licences, this is met by strikes or the threat of strikes. For this closed shop is one of the most potent in France, and it operates a lucrative black market: when a driver dies or retires, his licence discreetly changes hands at a going rate of some 80,000 francs. The drivers seek to justify their behaviour by claiming that a large increase in numbers, though it might solve the customer's peak-hour problem, would put most of them out of business, especially as fares have not been allowed to rise as fast as petrol prices and other costs. Yet more taxis could mean fewer private cars and thus far more trade for the taxi-drivers.

Meanwhile a visitor to Paris might be advised to take a bus or the Métro, rather than wait around for a taxi. Now that public transport has become so much more efficient and comfortable, the middle-class prejudice against it is beginning to wane; and already this has borne some fruit in the official campaign to limit car traffic. Fifteen years ago, London's public transport was far better than Paris', but now we have seen a sharp reversal, as London buses and tube trains get dirtier, slower and more infrequent. Is this a symptom of the two countries' changing fortunes, or at least of their attitudes to public services? In the 1970s London Transport invested only one-third as much as its Paris equivalent, RATP,[4] which also has a far more coherent long-term development policy. Moreover, the Paris passenger is paying only 37 per cent of the real cost of his ticket. The rest is met by a large RATP subsidy from the State, and lesser ones from the city, the region, and suburban communes, in line with the campaign to encourage use of public transport.

The bus service, till recently rather ramshackle, is now a joy. New and far more comfortable vehicles have been introduced and their numbers and frequency greatly increased. Down many boulevards and avenues there are now traffic-free bus lanes, seventy miles of them, so that along much of their route the green single-deck buses move at a spanking pace. Smart new bus-shelters have been built everywhere, with detailed bus-route maps; and you now queue in an orderly Anglo-Saxon manner, and no longer have to pull a numbered queue-slip from a machine and then wait like some convict for the conductor to call your number. Indeed there are no more conductors (unlike London), for all buses have automatic punchers, and the *carnets* of tickets are con-

4 The Régie Autonome des Transports Parisiens, responsible firstly to the State, also to the city and local bodies.

veniently usable on bus or Métro alike. In 1975 the RATP introduced a *Carte Orange* runabout season ticket, now costing 70 to 175 francs a month depending on zone, and valid on any bus, Métro or local SNCF train route in the Paris area. Its 1,350,000 subscribers give some idea of its success. Thanks to all these new factors, the total of passengers using Paris buses, which had been falling alarmingly for several years, has more than doubled since 1974 and is still rising. Quite a revolution.

Buses have long been acceptable to the bourgeoisie. But till recently the old Métro, with its nostalgic stench, prison-like automatic barriers, long Kafka-esque corridors and sad ticket-punchers like *tricoteuses* at the guillotine, had remained defiantly a working-class institution. 'So sorry I'm late,' says Marie-Chantal, archetypal French deb, in a Parisian joke of the '50s, 'but my brother Claude had taken the Jag, Pierre had taken the Mercedes, so I took the Métro – *tu le connais*?' London's debs have been cheerfully boarding trains at Sloane Square since W. S. Gilbert's day; but London's tube-trains with their plushy seating were for long a cut above even the first-class carriages of the Métro. So what would Marie-Chantal make of it today? She would find sleek new trains, rather less spartan, and many stations given a face-lift, with tastefully arty décor that mirrors their *quartier*: e.g. classical art reproductions along the platforms of the Louvre station. Gone are the ticket-punchers, the barriers, the stench; tickets can be bought in booklets, thus avoiding the need to queue, and the flat rate for any length of journey obviates ticket-collectors too. It also means that a longer journey can be up to four or five times as cheap as its London equivalent. Trains are far more frequent than in London, and the Métro is more popular, carrying 4.5 million people a day against London's 2 million. The only real snag is the long walk needed to change trains at some larger stations, up to six hundred metres.

Above all, the network has been greatly extended, with new express trains going far into the suburbs. Hitherto the Métro barely penetrated outside the Ville de Paris, but in the 1960s work began on the much-trumpeted new Réseau Express Régional (RER). Its first thirty-five mile line was finally completed in 1977 at a cost of 5,000 million francs, running from St-Germain-en-Laye via the heart of Paris to Boissy-St-Leger in the outer south-east suburbs. The journey from St-Germain to the Opéra takes a mere twenty minutes. This RER line links at some points with the old Métro, and its main stations – La Défense, Etoile, Châtelet Les Halles, etc. – are of a size and opulence rivalling those of Moscow. Châtelet-Les Halles is said to be the largest and busiest underground station in the world, a seven-acre cave-palace of space-age design. Here the old Métro's multi-junction of Châtelet forms an ensemble with the new Les Halles station, hub of the RER: a second RER line now runs from here into the far south-west suburbs, and in 1982 a short new section to the Gare du Nord will integrate with SNCF lines, allowing RER trains a twenty-seven-minute direct run from Les Halles to Roissy airport. This in fact is one of the most radical aspects of the new system: it is at last creating organic links between those old arch-enemies, the RATP (which operates the Métro and RER) and the SNCF (State Railways).

The old Métro was built in 1900 with a different gauge to the existing SNCF suburban lines, thus making integration impossible. It is said today that one reason for this was political: the State did not want a transport system that might make it easier for Red suburban hordes to surge into Paris, in time of unrest! Another reason was quite simply that the SNCF was jealous of its new rival and insisted on the different gauge. But today there is more rationality: the new RER does have the same gauge as the SNCF, and gradually the two networks will integrate so that the old main-line termini (Gares du Nord, de Lyon, etc.) will no longer be cul-de-sacs but part of a trans-Paris system. A start has already been made by linking the small Invalides and Orsay termini. How old-fashioned all this makes London look! It is as if a British Rail train from Surrey arriving at Waterloo could move straight on via the tube to King's Cross and out into Essex. No wonder transport experts agree that Paris is developing the world's best subway and suburban system. It is an expensive process, but it does seem to be bringing results. People are beginning to use their cars a little less in greater Paris; and despite the vast increase in car ownership, the traffic jams are less bad then twenty years ago.

Sociologically a number of Paris districts have been changing, under the impact of the builder's hammer or the iron whim of fashion. Centre-city living has always been chic, and recent expensive restoration schemes such as that of the Marais have accentuated this trend on the part of smart Parisians. Dukes and film-stars vie with each other to buy the elegant apartments in and around the Place des Vosges, where even a two-room flatlet may cost a million francs. The Ile St-Louis, where Pompidou lived, has seen a similar vogue. Elsewhere, the *haute bourgeoisie* retains its strongholds in the eighteenth-century *septième*, the nineteenth-century *seizième* and thoroughly modern Neuilly. But many districts have long tended to be more socially intermixed than in London, partly because of the way the Haussmann-era blocks were built, with flats of varying size and quality under the same roof. This was intensified by the housing shortage; middle-class people took flats where they could find them, and if the controlled rent was low they felt disinclined to move. So even today you still find many a 'good' family living at a 'poor' address, behind the Gare de l'Est for instance, or near Pigalle, and it confirms their reluctance to entertain at home. But rebuilding has brought changes. Many previously humble areas, notably in the four-teenth and fifteenth *arrondissements*, have been growing more bourgeois, just like Fulham or Islington; in Paris this is due essentially to new privately built blocks of flats and not to the conversion of older houses as in London. Other middle-class families have been moving to the suburbs, by necessity or by choice; and out to the west the glossy new luxury housing estates have been filling up with the new-affluent social *milieux* of computer programmers, P R whizz-kids and the like. Commut-ing has become a middle-class norm, and *la banlieue* is no longer such a term of contempt – except in the eyes of Marie-Chantal and her posh pals in Avenue Foch or the Marais.

The decline of the Ville de Paris' population does not at all mean that downtown areas are becoming deserted at night, as in some big Ameri-can towns or in the City of London. The population is still dense; also, central Paris with its glitter and street-life is still a powerful magnet for the pleasure-seeking tourist or suburbanite. Many central areas – the Latin Quarter, Montparnasse and St-Germain des Prés, the Champs-Elysées and Opéra districts, Les Halles, Montmartre, and the Grands Boulevards stretching eastwards – are lively till midnight and beyond with their terrace-cafés, restaurants, night-clubs, cinemas and so forth. But the character of some of these districts has been slowly altering. The Champs-Elysées has become more brash and commercialized; it is now the stronghold of the booming new trades of advertising and public relations, and of the fashion-model world, the movie business and the travel agencies. As the Edwardian elegance of Fouquet's dims into the past, so the giant new car showrooms and airline offices rise up beside it, and so do the fast-food eateries with their Americanized names, the multi-screen cinemas and the 'souks' and 'pubs'.

Perhaps too many tears need not be shed for the Champs-Elysées. More disquieting has been the 'Champs-Elyséefication' of St-Germain-des-Prés, a quarter that until the 1960s had provided such a contrast with the commercial glitter of the Right Bank. This enchanted kingdom of literary cafés and old street markets, satiric cabarets, bookshops, art shops and plain working Parisians, had always been something of an intellectual madhouse – but on its own authentic terms. Now it has been invaded by a new trend-conscious arti-smartness. Op-art boutiques in weird styles have swarmed down the boulevard; a multi-storey 'drug-store' of laughable brashness has planted itself right opposite the Flore and Deux Magots cafés where Sartre once held sway; and parking is a nightmare, as the big smart Citroëns slither on to the pavements of alleys built only for handcarts. Happily, by the late 1970s a counter-trend was emerging, as the banning of traffic from some narrow streets began to give the *quartier* back a little of its lost dignity.

The *cinquième*, around and behind the Sorbonne and the Panthéon, I find the most attractive part of Paris nowadays. Modern change has added to its vitality, without yet spoiling it. Some buildings down by the river have been expensively restored. Up on the hill, in a strange bohemian hinterland, picturesque squalor, cheerful modernity and academic traditionalism go hand in hand. *Risqué* cabarets and off-beat *bistrots* stand close to the walls of ancient colleges; in the crumbling Rue Mouffetard, ritzy cafés merge with old shops or stalls that evoke the Medina of Fez. And in the peeling old stone-floored houses of the *quartier*, impoverished artists and writers coexist with working-class families and with a few young émigrés from smart Passy homes who find it fun to deck out the romantic attics by stylish modern flatlets. Here the Paris of Mimi and Rudolf whispers its last enchantments. Montmartre, on the other hand, today hardly seems worth a mention. Artists no longer live there, and though the Butte with its steep steps and streets retains its visual charm, the area is in the grip of a vulgar tourist racket.

Paris today is emerging from a difficult period of transition. It is a much less depressing city to live in than the Paris I first knew in the 1950s, sombre with political crises and grimy façades. The years of neglect are over, and so are the years of too brutal expansion and renovation. The recent improvements in various public services have made daily life a little easier, and Parisian zest and glamour are reasserting themselves in a city that is seeking to reconcile tradition and modernity. It is still an immensely stimulating place for the visitor lounging in a boulevard café watching the world go by. But, as a place to work and live in, I am one of those who find it *too* stimulating. The fast tempo of life is wearing on the nerves: so much striving and hurry and sheer competitiveness in so crowded a space! This may be cheerfully invigorating in an area such as the Latin Quarter, full of tourists and students; but in the older commercial districts it leads to strain. In short, Paris today remains victim to the temperament of Parisians (see p. 374). Certainly they are less tense and brusque than twenty years ago, but they still find themselves caught up in a rat-race that breeds intolerance. Many of the more sensitive ones are acutely aware of this and of what Paris does to them, and so they try to insulate themselves within their home lives and small circle of friends; or they leave, for the more easy-going and generous-hearted provinces.

SOLVING THE HOUSING SHORTAGE – AT A FANCY PRICE

As late as the 1960s the housing shortage was still being described as 'national disgrace number one'. Today it is largely solved, but at a price. The French used to live in overcrowded and often squalid conditions, but cheaply; unable to find anything better, they spent their money on other things. Today housing is far more plentiful and comfortable, but prices have rocketed. The average share of family income devoted to it – to rents or mortgages, plus basic charges – has risen since the war from the incredibly low figure of 3.4 per cent to nearly 25 per cent, bringing France into line with Britain or West Germany. But the burden is very unevenly shared. While the very poor are helped by a new system of direct grants based on a means test, millions in the middle or lower-middle brackets find it increasingly hard to afford their neat new flats or suburban villas. Yet many affluent people are living in spacious older flats at controlled rents, costing maybe 5 per cent of their income. State housing policy has made repeated U-turns since the war, and its complex bureaucratic system of controls and subsidies has relieved some injustices but created others.

By the mid-'50s the housing situation had reached nightmare proportions, due to decades of neglect. Much of the trouble stemmed back to August 1914, when the Government froze all rents in order to protect soldiers' families from profiteering landlords. This was a fair wartime measure, but it was never repealed. So between the wars developers had little incentive to build, and in that period France completed only 1,800,000 new homes, a quarter of them reconstruction of war damage, while Britain and Germany each built over four million. Landlords equally had a pretext for making no repairs, so that many houses fell into premature decay, and the scars are still visible today. After 1945 the French then gave priority to industrial recovery, whereas Britain and Germany began massive rehousing right away: in 1952 France was still producing only about 75,000 new homes a year, one-sixth of the German figure. Yet the population was rising fast and farm workers and others were flooding into the cities. Poorer families lived huddled in one room, Moscow-style, and they had to face the appalling archaism of most lower-class housing: the 1954 census showed that only 10 per cent of all French homes had a bath or shower and only 27 per cent had flushing lavatories. Surveys frequently cited poor housing as the cause of divorce, crime, suicide, mental illness, infant mortality and the high abortion rate.

Finally, in the face of growing public outcry, the Government in the mid-'50s began to pump greater sums of money into new 'social' housing (the equivalent of Britain's council housing). This in France takes many complex forms, the commonest being the HLMs (*habitations à loyer modéré*) built by agencies run jointly by the State and local authorities with money from low-interest long-term Treasury loans. Under their crash programme, the rate of new building soared rapidly and in the 1960s was running at about 400,000 units a year, to peak at 550,000 in 1975. So quantitatively the problem was finally solved, helped by the fact that the private sector too began to boom when rents were freed on new housing for the open market. In twenty-five years, homes have been built for half the population, and every town is ringed with new blocks of flats; a common enough sight in the Western world, but something of an achievement in its sorry French context.

The early HLMs of the crash programme were of basic utility standard, with tiny rooms, minimal sound-proofing and often no bathroom. But steadily the norms have risen, and all flats built today have baths or showers and are sound-proofed. From its very low level, French housing has improved radically, as the figures show. Between the 1954 and 1975 censuses, the percentage of homes without running water fell from 42 to 2.8; without bath or shower from 90 to 29.8; without indoor flushing lavatories from 73 to 26.2; and a third of the dwellings without these amenities are old farmsteads, not in towns. Even so, today's figures are still unworthy of a wealthy modern nation, and they show that France still has some way to go before reaching the standards of other advanced countries of north-west Europe. Not only are rooms on average of smaller size than in these countries, but the ratio of people to rooms is one-third higher than in, for instance, Germany; in 1978, 17 per cent of French homes were still officially classified as 'overcrowded' (that is, with more than four people in three rooms). Nearly every home is full of modern gadgetry, such as washing-up machines, but space is so cramped that often there is hardly room to install them.

Many injustices have arisen from Government regulations artificially dividing unfurnished rents into different categories. Under a law passed in 1948, private sector rents are entirely free of controls on housing built since that date, but pre-1948 flats are subjected to strictly controlled rent increases. These in practice have been far outstripped by the inflationary rises in the new ones, leading to differentials of up to 300 per cent between flats of similar quality in the two groups. Moreover, pre-1948 tenants have security of tenure even on expiry of lease. If most of these were poorer people, the anomaly might not be so unjust: but many in fact are wealthy bourgeois families, clinging to the homes they have occupied for generations. In central Paris you find senior executives living in old six-room flats for 1,200 francs a month, the rental of a two-room new flat in the suburbs. These privileges give rise to various rackets. Sometimes a family in a large flat will sub-let one room furnished for as much as their entire rent. Or a big Paris flat may remain unused nearly all the year, its tenant a rich widow living on the Riviera. Or a flat may be sub-let furnished to foreign diplomats or other visitors at a colossal rent; this practice is illegal but connived at.

Another anomaly that appeared in the 1970s concerned the HLMs and other subsidized housing. The State was allowing their rents to rise so fast that the lower-paid workers for whom they were intended could no longer afford them, and many stayed in their old slums. As there was no means test for applicants, the HLMs were being infiltrated instead by skilled technicians or young professional people, thus benefiting from subsidies intended for the poor. The rent on a three-room HLM in the Paris suburbs is today around 800 francs a month including heating and maintenance, and since many of the newer ones are well built and well sited they make acceptable lower-middle-class homes. But the system was becoming both a waste of public money and socially unjust, and this was pointed out vigorously in 1975 by a Government commission headed by none other than Raymond Barre (the year before he became Prime Minister). He proposed that the method of financing should be inverted: subsidies should go not to the HLM agencies but to the occupants. Rents and prices could thus be raised to an economic level, but individuals would be helped to pay for them according to their means. Giscard accepted this plan, which became law in 1977. It has since been able to help many thousands of the poorest families, with grants often equalling half their rent or more. But it hits the lower-middle-income groups, who now have to pay the full price. It has also been unpopular with the HLM agencies and has led to a reduction in their building programmes, which for this and other reasons fell by half between 1975 and 1979. In fact, with the worst of the crisis now over, the Government has been cutting back on its overall aid to new public housing. For some years it has been trying to woo more private capital into building investment, but inevitably the response has benefited mainly the luxury market where developers can make higher and faster profits.

Now that the French are at last adequately housed, they are freer to pick and choose about the kind of homes they really want, and this has led to some striking changes. Above all, whereas ten years ago only 30 per cent of new building was individual houses and the rest was flats, today the proportion is reversed! In the crisis years the French submitted to new high-rise blocks as this was the quickest and cheapest way of solving the shortage; but at heart the Frenchman as much as the Englishman would rather have his own little house, and today private developers and public agencies alike are helping to give him just this. On the suburban housing estates, attempts are made to group the houses attractively into 'hamlets', thus avoiding either the monotony of ribbon-development or the anarchy of unplanned villas that scarred outer Paris between the wars. But in the countryside, rather too many commuter or weekend houses are being built at random, and this eats up farming land and in some cases spoils the landscape.

In all classes there is also a steady trend towards the buying rather than renting of new property. Before the war most urban flats were rented, but the percentage of French homes that are owner-occupied rose from 41 in 1962 to 50 in 1979. This satisfies the Frenchman's property-owning instincts, it provides developers with quicker returns and it was encouraged by Rightish governments for obvious political reasons. About one-third of HLMs are in the process of being bought by their occupants, and a few lucky ones are helped by a remarkably generous State mortgage system that works out cheaper than paying rent. In the private sector, however, mortgages are more of a problem. Building societies on the British model have never been developed in France, and only since the late '60s has the Government authorized private banks to operate the kind of mortgage system that can help a young couple without much capital to acquire a decent home. But this usually involves some initial savings-bank deposits, so that either the couple must wait some years to take possession, or else they must try to find the necessary down-payment from a bank at up to 17 per cent interest. Many middle-class couples today are spending 30 per cent of their income on mortgage repayments.

Matters have been made worse by the recent extravagant boom in the property market, as in Britain. Prices have been pushed up by building costs, by the growing scarcity of land in urban areas, and especially by the panic of inflation which drives people to invest in the security of bricks and mortar. And middle-range properties are the worst affected. A four-room family flat can easily cost 1.2 million francs in central Paris and up to 700,000 or so in the suburbs or provincial cities. The boom has also affected private rents, which were partially frozen during 1976–9 under Barre's counter-inflationary programme but have since again rocketed (except for the protected pre-1948 ones); rents vary greatly according to area, but on average a four-room flat may cost 3,500 francs a month in the *seizième*, 2,000 in Nice, Grenoble or a better Paris suburb such as St-Cloud, and 1,200 to 1,500 in Lyon or Montpellier.

Speculation over land and property has for many years been a major cause of the soaring rents and house prices. It has also limited the number and quality of HLMs, since so large a part of their funds has to be spent on the initial buying of land, whose prices have been rising very much faster than inflation. Today a square metre of land may cost 25,000 francs on the Champs-Elysées or in parts of Nice and Cannes, 10,000 francs in an average district of Paris and 3,000 francs or more in the suburbs; no wonder Chirac has such a struggle to build HLMs in Paris. For some years the Government has made efforts to limit speculation in areas marked out for special development schemes; notably in 1959 it set up entities today known as *zones d'aménagement concerté* (ZACs) and *zones d'aménagement différé* (ZADs), where the authorities have the power to forbid sales of land or to pre-empt. This has worked quite well for such schemes as the Villes Nouvelles, but these zones cover relatively small special areas, and elsewhere speculation has continued to flourish.

Under Giscard an attempt at least was made to check speculation in city centres, where prices were now so high that promoters felt obliged to build to a high density. This was threatening the character of some towns. So Giscard's Housing Minister, Robert Galley, prepared a law passed in 1975 that imposes a legal density limit of 1 (1.5 in Paris) in city centres; that is, a new single-storey building can cover the whole of a given site, but a two-storey building may cover only half the site, and so on. Town councils have the right to pre-empt central sites at market prices, also to impose special taxes on promoters breaking the density rules. The aim is that they should use this revenue for financing new green spaces, civic amenities and low-cost housing near city centres. The law, though in principle a step in the right direction, has not in practice been very effective. In a few cases it has thwarted ugly high-rise schemes and facilitated restoration; but in many others it has simply deterred owners from selling, thus making less land available. The Socialists came to power with plans for tighter curbs on speculation. However, their first action was over rentals: in January 1982 they put forward a Bill aimed at providing greater security of tenure for all tenants, not just those with pre-1948 leases. Landlords would now be obliged to grant six-year leases at pre-determined rents, and to submit to new national rules for the control of rent increases. The Bill was welcomed by tenants, if not by landlords. But many sceptics foresaw that it might simply lead to a shortage of rented accommodation, by dissuading owners from letting their propety – as has happened in Britain under parallel circumstances.

I have given here only the briefest outline of the story of French housing policy since the war, which offers a grisly spectacle of delay, incoherence, vacillation, machinations between rival bureaucracies, and political cowardice in the face of vested interests. A regime preoccupied with economic progress has never set a very high priority on social housing, which does not bring the same productive dividends as industry. However, Giscard did show a little more social concern than his predecessors (notably by adopting the Barre proposals), and finally the French have muddled through and most of them are now tolerably well housed; though if the market were better organized they would not have had to pay so high a price for it, in terms either of effort, patience or sheer cash. But at least a worker nowadays can usually find a flat near his job, thus avoiding long tiring journeys, and families are less ashamed to invite strangers to their homes. The French are becoming quite house-proud, and no longer so readily do they spurn home comforts in favour of food, holidays or other pleasures. Their expectations have risen; they no longer tolerate the old overcrowding, they want larger and better-built flats. In fact, today at least 10 per cent of new housing goes on what is officially called '*décohabitation*'; previously, in the poorer classes, a newly wed couple might have to remain living with one or other set of parents for some years, but now they expect, and generally get, a home of their own straight away.

The tempo of new building is slackening, now that the main needs have been met and the urban growth and birth rates are falling: 400,000 dwellings were completed in 1980 against 550,000 in 1975. If the total drops much lower it could be serious, for many slums still remain and each year some 200,000 homes are abandoned through decay. Significantly, this obsolescence embraces a great many of the HLMs thrown up so fast and cheaply in the 1950s: they have developed cracks or leaks, or are simply judged too ugly and primitive by today's working class. Many stand empty: some are due to be pulled down, others are being modernized. As regards older housing in general, and especially that in city centres, France like some other countries has now turned towards a policy of rehabilitation wherever possible, rather than demolition. This was the thinking behind the report of an official commission set up in 1975 under Simon Nora, a leading civil servant. He suggested that although many older buildings were beyond repair, in other cases it would be cheaper and also socially more liberal to modernize them rather than build new ones. He argued eloquently that to restore older housing would be to improve France's architectural heritage and re-animate city centres. The French no longer wanted to live in soulless suburban estates; they would be happy to live downtown if the housing quality and amenities were right. This policy is now being applied, slowly, as far as funds are available. And so today there are two trends, going in opposite directions. On the one hand, more people are wanting to move back to city-centre living, in the Latin tradition: rich people, as in the Marais in Paris, and poorer ones too when the housing is available. On the other hand, more people are wanting their own individual houses, amid greenery in the outskirts or within commuter range. What both groups reject, as Nora said, are the sad high-rise dormitories of the crash programme years. Town planning in France has entered a new era, and this we must now explore.

URBAN ENVIRONMENT:
THE YELLOW BICYCLES OF LA ROCHELLE

'The yellow bicycles of La Rochelle': it may sound like the title of a film by Jacques Demy, with Gene Kelly and Catherine Deneuve pedalling tunefully in the rain. In fact, the phrase has become a symbol of the New French Urban Ecology. In the latter 1970s many towns beside Paris have been turning away from grandiosity towards more human-scale projects: limiting car traffic, laying out parks, restoring old city centres, and so on. The vogue has been borrowed, a little belatedly, from countries such as Sweden and Holland. And in France the forerunner and pace-setter has been the graceful old fortified seaport of La Rochelle.

This former Huguenot stronghold with its fine Renaissance buildings has something of the quality of Bruges or Dubrovnik, and to my mind is the most attractive coastal town in France. But it was in danger of becoming a congested eyesore by 1971, the year the Gaullist mayor was defeated by Michel Crépeau, a forty-one-year-old local lawyer and Left-Radical, in alliance with the Socialists. Crépeau, a mixture of shrewdly ambitious politician and voluble idealist, promptly proclaimed his mission of 'restoring *joie de vivre* and gracious living' to La Rochelle. His first act was to veto a project already well in hand for a monstrous eleven-storey block of luxury flats along the harbour front. The developers had invested millions of francs and were furious; but as they had failed to secure a proper building permit they had no redress.

The new mayor then turned his sights on a projected giant suburb for 40,000 people which the Gaullists had planned. 'The land had been bought and work had started,' he told me in 1980, 'but I battled with the prefect and got the scheme radically reduced to 10,000 people. This cut-back cost me 20 million francs of the town's money, but I said it was better to be in debt for ten years or so than make people unhappy for a hundred and fifty years through bad planning! In place of one group of tower blocks I put an eighty-acre lake, so people can now go fishing beside their HLMs. The prefect and my predecessor had planned for La

Rochelle's population to double by the year 2000, to reach 200,000: but I said I'd rather have 100,000 happy citizens than 200,000 wretches in "labour-camp silos". At the time, I was looked on as a crazy and dangerous Malthusian, trying to limit growth; but I was simply the trendsetter of what is now official State policy and is considered normal in most towns. The Ministry no longer allows giant high-rise suburbs, nor big luxury blocks on harbour-fronts.'

A large boast, but not far from the truth. Crépeau found also that one big HLM estate built in the 1960s, Mireuil, still had very few public amenities and no *maison de quartier* (socio-cultural centre). 'I made it my *"zone à humaniser à priorité"*,' he said with a smile; 'we consulted the inhabitants on what kind of *maison* they would like, including the local nursery and primary school children. These kids produced drawings for us, and nearly all of them featured a red traditional house with curves and arches, surrounded by greenery and animals – in opposition to the grey concrete rectangles of their tower-block flats. So we gave the drawings to an architect – and now Mireuil has a low red-brick building with little round towers. There are even chickens and rabbits on the lawn beside it.'

Some may smile at this mock-ingenuous approach to town-planning. Yet any visitor is bound to be seriously impressed by what Crépeau has done for the historic heart of the town with its narrow arcaded streets, between the *mairie* and the fourteenth-century fortresses of the Vieux Port. Ten or so of these little streets have been banned to traffic and attractively paved over, while the old buildings have been handsomely restored, notably the superb Renaissance town hall. Crépeau commented to me in his characteristic style: 'All towns are now making traffic-free streets, it's à la mode – but *I* did it first. Giving back the street to the pedestrian is a return to pre-twentieth-century tradition. You see, all progress is the renewal of tradition.'

He had also to face the problem of traffic in the town as a whole, which teems with tourists all summer and like many old cities is ill-suited to cars. Crépeau looked at Amsterdam with its free bicycles, and at Orly airport he saw how easily a passenger picks up a luggage-trolley then leaves it where he likes. So he bought 250 bicycles for the unrestricted use of citizens and visitors, and had them painted bright yellow. Amid much publicity, the scheme was launched in August 1976. But unfortunately many of the cheaper second-hand bicycles broke down, and about forty others were stolen: not all Rochelais proved equal to their mayor's lofty civic idealism. So in 1978 the system was modified: the bicycles are still free, but they are now kept in special parks, and to use one you have to leave your identity card there in pawn with the attendant. Crépeau concedes that this is a bit of a setback for his initial utopian vision of collective property. However, the scheme basically goes ahead, every April to November; the fleet has been modernized and extended to 380 machines, financed partly by advertisements on frames and luggage-racks, and in summer they are just as popular with tourists as with locals. A party of Norwegians borrowed twenty for a week. The bicycles have done something to dissuade Rochelais from using their cars, though not as much as was hoped, and there are plenty of Frenchmen who regard the whole operation as little more than a gimmick, a gesture in the ecological struggle.

Crépeau would rather see it as 'part of a long-term process of civic education'. As an astute politician he knows also that the world-wide publicity has been useful, both for his own national career and for a town suffering from high unemployment. Among the hundreds of articles in the French and foreign Press, the *International Herald Tribune* devoted half its front page to an interview with Crépeau plus a photo of him riding a bike past the *mairie*. And the huge Crédit Agricole bank has not only supplied fifty bicycles as a gift but features the scheme in its international advertising. All this free publicity has brought the old Huguenot seaport a new fame as 'the city of *douceur de vivre*'; it is good for the tourist trade and – who knows? – it may arouse the interests of industrial investors too. As for Crépeau himself, his local ecological pioneering was richly rewarded nationally in 1981 when President Mitterrand appointed him Minister for the Environment.

His 'civic education' and 'gracious living' programmes at La Rochelle take various forms. Like Dubedout in Grenoble, he closely consults his neighbourhood committees on all municipal projects (see p. 316). He has taken the lead in France in initiating pre-sorted garbage collection and recycling of the refuse (paper, glass and plastic) and claims that the recycled paper saves 17,000 trees a year. Above all, he has made spectacular efforts for culture (see p. 334), raising its share of the town budget eightfold since he came to power, from 0.5 to 4 per cent. His achievements include the building of a 30-million-franc Maison de la Culture; the creation of a major museum of French historical links with the Americas; and, since 1973, an ambitious annual summer festival of modern art and music, international in its scope. Does his electorate, much of it working class, enjoy subsidizing this highbrow diet which is thrust at them? 'Of course there are grumbles,' admits Crépeau; 'the local bourgeoisie goes to Salzburg or Paris for its culture, and the workers want more money spent on football, so I'm not thanked for pushing up the arts budget. But the role of a mayor is to guide public opinion, not just follow it. Our duty is to combat the debased American-style society that is pushed at us via the TV screens, so it's necessary for democracy that I shove culture down my people's throats.'

There may be a flaw of logic in this Reithian concept of democracy. Yet the Rochelais in their vast majority are happy to accept the evangelistic do-gooding leadership of their remarkable mayor, discreet paternalism and all. They know that Crépeau *has* made La Rochelle a better town to live in than most in France, and he in turn pays tribute to their spirit: 'There are not many Protestants left here nowadays, Richelieu killed most of them; yet the Rochelais are still strongly marked by the Protestant tradition of reformism and open-mindedness; it's a kind of tribal memory. And it's made my task easier – could I have accomplished so much in the Midi?' The visitor, too, benefits from the ecology. Crépeau and his Left-wing coalition have succeeded in enhancing La Rochelle's innate quality of aristocratic grace, which blooms especially in festival time. Relaxed and cheerful the youthful crowds stroll down the arcades or through the traffic-free streets, against a backdrop of clean white stone buildings that present a remarkable harmony; and, as an added touch of elegance, all the numerous terrace-cafés have wicker chairs in identical style. In no other French town are the citizens so friendly, nor in so civilized a style; and just as I find the people of Bruges much nicer than other Belgians, so it seems to me that beautiful architecture does influence local temperament. As in some other cities with a very special history and environment, its people seem to inhabit a realm of their own, a city-state of the spirit, and are proudly aware of it.

No other French town has yet taken up free bicycles, but a number in their different ways are now following the ecological trend of La Rochelle. The movement is sporadic, sometimes feeble in its results, and by no means original to France which still lags behind some other countries in this field. But at least it marks a departure from the ethos of the '60s when big commercial projects dominated municipal thinking. Grenoble under Dubedout, not surprisingly, has been taking a path parallel to La Rochelle's, though with less *éclat*. The mayor has established a traffic-free zone in the old town round the Place Grenette and has developed public transport in a way that has greatly eased traffic jams; on the Dutch model, he is now also creating a network of lanes reserved for cyclists alongside main streets. A landscape architect has been hired to collaborate on all new building projects. But Dubedout's main effort today is centred on the restoration of poorer-class housing in the town centre. Making use of its pre-emption rights under the 1976 Galley law, the council buys up old decaying housing, rehabilitates it and resettles the inhabitants – mostly poor people – on the spot. It is a costly and slow process, and so far only one or two streets have been restored – 'But,' says Dubedout, 'our social policy is to resist the tendency for the downtown area to lose its residents or become a bourgeois ghetto.' Sound Socialism, and prudent tactics too for a council that fears losing its working-class electorate to the suburbs.

Motives may be mixed, yet it is certain that the Left's rise to power in so many big towns in the 1977 elections has boosted the ecological trend. In Rennes and elsewhere, new Socialist-led coalitions have been cutting back on mammoth downtown commercial complexes started before 1977, and instead are putting the accent on more green spaces and leisure centres; but in a time of economic recession this usually involves heavy increases in local taxes. At Besançon, the Socialist mayor has introduced an ingenious system of banning private traffic from a large section of the old town and replacing it with very frequent buses. This has been a success. Besançon is one of numerous older French cities with a dense knot-like structure (a core of narrow streets set on a hill or within a river loop) that presents the modern traffic planner with intractable problems and calls for drastic remedies. Another such town is Montpellier, where rampant urban growth had been clogging with traffic the elegant classical heart of the city. But since 1977 the new Socialist-led council has been extending the zone of pedestrian streets in the centre; as in other towns, the local shopkeepers at first protest furiously, thinking the ban on cars will harm their trade, then find to their delighted surprise that a little street with no cars actually attracts *more* shoppers. The new town council has also put into reverse the expansionist policies of its Giscardian predecessor under mayor François Delmas. He in the early 1970s had initiated a giant commercial and office complex right next to the town's charming central square, the Place de la Comédie. The new council has cancelled plans to complete it, and will use the vacant space for a low-rise estate of public housing amid gardens, designed by the influential Barcelona architect Ricardo Bofill. 'Montpellier has voted for quality of life and against the motor car,' I was told by Raymond Dugrand, the council's excitable and visionary new planning boss; 'Delmas wanted this little town to become a metropolis of half-a-million. He was crazy. But we shall give the people back their city.' As for Maître Delmas, who in 1978 became a junior Minister under Giscard, he regarded this tearing up of his plans with quizzical ambiguity from his office in Paris where he was . . . Secretary of State for the Environment!

Left-wing towns have no monopoly of ecology. Rouen under Lecanuet has carried out some remarkably elegant restoration and pedestrian precinct schemes, and so has Troyes where Robert Galley himself is mayor. And the Governments too have played some part, ever since the Pompidou era when ecology first became fashionable. In 1972 it launched what it called its *'politique des Villes Moyennes'*, with the aim of aiding towns of between 30,000 and 80,000 people to improve their town-planning and amenities. Some eighty towns have signed State contracts whereby they receive subsidies for urban improvements, and they include places as diverse as smart Annecy and Communist Dieppe, or Le Puy and Béthune (in the northern mining belt). The first *Ville Moyenne* to sign a contract, and one of the most successful, was the Aveyron's capital, Rodez. Today the streets of its medieval centre have been delightfully restored as precincts with multi-coloured pavestones, flower-pots and illuminated fountains, while the ramparts have been renovated and a slum improvement scheme has involved the restoration of old timbered buildings, the rehousing of some inhabitants on the spot, and the re-introduction of local artisan workshops and craft boutiques. Aesthetically the operation has been a success, but socially it has not worked out quite as intended, for rather more bourgeois families than planned have been allowed to snap up the renovated houses vacated by the slum-dwellers. For this, Rodez' Right-wing town council has come under fire from the local Left. In France today, town-planning is increasingly politicized, and so is local community life. But do the political zealots know what France's new urban society really wants?

COMMUNITY VERSUS PRIVACY:
FROM NEW-TOWN 'BLUES' TO NEW-TOWN 'REDS'

More than half the urban population today live in new suburbs or housing estates of one kind or another, posh or proletarian or both. The adjustment to the new styles of suburban living has not been easy, and its traumas tell us a good deal about the national character and modern French society as a whole. At first, the planners were heavily at fault. In the '50s and early '60s they made little effort to provide their austere dormitories with social and leisure amenities, and this led to epidemics of 'new-town blues', much aggravated by the temperament of the French, wary of new neighbours and community self-help. But the more recent suburbs have been much better planned and built, and their amenities now arrive at the same time as the housing; meanwhile the earlier estates have finally acquired amenities too, and little by little are discovering some kind of 'soul', simply through time and the growth of habit.

Slowly, and very fitfully, this displaced urban society is groping towards new forms of community living – either by the spontaneous efforts of little groups of pioneers, or else in a few cases through idealistic municipal action, as on an HLM estate at Grenoble, where Dubedout and his team have tried to create a 'utopian' society that goes to extremes of community integration. It is not easy; in France, disinterested attempts to create a more lively and caring local life still tend to fall victim either to public apathy and family-geared privacy, or else, conversely, to political extremism by those who see a crèche or a music club not as an end in itself but as a forum of the class struggle. Sarcelles, for instance, largest and most notorious of the earlier HLM suburbs of Paris, has thrown off its new-town blues only to catch a new virus, new-town Reds.

Our complex saga of the suburbs begins at Sarcelles in the late 1950s. Most initial post-war housing was thrown up piecemeal, but then the policy was launched of the *'grands ensembles'*, planned as self-sufficient entities each with their own shops, schools and so on. In some ways they were not so different from the New Towns that Britain had started some years earlier, save that they were built much closer to existing cities, their blocks were much higher-rise – and their planning was far less coherent. Sarcelles, the archetype, near Le Bourget airport, was started in 1956 and grew steadily, finally housing 40,000 people; yet for over fifteen years there was no *lycée*, and the big socio-commercial centre also arrived fifteen years later than scheduled. The criss-cross streets were given names like Allée Marcel Proust and Avenue Paul Valéry, but there was no poetry in the flat utility façades of their buildings. Sarcelles and other *ensembles* scarcely less ugly were built in the flurry of the crash housing programme, and little care was given to their architecture. It is true that, for the slum evacuees, Sarcelles in some ways was a paradise of modern plumbing and fresh air; it was allotted a fair amount of space, with trees and playgrounds, in contrast to the ultra-high density of much of central Paris. But this hardly atoned for the fearsome rectilinear concept, the austere gridiron of grey box-like blocks, from five to seventeen storeys high. Foreign visitors were horrified: Ian Nairn in the *Observer* castigated 'the intellectual arrogance and paucity of invention of this loveless, pre-cast concrete desert'. Sarcelles, in fact, sprang from a clumsy attempt by French architects to apply some of Le Corbusier's ideas without properly understanding them.

These aesthetic failings were matched by the administrative troubles of the earlier *grands ensembles*. Their construction was entrusted to public development bodies, but these were not given adequate funds for matters other than the housing, nor did they have proper powers of coordination in the manner of Britain's New Town Corporations. So all kinds of difficulties arose, as France's housing industry and its system of

local government both proved peculiarly ill suited to this kind of venture.
First, whereas the development bodies provided local roads and basic
utilities, they had no means of coercing ministries or State agencies into
providing other needed equipment, so the *ensembles* went for years with
a serious lack of schools, clinics, post offices, public transport and the
like. This was due to sheer lack of liaison, aggravated very often by
inter-ministerial rivalries and parsimony over funds. The Ministry of
Health or Education, for instance, might see no reason why it should
come to the relief of some new *ensemble* sponsored by the Ministry of
Construction. And on top of this, little foresight was shown in trying to
attract new light industries or other jobs to the vicinity of the *ensembles*,
whose working population thus had to face long tedious daily journeys,
made all the worse by the poor transport facilities.

The other major flaw in the system was that the new towns were
'parachuted' on to the territory of existing semi-rural communes, without proper coordination, and this led to endless conflicts and obstructions. Often the old commune objected to this giant parasite that had
arrived to destroy its peaceful way of life, and especially it resented
having to help pay for it. At Sarcelles, the mayor managed to block for
three years the building of the much-needed socio-commercial centre,
and the new inhabitants were the losers. At Massy-Antony, over in the
southern suburbs, the State authorities deliberately planted a *grand
ensemble* astride two communes in different departments, in order – so it
was said – to provoke maximum problems and so draw lessons for the
future. They certainly got what they wanted. The town was built by a
société d'économie mixte comprising State and private interests plus the
two existing communes, whose role for many years was largely obstructive. First, the Socialist mayor of old Antony rejected plans for a new
separate commune for the *ensemble*, since it would have deprived him of
some territory and power. Then the burghers of the sleepy old market
town of Massy, mainly small tradesmen, farmers and *rentiers*, began
systematic opposition to the new suburb, most of which was to be on
their domain. Building might never have started, had not the State in
1958 made rare use of its ultimate right to overrule a commune's veto,
and sent bulldozers out over the cornfields while the farmers were
harvesting. This did not make for happier relations. The mayor of Massy,
an old-style reactionary Socialist, retaliated by blocking for some years
the *dossiers* of some projects that needed his formal support, notably for a
sports centre. So the young slum evacuees were condemned to play
football on improvised pitches amid car-parks and vacant lots.

There were thus many reasons why life in the first new towns was
no paradise. Sarcelles even gave its name to a new 'disease': 'Sarcellitis'

(new-town blues), as stories filtered out of nervous breakdowns, delin-quency, and bored housewives resorting to part-time prostitution. Reporters were soon hurrying in droves to Sarcelles, Massy and other places, as the French in the 1960s suddenly woke up to the social problems of modern mass suburbia and were fascinated and disturbed by them. The *grands ensembles* came under heavy criticism, and their problems were analysed without cease in a stream of books, theses, conferences and sensational articles. The French, so conservative about their living patterns, found the new-town experience far more traumatic than the British. Life there was scrutinized as if it were the planet Mars.

The planners have since learned from their early mistakes, in terms of architecture, amenities and administration. Even at Sarcelles, the newer quarters built since the late 1960s are markedly less monolithic than the old ones, and the new blocks are no longer in linear form but harmoniously grouped. The design and quality of buildings show a similar improvement; whereas the older ones have barrack-like façades of stone and concrete, the new ones are gayer, with balconies, larger windows, and façades made of coloured synthetic materials. Though HLM costs must always be kept low, improved techniques and produc-tivity have finally made it possible to add a few frills for the same relative price. Likewise the newer HLMs now have larger rooms, a small bath in place of a shower-tub, and soundproofing that is still imperfect but less of a farce than in the day when *les bruits des voisins* were major causes of unneighbourliness and 'Sarcellitis'. Throughout France, after the horrors of the early period, many of the newer estates now show quite a pleasing sense of landscaping, design and detail.

The *grand ensemble* concept was finally abandoned in 1972, and most estates built today are very much smaller, and more carefully integrated into existing communities. Truly titanic planning did however have its final fling in the Pompidou period, when work began on nine *'villes nouvelles'*, five in the Paris region (see p. 263), others outside Marseille, Lyon, Rouen and Lille. They have been criticized for being too ambitious, several times the size of Sarcelles; but in terms of planning and quality they do mark a huge step forward, and their creators claim that their scale makes it easier to provide them with full amenities. They are inspired to an extent by the previously ignored British and Swedish models; one of them, Cergy-Pontoise, has hired British consultants.

The system of constructing these *villes nouvelles* was designed to obviate much of the feuding with communes or lack of liaison between ministries that had bedevilled the *grands ensembles*. In charge of plan-ning, building, land-buying and so on, each new town has its own State agency – rather like a New Town Corporation in Britain – with legal powers to ensure coordination between ministries. At the same time the communes are brought into the process in an intelligent and fairly democratic way. Each town is so vast that it spreads over several communes, and these are obliged to form a syndicate whose approval the State agency in turn is required to seek on all matters. The agency thus has two masters, the syndicate and the Government. If there are dissensions, and of course there are, the prefect arbitrates. Each commune keeps its usual powers within its old built-up area, but it delegates authority to the syndicate for all matters of equipment in the virgin zones where the town is being built. Complicated? – indeed it is; but it does provide a working balance between technocratic and citizen needs, while public responsibilities are at last clearly defined. There have been some frictions, especially where the syndicate has a Left-wing majority, but on the whole the system works effectively. A more rational solution might have been to carve out a separate new commune for the new town; but in France, where each commune is so jealous about its territory, this would not have been politically feasible.

These new towns really *are* getting their factories, offices, shops, schools, welfare and leisure amenities, at the same time as the housing instead of years later. Each town has considerable planning autonomy and has been encouraged to develop its own visual style. In many cases the modern architecture is varied and striking, and the density far lower than in places like Sarcelles. L'Ile-d'Abeau, south-east of Lyon, set out along a valley slope in the form of a series of villages, is especially attractive, while another success is Evry, south of Paris, with its cheerful multi-coloured flats. Its new town has only 10,000 inhabitants to date, but already the largest multi-purpose centre in France has been completed there, the Agora, with three theatres, a skating rink, dance halls, a library, youth centre and hypermarkets, all serving a wide area. Several new factories have opened near by, one of them using 80 per cent local labour. A recent opinion survey found that some 88 per cent of the new inhabitants were happy with their homes and with the local shops, while 72 to 77 per cent were satisfied with the schools and leisure facilities and the greenery. 'Like malaria, sarcellitis *can* be stamped out,' said a jubilant technocrat.

Cergy-Pontoise, twenty miles north-west of Paris, is taking shape on a splendidly spacious site overlooking a loop in the River Oise. The new city centre, a mini-Brasilia, preceded most of the housing; around its wide piazza there stand a number of imposing modern buildings including the new prefecture of the Val d'Oise and a bizarre asymmetric blue-and-green edifice of glass and steel that houses a cultural centre and the syndicate's offices. The new town today has 25,000 inhabitants, and this figure will rise steadily to about 120,000, balancing the existing 80,000 population of the fifteen old communes of its territory, the largest being Pontoise. The aim is that old and new will finally fuse into one coherent city, though there was much local reticence when the project was first decreed – 'We wanted to know with what sauce we were to be eaten,' I was told by the elderly mayor of the old village of Cergy, now vice-president of the syndicate; 'but the old communes now realize how much they benefit from the amenities of the new town, and they accept the giving up of some of their powers to the syndicate, which in turn has found a *modus vivendi* with the State development agency.' One of the successes has been that 40,000 jobs now exist at Cergy-Pontoise, thanks to the planned creation of offices and industrial estates. The new town has theatres and concerts, a large shopping-centre and a citizen group that helps newly arrived families. The housing spreads spaciously over a wide area in a variety of styles, some flats, some groups of villas, and it covers also a wide social range: many *cadres* choose to live in the new town, where house prices are at less than half Paris levels, thanks to the planners' legal curbs on speculation. Cergy-Pontoise has had its problems, but it is light-years away from early Sarcelles and most people are glad to be living there. They come by choice, not necessity. Already the town has the feel of being more than just a suburb; it stands on the edge of deep country, yet is in easy reach of Paris. It has some of the same quality as a British New Town such as Milton Keynes, plus a dash of provocative French modernism. It shows what French planners can do when they try.

These experiences suggest that the French can and will adapt in time to new suburban living, once given the right setting and amenities. And yet, if we look more closely, even in a place like Evry or Cergy, we find that many people, especially in the less educated classes, retain a certain rootlessness, a vague sense of isolation, however happy they may be with their new homes and the public facilities. This new-town problem is common to many countries, but is especially strong among the French with their traditional wariness about making new friends or pooling resources with strangers. Housewives without jobs grow bored in their easy-to-run little flats, yet they lack the Anglo-Saxon readiness to muck in, with women's clubs and self-help activities. This is a fair generalization, even though individual reactions of course vary greatly.

The problem was at its most acute in the early days in places like Sarcelles, and now it is easing as the towns improve and new habits slowly form; but it has not disappeared. Certainly those who have been rehoused from slum districts seldom regret the move: a sociological survey at Sarcelles in 1968 found that 80 per cent of the inhabitants were 'happy to be living there' once they had settled in. A little flat with all mod. cons. where the family can bolt the door and build its nest, a playground outside for *les gosses*, blue sky with no smog: these are their first priorities and these they have found. But once they look for contact with the world outside, they are victims of their own social inhibitions and of the profound French attachment to family rather than community. In their old slums, for all the discomfort, people were close to friends and shops they had known for years, and often to relatives too. Put them down in a new setting and they draw in their horns. Their first reaction is to close the door, enjoy the new privacy and comfort, and cling to what still remains familiar: the family cell. Friendly calls by neighbours are resented, or assumed to have some ulterior motive. And it takes years for a family to shed its emotional wariness towards regarding the *grand ensemble* as 'home'. Of course, within each new town there is always a small minority who think and react quite differently, and who create little cells of extreme animation. These are the pioneers, usually the more educated people, who far from drawing in their horns are inspired by the challenge of turning the concrete desert into a spiritual flower-garden. They may be Catholics, or Leftists, or social workers with a sense of mission. They busily create clubs and associations of all kinds, but their brave efforts do not always find a wide response.

The situation varies from town to town. One of the happier examples is Massy, which has come a long way from its difficult early days. Its former reactionary mayor has given place to a younger and far more go-ahead one, Claude Germon, also a Socialist but of the new school; and he and his team have worked hard to equip the town with its needed amenities and to try to imbue it with some community spirit. Its ambience, it is true, still suffers from its soulless rectangular architecture which Germon never ceases to denounce: 'Massy,' he told me, 'has the sad privilege of being a product of the Sarcelles era. Its crazy town-planning is not the fault of the council but of State technocrats who gave no thought for quality of life.' Yet Massy today has finally emerged as a real town, not beautiful but fairly spacious, with an interesting mixed population of workers, *cadres*, intellectuals and foreign immigrants. On a visit one afternoon in June, I was impressed with a sense of varied and cheerful activity. The big modern sports centre with its five swimming-pools was crowded. In one *maison de quartier* children were making marionettes and doing pottery; from the windows of the *conservatoire* came strains of violins; the municipal cinema advertised new films by Herzog and Olmi; and the shopping centre's boutiques were of Parisian standards. For this town of 45,000, I was told that the annual civic budget for culture is 2.9 million francs, excluding staff overheads.

Clearly, Germon has done much that a mayor can do to animate his town; and yet, my happy impression may have been partly deceptive. Massy has fifty clubs and associations of a social or cultural kind – from chess to sinology, from amateur choirs to the Cercle Celtique – but only one Massicois in five is a member of any of them, and the young bearded director of the Centre Socio-Educatif (civic cultural centre) told me sorrowfully, 'The vast mass of people don't do much in the evening, they're too tired after work, they slump in front of their TV sets, or if they want entertainment they go to Paris. Our activities at this centre are kept going just by a few enthusiasts. Yes, I think many people *do* vaguely feel the need for a richer neighbourhood life, but they don't do much about it. And there's hardly a soul in the streets after dark.' In all Massy only one café stays open after 9 p.m. (and that was closed for six months in 1979 for alleged drug offences). This indeed is one of the striking differences between a new town and a traditional one: the scarcity of cafés. It is due in part to new anti-alcoholism laws limiting cafés in new suburbs to one per 3,000 people, but more to the reluctance of *cafetiers* to try their luck in this milieu. Only at mid-day or apéritif time do they do much trade. The few cafés that emerge are mostly over-lit functional places where listless youths play with pin-tables. They lack the traditional café warmth to tempt the locals away from their TV sets, and in one sense this is the price of progress; the cosier their new flats, the less need the French feel to visit cafés in the evening (see p. 396). Certainly they are now visiting each other more readily in their homes than in former days, and more casually, especially the younger ones; but a certain Latin style of gregarious public life is disappearing, except maybe in the warm Midi. In a town like Massy, the gregarious evening animation comes mainly from the immigrants – Arabs, Antillais, Portuguese and others – who make up 19 per cent of the population. And yet, the Massicois are quite happy, in a complacent way. A middle-aged clerk told me: 'We sun-bathe on our balconies at weekends, we watch TV or drive into the countryside which is only ten minutes away. We like sport, but we don't feel the need for more club life for its own sake, the French are too *renfermés* for that. Personally, I don't see these new towns creating a new collective spirit in France.'

At a higher social level, on the smart new private residential estates, the French are at least becoming much more neighbourly within their own little circles. Out to the west of Paris, around and beyond Versailles, the spare land has been filling up with chic estates of California-style villas or luxury flats, estates with names like 'le Parc Montaigne' or 'la

Résidence Vendôme'. And here amid their tennis-courts, *piscines* and built-in barbecues, a new affluent French society of a new kind has been emerging: youngish couples working in the media, in modern business and technology, the kind you see sipping cocktails in the glossy-magazine advertisements. This society is less concerned with its roots than an older generation, less bound by the ties of the big clan family, more mobile, more preoccupied with material status symbols, in short, more Americanized. On the villa estates there are often no hedges between the gardens and no one minds; yet these same people, in their old Paris flats, would seldom have got to know their neighbours. A doctor with a new house in one of the up-market quarters of Cergy told me: 'We've become real friends with the people close by, we're always in and out of each others' homes for informal meals and drinks. But my wife and I take very little part in the organized club or cultural life of the *ville nouvelle*, we can't be bothered' – a common reaction. And so, within its self-absorbed little groupings, this new bourgeoisie of the suburbs is moving from French reticence to American patterns of casual neigh-bourhood friendliness. Progress of a sort, you could say – but a long way from the kind of brave new open community desired by the pioneers with a social conscience.

Is such a community possible? Well, since 1968 the pioneers have made one famous and spectacular attempt to create utopia in a high-rise HLM suburb – needless to say, at Grenoble (see pp. 153–61). Here Dubedout and his Socialist-led council have promoted the Arlequin district of the vast new suburb of La Villeneuve as a kind of social laboratory; with the help of special architecture and an army of social workers, their aim has been to break down some of the barriers of race and class and woo the inhabitants into a lively, caring community, integrated in various ways most uncommon in France. The results have been only partially successful and highly controversial; Grenoblois are divided on whether this is neo-Sarcelles or the glorious apotheosis of anti-Sarcelles. But curiosity has spread to all parts of France and beyond; and when l'Arlequin was first completed, in the mid-'70s, it drew a constant stream of sociologists, architects and town-planners, reporters and TV crews, politicians and professors. Pierre Frappat wrote in his book on Grenoble,[5] 'It was the Mont-St-Michel of all those who aspired to create a new society.'

So what then is this concrete Eden? Its town-planning, at first sight, is monstrous. As you drive south from central Grenoble, there rises before you this dense phalanx of multi-coloured twelve-storey blocks, in

5 op. cit., p. 357.

true neo-brutalist style. This outward aspect is all that most Grenoblois ever see of l'Arlequin and helps to explain its poor local reputation. But the true Arlequin needs to be judged from its inner side, *côté jardin*. Its origins lie with the big 'Olympic village' built nearby for the 1968 Winter Games, which was later developed into La Villeneuve, a *grand ensemble* of 40,000 people astride two communes; l'Arlequin, with 9,000, is just one district. Its main physical innovation is its mile-long central walkway or covered arcade, curving gently, giving access to the flats that tower above. On one side is a fifty-acre park and beyond rise the snowy Alps. All traffic is underground, or outside the central pedestrian area.

The very high density, in most towns today regarded as a fault, was here chosen deliberately in order to promote a womb-like feeling of intense animation and warm human contact, medieval-style – with the adjacent park as an airy escape. The flats too, which are of good quality and design by HLM standards, were conceived so as to facilitate contact; they are built on the now fashionable deck-access pattern, connected by passageways. This is supposed to help integrate the population, and 'integration' is the key word at l'Arlequin, integration of many different kinds of people, and of activities normally kept separate such as school and working adult life. In each tower block, the flats are of differing categories and prices, some cheaper HLMs, some middle-class homes for sale, with the aid of encouraging a social mixture to rub shoulders and make friends, thus avoiding the usual 'ghettos'. Special efforts have also been made to welcome and assimilate Arab families (largely working-class) and other immigrants. And in among the flats the planners have placed two old people's homes, a student hostel and a *foyer* for the handicapped, again with the purpose of reducing the segregations common in towns. France, a compartmentalized society, has long lagged behind Anglo-Saxon or Nordic countries in public efforts to assimilate weaker minorities into the community; so these initiatives caused quite a stir. One journalist summed up the municipal idealists' aims for l'Arlequin: '*A nous les Arabes, à nous les vieillards, à nous les fous!*'

The most radical innovation is that the local State secondary school is integrated with the *maison de quartier*; they share a building at the heart of l'Arlequin's shopping area, beside the main walkway. Here the school's library is also the public library; and the *maison*'s public self-service restaurant is also the school canteen. The *maison* has a theatre, a TV studio and video centre, an arts workshop and other facilities, all available under certain conditions both to pupils and public. Moreover, in this school as in l'Arlequin's five primary schools, parents are free to wander in and out of classes, or even to hold classes themselves, while pupils are encouraged to *tutoie* their teachers. This 'open-school' experiment, rare in any country, marks a revolutionary break with the hermetic French tradition of education, and has caused a mighty rumpus and much opposition from the teaching world (see also Chapter 7). L'Arlequin has also had difficulties with its open-door preventative medicine centre, which marks a similar break with rigid medical tradition; and with its community cable-TV project, as we shall see. Utopia is not built in a day, even in Grenoble.

However, in l'Arlequin's early years, in the after-glow of May '68, many idealists flocked to live there, fired by the challenge of building this new Jerusalem. A Parisian business manager took a simple job in adult education, while his wife ran the local pharmacy. A priest deserted holy orders to start a newspaper shop. Eight of Grenoble's town councillors took flats at l'Arlequin, and they were followed by hundreds of the city's *cadres* and intellectuals, many of them university or school teachers. A survey in 1977 found that no less than 54 per cent of the inhabitants were families of middle or upper *cadres* or professional people, all at l'Arlequin by choice. And of course this gave a somewhat artificial hothouse quality to the experiment of mixing of classes. The educated élites dominated social life, enjoying their roles of radical chic, while the working-class 'natives' stayed in the background. It was a parable of well-meaning neo-colonialism.

L'Arlequin has run into other troubles too. So eager has the town council been to make its 'social laboratory' a success that it has packed the place out with paid employees, 455 in all, many of them teachers, the rest social workers and *animateurs* of various kinds. This has had two results. First, l'Arlequin costs the Grenoble ratepayer twice as much *per capita* as an ordinary suburb, and this has added to the criticisms levelled at it. Secondly, and more serious, l'Arlequin for all its high ideals has failed to surmount one of the most basic of French failings: the stalemate of mistrust between officialdom and citizens. The paid workers jealously control the place, and discourage voluntary participation by the inhabitants, whose neighbourhood associations are thus thrown on to the defensive and become little more than pressure-groups for expressing complaints that this or that service is not running properly. And yet, if through staff problems or economy cuts some amenity is closed down for a while (as has happened, for instance, with the photo lab and the poster printworks), the residents will not take the initiative to run it themselves; they simply grouse. So the fault is on both sides. It is true that the inhabitants have their own active life of clubs and societies, with passionate intellectual debating sessions, and even housewives' rotas to help with baby-minding or visiting the sick; but this does not extend to any sense of sharing in responsibility for the general upkeep of their paradise. Oh, no, that is up to 'them', the authorities. And this feeling is equally strong among the élitist *cadres* and intellectuals, most of them Socialist and fully pro-Dubedout. They will eagerly hold a meeting to debate Iran or abortion reform; they will sign petitions of protest that the rents are too high; but it will not occur to them to club together to help tidy the place up – and it is now very shabby. The *maison de quartier* is run simply as a municipal service, and repeated attempts have failed to create a residents' committee to help supervise it. This failure of direct democracy may seem astonishing to an Anglo-Saxon, but it is very French; and to this extent l'Arlequin's laboratory test *has* yielded a clear and negative result.

The admirable attempt at racial integration has also had its problems. Grenoble more than almost any other French town has a policy of trying to ease the path of coloured immigrants, most of them Muslims from North Africa, who in recent years have faced increasing difficulties in France (see p. 469). At l'Arlequin, where one family in eight is from the Third World, the Indo-Chinese and Latin Americans (mostly middle-class) have assimilated easily, but with the Algerians and other Muslims (mostly working-class) there has been more trouble. The teenagers behave well in school, but out of class they tend to go around in unruly gangs, and most of the hooliganism and petty vandalism at l'Arlequin is blamed on them. Their fathers or elder brothers get noisily drunk at night in the local cafés and are simply not used to respecting European codes of behaviour: on my visit, I saw a car full of young Arabs careering down the central walkway, amid futile protests from the French standing by! Social workers and residents alike have made noble efforts over the years to help the Algerians to settle in: for example, housewives have freely given their time for holding French literacy classes for Muslim women, but this attempt at emancipation is often strongly resented by their Muslim menfolk. So, all in all, racial harmony at l'Arlequin is not quite what it was planned to be, even though it is still above today's French average. At the outset, Muslims and French were housed pell-mell together in the same blocks, in line with the integration ethos; but gradually a tacit *apartheid* has developed, much against the wishes of the town council, as European families move out of blocks dominated by Algerians and these become 'ghettos'. 'It's a sad fact,' one Socialist resident told me, 'that most of the social problems are caused by the Arabs. And it's a cruel irony that one of the most inspired features of l'Arlequin, this bid for racial integration, is in practice the main cause of the project's failure to fulfil its hopes. Just look at the tatty mess.'

I did look – and my mind boggled. This bizarre serpentine ensemble, unlike any other suburb in France, is a most odd mixture of imaginative humanist experiment and extreme urban degradation. The faults lie partly with the basic design, partly with the lack of upkeep. The flats themselves are fine, but the walkway is a hideous stretch of heavy concrete, covered with graffiti and torn remnants of posters, its op-art colour-schemes now faded and dismal. At the town hall, a member of Dubedout's team told me that State financial rules for HLMs were so strict that the money had not been available for making the public parts of l'Arlequin more attractive, and no doubt this is true. It is true also that the HLM agency responsible for maintenance spends hardly a franc on paint and tidiness; and yet, to do its job properly would involve a Sisyphean struggle against daily petty vandalism. Most of the letter-boxes have been smashed or their name-plates torn off. Even so, you would have thought that the residents could have done more themselves to keep their paradise in order; these hundreds of idealistic intellectuals could at least have banded together to spend some money on brightening the place up, or made some efforts to stop the damage; but no, they do not see that as their job.

L'Arlequin's local nickname is 'Chicàgauche', a clever double pun: and is it today much more than that, a fashionable Left-wing dream buried beneath the concrete and the ghetto vandalism? It is true that many of the early intellectual pioneers have departed, disillusioned. To share the life of an HLM suburb was a fine, generous idea in theory; but in practice they found it hard to put up for long with the daily nuisances, the noise, the delinquency, the lifts that continually broke down, the political feuding, the oppressive concrete. They have gone, but others have taken their place; and for all its failures, l'Arlequin remains some-where special. One young couple, teachers from petit-bourgeois back-grounds, living in a duplex flat with stunning views of the Alps, summed up for me the pros and cons of sharing in l'Arlequin's adventure: 'We were part of a group of ten couples, friends from our student days, who decided to move into this block all together when it opened. At first it was all very "utopian"; we had a real community, we even thought of pooling our salaries. But slowly individualism reasserted itself. The more upper-bourgeois couples tended to get fed up with l'Arlequin and moved off to little houses with gardens – and the newer arrivals now come here more because it's cheap than for any idealistic reason. So l'Arlequin is becoming "normalized". Yet it still *is* different. It's some-thing to do with the high-density architecture, which may be ugly but brings a feeling of togetherness. There's a far more neighbourly spirit than in most new suburbs, with far more casual dropping-in. People are always ready to baby-sit for free, or lend you things. And the old people and the handicapped are not made to feel left out; they're housed on the same passageways as us, on purpose.'

Others gave me similar reactions. Pierre Frappat, who lived at l'Arlequin for some time, said, 'One success is that there's more spirit of tolerance and compassion than in most French towns. The unmarried mother, or the Catholic priest who's got married, are not ostracized here; and delinquency is treated as a social disease, not simply a matter for the police. So Dubedout's ideals *have* left their mark. L'Arlequin may be far from a total success; but it's a failure only in the sense that people's hopes for it were pitched absurdly high in thinking that it could change society overnight.' Maybe what it has done is restore some sense of personal neighbourly concern, the warm contacts of old village society that normally wither when transplanted to suburbia. But l'Arlequin has not yet created a wider sense of community responsibility: even here, French hang-ups about authority remain too strong.

Not only in the new suburbs, but in all of France, local community life is today in a strange phase of transition, as the French confusedly re-examine the formal structures that have guided them for so long. This is a diffuse grass-roots movement, full of contradictions, varying from place to place, hard to identify clearly – but it exists. As we have noted elsewhere (see pp. 20 and 647), the French mood today is coloured by a disaffection for public institutions of all sorts, both State and non-State. Instead, there is a move towards more local, disparate and private forms of life; and this takes two very different forms, not easily compatible. First, the *repli sur soi*, the withdrawal into private fulfilments. Secondly, the sporadic citizen initiatives towards creating new kinds of community life, independent of the State or official bodies; they mark not only a bid to overcome loneliness, but also a groping towards new loyalties and commitments, as the old institutions lose their appeal. It is a most significant trend, but still tenuous and fragile.

Many a Frenchman will talk excitedly today about a new growth industry, '*la vie associative*', by which he means the local life of clubs, societies and other spontaneous movements that the Anglo-Saxon world has long taken for granted. But for the French, not normally a very clubbable people, this is something rather new, and the number of so-called '*associations*' has doubled since 1972, to reach a total put at 400,000. As in other countries, they are of three main kinds: leisure clubs, mainly for sport and culture; privately-created welfare bodies, for citizen self-help or for aid to the poor or weak; and committees for the improvement or protection of the local environment, many of them politicized protest groups.

How much does it all add up to? The French themselves, at least, believe there has been a change. At Orgeval, a large village twenty-five miles west of Paris, now in the commuter belt, a middle-class Socialist told me enthusiastically: 'Associations here are booming. They used to be the privilege of rich people, joining together to dispense charity to the poor, but now anyone takes part. For example, we've formed a committee to welcome new inhabitants and introduce them to the locals. Also, we had no sports ground, and neither the State nor the council would give us the money for it, so some of us grouped together, dug into our own pockets, and now we have all kinds of new sports clubs. And we've just had the village fête: the ladies did a classical dance, my son of twelve took part in a play, and I was so surprised to spend such a marvellous evening watching all this. It was fantastic to think that a lot of local people had spent months preparing it. Of course, to an Englishman, all this must seem very obvious, but in this country it didn't exist before . . .' Yes, I suppose I did find it obvious, and I am still not sure how far to be impressed by this new activity in France. Certainly sports clubs are booming, and so are the arts; but nearly always under official sponsorship, not private initiative (see pp. 25 and 636–8). And for every bright idea that succeeds there are ten that fail.

It is in welfare and self-help that the French are having most difficulty in adapting their traditions to the more informal needs of today. In a nation with little tradition of voluntary non-partisan public service, most welfare work has tended to be institutionalized, provided either by the Church and its *bonnes soeurs*, or else by official bodies – State or municipal – in a juridical manner. And in this legalistic land any private initiative is looked on with mistrust unless it secures the official stamp of approval by adhering to the complex legal statutes of the famous Law of 1901 that governs non-profit-making bodies. This is a shade inhibiting for anyone wanting to start up anything so simple as a crèche or an old folks' club. Also, an individual gesture of public service is often suspected of ulterior motives. A young housewife in a new middle-class Paris suburb told me that she was treated with some suspicion by the neighbours when, purely out of kindness and without seeking payment, she tried to start up a crèche. 'She must be a Communist, she's trying to get at us,' was the initial reaction of many bourgeois mothers who really would have liked nothing better than to be able to leave their small children in safe hands for an hour or two. But because she was not someone they knew, because she was acting 'unofficially' and was not a paid social worker, she was suspect. Finally the crèche did get going and was a great success, but it took patience.

Clearly the need has been growing for more voluntary work of this

kind, especially in the big new suburbs; here the traditional role of the
Church is in sharp decline, and paid workers are far thinner on the
ground than in a special place such as l'Arlequin. So, if the citizens want
to lead fuller and richer lives, they must do more to help themselves – or
that at least is the thinking of the new generation of pioneering do-
gooders now at work, in growing numbers, in urban France. They finally
seem to be making some progress, and the weekly *Le Point*[6] has written
lyrically about 'these new lady bountifuls in blue-jeans, these T-shirt
missionaries' who spend their free time visiting the old and sick, looking
after each others' children, running dressmaking classes, preparing
street festivals and trying to re-create in the H L M *milieux* some of the lost
warmth and solidarity of the old village societies. *Le Point* suggests that in
this new urban setting the French may at last be realizing that they
cannot leave everything to the State and town councils: 'The new wave
of voluntary work may mean that millions of citizens are today resolved
to look after themselves.' Brave words, but I heard a very different story
from a civic employee at Cergy-Pontoise who knows the United States
well: 'In our twin-town in Maryland,' she said, 'the associations do their
own fund-raising and virtually run the community: their role is far more
active than the town council's. But here, citizens are still not used to
helping themselves. When they form an association, it sits on its arse and
demands that every franc comes from the State and the communes. That
was true of our big spring festival: its committee made no effort to raise
money from the inhabitants, it expected us to pay for everything – *and* to
take the main decisions. In this kind of community action, the French are
still far less emancipated than the Americans.' From others, mainly on
the Left, one would often hear a different version in the Giscard era.
Their complaint: that the State was *too* interfering, wanting a finger in
every pie – 'Its officials are everywhere,' said one girl, 'keeping tabs on
each new association that springs up, trying to stifle the ones that are too
gauchiste and win control over others with enticing little subsidies.
We have to be wary.' Will the new Socialist rulers of France now live
up to their ideals, and leave local ventures to manage their own
affairs?

In a confused and varied situation, there is another aspect too,
rather depressing, that one finds in many a new suburb: community
efforts are often ephemeral, as the vigour of the few pioneers meets a
limited public response. The associations may go through an active
phase initially, in the form of residents' pressure-groups agitating for
better public services: but once the amenities are supplied, then interest

6 May 14th, 1979.

falls off and people relapse into cosy privacy. La Paillarde is a large new working-class suburb of Montpellier, built Sarcelles-style, without amenities, by the former Right-wing council. The city's new Socialist rulers have now at least provided it with a spacious new *maison de quartier*, but this is much under-used, as I was told by the municipal *animateur* in charge: 'It's ironic that La Paillarde had more sense of solidarity when things were going badly than today, now it's got the equipment it needs. At this *maison*, we find that people will come along if we offer them social and cultural activity on a plate, but they will not help organize it themselves – except for a tiny band of faithful volunteers.' In almost any new town it is the same little group of loyalists who circulate from one event to the next, and it is thanks to them that a visiting lecturer gets a decent audience, that the basketwork classes keep going, that an amateur drama group is formed. And a dynamic community life is nearly always due to the lead set by one or two strong personalities, whether paid officials or volunteers.

If the silent majority remains so passive, there could be one other reason that we have not yet evoked: politics. Most French people today are sickened by politics, by the hypocrisies and feuds of the parties and the bullying tactics of extremists. Yet a fair share of suburbia's new pioneers are politically motivated, notably on the far Left; and many of their community ventures thus become politicized, including those that have nothing to do with politics, such as sport or music. An attempt to launch a theatre group or a keep-fit class may develop into a dog-fight between Trotskyists and Maoists; so the average citizen stays at home and watches a Western on the telly. Better the mild malaise of new-town blues than the raging fever of new-town Reds?

The more positive side of this complex political picture is that many town councils, notably those led by Socialists or Left-Radicals, have been making laudable attempts to encourage direct democracy by strengthening the *comités de quartier*. Most larger towns now have these neighbourhood committees, either created spontaneously or sponsored by the council; and their roles vary. Some of them act as pressure-groups against the council. But in the more go-ahead towns – such as Grenoble and La Rochelle – the mayor has been urging the committees to play more part in the *animation* and upkeep of their quarter, and also to serve as a regular channel of communication between the citizen and the remote, impersonal *mairie*. The results have been variable. Michel Crépeau at La Rochelle operates a subtle paternalism. He scrupulously consults his committees on all civic projects; but as one of his senior councillors admitted to me, 'Our technique is so to prepare the ground that the citizens suggest to us what we already have in mind.'

At Rennes, the pattern is different. Here the previous *centriste* mayor, Henri Fréville (see p. 141), another enlightened paternalist, had in the 1960s set up a central 'cultural office' with *animateurs* in each suburb who created local civic units to run arts societies, crèches, old folks' clubs and so on. In its way this worked well, but it was judged insufficiently democratic by the Socialist-led council that took over in 1977, and they delegated the work of the office to the committees, most of them with Left majorities. 'That's all very well,' said one civic-minded Catholic who had played a key role in the Fréville scheme in his particular suburb, 'but we pay a price for this new democracy. When the committee meets, instead of getting down to practical tasks, it waffles endlessly about ideology and the future of the world. It will waste a whole meeting on wording some anti-nuclear resolution, rather than deciding how next week's old folks' outing is to be organized. Far less gets done than in the old days – and I've resigned.' A familiar French dilemma: can democracy ever be as efficient as benevolent technocracy?

In Grenoble, where Dubedout has made a real effort to involve the citizens in every municipal activity and decision, I heard a complaint of a very different kind from his right-hand man, Jean Verlhac: 'As Socialists, we try to encourage working people to play more part in running their *quartiers*, but we find them reluctant to come forward. Their lack of education seems to make them feel inferior, unable to express themselves or grasp the often technical decisions that need to be taken. And in practice a kind of screen is erected between us, the *mairie*, and them – a screen composed firstly of well-educated self-appointed demagogues in each *quartier* who claim to speak for the rest, and secondly of our paid social workers and animators who construe self-management as management by themselves, the professionals. They think *they* have all the answers; and so the power grip of the technocrat is spreading down to this humbler stratum – you see it at l'Arlequin. In France, it really is very hard to establish shared democracy, when élites always come forward and insist on running the show.' Significantly, in 1979 I heard a very similar comment on French civic life from a source far removed from the *mairie* of Grenoble: the Elysée Palace, under Giscard. Here the liberal-minded young specialist on local affairs, Alain Lamassoure, told me: 'In France a new type of grass-roots demagogue has emerged, who instead of going into local politics becomes the president of associations and ward committees. He's less the ambitious politico than a vainglorious busybody; at any meeting he monopolizes all the talk and claims to speak in the name of the community. And the others are too passive to shut him up. It makes it very hard for us, the authorities, to penetrate behind this verbose façade into true contact with the ordinary citizens, to find out what they really want, for example over public housing. This is not local democracy as we see it.' It is the usual French story, of the gulf between a huge apathetic majority and the dynamic, assertive few.

Many *comités de quartier* have arisen spontaneously for environmental defence. In some cases, they seem to be doing a useful job, enabling local people at last to take their own destiny in hand and force the aloof technocrats into real debate (see p. 342). And some residents' groups have achieved results, for good or ill: at Toulouse, one group secured indefinite delay of a plan for a throughway beside the Garonne, while in another suburb of the city, when the council announced plans for high-rise flats on a site previously scheduled as a park, the inhabitants put barricades of tree-trunks across the road in the classic French style and forced the council to back down. But without any such specific target the groups rarely survive for long; their horizons tend to be very parochial and their aims defensive rather than constructive. What is more, they regularly fall into the hands of Left-wing extremists, especially in a town where the council is Right of Centre – and here again an exemplary case is Toulouse. Its twenty-five *comités de quartier* are solidly Leftist, and they issue tracts denouncing the council's schemes: 'This new town-plan is tailor-made to suit the rich and swell the profits of the speculators, while exiling the working class to the far suburbs . . .', etc. The mayor, Pierre Baudis, throws the weight of his own civic apparatus into combating the influence of these groups, and so community action in the city degenerates into a running political dog-fight – and the inhabitants are the losers. The local youth and culture centres (*maisons des jeunes et de la culture*) have provided the main battlefield, as Baudis seeks to squeeze out the autonomous Leftist ones and implant his own network in the suburbs. At one such centre on an HLM estate, a defrocked Franciscan with *gauchiste* views took charge of the place and started progressive discussion groups on moral and social problems such as free love and worker-management. These were a great success. But Baudis took fright at this dangerous Leftism in a centre that formally was under the council's tutelage, and he tried to close it. There was a local outcry, and finally the *mairie* backed down – a rare example of spontaneous public action of this kind in Toulouse. But in other cases Baudis has been more successful.[7]

Throughout France, there are countless cases of useful community projects being sabotaged by political feuding. At Massy, the Socialist council with the aid of the State built a large socio-cultural centre, and in a democratic spirit handed over its daily running to an association. But

7 See my book *A Tale of Five Cities*, Secker & Warburg, 1979, pp. 315–19.

this body fell into the hands of extreme-Left groups, who used the centre to propagate their own views, thus alienating most of its habitués. There were constant conflicts with the *mairie*. Finally the mayor felt he had no choice but to kick out the association, and the centre is now run by a delegation of civic councillors: a defeat for direct democracy.

Far worse has befallen the national experiment in community cable-TV, which the Giscard Government sanctioned on the pattern familiar in North America. Eight new towns including Sarcelles, Cergy-Pontoise and Villeneuve (Grenoble) were duly equipped with cable networks, and it was agreed that the trial programme would be run by associations. At Cergy, Leftists got control of the associations and their output followed a predictable pattern. Asked to do a consumer programme on holidays, they turned it into an attack on capitalist tour operators; asked to present a consumer advice programme on local clinics, they made it an assault on the State health service; and so on. In Grenoble the trials went more smoothly at first, but similar difficulties began to arise. At Sarcelles, before trials ever started, the Communist town council made a powerful bid to seize control of a system intended to be run by an association in a non-partisan spirit. So the net result of all this was that the Government, not surprisingly, cancelled the entire experiment. The eight cable networks today remain, unused. There are cynics who say that the Giscard Government, always wary of sacrificing its TV monopoly, had sanctioned the trials knowing full well that they would run into these problems and would thus demonstrate that local TV of this kind was not feasible in politicized France. In any case, a venture of real potential value to local communities was destroyed by the French inability to abide by the rules of '*le fair-play*'. And again the moral might be that the general public itself is too passive and un-public-spirited to forestall the extremists by stepping in to take its own responsibility for such a project. Anyway the Socialist Government now has plans for relaunching the scheme, which might stand a better chance of working in the new French climate.

Less crudely and aggressively than the *gauchistes*, but far more methodically, the Communists too have been dragging politics into every corner of local life, as part of their national strategy, at least in the 1977–81 period (see p. 634). If there is any little club in any little village that seems ripe for infiltration – be it of fly-fishers, trombone players or entomologists – they will seek to take it over and run it for Party ends. And naïve is the entomologist who thinks that the main purpose of his club will still be to catch butterflies! It is true that the Party has a sound record of civic administration in those towns which it has ruled on its own for some years, such as Le Havre, where it has built up its own tight network. The trouble today lies in those many towns where it is in uneasy coalition with the Socialists, and especially in those places where it has newly taken over the *mairie* and is still battling to complete its infiltration of local society. For example, at Sarcelles.

Like Massy, Sarcelles today has come of age, shaken off its blues and become a real town; not beautiful, but lively. People are quite contented, even proud of the place, and indignant if you mention 'sarcellitis'. There are swimming-pools and hypermarkets, a synagogue, factories and music schools. On my last visit, old men were playing *boules* in the public gardens, as if in the Midi; the Red municipality was organizing a chamber concert in a church; and the Amicale Antillaise was holding a gala, full of dusky ladies in gorgeous headdresses – Sarcelles is vividly cosmopolitan. But, if you look a little deeper, you soon see that the town is riven by a conflict between the Communists and the rest, as the Party strives implacably to add Sarcelles to its ring of safe bastions in the Paris Red Belt. And at present only 32 per cent of the town votes Communist, leaving the Party uncomfortably dependent on its Socialist partners in the *mairie*. So, under mayor Henri Canacos, a dour technical worker, the Party has been systematically taking over the town's community life; and the non-Communists are generally too easy-going and divided to put up strong opposition – a parable of the Western world today. Of the hundred or so associations, the Party now controls two-thirds, including most of those for sport and culture. The gymnastics club has split into two, like Berlin. And as the town council controls the sports centres, it can and sometimes does deny their use to clubs not of its colour.

One *maison de quartier* succeeds in holding out against the Party's offensive. It is run by a residents' association on which the Party – to its fury – has not been able to gain a majority. Its guiding spirit is a Jewish pharmacist who is not on speaking terms with the Communists: he refused to go into the municipal library with me. 'This town is being ruined by politics,' he told me; 'voluntary workers are leaving the place in droves, for if they don't hold a Party card they get victimized.' However, a Protestant pastor manages to run a successful youth and culture centre in his Reformed Church, but at first it was not easy: the municipality tried every dodge to prevent him opening the centre, including a lawsuit – which they lost – alleging that he had no right to the land. Most Sarcellois, fairly unpolitical, show little taste for these power battles that rage around them; they simply want to enjoy life. But the polarization inevitably affects them, and leaves them vaguely uneasy and annoyed.

The Party's main local adversary is the SCIC (Société Centrale

Immobilière de la Caisse des Dépôts), the big State-backed development company that built the new town and is still responsible for its public housing and some equipment. The mayor repeatedly accuses it of every capitalist sin in the book, such as evicting tenants behindhand with the rent; and for years he has carried on a battle with the SCIC over Sarcelles' big shopping centre, where certain commercial muddles and errors of judgement were exploited by the Party as a scandal of embezzlement. However, the crucial power struggle at Sarcelles is over housing, for housing means electors, and the Party's basic strategy is clear. It wants to develop Sarcelles as a sure and solid fief, like some other Red suburbs such as near-by St-Denis, but for this it needs more voters than its present 32 per cent. So on the communal land of old Sarcelles, outside the new-town area, the council is building new high-rise HLMs, and there it discreetly places its own faithful by a transfer of inhabitants from places like Argenteuil and St-Denis where the Communist vote is in easy surplus. This is national policy. The Prefect has only limited powers to thwart this devious operation, though the SCIC tries to do its best by stepping up the building of more middle-class housing within its own domain of the new town. Such is the sinister *Realpolitik* of many a French housing programme.

Sarcelles is an extreme but not a unique example. In many towns where the Communists are active, whether or not they control the *mairie*, community life suffers from endless political tussles. At Grenoble, Party militants at first fought hard to sabotage the Arlequin project; but they have calmed down since joining Dubedout's coalition in 1977. Generally speaking, in a town where the Communists are the weaker partners within a Socialist-led coalition – as at Grenoble, and Rennes, Montpellier and elsewhere – the tactics of the Party today are to be fairly acquiescent and cooperative on the level of council affairs, but to militate behind the scenes at neighbourhood level. Crépeau has suffered from this at La Rochelle. Very reluctantly he brought the Communists into his coalition in 1977, and has since had little trouble from them within the council itself, but he has to be vigilant; the Communists are constantly manoeuvring to get control of the *maisons de quartier*, and also of the town's cultural life. Robert Kalbach, a senior councillor, virulently anti-Communist, told me: 'The only way to deal with these bastards is to be tough and stand no nonsense. Luckily, in the council, we are twenty-six and they are only eleven. In its cultural commission, which I chair, I faced constant heckling from a young Stalinist firebrand who wasted meetings by lecturing me about wicked imperialists in Africa, etc. So I went to the local Party boss and complained about this breach of "coalition spirit", and it worked – the young man has since shut up!' These tensions are common throughout France, and sometimes they burst into the open. At Angers and Brest, two of the larger towns taken over by the Left in 1977, the Socialist mayors finally lost patience with their dear Communist allies and in the winter of 1979–80 removed them from all municipal posts of responsibility, thus virtually placing them in opposition on the council.

It is true that since the coming to power of the Left, in 1981, the Communists have grown rather more docile in local affairs, at Sarcelles and elsewhere. After all, they have now outwardly healed the breach with the Socialists, by entering their Government. Also, their vote slumped so badly in the 1981 elections that they have been forced to rethink their strategy. This has pushed them on to the defensive, and their mood has grown quieter, for the time being, in many towns. But it is unlikely that their basic strategy has changed, or that they will cease trying to exploit every advantage against their Socialist rivals.

There are many sides to the argument about whether or not community action should be politicized. Of course it is true that many Left-wing activists, Communist or other, are warm-hearted people who are not solely bent on revolution but also care about social aid and culture, even within the existing context of society. But the familiar problem is that often they confuse ends and means. At Sarcelles I met a young militant, neither Communist nor *gauchiste* but Left-wing Socialist, and he told me that he was active in promoting crèches, arts clubs, visits to the sick and elderly, and similar voluntary services. Splendid, I said. He explained, 'Yes, we see these activities as an essential means of arousing public consciousness to the evils of the Government and capitalism, so that the masses can be mobilized for *la lutte des classes*.' I gulped, and replied that I thought a crèche was for helping young mothers, an arts club was for those keen on art, and visiting the old and sick was a matter of human compassion, not a ploy in some political crusade. My young friend sincerely saw the two levels of action as equally important, and inter-dependent. For him, a crèche was both for helping mothers *and* for helping revolution. But a great many people, myself included, simply do not agree with this. Our argument is that the baby goes out with the bathwater if non-political activity is constantly being harnessed for political ends. It creates endless conflict, over matters where it ought to be possible to achieve simple human consensus. If mothers want to help each other mind their children, or if a group wants to gather to play chess or sing madrigals, let them be free to do so *for those ends*, without first having to argue on whether the chess-boards and the music-sheets and the children's toys are the products of a wicked capitalist conspiracy. But here we are in face of two fundamentally different views of society. My empirical conclusion is this: a great many ordinary French people today are sickened and revolted by the constant dragging of politics into the non-political, and this is one of the main reasons why so many of them withdraw into their own circles of privacy and why community activity in all its forms remains so fragile and so ill-attended in France. Political association is the enemy of *les associations*.

CULTURE IN THE PROVINCES: FROM MALRAUX'S 'MAISONS' TO THE NEW OPERATIC SNOBBERIES

An average spring evening in an average city, Toulouse ... a local chamber group is playing Mozart in the floodlit courtyard of a pink Renaissance palace, the *cinémathèque* is showing Herzog, Verdi is at the opera house and Sartre at the civic theatre, while the Centre Culturel has a 'trad' jazz concert and a modern sculpture exhibition ... Whatever the limitations of their community life, the French at least are ready consumers of culture when it is offered to them, and the post-war cultural revival of the provinces has been as marked as in Britain, save that, as you might expect, it has been due a little less to private initiatives and more to official policies, leading to the inevitable conflicts.

Until about 1950 the gulf between Paris and its 'desert' was nowhere so evident as in the arts and intellectual activity; almost any ambitious creative artist or performer, in any field, would make for the limelight of the capital. But the tide has since turned. The swelling of the provincial ranks of teachers, *cadres* and students has produced vast new potential audiences, while the rise in prosperity – at least till recently – has made new funds available, and the State has weighed in with sizeable subsidies as one facet of its *aménagement du territoire*. Of course, Paris still exerts its lure; much of the best culture on offer in the provinces is still imported from the capital or abroad, while the home-grown product is of variable quality. But, increasingly, talented creators are prepared to stay and make a career outside Paris. The post-war drama revival has been followed in the 1970s by an amazing renaissance of music in France (see pp. 603–14); and, in summer, arts festivals of all kinds are everywhere.

In the very early post-war years a few talented young actor-producers decided to forego the Parisian rat-race and set up 'reps' in other cities. This was one more token of the spontaneous rebirth of France in that period, following the inter-war years when provincial theatre was virtually dead, killed by local apathy as much as by the cinema. For these early pioneers the struggle at first was tough, but soon the State and some councils were providing regular grants and today at least fifty subsidized companies have fixed homes outside Paris. Much of the liveliest French drama now comes from the provinces. Many com panies go on tour to Paris and abroad and a few have won international fame, notably Roger Planchon's theatre in the Lyon suburb of Villeur-bannc. One typical success has been that of the Comédie de l'Ouest at Rennes, now renamed the Théâtre du Bout du Monde, which since 1950 has patiently created an audience for serious drama in a region with little such tradition. Eight towns in the north-west have even built theatres to house its tours, which take Brecht, Arrabal, O'Casey, Shakespeare, Strindberg to the far corners of Brittany, as well as visiting Britain, Germany, etc. In the early '60s *Look Back in Anger* caused a furore in Brittany and set Catholics distributing tracts against it, but times have since changed: 'When we first put on Beckett, people were horrified,' said the company's director, Guy Parigot; 'nowadays the *lycées* come and ask us to do his plays. He's on the *bac* syllabus.'

Most of the leaders of this post-war wave have been men of the Left. Planchon was much helped by the Left-wing council of Villeurbanne when he first began his remarkable experimental theatre there in the '50s. He went all out to build up a working-class audience, staging lunch-hour excerpts in factory canteens, and in the evenings bringing workers by busload to the theatre on its hilltop above the ochre tenement-towers of this unlovely suburb. The bourgeois theatre-goers of adjacent Lyon, snobbiest city in France, at first ignored this young Bolshevik crank. When he became famous and began to do seasons in Paris, the Lyonnais, surprised, would go and watch him there; but few would venture in their glad rags to sit among the workers on their own back doorstep. Finally in 1972 the Government honoured this brilliant pioneer by allowing his company to take over the mantle and the title of the Théâtre National Populaire which the late Jean Vilar had founded in Paris (see p. 549). Planchon's 'TNP', still at Villeurbanne, is thus officially recognized as France's foremost drama company after the Comédie Française. It is the apogee of the provincial revival, and it has encouraged others. At near-by Grenoble in 1979, in the huge Maison de la Culture, I saw the most ambitious and technically brilliant production of a modern play that I have ever seen outside a capital city: *Les Can-nibales*, conceived and directed by Georges Lavaudant, the ascendant local genius. His sweeping vision of civilization in decay, against a backdrop of the winking lights of Manhattan, drew a rave review in *Le Monde* for its 'tenderness, refinement, generosity . . .'

Many of the early post-war 'reps' had no adequate theatre, and in many sizeable towns the live arts were badly housed. This inspired de Gaulle's Minister of Culture, André Malraux, to embark in the early 1960s on his grandiose policy of building a network of huge multi-purpose arts centres, the notorious Maisons de la Culture. The project has been far from a total success. After a promising start the centres ran into various troubles and in the 1970s the building of new ones was largely halted. But a number still operate, and the experiment is so interesting that its story is worth telling. The basic formula is one of State/municipal partnership; if a town agrees to have a Maison, then council and State go roughly fifty-fifty on building costs and annual subsidies, while an artistic director is in charge of programming. He is responsible to his two patrons, and to a local supervisory association where the general public is also represented.

The enigmatic Malraux, successively man of the Left, man of action, visionary mandarin of art and prophet of Gaullism, was a somewhat unbalanced fanatic with his own very special ideals, and many of the strands of his thinking were evident in his scheme for the Maisons de la Culture. These, he declared at the outset, would enable France 'to become again the world's foremost cultural nation' (what an admission, that she had ceased to be so!). It was his lofty aim that they should present only works of quality and spread Paris standards across France – 'Soon,' he claimed, opening a Maison at Amiens in 1966, 'this hideous word "provincial" will have ceased to exist in France.' His second aim was to destroy the notion of culture as a bourgeois preserve and draw a new social class into theatres and art galleries. The Fifth Republic, he said, must do for universal culture what the Third had done for universal education. Here spoke Malraux, man of the Left, with ideas not so very different from those prevalent in Britain. But Malraux, mandarin of art, went further: art was a means whereby the soul attains to God (see his later works such as *Les Voix du silence*), and so with a Gaullist missionary zeal he sought to colonize the French desert with this divine truth. It was therefore a matter of doctrine that the Maisons should be highbrow and not offer a place, as many would have liked, for mere entertainment or for local amateur productions. The Maisons, quoting Malraux again, were to provide for 'interpenetration of the arts', with many activities under the one roof: thus a film lover, once drawn inside, might begin to take an interest in sculpture, or an opera fan in poetry. But this sensible idea did not solve one of the basic contradictions of the whole policy. The highbrow doctrine was hard to reconcile with that of bringing culture to the masses. It presupposed that workers must needs love the highest when they see it, and would flock in. Which of course they did not.

Malraux's doctrine also rapidly brought him into some conflict with his partners, the town councils, who were well aware that their electors might not be too keen on the austere diet proposed to them. It was to Malraux's credit that, regardless of politics, he chose as artistic directors the best men available – and not surprisingly most of these were Leftist anti-Gaullist theatre men, of the stamp of Brook or Wesker. Some of them soon fell out with their local council; the first serious conflict arose in the mid-1960s at Caen. Here the director, Jo Tréhard, a lively young Left-winger, launched a programme of *avant-garde* plays, concerts and debates, and picked up eager audiences from the 'new wave' of Caennais, the university students and the scientists and *cadres* from Paris. The Maison with its fine modern theatre, art gallery and lounge-bar, provided Caen with the cultural focus it had lacked. But the older bourgeoisie were furious with Tréhard's policy. Their idea of theatre was operetta and boulevard comedies on tour from Paris; that was what they'd had before the war. And the Right-wing council supported them, with an eye on their votes, and began to plot Tréhard's removal (it shared with Malraux a power of veto over the director). At first Tréhard survived by making concessions: 'I put on *The Merry Widow*, to appease the council, though I'm ashamed of it,' he told me. But then came May '68 when Tréhard sided with the rebels, and the council found this too much and secured his removal. The State replied by suspending its funds, so the building ceased to be a Maison de la Culture and became a routine municipal theatre. In 1969 I found it locked and empty at 7 p.m., a time when it had normally been full of students. Posters announced an insipid boulevard comedy for the following week. And Jo Tréhard I found gamely trying to salvage the wreckage of his policy (with modest State help) in a tawdry church hall in the suburbs. It seemed a local tragedy worthy of Brecht.

There were similar disputes elsewhere, either over politics or over 'brow', or both (and while the highbrow minority may be a little larger in France than in Britain, the average middle-class Frenchman is scarcely more devoted to 'culture' than his English counterpart, even if he pays greater lip-service to it). At Bourges in the 1960s, the Maison de la Culture revitalized the life of this sleepy old market town; bus companies even revised their time-tables to take villagers back home at night. The director, Gabriel Monnet, offered an eclectic programme to suit many tastes, including the staging of French premières of new experimental plays. But despite his local popularity he too ran into trouble in that fatal spring of 1968, when he allowed his Maison to be used for talk-ins by student rebels. The conservative mayor of Bourges forced his dismissal. Especially in the aftermath of May 1968, the Maisons fell easy prey to the French talent for extremism and lack of compromise; frequently they were denounced by the bourgeoisie as hotbeds of Leftism, yet boycotted by the *gauchistes* as being too 'institutional' and part of the Establishment. The directors were caught between this cross-fire. One told me, 'The Catholic middle classes think I'm an atheist or Communist because I like modern drama, while some Left intellectuals despise me for working with the Government (which in fact I oppose).'

These quarrels have subsided in the 1970s. Since Malraux left the scene in 1969 the State's role has become less evangelical, and directors have mostly come to terms with their public and with local councils. The fifteen Maisons today in operation – at Grenoble, Rennes, Reims, Le Havre, Amiens, etc. – are far fewer than originally hoped for, but they do perform a service, they draw audiences, and their frictions are less acute than in the 1960s. In an age of budget cuts and soaring costs, their problems today are less political than boringly financial.

The Maisons de la Culture were in some ways a brilliant idea; but most people today agree that these 'cultural cathedrals' were built on too unrealistically grandiose a scale. The Maison at Grenoble, the largest, cost 30 million francs in 1968; a palatial but unlovely edifice of glass and concrete, far grander than London's Royal Festival Hall, with three separate theatres, one with a revolving auditorium. The big Maison at Rennes also has three theatres, a cinema, art gallery and much else. The Maisons' audiences are adequate – the larger theatres are usually full for the more popular shows – but the oppressive scale of the buildings does not make for a warm inviting atmosphere. So this is one reason why they have failed to fulfil Malraux's aim of wooing the working class to culture; workers account for only 2 to 3 per cent of audiences. They seem to have been frightened off by the cathedral-like nature of these *temples de la culture* – dare the uninitiated enter? Probably this cannot be solved without changes in French education, which has hitherto given the working class a sense of exclusion from bourgeois culture (see pp. 472–93).

The size of the buildings leads also to high overheads, and this today is causing grave problems. At Grenoble there is a full-time staff of eighty-four, at Reims seventy-six, at Rennes seventy, including the cleaners, electricians, secretaries and others needed to keep these palaces fully functioning (and the Left-wing unions go on strike at any hint of cuts). This severely limits the amount of money available for programmes. At Grenoble, 28 per cent of revenue comes from box-office and the rest from State and local subsidies (9.2 million francs in 1978); but of this total income over 50 per cent goes on staff wages, a further sum on upkeep, leaving only 31 per cent for supporting artistic creation. And this is better than average; at some Maisons, wages and maintenance account for 80 per cent of spending. Yet such is the stern arithmetic of subsidized culture, anywhere, that if seat prices are to be kept within the means of the less well-off, then any performance however popular will run at a deficit and need its share of the subsidy. This applies especially to opera, orchestral concerts, large-scale drama and even to a star one-man show. 'It's an absurd irony,' said the director of one Maison, 'that we could play *Carmen* or *Tosca* to full houses for four nights, but we can't afford it, so we have to limit the run to two nights – and lots of our subscribers can't get seats. The more successful a show, the more it would cost us.' I heard the same story everywhere. And so, as subsidies (until 1982) have not been keeping pace with rises in costs, the Maisons have been forced to reduce their already sparse programming, and hence are used far below capacity. At Amiens, I found that each of two fine modern theatres had a live show on average one night in six. The picture is the same at Grenoble, Rennes and elsewhere, and the prime reason is lack of budget rather than of audience. So, when there is no evening performance, the Maison is virtually deserted, for it rarely has the appeal of a social centre. At Grenoble, a big town with over 30,000 students, I found the Maison locking its doors at 9 p.m. as the last few customers left the large, overlit, uninviting cafeteria, and I compared this with the jolly club-like ambience of many far more modest arts centres in Britain, or indeed in some other French towns. It is a sad failure of planning. A much smaller centre, more attractively designed, with lower overheads, could afford more activities, and become more of a cultural club, less of a cultural discount warehouse.

So what is the answer? Seats even for an opera rarely cost more than about 15 francs, so there are those who argue that prices should be raised drastically. But State and Left-wing councils are both against this solution, which would deter the kind of people (students and workers) whom the Maisons especially seek to attract. Another suggestion is that the Maisons should be opened out to much wider uses: to business conferences or touring variety shows which would help pay for their overheads; or to local amateur activities which could share their under-used facilities without costing public money. In one or two towns, civic arts centres that have chosen to remain outside the State scheme are going ahead on these lines, notably at St-Etienne. Here the State helped to build a large Maison de la Culture, but the mayor then changed his mind and decided the town would run the place itself, in its own way, without State aid. It is used for professional theatre, art and music, yes, but also for congresses of doctors, farmers, trades unionists and the like, as well as for adult education classes. A sensible compromise, in some ways, but a blasphemy in the light of the purist Malraux doctrine, to which the State-funded Maisons must still adhere at the risk of appearing dog-in-the-manger. 'A Maison de la Culture is not a public garage,' said one director, primly; and in Amiens I found *The Merry Widow* on tour relegated to a local cinema while the Maison's larger theatre stood empty. It is a highly debatable policy. Do you give people what they want, or what you think good for them?

It is true that, since Malraux left, the highbrow policy has been discreetly relaxed to the extent that Maisons can now invite cabaret artists and pop singers of the more respectable kind (Devos, Moustaki etc.) and these always draw full houses. The Maisons can also stray into cultural education, with art and music workshops for children, and suchlike. But amateur dramatics or singing clubs? – no, these are still taboo, and so *a fortiori* are popular galas or do-it-yourself folklore. The argument – a very un-British one – is that professional and amateur standards must be kept distinct. One cultural official told me that he had been appointed to run a small Maison in a new town near Marseille: 'The mayor was delighted to get his 50 per cent State subsidy, but had no idea what a Maison de la Culture was for. He was furious when I wouldn't let him fill the place with majorette parades. Finally he got rid of me, and his State subsidy, and now he runs the place as a kind of *salle des fêtes*. It keeps most people happy. But where its own funds are involved the State must retain some control, or many of these councils would run their Maison as a glorified Rotary-Club-cum-funfair, with an eye to their own re-election.'

Despite their unwieldy size and shaky finances, in cultural terms the Maisons cannot be written off as a failure.[8] Perhaps the best today is the one at Rennes, whose director believes in a serious but eclectic programme. In a single typical month, February 1979, he presented the Bolshoi Ballet (no less), the Stuttgart Philharmonic playing Beethoven's Ninth, Guy Parigot's local State-backed 'rep' in a minor Brecht, a Belgian company with a new German play, three chamber concerts, films by Ozu and others, a modern art exhibition from the Maeght museum near Nice, a lantern-slide lecture on Japan, readings from Roland Barthes, a play for children, and various Parisian *chansonniers* including Guy Béart – nearly all of these for just one, two or three performances each. Here, as elsewhere, most of the material is imported from outside (often from abroad), save for the work of the local 'rep' and any other local drama or music groups of professional standard.

The Maisons de la Culture are only a small part of the overall cultural life of the provinces. Some towns, such as Toulouse, have preferred to forego State aid and open their own smaller arts centres; others, such as

8 The Socialist Government's doubling of the State culture budget for 1982 may now revive their fortunes (see p. 616).

Lyon and Strasbourg, have renovated their existing theatres, concert
halls and opera houses, where activity booms. In any event, in 1971 the
Ministry gave up the policy of building 'cathedrals', in favour of new
centres of a more modest kind; in some towns, a few small buildings are
dispersed around residential districts, in the hope of getting closer to
local audiences. About twenty-six towns now have these new-style
Centres d'Animation Culturelle, or mini-Maisons, and they are working
quite well, notably at Annecy, a brilliantly lively place where several
cultural bodies banded together and secured State aid. At Tarbes, down
near the Pyrenees, there is even a new arts centre inside a hypermarket,
part of the idealistic Leclerc chain (see p. 399). This gives a new twist to
the notion of 'interpenetration' (if hardly as Malraux conceived it), as
culture hopefully entices new clients to the store, or shoppers in turn can
stay on for a chamber concert or *Waiting for Godot*. On occasions, actors
have even staged impromptu playlets or cabaret acts down among the
grocery counters, to the surprise of the housewives with their trolleys.

This is very much in line with the new French trend in the 1970s
towards a more spontaneous and local kind of culture, with the accent on
animation, that favourite French word. It is a break-away trend from the
established Malraux doctrine, so there are now two movements in
parallel. On the one hand, there remains the formal French tradition of
spoon-fed professional culture – in opera houses, theatres or Malraux-
esque 'cathedrals' – whether the material offered there be classical or
modern. On the other hand, the 1970s have seen a flowering – as in
Britain – of all kinds of very small-scale, very local activities, now more or
less encouraged by a State that recognizes after all that small can be
beautiful. Over five hundred little troupes of young professional actors
have sprung up across France, often ephemeral, always struggling on a
shoestring, seldom with a theatre of their own; but about a hundred and
ninety of them receive some State aid. In Brittany, for example, Guy
Parigot's company had the field to itself till recently, but now has a score
of little rivals, such as the well-named Théâtre de l'Instant at Brest. From
its base in a poky HLM flat, this intrepid group of nine actors sallies forth
on its 'civilizing mission' to a town with scant knowledge of modern
theatre, and introduces to it Weiss, Stoppard, the inevitable Brecht and
others far more obscure. 'For two years we almost starved,' said the
leader, Bernard Lotti; 'we acted where we could, in the back-rooms of
cafés. But now we're just beginning to get recognized.' This group is
'serious' about intellectual theatre; but other troupes, more Leftist, have
a more populist approach, and they tour the HLM suburbs with their
own home-grown little plays on local life, in a language they hope the
workers can understand. It is their bid to bridge the notorious cultural

gulf that has kept the working class away from the 'cathedrals'. The movement has now spread to the civic *maisons des quartiers*: at one; in Rennes, the staff *animateur* created an amateur drama group which wrote and acted a playlet about housing, with the chorus, '*On a des HLMs, Vive la Bretagne!*' These homespun attempts to relate culture to local daily life may seem old hat to a British reader; but in France, dominated for so long by the reverential approach to '*la culture*' taught in schools, it is all new and exciting. Amateur drama, and amateur concerts, do not have the same solid tradition as in Britain.

Though the State still does not want this non-professional activity to defile its Maisons de la Culture, it is now keen to help it elsewhere. The Ministry of Culture is now putting a special stress on extra-mural education and what is called 'le socio-culturel', and its *animateurs* are everywhere in their hundreds, organizing a festival here, starting up a pottery class there, allotting funds judiciously to any new spontaneous project that seems to deserve it. More than ever, the *animateur* is now a member of a key French profession; he has no real equivalent in the Anglo-Saxon world, but he is the man who breaks down public apathy, stirs people into happy activity, and in many places he is filling the gap left by the sharply declining roles of the *curé* and the *instituteur*. Rural animation in particular is now *à la mode*, and in the Ardèche young *installés* (see p. 254) have been given State funds for going round the schools and youth clubs, reciting their own or traditional poetry, and urging the peasants to write poems too! Apparently it is a success. Town councils, too, have been jumping on the *animation* bandwagon, particularly in Grenoble which has four hundred paid *animateurs*, fanning out from the Maison de la Culture to bring the message of cultural self-help to the lonely suburbs. But all this raises a giant quarrel of doctrine. What is the purpose of culture? For some people, this kind of *animation* is an essential means of bringing an alienated working class into the cultural fold of the nation. For others, it is irrelevant to the true creative role of an artist or actor. Bernard Lotti in Brest was scathing: 'The *animateurs* here consider us too aesthetic and highbrow, too cut off from "the people". But for me, it's a pure waste of my time to go round the schools and suburbs giving drama classes. We need the cash so we have to do it, as the Left-wing council will more readily give us money for this work than for our serious plays, which it thinks a luxury. This animation vogue has gone too far: it's sad to see theatre being debased into occupational therapy.'

This may be the view from Brest; but most big towns of all political shades remain far readier than in Britain to spend large sums on culture to suit every 'brow', often up to 10 per cent or more of the civic budget.

Of course the odd voice is raised that the funds could be better devoted to new schools or housing, but seldom is the spending of ratepayers' money on the arts the electoral suicide that it can be in Britain. Culture is in demand; it is also a matter of local pride, a status symbol, like having a good football team. In Toulouse, the opera house and its large regular company received 3 million francs from the State in 1977, a mere 2.3 million from box-office, and the balance of its deficit – 17.3 million! – from the city. For the regional orchestra, the proportions were not very different. These are astonishing figures, especially as the opera plays to 98 per cent capacity (see p. 609).

The nature of the State/municipal partnership for arts patronage has shifted in the past decade or so. The State is still very active in certain fields; but, increasingly, big towns have been taking charge of their own programmes, with the State simply providing a back-up of funds. Grenoble under Dubedout – yes, again Grenoble – provides the star example of how a city's cultural life has been revolutionized in the past fifteen years. When Dubedout took over in 1965, the arts activity of the home town of Stendhal was little less fossilized than the relics in the local museum: a moribund music *conservatoire*, a struggling 'rep', a few traditional Catholic youth *fêtes* and endless tours of boulevard comedies and Viennese operettas that fully satisfied the older bourgeois public. But the newly arrived younger élites of this boom city were far from satisfied; they were by now demanding a more up to date and stimulating diet. And they soon got it. The man Dubedout put in charge of the town's culture was the remarkable Bernard Gilman, a self-educated ex-worker turned primary schoolteacher, from the Nord, with a taste for modernism allied to democratic ideals on the need to open culture out to the masses. Helped by a trebling of the council's budget for the arts (it is now 13 per cent of the total), he and his team set to work on the Great Leap Forward. First came the Maison de la Culture, opened in 1968. Then the *conservatoire* was enlarged and revived, and complemented with a new civic musical centre and full-time chamber orchestra. The fusty old Musée Dauphinois was modernized, to become a live centre for local artists and their work. The old municipal theatre, too, was given a face-lift and today operates a varied programme parallel to the Maison de la Culture: it takes a number of touring comedies and musicals, for which there is still a steady bourgeois audience, but it also puts on, for example, *café-théâtre* satire, Indian dance troupes and certain local amateur productions that are taboo at the Maison. Gilman also greatly extended the public library system, which in France as a whole is still so backward and ill-equipped that only 3 per cent of citizens borrow from their local library, against 30 per cent in Britain. But in Grenoble the figure has risen to over 15 per cent. The town has a central library with 500,000 books and 15 branches.

Equally important, Gilman sought to bring culture out from its temple-like enclosures, into street and suburb. In the public squares he placed modern sculptures by Calder and others, to the fury of older conservatives. He launched a summer open-air festival, *La Ville en Fête*; every June, in courtyards, squares and piazzas, there are plays, concerts, poetry recitals and debates on topical subjects such as abortion reform. Gilman also experimented with a series of lunchtime drama and music events, which surprisingly found audiences, proving that the long French family lunch is no longer so sacred, even in the provinces (see p. 394). Above all, Gilman sent his *animateurs* out into the suburbs, to the youth clubs and *maisons de quartier*. Here he organized street festivals, and free classes in weaving for Muslim women, a minority rarely given any special attention by French authorities. He encouraged itinerant groups of 'socially committed' professional actors, notably the Théâtre de l'Action; their technique is to live for a while with a particular social milieu, then devise plays on its own themes, expressed in its own language[9] – for example, about housing problems or delinquency. In a bare school hall at Villeneuve, I sat with a working-class audience at one of these performances, about clandestine abortion. It was not exactly of TNP standard, but it was original.

This vital and varied new cultural life in Grenoble was prompted by Dubedout and Gilman, but it soon developed a momentum of its own as various spontaneous activities grew up too. The policy of the council has been to set a lead, but not to dictate or control too much, and to encourage diversity and citizen initiative. That is fine; but, this being France, it has led to all kinds of petty conflicts and jealousies, the creation of rival cliques, and a duplication of resources. The Conservatoire, for instance, virtually refuses to cooperate with the new Centre Musicale, which it sees as an upstart rival. And the Maison de la Culture complains bitterly – much more than in Rennes – that Gilman's 'diversification' policy has been stealing its audiences and adding to its already grave financial troubles. The Maison in its turn is heavily criticized by both Right and Left. Many bourgeois will not set foot there because they consider the programmes too politically slanted. The extreme Left, on the other hand, denounces the Maison for being 'run by an élitist clique who turn it into a highbrow ghetto, out of touch with popular needs'. In other words, there is Left, and left. The 'élitist' argument is levelled especially against

9 This is very similar to the methods of the new populist theatre groups in Newcastle-upon-Tyne, who go to the workers and then 'tell their own life-stories back to them'. See my book, *A Tale of Five Cities*, Secker & Warburg, 1979, p. 235.

Georges Lavaudant, whose brilliant creation *Les Cannibales* I described earlier. He is the ambitious director of the Centre Dramatique National des Alpes, the State-funded 'rep' that uses the Maison as its base. He is on the Left, but in a very intellectual way, and his personal links and sympathies are less with Grenoble's *hoi polloi* than with Leftist luminaries of French theatre such as Planchon and Vitez. As someone said to me of this gifted but arrogant young man, 'Lavaudant goes for quality, and he's far more concerned by what the Paris critics write about his shows than by whether local people enjoy or understand them.' Lavaudant in turn is fiercely hostile to the Théâtre de l'Action, which he considers a bunch of woolly-minded mediocre amateurs, undeserving of public subsidy. So we are back to the familiar conflict between the élitist and populist concepts of contemporary culture. Is the role of a Left-wing artist to communicate with the masses in terms they can follow? Or to express his own complex ideas in his own way, and risk appealing only to a chosen few? At all events, in July 1981 Lavaudant was appointed as director of Grenoble's embattled Maison de la Culture, where he will be obliged to take account of local box-office needs, as well as of his own ideals of artistic quality. Many Grenoblois think him an odd choice for the job.

Many towns besides Grenoble have been facing these problems, especially as the culture-going public itself has been tending to polarize: on the one hand, an older middle-class audience wanting the known classics; on the other, a younger generation, searching for the new, the experimental, maybe the politically provocative. In a provincial town, it is not easy to satisfy all tastes at once when resources are limited. At La Rochelle, Michel Crépeau in 1973 launched an annual summer festival of contemporary music and art, all very highbrow and international. With local and State subsidies it did quite well, and began carving itself a modest niche on the Salzburg–Aix–Edinburgh circuit. But then a Communist took over the local Maison de la Culture, and he pointed out that very few Rochelais workers had the slightest interest in the festival's arty offerings, which were diverting civic funds from *his* centre. Crépeau, under fire from his Communist partners on the town council, felt obliged to back down and make the festival more 'popular'. Maybe this was unavoidable; surely, in a smallish town, a festival must either keep in touch with popular taste, or else became a major élitist venue *à la* Salzburg, as La Rochelle never quite managed.

The revival of the vogue for grand opera (see p. 609) is causing similar dilemmas. Thirteen towns now have full-time companies; and opera is now so popular, and such a civic status symbol too, that many big towns without their own companies feel the need to mount their own short operatic seasons, at absurd cost. The Communist-led council of St-Etienne spends 2 million francs a year on five homegrown opera productions, each presented for *one performance only* (the budget would not run to more). Artistically the results are mediocre, as many members of the chorus and orchestra are amateurs: but the Stéphanois regard 'their' opera as essential to the town's prestige, and even the Party goes along with this. (St-Etienne would do better to stick to winning football cups.) Even Grenoble has also succumbed to the temptation of operatic prestige. When it stages *Carmen* for five performances the Maison's big theatre is full, but the 600,000 franc subsidy is a lot of money. So, rather than trying to excel in every art, would not Grenoble be wise to forego its own production and instead play host to opera tours from near-by Lyon, whose company is one of the four best in France? What! – be spoon-fed by its despised rival city? That would be like asking Belgium to stop making beer and buy it all from Germany. No, if Lyon produces opera, then Grenoble must do so too, whatever the cost.

In some towns, operatic prestige-hunting has led to political con-flicts with those preferring other, less costly arts – notably at Nancy. This historic city has an old operatic tradition which since the war was gradu-ally crumbling into decay. Instead, Nancy began spontaneously to shine in other, more modern arts. In 1962 a young local Socialist, Jack Lang, founded an international festival of experimental drama which has since become famous as one of the leading events of its kind in the world; each year it has attracted forty to fifty troupes from every corner of the globe, and 200,000 visitors. Then in 1973 some other young Nancéiens started an international biennial jazz festival which has had an almost equal success; guest artists have included Dizzy Gillespie, and there are count-less concerts in the streets, in schools and hospitals. Both festivals have enjoyed sizeable civic subsidies. But in 1977 a new mayor took power, an elderly Right-wing figure, Claude Coulais, and he decided that a revival of opera and ballet would be better for the city's gracious image – and more popular with his bourgeois voters – than all those messy long-haired types disturbing the place with their noisy music and subversive Leftist drama. Better Berlioz than the Bread and Puppet. So Coulais hired a prestigious new director for the civic opera house, Jean-Albert Cartier, who brought with him a leading State-backed modern ballet company, of which he was already in charge. Helped by vast subsidies, Cartier has renovated the opera company and now stages lavish productions, in a bid to outdo the distinguished opera at Strasbourg, Nancy's much larger rival. 'My sole aim is top international quality,' the arrogant Cartier told me. For his opera and ballet, Coulais gives Cartier over 30 million francs a year, which has meant pushing culture's share of the city budget up to 15 per cent, a French record. It has also meant severe cut-backs in the subsidies for the two festivals. As a result, the jazz festival in 1979 had to reduce its scope from ten days to four, and the drama festival's future was in doubt.

The organizers were furious with Coulais. 'That bourgeois swine is killing the cultural life of this town,' Lang told me in 1979; and Raymond Sauna of the jazz festival added, 'Ten days of jazz in the streets, giving pleasure to 100,000 people, cost the town no more than the décor alone for one Verdi production. It's a criminal switch of priorities.' So Nancy has become the scene of the sharpest cultural policy conflict in France. Cartier's operas are good, yes, and they are popular with a certain public; but the jazz and drama festivals not only appealed more widely and were infinitely less costly, they were also unusual achievements (notably the drama festival); whereas Coulais now is simply adding one more decent opera company to the hundreds already existing in Europe. What is the point of Nancy trying to rival near-by Strasbourg? In a time of economic crisis, is a town of a mere 100,000 people justified in such extravagant *folie de grandeur*? Many Nancy ratepayers, not only those on the Left, are hoping that in the 1983 local elections their mayor will meet his *Götterdämmerung*. Meanwhile, Jack Lang has already begun to win a sweet revenge, for in May 1981 Mitterrand appointed him Minister of Culture (see p. 615). This puts him in a position to use State funds for rescuing the drama and jazz festivals, and also to ensure that very little money from his Ministry's budget, if any, come the way of Coulais.

ECOLOGY IN FASHION:
GISCARD DID HIS BIT, THEN WAS STRUCK
BY ANTI-NUCLEAR BLAST

Militant ecology groups – 'the Greens', as they are called – have never made the same impact in France as in, say, West Germany or the United States. But by the late 1970s they were quite active, often doing battle with the police in their efforts to save some village from a planned nuclear station or a pastureland from an Army firing range. And they are still active today. These militants may number only a few thousand, and many Frenchmen may disagree with their anti-nuclear aims or dismiss them as fanatics. Yet they are also a portent of the growing public concern about ecology and the preservation of nature. For a long time this problem seemed less acute than in some countries because, after all, France has relatively so much space. And the French were probably right, in the post-war decades, to set their first priority on modernization. But today they have become aware that industrial growth in turn creates its own hazards.

Since the early 1970s France has had her share of doom-men writing doom-books, preaching what in a sense are the opposite of Gravier's warnings: that the 'French desert', having been made to bloom, might return to being a desert, this time not through neglect but over-exploitation. The wide open spaces are not inexhaustible. Already many a beauty spot has been sacrificed to a new factory or refinery; pollution has been allowed to spread because the cost of checking it might harm productivity; and at least until Giscard's day the regime connived too readily at ugly new building on beautiful coastlines such as the Côte d'Azur.

Public opinion in the past decade or so has become far more sensitive to these issues. In 1969 a public campaign dissuaded the Government from allowing a promoter to build a smart ski resort in the Vanoise National Park in the Alps. Later, another campaign induced the Government to ban the siting of a new oil refinery in the Beaujolais wine country. As an indication of how local opinion has been shifting, a Socialist teacher in a small village near Montpellier told me in 1980: 'A few years ago the mayor wanted to turn this place into a commuter suburb, full of chic villas. I stood against him, but was defeated. But now I find that the mayor has come to accept the ideas that I defended; he's even discovered the charm of old houses he'd planned to knock down. So the expansionists have steadily become ecologists. It's due in part to the influence of the media.'

De Gaulle's Government showed little concern for these matters. Its creed was expansion and profit. But even under Pompidou there were signs of a change. In 1971 he created a Ministry for the Environment – the term was then coming into fashion – and this began to spend its limited budget on buying up small bits of coast, on mobile teams to check noise, on anti-pollution devices, and so on. It was a start, but it only nibbled at a huge problem. Although air pollution in the Paris area has been reduced, river pollution of the Seine below Paris remains severe. And on the Mediterranean the problem is worse. Here the new industrial complex at Fos has been pouring tons of sulphur dioxide daily over the Fos/Marseille area with its 2.5 million people. Yet the Government has faced a dilemma: if it imposes stricter anti-pollution rules, will it not frighten away the new industries it has been so anxious to entice? There is a tax on pollution, but many firms have found it cheaper to pay this than to install costly anti-pollution devices; so they have a virtual licence to pollute. Of course the whole Mediterranean has been clogging up with filth from industry, sewage and tankers, the Italians being the worst offenders. An international campaign led finally to the Barcelona and Athens agreements of 1980, and in line with these the French Government at once promised to spend 1,500 million francs over ten years on cleaning up its south coast; high time too, for the luxury playground of the Côte d'Azur had become one of the slimiest stretches of coast from Gibraltar to Suez. Today, all French beaches are subject to elaborate pollution controls, and the number of sewage plants has been doubled since 1970; this has brought an improvement to all French coasts (leaving aside, of course, the Brittany tanker disasters), but there is still much left to be done.

Giscard came to power on a wave of environmentalist feeling. He was both a modernist and a nostalgist, a believer in post-industrial Le Corbusian concepts of factories-amid-meadows, but also in conservation. And when in 1975 he produced his famous slogan, 'a more human kind of growth', it undoubtedly found a genuine public response. He at once launched various actions. Notably, he set out to save France's beautiful coastline, for as well as beach pollution there was serious over-building: an official report on the Côte d'Azur property boom had warned that this coast from Marseille to Italy was 'being gradually obstructed by a wall of concrete'. Notably, between Antibes and Nice a curving wall of holiday flats, twenty-two storeys high and half a mile long, had arisen beside the beach, scarring the landscape. It was too late to pull this down, but Giscard did veto or rescind permits for some other plans for mammoth 'marinas' or leisure complexes on this coast. He put a brake also on the activities of the notorious Guy Merlin, who had become France's leading property developer by building 'walls of concrete' along parts of the Normandy and Vendée coasts and elsewhere. Appealing to the *petit-bourgeois*' growing desire for his own holiday flat by the sea, Merlin threw up ugly six-storey strips along some of the finest unspoilt Vendée beaches, and destroyed some near-by woodlands too. Commercially, it was all a great success. At first local *notables* welcomed Merlin, glad at the prospect of more tourists in this not-so-prosperous area, but some of them later regretted it. Merlin was accused of creating 'human rabbit-hutches' and of 'Sarcellizing' the coast. Finally he was forced to modify all his future projects.

All over France stable doors were being shut, even if some horses had escaped. In 1975 the Government created a Conservatoire de l'Espace Littoral for the entire coast, modelled on Britain's National Trust. With a modest budget it has had a little success in buying some of the lovelier stretches of threatened coastline, tidying them up, then reselling them to communes, holiday clubs or other bodies, on condition that they develop them aesthetically. Parts of the Ramatuelle peninsula south of St-Tropez have been thus preserved.

In some places, eyesores are still being built. But in Aquitaine, at least, a new coastal project is proving a relative success. Here, along the

150 miles of open beach from the Gironde to Biarritz, the Government since the mid-1970s has been doing what it did earlier for the Languedoc, but this time in a gentler style. The huge Languedoc resorts (see p. 146) were very much a product of the 1960s; they may not please all tastes, but at least they were coherently planned and equipped. However, such gigantism is now out of favour, and the Aquitaine scheme reveals the shift in policy. Once again a Government agency masterminds the operation, checking speculation, buying up land; but this time there is more accent on conservation of landscape and natural resources. Nine new tourist zones have been marked out, but these are being integrated into existing resorts, such as Lacanau and Hossegor, rather than built Brasilia-like on their own as at La Grande Motte. New holiday property is restricted to three storeys and low density, and is placed either just inland – around the lakes and forests of the Landes – or perpendicular to the coast, not parallel. Fine for the environment – but so much so that much of the required private investment was at first frightened off by the strict conditions. One promoter said, 'The Germans, our best flat-buying clients, want to be right on the beach or they won't come.' Finally, after a few concessions by the planners, some investors were found and building started. The project has been criticized for the delays, but not quite fairly: as the technocrats in charge have pointed out, there is no hurry, and it is wiser to spend time first on the environment than throw up eyesores which are later regretted.

This approach is typical of the ethos among planners that came into fashion with Giscard. When in 1975 I toured the entire Atlantic coast and then reported my findings to the head of DATAR in Paris, his first question was, 'Do you think we are doing all right? – are we succeeding?' I was about to reassure him that, yes, the new factories I had seen at La Rochelle, Bordeaux, etc., seemed to mark a step forward, when he added, 'I mean, shall we save it, that coast?' Even five years earlier, he would have asked first about the factories. But in 1975 recession had hardly begun to bite; later, with unemployment rising fast, factories again became the first priority. So this was the basis of Giscard's dilemma. He was sincere about his 'quality of life' policy: but he also had an economic crisis on his hands, and felt that he must concentrate on measures to attract new investment, reduce energy imports, and so on. As his ecological critics pointed out, the two strategies were not always easily compatible.

During his seven years in power, what did he really achieve? His coastal measures brought some results, and so did some of his efforts for urban environment, examined earlier in this chapter. In rural areas, the Ministry for the Environment had a little success in checking the scattered building of villas and holiday homes that had been eating up farm land and often spoiling the landscape. There was also a national campaign against noise, which included the erection of sound-proof barriers between motorways and housing areas, and tighter rules on the use or manufacture of high-decibel equipment, from motorcycles to vacuum cleaners.

The overall record under Giscard was still modest: but at least the various problems were now being discussed and tackled at official level, as had not been so in the 1960s. Yet the ecologists remained sceptical. One of their leaders told me: 'Giscard has achieved something with the coast, yes, but otherwise his actions have been little more than cosmetic. He is too obsessed with the economy: he won't accept that we may have to settle for a simpler life-style.' Yes, but to this it could be answered that Giscard was at the mercy of the French people, who in their vast majority wanted it both ways: 'quality of life', but without any drop in personal consumer spending or job prospects. And Mitterrand today has inherited the same dilemma. Only a tiny minority of the French are yet prepared to put their ecology into practice and live very simply: for example, the young settlers in the Cévennes (see pp. 248–57).

The ecology movements had some justification in complaining that, in their handling of major pollution dangers, the authorities under Giscard often behaved with inefficiency and lack of foresight. In 1967–80 the north-west coast of Brittany suffered six times from oil spills and tanker accidents. The worst of these disasters, and the worst of its kind in the world, was in March 1978 when the wreck of the *Amoco Cadiz* sent 220,000 tonnes of crude oil over a 120-mile stretch of rocks and beaches, causing serious damage to fishing, wild-life and tourism. At the time the Government had ready on paper an elaborate scheme for early warning and rapid counter-measures; but the practical machinery for putting them into action did not exist. So the Breton coast suffered far worse than it need have done. In 1980, when another wrecked tanker threatened the area, the Government's vaunted 'Polmar' emergency system still seemed to be working inadequately. So more oil was poured on the troubled waters of Bretons' habitual hostility to Paris.

Virtually unheard of in the 1960s, the ecology groups ('*les Verts*') have gathered pace more recently. Some were born of the May '68 revolt, others were influenced by Californian models or the effects of the energy crisis; nearly all reflect a new generation's disenchantment with the older parties and their ideologies. The ecologists are fighting on many fronts. Nuclear stations have been their main target, especially under Giscard; but you also find them campaigning against uranium mining, motorway projects, chemical pollution or any building scheme that threatens the landscape. They urge town councils to recycle their refuse; they promote organic farming; one group holds an annual *'Salon de l'anti-Automobile'*; others fight to preserve wild-life from France's huntsmen hordes. The movement is highly diverse, which is both a strength and a weakness. About a hundred and fifty organizations exist on a national level, plus another two thousand or so purely local ones which sometimes score notable successes. In south Brittany an elderly aristocrat runs a society for protecting wild-life in the lagoon-like Gulf of Morbihan: 'The sport of hunting from boats was wiping out the barnacle geese,' he told me; 'so we lobbied the Ministries and finally got it banned here. Since then, we reckon the number of these birds has risen again from 400 to 20,000. So we saved them from extinction just in time – and it's thanks to a shift in public opinion. Ten years ago, the State would never have bothered to help us.'

The ecologists have some well-known protagonists, such as Commander Cousteau, the underwater explorer. And from time to time they make some impact in local or national elections. In the presidential election of 1981 their persuasive young leader, Brice Lalonde, scored a creditable 3.9 per cent, coming ahead of all the other minor candidates, even ex-premier Michel Debré. The ecologists claim that their steady pressure on the Government has yielded some results, such as a law obliging all new building projects to be preceded by environmental studies. But politically their impact is weakened by the fact that – like most French protest movements – they are splintered and quarrelling. Of the main groups, Les Amis de la Terre (Friends of the Earth, part of the international body) is at loggerheads with its newer rival, the Mouvement d'Ecologie Politique, while both are viewed critically by the less political Nature et Progrès. It was only after much public haggling that they all agreed on Lalonde, leader of the 'Friends', as their joint candidate for the 1981 elections.

The ecologists are vigilant in defence of their causes. But the trouble with many of their local field crusades is that they rapidly get confused with other issues and notably – at least under the Gaullists or Giscard – with the long-running feud between the French public and a technocratic State. Under Giscard, a common scenario was this. The State in its high-handed way would announce some project without proper consultation. The local population would object and *les écolos* would leap to their aid; the State then dug its heels in, and there ensued a battle of wills; in the process, the real ecological issues tended to get submerged beneath the weight of popular fury at the technocrats' arrogant tactics. By law a public enquiry had to be held locally; but this was purely consultative and often no more than a formality. If the enquiry revealed massive local opposition to the project, the State was much less likely than in Britain to take account of it and back down. This is what angered people so much. So the real ecological debate was not conducted on its merits. The Socialist Government, by taking fuller account of local views, now hopes to break this pattern, which is rooted in French tradition. It may not be easy. Let me give some examples of it, under Giscard.

In 1979, at Castries, a big village east of Montpellier, the State-owned Gaz de France company carried out some discreet seismic surveys, then suddenly announced it was planning to use some natural underground cavities as a storage reservoir for 400 million cubic metres of gas. The population, aware of geological faults in the area, formed a committee to fight the project. They sent a petition with 4,000 signatures, but at first Gaz de France's technocrats refused even to discuss the matter. One of them said, in effect, '*We* know what we're doing, *you* don't, it's not your subject. Don't try to know, just trust us.' But the company said it would hold a public enquiry in local town halls, as it was obliged to do by law. One leader of the committee, Jean Joubert, an ecology-minded professor, gave me the rest of the story: 'We knew the enquiry would be a pure farce, so we all decided to boycott it, including the mayors. They sent the enquiry documents back to the prefecture. Then came weeks of suspense, and finally we learned that Gaz de France had dropped the project. The reason they gave was that their seismic surveys had indeed revealed faults. But these had been done months ago, so we felt sure that much of the real reason was our petition and boycott. They simply didn't want to lose face by admitting they had backed down under pressure. They were very arrogant about the whole thing, but we scored a victory over their arrogance: we proved that popular action of this kind *can* bring results. Usually, in such conflicts, the State wins – but the danger is to believe that the citizen can never win, for people then lose the courage to fight.' I said, fine, but surely the gas was needed and would have to be stored somewhere? 'Yes, it's probably needed in a way,' said Joubert; 'but maybe we should change our way of life entirely, and depend less on gas and oil.' '

A better-known example is the much-publicized Larzac affair. In 1971 the Army bluntly announced its intention of extending from 7,000 to 42,000 acres its tank firing range on the Larzac plateau, in southern Aveyron near Millau. The 103 sheep-farmers involved were due to be compensated; but they did not want to be driven off their ancestral acres, so they began to resist. And their cause was quickly taken up by scores of ecology and anti-militarist groups all over France, as well as by the

Occitan regionalists who regard Larzac as part of their domain and are always eager for a chance to hit out at Paris; their *oc* slogan, *'Gardarem lo Larzac!'* (save Larzac) has been daubed across the Midi. About a hundred 'Larzac committees' were formed in France, and money was raised for buying up empty farms due to be requisitioned. Young ecologists, by way of peaceful protest, would lie down in the path of tanks. In fact of this unexpected barrage of opposition, and finding its plans obstructed by ingenious legal obstacles, the Army prevaricated; and so the dispute went on, year after year. Larzac had become a national crusade, a pilgrimage centre drawing thousands of sympathizers each summer to take part in the protest and listen to lectures on anti-militarism and ecology.

The evolution of the affair is significant. It began as a simple local movement of self-interest, by farmers not wanting to leave their land. It was then taken up as an anti-Paris regionalist issue and a test case for ecology: the 'Greens' who jumped on the bandwagon became more militant about Larzac than the local farmers. And from this it developed into a battle against the State, as the Ministry of Defence made all the usual blunders of failing to consult, failing to state its case clearly or indicate the compensation terms. 'We are not against French national defence,' said one farmer; 'what angers us is the way the plan was decided in secret, then imposed on us.' And an official at the local prefecture told me, 'Yes, the Government has handled the affair stupidly and arrogantly. We've now learned some lessons about farmers' feeling for their land and the need to treat this with more respect. But, ecologically, the problem is a false one.' As in other such cases, the Government was caught in a dilemma. If it bulldozed the scheme through, as it could, then it would create martyrs and risk even greater unpopularity; if it backed right down, it would appear weak and so encourage similar protest campaigns elsewhere. Hence the prevarication, for pride was involved. Mitterrand however was not bound by this. Like any incoming ruler, he was in a position to change his predecessor's policy without loss of face. So, as a gesture to the ecologists and regionalists, one of his very first acts in May 1981 was to cancel the Army's scheme for a larger firing range at Larzac.

The Giscard Government did show greater firmness of purpose in the case of my last and most important example: the anti-nuclear movement. Giscard regarded his ambitious nuclear programme (see p. 80) as an absolute national priority, and was determined not to be deflected by the demonstrators who were growing more vocal and violent. Hence the anti-nuclear lobby made scant impact on policy, as compared with the three-year German moratorium on building new power stations or the

American halt on reprocessing. The Government was able to point to the opinion polls, showing a vast majority still in favour of nuclear power. However, by the mid-'70s concern over health hazards was growing in some quarters, alimented by a report in 1976 from a team of scientists working for the Government, who called for a three-year halt in order to study safety. They alleged that the new reactors were badly designed, and no proper thought had been given to waste disposal. The Government denied that the health hazards were so grave; and went ahead. Whenever there were protests from the population close to a proposed site, officials would react with a cynical shrug: 'The Frenchman is all in favour of nuclear reactors – so long as they are not near his own village. That's normal. Our job is to put the national interest before local qualms.' But the protests were not solely local. The first serious incident was in July 1977 when 30,000 demonstrators from various countries clashed with riot police at the giant plutonium reactor, Super-Phénix, being built at Creys-Malville east of Lyon. One protester was killed, and at least a hundred and five people were injured including some police. The authorities were quick to point out that the 'trouble-makers' appeared to have been led by a commando of German extremists, members of a new breed of roving European ecology troopers. At all events, work on Super-Phénix went ahead.

After the 1979 Harrisburg scare the anti-nuclear lobby returned to the offensive more sharply, pointing out that France was using a similar kind of nuclear fission to Harrisburg's. The next battlefield was in sensitive Brittany, where the Government was keen to build a power station as the region produces only 6 per cent of its own energy needs. A site for a huge 5,200-megawatt station, to be one of Europe's largest, was selected on the rugged coast of the Cap Sizun promontory in western Finistère, near the village of Plogoff. The Brittany regional council and the Finistère *conseil général*, both with pro-Government majorities, voted in favour of the project. They reckoned it could bring valuable new jobs and investment to one of the poorest corners of this struggling province. But Plogoff itself thought otherwise. The mayor complained that the first he heard of the plan was by reading the newspapers, and all his villagers backed his protest. As at Larzac, the ecologists took up the cause, and so did the regionalists, and the stage was set for another showdown with the State. Electricité de France, in charge of the project, produced some soothing literature to explain that the station would be down by the shore over a mile from the village, and there was no danger. The locals were not satisfied. And in the summer of 1979, as EDF's field studies went ahead, so did the regular protest rallies. I attended one on Whit Sunday, a good-humoured, relaxed affair with a holiday spirit, and *les flics* discreetly out of sight. Young ecologists, many of them teachers or students, had come in their thousands – by car – from all Brittany and elsewhere. There were children with T-shirts, *'Halte à l'industrie nucléaire'*, and other kids with balloons inscribed, *'Danger, radio-activité!'* There was a variety of posters and banners, such as *'Oui aux moutons, non aux neutrons'*, and lots of Breton nationalist flags and slogans. On the site itself, some villagers were starting to build a sheep-pen, in an effort to prove that this barren stretch of moorland was in fact farmland and therefore, by law, not to be tampered with. A jolly Sunday outing, despite the sinister undertones.

EDF were not moved. In February 1980 the ritual public enquiry was due to begin, and by now the villagers were seriously worried. They knew that in other such nuclear enquiries local rejection had counted for nothing: at Nogent-sur-Seine, near Paris, 45,000 voted against, 1,500 for, yet the power station went ahead. So, knowing of the success of the gas storage affair near Montpellier, the mayors of Plogoff and three adjacent communes decided on a boycott and closed their *mairies* to the enquiry. But with nuclear power at stake, the State was not going to yield. It conducted the enquiry itself, by setting up mobile 'town hall annexes'. At this point, the villagers' wrath exploded. The 'annexes' had to be protected by 600 armed gendarmes backed by riot police and paratroopers, and for six weeks the Bretons and ecologists fought a pitched battle with them, hurling rocks, Molotov cocktails, even a time-bomb. *Les paras* charged, amid tear-gas; fourteen arrests were made. In the chill winter gales, the mood was utterly different from that of the sunny protest back in June. The Bretons, tough, passionate and intransigent as ever, were not only protesting against nuclear power but giving vent to their long hatred of Paris; so the battle of Plogoff became a symbol of Breton resistance and the two issues merged into one. France's ecology leaders were there too, adding their fuel to the flames.

The Government stuck to its guns. When the mobile vans and the troops had departed, the enquiry commissioners simply ignored the boycott: they noted that no votes had been registered against the project, therefore it should go ahead. And by the time of the 1981 elections the survey work was just starting. The Government may have been shaken by the Plogoff affair; but it judged that to yield would have set a dangerous precedent. The villagers, on their side, may have had a case, but there was also a case against them, summed up to me in 1980 by one pro-Giscard Breton leader: 'Of course no commune will ever vote for a nuclear station on its soil, that's normal human selfishness. So the decisions have to be taken on a wider level – and please note that the Breton elected leaders have voted *for* the project. Even towns twenty miles from Plogoff are in favour; they know the boost the station will give to our economy. Only Plogoff and its neighbours are against – but what right have a few villagers to dictate to all Brittany, let alone France? And it's wild and illogical of Bretons to scream at the Government to help their economy, then reject their plans to do so. Where else is our energy to come from? The anti-nuclear boys and girls drive in their little cars to the demos; they'd be the first to moan if France had no fuel left. There's a lot of hypocrisy in ecology.'

Mitterrand, on coming to power, promptly put a stopper on the Plogoff project, and on four others where work was about to start. This was in line with Socialist plans for scaling down the nuclear programme (see pp. 81–2). It was also an important gesture to show that the new Government would not treat local feelings so high-handedly as the previous one had done. Ecologists, and Breton villagers, heaved a sigh of relief. But wider problems still remain. In general terms, the Socialists' environmental policy is not likely to differ greatly from Giscard's: the campaign will go ahead to protect nature, check pollution and so on. The main difference is likely to be one of style and approach, for the Socialists had indicated that over any new scheme, nuclear or other, they will now take far more care to consult local opinion honestly, and will try to avoid foisting a project on an area against its will. The arrogant technocrat will have to change his ways. So far, so good. But Mitterrand will have to find ways of reconciling his fine intentions with economic realities. Already in August 1981, when the new Government began to press ahead with its modified nuclear programme, it was facing violent demonstrations from the out-and-out anti-nuclear brigade, and Brice Lalonde claimed, 'You have betrayed us.' If on a lesser scale, Mitterrand may well inherit some of the same troubles as Giscard.

The French, having won through to the affluent society, are now looking beyond it to something else, more deeply fulfilling, but without being ready to sacrifice affluence. Tired of the State and its aloof Giscardian technocrats, they have been groping towards more democratic and informal styles of local community, and have now elected a Government which promises them more of just that. But, in France, local autonomy can often lead to endless quarrels, as we have seen in this chapter. In deciding so boldly to decentralize the Socialists are taking big risks. Can they establish the climate of trust that will enable it to work? These are big issues, and we shall return to them at the end of this book.

Chapter 6

DAILY AND PRIVATE LIFE:
TOWARDS A MORE OPEN SOCIETY?

The economic transformations of the post-war decades have had a diverse impact on the fabric of private and daily lives, on leisure habits and on social patterns. As individuals the French have adapted with eager appetites to certain modern life-styles; but, as we have seen in the new suburbs, changes involving basic social attitudes are often harder to accept. The holiday and weekend habits of the French, even their cherished gastronomic traditions, have evolved much more radically than their class structures; and not surprisingly they took to hyper-markets more easily than to abortion reform. But the leaven of social mutation is now at work. While the confident '60s brought striking material changes, the seemingly sombre '70s have finally yielded their own harvest of social and psychological change: in greater equality for women, much greater sexual tolerance, freer relations between parents and children, a growth of informality in daily contacts, and much else. Slowly the French are emerging from their old formalized rigidities towards a more open society. But the black spot, as the politicians know, is that wealth and opportunity remain much more unevenly shared than in other countries of France's high rank. The crusade is on for better 'quality of life', but how far can it go without better quality of lives?

FEMINISM WINS A BATTLE – BUT NOT
AT THE PRICE OF FEMININITY

One silent revolution of the France of the past twenty years has been the progress of women towards fuller emancipation, legal, professional and sexual. It has happened later than in most advanced countries. Only in the 1970s did women begin to make an impact in politics, or was abortion made legal and female contraception at last widely practised. Only in 1980 did the Académie Française, that bastion of male chauvinism, admit its first woman member, the novelist Marguerite Yourcenar. And until the 1964 Matrimonial Act, a wife still had to obtain her husband's per-mission to open a bank account, run a shop or get a passport, while much joint property was legally the husband's and the divorce courts were obliged to regard a wife's infidelity as more serious than a man's. Only in

1975 and 1979 did further laws remove the last remaining inequalities in matters of divorce, property, and the right to employment.

The latent *machismo* of a Latin society with Catholic traditions may help to explain these delays. But what is more curious is that French women themselves, whose social role in some other ways has always been so strong, did not show much interest in this kind of legal equality or in sharing a man's privileges – at least until very recently. Theirs has been a half-hearted revolution, save for the work of a small and untypical band of feminist pioneers. Even the 1964 Act was not especially popular with women, as one feminist told me: 'Many of them felt it implied a mistrust of the husband. They were little concerned with legal equality, but would rather use their charms on a man to win their way.' Since then, times have been changing: but even today the Frenchwoman prizes femininity above feminism; and all the foreigners' silly clichés about her, seductive, chic and sexy, spring from this abundant truth.

Socially, women in France have rarely been segregated or treated as inferior, as in some southern countries. The Frenchwoman regards herself, and is regarded, as the equal of man – *equal, but different*. Given an opportunity to play the same role as a man, in public life, she has often shied away in fear of losing her femininity, and men have cheered her for it! Cliché or not, this has been the land of *la petite différence*, not the land of suffragettes, nor of the women's clubs beloved of Anglo-Saxon amazons. A woman has seen herself in relation to family – where her role is powerful – and to individual men, rather than to other women or the community as a whole. So it is not surprising that the modern 'Women's Lib' movement in its more militant form has never been more than very marginal in France, and unpopular: influential feminists have taken care to remain very feminine. However, in the past decade or so a milder and different kind of feminism has now taken root among the new generation, as one result of May '68. French girls today expect equality of rights and career prospects, equal personal freedom (sexual and other), and equality in marriage: they no longer expect their husband to take all the decisions and do none of the chores. They resent, and fight against, *machismo*. But they do not want to become the *same* as men, and they certainly do not hate or shun men, like some militants. They want it both ways. They want a fully emancipated life, yet also to be courted, flirted with, told they are beautiful. Today it remains as true as ever: feminism must not be at the price of femininity.

Frenchwomen were given the vote in 1945, by the Liberation Government under de Gaulle (not himself a noted feminist). But though not legally barred from any office of State they have seldom rushed to enter active politics. After an initial burst of post-war feminist enthusiasm their numbers in the National Assembly dropped steadily from 30 in 1945 to 10 in 1977 (against 26 British women MPs by that date); and in all the shifting Ministries of the 1945–74 period, only 3 women reached even junior office. It seems that this was due equally to male bias and to women's own disinclination: traditionally they have preferred to wield influence behind the scenes – with de Pompadour as their proto-type, not Jeanne d'Arc – and I am sure that Madame de Gaulle had more influence on French affairs than all the women politicians together of the 1945–74 years. However, Giscard, a genuine champion of women's causes, tried an entirely new tack when he came to power. He brought women from outside politics into his Government. Simone Veil, a brilliant and liberal-minded lawyer, became Minister of Health, and was so persuasive and successful (see p. 366) that the polls were soon showing her as the most popular Minister ('The best man in our team is a woman,' Chirac is said to have remarked). In 1979 Mme Veil moved on to the even more exalted post of President of the European Parliament. Giscard also brought in Françoise Giroud, the well-known editor of *l'Express*, to a new post of Secretary of State for Women's Affairs. By 1976 there were five women in the Government, claimed as a world record. But the most prominent were not career politicians; they had been co-opted, like technocrats. Giscard had shown that women can be effec-tive in government: he had not proved that a woman in France is able, or willing, to fight her way up the party hierarchy like Mrs Thatcher.

The Socialist leaders, who today are strong espousers of women's rights, have made real efforts recently to promote women within party ranks. And in the 1981 elections this finally bore some fruit: the total of women deputies then rose to 26, its highest figure since 1945, and of these 19 were Socialist, compared with 3 Communists and 4 on the Right. But women still account for a mere 5.3 per cent of all French deputies. Why is this figure so low? Today it appears to be due less than in the past to the reluctance of women to come forward, and more to an enduring *phallocracie* (French for 'male chauvinism') among Party activ-ists, who fear that women will not pull in the votes. This at least is the view of most women in politics, for example, the Socialist Edith Cresson, a bouncy feminist, now Minister of Agriculture: 'Most men still do all they can to keep us out,' she told me: 'The convention persists that politics is a man's affair, for discussions in *bistrot* or parliament. A woman who pushes herself forward is *mal vue*: if she "gets herself talked about", well, that's an innuendo. I can tell you, life is hellish here for a woman in politics, unless she's old and ugly, and that has other draw-backs. Mitterrand has been trying hard to break the phallocratic traditions of his own rank-and-file, but few local associations will accept women candidates. They think we have less chance of winning. And yet the party is dead keen on women's rights – it's absurd. Men often tell me, "You're too pretty to be in politics, my dear" – it's still a common attitude, and I feel like slapping them in the face.' But there are signs of progress, as Mme Cresson must admit. In the 1979 European elections all parties made a special effort for her sex, with the result that France's 81 MPs at Strasbourg include 18 women, only 4 of them Communist. In local affairs, the proportion of women councillors has risen from 2 per cent to 8.7 per cent in twenty years. And in 1980 Giscard's new Minister for Women's affairs, Monique Pelletier, pushed through Parliament a law obliging parties to include at least 20 per cent of women on their lists for the 1983 local elections – quite a breakthrough. In 1981, Mitterrand's first Government included 6 women among its 44 members, a new record.

Though women may still have a tough time in politics, in many other careers there is now virtual equality. Long gone are the days when a girl of good family was expected to lead an idle life at home before marriage: she now gets a job. At universities the proportion of girl students has risen from 25 per cent in 1930 to 46.4 today; 15 per cent of students at ENA are girls, and 10 per cent at the Ecole Polytechnique, till recently a male preserve. The first girl ever to enter 'X', in 1972, came first in the passing-out exam! In the liberal professions women's numbers have also been rising, and now make up 23 per cent of the total: 34 per cent of young doctors are women. There is a woman prefect, a woman general, and there was recently a woman ambassador. Only in industry and big business is there still a masculine bias against women in directors' chairs: but here too they are infiltrating, for example the dynamic Mme Gomez, chairperson of Waterman (France). In the educated classes, far more women are at work than before the war: conversely, in the poorer classes, where habitually wives had gone out to work, the rise of prosperity has enabled many of them to give up their jobs and devote themselves to the home. In this milieu, to have a wife who does not work is often a status symbol. Yet women account for a higher percentage of the total labour force in France (39.2) than in Britain (38.6) or West Germany (36.7).

The energetic ladies in Giscard's Government had quite a success with pro-feminine reforms. Their record included the legalizing of abortion; fairer divorce laws; sixteen weeks' paid maternity leave and other measures to help young mothers; and steps towards the ideal of equal pay for equal work, where France is now ahead of Britain and West Germany. Sexist discrimination, for example in the wording of job advertisements, is not yet formally illegal as it is in Britain: but in practice the courts have power to impose fines in such cases, and sometimes they have done so. The Giscard regime had its failures too – many of Mme Giroud's bolder proposals were never applied – but its overall achievement was enough to steal the thunder of the small but militant 'Women's Lib' movement which emerged in the 1970s, stimulated by the events of May '68. This movement has made some impact when fighting for specific causes: it has helped battered wives and has organized women's strikes in factories. But its aggressive stance, denouncing male 'tyranny', has never gone down well with French women as a whole and today its influence is minimal. Similarly, thirty years ago, Simone de Beauvoir's *Le Deuxième Sexe* was well received in some intellectual circles; but when she lectured her compatriots on how to escape from their 'self-imposed inferiority', they paid little attention.

One fully emancipated Parisienne told me: 'We have never felt the slaves of men, we have our own power. American-style Women's Lib has little meaning for us.' The more moderate French feminists, and they today are numerous, have a different and more subtle approach from that of the Women's Libbers. '*Le droit à la différence*' is one of their slogans, and while demanding full equality of rights and opportunities, they also put the stress on a woman keeping her feminine qualities. In France, men and women alike have a fear and contempt for the bossy, masculine type of woman, and Frenchwomen who emerge as leaders of their sex are usually exquisitely feminine people, such as Mme Veil herself. Christiane Collange, a leading journalist and a most attractive woman, told me: 'Whenever I make a speech about women's rights, I'm always careful to look *soignée* and appealing. The shock-haired, bra-burning kind of feminism gives people here the willies.'

French women today are emerging from a transitional phase. From the old dependence on a man's world they are moving towards real emancipation, and are not finding the change so easy. Mme Pelletier told me in 1979: 'Compared with even ten years ago, women today are very demanding. They want everything – a husband and kids, but also a job, a full social life, and an active say in politics. It's hard to combine it all.' Twenty years ago in the bourgeoisie there was still a certain prejudice against the young housewife, however gifted, who left her small children with a nanny or *au pair* girl and continued a full-time job. But in the 1970s a new generation had swung round to the opposite dilemma, already familiar in Britain, that of the young graduate wife at the kitchen sink, guilty and frustrated at wasting her education. So the vogue grew for having jobs. But in practice many young wives have found it a great strain, both physically and psychologically, to combine a career with running a home, especially in Paris where the tempo is so fast and standards so exacting: office hours are long, bosses are demanding, and a husband will expect everything just perfect when he wants to entertain. So now there are signs of a trend back to the kitchen sink. 'Should a wife and mother work?' has become a public debate. The Giscard Government, in an effort to help wives out of this dilemma, launched a campaign to persuade firms to offer more part-time jobs; but in a period of recession this was not easy. Giscard's feminist leaders, Veil, Pelletier and others, always fought hard for the woman's right to a job and a career equal to a man's, and the new Socialist Minister for Women's Rights, Yvette Roudy, is now doing the same with even greater zeal. But national conditions have been changing, due both to the rise in unemployment and the fall in the birth-rate (see p. 15). Fewer jobs are available, and more babies are needed: so Governments have been increasing the incentives, in the form of allowances, for wives to stay at home and breed and feed. It has put Ministers in a moral dilemma, and has angered the feminist movements. France's young wives share in the dilemma.

Among younger French people, the greatest change of the past decade is one that is hardest to define, for it concerns the nature of 'the couple', the intimate power-balance between man and girl. Here, it is the man who usually is finding adjustment hardest, for his *machismo* is now in question. Traditionally, in this Latin society, women have exerted their greatest power within the family or in relation to one man, or to individual men, rather than to the community. To live for one man, to use feminine charm or guile to persuade or please him: this may be a woman's instinct in many societies, but especially it has been so in France. It may have brought its ecstatic rewards, but it has also made French women vulnerable and subject to strain. For French men, those notorious egotists, have exploited their advantage both emotionally and in practical ways, down to refusing to help with the chores because it is thought unvirile. Both before and after marriage a woman has usually had to fight harder than in most countries to keep her man's interest in her; and though this has certainly been one reason why older French women often remain so chic and sexually alert, it may also explain those tense, sharp expressions, the hard lines round the mouth. They lack the puddingy relaxedness of English matrons.

This has been the traditional pattern, but in the past ten or fifteen years a younger generation of French girls has rebelled against it. This is the generation influenced by British and American societies via the media, by May '68 and other youth explosions of the '60s, by the arrival of the pill, and many other factors. Today, if her man behaves with thoughtlessly arrogant *machismo*, a girl will simply walk out on him. She expects the same degree of sexual freedom as a man; and, conversely, the same degree of fidelity *from* a man. She no longer accepts that his peccadillos are more forgivable than her own. Inside marriage, she demands equality of decision-making, and equal control over shared finances; and she insists that her own leisure interests, her own cultural or other needs, be taken as seriously as her husband's. Men have reacted in various ways to this onslaught. The younger ones generally adapt, so that the boy-girl *camaraderie* of their student days is carried on into marriage where they are now much readier than in former days to share the housework and the baby-minding, or allow a wife to develop her own interests. Older or more conventional men may at first resist, but they too will often adapt in time. In a TV programme on the subject, one man described how his young wife announced that she was bored with sitting at home all day, she intended to learn a language and take up music lessons. 'For the first few weeks, I was appalled,' he said; 'I complained that she was never there when I needed her, the house was in a mess, and so on. But finally I realized that my wife had revitalized herself and found her personality. It was like a new honeymoon.' Today there is greater comradeship and sincerity in marriage, and the old-style arranged marriage has long disappeared.

I find it very noticeable that younger French women are more relaxed, more confident, less brusquely defensive, than their mothers' generation used to be. And the older ones in their turn are influenced by this basic change and are becoming gentler too. Yet the emancipation has not been at the price of femininity – 'How could it be?' said one feminist sharply; 'femininity is not something one loses like an umbrella.' The French game of flirtatious badinage between the sexes continues as before, enjoyed by both sides. And the Frenchwoman, in becoming emancipated, has not lost her *mystère* nor her natural feminine reserve and subtlety: socially and sexually she does not brashly assert herself as many Americans do. Her problem today, however, is that while individual relations may now be more equal, in public and working life the spirit of male chauvinism does not die so easily. For example, as the feminists point out angrily, school textbooks have not yet updated to take account of the changing role of women: the picturebooks used in State primary schools still show the woman beside the stove or cradle, or as hospital nurse or secretary, while the surgeon or executive she works for is always a man. Feminists complain also that the fine new laws on divorce and employment, giving equality to women, are not always properly applied by an older generation of judges and *patrons*. And the average French boss still tends to treat his secretary as a ninny, unworthy

of his trust or of responsibility (see p. 645). It will take another generation
– and maybe longer – for French male society as a whole to adjust its
attitudes and forget its old *phallocratie*. But now that even the Académie
Française has begun to admit women, the citadel is surely crumbling.

The sexual attitudes and behaviour of French girls have also been
changing dramatically, though the new permissiveness is still very
recent, more so than in many countries. As late as the 1960s, all the
evidence was still suggesting that French unmarried girls as a whole,
especially in the provinces, were still among the most virginal in Europe,
outside Italy and Spain. Of course the old idea of France as the land of
unfettered *amour* had always been one of the silliest of foreigners' clichés.
It sprang largely from the tourists's inability to distinguish between the
strict codes of French domestic life (which usually he never saw) and the
manifest tradition of public tolerance which has always readily sanctioned conspicuous minority activities such as Montmartre night-life or
the free-living world of the Left Bank bohemia. If you were on your own
and outside society, then the guardians of morality would ignore you,
and so for many decades Paris was a favourite refuge, and indeed still is,
for foreigners wanting freedom and privacy. But if you belonged to one
of the rigid compartments of French society, then you had to obey its
hypocritical rules.

Well into the 1960s the old codes of this Catholic society remained in
force, at least on the surface. According to a survey in 1960 by the Institut
Français d'Opinion Publique, more than half of French mothers still
thought a girl should not be allowed out with a boy till she was nineteen,
and many still acted on it. And only 27 per cent of girls said they
approved of pre-marital sex even between fiancés, while 70 per cent of
married women under thirty *claimed* to have been still virgins on their
wedding night. Maybe not all were telling the truth: yet there is a true
story that when, in Lyon in 1962, a dead baby was found in a hostel for
working girls, and all 144 inmates agreed to a police request that they be
examined to see who could be absolved from suspicion, all but seven
were found to be virgins.

However, in the wake of the Nordic countries, sexual freedom
finally began to spread. Parents became readier to allow their daughters
to go out with boys; young people got more leisure and money for going
off together; the younger clergy grew more liberal about sex. In some
student circles, relations were very free by the mid-'60s. At first, many
French girls seemed unsure whether they really wanted this new freedom: this was true of Catholics and agnostics alike and for some it is still
true today. Generally *sérieuse* and romantic, with part of herself the

Frenchwoman welcomed the growing climate of frankness between the sexes; but another part of herself remained under the shadow of various complexes and conventions, the legacy of Catholicism.

But the past decade has seen a further big change, essentially among the very young and in parental attitudes to them. This has come from foreign influences, from the freeing of legal controls on contraception, from the steady decline in the role of the Church, and maybe from other factors too. France's leading sexologist, the liberal-minded Dr Pierre Simon, told me in 1980: 'At the time of my last major survey, in 1972, the average age at which a French girl first had full sexual intercourse was twenty-one; but since then all has changed, utterly. It's now the "done thing" at school to sleep around, and teenage girls treat boys as sex objects in a free market, just as boys treat girls. Teenagers are now most of them very promiscuous for a while, but sex in this phase is rarely linked with love or even eroticism: it is simply an exchange, a means of communication and self-discovery. Real love comes later, after twenty or so, and with it fidelity and true eroticism. Virginity is no longer considered a virtue, except by some parents, and most girls think of it as something they *ought* to lose. Today only 5 per cent of French of either sex are still virgins at twenty-five, and mostly these are the "old maids" who will stay virgins all their lives. In general, sexual freedom in France has now reached the same level as in Britain, Germany or Sweden – and that, for this so-called Catholic land, is quite a transformation.'

Of course it would be wrong to infer from this teenage revolution that every adult woman has become *légère* overnight. Most of those in their mid-twenties or older are still *sérieuses* and will not give themselves except for love. Moreover, the liberalization is far less evident in small towns or rural areas than in Paris or other big cities; and group sex or wife-swapping sessions are still far less common than in America (in Paris, there are two or three places where for 400 francs or so a head you can share in a *partouze*, or organized orgy, but it is all very discreet and anonymous). Some social classes, too, remain more strict than others. Working-class families (under the influence of the prim Communist Party) tend to retain a sterner morality, and a tighter watch over their daughters, than the middle classes. But in nearly all milieux the days are gone when the average father would expect to lead his daughter a virgin to the altar. Gone too are the days when the young bourgeois, after sleeping around with *filles légères*, would expect the girl he marries to be a virgin. There are simply not enough virgins left; and most parents have given up the unequal struggle of trying to prevent their daughters from doing as they wish. Hitherto, as in any Latin or Catholic country, virginity in males eyes has been something of a sacred property; but many

French girls at heart were readier for sexual emancipation than male society would let them be – and now they have won.

Twenty years ago, in a Catholic family, if a girl of seventeen or so wanted to have a love-affair and her father opposed it, she would probably yield to his authority: today, if thwarted, she simply leaves home. It can still cause anguished dramas, though most parents are rapidly learning tolerance. The easing of the housing shortage has now made it far more feasible for very young people to find a flatlet of their own away from the parental nest, and today hordes of young couples live together outside marriage. In the middle classes, this has even become less the exception than the norm! According to one survey, of those married in 1977, 44 per cent had lived together first, against 17 per cent in 1969 – and this 44 per cent would be well over 50 per cent in the bourgeoisie. But except in bohemian or student circles the cohabitation is usually done discreetly, for middle-aged provincial society will not yet accept that such liaisons be flaunted. However, Giscard's liberal Government has now officially recognized the status and rights of '_le concubinage_'.

In the post-war years, marriage was the great ideal and couples were marrying younger than before 1939. But now they are turning against this institution. The number of marriages fell from 416,000 in 1972 to 340,000 in 1979, while according to a recent Church-sponsored survey, around 60 per cent of people between twenty-one and thirty-four 'do not think it worth going through any marriage ceremony'. One leading feminist, the writer Benoîte Groult, told me: 'It is simply not true any more than a girl is keener than a man on settling into matrimony. The girls, above all, are now the ones refusing to marry, terrified of being caught up in the traditional role of housewife.' If a couple living _en concubinage_ do decide to legalize their union, it is often to please their parents. Or in very many cases they take the step when they start a child – and maybe not even then. This can cause problems. I have friends in a small town in the north, surrounded by relatives. Their daughter went to university in the Midi where she fell in love with a fellow-student, and there they settled down as a couple, passed their exams, got jobs locally – and had a child. They were devoted to each other, but against marriage on principle. 'It's horribly embarrassing,' the girl's mother told me; 'Alain and I are quite liberal, _we_ don't mind. But we can never let Jeannine come here for a visit when there's been no wedding – the neighbours, our own parents and all our family would be scandalized. We'd never live it down – this is _la province_!' Later, after much persuasion, the couple did get married. I have not seen my friends since, so I do not know how they have managed to explain away the tiny tot aged two.

Inevitably, the old moral conventions still carry weight with older people. Yet in many respects the social codes have become more tolerant. Divorce has not only become much easier, it is now so prevalent that rarely does it carry any stigma. According to the surveys, religious conviction or fear of scandal or family dishonour are no longer the main factors inhibiting divorce, if a marriage is on the rocks; fear of harming the children, or of financial distress or loneliness, rank higher. In this secular State, divorce has never been a great divisive issue as in Italy. The figures for it rose steadily in the post-war years, to level off at about one marriage in ten by the early '70s. Then in 1975 an easy form of dissolution by mutual consent was introduced, rather as in Britain, and this now accounts for one-third of divorces. One marriage in six today ends in the courts. Another sign of growing tolerance is that the unwed mother with an illegitimate child, though still socially frowned on, is no longer such an outcast: officially her title is now *mère célibataire*, she can legally call herself *Madame* if she wishes, and there are plenty of State and private agencies to help her with her problems and her child care.

Traditionally in France, the pre-marital affair has always been much less common than the extra-marital one. Under this code, the open season would begin after marriage, and to abduct deceitfully thy neighbour's wife would be less shocking than simply to sleep with his unattached daughter, a topsy-turvy morality, you might think, but fully in line with the high store set on virginity. Times of course have changed, but there are still many people who resent this national image of adulterous intrigue, fostered in countless novels and films from Flaubert to *Cousin Cousine*: when Jean-Luc Godard made a film about a modern Bovary with the title *La Femme Mariée*, the Gaullist censors sprang to defend French marital honour and made him change '*La*' to '*Une*'. More to the point, some people today suggest that adultery has grown less common, now that fewer marriages are 'arranged', divorce is easier, and men and girls have far more scope for sowing their wild oats before wedlock. It is far from certain that this is so. The growth of travel and secondary homes may well have encouraged infidelities, at least in the bourgeoisie where adultery is more usual than in the working-class. According to a remarkable sociological survey reported in *Elle* magazine in 1980, of the wives questioned, aged between twenty and fifty, three out of four admitted to adultery and a third of these said they had made the running in the affair, quoting sexual desire as their main incentive. Nearly 25 per cent said they were openly looking for an adventure because their husband was boring. So Godard's initial title may have been right.

Despite this behind-the-scenes activity, the French have always tended – at least until very recently – to be exceptionally discreet about their love-affairs, even when both partners are unmarried and it is not a question of trying to keep up appearances or to avoid hurting someone else. This is changing among the new generation, and it has never been so in the Paris intellectual world; but in most circles it is considered vulgar to 'flaunt' your liaison by moving openly as a couple, however free you both may be. When I told an upper-class Parisienne how disconcerting I found it, when with a group of unmarried French people, that one could never tell who was involved with whom, she said: 'Don't worry, nor can we. In France, we like to keep people guessing. My private life is my own; I'd hate other people to know what I was up to, they'd simply gossip and make it seem cheap.'

You can call this discretion a sign of civilized delicacy in a society. In France traditionally *il y a des choses qui se font mais dont on ne parle pas.* Many Ministers or other public figures have mistresses, *c'est normal*, but a public man's private life is his own business so long as he is discreet and does not step outside the law. He can be a homosexual, or an arch-philanderer, and there may be jokes about it in private, but it will not be held against him in his career. When in 1975 Giscard's alleged nocturnal doings began to raise criticism, even in the Press, it was less because he was thought to be immoral than because it was feared that his work might be suffering! Anyway, it all rapidly blew over, and was forgotten. And in France, a John Profumo or Jeremy Thorpe would never be held up to public scrutiny for some minor and irrelevant peccadillo and be forced as a result to sacrifice his political career. Even the divorce cases of well-known people usually take place in private in France, and though they may cause gossip among their friends, they are rarely reported in the Press.

Civilized delicacy, yes, even if it includes an element of hypocrisy. But at least the climate of intrigue helps to keep the French romantic temperature running high, with the titillation of *fruits défendus*. It relates to the traditional French male attitude to women, as prized possessions to be courted and desired but also protected from other men. Therefore, as an essential alibi of a male society, *amours* must be discreet. Despite the new sexual freedom and equality, a hangover of this Latin mentality persists, at least among the over-thirties. Even today, a woman must not be too brash or assertive, she must use guile to achieve her sexual ends, or she will not be found attractive, and what she treasures above all is male appreciation of her femininity. This she is given, abundantly. It might even be claimed that the French have the ideal balance between Italo-Spanish female subservience and the Americo-Nordic destruction of the prized *petite différence*. Many women, at least, think so. An English girl who has lived and worked for some years in France told me: 'In England when you're working in an office with men, they either treat you as just silly, or if you're good at your job they forget you're a woman. In France, they manage to treat your work seriously *and* flatter you as an attractive girl, and I prefer that.' A Parisienne in her forties, back in Paris after some years in London, said: 'One feels much more a *woman* in France. Men aren't frightened of the other sex as in Britain, you're gently pestered all the time, it's nice. There's also still a certain courtly aspect, a subtlety and delicacy, at least in my generation.'

The Frenchman's demonstrative delight in female company gives to relations between the sexes a certain romatic tenderness and intimacy that is not always equalled in countries with an older record of emancipation. The Frenchman may often be a sexual egotist, but his egotism is not brutish or in-turned. Partly to flatter his own vanity and sexual power, he is more sensitively concerned than most males to see that his woman, too, is fulfilled: and *donner le plaisir* is for him as important a part of love-making as his own satisfaction. Hence his reputation as a good lover, usually justified. There can be drawbacks, however, to this idyll between the sexes. Among the over-thirties, not only can women be made vulnerable and even strained by the emotional dependence on male egotism; but men are less easily prepared than in Anglo-Saxon countries to treat them as friends or ordinary social equals. Some women regret this lack of easy-going camaraderie: in France, a close friendship between a man and a woman does not so often develop without ceasing to be platonic or at least giving rise to gossip. A girl who knows both Paris and London said to me: 'In London, if a man takes me out to dinner, I know I can ask him up to coffee in my flat afterwards, out of politeness – and it needn't mean any more. A Frenchman will always take it as *une invitation*.'

The Frenchwoman today is often unsure which male attitude she prefers. In a way she is pleased to be reminded so continually of her femininity: she regards a suave pass as rightful *hommage*, and the English approach she may find boorish and unflattering. But she has also come to want the advantages of an Anglo-Saxon style equality and emancipation, and that is the path which the new generation have now chosen. A very young divorcée told *Elle*: 'I lived for two years with a boy. He saw it as a one-way exchange. I agreed to share his life, take an interest in his work. Not he. My concerns were unimportant to him the moment they were mine. So I left him.' This difference of generations makes it hard to generalize about French women today. Those in their mid-thirties or over are still bound, half gladly, half resentfully, by the traditional feminine role. The younger ones have struck out with a new assertiveness, a new independence, and the males of their own age seem to be accepting it, as *machismo* beats a doleful retreat. But is mystery and romance to be lost in the process? It may be too soon to tell, though Dr Simon, an optimist but also an expert, does not think so: 'Today's teenage girls may have given up chastity for a male kind of promiscuity, but when they emerge from it they are still immensely feminine. The roses and moonshine of romance are still potent in the new France – and that gives poetry to life. Sexual freedom does not destroy it.' So young womanhood appears to have won its revolution, and intends to consolidate it with an emancipation – sexual, social, professional, even political – that does not involve any sacrifice of *la petite, et précieuse, différence.* The modern French girl wants her own kind of freedom. She detests the penis-envying extremists, she does not want to be an amazon in the Crusades. She still wants to be serenaded by her troubadour – but not kicked around by him.

ABORTION AND BIRTH-CONTROL REFORM: BETTER LATE THAN NEVER

The belated legalization of contraception, and then of abortion, has been a major factor behind women's great leap forward of the past decade. Psychologically and practically, it has liberated them from so much. It lies at the basis of their new pre-marital sexual freedom, and inside marriage it has helped them to order their lives as they would wish. But these advantages are still bitterly contested, both by old-style Catholics in the name of morality, and by nationalists alarmed at the falling birth-rate.

Until the early '60s birth-control was almost as taboo from public discussion as in Franco's Spain. Ever since 1920 this secular State had imposed anti-contraception laws which liberals described as 'criminal', or 'medieval, compared with the family-planning policies' of Tunisia, France's former protectorate'. And it seemed that nowhere did the unemancipated Frenchwoman suffer so much from society as in her own intimate privacy. But in the 1960s the campaign of a few pioneers forced a breach in the curtain of social prejudice and brought the whole issue into the open. Since then, a revolution has taken place, in a climate of national controversy. Abortion reform came in 1975, not unduly late for a Catholic country (this was actually a year ahead of West Germany, and only two years behind 'liberal' Denmark). What is more startling is that not until 1967 was there repeal of the archaic law banning contraception.

The aim of this law passed in 1920 was not religious but demographic: to help repair the human losses of the Great War. It prohibited all publicity for birth-control, including advisory clinics, and it forbade the sale of contraceptives except for some medical purposes. It soon came to be frequently side-stepped and finally was overtaken by most educated opinion: but over the years it caused untold hardship and frustration, especially to poorer people who could not afford the luxury of visits to gynaecologists abroad. Decades after the invention of the diaphragm, most French couples still resorted to the time-honoured methods of *coitus interruptus*, vaginal douches or periodic abstinence, or they turned to clandestine abortion. Deaths from clumsy self-abortion ran into thousands a year. Abortion was legal only when the mother's life was in danger, and most doctors interpreted this with a cruel literal-ness. In one case a woman of thirty-nine who had had four miscarriages, four still-births and seven live births, four of them producing abnormal children, had great difficulty in persuading the doctors to sanction an abortion when she was pregnant for the fifteenth time and acutely ill.

A few thousand rich and informed women would avoid these prob-lems by visits to private doctors in London, Geneva or Morocco, for their diaphragms or abortions: *'Elle va en Suisse'* was a stock whispered joke in Paris salons. But most couples had neither the means for this nor, more relevant, the knowledge or initiative to take other, less costly steps, such as finding one of the few French doctors who would discreetly help with birth-control. And millions of working wives, faced with the horrors of raising a large family under French housing conditions, came to regard sex and their husband's desires with panic, and greet the menopause with relief. So this was one main reason why the sex-life of the French, despite their romanticism and their warmth and skill as lovers, was in those days not always the paradise of fulfilment that foreigners imagined. But few writers dared say so.

In 1956 a courageous young woman doctor, Marie-Andrée Weill-Hallé, was the first to declare war on the 1920 law by founding the Mouvement Français pour le Planning Familial. Its first advisory clinic was opened in 1961, in avant-garde Grenoble, and by 1966 there were nearly 200 all over France. The Government turned a blind eye: though the clinics were illegal, Ministers were anxious to avoid a showdown with informed opinion that might make them look ridiculous. So a tacit truce was observed between M F P F and Government; but the former, in order to keep its side of the bargain, had to resort to the most bizarre procedures in order not to flout the law too openly. When a woman visited one of its clinics, she was put in touch with one of the 1,500 or so French doctors who agreed to work with the movement, and he would probably fit her for a diaphragm. But the sale or import of these was illegal. So, by an arrangement with the international movement, the woman sent a ten-franc postal order and her prescription to a clinic in London, which then posted her the cap in a plain envelope. Sent singly, by letter post, they usually escaped customs checks; initial attempts to import them in bulk packets often led to seizures. Dr Pierre Simon told me: 'Whenever I went to London, I would bring back dozens in a suitcase for my patients. Once, the customs officer at Orly inspected my case, and they dropped out over the floor. The women near me giggled sympathetically, and then the officer laughed too, and told me to clear out quickly or he'd get into trouble.'

This was not the only example of the Government's hypocritical handling of the 1920 law. On the pretext that they limited syphilis, male condoms had always been freely on sale in chemists' shops; and even the pill began to be available in the mid-'60s, on prescription – officially, for curing a variety of obscure diseases. The Ministry of Health would privately encourage the MFPF. Hypocrisy was clearly better than repression, and there were some who argued that so cleverly had the law been turned by usage that it scarcely needed reforming. But this was not really so. Not only did the law add greatly to the hesitance of doctors and manufacturers, but the MFPF could never publicize its clinics. It had to rely on 'bush telegraph', mainly among the bourgeoisie; and class barriers and female reticence to talk about sex were such that most working women never knew of their local clinic. The movement has been a remarkable and rare example in France of effective unofficial civic action on a national scale; but, lacking official funds, it had to rely mainly on voluntary staff working in obscure premises.

Reform had originally been blocked by Catholic opinion, but the 1960s saw a steady change of heart among rank-and-file Catholics, both laymen and priests. The latter ceased coming to family planning meetings to heckle and protest; many of the younger ones even began to advise their faithful on how to seek birth-control advice, while many of the MFPF's own leaders were practising Catholics. But as the Vatican remained firm against contraception, the French hierarchy had to follow suit, at least outwardly, and this in turn carried weight with loyal Catholics in the Government, not least de Gaulle himself. Catholic opinion was by now sharply divided; but for various reasons, partly electoral, the Government remained wary of offending the diehard faction, one of whose leaders was that *éminence grise*, Madame de Gaulle. It prevaricated, clutching at straws of medical doubt about the pill or the coil as alibis for inaction. However, by the mid-'60s the national conspiracy of silence was shattered. There was a crescendo of debate about birth-control, in the Press, in polemical articles by feminists in papers such as *Elle*, and even on State TV where admittedly the evidence was sometimes slanted in favour of the *status quo*. The Socialists by now were demanding reform, and even demographers were openly doubting that the 1920 law was any longer relevant to keeping up the birth-rate. In face of this mounting tide of public opinion, the Government finally capitulated. It allowed a progressive-minded Gaullist deputy, Lucien Neuwirth, to put forward his own reform bill which with discreet official support went through Parliament late in 1967.

This was not quite the end of the battle. Some Ministers hostile to the reform then tried to sabotage it by withholding their signatures from the decrees needed to put it into force. Thus the authorization of the sale of the coil was held up for five years, and similar tactics delayed the decrees legalizing birth-control publicity and setting up a national advice centre. But finally the repeal of the 1920 law was fully operative, in practice as well as in theory, and today contraceptives and advice on their use are as easily available as in most countries. The pill rightly requires a doctor's prescription, but not parental approval even in the case of girls of fifteen. In this respect the new French law leapt ahead of custom in Britain, in drawing no formal distinction between the married and unmarried. Its authors accepted that the latter are just as much in need of contraceptives, and today these are available free on the health service, for women of any age, with the proviso that a doctor can use his discretion over prescribing the pill.

At first there seemed a danger that doctors, even more than politicians, would succeed in sabotaging the new law. Before it was passed, only 4 per cent of doctors had collaborated with the MFPF, and the vast majority of this conservative and cautious profession had either opposed birth-control or hoped that if they ignored it, it would go away. Twice in the mid-'60s the Conseil de l'Ordre des Médecins, the supreme medical body, had declared formally that contraceptive advice was none of a doctor's business. But after the law came into force, things began to change rapidly. Young doctors actually took the trouble at last to learn about modern birth-control; and today only about 5 per cent of GPs, mostly older Catholics, refuse to collaborate with the new law or give practical advice to their patients. Consulted by a worried and ignorant girl, they may give her a lecture on the joys of motherhood or the duty to be chaste, and send her away. But she can usually find someone else to help her.

More surprising maybe than these masculine reticences was the initial reaction of women to the new law: they proved slow at first to take advantage of this offered liberation from anxiety and restraint. This same

hesitance had been apparent since the early days of the MFPF. Back in
1962, according to one survey, 57 per cent of women favoured the sale of
contraceptives, and of the rest only one in four was opposed for moral
reasons: yet when it came to applying these views to their personal lives,
they held back. Old-style, anti-sex Catholicism was already in retreat,
but it had left behind a legacy of semi-conscious guilt and prudery, even
among women professing themselves atheists. Dr Weill-Hallé told me:
'If for so long we lagged behind in Britain in family planning, the reasons
were less legal or moral than psychological. The first task of our staff at
the clinics was usually to *déculpabiliser* a new client, to rid her of her
complexes about coming to see us.' In those days, a woman who ventured to try out a clinic and was satisfied (as nearly all were) might still be
unlikely to recommend it to her friends: it was as if she had discovered
some secret opium den, a source of guilty delight. This seemed to
illustrate, once again, the lack of club-like solidarity among Frenchwomen: were it not for this, the bush telegraph might have spread more
rapidly, and reform might have come sooner. The prejudices waned first
in the middle classes, while working-class wives remained reticent far
longer. There was a political element here, since official Communist
policy for many years was to oppose birth-control as a capitalist trick to
reduce the numbers of the proletariat. The MFPF, a private bourgeois-
led enterprise, was suspected as being some stratagem of the Patronat.
But since the early '70s the Communist Party – for electoral reasons, it
seems – has swung in favour of contraception, as of abortion, and this
has paved the way for a steady change in working-class attitudes.

In 1968, a year after the passing of the new law, less than 4 per cent of
women aged between fifteen and forty-nine used the pill, and a mere
handful the coil. After a slow start, the numbers have climbed steadily,
and today over 22 per cent of women in this bracket are on the pill, while
9 per cent (a higher proportion than in Britain or the United States) use
the coil. A further 12 per cent of couples stick to *coitus interruptus*, while
11 per cent use the male sheath. All in all, some 67 per cent of women of
child-bearing age today practise some kind of contraception, old or new;
and of the remaining 33 per cent, if we exclude the infertile, the absti-
nent, the pregnant and those trying to become so, we are left with very
few women indeed who are simply incautious. France today claims to be
on the same level as other advanced countries, and this is quite a
dramatic change in one decade. Women may vary in their views on this
or that method, but they have nearly all come to accept contraception as
normal: over 90 per cent, according to the surveys, now favour it.

Of course there are still problems. Many teenagers in particular feel
that information about birth-control is still inadequate, and they blame

equally the health service, the media, their parents, and their school-teachers. Sex education in schools was not made compulsory until 1976, and in many places is still rudimentary. And while an increasing minority of modern-minded mothers now take their sixteen-year-olds to the family doctor ('Please put her on the pill before she gets into trouble'), in a majority of families the subject is still taboo between parents and children. 'I'm taking the pill but I have to hide it, Papa would be horrified,' says many an adolescent. Many parents, while in favour of contraception for themselves, vaguely resent it for having made sex too easy for their daughters too young; and though they know they cannot prevent it, they will not face up to facts and help educate their children to be prepared. But this is a common drama in many countries.

In general, the birth-control revolution provides a good example of how the French today, after a painful tussle with their own traditions, have finally adjusted to modern reality. The drama has been typical of the manner in which many social and economic changes have been taking place. First, an intolerable situation is allowed to build up without anyone taking action. Then a handful of pioneers set to work, and progress slowly follows, haphazard, empirical, unauthorized, usually resisted by the strong social forces always at work to protect the harmony of the *status quo* against conflict. Then, finally, legal or structural reform is sanctioned, not so much to facilitate as to regularize changes that have already taken place.

Much the same has happened more recently in the case of abortion. Their legal battle for birth-control won, the pioneers turned their attention in the early '70s to abortion, where France's legislation was on much the same repressive level as that of Germany and Italy. In the 1960s the number of clandestine abortions was estimated at 700,000 to 800,000 a year, many of them clumsily performed: the figure dropped after the spread of contraceptives, but in 1974 was still running at maybe nearly 500,000. Only a minority of women, about 30,000 a year, had the funds or know-how to go to that new Mecca of abortion, Great Britain. As with birth-control, the Government for years was afraid of legalizing abortion for various political reasons: not only was the opposition from the bishops and old-style Catholics far stronger in this case, but there was a clear hostile majority among the pro-Government parties in Parliament, and the Ordre des Médecins too was far more wary than over contraception. A 1972 survey showed that over 40 per cent of doctors were opposed to abortion even in the case of rape or incest when the girl was under fifteen, and 39 per cent would not approve it even if a foetus were found to be seriously malformed. Public opinion was more advanced: 91

per cent favoured abortion in the case of a malformed foetus, or if the mother's mental or physical health was in danger.

The 'Bobigny affair' in 1972 helped to mobilize this opinion behind the growing campaign for reform. A girl of sixteen in this Paris suburb was arrested and prosecuted for getting an abortion as a result of rape. She was defended, with brilliant success, by the well-known radical lawyer, Gisèle Halimi, who tiraded in court against the cruelty of the existing laws. As soon as Giscard came to power, he saw that reform must be delayed no longer, and instructed Simone Veil, his Health Minister, to prepare a bill with all speed, which she eagerly did. Polls were now showing 73 per cent of the French (and far more women than men) in favour of reform. But there was also an active anti-abortion lobby, 'Laissez-les-Vivre', which denounced Mme Veil as 'an assassin', while many Gaullist and Giscardian deputies were opposed either on religious grounds or else – like Michel Debré – because of the feared threat to France's already waning birth-rate. However, Giscard was determined to push the bill through even if it meant splitting his coalition – which it did. In November 1974, on a free vote, two-thirds of the Gaullists and their allies opposed the reform, and it was passed thanks only to the support of the Socialists and Communists!

The law gives women married or single the right to claim an abortion within the first ten weeks of pregnancy: after this, termination can take place only if there is judged to be grave risk to the health of mother or child, verified by two specialists. There are some other restrictions too: minors (under eighteen) must obtain parental consent; a woman must have been resident in France for at least three months; and she must first be interviewed by a psychiatrist to establish that the abortion is desirable. Abortions are not free, but the State's guideline fees of around 700 francs in public hospitals or clinics are in theory at least within the means of most women and far below the old illicit back-street rates.

The application of the law has had its teething-troubles, as was to be expected, and by the end of its initial five-year period it was working variably. In 1979, there were some 180,000 legal abortions under the new scheme: 33 per cent of the women were unmarried, and 45 per cent under twenty-five. The estimated total of illegal abortions was down to 120,000, with far fewer women now going abroad or resorting to the back-street hacks. This was progress, helped along by the continuing spread of contraception which had cut the overall figure by at least a third in five years. But today there are still problems, due partly to shortage of hospital facilities, and especially to the fact that many doctors, nurses and hospital directors are refusing to cooperate. They have the right to invoke a conscience clause, and many of them do. Dr Simon, himself a leading freemason and hostile to Catholic morality, told me in 1980: 'The head of a hospital can forbid abortions on his premises. So, in some such cases, liberal doctors have built little hut-like clinics in the grounds just outside – like the segregation of lepers in the Middle Ages! Too many of our senior doctors still carry the Middle Ages around with them, that's the trouble.'

Some hospital chiefs claim that they lack the staff, beds or facilities for what they regard as an unnecessary operation since it is not curing sickness. Some hospitals will accept only single teenagers, or mothers aged forty with several children: but this is against the spirit of the law, which in theory gives the woman first choice on whether to have the child or not. Many doctors find excuses for delaying the abortion beyond the ten-week limit, after which the woman may have to resort to less legal means, or go to Britain where the limit is eighteen weeks. All in all, the situation today is easiest in Paris and other big cities, where a woman usually can find a State hospital that will help her, if she looks; but in smaller towns it can be much harder, and in 1979 there were some fifteen departments where doctors' hostility was still making legal abortions virtually impossible. In such cases many women are obliged to turn to the private clinics, where charges are at least twice the 700-franc guideline in the public sector, and for a working girl this is not a small sum. Given the mentality of the medical profession, its various reticences are not surprising. But matters *are* slowly improving: at least the number of deaths through clumsy self-abortion has fallen sharply.

In November 1979 the law came up for re-appraisal by Parliament after its trial period, and much the same bizarre scenario was re-enacted. In the run-up public debate, the *'Laissez-les-Vivre'* lobby again denounced the Government 'assassins', and the bishops this time were more vehement than before, calling abortion 'an act of death'. They were now under strong pressure from the reactionary new Polish Pope. The Ordre des Médecins, at least, was now much less hostile, recognizing there could be no return to the *status quo ante*. But in the Assembly the Government again had to rely on Socialist/Communist support to get the law reconfirmed, as most *majorité* deputies voted against it. Again the Debré lobby pointed to the falling birth-rate, while the Government countered with the view that this fall had begun long before abortion reform and was due mainly to other factors. 'In a free modern society,' said an Elysée spokesman, 'it is no longer possible for a nation to increase its population by forcing women to have children they do not want. It must find other incentives.' And the opinion polls now show two-thirds of the public to be of the same view. In July 1981 the Socialist Minister for

Women's Rights, Yvette Roudy, pledged herself to ensure that the abortion laws would at last be fully and properly applied.

Dr Simon, who has much influence in Government circles, is optimistic: 'The problem will sort itself out within ten years or so, when the younger doctors have adjusted to the new realities and the old ones have retired. The great thing is that our legislation is now on the same civilized level as in Britain or America. The law in France was hitherto out-of-date compared with popular practice and opinion, but it has now actually leap-frogged ahead, for the time being. The public is still rather more confused and divided than in some modern countries, but it will catch up in time.' So a battle for social justice has been won, and France now holds an honourable place in the European league table of recent abortion reform. If only Giscard's Government had shown such courage in all other matters . . .

FAMILIES, FRIENDSHIP, FORMALITY: THE MYTH OF FRENCH INHOSPITALITY

Daily social relations in France have always been dominated, more than in Anglo-Saxon countries, by family ties. The family has appeared as the focus of the individual's loyalty and affection, of his economic interest, and even of his legal duty, for the rights and obligations of the family were defined in the still operative Code Napoléon of 1804. Many an older Frenchman has spent his youth in a world where he was expected to regard cousins, uncles and grandmothers as more important to him than friends of his own age, and where the family's needs and demands were put before those of the local community or even of the State: 'I cannot pay my taxes: you see, I've a duty to support Aunt Louise,' has been a common French attitude.

The main change since the war is that the focus of loyalty has been steadily narrowing from what sociologists call the 'extended family' to the 'nuclear family': from the big multi-generation clan to the immediate home cell of parents and children. The trend varies from class to class. In the property-less lower bourgeoisie the nuclear family has long held more importance than the clan: but in rural areas the big patriarchal peasant families have been losing their influence as the young drift away to the town. And in the upper bourgeoisie, as property gives way to income, as family managements disappear and sons disperse to new salaried careers in other parts of France, so the tight network of the big family gathering, subject of a thousand bitter novels, has become less necessary for the individual's future and security, and also less easy to maintain. Many younger couples are today likely to prefer pleasure travelling, or a weekend cottage shared with a few close friends, to the traditional big family reunions on Sundays and in August. It is hard to be precise on this subject, for French sociology, though abundant with data about working relations and economic habits, shows a typical French reticence about invading family privacy. So I cannot state for sure that the average bourgeois, say, meets his uncles and cousins 5.7 times a year against 13.8 times in 1938, though this might be so. But even this putative 5.7 would still be near the European record.

Once a friend of mine, a young civil servant, invited me to spend Sunday in his parents' prosperous country home near Paris. There I met four generations of them, from his grandmother of ninety-two to his own children and their hordes of little cousins, twenty or more people, and myself one of the only two outsiders. It was delightful, relaxed and very French. On another occasion a girl teacher of twenty-five told me, 'I had to cancel my holiday in Greece this summer: you see, my grandmother got ill and my mother was worried.' I doubt if her English equivalent would often display such a sense of duty. In other words, though clan loyalties towards more distant relatives may be waning, an adult's ties with his own parents and even with *their* parents often remain remarkably close. And if many younger people are today trying to lead more emotionally independent lives, it is often not without a sense of guilt, or an awareness of the pain it causes to their parents who cling to a different family tradition. This may be so in any country: it is especially sharp in France.

In all classes, couples no longer accept so readily that an elderly widowed parent should come to live with them: granny or grandpa is now expected to stay in a flat of her or his own, especially now that the housing shortage has eased. This has caused a good deal of heartache; but officialdom has finally come to recognize this new more independent status of the elderly, and has begun to help. While old age pensions have at last been raised from their previous miserable level (see pp. 384–6), thousands of town councils have been building hostels and *foyers* for old people. Society is finally accepting that its elderly are no longer solely a family responsibility, and in recent years some 10,000 clubs for old people have been created – a new departure for France – many of them under private initiative. The old people themselves are adapting to the change, and are even beginning to group to build their own social life. You see busloads of middle-class widows, going on outings and holidays together, spending freely – an American phenomenon that belatedly has hit France.

After the war the rise in the birth-rate, *le bébé-boom*, did as much as anything to strengthen the prestige and social importance of the younger nuclear family. Baby-making and baby-rearing came to be regarded as a kind of prestige industry, as in Russia, and the young mother filling her HLM with tots and nappies was saluted as of more value to the nation than the old family patriarch or matriarch. Stimulated by the large child-allowances, the average size of families swelled after the war. These factors, plus the typically Latin adoration of small children, led to a veritable *culte de l'enfant*, as the new suburbs pullulated with the kind of images of fecundity that Agnès Varda satirized in her film *Le Bonheur*. But for more than a decade now the birth-rate has been falling steadily, as in other Western countries and for much the same reasons (see p. 15). Giscard's Government anxiously reacted with special new measures, such as even larger allowances for families with more than two children. So in official eyes baby-making is still a prestige industry: but in the eyes of the public the baby-cult is over. Sociologists find that most young couples still seek a first child almost instinctively (*l'enfant biologique*) as a means of proving their fertility and assuring their reproduction: but, in today's uncertain world, they will think twice about having even a second child (*l'enfant économique*). This is true especially in the middle classes.

Families today may be smaller; yet curiously the past few years have seen a new strengthening of the links that bind the nuclear family, after a tense period of transition. Around 1968 French teenagers kicked over the traces of traditional parental authority, more suddenly and sharply than in most Western countries (see pp. 518–26). This was a blow to the nuclear family. But today, having asserted their right to independence, young people are moving back to closer emotional ties with their parents, on a basis of greater equality than before. So the family today is united less by constraint and convention than in the old days, and more by genuine need and affection. In practical terms, a boy or girl of nineteen or twenty is less likely than in the '60s to be still living at home; but he or she will still keep in close touch with parents, pay frequent visits, and probably confide more readily than in the old days. The generation conflict has subsided, now that youth has won its rebellion. And whereas the youth of the '60s rejected the values dictated by its parents, today's adolescents are turning again to the family as a bulwark and a source of comfort, since they no longer find solid values in the public world outside. The fears created by rising youth unemployment have increased this homing trend. And so the new-style liberated family regains a new importance, as a point of anchorage in a shifting world.

Since their first loyalty has always been to family, when it comes to friendship the French tend to be more selective and reticent than the casually gregarious Anglo-Saxons. Their conceptions of friendship differ from those of the British, and this can cause confusion: though more loquacious, they are also more *socially* reserved. There are three levels here. First, a Frenchman will more readily strike up a chat with a stranger in a train or café: there may be a passionate discussion, but it will remain anonymous; personal questions are not asked, and there is no presumption of acquaintanceship. On the second level, the British and Americans are certainly more pally and open than the French at making new acquaintances, developing them quickly into friends, asking them home, calling them 'Bill', swapping personal details. The French admit this: they know they are wary of new friendships, in a society still based so much on mistrust (see p. 642), where the initial reaction to a stranger is often one of suspicion (*'Qui est-il donc? – on ne le connaît pas.'*) and much chatting-up has to be done before this is overcome. Yet the French consider the Anglo-American style of so-called friendship very superficial, an undiscriminating chumminess which, they claim, is an aspect of our *emotional* reserve, a façade to hide the fear of real friendship. They distinguish more sharply between acquaintances and – the third level – *Les vrais amis*, few and select, and here they consider they outclass us in terms of emotional depth and subtlety. The French do not make true friendships lightly, and most of these are formed in youth, or slowly over the years among professional colleagues. Once made, they tend to be enduring and loyal; but the reserve against breaking the ice with new friends can lead to a stiff atmosphere, notably in office life. Except at senior executive level, office colleagues do not often try to meet each other socially, and casual friendship is rare between staff of differing grades. Thus the social ambience of the traditional French office is less chummy and relaxed than in Britain, and this can make life lonely for anyone who arrives to work in a new town, especially Paris, without existing friends. However, the pattern has been changing in the past decade, among younger employees and in new-style offices open to American methods, such as those dealing with the media.

Under the impulse of a younger generation, there has been a steady easing of the social formality and ceremonial that has always been such a feature of daily human contact, in many aspects of French life. True, an Anglo-Saxon may still raise his eyebrows at a respect for hierarchies that can seem almost Teutonic. Any ex-chairman expects to be addressed till his death as 'Monsieur le Président', and letters still ask you to agree to the assurance of most distinguished sentiments. Though the French can be stimulatingly outspoken and unconventional in the voicing of opinions and in conversation, they can also be oddly conventional about manners and behaving *'comme il faut'*. In one sense, this is the outward sign of a snobbish society that respects a person's position and diplomas more than what he is ('Ah, Monsieur est polytechnicien!'). But in another sense, the formality should not be mistaken for coldness: courtesy may be stylized among older people, yet it can be a channel for expressing warmth. The habitual 'Cher Monsieur' does not mean 'Dear sir': an older Frenchman will often call his buddies just that, and it can be rather cordial, like 'mon vieux'.

Anyway, for some years now a younger generation has been showing impatience with the old formal approach and is setting less store by titles and decorum. Today there are fewer ceremonial banquets with speeches, and far more informal home entertaining. Among the new cadres, a new free-and-easiness is emerging which can be traced in the new leisure and holiday habits such as the Club Méditerranée, and in the trend towards casual clothes, casual décor and entertainments, and what the smart 'ads' call 'une élégance vraiment relaxe'. It is true that the French sometimes find it hard to be spontaneously relaxed in this new style. I know one upper-class family who have got with-it by eating snack suppers sitting cross-legged on the floor amid their Louis XV furniture: but this develops a ritual of its own, rather self-conscious. However, gradually the French are making the transition, as one generation succeeds to another, and I would say that today among their own friends, guests and family, the under-forties are virtually as informal as Anglo-Saxons.

The use of Christian names has also been increasing steadily and today is far commoner than in Germany, though by no means yet as universal as in Britain or America where the coinage has been debased into virtual meaninglessness. Again, this is a matter of generation. I have a friend in his fifties who only after several meetings cautiously dropped the 'Monsieur' and called me 'John', whereas his son of thirty did so right away – and this is typical. 'Tu' provides an alternative step towards friendliness; and men will often call each other tu but stick to surnames even when they are good friends, especially if they have been at school or in the Army together. Tutoiement used to be largely restricted to this male camaraderie and to family life, but now it is almost universal among students and teenagers, and is spreading fast in the newer professions, among younger cadres, and in Left-wing circles where it is a conscious anti-bourgeois gesture. In the upper bourgeoisie, by contrast, you even come across some older married couples who call each other vous, by an old tradition; and in this class, though a man is far more likely than twenty years ago to know the wife of a friend or colleague by her Christian name, to call her tu might still give the wrong impression. Women are usually more formal than men, even with each other. I know two married couples in their fifties where the men are firm friends and use surnames and *tu* with each other, while the wives, though they know each other quite well, say *Madame* and *vous*. But, between their grown-up children, it is 'Jacques', 'Odile' and *tu*.

The French have a reputation, quite unjustified, of not entertaining in their own homes. Most Anglo-Saxon horror-stories about this alleged inhospitality are based on stays in Paris, where it is true that daily and business life is so hectic that many families prefer to hug their privacy to themselves: but go to other areas, and you will find a people as welcoming as almost any in Europe. And even Parisians, when they get round to it, are now entertaining much less stiffly and ceremoniously than in the old days, except maybe in a small 'fashionable' milieu. Most younger people, freeing themselves from the formal standards and obligations of their parents, have become far more casual and informal in inviting friends as well as relatives to meals, and are thus readier to do so more often. They will frequently extend an invitation to supper at a few hours' notice, although they may add, apologetically, *'ça sera à la fortune du pot'*, as if half-ashamed at betraying the old ceremonial standards. How much they entertain may depend on where and how they live. The deeper you go into country areas the warmer the welcome, and sometimes I have found young farmers almost embarrassingly hospitable, as in Greece: *'Mais restez chez nous jusqu'à demain, vous pouvez coucher dans le grenier.'* Even in big towns the hospitality can be overwhelming. On a five-week research visit to Toulouse, a city where I had no friends when I first arrived, I was asked home to lunch or dinner by *seventeen* French families, some of them several times; and on a six-week provincial tour for this book, I was invited to a meal in *thirty* different French homes, half of them by people I had not met before, and in ten cases was asked to stay the night. I say this not to boast, but to set the record straight, for foreigners often have a false picture of the French. In nearly every case I found the welcome spontaneous, cordial and unpretentious – very often a family meal shared with the children, truly *à la fortune du pot*.

My only criticism is that the French have the disconcerting habit of offering you either a slap-up meal or not even a glass of water. Of course if you are specifically invited by a friend to *prendre un verre à la maison*, it is different; but in my job I frequently arrange to call on people *chez eux*, where we chat cordially for an hour or so, during which time not even a coffee or a beer is proffered. They are not being mean: it simply does not occur to them. Then, as I get up to go, my host says, *'Mais vous restez dix minutes prendre l'apéritif?'* – by which time it may be too late, if I have another appointment. It can be trying, at the end of a hot and tiring day, when one could really do with a drink. So my policy is either to get up to leave ten minutes before I need to; or else to arrive flustered, saying, 'I'm *so* thirsty – have you just got a glass of water?', which usually shames them into bringing out *le scotch*. In most other countries, a drink or a snack of some sort is offered as soon as a guest crosses the threshold, but not so in France – and the same applies to office meetings, where a visitor is not plied with cups of tea or coffee as in Britain, Germany, or Slav or Arab lands, or elsewhere. True, a few senior executives now follow the Anglo-American habit of keeping a drinks cabinet in their office for special guests, but this is not yet common. As an example of French behaviour at its most extreme, I remember well a day my wife and I spent touring the Burgundy vineyards for the BBC at harvest-time. We called on a number of leading growers and shippers who showed us their *chais*, their cellars and tasting-rooms, and were most friendly: wine, wine everywhere, nor any drop to drink were we given all day! But one grower, a Chevalier du Tastevin, invited us to come as his guests two days later to one of the famous banquets at the Clos de Vougeot, where we ate and drank royally as rarely in our lives.

This is a digression from my subject, which is that the French are more hospitable in the provinces than in Paris, where a friend is likely to bid you *au revoir* with, '*Il faut que tu viennes dîner à la maison, on te fera signe*', and then do nothing. Yet even Parisians can be quite different, once away from the frenetic big-city rat-race. I knew an English married couple in official jobs in Paris who became friendly with two French civil servants. There were cordial business lunches, and sometimes the couple asked the French to parties and were then assured, '*Vous devez dîner chez nous*', etc., and of course nothing happened. Until, one day, the English couple and both the Frenchmen and their wives found that by chance they were all going to spend August in villas in the same part of Auvergne. Holiday addresses were exchanged, and the usual promises of hospitality, which the English took with a pinch of salt. But lo! – in Auvergne, the phone rang, dates were fixed, their French hosts piled lavish meal upon lavish meal with the utmost grace and warmth. The English had broken through the barrier: they were *des vrais amis* at last. But, back in Paris, the iron curtain descended again. Of course, this is a big-city disease not confined to Paris: the French in London have just the same grievances, and Jilly Cooper has said that 'You must come to dinner soon' is Londonese for 'good-bye'.

In Paris, at smart 'society' level, the tradition of formality still powerfully persists. Here dinner-party habits can still be Edwardian by most London standards, with printed invitation cards, probably evening dress white-gloved hired waiters, rigid conventions about serving the correct food and wines; and, very possibly, much of the expensive silver, glass and china will have been borrowed for the occasion from relatives! Here the notion lingers that, if you are to give a party in your own home, then it must be done perfectly or not at all, and so it is not done very often. 'I can't have anyone to dinner this month,' said a leisured housewife, 'you see, my maid has hurt her leg,' while another gave the excuse, 'I'm re-covering my sofas.' It is true that the formal tradition is now under encroachment. On the one hand there is, and always has been, a small moneyed arty-smarty milieu where parties are held with a bizarre bohemian show-off extravagance that relates back to Misia Sert and the *Belle Epoque*. On the other hand, in the upper professional classes just below 'society' level – the world of successful architects, lawyers, bankers, surgeons and the like – entertaining is less elaborate and *mondain* than it used to be, save on special occasions such as weddings. A sophisticated Parisienne who has moved back into this world after some years in London noted the difference: 'People are now readier to invite you to supper on the spur of the moment, or to give an informal buffet party at a few days' notice, and I like that. But even in this more casual style, Parisians still expect excellence: you have to provide the best of everything, all elegantly laid out, and this takes time and money, so people don't entertain very often. Above all, compared with London, social life is very cliquey. People stick to their little circles of close friends, with whom they are truly warm and sincere, but they rarely seem to care about meeting new people outside their own circle – they're too busy, too tired, the tempo in Paris is too exacting. So there's far less gregarious interchange than in London, less sense of lots of overlapping circles where you move easily from one to another – and this makes life hard for an outsider, coming to live here without a ready-made circle.' When people do throw a party, which they do less often than in London, they tend to invite their own kind: you are far less likely than in London to find all types rubbing shoulders easily together in the same room, go-ahead bankers, left-wing thinkers, way-out artists. Doctors will invite other doctors, and so on. A friend told me that at one Paris buffet party for twenty-five couples, two-thirds of the men were Inspecteurs des Finances. It is one aspect of the abiding social divisions in France, which only very slowly have been giving way under modern post-war influences. Will the Socialist regime, as it intends, now accelerate the pace of change? This we must now explore.

SHARING THE POST-WAR AFFLUENCE:
SOME CITIZENS HAVE MORE 'ÉGALITÉ'
THAN OTHERS

The post-war rise in prosperity has been most unevenly shared, in this
land where material inequalities have – till now – been greater than in
almost any other advanced industrial nation. This is the challenge now
facing Mitterrand. Giscard's regime, it is true, made some efforts to
reduce real poverty by raising pensions and the minimum legal wage; it
also tried to increase equality of opportunity through school reform. But
it largely failed to attack the wealth, power and privilege of the small
upper stratum that has long dominated France – and was this any great
surprise, seeing that Giscard and his family were supreme products of
this caste?

The United States, too, has its extremes of wealth and poverty; but it
also has far greater social mobility, and thus more freedom of opportunity, than an older society like France's where despite the dramatic
changes in life-style many class divisions remain remarkably rigid. This
is a matter of psychology as much as of economics. The British, for
example, are far more class-*conscious* than the French, but today in my
view they are less class-*divided*. In Britain, with its post-war social fluidity, the classes are fascinatedly aware of each other on a personal everyday level. In France class distinctions are taken very much more for
granted and are rarely discussed with the same human interest. Certainly there is more mobility than before the war, and children of all
classes now mix in the same State schools till fifteen; but there is little
sense of a classless meritocracy where a worker's gifted son can rub
shoulders with a banker's or a general's. The bourgeoisie retains much of
its aloofness, its ignorance of the lives of workers or peasants, and the
different strata mix little. According to one survey, of the 2,500 most
famous or powerful people in France today, only 3 per cent have come
from working-class homes.

The new Socialist Government is pledged to modify all this, but it
can only be done progressively. In the meantime, you have only to
wander round France to notice how the workers, despite their new
prosperity, are less assertively emancipated than in Britain. There are
some parts of west-central Paris that still have the air of elegant upper-
class preserves in a way that is true of no part of London, not even
Belgravia. Workers in France, even when they can afford it, are reticent
about thrusting forward to share in the bourgeoisie's own public world
of smart shops, cafés and theatres, and their own tastes are not publicly

catered for on the same scale as they would be in the United Kingdom.

The causes of these abiding rigidities lie deep in French history and character. The desire to avoid open conflicts has led to a protective formalization of life which has pushed each class into its fixed place. Conflicts take the form of political demands, *prises de position*, ritual mass rallies: the taking of pot-shots from behind sheltering barricades, rather than the British hand-to-hand jousting. A French worker may resent and fear the alien bourgeois world, but when he meets a bourgeois he is likely to treat him naturally as a simple fellow-citizen, without the chip-on-the-shoulder awkwardness common in Britain. For, paradoxically, the tradition of civic *égalité* remains real and strong, and it leads to a mutual respect between all individuals when regarded as citizens rather than as members of a class. This produces a kind of legal fiction that the gross inequalities of income, opportunity and way of life do not exist.

Class patterns are certainly changing, but less through a merging of different classes than a blurring of the outward distinctions between them. Under modern conditions their interests and habits are drawing closer. A skilled worker may own the same kind of car as a bourgeois, and off duty he may dress much the same way; the new working generation has given up its old class 'uniform' and is dressing like the middle class, so it becomes harder to tell them apart. But the real barriers remain; the bourgeoisie succeeds in retaining control of certain professions, and the lower classes remain reticent about trying to enter these via the supposed equality of education. There is still a feeling of 'us' and 'them'. A worker's son may enter the white-collar lower-middle class by training to be a primary teacher or *fonctionnaire*, but he will rarely aspire to be an engineer or doctor. For a family to change its class takes two generations. A man's accent will not give him away so quickly as in Britain, but his family background clings to him more closely.

Inside these barriers the character of each class has been changing, and nowhere so much as in the aristocracy. In pre-1914 days the French nobility set the tone in France and all Europe for taste and gallantry. But in the past decades the nobility has been pushed into the sidelines of national life, though not extinguished. Few young writers or artists seek their patronage today. Yet many of the great families, the de la Rochefoucaulds, the de Cossé-Brissacs and the rest, have managed to keep their identity and their pride by coming to terms at last with the modern economy. In the nineteenth century their lordly code of values led them to scorn business, and so they let the new empires of banking, industry and technocracy fall into the hands of the bourgeoisie. Today, late though not quite *too* late, they have been taking up salaried posts in these milieux, as the only answer to financial ruin. Economically the nobility is thus merging into the upper bourgeoisie, just as in the last century many bourgeois families succeeded in merging into the aristocracy and prefixed the lordly 'de' to their names.

With their landed fortunes eroded by inflation, taxes and social changes, aristocrats often have to devote part of their new industrial incomes to the upkeep of their cherished family *châteaux*, if they want these to remain habitable. Other *châteaux* are falling into ruin or have been sold; a few, the historic ones, are helped along by State grants. A family may spend weekends and part of the summer in its *château*, and most of the year in its Paris flat, usually in one of the dignified older quarters such as the Faubourg St-Germain. Here the great families for the most part live discreetly and unflamboyantly, clinging together in their own exclusive social world, inviting each other to formal cocktail parties or an occasional ball or banquet with echoes of past glories. And the rest of France tolerates and ignores them. For although the French public adores foreign royalty or the idea of an English *milord*, it cares not a jot for its own nobility, whose doings find little place in French gossip-columns. It is one typical facet of the stratified privacy of French society. Snobbishness certainly exists, but not in the national limelight; it is provided by those bourgeois social-climbers who do still hanker for *la noblesse* – 'Moi, *je suis reçue par les de Rohan-Chabot!*' said one insecure middle-class girl I know, in tones of pride. But if the rest of France lets them be, if they are not constantly Hickeyfied like Lord Lichfield, perhaps this privacy has helped the aristocrats' own true qualities of *finesse* to endure. Many of them are cultured and gentle people, less grasping than the bourgeoisie, and often politically liberal. Increasingly today a minor aristocrat such as a count or baron will no longer use his title in public or professional life and is called simply 'Monsieur'. But he retains it in social life, among his friends, and his pride in his family name remains deep. The big clan family may be on the wane in France, but the nobility is one of its last strongholds.

The equivalent of the English upper-middle class is in France divided between the *grande bourgeoisie* and, just below it, the *bonne bourgeoisie*. De Gaulle was a typical product of the former, as Mitterrand, an ex-lawyer and son of a businessman, is of the latter. These professional and money-making strata retain most of their power as the ruling élites of France, yet the bourgeoisie's nature is changing as France changes. Traditionally its strength was based on property, passed on through family hands and so necessitating close family loyalties and careful marriages. Today the bourgeois family firm is yielding to the managerial corporation, so the upper bourgeoisie now relies increasingly on income from élite salaried positions; and as it still dominates the higher rungs of the educational ladder, a near-monopoly of these jobs is well within its grasp (see pp. 82–92).

The upper bourgeoisie still makes strong efforts, largely successful, to preserve its social *milieux* against *parvenus* from lower down the middle classes. However, a new middle-middle class has arisen, and its numbers and influence have been growing fast without necessarily bursting through the barriers above. Economic expansion, especially of the new tertiary services, has thrown up from the ranks of the lower bourgeoisie a new group that lacks inherited property but has achieved affluence: sales and advertising executives, skilled technicians, *cadres moyens* in modern firms, and those shopkeepers, artisans and small industrialists who have modernized and moved with the times: men like the master-butcher whose lavish party I attended in one small town. Twenty years ago he had one modest shop: now he owns a chain of big ones, and lives in high *nouveau-riche* style in a new country house with a swimming-pool. This is an assertive status-seeking world of new social mobility, more than half in love with American and German material values. But elsewhere in the middle classes the rise of prosperity has been more uneven. Many older people, their savings or investments eroded by inflation, and no longer so able to count on help from their family, are living in genteel poverty. And much of the traditional *petite bourgeoisie* has slumped into decline, notably the less enterprising artisans and small traders outclassed by the new consumer economy. Even the *petits fonctionnaires* in public service (postal workers, clerks, primary teachers) have seen their wages rise less fast than in the private sector. Their ranks have now been infiltrated by the sons and especially the daughters of the peasantry and by some workers – young people who prefer soft jobs as clerks or typists to the drudgery of farm or factory.

One of the few really striking post-war changes in class structure is that medium-sized farmers are now largely integrated into the commercial middle class (see pp. 206–7), so that the former sharp distinction between *paysan* and *citadin* has been fading, as the two grow closer in life-styles and knowledge of each other. But the other sharp distinction, that of *ouvrier* and *bourgeois*, is proving far more resistant to change, since it derives not only from mutual ignorance but from the direct economic and social subordination of one class to another. It is true, as I have suggested, that the workers are picking up bourgeois habits. Nowadays they watch the same TV programmes – a great leveller – and sometimes go on the same kind of holidays, while the young frequent the same local discos. And in their new flats the workers are developing the same property-owning instincts and material aspirations as the bourgeoisie. The working class has also become less homogeneous: its better-paid upper echelons, such as the envied *'métallos de chez Renault'* and other skilled workers, are forming new proletarian élites who, without becoming middle class, often find that their interests are closer to those of the factory's junior *cadres* than of lower-paid workers in less go-ahead firms. And yet, despite exceptions, the broad mass of the French working class still lives in a social world of its own; and especially this is so in its ghetto-like strongholds, the older industrial areas such as the Lorraine steel basin, St-Étienne, parts of the Nord, and the Paris Red Belt. During the boom years of the '50s and '60s there was a certain decline, as in Britain, of the old emotional solidarity of class, born of hard times. But in the late 1970s the rise in unemployment under a hated Right-wing Government brought back some of that feeling, and the Communist Party in its new tough mood strained every nerve to build on it. Rightly or wrongly, the working class under Giscard's regime felt alienated and excluded from the mainstream life of the country, from the Government, from culture, from business, and from other centres of power save where the Party locally controlled a town hall. It remains to be seen how far the Socialist regime can now cure this sense of alienation.

If I have drawn a somewhat severe picture of French class divisions today, it is because change has until now been less apparent than in Britain. One reason often advanced for the sharp social changes in post-war Britain is the enforced mucking-together of wartime; the French did not have this kind of experience, being split up and paralysed by the Occupation (even though in other ways this was a useful catalyst). But today, a generation later, the social rigidity is due more than anything to the way the bourgeoisie has managed to retain its domination of the upper-secondary and higher education systems. Strange as it may seem, education in France for the over-sixteens is in many ways even more closely divided on class lines than in Britain with its public schools (for this and the Haby reforms see pp. 472–93). The proportion of university students from workers' homes is far lower than in Britain and has actually been falling – from 13 per cent in 1974 to 9 per cent in 1979. And inside the middle class the cachet of a Grande Ecole diploma often produces a further distinction (see pp. 82–92). These gradings stay for life: once a *cadre* always a *cadre*, and opportunities for an able man to win promotion from the shop-floor or from junior clerical ranks have been improving only slowly and are more limited than in Britain.

Giscard's Government did make some efforts to reduce these inequalities. Its new stress on adult vocational training (see p. 480) has made it a little easier for a bright shop-floor worker to secure advancement in his firm; and the Socialists are now taking this further. Above all, under the Haby reforms of 1977 the junior classes of *lycées* are abolished and all pupils follow the same general course until fifteen: this is supposed to encourage more workers' children to accede to higher education. The results may not be apparent for some years. But, whatever the effect of official action, the real problem in French class structure is this: while in the middle and lower-middle strata a new fluidity has been developing spontaneously, at the two extremes – the hard-core proletariat, and the upper-bourgeois élites – the rigidities have till now persisted. Farmers, tradesmen, skilled workers, junior *cadres*, are intermingling more than ever before; the rural exodus and the mass rehousing have played their part in this, as the new suburban estates provide the different groups with new social contacts that they never knew in their old homes. But this is not the main issue. While Giscard may well have been sincere in seeking to improve prospects for workers, he made little headway in the harder task of loosening the dominance of his own élite class. And indeed how could he, even assuming he wanted to, given the obstinate resistance of his own political allies? All the studies show that under Giscard the same self-perpetuating castes continued to enjoy a near-monopoly of the main positions of power and influence: the technocratic class via the Grandes Ecoles; the upper strata of the liberal professions; the wealthy industrial and banking families. At least this was a kind of meritocracy, where the more brilliant members of these castes were the ones acceding to the top posts, even in private industry; but it was a narrowly based, self-selecting meritocracy, awarding itself high salaries and high privileges. And it is the dominance of this élite, more than anything, that explains why the new-affluent France has remained till now one of the most unequal of Western societies, alike in terms of opportunity and of wealth. Again, how far will the Socialists now pursue their plans to modify this structure?

The inequalities must be seen in perspective, for it is also true that all classes have shared in the prosperity boom of the post-war decades. Living standards have been rising faster than in most other West European countries, though admittedly from a lower starting-point than in some such as Britain. So how does France today compare in affluence with her neighbours? It is not an easy question to answer precisely, in a period of high inflation and fluctuating currencies, and especially in view of the social disparities. We should also beware of taking statistics too literally, for they can be misleading (the French, who adore using them, sometimes call them 'an elegant way of telling lies'). But for what they are worth here are some statistics from official sources (OECD and EEC). The real purchasing power of the average French worker's salary rose by an estimated 170 per cent in 1950–75, and in the middle and upper income groups it rose slightly faster still. According to other figures, overall private consumption rose by 174 per cent in 1950–74. The increase has of course slowed considerably since the latter date, but even in 1975–8 real incomes were still rising at an average 2.4 per cent a year, and only with the onset of the new recession in 1979–80 did a very slight fall become apparent. Average real spending power has roughly trebled since the late 1940s, the date by which it had regained its pre-war level.

So how does this place France, internationally? The statistics are surprising. In 1979, according to the latest OECD figures, France had an annual gross domestic product per capita of $10,680, behind a number of other advanced countries such as Switzerland ($14,970), Denmark ($12,940), Sweden ($12,820), West Germany ($12,450), Norway ($11,470), Belgium ($11,000), but just ahead of the United States ($10,650), Holland ($10,620) and Canada ($9,580), and far ahead of Japan ($8,620), the United Kingdom ($7,170), Italy ($5,690) and Spain ($5,310). As a guide to living standards these figures can be misleading, for they also reflect the strength or weaknesses of currencies at a given moment: sterling, for example, soon picked up strongly from its low 1979 level, so that by 1981 Britain was no longer trailing behind France so dismally as the figures above may suggest. We must also deduct the differing proportions of national production ploughed back into investment (higher in Germany than France, and lower still in Britain) and then take into account the differences in the cost of living, which by 1980 was about 15 per cent lower in France than Germany and 15 per cent lower again in Britain. From these various calculations it may be fair to say that, of these three peoples, the British were until about 1960 the richest and are now much the poorest, while the Germans have moved from third to first place. But we still have not fully answered the question about living standards, which depend not only on purchasing power but on factors inherited from the past, notably housing: the owner of a cottage may rise to the same level of income as his neighbour in a mansion, without thereby having the same standard of living. This is why some French middle-class families still *seem* to be less comfortably off than their British counterparts, despite higher spending power: they are less well endowed with a legacy of good housing. And they still choose to spend their money in different ways. Although the styles of living and consumer habits have been drawing closer, the French still spend more on pleasure and expensive gadgets, and less on home comforts. But the gap is narrowing, and now that their housing has improved the French have moved clearly ahead of the British in prosperity in the past decade or so.

The upper bourgeoisie in particular today live far better than in Britain and just about as well – though in a different style – as in Germany or in America. In addition to their higher incomes, another reason for their advance over the British is that they rarely inflict on themselves the same burden of high private school bills. Many a family can thus afford two long holidays each year, and plenty of smart clothes and dining out. A British doctor who in 1980 went to stay with a colleague of the same professional level in Lyon was amazed: 'With two sons at public school, we can hardly afford foreign holidays; I have a four-year-old Cortina, I buy a new suit once every two years at most, we have no help in the house, and our friends are given Spanish plonk for dinner, with a glass of ordinary Scotch first if they're lucky. As for my French host, he drove us around in his brand-new Citroën CX, his wife wore Yves St-Laurent, and a maid served us at dinner in their luxury flat overlooking Lyon where his drinks cabinet had six different malt whiskies. They seemed to think nothing of spending 300 francs a head *chez* Bocuse, and were leaving the next month for two weeks in the Caribbean.'

This may change under Socialism. Moreover, you have only to look further down the social scale to see that the new wealth is shared more unevenly in France than in either Britain or Germany, as is indicated by this table prepared by the Confederation of British Industries, of average monthly net salaries (in £ sterling) in 1979:

	France	Britain	Germany	Italy
Managing director	2,818	1,051	2,645	2,089
Sales manager	1,529	655	1,323	1,283
Skilled worker	472	399	624	312
Unskilled worker	342	329	503	234

So a German is much better off than a Briton at every level: in France, where the range is much wider, the better paid are as rich as in Germany and the lower paid are as poor as in Britain. In practice one has to add in other factors too, such as the higher French welfare allowances, so that the real income range is not quite so much greater in France as might appear. Even so, during the Gaullist boom years in particular the rich were getting richer faster than the poor. Rapid expansion under a liberal economy favoured those with high salaries, or running their own businesses, or with special technical skills. However, since 1968 the gap has been narrowing again. From 1970 to 1978 the average spending power of a worker rose by 33.2 per cent, against 17.9 for a *cadre moyen* and 14.9 for a *cadre supérieur*. According to official statistics, the differential between workers and senior *cadres* as a whole fell from 4.6 in 1967 to 3.4 in 1980 (though other sources, such as the CBI table, suggest that the real range may be wider). Various factors explain the new trend. The workers won big increases as a result of the May '68 strikes, and since then union pressure in a period of high inflation has helped them to develop their incomes more easily than the *cadres*, who now complain bitterly they are being squeezed. It was also Giscard's policy to help the least well-off. Old-age pensions, once miserably low, were at last raised radically (retired people saw their real incomes go up by 52.7 per cent in the 1970–78 period), while the better-off bore the brunt of increases in social security contributions.

Above all, the official minimum legal wage, which aims to protect the lowest-paid against exploitation or near-starvation, was raised during the 1970s with something approaching generosity. For years after the war it did no more than keep pace with rising costs and in May '68 barely exceeded two francs an hour. Its regular increases since then have moved much faster than inflation, and by May 1980 the SMIC stood at 13.66 francs an hour, enabling a *smicard* on a forty-hour week to earn some 2,380 francs a month – no big deal, but at least allowing a simple manual worker to look for more than subsistence living. However, the other side of this coin is that recession has led to short-timing in many firms, and as many *smicards* are paid by the hour their real take-home pay has tended to fall. At all working levels, from the SMIC upwards, rising unemployment has led to much new hardship: for of those out of work, not everyone qualifies in practice for the indemnities which in theory are so high (see p. 107). Add to these the small farmers, artisans, and others among the less successfully self-employed, and there is still plenty of poverty in France.

Differentials may be falling, yet they are still far above the north European average. And income statistics give only part of the picture. They gloss over one notorious injustice: not only are rates of income tax relatively low, but the self-employed can indulge happily in that ancient French pastime, tax evasion. It is this, as much as anything, that leads to the gross inequalities of wealth. Partly because of the difficulty of getting the French to pay direct taxes, the State has long put its main emphasis on indirect taxation, such as high VAT. But this can be socially unjust, for consumer taxes hit rich and poor alike as a progressive income tax does not. It is reckoned that only 20 per cent of French fiscal revenue comes from income tax, and 60 per cent is in no way related to the level of an individual's wealth. Moreover the wage-earner, representing 55 per cent of all earned income, pays 84 per cent of all income tax – this gives some idea of the degree of evasion by non-wage-earners. It is believed to deprive the exchequer of some 60,000 million francs a year, almost as much as the total revenue from income tax. Successful lawyers, actors, private doctors and others can make huge sums and declare only a small part for tax, and this is connived at by the inspectors. They lack the staff or machinery for making proper checks; and, anyway, too many highly placed friends of the Government benefit from the *status quo*! Wealthy individuals are still checked on average less often than every twenty years, so the risks are well worth taking.

Evasion apart, even statutory taxes on wealth such as death duties and capital gains tax have till now been lower than in most advanced countries. In 1976, in the face of Gaullist opposition, Giscard did manage to get a mild capital gains tax through Parliament. It was little more than a gesture, as the income it has since provided for the Treasury is minimal. But the furore it caused on the Right – when most other Western countries have long had far more extensive taxes of this kind – showed how savagely the French wealthy classes would fight to defend their yachts and tiaras. Then in 1979 a Government commission dared to propose a doubling of the rate of death duties on larger fortunes. The ceiling for this tax in France was then a mere 20 per cent, compared with 35 in Germany, 70 in the US, 75 in Britain; and death duties earned the Treasury only one-sixtieth as much revenue as VAT. But this proposal too came under heavy fire from Giscard's own allies, and was shelved. So, in short, by 1981 the very rich in France were still sitting very pretty. An OECD report in 1976 indicated that the top 10 per cent of Frenchmen earned 30.4 per cent of all take-home income, while the bottom 10 per cent earned 1.4 per cent, or 21.7 times less. The equivalent ratio, said OECD, was 9.4 times in Britain, 9.7 in Sweden, 10.8 in West Germany, 12.7 in Spain and 18.02 in Italy. So OECD depicted France as the gold-medallist of inequality. It is true that the gulf in terms of owned wealth (as opposed to income) has tended to be slightly less than in Britain, where 1 per cent of the population owns 32 per cent of all wealth (in France, 26 per cent; in Germany, 28 per cent). But this is a legacy of Britain's mighty past. In newer-rich France, the wealth gap actually widened in the boom years: from 1953 to 1980 the assets of industrialists and professional people accrued twice as fast as those of workers.

By 1981 it seemed clear that only a change of regime would radically change the situation. Giscard, when I went to see him at the Elysée, said he regarded the wealth gap as one of the major French problems still to be solved. I am sure that he was sincere in wanting to create a more equal society. But it seemed unlikely that he could get far simply by chipping away at the areas of greatest poverty; and he clearly lacked the courage, and the necessary allies, to attack his own personal milieu – the world of wealth. Then the Socialists came to power with a programme of redistribution of riches. Straight away, in June, they introduced some quick measures to show they meant business. They raised family allowances by 25 per cent, old age pensions by 20 per cent, the SMIC by 10 per cent.

They slapped a new 25 per cent supertax on the 100,000 highest incomes, and they put new taxes on expense accounts, yachts and luxury hotels. But this was only a start. Mitterrand announced more radical measures for 1982, including an increase in death duties and an intensified campaign against tax evasion. In the budget for 1982, the income tax structure was remodelled so as to penalize the higher-paid and ease the burden on poorer people. Above all, a new annual wealth tax was now to be applied to those (about 150,000 households) with possessions valued at over 3 million francs: this was to be on a sliding scale, starting at 0.5 per cent and rising to 1.5 per cent annually for those with fortunes of over 10 million francs. Of course there was an outcry, and the Right did succeed in forcing Parliament to dilute some aspects of the tax. Moreover, after strong lobbying by artists, dealers and art-collectors, Mitterrand personally intervened to decree that all works of art should be exempt. The art world had pointed out, fairly enough, that the tax might lead to many French art treasure being sold abroad and thus would hardly help French culture.

Even in its modified form, the wealth tax is one of the toughest in Europe. The Socialists' package of fiscal measures has caused cries of alarm to go up from Neuilly and the *seizième*, from country *châteaux* and Côte d'Azur villas, and many people have reacted by trying to smuggle their capital or their valuables out of the country, often to Swiss banks. So the rich in France are now being hit quite hard, for the first time since the war, and are having to cut back on smart clothes, expensive holidays and lavish entertaining. The worst extremes of the wealth gap are being closed, and France is moving towards the North European average. But there will still be plenty of inequality. And the bourgeoisie is still likely to remain better off than in Britain.

LEISURE AND CONSUMER MODES: 'LE WEEKEND' IN A RURAL DREAM-NEST

To paint too dark a picture of the inequalities might give a false impression. For, viewed from another angle, the remarkable rise in living standards since the war has benefited nearly all French people, albeit unevenly; and only since 1979 has recession begun to dent the surface of the new affluence. France's post-war consumer revolution, as in other countries, has brought great changes in spending and leisure habits, and the workers have shared in this. They are eating far more meat than before the war, and have even been adopting the middle-class habit of saving part of their earnings. Cars, television, summer holidays by the sea and other new 'privileges' have been altering their lives.

If in their family and private habits and social attitudes the French are still uneasily torn between old and new – as we have seen – they have shown fewer complexes about adapting to the more practical aspects of modern affluence. After some initial consumer resistance in the 1950s, they have since thrown themselves into *la civilisation des gadgets* with a hearty materialist appetite (and only recently have some younger people begun to question it, again as we have seen). The figures show the advance in modern household equipment in France and how it compares with other countries (source: EEC):

Percentage of homes equipped with:	France			Bel-gium	Other countries (November 1978)				Italy	UK
	1954	1970	1979 (January)		Den-mark	Ger-many	Hol-land	Ire-land		
Passenger car	21	56	68	70	57	63	67	65	70	55
Refrigerator	7	79	93	90	77	97	97	81	88	87
Deep-freeze	0	0	23	52	54	55	43	20	25	37
Dish-washer	0	2	13	14	16	16	10	7	17	4
Clothes-washer	8	55	76	75	52	88	88	64	87	72
TV (any kind)*	1	69	88	95	97	112	108	72	106	70
TV (colour)	0	0	31	50	50	56	60	26	15	33

* Figures include homes with more than one set.

If we look at the breakdown in France by social category, one interesting fact is that lower-income families possess almost as much of this equipment as the more privileged ones – with the exception of dishwashers, which are seven times commoner in upper-bourgeois than in working-class homes. But automatic clothes-washers are owned by virtually as many workers (84 per cent) and farmers (86.8 per cent) as *cadres supérieurs* (86 per cent); 77 per cent of workers have cars, above the national average; and 67 per cent of farming families own a deep-freeze. The senior *cadre* spends only twice as much more on food (at home) than the unskilled worker; on the other hand, he spends fifteen times more on holidays, dining-out and leisure.

Food and drink today account for no more than 23 per cent of the average family's budget, compared with 50 per cent before the war and 38 per cent in 1959. Spending here is still rising in real money terms, but not as fast as it has done in other sectors. For instance, private spending on transport, travel and telephones has more than tripled in real value since 1950, and its share of the family budget has increased in this period from 5.4 to 13.1 per cent. The sector described by the statisticians as 'health and hygiene' has risen equally fast, from 5.9 to 12.3 per cent: so the French have got cleaner, and much more diet-conscious. Spending on clothing, homes and leisure has seen similar increases; and within the leisure bracket, café- and restaurant-going are in relative (but not absolute) decline compared with the rapid advances of television, cars, sport and holidays. These dry statistics confirm that affluence has pushed French spending habits closer to British or American models. Relatively the French still place more emphasis on enjoyment, but their former reluctance to spend their money on useful possessions has waned sharply.

This at least was the picture until recession first began to hit real incomes in 1979, when its initial impact on these habits was rather curious. Most French people seemed to adopt an epicurean attitude. They put less money into savings, and they made economies in routine expenses such as clothes and food: sales of expensive cuts of meat fell noticeably. But they continued to spend as much as before on their special new consumer indulgences – maybe owning a smart car, or a boat, or a country villa, or taking exotic holidays, or following some sport or hobby. The sociologist Bernard Cathelat commented: 'The hedonistic, instant-pleasure ethic of the boom years still strongly persists, despite changing conditions. So we see a divorce between two types of consumption. On the one hand, basic utility spending, where people try to make cut-backs. On the other, motivated spending for pleasure or consolation, psychologically essential. This is the escapist dream element that each of us seeks to preserve, and it seems to be affected least by the crisis.' The Italians, even more Latin, have reacted in the same way. Fun first, caution afterwards, for maybe tomorrow we die.

During the boom years, the French steadily increased the share of their budget that went on their homes, not only on rent and mortgages (see p. 289) but on comfort and equipment too. The proportion spent on the home (25.5 per cent) is now as high as in Britain. *Le bricolage* (do-it-yourself odd-jobbery), which used to interest the French so little, has now become a major pastime, linked with the growth of individual housing and the middle-class vogue for buying up derelict country villas for weekends. Outside many towns you see big new 'garden centre' supermarkets, and they do a roaring trade with a new generation of gardening enthusiasts. Even in respectable suburbs, a bourgeois husband no longer considers it undignified for the neighbours to see him mowing the lawn or painting his own front door on a Sunday. One curious side-aspect of this new emphasis on the home and comfort is the rapid growth in the number of domestic pets owned by town-dwellers. In numbers, the French here have even overtaken the British: they own 8.2 million dogs, 6 million cats, 6.5 million caged birds, while production of petfoods rose startlingly from 21,000 tons in 1965 to 339,000 tons in 1978. You see huge hoardings, *'Wiskas* [sic], *elle aime la qualité'*. It may not yet be true that the French, like many Britons, prefer pets to people: but the psychologists have plenty of explanations for this new craze. Now that adolescents claim their independence so much earlier, the pet becomes a substitute child, with the added advantage that you do not have to worry about its career future, and you can talk to it without provoking a quarrel. A nation that still turns a blind eye to industrial cruelty towards animals for slaughter (e.g. imported horses) is nonetheless kind towards its own pets. The Government, always alert in these matters, even created a feline identity card in 1978.

In some respects the French seem not quite sure how to deal with their new domestic affluence. Consider furniture and décor. Many sophisticated couples with a smart modern flat show a bias against filling it with modern furniture, and go out of their way to install antiques, real or 'repro', often with incongruous results. Modern designs, readily accepted in the office or restaurant, are regarded by many older people as cold and unfriendly in the home – witness Tati's satire *Mon Oncle*. But this bias has been steadily declining, and many well-to-do people now have new flats most elegantly furnished in a modern manner, often with Scandinavian influences. But the French are still drawn more strongly than the British to their own classic tradition, to those spindly straight-backed Louis XV chairs and formal settees that decorate so many bourgeois salons. The French have little equivalent of the comfy vulgarity of English pre-war style: their taste is either for the classical or the ultra-new. Neither in furniture nor in domestic décor have they yet found a satisfactory modern style of their own. But a few innovators are at least now trying, with some successes. Parisian décor is at its best when using glittering surfaces of glass and metal, and then in its flamboyant way it often achieves an elegance and lightness that outclasses London.

In the important French domain of clothes and fashion, affluence has brought an increase in the general level of public taste, paradoxically, just at a time when Paris has been losing some of its pre-eminence as world trend-setter. But the true *milieu* of Paris *haute couture* has always been restricted to a few thousand rich society women. Maybe this world has lost some of its lustre, yet at the same time good taste has become more democratic and has spread much wider. Many of the simpler of the new fashions are nowadays quickly copied and mass-produced by the big stores like Le Printemps, at prices within the reach of secretaries and even factory girls; and, ever since the war, papers such as *Elle* and *Marie-Claire* have been drumming notions of elegance into the heads of ordinary Frenchwomen who, as a general breed, never had any special claim to be very well dressed. The ordinary girl certainly dresses more elegantly than twenty years ago. So French *chic* is not a myth: in fact it can be argued that since French women as a race, often sharp-featured or flat-chested, tend to be less beautiful than, say, Italians or Scandinavians, they try all that much harder, with clothes and cosmetics, to make up for what nature has failed to provide.

Elle, Marie-Claire and one or two similar magazines can also take some of the credit for improvements in décor, housekeeping skills, and especially hygiene. Just before the war, when Frenchwomen were among the dirtiest and smelliest in Europe, *Marie-Claire* took the lead in a campaign to get them to wash more. After the war this developed, other papers joined in, the public responded, and the rise in the sales of soap, deodorants and toothpaste has been phenomenal. If the provision of bathrooms in the new flats has been one factor in the new cleanliness, the women's magazines can claim a share in the triumph too. Marcelle Auclair, founder of *Marie-Claire*, told me: 'French girls used to disguise their dirt with powder and make-up on top of it. Now they wash properly, and clean their teeth. Haven't you noticed how the Métro stinks much less than it used to?'

Flip through these magazines' pages, or even those of a more newsy glossy such as *Le Point*, and many words will stand out strangely in the advertisements: '*Le temps d'un long drink . . . immeuble de grand standing . . . le business car . . . le short de football . . . la mode made in Timwear . . . dressing-room aménage . . . l'après-shampooing . . . une star est interviewée . . . stéréoplay.*' These, and many others, I culled at random from *Marie-Claire, Le Point* and *l'Express* in 1980. Whatever has been happening to the language that Proust and Balzac spoke? The massive invasion of French by Anglo-Saxon words in the 1960s (*franglais* it is called) caused a great intellectual outcry, and a Sorbonne professor, Etiemble, wrote a book denouncing it. But I think the invasion has been often misunderstood. It is not that ordinary French people have been voluntarily abandoning their language: rather in the 1960s they were the victims of a commercial conspiracy. Modern techniques of advertising and public relations arrived late in France, but then swept through the land with hurricane force; and the experts decided that the French could be conditioned to accept a commodity as new and smart if it were given an Anglo-Saxon name. The clothing and cosmetics worlds virtually adopted English as a *lingua franca*, and house-agents for a while did so too. Some of this inevitably spilled over on to journalists and others who picked up the new habits of speech, but only superficially: though some ads may still speak of *un drink* and *le shopping*, a Frenchman is still more likely to ask you to *prendre un verre* and his wife will *faire les courses*. If they do use English words, it is often as a kind of joke. In fact, during the 1970s the advertisers' craze for *franglais* has waned considerably. It was a mode, now well past its peak.

However, *franglais* has left its mark in several ways. There has been a more permanent incursion of English terms into the everyday vocabulary of French business and technology, where words like *le marketing, le cash-flow, le pipeline*, have become common currency simply because no one has invented adequate French equivalents. The Giscard Government became alarmed at this trend, and helped Parliament to adopt a Bill put forward by a Gaullist deputy, Pierre Bas, that from January 1977 has made virtually illegal the use of foreign words – where French alternatives can be found to exist – in advertisements, official documents, and even on radio and television. The law was greeted with some derision in the Press, which pointed to the absurdity of trying to impose legal curbs on anything as spontaneous and fluid as language. The British laughed at it as a typical bit of French legalism, and in *The Times* Bernard Levin wrote a leader in French lamenting, as a francophile, 'this cultural crime of a crackpot nation that will impoverish its own tongue through this protectionism'. But in practice the sillier and more repressive aspects of the Bas law have never been applied: radio announcers still refer to *le weekend* without being sent to prison for a year, as in theory they could. The law is used mainly for sensible consumer protection, to ensure for example that instructions on imported goods carry translations, so that the public knows what it is buying and how to use it. In fact only once has a firm or individual been brought to the courts and fined, and this was British Airways for failing to print a French version of the 'conditions of contract' appearing on the tickets it sells in France. It has since complied.

One can understand French sensitivity about their proud language, but the *franglais* issue was much exaggerated, and happily the furore has now died down. Surely a language will wither unless it is in constant evolution, fertilized from outside – and it is now the turn of the French to import English words into daily speech, just as English was so much enriched by countless French terms in past centuries. The French must accept this: as we British say, *noblesse oblige*. As we have cafés, so the French now have *le snack*; as we have maîtres d'hôtel, so they now have *le barman*; as we have maisonettes, so they have *le parking*; and so on with scores of other words that have been slipping quietly into daily use, such as *le weekend, un leader, le duty-free,* and *le* now popular *jogging.* Admittedly, the French sometimes borrow falsely, and English eyebrows may be raised at such quaint terms as *un recordman, un tennisman, le footing* (walking), *un pull* (pullover), *un smoking* (dinner-jacket), and *grand standing* (house-agentese for 'up-market'). Equally ludicrous, in a way, are some recent official efforts to squeeze out *franglais* by fabricating French equivalents. This often flops because the French language is not sufficiently supple and concise: *le cash-flow* does not convince when turned into *le marge brut d'autofinancement,* and who will bother to talk about *un appareil de forage en mer* when he has *un oil-rig*? Some Gaullists even thought the answer, when all else failed, was to Gallicize English spellings, but their *beuledozère* soon ground to a halt. A limited degree of *franglais* is here to stay: it will be assimilated and forgotten, as we have forgotten that 'restaurant' is a French word. And as more of the French learn to speak good English, as they are now doing (see p. 467), so they may be more likely to conserve their own language properly and cease to confuse the two.

The very fact that the French have no word of their own for 'weekend', and have had to borrow the English one, is significant of changing attitudes to leisure in the new France. The French are a hard-working people, in their own not-always-so-constructive way; and though traditionally they have set high store by *le plaisir* – self-indulgence in intervals between toil and duty – only with post-war affluence have they come to embrace the modern concept of *le loisir.* This has now acquired the status of a *valeur,* like work, and officialdom has shown a new concern with helping people to use their free time positively. In many of their new leisure habits, as in so much else, the French have been drawing closer to other nations, through the spread of television, discothèques, hi-fi, weekend pleasure motoring, various sports and much besides – 'Modern leisure will be uniform and mutually imitative', said one sociologist. In fact, apart from *boules* in the Midi and the abiding penchant for long meals with much chatter, it is hard to think of many French pastimes which remain specifically French. Yet in some respects their *attitudes* to leisure still differ from the British, notably in the way they like their free time divided up: that is, since the war they have shown a preference for longer annual holidays rather than shorter daily working hours.

The French take the longest holidays in Europe, and they live for them quite obsessively, as we shall see later in this chapter. In addition, the number of official *jours fériés* (July 14th, May 1st, November 1st and

11th, and the rest) has been growing and now accounts for ten days a year. And whenever one of these falls on a Thursday or Tuesday, many a *cadre* will *faire le pont* by taking the Friday or Monday off as well, to give himself four free days in a row. Yet this does not mean that the Frenchman fails to work hard, merely that he works differently. Executives and professional people will frequently stay in their offices from 9 a.m. till 7 or 8 at night, but also take five or six weeks' holiday a year. However, there have been some changes in recent years, affecting all classes. First came the spread of the weekend habit, with the giving up of Saturday work in offices and factories. This was closely followed by a widespread shortening of the long lunch break, at least in Paris and northern cities. Finally, in the past three or four years, under the dual impact of the unemployment crisis and the changing mood of French youth, employees have at last begun to press for a shorter working week.

Le weekend has now become a sacred social institution, but only fairly recently. It was not until 1966 that an experiment began in Paris ministerial offices to give up Saturday morning work in favour of longer daily hours. It was welcomed and generalized, and was rapidly followed by the closure of nearly all factories on Saturdays with the full support of the unions. Shops remain open all that day but many close on Monday instead, for the five-day week is now seen as a universal right, and the French are not very good at staggering. The middle classes go away for the weekend far more than they used, and some workers are now doing so too. Many more families in all classes might have done so sooner, were it not that the French have traditionally inflicted on themselves the illogicality of State schools staying open all Saturday but closing one day mid-week. Pedagogic reasons were given for this (children were said to need a break from hard study) and many parents too were in favour: especially in working homes, parents were often quite glad to have *les gosses* out of the way on Saturdays. However, reforms since 1969, while keeping the Wednesday break, have aimed to lighten the burden of classwork by allowing junior schools to close all Saturday and *lycées* to finish at noon. For many families, this has given new scope to the weekend getaway craze.

You have only to stand beside one of the main roads out of Paris, at 7 p.m. on a summer Friday, to see the extent of this vogue. Even back in May 1958, at the height of the crisis that brought back de Gaulle, the sight of that army of cars, piled high with suitcases, cots and children, misled a British reporter into writing a scare story about the threat of civil war: 'Mass flight from Paris begins' ran his front-page headline. Today, as in 1958, it is not the threat of paratroops from Algiers, but the strains of daily city life, that incites so many people to make for the weekend quiet of the country, and as likely as not they will go neither to a hotel nor to relatives but to their own country cottage or villa. The *résidence secondaire* has become something of a cult among middle-class Parisians and other city-dwellers. Many are old farmsteads, left empty by the rural exodus and now sold to bourgeois owners who smarten them up. Others are new weekend villas for the well-to-do, or seaside flats. With over 2 million of these secondary homes, France holds the world record: one family in nine owns one, against one in fifteen in the United States, one in a hundred and forty in Germany, one in two hundred in Britain. In the Yonne department, not far from Paris, 20 per cent of all housing falls into this class; but you also find quantities of it much farther afield. From Paris, from Lyon and other cities, people will cheerfully drive hundreds of miles each weekend, arriving back late on Sunday, exhausted from crawling through the traffic-jams of similar migrants: the price they pay for their dream-nest, the ideal escape from weekday reality. It ties in with the new trends of ecological back-to-nature and the hedonistic or spiritual search for privacy. It is also a shrewd investment, with demand rising faster than supply. Many a rural ruin has increased its price tenfold in as many years.

If weekends are now more important, lunches are less so. The leisurely two-hour family lunch, weekdays included, is one hallowed French tradition that is in decline under the *force majeure* of suburban commuting and economic change. This has habitually been the main meal of the day, with children coming home from school and husbands from work – and so it still is, in many small towns and rural areas. But the cities have seen big changes.

For some years after the war, Paris still went dead from midday to two o'clock: even the banks and the big stores closed. But then, as the drift to the suburbs grew, Parisians reluctantly came to accept that the lunch-break must be made more flexible. A growing number of employees faced the invidious choice between a long trek home in defiance of sense, or else a cheap lunch near their work (if they could find one) followed by an hour or so killing time. Managers, too, with their new American business ethos, came to realize what a drag the long break could be on a modern economy. So a few firms began to introduce a uniform one-hour lunch for more junior staff, with earlier evening closing. This was generally popular, though conflicts were sometimes acute: many firms delayed the change for years because it was strongly opposed by staff who did live fairly close, and staggering of hours to suit both sides was not feasible. Older people in particular often grumbled at having to alter their habits: 'The change has upset my family life,' said a saleswoman; 'I used to get home in time to cook a big hot lunch for my husband and children, who go to school near-by, and we'd have a cold meal at night. Now I have to stay and eat in the canteen, my family get the *femme de ménage* to cook them lunch, and I make myself a hot meal in the evening.' But change was finally accepted. The past twenty years have seen quite a revolution in Greater Paris, where the percentage of employees going home for lunch has dropped since 1958 from 60 to 15, at which point it has levelled off: most factories and many larger offices have opened canteens, while down-town snack-bars and cafeterias have sprung up to cater for those with limited means. Most central banks and shops, though not all, remain open; and only executives now take long business lunches (or use them as an alibi).

In the provinces, too, most larger or newer factories now have short lunch-breaks, canteens, and earlier closing, and this is generally popular with staff. But in other respects the provinces have moved more slowly than Paris, notably in the drowsy Midi, so close to Spain and its siestas. In Toulouse, even the big new hypermarkets tend to close for two hours, and it is hard to get a hair-cut, or even find a bank open. In smaller towns, every shop and office closes, including the post office. All this is changing, but very slowly. The long lunch can be most agreeable in one's own life, and I have spent many a boozy time with friends in the sunny Midi, at an hour when Paris and London are hard back at work: but the practice is irksome when everyone else is doing it too, and you cannot even buy a loaf of bread.

Lunch habits may have been changing under force of necessity in Paris and some other places. Yet even when they get home from work earlier, the French remain very conservative about their dinner hour: in most social classes it is set for 8 p.m. or at earliest 7.30, and they will rarely shift it earlier in order to spend a full evening doing something else. Evening events, such as club meetings, cinemas or theatres, therefore do not start until 9 o'clock or possibly 8.30, and as many people have to get up early for their work, most organized leisure activity is left for the weekend (if indeed people have not left for their country retreat). All this may help to explain the relative lack of club-type activity described in the previous chapter.

Personal spending on leisure has more than quadrupled in real terms since 1950. One symptom is the immense development of horse betting, known nationally as *le tiercé* (three-horse bet): though still less of an obsession than in England, its turnover has reached 26 francs a week per head. The letters 'PMU' outside a café means that it houses one of the 3,000 branches of the Pari Mutuel Urbain, the semi-public body that controls all betting in France. Another trend towards the British pattern is that leisure money is now spent increasingly on possessions: the French are buying ten times as many music records or cassettes as in 1950, eight times as much photographic and film material, five times as many musical instruments. Yet the share of café-going in the average leisure budget has dropped from 40 to 22 per cent. Thousands of little old *bistrots*[1] have gone out of business; others struggle on, with falling custom. Of course, in the centre of Paris and other cities the larger modernized terrace-cafés and brasseries still do a brisk trade at certain hours: but they have lost some of their old importance as centres of social life and gossip. Their old *habitués* spend more of their time at home. Many cafés, faced with a decline in their trade in wines and spirits, are now trying to diversify their appeal. Some have introduced juke-boxes and pin-tables (known as *le baby-foot*), and so fill themselves with strident youth, at the risk of driving away staider clients. Others, in parts of the Midi, are becoming mainly venues for games of *boules* or *pétanque*. Some cafés in poorer areas have installed TV, for clients who still lack a set or want to get away from home, and here the men sit hushed all evening in the semi-dark – what a change from the old days of public chatter! They drink less, argue less and have become, you might feel, more docile and less picturesque.

IN THE SHADOW OF THE HYPERMARKETS:
WHAT FUTURE FOR THE LITTLE SHOPS?

The consumer revolution of post-war France is nowhere so evident as in the retail trade. The French – who so often act by extremes – have moved in one leap from the little corner-shop to the biggest hypermarkets in Europe: on the outskirts of many a town today you see these vast American-style emporia, brashly inviting with lights and music, as ready to sell you a TV set or an off-the-peg suit as a packet of frozen snails or a pot of caviar, and offering a range of fruit and vegetables as fresh and varied as in any street market. These highly efficient stores are the outward sign of a dramatic change of mentalities among many French shopkeepers, a milieu previously so stick-in-the-mud and uncompetitive. And the housewife, though at first torn in her loyalties, is now a happy customer. A battle has been won for modernism, once again, maybe, at the price of a certain picturesqueness.

France's small-tradesman class emerged from the war with a muddy

---

1 In English this word, without its final 't', is taken to mean a small French-type restaurant: in France, it is more correctly used to mean a little café selling wines and often, but not always, some simple food.

black-market reputation. 'Les BOF' (*beurre, oeufs et fromages*), the old generic term for dairy shops, became a phrase of contempt to denote a whole selfish crypto-collaborationist class of petty shopkeepers, vividly described by Jean Dutourd in his novel *Au bon beurre*. After the war the reputation changed but scarcely improved: in 1955 this was the class that provided the Right-wing rabble-rouser, Pierre Poujade, with the hard core of his support, in opposition to the growth of big industry. With competition as their enemy, their aim was to keep prices and profit-margins high even if it meant selling less, and few stopped to consider that a reverse policy might yield better results. Their archaism was as great as in small industries and the food-produce markets in those days. And for some years they held their ground. France's first real super-market was not born till 1957, but today there are over 4,000, accounting for 60 per cent of the sales of regular packaged foodstuff. For better or worse, a new spirit of salesmanship and competition has come in, entirely novel for France, and today more showy and aggressive than in Britain.

Government reforms, foreign influences, the growth of the new suburbs, have all played their part in pushing these changes forward. But the original catalyst was an inspired young grocer, Edouard Leclerc, in a small town in Brittany. Had it not been for his persistent crusading since 1949, the old order would never have cracked so easily. He was the first with the courage to use discount methods and so challenge the conspiracy of industry, shops and middlemen to keep prices high. Leclerc has been one of the truly amazing figures of modern France, variously likened to St Vincent de Paul, Danilo Dolci and Rasputin.[2] Whimsical, boisterous, conceited and religious, he entered commerce with a driving sense of social mission. Today he owns only two stores himself; but he presides over an association of 350 others all over France, large and small, that use his name and apply his methods. The secret is to buy direct from the maker or producer and sell to the public with profit-margins as low as possible. In Britain or the United States this might seem either very obvious or some kind of sales trick. In the France of the '50s it was an innovation, and went some way towards forcing other shops to bring down their prices too. And though Leclerc himself has now moved his crusade to other fields, there is no denying the key role that he played in preparing the way for the hypermarkets and the new spirit in commerce.

In a land where shops are usually handed down from father to son, Leclerc could hardly have come from a more unlikely background. His father was an army officer and gentleman farmer, and young Edouard

2 Or indeed a more successful Freddie Laker.

was destined for the priesthood. But after ten years in Jesuit seminaries he quit, partly because he already felt his true vocation to serve his fellow-men by smashing a 'wicked' system. In 1949, aged twenty-three, he opened his first little barrack-like store in his home town of Landerneau, near Brest, and began by buying biscuits from a near-by factory and selling them at 25 per cent below usual prices. Soon he was dealing in the whole range of groceries. At first the local tradesmen laughed at this crazy young amateur: but the public flocked in, and Leclerc's turnover shot up. By 1952 the Breton tradesmen were alarmed and made their first combined effort to destroy him. They used the weapon which has since been used against him and others many times: they persuaded manufacturers and wholesalers to threaten to stop supplying him.

For fifty years there had been a *de facto* system of price-fixing in France. Industry set the minimum prices of its goods and boycotted any shop that went below them. The shops liked the system, for it prevented tiresome competition. Theoretically it was illegal, but never prosecuted, and it benefited everyone except the consumer. No one until Leclerc had dared challenge it. Soon his supplies began to suffer from the boycott, so he wrote to the Government to protest and explain his aims. Ministry of Finance officials had barely heard of this strange idealist in far Brittany: but his plight happened to chime in with some of their own preoccupations for checking inflation. In 1953 the Laniel Government in one of its rare moments of effectiveness signed a decree that strongly reasserted the illegality of imposed prices and refusal of sale. This, reaffirmed later by the Gaullists, remains the key to all post-war progress in distribution. Without it, Leclerc would have perished and the supermarkets would have had far more difficulty in starting.

Leclerc now began to carry his campaign outside Landerneau. A few likeminded shopkeepers rallied to him, and so the chain of Centres E. Leclerc started to spread across Brittany, then to Grenoble where its success was spectacular, then to Paris. By 1960 there were 60 Leclerc centres, and a few other new discount shops had dared to copy his methods. The national grocery trade by now was really scared, and so were the *Grands Magasins* (big department stores) and their chain-store subsidiaries. Monoprix, Prisunic and others, with their hundreds of local branches, are the equivalent in France of Woolworth's or Marks and Spencer; and they owed much of their prosperity to the fact that, while charging prices only a little below those of the *boutiques*, they did their own wholesale buying and so could make a double profit. This might involve a total mark-up of 50 per cent, compared to Leclerc's 8 to 12 per cent. These stores declared war on him. First they tried the American tactic of the 'loss-leader', publicized shock reductions on a few mass-selling articles. Leclerc hit back by extending the range of his own centres from groceries to textiles, where French mark-ups were often absurdly high, up to 100 per cent. When his textile stores spread across France, with 30 to 40 per cent discounts, they had an obvious success.

Today, in his fifties, he presides over his association of the 350 separately owned Centres E. Leclerc, of all sizes from hypermarkets to modest *supérettes*. The owners form a strange and motley brotherhood in the world of commerce – they include an *énarque*, a former CGT unionist, ex-farmers, an ex-civil servant from Algeria – for Leclerc believes that outsiders like himself will often more readily follow his ideals than regular tradesmen. Each new member signs a 'moral contract', promising not to raise margins more than strictly necessary, and those who break this rule are expelled. Leclerc never intended to be more than a catalyst. His aim was to provoke, and to pioneer methods that the larger, more commercial chains could copy, and that is what they have since done.

Leclerc set out with the dogma that it is immoral for a shop to spend money on gay and expensive décor and equipment, and then pay for it by raising prices. His own supermarket in Brest was initially of an austerity that East Berlin in the late '40s might have found hard to beat: a tawdry warehouse piled high with packing cases. It is true that some new supermarkets go to the opposite wasteful extreme, then wonder why they make a loss. But the better chains, such as Carrefour, have now proved that you *can* combine low prices with a bright and cheerful setting; this is what the customer expects, and the Leclerc stores have been obliged to follow suit. There is little of the grim warehouse about his centres today: a new supermarket I visited in Boulogne-sur-Seine in 1979 was not only neat and bright but had a most dazzling array of delicatessen, sausages, cheeses, wines, patisserie, of an opulence that might have made Harrods envious. That is France.

The impact of Leclerc in his own Finistère stronghold was such that over a thousand small shops closed there in 1954–67, and it is not hard to see why. While a small shop might buy 100 kilos of vegetables a day from a middleman, Leclerc would bring five tons on a lorry direct from the Nantes central market and undercut the local shop by up to 70 per cent. Once he brought in 300 tons of Bulgarian strawberry jam by boat to Brest, and sold it at far below usual prices. When a local chain-store manager later asked his Paris head office how they had missed such an attractive import deal, he was told, 'We tested that jam, and found it unfit for consumption.' 'But Leclerc's been selling it for a year and no one's got ill.'

It is a joke that Leclerc likes to tell. Half his crusade has been deadly earnest; half is schoolboy spirits, Robin Hood against the bad barons. And he enjoys mockingly exploiting the legend he has helped to create of himself. Half the time he is campaigning across France or the world, and the other half he spends quietly with his wife in a *château* they have bought near Landerneau, his other luxury a Mercedes which he changes each year. He has clear blue eyes, a cheeky smile, a soft excited voice, and a very personal manner as if he were letting you into some secret. 'Maybe what I'm doing is close to religion,' he told me; 'it's economically viable charity. I admire Christ for chasing the tradesmen from the Temple . . . in the struggle for happiness one finds the sense of eternity . . . God is a river of life that flows through all . . .' In public speeches today, he adopts a prophetic, apocalyptic manner, *à la* Malraux: at a recent Press conference in Paris, he intoned for an hour about the rise of Islam, the agony of Europe, the archaisms of our society, the need for a new vision – and some of the journalists were giggling. But he was probably half laughing at himself too.

Today he leaves the daily affairs of his association to others, notably his talented son, and goes chasing off on various new crusades. He has helped fishermen to fight their middlemen by organizing fish-stalls at wholesale prices outside Métro stations, as a way of alerting opinion. He has travelled to advise Governments on distribution reform in Spain, Bulgaria, Africa. He has bought a large slaughterhouse in Brittany, and has also launched into grandiose plans for transforming Breton farming through mass-scale greenhouses. He has many enemies, and some people today think he has become a crank and a windbag, but others still find sound sense behind the flamboyant half-tongue-in-cheek verbiage.

Leclerc was the forerunner of a wider supermarket movement that finally made its breakthrough in France in the 1960s, after a slow start. It was the French who had invented the modern department store, with the opening of the Bon Marché on the Left Bank in 1852. This was followed by Printemps, Galeries Lafayette, and the other Paris giants that are still there today. They began to form branches in the provinces, and chains for cheaper goods: Prisunic belongs to Printemps, and Monoprix to the Galeries Lafayette. But these big stores and their chains were eventually overtaken in scope and efficiency by their Anglo-Saxon counterparts. Their growth was stunted by their high-price policies and their *ententes* against competition. Then in the late 1950s the growth of the new suburbs and of spending power gave the cue for the appearance of the first self-service stores. Though influenced by Leclerc, their ideas and techniques were borrowed just as much from the United States –

from the famous sales courses given by Bernard Trujillo of the National Cash Register Company at Dayton, Ohio.

With the aim of selling more cash registers in France, the NCRC began to invite Frenchmen to Dayton, where Trujillo preached his doctrine of large stores, rapid turnover and loss-leaders. Thousands of French shop executives listened in amazement to this gospel, and back home some of them began to try to apply it. The change started to make its impact around 1959. This was the time that Léon Gingembre of the PME (most of whose members are tradesmen) was breaking with Poujadism to face up to the Common Market, so it all fell into place. I met one store-owner who had been a strongly Poujadist believer in the small shop. Then he went to Dayton three times. Four years later he had a new supermarket outside Paris, with gaudy lighting and rows of clicking registers. The aggressive sales atmosphere was reinforced by megaphones blaring details of the latest bargains. It was centuries removed from the old *épicier du coin*: yet, regrettably or not, its noisy materialism seemed as typically 'French' as the quiet, unambitious order now passing away.

This change was one of the most eye-catching aspects of the economic modernization of France in the 1960s. A new breed of shop executive arose, believing in Trujillo and Leclerc. And those who feared that the conservative French housewife could never be wooed away from her local grocery, with its human contacts, were soon proved wrong. The number of super- and hypermarkets, nil in 1957, rose to over 1,000 by 1969 and 4,800 in 1982, while their share of the total retail trade moved from 4 per cent in 1969 to 34 per cent in 1982, including 60 per cent of major packaged foods. Supermarkets may be more numerous in Britain than in France, but they are not as large. The French, in this as in other fields, acquired in the 1960s the American taste for gigantism. Not content with the word *supermarché*, they coined *hypermarché* to denote the giants with over 2,500 square metres' selling space: Carrefour's new ones outside Marseille and Fontainebleau, each with 22,000 square metres, are claimed to be larger than anything in America. There is nothing quite like these stores in Britain. You can find them on the periphery of any sizeable French town, where the land is relatively cheap and there's plenty of room for car-parking. Behind a row of up to 70 check-out desks, the lights blaze down on a garish emporium that sells furniture, toys, electrical and kitchen goods, as well as every kind of food and drink in mind-blowing profusion. The delicatessen counter may be 50-metres long, with 100 kinds of fresh cheeses. The stores have attractive cafeterias, and are usually open till 10 p.m. On Saturdays the whole family comes to pile its week's supplies on to a giant trolley that the husband will hardly have the strength to wheel out to the car. It is all a far cry, not only from the *épicier du coin*, but even from the modest Sainsbury's.

The most dynamic and successful of the new chains is Carrefour. It was founded in 1960 by a small shopkeeper from Annecy, Marcel Fournier, who borrowed some ideas from Leclerc and others from Trujillo and applied them on a large scale with tremendous flair. In 1963 he opened the first *hypermarché*, near Orly airport, and attracted a diverse clientèle. Some were local tradesmen who actually found it cheaper than buying from their own wholesalers, partly because they could avoid tax declarations! One café-owner would carry away 80 bottles of Pernod a week and never ask for receipts. Today France has 403 hypermarkets, of which the Carrefour group runs 45.

There are six or seven main supermarket and hypermarket chains, and the price wars between them are loud and ferocious, especially now that the housewife is watching her budget more closely. When in 1979 Carrefour hired a market survey firm to produce reports showing that its own prices were lowest, Leclerc hit back angrily, accusing Carrefour of 'cheating' and 'misleading the public'. Such battles often hit the headlines. In fact, according to the consumer associations, the Leclerc centres are the cheapest of all, with mark-ups averaging 12 per cent: Carrefour follows close behind. In the older chains such as Monoprix, mark-ups are still well over 20 per cent; and independent surveys suggest that prices of food and other mass consumer goods are on average 10 to 14 per cent lower in the super/hypermarkets than in small shops. So the housewife has definitely benefited from the retail trade revolution of the past twenty years. If some French products still seem expensive by British standards, this is due less to high profit-margins in the shops than to high VAT and the backwardness of the food-processing industries.

During the boom years, while many small groceries and hardware stores were killed off by the supermarkets, at the same time the rise in consumer spending produced a crop of new luxury specialized shops, often in multi-boutique suburban 'commercial centres'. This indicates how diversely France's myriad small shopkeepers have reacted to the retail revolution. An intelligent minority have realized they can actually benefit from it, if they adapt to fulfilling specialized needs when a new supermarket appears on their doorstep. In the shadow of many a hypermarket, little general stores have been replaced by coiffeurs, dry-cleaners, or boutiques selling jewellery, modish clothes or quality leather goods, often doing a roaring trade. They profit from their big neighbour's proximity and share some of its clients, without competing with its goods. One owner told me: 'I used to sell general hardware, now I've switched to antiques and I'm doing fine. There will always be things that a small shop can do better than a large one – personal repairs and services, or luxury goods where cut-price is not the main object. American experience proves this.' What is more, the recent ecological vogue has now restored a certain popularity to the smaller shop, whenever its prices can compete with the big ones. Carrefour, alert to this new mood, is even planning its own chain of smallish stores.

The total of small tradesmen (of whom about half are retail shop-keepers) fell from 943,000 in 1954 to 771,000 in 1975 and is still falling. Of course there are some little grocers that still do well, especially if there is no supermarket too close: they serve a purpose for *ad hoc* or last-minute purchases, in between the major expeditions. In Paris and some other cities, a growing number of these shops are being taken over by North African families, prepared to stay open late in order to remain viable – the same phenomenon as with Indians in Britain. But the traditional inde-pendent French *petit épicier* is a dying species, above all in older suburbs, and in rural areas where the farm exodus too has hit his trade. It is easy to find extreme examples of his *malaise*: the dingy general store that ekes out a bare living by selling everything from tin-tacks to poor-quality fruit, and often acts as a café too for its few faithful clients. Such people have neither the means nor the psychology to adapt, and they are gloomy about the future. Most of them are elderly, and their children have moved into salaried jobs.

Government policy – as with farming – has been to try to protect this dying class from too much hardship while at the same time encouraging the modern sector. In the mid-'60s one weapon it used to modernize commerce was fiscal reform. Hitherto, while manufacturers paid a high value-added tax, shops were subject merely to a 2.75 per cent local tax on sales turnover, irrespective of profits, and this was no incentive to reduce profit-margins. The shopkeepers' lobby fought with success for years to keep this system, while Leclerc lobbied for reform. Finally in 1965 the Government did bring in a law abolishing the turnover tax and extend-ing VAT to commerce, in line with what is now standard EEC practice. VAT, a direct tax on profit-margins, ranges today from 33 per cent on luxury goods to 7 per cent on most foods. However the law did contain major concessions to the smaller shopkeepers. Those with a low turn-over (about half the total) are entirely exempt from VAT, while others in a medium range are assessed for a modified tax on a lump-sum basis.

Despite these concessions, France's small shopkeepers remained far from satisfied, and soon after May '68 a militant minority turned to violence, in a desperate crusade against the supermarkets. A 'neo-

Poujadist' movement of some ferocity sprang up north of Grenoble and soon spread across France: its leader was a young café-owner, Gérard Nicoud, who saw that the students and workers had won something through their violent tactics in May and so decided to copy them. He and his followers raided local tax offices to burn documents, they blockaded main roads, assaulted Ministers, sent out pirate broadcasts. When a Carrefour hypermarket near Lyon went up in flames in 1970, sabotage was whispered, though never proved. Nicoud considered himself a martyr for a noble cause, and several times went to prison. He was compared to Poujade, but was really very different. Poujade was an old-style demagogue who moved into politics; Nicoud was more of a modern-style extremist, despising politics, a kind of Right-wing *gauchiste*. Yet Poujade, though less violent than Nicoud, was in fact more reactionary. He wanted French commerce to stay as it was. Nicoud, fascist though his approach might be, was more progress-minded. He accepted the need for small shops to become modern and efficient: but he wanted them to be helped to survive, and he charged the Government with trying to kill them by siding with the supermarkets. He was a typical product of the post-'68 period, as Poujade and Leclerc in their very different ways had been of the 1950s.

Pompidou's Government grew alarmed at Nicoud and his supporters. It was anxious to avoid riots and disorders in a pre-electoral period, so in 1972 it decreed a series of measures to help small traders, on the lines demanded by Nicoud. Some of these decrees were humane and reasonable: others were blatant vote-catching. The Government also appeased the small shops by forbidding the big ones to practise 'loss-leaders' and, notably, by making it much harder for them to get building permits. In 1973 the Minister of Commerce, Jean Royer, a notorious reactionary, pushed through Parliament a vote-seeking law that made further expansion by the hypermarkets extremely difficult. Under this law, a firm wanting to set up a new store of more than 400 square metres in a small town, or more than 1,000 square metres in one of over 40,000 inhabitants, must first submit its case to a special local committee. Since, under the law, the committees are composed largely of local tradesmen and their allies, they usually say 'no' to the application; and though the Ministry has the last word, it does not often override them.

In 1973–6 Carrefour was able to start building only two new stores in France, and both of these were on sites vacated or sold to it by other firms, i.e. already marked out as supermarkets. Denis Defforey, Carrefour's new director-general, told me: 'The Royer law makes it hard for us to expand. We can do so only by building extensions to our present stores, or by taking over permits already granted to other firms that have since gone broke. It's all very retrograde, and the consumer is the loser.' Today the creation of larger hypermarkets is still largely banned: but the situation has eased for supermarkets in the 1,000 to 2,500 square metre category, for these are considered less of a menace by the small shops. They can often get a licence, if they lobby the Ministry hard enough. Government policy today is to try to hold a balance: on the one hand, not to restrict too much the modernization of commerce, useful in the fight against inflation; on the other, not to provoke a sensitive French minority, representing perhaps a million votes. The conflict between the very big new stores and the little ones has been far more dramatic than in most other EEC countries: it illustrates clearly the dilemma of France in transition.

In the earlier post-war years it was partly the consumer's own fault that French retail prices were not lower. The housewife grew so used to inflationary price-rises that she ceased to question them, and in a land so snobbish about quality, anything cheap came to be regarded with suspicion. In the 1950s the Government carried out the experiment of cutting cheeses in identical halves in a number of shops, and giving them different price-tags: most people chose the dearer halves. With price-fixing so widespread, the notion of a valid 'bargain' never really developed. Then Leclerc and other new influences did help buyers to become more price-wise, but for many years they were handicapped by the scarcity of advice from consumer bodies. Consumer protection made a much slower start in France than in Anglo-Saxon countries. Right up until the 1970s the few private consumer associations were too small, too poor and too split by petty rivalries to make much impact, and they found it hard to attract members. This was hardly surprising: the French have always been notoriously bad at this kind of spontaneous civic initiative and have expected the State to take the lead. However, the past decade has brought remarkable changes.

A forerunner of the modern French consumer movement was an inspired venture started in 1954 in the specialized sectors of photography and household electrical goods. André Essel, a thrusting ex-journalist, founded a body with the snobbish-sounding name of the Fédération Nationale des Achats des Cadres. This began primarily as a discount store, in a field where mark-ups were very high: by buying wholesale Essel was able to undercut other shops by 20 per cent or more, and his turnover rose dramatically. He was the Leclerc of the Leicas (or, you could say, the Laker of the Leicas). The other unusual aspect of his venture was that he did regular scientific testing of the goods that he sold, and published the results in FNAC's monthly consumer magazine, *Contact*, which existed partly to publicize FNAC wares but tried to be objective too: on one occasion it advised subscribers against buying FNAC's top-selling photo flashgun when it detected a fault. Today, FNAC is a mammoth enterprise and somewhat the victim of its own success. It has expanded into other fields, notably sports gear, books and records, and its two new bookshops at Montparnasse and Les Halles are among the largest in Europe. They too are discount stores. FNAC has eight branches in the provinces, as well as a cultural club that sells theatre and concert tickets at reduced prices and organizes its own debates and shows.

The FNAC, though valuable, was never a true consumer body: but it did play a part in stirring up the Government to take a step that in some other countries has come from private initiative, that is, to create an Institut National de la Consommation, in 1970. This now publishes a monthly magazine with a sale of 300,000, *Cinquante Millions de Consommateurs*, giving consumer advice of various kinds and printing comparative test reports on a wide range of brand goods. Finally, during the 1970s, the consumers themselves rallied to action. One of the older independent bodies, the *Union Fédérale des Consommateurs*, has now moved strongly into the front of the scene and it too has its monthly paper, *Que Choisir?*, also with a 300,000 circulation, mostly by subscription. These two bodies and their magazines are in fruitful competition. The INC with its *50 Millions* is liberal-Giscardian; the UFC with its *Que Choisir?* is moderate Leftist, and was fearlessly critical of many official policies under Giscard. *Que Choisir?*'s test reports have also infuriated many industries, which in France are not yet used to this kind of scrutiny. Its deputy editor told me: 'The food and drink firms especially hate being tested. We ran a report on wines, in which we said that some of the cheaper brands of table wine contain asbestos, due to their production process. We reported that some medical experts, though not all, consider asbestos harmful, and so we advised our readers not to buy certain brands, which we named. The wine merchants' federation then took us to court, demanding 5 million francs' damages for those firms. But the court upheld our right to make such tests and to warn the public of possible dangers. It was a great victory for consumer defence in France.'

Above all, the UFC is a grass-roots movement with 160 local branches throughout France; and of its members, 45,000 are *militants* who voluntarily assist with surveys into public services of all kinds. They help to compile reports, say, on the railways or postal services, or the behaviour of doctors, house-agents or insurance companies. In all this, the UFC has drawn some inspiration from the Consumers' Association in Britain, publishers of *Which?* Voluntary civic action of this kind is still quite novel in France. Probably it owes a good deal to the ideas generated by May '68, and is linked also with the more recent growth of ecological movements and of *la vie associative* (see p. 313). So, after its late start, consumer self-defence is at last becoming organized in France and a force to reckon with. In my first book on France, in 1968, the sub-chapter parallel to this one was entitled, 'Wanted, a French *Which?*'. The request has been answered.

The new consumer movements have notably been crusading against phoney or misleading advertising, where the regulations in France used to be very lax. In the 1960s one cinema advertisement for sweets featured lorry-loads of milk and butter, but the sweets were found to contain neither. The Government has since tightened the legislation, on the lines of the Trades Description Act in Britain. But, at least until recently, the new laws too often remained a dead letter and action in the courts was rarely successful, as the consumer bodies were so much weaker than the big commercial firms with their high-powered lawyers. However, some astonishing programmes on State radio and TV – of all places – have helped to swing the balance in the consumers' favour. First a TV producer, Jean-Pierre Guérin, ran a satirical series worthy of Esther Rantzen, showing up the silliness of some phoney advertising. For example, an 'ad' for Samsonite suitcases, 'the strongest in the world', showed an elephant standing on one of them and leaving it intact. So Guérin found an elephant to perform this act in front of his cameras – and the suitcase was squashed flat. But after a few clever *coups* of this kind, industry put such pressure on State TV that the programme was suspended.

A more successful campaign in the same genre, which actually survived for six years, was carried out on State radio by Anne Gaillard, a producer-presenter with a dauntingly aggressive manner. She and her staff would go into shops and make clandestine tape-recordings of the often absurd claims made for their goods by the sales assistants or shopowners, and then play back the tapes in the studio to the highly embarrassed manufacturers – 'Monsieur, you've heard this pharmacist telling us that your drug makes people younger – how do you justify this scientifically?' Gaillard also exposed the misleading wording and illustrations on many processed foods, for example a baby-food tin with a picture of a lot of green beans and a little corn when the real proportion was the reverse. She was diet-minded, constantly urging her 3½ million regular listeners to avoid certain brands too rich in butter, sugar or starch; and, like Guérin, she was not afraid to quote brand names – a daring innovation in State broadcasting. Coca-Cola, Nestlé and other giants fell under her flail. Her daily sixty-minute programme was highly popular, but in the end it was silenced by the Patronat's subtle pressures. 'One problem,' she told me, 'was that industry and some Ministers thought me a subversive Leftist, whereas the Left criticized me for failing to condemn capitalist society outright. In fact, I was apolitical: I was preaching reform of certain faults, not revolution. But in France you always get categorized.' An all too familiar French dilemma.

Gaillard and Guérin lost their battles to stay on the air; but their movement is gradually winning the wider war. Thanks to them, and to *Que Choisir?* and others, the public has now become more exacting about the authenticity of products, and more concerned with real quality rather than mere snob-appeal. In the 1960s, the fear was often voiced that the new mass-market would bring with it too great a loss of quality and variety, and one of the arguments flung against Leclerc and Carrefour was that they were ushering in an un-French uniformity. This danger has not been entirely averted, but at least it is being tackled. Of course, as in other countries, many new mass-produced goods are shoddy or tasteless. But the French, with their traditional concern for individual style, are slowly educating themselves in how to adapt this from the age of the lone craftsman to that of the big store or factory. One example, to be explored in the next sub-chapter, is the surprising new marriage between *grande cuisine* and the mass deep-freeze. As in many fields, the issue for this nation is how to modernize without losing the essential French qualities.

There are still some specialized sectors of the retail or servicing trades where cartels or vested privileges keep prices high, and consumer bodies or Leclerc-type innovators can do little about it, without Government action. Opticians operate a powerful cartel. Watch-repairers and master-butchers each have their *ententes*, fixing prices between them and making it hard for any outsider to undercut them. These and other trades have this in common, that they demand some special expertise, and in some cases special diplomas. They can therefore dig their heels in when any Government tries to reform them. 'They represent the worst aspects of the medieval guild spirit,' one State official told me, 'and they may be the last strongholds of the bad old France to be swept away.' The worst such case is pharmaceutics. In France the chemists' shops have the highest prices of all, for they cling tenaciously to an old privilege that forbids the sale of their goods in other kinds of shop; and they exploit this through a price-fixing cartel with high minimum mark-ups. Cases have been quoted of the same drug costing four times as much in a shop as when sold wholesale for medical purposes. Reform commissions have proposed that the monopoly be removed and a number of ordinary chemical goods and medicines be authorized for sale anywhere, as in many countries. But the Government has never dared act: the chemists are powerfully organized, and are in league with the industry which in its turn complains that the Government is killing its profitability by refusing to free prices as in other sectors (see pp. 52–3). The cartels in drug manufacture are a European-scale problem, of immense complexity, and the European federation of consumer associations is now preparing an inquiry.

THE VOGUE FOR
'LA NOUVELLE CUISINE':
GASTRONOMIC DECADENCE OR RENEWAL?

La gastronomie, that most revered of goddesses in the French pantheon, is today a kind of damsel in distress, rescued in the nick of time, by Paul Bocuse in shining armour, from the dragon of snack-bar modernism. Or that is how an apostle of *la nouvelle cuisine* might put it. The reality is rather more complex. Traditional French good eating has suffered many changes in the past decades and has come under various conflicting pressures, pushing it simultaneously towards decline and recovery, and a foreign visitor may at first be baffled by what he sees, hears and tastes. On the one hand, bars in central Paris serving *le fast-food* and *le hot-dog*; lengthening frozen-food counters in the supermarkets; and restaurant standards, once so dependable, now more erratic. On the other, much talk of a renaissance of cooking and of the French passion for food; as witness of this, quality restaurants fuller than ever of discerning French clients paying high prices; and the chefs of the so-called *nouvelle cuisine*, Bocuse and others, enjoying an idolatry and publicity equal to that given to film-stars or celebrity musicians.

So what is happening? Answer, a curious new polarization of the individual's eating habits. The French, at least in the middle classes, used to eat serenely well as a matter of course every day, especially in their homes. But a modern nation in a hurry no longer has such time or concern for serious daily cooking and eating: both at home and away from it, routine meals have become more simple, slapdash and utilitarian. And ordinary restaurants, faced with soaring costs, have been cutting corners, using mass-production techniques and second-rate processed foods, and their clients accept it. In this sense, standards have been slipping, especially in big cities. Yet the Frenchman's gastronomic zeal is not dying, it is simply taking a new turn; increasingly he is channelling it towards the once- or twice-a-week occasion, the really good restaurant meal with his beloved, the ritual Sunday lunch, the dinner-party at home for a few friends. And here he is as exacting as ever. This is a facet of the 'new hedonism' of the '70s and '80s, just as the utility trend was born of France's modernization in the '60s. So the French in their food habits, as in so much else, are moving closer to other nations. Good eating is becoming less regular, more special. But the change is relative. In the provinces and rural areas especially, with their wealth of tradition, the French still eat far better than any other people; and they still talk and think about food to an amazing extent, comparing in detail this week's *civet de lièvre*, say, with last week's in a way that the British might find boring or in bad taste. The issue today, however, is whether this grass-roots tradition of quality can continue to survive the new, erratic city eating patterns and the growing pressures of industrial catering and food-processing. The *nouvelle cuisine* gourmets are confident that it can. Some others have doubts.

In the difficult years before, during and just after the war, the Frenchman – so it seemed – clung to good eating partly as a compensation and a constant in a shifting world: his *cuisine* went on tasting the same, it did not turn sour or betray him as so many ideals of liberty and patriotism had done. But them in the boom years he came to feel less need for this kind of solace; or if not, so many other material compensations became available too. Television, cars, foreign holidays, smarter flats and other possessions all developed new rival claims on his attention and budget – and especially on his wife's time. In the middle classes, far fewer wives now have servants than before the war, more have jobs, and life is more hectic. So today the *bourgeoise* will sooner toss a couple of steaks under her electric grill than spend hours over a *plat mijoté* as her mother or her mother's *bonne* would have done. Some young wives also feel the need to assert themselves by refusing to be a slave in the kitchen. Henri Gault, top French gastronomic writer, told me: 'A wife's preparation of a really good meal for her husband each evening used to be a kind of making love. But a woman no longer feels it necessary to show her love in this way, and a man no longer expects it. They eat a plate of ham or pasta, and watch TV.'

There was even a period, in the '50s and '60s, when many younger middle-class people took a conscious pride in reacting *against* their parents' self-indulgent gourmandise. This was the intellectual, anti-gourmet era. But it ended with '68; and today many younger people, free of such guilt-feelings, are returning to *cuisine*. Just as in the 1930–50 period, this could well contain an element of consolation in a new time of anxiety. But the new trend extends only to dining-out, or to special meals at home. So, for its average meal, the younger middle-class family today does not eat much more excitingly at home in France than in Britain (where standards have risen so much since the 1950s). It still however eats a little differently: table wine is far cheaper, fresh French bread is uniquely and compulsively chewable, and the French still show far more flair in preparing salads and *crudités* and cooking vegetables. But the family *pot* of which you are invited to *prendre la fortune* will probably be no more than a conventional roast veal or chicken dish, followed by cheese and fruit; the housewife rarely bothers with complicated desserts. When she entertains her friends, she will probably stick to a classic recipe, or possibly try out an 'amusing' foreign dish discovered on summer holidays (*paella* or *moussaka* for instance), or go modishly for *fondue bourguignonne* or American-style barbecues.

The housewife still has a far wider variety of fresh foods to choose from than in most parts of Britain, available in shops all open till eight or after. But after a long resistance she is now thawing towards frozen foods. For many years after these entered Europe, in France tradition prevailed: shoppers shunned goods which they felt lacked flavour and freshness, so grocers did not stock them. Even today, the French eat less than a third as much frozen produce as the British or Germans: but the figures are creeping up by 15 to 20 per cent a year. The main difference is that while in Britain the big-selling frozen foods are ordinary things like peas, beans or fish-fingers, the French prefer much more complex and expensive deep-frozen pre-cooked dishes such as *cassoulet* or *bouillabaisse*. So at least they are transplanting their own gastronomy to the deep-freeze rather than merely aping Anglo-Saxon tastes.

There was however some aping of Anglo-Saxon models in the mass-catering field, when the shortening of the lunch-break and other modern influences began in the 1960s to throw up a rash of new snack-bars and self-service cafeterias in Paris. The cafeterias have been fairly successful. They may adopt silly *franglais* names like *Le Self des Selfs* (off the Champs-Elysées), but at least the food they offer bears some relation to classic French dishes (you can get maybe *choucroute* or *petit salé aux lentilles* for about 15 francs) and though mass-produced it is edible. These are crowded, cheerful places, popular with office-workers at lunch-time, and they compare very favourably with their English equivalents. But the French have also tried to import British and American hamburger-bars and counter-service snack-bars, without managing either to run them properly or adapt them to French taste. A chain of Wimpy Bars emerged under licence from J. Lyons, offering *un wimpy avec chips* and other such delights, but it never really caught on. A few McDonald's have now appeared in its place. The French catering industry has never shown much skill at this very American style of packaged operation, so the quality is poor and the public are not interested. The danger, which seemed so real in the late '60s, of a mass invasion of France by this kind of cheap-eatery has now – mercifully – receded. *Le fast-food* remains a marginal intruder, appealing mainly to tourists; and the Parisian typist, if she does not want to queue in a cafeteria, will probably content herself with a salad, an omelette or a French-style sandwich (half a *baguette*) in an ordinary café.

It seems inevitable, and no bad thing, that the French should want to move over to the light-meal habit for at least one of their main meals of the day. It should be possible for the light snack and true gastronomy to coexist, each for its own occasion. France has long been a nation of over-eaters, where the middle-aged *crise de foie* has been an occupational disease, and where too much stress has been set on the convention that a meal must, *de rigueur*, contain three or four full courses. Today, with the nervous speeding-up of life, far more care is being given to dieting. People are tending towards smaller and less complex daily meals, with fewer rich sauces and more emphasis on good-quality meat cooked simply, or on simple if expensive raw products: the consumption of oysters has risen hugely. It was this change in public demand, as much as anything, that paved the way for the 'Great French Gastronomic Revolution' of the 1970s.

Enter from the wings, noisily, *la bande à Bocuse* – 'Bocuse and his gang', as they have been called. So much ballyhoo has surrounded *la nouvelle cuisine française*, both in France and abroad, that it is not easy to assess it fairly. It has been described, justly, as the first major development in French gastronomy since Escoffier. Bocuse himself has been on the cover of *Newsweek*, while a *Time* cover-story in 1980 was devoted to Henri Gault and Christian Millau, the all-influential tandem of food critics who first coined the phrase '*la nouvelle cuisine*'; they believe passionately in this new style and have done as much as anyone to propagate its vogue with a well-to-do public. But it must be made clear that the vogue is a limited one. This new style of cooking, usually expensive, marks a revolution in *haute cuisine* which has profoundly affected the top one per cent or so of restaurants: but it has had little influence on the rest, or on home cooking. Its likely long-term impact on France as a whole must be seen in this context.

This 'new cooking' is a highly inventive approach to *cuisine* that reduces to a minimum the rich, high-calorie ingredients such as cream, egg-yolk, sugar and brandy which have decked out so many of the great classic dishes. It spurns heavy sauces that mask the taste of the meat, spurns flour and other starches too. It is a return to a lighter, purer style, using the best raw materials and cooking them in their own juices. It relies on very fresh ingredients, rapidly cooked almost in the Chinese manner, and daringly blending flavours: thus a purée of mixed spinach and pear preserves the fresh taste of both. Above all, it encourages the chef to deviate from classic recipes and use his flair for inventing new blends. Bocuse's menu contains such innovations as lobster with lettuce hearts, sea bass with seaweed, sweetbreads mixed with crayfish, while Alain Senderens at L'Archestrate in Paris offers cooked oysters with leeks. This kind of cooking requires much time and skill, and it depends on best quality produce, for no longer can inferior meat be disguised by rich sauces. Hence the expense. Most of the better *nouvelle cuisine* restaurants are in the range of 250 to 350 francs a head.

The initial impetus for the revolution came more from the owner-chefs themselves than from public demand. A few young ambitious ones felt that classic *cuisine* was growing as weary as last week's joint. They were bored with churning out the same old dishes and wanted to express themselves with something new. At first their traditional clients were suspicious, but some were soon seduced by the dietetic appeal of the new cooking. One of its leading initiators, Pierre Troisgros at Roanne, told *Esquire*: 'Our customers nowadays do not want to get up from the table feeling as if their bellies were filled with lead ... Why must the grand pleasure of a great dinner always be associated with gaining weight? Our challenge today is to continue to provide the delight and excitement of *haute cuisine* without its excesses of richness and weight.'

The true pioneer was the late Fernand Point of Le Pyramide at Vienne, the most inspired French owner-chef of his day. From the 1930s he had been experimenting with a new lightness of style which he saw as a return to the true, simple pre-Escoffier tradition. He attracted a few disciples, and one of them in the 1950s was the young Bocuse whose family owned a modest *auberge* beside the Saône just outside Lyon. Bocuse, most people today would agree, is not himself the greatest of the new cooks; a few others have surpassed him in brilliant creativity. But it was his magnetic personality and powers of leadership that rallied a new generation of chefs to apply and to spread abroad Papa Point's philosophy. That is his greatest achievement.

When his father died in 1959, the ambitious Paul planned to turn the *auberge* into a luxury showpiece for the new cooking. He was his own master, but he needed wider support (Point was now dead), and all around him in France he saw that the top restaurants were not in the hands of cooks but of businessmen who often knew little of *cuisine*. The chef was a mere employee, forced to cook as he was told. Bocuse was fired with a sense of mission. He encouraged the best young chefs to open their own restaurants where they could practise this *nouvelle cuisine* which for him was a religion. Gradually he succeeded. It was a liberation movement, a revolt of the serfs. Today, thanks to this Castro of the cookpots, fifteen of France's eighteen three-star (in Michelin) restaurants are chef-owned, against a mere two or three in the old days – quite a revolution. 'Today, cooking belongs to the cooks, we're no longer ser- vants,' Bocuse told me; 'the cook now goes into the dining-room to meet his guests, he's not hidden away in some basement.'

Another success of Bocuse has been to create a new fraternity and friendship among leading chefs. In the old days in France, this little *milieu* used to seethe with suspicion: the cooks were jealously hostile to each other, they seldom met and each would guard the secrets of his recipes. But today the jolly *bande à Bocuse* – those who share his philos- ophy – not only wine and dine together, run joint businesses and publicity ventures, travel abroad together, but also pool their creativity. Bocuse's own menu accredits twenty of its dishes to his friends – *loup aux algues Michel Guérard, pâté d'anguilles Roger Vergé*, and so on. So today an élitist owner-chef of a new stamp has emerged in France: sophisticated, much-travelled, sometimes arrogant, an artist who is also a public figure and sees himself as the peer of a master-architect or star orchestral conductor. At the end of the evening he emerges proudly from his kitchen, high-*toque'*d, sits to take a drink with his guests, and is applauded as if he had just brilliantly rendered *Othello*. Today, nearly all the most highly-starred restaurants in France are run by this fraternity. Significantly, nearly all are in the provinces.

Bocuse himself is an astonishing figure, Rabelaisian, full of para- doxes, a whimsical *provocateur* who has outraged many people by using bizarre showmanship and PR gimmickry to promote the *cuisine* that he takes seriously but not solemnly. He travels the world as ambassador for French cooking: yet he still plays schoolboy pranks on his friends, such as sending a gift of flowers wrapped round the rotting entrails of a hare, or importing near-naked strip-tease girls into a smart Paris party. He gets terrific fun out of life. And at least he has made the backroom job of chef look glamorous, which helps all his colleagues. When he went as guest of honour to the Elysée, to prepare and eat a special meal with Giscard, it was front-page news.

In the temple of French gastronomy he is at once high priest and iconoclast. He is known as 'the Emperor', and it was in some awe that I went myself to Lyon to prepare a radio profile of him for the BBC. But I found him extremely easy, warm, funny, unpretentious. He says out- rageously conceited things, but with a merry twinkle in his eye (like Edouard Leclerc). In his mid-fifties, he is tall and burly, a powerful presence, with the beaky nose and sharp eyes of a proud Gallic cock. A quick-fire intelligence, but with little conventional culture: his restaurant's opulent furnishings are in *nouveau-riche* taste, the mediocre paintings clashing with the *chic* of the *cuisine*. On the main wall hangs a big portrait of the Emperor, in his high chef's hat, cutting up an onion. Had I paid the bill, I would have left 300 francs or so the poorer, but I was Bocuse's guest and he set before me three of his most famous dishes – the truffle soup he created for Giscard, a sea bass in pastry with lobster mousse, and a fat chicken stuffed with diced vegetables and cooked inside a sealed pig's bladder. They were delicious, but how many people can afford to eat at this level? 'Of course,' said Bocuse, 'I too would hate to lose the robust French country dishes such as *cassoulet*, *choucroute* and *tête de veau vinaigrette*: they are our heritage, and there will always be a place for them. But in *haute cuisine* we must move forward, and the secret is to apply what I call *"la cuisine du marché"* – you cook according to what you find in the market. My ideal is to find the fridge completely empty at the end of the day, and then I start again in the market and build the menu round that.'

Bocuse in his kitchen is something of a dictator, with a quick temper – like many great chefs. When he is on his travels, which is often, his head chef deputizes. But when he is around, his presence is felt. His is still a family concern, with his wife and married daughter acting as receptionists. But he finds that guests can be a strain: 'There was this big family party of Germans this evening, nice people, they'd been planning to come here for years. But before the meal they made me sit down and pose for a dozen photos with them – "please go and sit next to granny" – click click – "Now hold the little boy's hand" – click click. It's sympathetic in a way but it's tough. I have to keep my cook, but I find myself asking: do people come to eat chez Bocuse, or merely to see Bocuse and be able to show off their photos?'

He has become a tourist attraction, like Napoleon's tomb. You could say he has brought it on himself, through his tireless globe-trotting publicity. And this is the source of other criticisms too: some people feel that his restaurant's quality has begun to suffer a little from his absences and his diversification. The list is amazing. He is under contract to advise Air France on their flight catering; he is an official consultant to the Ministry of Tourism; he runs gastronomic sea cruises; he part-owns a firm that markets Beaujolais, and has lent his name to helping a Lyon subsidiary of Joe Lyons to market charcuterie. He operates a cookery school in Japan, and often flies there or to America, to lecture or to cook special banquets for gigantic fees. Once he smuggled past the US customs some pigs' bladders tucked in his jacket-sleeves, so he could prepare his chicken speciality for some New York feast. He is in Singapore this week, Munich or Abidjan the next – the Kissinger of Cuisine, he's been called. So he no longer has so much time to invent new dishes. Of course, his global evangelism is not just for his own glory: he does it for *la nouvelle cuisine*, and also for France, to promote her reputation as *the* land of gastronomy. This is one reason why he is so popular with the French: he is seen as a national prestige symbol, like Tabarly or Yves St-Laurent.

Bocuse and his friends have now succeeded in 'imposing' their style of cooking on the vast majority of France's top restaurants. Leading chefs who ten years ago were serving only classic dishes have now 'seen the light' and added *nouvelle cuisine* inventions to their *carte*, either so as not to be left behind by fashion, or because they genuinely find the new cooking more exciting. The latter case is true of the great Haerberlin brothers at the Auberge de l'Ill near Strasbourg, who still offer a classic fillet of venison but have now thought up such wonders as mousse of frogs and salad of baby rabbit with artichokes and truffles. 'Exquisite, miraculous,' raves the Gault–Millau annual guide, awarding the Haerberlins its top rating. Gault and Millau, supreme arbiters of taste, hold it as a dogma of faith that the new cooking is superior to the old, and the symbols in their book assertively signal this to the reader: red for the new, black for the old. Of the guide's 22 highest-rated recommendations in 1981, *all* were *nouvelle cuisine* places except Lasserre and La Marée in Paris! The Kléber guide, also influential, takes a fairly similar line. Both books have demoted such illustrious Parisian temples of tradition as Le Grand Véfour and Maxim's, the latter now considered little better than a museum-piece of Parisian history. Kléber's editor told *Esquire*: *'La grande cuisine* has virtually disappeared. The *grande luxe* restaurants of Paris . . . represent nothing except *grande luxe*, maintained mainly by wealthy amateurs who are in no sense connoisseurs.' The cautious Michelin guide has been slower to react; but even of *its* top recommendations (two or three stars), three-quarters now practise the new cooking.

Many gourmets and critics resent this 'tyranny' of the new chefs abetted by the guidebooks. The revered Robert Courtine ('La Reynière' of *Le Monde*), doyen of the old school of food critics, considers the new cooking *'fin de race'* (decadent) and prefers simple, classic regional dishes. And so in their hearts do many discerning diners-out. They may have tired of *haute cuisine* and its rich sauces: but they would rather have an honest, copious, time-honoured *cassoulet* or *coq au vin* than many of the more chi-chi of the new inventions, usually served in miserably small helpings. So why has the new style caught on so widely with a monied public? – because, in the right hands, it can be very brilliant; because of the dieting vogue; and because in a certain social *milieu* the French are always suckers for novelty and trendiness. And the chefs lean back and enjoy it. Some of them, with the sincerest of intentions, have taken the style a stage further. Michel Guérard, notably, has invented what he calls *la cuisine minceur*, and is now running a kind of luxury health-farm for gourmet-minded slimmers in a country hotel near Pau, where you can combine exquisite eating with an intake of less than 500 calories per four-course meal. His mayonnaise without oil has won rave notices. When I telephoned him, the receptionist said, 'The Master is holding a seminar, please ring later.' Guérard, Bocuse and co. do indeed see themselves as *maîtres-à-penser* of one of the greatest of French arts. They have run five-day gastronomic cruises aboard a liner off the Côte d'Azur, complete with lecture courses.

The inventions of *la nouvelle cuisine* are so diverse – ranging from the sublime to the ridiculous – that it is hard to generalize on its real value or its likely future. It must be said, in its defence, that it is not a full break with tradition. Many of its better dishes draw inspiration from classic Oriental cookery, or from pre-Escoffier *cuisine* in France. Some are no more than clever variations on older recipes; and on very many menus, such as Bocuse's, you find new and old dishes coexisting, new and old styles blending with each other. Certainly Bocuse is right to assert that gastronomy, like any art, cannot afford to stand still, it needs to renew itself. The only trouble, as he freely admits, is that the wilder experiments can often lead down a blind alley, just as in modern music or painting. *Nouvelle cuisine* can be splendid in gifted and responsible hands: but, as with any liberation movement, it has led to excesses by the rank-and-file. Food is now so fashionable that any young man who likes to cook opens his own restaurant and follows the new trend, but often without having the basic skills. The licence to invent has produced absurdities, as new chefs bid to outdo each other in the heady quest for stardom, and Gault himself recognizes this: 'Young cooks striving for instant fame are doing horrible things in the name of the new cooking, like serving raw sweetbreads, or putting steak with strawberries. The cult of innovation for its own sake is silly – in this, as in other modern arts.'

For my own money, I still prefer the more robust tastes of maybe less healthy dishes of the good peasant casserole type, *bien mijotés*. *Nouvelle cuisine* is too often chi-chi, in my humble view. Tiny strips of meat served beside bland purée of chestnut or spinach; multi-coloured vegetable terrines, looking decorative but tasting of very little; minced partridge, wrapped in a lettuce leaf and shaped to form a cake – no, give me a pungent *bouillabaisse* or a rich oily salad, any day. Moreover, *nouvelle cuisine* is so much in love with luxury ingredients – lobsters, truffles, foie gras – that it is outside the range of most purses. It could in fact be provided more cheaply, if simpler natural produce were used: but the middle and lower-range restaurants show little sign of adopting it, for *their* public is not very interested. And even the rich, who will eagerly dine out *chez* Senderens or Vergé, are rarely prepared to try out the new cooking in their own homes – despite the bulky tomes of recipes produced by Bocuse, Guérard and others. These seem little more than bedside or coffee-table books, *très snob*, providing a vicarious mouth-watering thrill, like reading classy pornography.

Many practitioners of the new cooking now predict that the vogue for experiment will very shortly wane. So *nouvelle cuisine* will settle down as a permanent modification of *haute cuisine*, but its practice may not spread more widely. Yet its legacy will indeed have been positive. It has had a vast influence abroad, helping Americans, Germans and other barbarians to become more gastronomy-minded. In its way, it has done a good PR job for France abroad; and at home it has helped give a needed shot-in-the-arm to a flagging gastronomic tradition. The film-star exposure of the new chefs, excessive though it may be, has at least helped to revive a wider public interest in food: it has made the French more aware of the necessity of protecting their heritage from the new hazards of industrial mass-catering. Ten years ago, there was a growing shortage of good young chefs. Many a son of an old *patron-chef* had left to take up office or factory work, with its easier hours, rather than follow in papa's rigorous footsteps. But now this has changed, for better or worse. In the hotel schools, until recently, training to toil in the kitchen was held in lower prestige than training to be a waiter, the classic royal road to the good executive jobs. But today the more ambitious students want to be cooks. They have Bocuse to thank for creating a new brand image.

A large part of the middle class is not actively interested in food; it eats well from time to time simply as a matter of tradition. But in line with the 'new hedonism' an important minority of youngish well-to-do people has now become consciously food-crazy in a new way: Gault says that the average age of the readers of his monthly magazine is thirty-two. These are the 'food bores', as some might call them, who to prepare a dinner-party (albeit non *nouvelle-cuisine*) may spend hours trekking around Paris for the finest produce sold in special shops – 'My dear, where *can* one buy bread except *chez* Poilane?' As in Britain and America, sales of cook-books have soared, and in France one reason is that after the war many middle-class urban mothers ceased handing on their culinary lore to their children, who are now having to learn it for themselves. One classic, *La Vraie Cuisine de Tante Marie*, has sold ten million copies.

'Dining-out has dethroned the show-going habit,' writes *Marie-Claire* with a touch maybe of hyperbole, though given the current state of the Paris theatre it is not so far from the truth. 'The restaurant itself becomes a show, lasting for hours, with the diner himself in a small walk-on part.' In the evenings, the better or more 'amusing' restaurants are fuller than ever, despite crisis; and while some people go with a gastronomic fervour, others are looking equally for *ambiance*. In the old days, most of the good restaurants popular for dinner were sober, brightly-lit places, either conventionally elegant (like Fouquet's) or plain and shabby (like many of the greatest *bistrots*). But then in the '60s a new atmospheric modishness crept in, as in Chelsea. To meet a new youth demand, many Quartier Latin or Ile St-Louis restaurants updated their décor in a mock-rustic or arty-crafty style, often installing canned music or a guitarist. The *cuisine* rarely rose above the level of *viandes aux herbes de Provence grillées au feu du bois*, but a '60s *jeunesse dorée* did not care. The vogue was for 'intimate' restaurants with *ambiance*, open very late and helped along by dim lights or candles: yet in previous days the French thought it barbaric not to see clearly what they were eating. This '60s trend still exists, and some new showy gimmicks still appear: one large and popular new fish restaurant at St-Germain-des-Prés has a huge screen across one wall, showing a succession of lantern-slides of seaside scenes, rather attractive. But with the return to more serious eating, the vogue in the '70s has been for the refurbishing of the classic *bistrots*, or else for pretty restaurants with mirrors in the very trendy *'style 1900'*, many of them offering *nouvelle cuisine*. At the cheaper end of the scale there has also been a rash of new 'formula' restaurants with the briefest of fixed menus: maybe just a salad with walnuts, an *entrecôte* with a light sauce, and a choice of creamy desserts. For a quickish meal in the 60-franc range these are pleasant and useful, though their standards vary.

One side effect of these new trends is that hitherto despised foreign *cuisines* have been coming into their own in Paris. The French (who rarely get as far as Peking) have always been acutely conscious of other nations' culinary inferiority, and gourmets would seldom accept even the best Italian or Hungarian dishes as much more than quaint or exotic. But today an amusing exoticism is just what many people want. Of course there have always been some foreign restaurants in Paris, notably those nostalgic little Russian ones that arrived after 1917; but they formed a kind of ghetto, patronized mainly by national exiles. Now some foreign food is *à la mode*. First came the Tonkinese and Cantonese restaurants, of which there are now 2,000 in Paris alone, popular with weight-watchers and budget-watchers alike. Then came the wave of *pizza* houses, all Chianti-flasks and Amalfi posters and waiters in Neapolitan costume (many of them Corsicans) singing *Torna a Sorrento*. These places are ubiquitous, crowded, and good value. Now, Spanish, Greek, Moroccan and even Japanese restaurants are spreading in Paris, while the *pieds noirs* have imported *couscous* and *méchoui* to hundreds of menus throughout Paris, and a few Chinese and Italian ventures have appeared in provincial towns where foreign food was hitherto unknown. Tourists on their foreign holidays have been discovering that Mediterranean, Levantine and Austro-Hungarian food is not as coarse or unsubtle as they have been told; and so, back home, they carry these new tastes into their own dining-out. And although these foreign restaurants fill a far less crucial need than in Britain, I think they have added spice and variety to the Paris scene.

Most of these places are good and authentic, run by their own national chefs. Others, notably the slick new quasi-Anglo-Saxon ones, have less to do with gastronomy but are quite funny. The glossy Parisian 'drugstores' tend to offer a mixed Franco-American menu including barbecued spare-ribs, 'club sandwiches', hamburgers and *Chien Chaud dit Hot Dog* – and this for their French public, not just tourists. Many a large town or smart suburb now has its 'drugstore'. It is easy to laugh at them, but in fact they perform a useful service and the food often tastes better than the silly menus would suggest. The salads and ice-creams ('*le Hawaii cup*') bear a strong transatlantic imprint, but the *plat du jour* is usually decently French. The 'drugstores' are open late, Sundays included, and offer a range of facilities in their little *boutiques*. It is highly convenient to be able to stroll in at midnight, and buy a novel or razor-blades or records. Where in an English town can you find such service?

As for the British, for decades our island *cuisine* was a stock topic of mirth in Paris. But in the '60s the Parisian passion for mimicking (inaccurately) all things English began to scale new heights. In Paris, Lyon, Toulouse, as in other towns across Europe, so-called 'pubs' appeared, implausible baroque pastiches of Victoriana. At one such place on the Left Bank a well-dressed crowd (French, mind you) could be seen gobbling *le London Lunch* (*rosbif et Yorkshire pudding*), *le Buckingham salad*, *le rice crispies* and *le Toffy cup* (*sic* – toffee ice-cream) and maybe washing it down with one of nine recherché blends of tea at 5 francs or so a pot, just as in an English pub! The food was grotesquely unlike the real English thing. Finally the French public twigged to this, and the 'pub' vogue is now past its prime. Some have closed, others now simply sell beer and other drinks. One straw in the wind: the Red Lion on the Champs-

Elysées, which tried so hard to introduce *le beau monde* to shepherd's pie, was in 1979 replaced by a good French 'formula' restaurant.

Another happy sign is that the sillier aspects of this recent Parisian trendiness have scarcely affected the provinces. These are not only the heartlands of *nouvelle cuisine*: they remain also the bastions of sound regional *cuisine* in all its diversity, both *paysanne* and *bourgeoise*. Although value-for-money may have declined at tourist-traps along main roads, there are still thousands of small family-run hotels and restaurants throughout France where you can eat excellently for a mere 50 francs or so, and they are well patronized. To quote one example among dozens: in 1980 at the modest Le Rossignol (one crossed knife-and-fork in *Michelin* in Sarlat (Dordogne), for 32 francs *prix fixe* I had a rich and meaty country salad, a copious *coq-au-vin* in the true style, and home-made apple pie – surrounded by family parties enjoying their Sunday-lunch outing. Another positive factor is that the working and petty-bourgeois classes still seem to care about their food. In Britain, 'civilized' eating is an import confined to a small educated class: in France, for reasons of tradition, the practice is far more general, and at the lower social levels the gulf between standards in the two countries remains immeasurable – compare a *relais routier* for lorry-drivers with a British transport 'caff'! In many factories, unions and works committees are more demanding about the quality of the canteen's food than almost any other aspect of working conditions, and I well remember eating a splendid *cassolette des fruits de mer* as the *plat du jour* at Motorola in Toulouse. At home, working families now have the money to buy more meat and fresh vegetables than before the war; and as the working-class wife, unlike the *bourgeoise*, is now less likely to have a job, she may spend more time on proper cooking. Henri Gault told me: 'Wives in this class still cook a *pot-au-feu* or *boeuf en daube* for the evening meal, and their husbands expect it. But in the *grands ensembles*, where the workers *s'embourgeoisent*, this is disappearing.' Yet though many French may have become negligent about gastronomy, they still have it in their bones, as the British do not. Officialdom, State or municipal, still expects high quality from its cooks at all functions. Recently in the Ardennes I went to a routine dinner at the prefecture for some local dignitaries: we had turbot in champagne, stuffed quails, followed by superb cheese and an orange soufflé – all magnificent. Does an English council ever entertain like that?

The threat to good eating in France appeared very real in the late '60s when I wrote my previous book, and my conclusions were gloomy. Jacques Borel, the dynamic tycoon of mass-catering, told me then: 'Restaurants today should be run by accountants, not by *patrons* who see themselves as artists. In France, as elsewhere, the future is with the big chains; and if Paris today is copying New York, the provinces tomorrow will copy Paris.' As Borel's steak and hamburger bars began to spread across France, many gourmets feared he would be proved right. Since then, however, French innate taste and concern for individual quality have made a certain come-back. The vogue for blind copy-catting of Anglo-American modes is in retreat, so chauvinism does have its uses! And Borel himself has come a financial cropper and gone off to his cherished America. So the decline has in some ways been averted – but how long can the revival last? It still appears fragile, given today's economic pressures and the new polarized eating habits. Many restaurants of all kinds are still full and doing well, both the starred luxury places and the little family *bistrots* alike. But of France's 50,000 or so restaurants, very many others are in the grip of a *malaise* – the ordinary places in suburb or back-street which are not praised in the guide-books nor especially well thought-of locally. They are afflicted by rising costs, especially staff costs, and if their clients fall away their standards slip badly. Many of these places are doomed to go out of business, like the small shops and farms. And if the polarization of personal eating patterns continues, as seems likely, then restaurants too will become ever more polarized: on the one hand, the various types of good restaurant, for dining-out and business lunches;[3] on the other, a growing number of cheaper functional places, which may not be Americanized hybrids, but will be self-service cafeterias and simpler 'formula' restaurants whose standardized menus help to keep down costs. These places, as well as the French family in its home, are likely to draw increasingly on convenience foods, frozen or packaged. And added to this is the hazard of growing normalization of foodstuffs, *quid pro quo* of the modernization of agriculture. The broiler has begun to oust the farm-reared chicken; fertilizers and machine-sowing are making fruit and vegetables larger and more handsome but not always more succulent. This particular American-style trend is not so easy to arrest. And so, in day-to-day eating, as opposed to the more special occasions, there may be a further decline in quality.

There is one possible remedy, today much advocated by Gault and Millau. Might it not be feasible to make industrial labour-saving techniques into the ally of real cooking, not its enemy? Methods of dehydration and deep-freezing have been rapidly improving, and a *cassoulet* pre-cooked in large quantities in this way under the guidance of a

3 However, in 1981 the Socialist Government introduced a special new tax on all business entertainment expenses, and the trade of this kind of restaurant at once began to suffer.

master-chef can be almost as good as the real thing, whatever purists may fear. Christian Millau told me that a dish expertly pre-cooked, then properly frozen and defrosted, was barely distinguishable from the same dish freshly cooked, and generally better than average restaurant fare. He saw this as an inevitable prospect for the future, and as a gourmet he was not distressed by it. The housewife and the ordinary restaurateur alike, maybe at some cost to their pride, could raise the quality of their average daily meal if they used these methods, stocking their deep-freezes with these dishes. Already, some French firms are pioneering in this field, allying science to art and quality: Michel Guérard now has a tie-up with the French branch of Findus, to supervise the mass-production of special recipes of his own. There are some who feel that one day it may be as unusual to prepare a fresh dish of this kind as it is today to buy hand-made clothes or furniture. .

Even so, may not something be lost? For centuries the greatness of French *cuisine* has depended on its daily grass-roots tradition: its genius has grown from the marrow of the nation, like music in Germany, sport in Australia, art in medieval Italy. What will happen if the art of home-cooking is gradually lost, and gastronomy is practised only by an expert band of specialists, the master chefs, whether beside the stoves in their luxury restaurants, or in their factory laboratories? This is so alien to the French tradition that it is impossible to predict what would happen to quality. Bocuse has 'given cooking back to the cooks', but cooking belongs also to the people – to *tante* Marie in her farmhouse, preparing her chicken stew, or to the young housewife in a hypermarket, choosing exactly the right cut of meat for Sunday's garlicky roast lamb. Just as a nation that plays no music will produce few great musicians, so the French will not continue to eat well unless they also know the secrets of food and can share in its practice. In an age of changing life-styles, French gastronomy is still at a crucial turning-point: Bocuse has won a battle against decline, but he has not yet won the war.

THE HOLIDAY MANIA:
HAPPINESS IS A STRAW-HUT 'VILLAGE'
WITH 'LE CLUB' IN GREECE

As national indulgence number one, *cuisine* has now come to be rivalled by a new French obsession, even more widespread. 'We are the first to have made holidays a national institution, a collective dream,' said one Frenchman; 'psychologically, we think about them all through the year.' Of course others do so too: the post-war growth of tourism is not confined to the French, and the number of people who take holidays away from home remains lower in France than in Britain or some other nations. But there are few countries where the annual urge to get away from it all has grown quite so powerful. In London, many of us work peacefully through all the dog-days of summer; in Paris by the end of June people are talking of nothing but *les vacances*. Economic crisis since the late '70s may today be forcing the French towards less expensive kinds of holidays: yet it has also intensified their craving for escape from daily cares.

Before the war, long holidays were the preserve of the well-to-do. Now French wage-earners have secured for themselves the longest annual paid leave in Europe: in 1936 they won the legal right to two weeks' *congés payés*, a third week was added in 1956 and a fourth in 1965. The Socialist Government in 1981 then added a fifth, whereas in Britain the legal minimum is three. The numbers taking holidays away from home each year (51 per cent of the population) are twice as great as in 1939. But as this figure shows, there are plenty who still feel excluded: in any given year 53 per cent of workers do not leave home on their paid leave, usually because they fear they cannot afford it. The proportion of farmers going away on holiday has doubled since the 1960s but is still only 17 per cent. True, if you live in the country the urge may not be so great, but farmers too are growing restive: '*Nous aussi, nous voulons voir la mer*' are the placards you sometimes see in summer along the routes to the crowded beaches.

The strongest element in the holiday cult seems to relate to the new 'back to nature' urges of the French. Previously the city-dweller often felt ill-at-ease in the deep country with its alien peasantry: he preferred urban resorts like Biarritz with casinos and promenades, or else the orderliness of some family villa or *château*. But today the vogue is for going native, and millions are happy to lose themselves amid the lonelier mountains or beaches of this large and still largely unspoilt land. Hotels with their soaring prices have lost ground heavily to the cheaper craze for *le camping*: the numbers who practise this have risen since 1950 from one to six million a year, and though in August it may look as if all of them have flocked at once to the Côte d'Azur, in fact there are plenty elsewhere too. Skiing, sailing, cycling and other holiday sports have also increased hugely in popularity. And whereas the less sophisticated Englishman often likes to re-create his home environment on holiday, in his well-equipped caravan, his Butlin's camp or his cosy boarding-house, the modern Frenchman tends to prefer as complete a change as possible, to wear as little as weather or decency will allow – or even less – and to scrabble amid pine-needles in a tent. On many beaches, nudism is now all the rage.

The holiday 'back to nature trend' pre-dated the newer ecological tendencies of the '70s; and like them it seems to mark a reaction against too rapid urbanization and maybe a subconscious national desire to compensate for the desertion of rural traditions. Sociologists are thus unsure whether this frenetic urge to escape to a different life is a token of healthy adventurousness or of maladjustment. One of them, Michel Crozier, has blamed the holiday mania on the tensions of French society and office life where 'no one is truly at ease, and so the French *need* holidays more than, say, the Americans'. Many people are thus looking not only for change and relaxation, but for a social liberation and fraternity they do not always find in their own lives. Many of course do still take the long traditional family holiday amid lots of relatives, in *grand'mère*'s villa in Auvergne or *tante* Louise's Norman *château*: but this habit has been yielding ground to a newer emphasis on holidays at once more collective and more individual: the camping-site, holiday club or big skiing party, where everyone in theory is democratically equal, yet liberated from the emotional ties *chez tante Louise*.

The French also now tour outside their own frontiers as much as the sun-starved British, and this never used to be so. One reason could be that, although still chauvinistic, they are less insular than they used to be; they have become more aware of other peoples and curious about how they live. The growth of air travel and motoring have obviously played their part too, and so has the easing of currency restrictions. French tourist spending abroad rose sixfold in the 1950s, and by 1980 one holiday in four was taken outside France, a higher proportion than for Britain where the tradition of foreign travel is greater and the climatic incentives for it far stronger. French tourists today spend as much money abroad as France's own tourist industry earns from its millions of foreign visitors; and this is quite a change, for a country that itself has always been such a tourist venue. Two million people now go annually to Spain (day-trips excluded) and a minority venture much farther, to Morocco, Israel, Greece (now flooded with French philhellenes) or even to Mexico or India. The United States especially is now popular, attracting some 350,000 French in 1980.

When the economic climate changed in the mid-'70s, at first it seemed if anything to add to the holiday mania. As with some other pleasures, the French spent more money than ever on their holidays, maybe as a kind of compensation. Only in 1979–80, when real incomes began to dip slightly, did many people start to make economies: they went away for shorter periods, or less far afield, or they cut back on luxury frills such as night-clubs. The hotels suffered; the camping-sites grew fuller than ever. And for the first time since the war the migration abroad declined slightly, the main victim being Spain with its prices now almost as high as in France. And yet, holiday habits overall remain less affected by the crisis than one might have expected. The middle and upper classes are still carrying on much as before. Here, the trend for some years has been towards more unusual, varied and active kinds of holiday. A growing minority of people are less ready to spend long weeks beside a beach or in a country villa: they may opt instead for a cultural tour of Mexico, or trekking in the Himalayas, or swapping ideas with students in Budapest or Boston; or if they stay nearer home, they may want a holiday devoted to painting, riding or even archaeology. Some arrange these things for themselves; others turn to the new entrepreneurs of 'liberated but assisted holidays', where a guide organizes the mechanics of the operation while leaving the clients as free as possible.

All that I have said about the new French holiday ideals could be summed up in one magic phrase: Club Méditerranée. This is the Great French Dream made reality, sorely deserving its French Scott Fitzgerald. Its vast success with the French themselves reveals a good deal about their spirit today. But it has also spread around the globe and attracted other nations, thus becoming a mass export of French stylishness, sensuality and fantasy. Arguably it is the most original and creative large-scale holiday venture the world has yet seen.

It began in 1950 when Gerard Blitz, a tall blond athlete from Antwerp, started a small informal holiday-camp on Majorca. The idea snowballed and became a permanent holiday club, currently providing 600,000 people a year with holidays, just under half of them French. The Club and its affiliates operate more than a hundred 'villages' around the world (you must never call them 'holiday camps'), and it has cleverly diversified to suit varying tastes and purses. It still has fourteen of its famous original straw-hut summer villages around the sea that lends the Club its name; but it has also moved up-market, and the majority of its villages now are more solidly built in bungalow or hotel style; many are open all the year, and twenty-two are in winter ski-resorts. Blitz has long retired, and since 1963 the Club has been run by Gilbert Trigano, an equally remarkable man; like Edouard Leclerc, both have brought the visionary touch to a cut-throat competitive field, and today the Club applies skilful organization and packaging ('the computer is never far from the palm-tree') to the Blitz/Trigano philosophy of human happiness.

'Adventure is dead and solitude is dying, in today's crowded resorts,' wrote Blitz. 'The individual has a horror of promiscuity, but he does need community. So we give him a very flexible holiday community where at any moment he can join in or escape – a strange cocktail of *la vie de château* and *la vie de sauvage*.' And Trigano told me recently: 'Holidays provide a liberation that enriches the rest of daily life. The Club has broken down certain barriers; it gives a man or woman the right to be ridiculous, to try anything. It is an outlet for true individualism amid community, and the two are complementary.' So the Club's villages were early developed to satisfy certain French desires: sophistication amid return to nature; individualism amid camaraderie; a blend of sport, sensuality, culture and exotic foreign settings; a harmless once-a-year escape from the barriers and tensions of society into a never-never-land fraternity. Today this is still the ideal even though, victim of its own success, the Club inevitably has veered from spontaneity to prepackaged primitivism, and also towards greater comfort.

Borrowing the enchanted model of the Polynesian village, Blitz and Trigano built their colonies on the tracks of another no less romantic tradition, the Odyssey. The prototype is at Corfu (Corcyra) near Ithaca, others are on Djerba (authentic island of the lotus-eaters), at Foca not far from Troy, at Palinuro, at Cefalù beyond the Sicilian straits of Scylla and Charybdis, at Al Hoceima in Morocco towards the pillars of Hercules – as well as in Israel, Spain, Yugoslavia and elsewhere. There is even one in the Tahitian motherland itself (patronized mainly by Americans).

The villages vary in style, but the basic formula remains the same. All money is banked on arrival, and no cash changes hands in the village save in the form of pop-apart beads worn like a necklace, for buying bar drinks. Meals, served in elegant patios, are gargantuan and excellent, with unlimited wine included in the fees. All the tables are for eight and conversation is general, club-style, with no introductions. In many Mediterranean villages you sleep down by the beach in little round thatched huts; and some of the more dedicated Club members go around all day in next to nothing but a *paréo* (gaudy Tahitian sarong), uniform of the new utopia. In some tropical villages you can also wear flowergarlands. Phoney and embarrassing? Maybe to some people. But the appeal to the imagination, and to the craving for a kind of comradely naturalism, is real enough. The staff, known as Gentils Organisateurs (GOs), mix on equal terms with the Gentils Membres (GMs), sitting with them at meals, dancing with them, often calling them '*tu*', and maybe trying to imbue them with *le mystique du Club*. Yet (unlike in some holiday camps) no attempt is made by the GOs to force individuals to join in activities. You can skulk in your hut all day, or wander alone into the hinterland, and no one will mind or notice. And there is plenty to do for those who wish it – nightly open-air dancing and sing-songs, sports from water-skiing and sailing to judo and volley-ball, all included in the basic fees. For an extra charge you can go on sight-seeing excursions of anything from a day to a week, so the village can be used as a base for group exploration, say, of classical Greece or the Sahara. There are also daily open-air concerts of classical records, as well as a few lectures, and in some villages a supply of live culture in the form of touring drama or dance groups, or chamber orchestras performing in bathing trunks under the stars. The Club's appeal is middle class, and it is as different from Butlin's as Rupert Brooke from Ken Dodd.

In its earlier pioneering years the Club was entirely youthful and exuberant, everyone was on '*tu*' terms (amazing, for France) and the back-to-nature quest was for real. On my first Club holiday, at Cefalù in 1967, I was quite stunned by the euphoric spirit, the sense of together-ness, and by the readiness of G Ms to participate spontaneously with the G O *animateurs* in the nightly task of getting the party going. This atmos-phere still survives today in a number of the straw-hut villages, where the G Ms tend to be young in age or in spirit. But the Club is now so well known that it has also become popular with many of the kind of people who in the old days were suspicious of it. It is no longer just a mad adventure by a few uninhibited initiates. In moving up-market, it is now attracting also an older and more sedate clientèle, at least in some of the newer, more luxurious villages. Today the plumbing is better and the *paréos* fewer; the organization is smoother, and the spontaneity less evident. Many G Ms stick to '*vous*'; and the G Os now have to be careful whom they call '*tu*', for it can cause offence with older G Ms. The Club, in becoming a venerable institution, has inevitably lost something: but it remains a unique and fascinating venture, brilliantly stage-managed, hypnotic in its sheer sensual impact. And no village is quite like another, as I found when visiting four in Greece in 1979.

Et in Arcadia ego. Bleary-eyed, one late August dawn, my wife Jenny and I and a hundred other G Ms arrive a few score miles north of Arcadia – at Patras airport – on a Club charter from Paris. Buses take us to Aighion on the Gulf of Corinth, an average-sized village (680 beds). Here we are greeted musically by the assembled seventy GOs, including Pascal, chief *animateur*, a funny-sad clown in a big green hat. We are allotted a hut called Meduse, near the beach. Other G Ms have huts with names like Styx and Zorba. After breakfast, we new boys and new girls are given a pep-talk on the beach by bearded Mouche, the young *chef-de-village*, looking like a Greek god, in a robe with sun-patterns on it. He tells us that the aim of the Club is that we should all be very nice to each other (which the French need to be told as they aren't always nice to strangers, though here they seem to manage it).

Here is a typical day. After waking, a quick visit to the communal *lavoirs*, where it's unnerving to shave while a luscious blonde in a bikini beside me is cleaning her teeth with an electric brush. Breakfast (nearly everyone in swimsuits) is an amazing meal, as always at the Club, a world away from the usual French *petit déjeuner*: you help yourself from a long buffet laden with melon, yoghourt, *feta* cheese, *halva*, smoked fish, honey, fruit, or you fry your own bacon and eggs. You can have coffee, juice, or indeed Greek wine. Then we take a walk round the village which is beautifully landscaped on a wide slope full of flowers and olive trees. Then a sunbathe by the idyllic crescent-shaped *piscine* where most of the girls are topless. The jokey GO head of sports, who calls himself 'Radio Connerie', is noisily organizing tugs-of-war and other water-games which make it hard to bathe in the pool. Lunch in the terraced patio under the vine-creepers is another lavish help-yourself buffet: *dolmades* and other salads and *hors d'oeuvres*, a barbecue of chops and red mullet, various Greek dishes such as *moussaka* (dinners, by contrast, are classic French). At our table for eight, a shy Dutch girl doctor, some enthusiastic Germans and a museum curator from La Rochelle and his art designer wife, both passionate about classical Greece (significantly, the straw-hut villages often attract a more interesting type of GM than the newer, posher ones). After lunch, the hypnotic rhythms of *sirtaki* music invade the still air, and some of us go down to the open-air dance floor for our daily *sirtaki* lesson from an ebullient Corfiot GO.

At the big outdoor bar by the pool we drink *ouzo* (price: three gold beads, one black one) and amusedly watch a grotesque bulky Belgian being rejected by a girl from Nancy. Then, for an inside view on Club life as seen by the GOs, we talk lengthily to Andrew from Nottingham, chief water-skiing instructor. He says the GOs tend to get bored and exhausted by the end of the season and enjoy playing harmless hoaxes on the GMs. 'Last week we advertised "come and see the sun rise in a boat", and 200 GMs signed on. We woke them before dawn and they crowded on the jetty. Then two of us came by in a dinghy and slowly raised up a cardboard sun, lit from behind by a torch. There was utter silence, then laughter. Some GMs were really angry, and threw us in the water.' Andrew with his curly blond hair and his virility-symbol speed-boats is all the rage with the teenage girl GMs, and I find his boasts about his string of seductions entirely believable. 'I've had parents clamouring outside my hut that I give them back their fourteen-year-old daughter.'

At six there is recorded Brahms in an area known as l'Odéon, an open forum by the beach where we gaze at the silent sea as the sun sets and the Double Concerto finds a more perfect setting than any concert hall. Then dinner, this time French food served at the table; we find ourselves sitting with three young Parisian *cadres* and their girls, typical hard-core GMs, swapping anecdotes about previous Club holidays like veterans telling campaign stories (*'Moi, j'ai fait Cefalù en soixante-seize, c'était sensass!'*) but, significantly, not saying a word about France or their other lives back home. Later, hundreds of us crowd round the dance-floor/amphitheatre as the nightly *animation* begins. Pascal and the other *animateurs* embark on some carefully rehearsed pranks and lead us in jokey games, and at last there is a touch of Billy Butlin. The GOs, whatever their daytime job, are required also to be actors in the evening, and tonight some thirty of them give us a Western show, cowboys and Indians, miming and mouthing to recorded music. A few GMs join in the *animation* – notably an ugly little man with cropped hair and a toothbrush moustache whom Jenny and I have dubbed the 'Bank Clerk' (he probably is one). He arrived looking so drab, and now his inner personality seems to have come alive, as he leads us all in a riotous chain-dance, wearing a comic hat with a flower in it.

The next day Jenny and I take a ferry boat to Corfu for our next, utterly different, Club experience. This is not the famous straw-hut village of Corfu-Ipsos, but a newer luxury 600-bed hotel which the Club has rented close by, called Hélios. Each room even has a bathroom! Fees (for early September 1979) are 1,290 francs a week, against 730 francs at Aighion or Ipsos. However, the drawback is that this ugly eight-floor building, conceived for the ordinary hotel trade, works entirely against the Club's kind of *ambiance*. Added to this, the respectable well-heeled GMs, many on their first visit to the Club, are on average ten or fifteen years older than at Aighion, and older still in spirit; few are of the kind to make whoopee in a *paréo*. The large contingent of Germans, Italians and others tend to keep to their national groups; there are no xenophobic tensions, but the language barriers add to the reserve. The GOs have an uphill task creating *le vrai ambiance du Club*.

But Hélios has one star asset: its *chef de village*, the incredible 'Tonton Jean' (Uncle Jean). This professional actor and theatre producer is determined to overcome the village's innate handicaps; he runs it as a one-man show, a non-stop spectacle of bravura gimmicks and classy drama. Shaven-headed, athletic, often bare-chested, he is a manic extrovert on an ego-trip, and he is everywhere at once – down by the *piscine*'s snack-bar shovelling *taramasalata* onto GMs' plates, then up in the main dining-room giving us all a pep-talk on the day's programme, then down on the jetty exuberantly welcoming new arrivals. The GMs adore him, the GOs find him a trifle despotic. He and his wife Annie, herself an actress, had a tough time in the Paris *café-théâtre* and fringe theatre world. Then he joined the Club as an *animateur*, and rose to become head of its Animation Department, in charge of showbiz in all the villages. Next he was sent to problem-child Hélios, with a big budget for *animation*. 'It's marvellous!' he tells me; 'in our little Paris theatre we had a handful of actors and small, uncertain audiences. Here, I have a captive audience of up to 600 G Ms every night, and ninety G Os I can use as actors or extras.' So, in his outdoor theatre beside the hotel, Jean can now realize his frustrated dramatic ambitions, with a series of shows of high ingenuity and professional standard. On our five nights at Hélios, he does a Feydeau farce (stars, Jean and Annie), *Irma la Douce* (stars, Jean and Annie), and two large-cast spectaculars with echoes of Cecil B. de Mille and Hal Prince. The ritual weekly presentation of all G Os to newly arrived G Ms is called 'The Gods descend from Olympus', a pageant of blazing torches and robed figures, with a jokey commentary, and Jean as Zeus. The weekly last-night show, before the charters leave for Paris, is 'La Légende des Siècles', an ambitious 'historico-erotico revue' with clever lighting effects and back projections; the red-headed village *coiffeuse* is Joan of Arc, the head of sports ('Naff-Naff') is Cro-Magnon Man, a naked *hôtesse* from Martinique is Empress Josephine. G Os cascade across the stage for ninety minutes in a profusion of costumes, and then Jean takes rapturous curtain-calls as if this were an Opéra *première*. But pity the G Os who've been up rehearsing till 2 a.m., on top of their daily duties of, say, doing the accounts or teaching sailing.

Tonton Jean's other *coup* is the stunning method of bidding welcome or farewell to each group of G Ms. From the airport, a new contingent is brought to Hélios not by bus but straight across the bay in the Club's motor-yachts. As they approach the jetty, teams of G O water-skiers weave in and out of the yachts, carrying aloft the group's national flags, while loudspeakers blare out the jingly village signature-tune; and there on the jetty are Tonton and topless G O lovelies, some flower-garlanded, ready to kiss the newcomers. Bedraggled and bemused after a dawn flight from, say, Brussels or Munich, they are led up the steps, amid applause, for an *ouzo d'honneur* with Jean beside the pool. A dazzling way to start a holiday. And at the end, they get a send-off in the same style. The G Ms are pleased with all this, as they are with the theatre shows and the usual lavish food. But they are passive consumers and spectators, and some are a bit out of their depth amid the Club's rituals, at least at first. So Annie gives a tactful pep-talk to each new group (many with a strong sprinkling of matrons in their fifties): 'You must realize, this is *not* a hotel, it is a club – so there are no phones in your rooms, no locks on your doors. We like everyone to use Christian names, but don't feel that you *have* to use "*tu*" if it makes you uneasy.' Most GMs accept this *règle du jeu*; but a minority react badly. They complain at having to share tables of eight with strangers, or at 'the indignity of eating with the servants'! 'What cheek,' says a Lyonnais lawyer in his fifties; 'the young girl who teaches windsurfing expects to call me Pierre.' And many of the young GOs, after doing their best to create the true Club *ambiance* and then being consistently cold-shouldered or patronized by older or snootier GMs, finally react by withdrawing into their own cliques. Such are the perils and problems of the Club's up-market move.

Jenny and I are now glad to get back to the world of *les cases* (huts) – the true aristocrats of Le Club, of all ages, are those who prefer the youthful *mystique* of the straw-huts, and look down on those *arrivistes* who make for the comfort of the hotel-villages! So a group of us leave by boat for the little *village-annexe* on the mainland: Parga the enchanted. Nothing much save forty huts in an olive grove, a sandy beach in a little bay, a few windsurfers and sailing boats and three very young GOs. As we disembark the sun is blazing, and the hi-fi is playing Parga's romantic theme-tune, 'Kaleméra', a Greek melody. Nearly everyone is in *paréos*, rare now in the big villages. We are offered a *sangria d'honneur* by Patrick, *chef-de-village*, ex-actor, clad in the lowest-slung *paréo* I've ever seen, kept up by will-power. I tell Jenny, 'This is the *real* Club, at last!' We are shown to our ultra-primitive hut by Sally, young music graduate from Edinburgh, whose role as GO is Girl Friday – *hôtesse*, accountant, nurse and pianist. Our fellow-GMs, a select band of paradise-seekers, include a Parisian orchestra conductor and his family, a Grande Ecole student, an English headmistress. Some of us go by boat to a secluded creek where we can bathe nude and display our *gentils membres*. As is well known, this sport poses problems in Greece, where even bare breasts are still banned on beaches and the Club is often having trouble – especially as the French today regard toplessness as a sacred human right.

As dusk falls, the Parga scene is magical. Flowering oleander and mimosa surround the wide sandy patio beside the bar, where ping-pong, *boules*, impromptu *sirtaki* and much *ouzo*-drinking are all in progress. The hi-fi softly plays 'Kaleméra'. At dinner we sit with two factory workers from the Midi – there is democracy in paradise. The food, prepared by proud local Greeks, is even more lavish and succulent than in the big villages – seven-course dinners; Greek buffet lunches with every kind of fish and salad; amazing breakfasts with jelly, peaches, watermelon, figs. Only the local wine is fairly ghastly. After dinner it grows chilly, we light a camp fire on the patio, we wear our *paréos* like shawls to keep warm. With Sally at the piano, Patrick sings 'Raindrops

are falling . . .' and Serge Lama; Jacques from Blois recites his own
love-poems. This is our *animation*, a far cry from Tonton Jean. The idyllic
family atmosphere leaves me speechless, we are all touched by grace;
indeed, all day at Parga the mood has been dreamy, poetic, intimate,
lotus-eating. Parga is a rare surviving example of the true early spirit of
the Club, of Blitz and his utopia-seeking pioneers.

And so, Jenny and I return to Paris, drugged and brainwashed by
two Greek weeks of gregarious sensuality. We wander around Neuilly,
suffering from withdrawal symptoms. Why do the people in the street
not say 'bonjour' as we pass them? As I wash my car, why do the
neighbours not come up to help? What's wrong with these people?
Socially, as well as physically, the Club is a drug from which one
re-adjusts only slowly. Like Meaulnes, we yearn for our lost domain. Of
course, there's always next year, with honey-dew and the milk of paradise again included ad lib in the basic fees. But in the meantime, how to
live?

So this leads to the question: Of what value is this never-never-land
to French society? What influence has it had, or could it have, on French
social structures and behaviour during the rest of the year? This may
sound a ponderous question to ask about a harmless summer frolic, but it
is not an irrelevant one, even if the answers are hard to assess now that
the villages differ so much. The Club's French clientèle is substantially
middle class, down to clerks and artisans but with very few workers. In
its French context this is not surprising, even though straw-hut prices
would not be outside a skilled worker's means. So as a social catalyst the
Club has its limits: and yet, within its broad middle-to-upper range the
Club may well have played some part in the loosening up of French
rigidities and formalities over the past twenty years. Some sociologists
actually believe so.

In one sense, the Club is a therapy that involves some social make-
believe. Its officials enjoy telling the story of two men who struck up a
warm friendship over Samos wine and deep-sea diving at Ipsos: only on
the way home did they swap names and addresses, to discover that one
was a director and the other a night-watchman in the same factory. But
we are not told what happened to this friendship when they got back
home; and one managing-director GM has been quoted as saying, 'I got
friendly with one of my clerks: it was all right at the Club, where
everything's so free and easy, but it did make it harder to keep up *les
convenances* back in the office.' I have found it noticeable that the French
GMs, more than the foreign ones, prefer to remain anonymous and not
discuss their jobs or backgrounds with each other. They want to forget

about France; exchanging visiting-cards is not done. Nor has there been much pressure from members for Butlin-style winter get-togethers in France: one or two Club attempts at these failed because they showed up the social differences that were masked in the villages, and Blitz himself once told me with disarming frankness: 'The Club's success is due to its divorce from daily life. We found that trying to hold meetings in Paris lost us the credit we had won in the villages.' Indeed I have often thought of the Club as a kind of compensation-world, almost a Jean Genet territory where men and girls act out the fantasy roles they cannot manage in their own lives – classless democrats, cultured pagans, noble savages, high-spirited friends-to-all-the-world.

But in the past decade France has evolved; as we have seen, the French have become less formal and uptight, in entertaining, in using *tu* or Christian names, in office relations, and so on. Millions have been GMs at least once, and it could just be that some of the Club's informality has rubbed off on their behaviour during the rest of the year and so the Club *has* had an influence. But whether or not this is so, French life has patently been catching up with the Club, as Trigano told me in 1979: 'In the '50s we were in advance of our age, but today it comes to meet us. In those days the gulf between the Club and the new GMs who joined us was so great that we had to create a shock, such as insisting on *tu*. But today Monsieur Dupont is himself readier to be *"toi, Jacques"*, so we don't need *tu* so much. It's France that's changed.' So it may be that the appeal of the Club as a Jean Genet land has diminished a little, now that in daily life the rigidities are less severe. It is ironic that growing French informality has made the informal Club more subdued.

The Club does still come in for plenty of criticism, especially from Leftists, for creating a fictitious world. At Aighion, a GM girl student from Besançon told me, significantly: 'This place is nice in its way, but it's contrived – all these GOs with their PR smiles. It's a shame the Club's *ambiance* is confined to holidays for the affluent; where it should be is in every street and suburb of France, all the year.' I said I couldn't agree with her more – but whose fault is it? She should read the section of this book on the problems of creating *ambiance* in the new suburbs. When I told Trigano of her remarks, he said, 'Yes, I agree too. In fact, we proposed to the Government and to some mayors that we should set up *écoles d'animation de la vie quotidienne* in a few towns, so that all France could gradually become one non-stop Club Med in spirit! But no one has dared take us up on it.' Meanwhile the Club continues to serve as an annual middle-class therapy; a painless mini-lesson in civism, a forum where strangers can be nice to each other without the mistrust common in France – 'a kibbutz without the work', it has been called. 'The Club,' Trigano says, 'sets a model that should be contagious through the rest of the year.'

The success of the whole cunning operation depends above all on the GOs. Its supreme innovation, its masterstroke, is to make it seem that the staff are on holiday along with their clients. Of course, *ars est celare artem*; to do his job properly, the GO must work hard and skilfully. It is a highly popular job, not too well paid but attracting hordes of applicants, not surprisingly. New recruits have usually already trained or worked elsewhere as sports instructors or actors, or *animateurs* for youth clubs or town councils; nearly all are in their twenties; about half are foreign; and many *hôtesses* or excursion leaders are from a classy Paris background, for to be a GO can carry a social cachet. The Club then puts recruits through its own training courses, and in Trigano's words 'has created a new profession', closer to the classic animateur than to the hotel employee.

In France, as abroad, the Club has an oddly mixed reputation. In some milieux, a holiday with it is a chic status symbol; in others, people do not even dare tell their friends they have gone. Once in Paris I was with three very superior couples – a cousin of Giscard's, the then head of DATAR, and a well-known count, plus their wives, all close friends – and where were they about to go on holiday? – to the Club, at Foca in Turkey! And yet, a young member of Giscard's personal staff at the Elysée told me that he too had been with the Club, in Morocco, and was upset by the atmosphere of gluttony in a poor country, and by the ethos of *'bouffer, baiser, bronzer'*. So it is a matter of individual taste. The fastidious might not like the togetherness and *animation*, so maybe the Club is not for them; but surely without *animation* the villages would be rather dull. In my own view, the Club does achieve a certain basic good taste and freedom from vulgarity in the way it is conceived and run. For instance, the hundreds of straw huts or bungalows are dotted irregularly among the trees in a way that pleases the eye and preserves the environment; from half a mile offshore at Aighion or Ipsos you see nothing but trees. And basically I agree with the view of one senior GO: 'Only the French could have succeeded with a holiday formula like ours. In Italy, the position of women would have made it difficult, while the Germans or British would have turned it into jolly boy-scoutism for adults. Our French individualism saves us. Despite all the foreign GMs, the Club's style remains French.' But as the Club expands and diversifies, what will happen to its original spirit? Those anxious to preserve the early back-to-nature ethos are heartened by one recent trend: after some years of a move towards more comfort, the straw-hut villages are today coming back into greater popularity, and their level of occupancy has caught up with that of the *villages en dur*. The reasons may be partly economic, but Club officials believe that even more they are 'ecological'. Many senior *cadres* and others are more than ever seeking a real break with their city life-styles, and so they go for the straw huts and their *ambiance*.

Small, dark, always shirt-sleeved, the sixty-one-year-old Jewish whizz-kid who propels the Club's expansion is a strange mixture of social visionary and astute businessman. Son of a grocer, Gilbert Trigano left school at fifteen, later joined the Communist Resistance and for a while worked for *l'Humanité*. He then switched to the camping equipment business, and thus he met Blitz and joined the Club in 1954. He has long broken with the PCF and today says he hates all political parties and 'isms', but he still holds to the ideal of a comradely classless society and claims to hate private property. 'The happiness of the individual is ensured by the collective use of wealth,' he says. For him the Club's villages are an attempt to embody this principle, though he does add: 'The Club gets no subsidies, and in the tough competitive world of tourism we cannot be philanthropists. I am not ashamed of making profit.' But has he possibly compromised with his ideals, in being lured up-market rather than sticking to a more 'social' kind of tourism? There are some who think so. The Club is now a public company with a 75-million-franc capital and shares quoted on the Bourse, most of them belonging to big banks. One by one it has absorbed a number of its imitators and rivals, and is now the largest French-owned hotel chain and the world's largest non-American one after Trust Houses Forte.

Above all, Trigano is now aiming hard and with success at an American mass market, helped by a tie-up with American Express. The nine villages in the Caribbean, Mexico and the Pacific are now mainly for Americans, and the first language in these tends to be English, while the Club has just opened a village in the USA itself, in Colorado. In 1978, 13.8 per cent of all GMs were American (48.7 per cent were French, 11.5 Italian, 6.9 Belgian, 3.5 German, only 0.6 British). Needless to say, the Club's formula appeals very readily to the open American temperament, given a few adjustments of language and comfort (Americans do not care for straw huts); but the basic style remains French. The Martinique and Guadeloupe villages are especially popular with American singles, and the atmosphere even on the outward planes from New York is said to be electric. One Club executive has put it: 'America is still an old-fashioned country in its methods of tourism, so we are exporting our techniques to them, just as France has imported American know-how in other fields. The Club is an authentic French penetration into the US sphere, just as IBM penetrates into France.' And why not? One of Trigano's policies today is to export the Club to a new clientèle in far-off countries by implanting villages on their doorstep. Thus a new village in Mauritius appeals to South Africans; Brazilians are discovering the Club for the first time, thanks to a new village in Brazil; and so on. Trigano, like Queen Victoria, rules an empire on which the sun never sets.

He makes a number of claims for the Club. One: it is doing its bit to spread international amity. Another: it has been influencing the rest of the tourist industry – 'They flatter us by trying to imitate us. People no longer build big classic hotels along the coast: they try out the bungalow style, maybe with some club-like features.' These claims are not too far-fetched, and nor was Blitz' assertion that the Club 'is the pilot-organization of Europe's leisure, laboratory for the holidays of the future'. But as the Club tries hard to be all things to all men, what will happen to the dream that first impelled Blitz and his fellow-pioneers to seek the Happy Isles? As the Club's computers colonize the palm-beaches of the world, let us hope that the sun never sets on Parga and its wine-dark sea.

There are echoes of the Club's atmosphere in some of the ordinary public camping-sites in France, especially along the less urbanized westward stretch of the Côte d'Azur from Cannes to Cassis, where the gaudy blue-and-orange tents fill the pine-forests for miles. The whole trend on the Riviera since the 1950s, for rich and not-so-rich alike, has been away from the Edwardian sedateness of Menton or Monte Carlo and towards the St-Tropez or Ile de Porquerolles pattern – film-stars with sand between their toes, pine-needles in your *soupe de poissons*, nudists among the rocks, a juke-box idly blaring Serge Lama in the sun, and all the paraphernalia of *le camping élégant* which the French are able to manage with a lithe Latin flair. The 'topless' revolution of the '70s has been amazing and is one more sign of France's new permissiveness. Even staid resorts like Nice and Deauville now sanction bare breasts on all their public beaches, while in many French seaside towns today you see topless girls not only on the beach but in shops and cafés. Public opinion now largely accepts this: the few conservative mayors who have tried to ban breasts have simply seen their town's holiday trade slump. Total nudism too, male and female, has been creeping in along some beaches, though this is still formally illegal outside the nudist camps, and sometimes fines are imposed. The nudist camps themselves are booming, especially on the Languedoc coast (see pp. 145–8).

The French have increasingly been drawn to the seaside (46 per cent of all holidays were spent there in 1978, against 23 per cent twenty years earlier) and to the mountains (17 per cent in 1978, 10 per cent in 1958), though the latest recession has brought some revival of holidays spent in the country among friends or relatives or in secondary homes. Sea and mountain provide the main setting for the tremendous growth of sport in France. The number of private sailing-boats and motor-yachts rose from 20,000 in 1960 to 475,000 in 1979: today the Côte d'Azur is so jammed with yachts in summer that some ports have instituted parking-discs for them as for cars. Skiing is also immensely popular: some four million go on holiday to the ski-slopes each year (excluding day-trippers from towns such as Grenoble) and 10 per cent of these are working class. The French Alps are the favourite venue, followed by the Pyrenees, Vosges and parts of the Massif Central (used especially for Norwegian-style long-distance skiing). The building of new ski-lifts and hotels in smart Alpine resorts such as Megève and Les Arcs has meant big business for financiers and developers, and some well-to-do Parisians have now picked up the New York habit of making long car journeys for weekend skiing.

The new hedonistic and ecological trends in France have brought a huge increase in the individual practice of sport for fitness or pleasure. The French today are more *sportif* than the British; or at least they are more devoted than the British to participation as opposed to spectator-sports. True, the annual Tour de France cycle race is a mammoth spectator-sport, and so are the big car races and league football. But France's sporting clubs claim a total of over four million *licenciés* or certified active participants (three times the 1967 total), while sales of sports and other outdoor gear have risen more than fifteen-fold since 1960. Amateur footballers number over 1,300,000. Tennis, formerly considered a sport of the rich, is now more democratized: the number of courts has tripled in ten years. Fishing too has increased in popularity, and so till very recently did hunting. *La chasse* is generally conducted with a rifle, not horse and hounds: formerly it was the preserve of peasants and gentry, as in Renoir's *La Règle du jeu*, but after the war it spread more widely, and so many urban amateurs took to the woods on Sundays with their guns that the accident-rate soared and tighter licensing laws had to be enforced. This, and the growing scarcity of game, has now reduced the total of huntsmen from 2.3 to about 1.9 million. But today's great boom is in horse-riding, a sport that ideally combines physical exercise and communion with the world of nature and animals. The numbers who belong to riding-clubs or join riding excursions have risen tenfold since 1972, to reach 300,000.

In international competition the French show up better at individual than at team sports, as you might expect. They did poorly in all the recent World Football Cups and their post-war summer Olympic record has been generally disappointing, due partly to failures of team training and morale. Their few gold medals have mostly been for aristocratic and individual sports such as horse-jumping and fencing. At Munich in 1972 they were placed seventeenth with two golds; at Montreal in 1976, eighteenth with only one. Then at Moscow in 1980 they actually came eighth with six golds, ahead of all other non-Communist countries save Italy: but in the sorry Moscow context, this might not be anything to boast about. Front-rank French athletes are rare: but when they do emerge, like the runner Michel Jazy and the swimmer Christine Caron a few years ago, they are lauded as national idols. When in 1976 Eric Tabarly again won the single-handed transatlantic sailing race, his return to Paris produced a hero's ovation from a huge crowd on the Champs Elysées, like a Roman triumph, and there was similar excitement in 1980 when he broke the transatlantic speed record: a mystique in France now surrounds this taciturn naval officer, and it is he who has inspired so many thousands of young Frenchmen to become sailing fanatics.

For many years public participation in sports was limited by lack of equipment. More recently, the State and town councils have at least made a big effort to provide public swimming-pools, and nearly every little town now has its civic *piscine*. But there is still a shortage of sports grounds, especially in the *grands ensembles*, and only very recently has sport in schools begun to be taken seriously. In 1979 the Ministry of Youth and Sport launched a scheme for putting all children of eight to thirteen through a series of tests, with a view to spotting and then training future champions: this was generally welcomed, though some people criticized it as smacking too much of the ruthless East German system. The past years have seen other new ventures too ('snow classes' for poorer children, and State-subsidized skiing holidays for young workers), but funds are limited, and there are frequent complaints that the best ski-runs fall into the hands of tycoons charging high prices.

The great holiday boom has been unevenly shared: one person in six in the eighteen to thirty-four age-bracket has never been away on holiday in his life. Right-wing Governments, it is true, did make growing efforts to create cheap holiday-villages and hostels in deserted rural areas, and to develop *colonies de vacances* under trained monitors for poorer children whose parents cannot afford holidays *en famille*. More than a million children visit these colonies annually: you see them all along French beaches in summer, a touching and slightly pathetic sight.

Now the new Government plans to put far more public money into 'social tourism' for the less well-off: holiday camps, subsidized skiing trips, and the like.

If only the French public could be induced to spread its holidays over a longer period of the year, fuller and more effective use could be made of such cheap tourist amenities as do exist. Many hostels and camps are over-subscribed for July and August and at Christmas, and empty much of the rest of the time. Yet many a Frenchman will stay at home rather than change his habits. Holiday-making in August is typically one of those rooted French traditions that is proving hard to alter, however unrealistic it grows as the tourist numbers swell. Some 80 per cent of French summer holidays are taken between July 14th and August 31st, against 70 per cent in Britain and 60 per cent in Germany. Industrial production falls by 40 per cent in August, against 10 per cent in Germany where factory holidays are officially staggered from one *Land* to another.

Anyone who has lived in Paris knows how the city goes to sleep that month. It is the time that tradesmen in particular choose for their annual bolt to the country: you can stroll pleasantly in empty streets, but your favourite *bistrot* may well have closed, and in some districts you may find it hard to get a haircut or shoes repaired, or even buy food. In the prosperous classes, mothers and children generally depart for six to eight weeks at a stretch, leaving breadwinners behind for part of the time in silent flats, possibly up to no good. The nation's business slows to a crawl, and those who are still at work often pretend to their friends they are not there. Until recently, in the bourgeoisie it used to be such a sign of failure to stay in Paris in August that spinsters in genteel poverty might spend the month like hermits behind closed shutters rather than show that they could not afford to leave.

Meanwhile the summer traffic-jams and casualties mount up along the tourist routes, on the way to the overcrowded beaches. At the time of *le grand départ*, the last weekend in July or the first in August, more than two million cars are moving south. In recent years the Government has launched an operation called *Bison Futé* (the wily bison) which advises motorists on alternative routes and peak hours to be avoided, but this only partially limits the jams. If you leave Paris at 3 a.m. and go by secondary roads, you may still find yourself queuing for long hours at the approaches to the Pyrenees and Provence. Above all, the tourist industry is the victim: hoteliers in resort towns, faced with rising costs, find it ever harder to balance their budget with the season so short. It is the single gravest problem they face today.

There are those who argue that staggering might not after all be the best solution; that, maddening though it may be for holiday-makers and the holiday trade, the August concentration has its business convenience for France as a whole. Everyone knows where everyone else is: away. And the corollary of the August holiday is that for all the rest of the year people are at work simultaneously, which makes planning easier. This is not however the Government's view, and probably it is right. For some years it has led a campaign for the wider spreading of holidays, though with minimal success: the percentage starting their summer break before June 27th or after August 28th has risen merely from 12.7 to 15.1 per cent since 1969. Although a few big firms have been induced to close their plants in July rather than August, most others have refused to do so for commercial reasons: they must close when their suppliers and dealers close. It is a vicious circle.

Government policy is now to induce some staggering of school holidays, in the hope that this will influence families and business people too. Since 1970 the school year has been redivided into two long semesters on the German or American pattern, with a two-week break in February. Industrial workers too, under a recent law, are being encouraged to take at least part of their holiday in February. With the growing popularity of skiing, this has had some effect, and just a little of the August crush has now been diverted to the winter – but not to June or September which remain largely taboo, even though the weather can then be at its best. Just a few middle-class people are now becoming readier to take their main summer holiday then, attracted by the off-season rates, and these include the G Ms with whom I romped in Greece early in September: but they are only a small minority. However, the Socialist Government has now promised to make renewed efforts to persuade people to stagger their holidays, including offering travel subsidies to those prepared to go in May or June, or in winter. Will the Socialists have any greater success?

Independently of any State initiative, in central Paris itself an increasing number of theatres, shops and restaurants have come to realize what lucrative tourist trade they lose by closing all August: today nearly half the city's theatres remain open that month. But in the suburbs, where there are no tourists, the blinds are still down. The main obstacle to staggering is now purely that of habit. According to an opinion poll taken by the IFOP (Institut Français d'Opinion Publique), 49 per cent of families say they would be willing in theory to take their holidays in June or September, but in practice they do not do so. The French are individualist about nothing so much as the right to share the same herdlike conventions.

The French, who used to seem so sedentary, have since the war become a restless people; and the recent rise in fuel prices has scarcely altered this. Ring up a businessman, even quite a lowly one, and he is sure to be just back from Bordeaux, or just off to Geneva, or on the point of driving his family 200 miles for a short weekend. 'Where are you going for Easter?' I asked a Parisian recently: 'I'll drive to Italy,' he said, while a generation ago it might have been Fontainebleau,' and my dentist is driving to Prague, and my lawyer's taking his mini-bus to Nice.' The only effect of the energy crisis has been to slow the annual increase in total car usage from 6 to 3 per cent: a car still does on average 13,500 kilometres a year. Few people in Europe are so car-mad. Not only do they have one of the highest levels of car-ownership, but they react emotionally to cars as to women: '*Une voiture, Monsieur, est comme une femme*,' my *garagiste* once told me when I complained that my Renault's performance was varying mysteriously from day to day. Snobberies about certain makes of car have their own elaborate and shifting scales of values. Foreign cars are smart (if less so than in Britain), and their share of the market has risen to 21 per cent. Some British cars have prestige-value, notably Rovers and even Minis. Mercedes and BMW also score high, but Italian sports-cars are no longer so fashionable. Among French cars, large Citroëns have a cachet for stylishness, and Peugeots for reliability (see pp. 62–70). Though Panhard and Renault were among the great pioneers, the French today care little for veteran cars.

The energy crisis has at least made the French drive more carefully. Habitually they have always liked to drive fast, using their brakes and taking chances, and the price they paid for this was an accident rate that by 1972 was causing 16,600 deaths a year, twice the British rate and about the same as Germany's. Nearly half of fatal accidents were caused by drink. But plans to increase penalties for drunken driving, or to tighten the very liberal speed limits, caused such an outcry that they were shelved. Then, at the end of 1973, the need to save petrol did finally give France the cue to introduce new speed limits, like many countries. These were found also to be reducing the accident rate, so they were retained even when the threat of oil scarcity eased: today they are 130 k.p.h. on motorways, 100 on dual carriageways, 90 on other country roads – around the European average. The Government recently has also step-ped up its campaign for road safety. Seat-belts are now compulsory at all times. Breathalyser tests have been introduced, to the fury of drivers: their motoring clubs have pointed out that of those subjected to the tedium of random checks, only 1 per cent are in default of the alcohol limit. So the tests now tend to be used only when a driver has been stopped for speeding, or after an accident. But the new much tougher penalties do seem to have succeeded in making the French more cautious about drinking before driving. That cherished half-bottle of wine with a meal is still safe, it will not bring you above the legal limit. But gone are the days when a driver might follow it with two cognacs.

The fatality rate is now down to 12,000 a year, a certain achievement. 'But that's still 12,000 too many,' said a spokesman: quite apart from the human suffering, the material cost to the nation of road accidents is put at 40,000 million francs a year. So the speed limits are now being enforced much more strictly, especially at those danger-points where drivers tend to ignore the signs to slow down at a curve or crossing. Fines are 300 francs and upwards, and the police have the right to exact cash on the spot. In serious cases they can also remove the driver's licence for a period of days or weeks – this happens constantly – and he has to complete his journey by other means. So the French do now drive more prudently, but there are still the few crazy ones. On one motorway, a radar control found a driver doing 232 k.p.h., but at that speed the police could not even read his number-plate, so he got away. Drivers who do get booked give all kinds of excuses, and I especially sympathize with this one: 'My car isn't built for driving slowly: send the fine to the manufacturer.' Once a man who had driven all night from Strasbourg was stopped for speeding near Cannes. The police confiscated his licence, so his wife took over the wheel. 'Thanks, officer,' she said, 'you've done a good job. He never lets me drive.'

THE WELFARE STATE:
A COSTLY NEW CRAZE FOR HEALTH

What of the many millions who cannot possibly afford a new Mercedes, or the delights offered by Bocuse or Trigano? Has France done as much as other Western countries to build up a modern Welfare State, and thus to protect her weaker citizens and provide some compensation for the gross inequalities of wealth? The answer is a very qualified 'yes'. In the earlier part of this century France was slower than some of her neighbours to develop social legislation, which did not make a real start until the Popular Front regime of the 1930s. But since the war there has been huge if uneven progress: public hospitals have improved out of recognition; and the overall Social Security budget is around the EEC average. It accounts for 18.5 per cent of GDP, below the German figure (21.6) and even the Italian (19.6) but above that of Britain (16.7), the nation that pioneered the modern Welfare State but has now slipped back.

Statistics however are not the only guide. Some practical aspects of public welfare remain less developed than in Britain, in that they do less to help the most needy. The main difference is that Social Security is much more employment-related. Contributions are linked to salary, with employers paying the bulk (58 per cent), employees only 19 per cent, and the State the rest. This may seem very democratic, but it tends to discriminate against the non-employed. Of course Social Security does have its humane content: but its priority has been set on helping those potentially useful to society, notably young mothers, and workers. If you are old, or handicapped, or chronically unemployable, and thus of less economic value, then relatively you are less well looked after than in Britain. Only in the '70s has this begun to be rectified.

Typically, the strongest feature of the French system is the family allowances, the highest in the EEC: they account for 20 per cent of all welfare spending, against 10 or 11 per cent in Britain and Germany. So great is the Government's desire to raise the birth-rate that if you have only one child you get no help; allowances start with the second child, and soar high from the third one onwards. A three-child family on the modest income of 50,000 francs a year draws at least 1,250 francs a month for them. In addition, a mother gets a generous grant if she forgoes a job and devotes herself to the home. And in 1980, in a further bid to revive the flagging birth-rate, the Government introduced a new 10,000-franc lump-sum payment for a third child and each subsequent one. Over four million families benefit from these various bonanzas, and over two million also receive State housing subsidies, financed by a direct levy on employers. In many workers' homes, allowances add more than 50 per cent to the husband's net wages.

However, in the case of other forms of benefit the picture is different, for it is here that the job-related system works unfairly. As we have seen (see p. 106), of France's current army of unemployed, those who have paid their social contributions for some years are treated quite generously, but those who have not – mainly of course the very young – get little from the dole. The same kind of discrimination affects old-age pensioners. Until the 1960s the aged were the poor relations of the welfare system: the basic pension was so low that many old people lived in dire poverty, unless they were able to get help from their families or from religious charities. Today, an earnings-related pension scheme that started in 1945 is finally bringing proper results, for most old people have now paid their contributions long enough to benefit from it. But this does not always help the former self-employed, nor those who for some reason have missed out on their contributions: they often have to make do on the legal basic pension for over-sixty-fives of a mere 1,200 francs a month. The old are certainly better off in France than they used to be (see p. 384), but there are still pockets of real misery. The trouble is that old people, though they have the vote, do not form an organized lobby like vinegrowers or small shopkeepers, and so they have little political clout. And the same is true, in a different way, of the handicapped. Until fairly recently, France's economy-oriented welfare structure tended to leave the care of the old or handicapped to voluntary bodies, often religious, or to the family. Giscard in 1975 then produced a wide-ranging law to help the physically or mentally disabled: *inter alia*, it gives grants to firms that will offer them special sheltered employment. But this law, however worthy its intentions, has been criticized for keeping the handicapped in a kind of ghetto. Less is done than in Britain or Scandinavia to try to integrate them into society. If they are not able to live a family life, then they tend to be tidied away behind the walls of institutions, by a society that would rather not be reminded of them. It is in this context that Grenoble town council's initiative at l'Arlequin is commendable (see pp. 308–13).

As in some other countries, the Government for years has been generous in allowing the Social Security budget, and especially the health budget, to rise much faster than national income. During the boom years this posed little problem, and indeed was valuable in order to remedy some of the archaisms of the health service. But by the mid-'70s Social Security had built up a serious annual deficit, and a Government now austerity-minded became worried. What was the answer? Employers were reluctant to pay more, pointing out that social security charges already added over 40 per cent to their wage-bills, more than in other countries. Nor was it feasible to increase the public's contributions too greatly. So the Government launched a campaign to make economies in the health service, including the checking of various abuses that were causing overspending. This led in 1979–80 to a long conflict with French doctors that endlessly filled the headlines.

The national health service began, as in Britain, just after the war. For a long period it remained very far from adequate. Doctors and nurses were too few, and the building of new hospitals did not keep pace with urban growth: most of them were overcrowded and fearfully old-fashioned. But in the past ten or fifteen years a well-funded crash-programme has radically improved the situation, so that French hospitals today are on average more modern and efficient than in a Britain at grips with its NHS crisis. As with public transport in London and Paris, it is quite a reversal of roles! There are few waiting-lists now for beds in public hospitals; nurses are more plentiful, and their morale is much improved; a computer system saves muddles and delays, and helps the staff to serve the patient more smoothly. True, under the French system a national health hospital patient may have to pay up to 20 per cent of his

bill, but this is not the case for more serious illnesses where hospitaliza-
tion is free. One sign of the all-round improvement in the medical
service, and in hygiene in France, is that between 1950 and 1976 the
infant mortality rate dropped from 53 to 13 deaths per 1,000 births. Here
France has now moved ahead of Britain, Germany and the United States,
and is close behind Sweden and Holland.

In relations with the family doctor, as with hospitals or specialists,
the basic structural difference from the British system is that the patient
pays his doctor direct for each consultation, and must then apply to his
local Social Security office for a refund – like paying your garage for
repairs and then claiming from insurance. This involves some delay and
much form-filling. Moreover, the refund is not total: it is only 75 per cent
of the 55 franc fee that GPs are authorized to charge (specialists get a little
more). So the health service in France is not entirely free, but the 25 per
cent margin does dissuade some people from consulting their doctors
unnecessarily. And the doctors themselves are especially attached to a
system which, as they see it, safeguards the independence of their liberal
profession and prevents them from becoming 'mere civil servants' like
British NHS doctors. The GP can move around as he wishes and
chooses his patients: his relationship is solely with them, and not with
the *Sécurité Sociale* which is simply a kind of State insurance company.
His only commitment is to stick to the agreed fees (admittedly, he does
sómetimes overcharge), and only if he works in a public hospital does he
become a State employee. About 85 per cent of French GPs participate in
the service (the rest have private patients). It should be added that
prescription charges must also be paid direct to the chemist, and are then
reimbursed at a standard 70 per cent – some more, some less, according
to the drug.

The medical service is now of so high a standard that it has become
very costly for the State, even though the patient pays a share. Much of
the huge Social Security deficit has been due to increased health spending, which from 1950 to 1980 rose from 3 to 7.5 per cent of GDP (the
figure for Britain is 5.2, for Germany 6.7); and given the rise in GDP over
that period, it means that in real terms the French are spending per head
about six times as much on their health as thirty years ago. One factor: as
in other countries, hospitals are now using far more expensive and
sophisticated equipment, for transplants, brain surgery and so on.
Another factor, much less justifiable: many doctors are over-prescribing
expensive drugs, sometimes in tacit conspiracy with the pharmaceutical
industry from which they may get pay-offs of a kind. And as many
costlier drugs are reimbursed at 100 per cent, the State foots the whole
bill. But this drug boom is partly the patients' fault, as well as the doctors'

and the industry's. One curious trend of the France of the '70s is that the French have become far more fussy about their health: it seems to be one more aspect of the move towards ecology and private fulfilment, noted throughout this book. The French today hold the world record for the number of medicines bought, both on and off prescription: consumption per head is three times higher than in Britain, and 50 per cent above the American level! 'We've become a nation of hypochondriacs,' one doctor lamented to me. So the public forks out readily for its own modest share of the prescriptions, and the Ministry of Finance tears its hair.

When in 1978 the Social Security deficit reached a titanic 27,000 million francs, Barre could stand it no more. Simone Veil, Minister of Health, was obliged to put her famous popularity at risk by forcing the public to swallow the pill of a big rise in contributions. But the Government did make the rich bear the brunt: a worker earning 3,000 francs a month saw his quota rise by 15 per cent (from 238 to 276 francs monthly); a *cadre* with four times that income now had to pay out 54 per cent more (674 instead of 438 francs). This had some effect on the deficit, but not enough. So the Government moved next to make economies in the health service. It managed to get public hospitals to trim their spending, without any real reduction in quality. Then it turned on the doctors and asked them to help too. It produced a plan that would penalize those who over-prescribed. And it proposed a complex new two-tier system for G Ps, whereby a patient by paying extra could secure better attention. The doctors reacted angrily to this scheme which, they said, would create 'one medicine for the rich, another for the poor', alien to the spirit of the health service. They also feared a drop in their incomes, for the Government wanted to freeze the basic consultation rate at 40 francs. So in 1979–80 there ensued a year-long wrangle between the Ministry and the main medical union, during which the doctors three times went on one-day strikes – the first time this had ever happened in France.

The doctors were really giving vent to a wider sense of grievance and malaise. So popular did their profession become in France's boom years that, previously too few, they are now too numerous except in some country areas. In 1965–80 their numbers grew from 86 to 178 per 100,000 people, which puts them roughly on the EEC average, ahead of Britain (152) but behind Germany (204). And despite the *numerus clausus* set up in medical faculties since 1968 (see p. 502), the total is still rising. So, in what is virtually a free market, many a G P is having to fight harder to get enough patients to make a living. He has also seen his costs rise much faster than the fees he is authorized to charge, and many a doctor has complained of a fall in real earnings. It is a profession with a very wide income range: while the average is a comfortable 200,000 francs a year, a surgeon or a GP in private practice can easily reach 600,000, yet many health service GPs in industrial areas exist on 80,000 to 100,000 which is low for a liberal profession in France. Overstretched and harassed, working often a 60-hour week, many doctors are having to take on part-time extra jobs in order to keep up their living standards. As one of them said, 'The golden age of our privileged profession may be nearing its end.'

In 1980 the Ministry agreed to raise the basic fee to 55 francs, and the doctors in turn accepted a version of the two-tier system. So the conflict subsided. But then in 1981 the Left came to power with rather different views on the health service. Among other measures it proposed to cancel the new sliding-scale system and to insist that all GPs (except private ones) charge the same rates: this, it felt, would prevent some public patients from getting better treatment than others. It also did away with private beds in State hospitals, and prepared to set up a national network of 'integrated health centres' where doctors and nurses would work in groups. Never happy under Giscard, the medical profession now took even greater fright. Was the Left planning to destroy the French doctor's basic freedom, to turn him into a civil servant *à l'anglaise*? These fears were not lessened by the fact that the new Minister of Health, Jack Ralite, was a Communist, albeit a mild one. So today the French health service is rethinking its structures and principles, as well as its financing. No one has yet quite come up with the solution as to how, in a time of recession, this affluent society can best continue to preserve the high level it has achieved for its medical services. But some things are clear. Ways must be found of checking the rise in doctors' numbers. Doctors must accept that they should prescribe fewer drugs, as already many of them are doing. Above all, the French public must tone down its new craze for medicines, and must stop going to the doctor for pills for every ache or sneeze. On this, nearly everyone is agreed; but, as with the staggering of holidays, it is not so easy to achieve.

On another point all are agreed: more should be done to combat alcoholism, which Giscard himself described as 'the worst of all French social scourges'. But they have been saying just that for many years. A vigorous official campaign against alcoholism ever since 1954 seems to have borne some results, but it is hard to tell just how much. On the one hand there are some encouraging signs: the huge increase in the sales of soft drinks, the disaffection of many young people for their parents' style of heavy drinking, and the decline in inveterate alcoholic café-going. On the other hand, many people are simply transferring their drinking habits from the café to the home. Deaths from cirrhosis of the liver or alcoholic excess (delirium, polyneuritis) still run steady at about 21,000 a year, and to these must be added another 20,000 or so deaths from other alcohol-induced diseases, though as these are mostly old people it could be argued that the figures relate more to past habits than to present ones. The more encouraging fact is that alcoholic consumption per head has been declining steadily, by almost 20 per cent since 1951. But the French are still the world's heaviest drinkers: 16.4 litres of 'pure' alcohol per head per year, followed by Luxemburg (14.4) and Portugal (14). Other figures are: Germany 12.4, Italy 12.1, USA 8.3, Britain 8.2. At least, prosperity in France has brought an improvement in the quality of what is drunk: consumption of champagne, whisky and good wines has soared, while that of the old liver-rotting strong coarse wines and *eaux-de-vie* has dropped.

Pierre Mendès-France, as Prime Minister in 1954, first gave official status to the anti-alcohol campaign, and won himself a good deal of derision for his milk-drinking image. But the permanent High Commission he founded is still very active, and seems to have done something to wean younger people away from the traditional French ideas that wines and spirits are actively good for health and that not to drink is unmanly. The Committee prompted the distribution of literature to all schools, not advocating teetotalism but warning against excess. This campaign led to riots in wine-producing areas like Languedoc, but it did make some positive impact: according to one survey, only 38 per cent of young people now think wine is essential to health. Giscard in 1979 gave a new boost to the commission's work by appointing a 'Monsieur Anti-Alcohol', an expert charged with devising a national strategy for the 1980s.

Several measures have been pushed through Parliament since the 1950s. One, strongly fought by the wine lobby, forbids cafés and restaurants to serve alcoholic drinks to minors under fourteen, or unaccompanied minors under sixteen: it is frequently winked at, notably in the case of wine or beer with meals, but it does limit the kind of thing that horrified me when I first lived in France, the sight of babes of two or three in cafés being given full glasses of undiluted wine by their parents. A newer law forbids the serving of spirits to under-eighteens. The frequency of cafés in new suburbs, and in the vicinity of schools, is also now severely restricted.

The problem is still huge, mainly in older slum districts and backward rural areas. You see few merry drunkards in the streets in France, because wine and *eau-de-vie* do not have that kind of effect, they strike deeper; and the French are heavy drinkers not so much through neurosis or unhappiness, like many Anglo-Saxons, but from sheer ancestral habit. It is reckoned that nearly a million French adult males drink more than two litres of red wine a day, and another three million drink more than the litre a day that the doctors concede as a safe maximum for a manual worker. Some two million adults are medically classifiable as alcoholics; two-thirds of mentally handicapped children are born of alcoholics; and 25 per cent of divorces and suicides, 40 per cent of juvenile delinquency, 50 per cent of cases of homicide are said to be due to alcoholism or excessive drinking. More than 37 per cent of the men and 14 per cent of the women in public hospitals are alcoholic cases. And yet, in a land where four million people derive their living from the wine and spirits trade, every step towards reform is strongly opposed. Often the wine lobby will invoke lofty national sentiments to defend its interests: 'It is wine that helped the French *poilu* to win the Great War,' said a deputy in Parliament. Such speakers often invoke the idyll of the innocent small farmer.

One dubious idyll is now definitely ending – that of the *bouilleurs de cru*, or home-distillers. Millions of farmers traditionally had the right to produce for their own consumption up to ten litres of tax-free *eau-de-vie* each year from their own fruit-trees or from the *marc* (pulp) of their wine-harvest. Many also distilled secretly a great deal more than this, and a total of some 400,000 hectolitres found its way illicitly on to the market each year, bringing tidy profits to all concerned. Mendès-France tried in vain to bring the *bouilleurs* to justice: he found the lobby against him too powerful. But in 1960 the Gaullists managed to steamroller through Parliament a law enabling them to decree that henceforth the home-distilling privilege would no longer be passed on by inheritance or sale of property, but must end with the death of its owner. So the privileged *bouilleurs* have been slowly dying out and are down from two million to 800,000. This has also greatly reduced the illicit distilling. Anyone with a few vines or fruit-trees still has the right to distil up to ten litres a year for family use, but he has to pay tax on it. In practice, as a cause of alcoholism, the problem now is only a marginal one.

Red wine, not *eau-de-vie* or other spirits, is by far the biggest source of alcoholism. And the scourge is worst, strangely enough, not in the vinegrowing regions of the Midi but in Brittany and the Nord where no vines grow but much cheap plonk is imported. In Brittany the alcoholic death-rate is eight times the national average, and many men drink a gallon of red wine a day. One problem is that, in poorer districts, much social and even economic life revolves round this habit: business transactions are regularly conducted over a litre of *rouge* in a café, and in one fishing-port a merchant navy doctor had to set up his surgery in a café.

Alcoholism is thus a different kind of problem in France from Britain or America. It is essentially linked to social backwardness in rural or slum areas, and is nourished by the cheapness of strong red *vin ordinaire*, still only two francs or so a bottle. Among sophisticated people, excessive drinking of whisky or cognac through stress or neurosis is less common than in many countries. So education, rehousing, the rural exodus and other factors are very slowly limiting the evil of their own accord. Already, in the middle classes, the convention that no meal is complete without wine is losing some of its force, and at lunch-time in restaurants you often see people sitting down with just mineral water. Since 1959 the consumption of mineral waters has almost trebled, and that of fruit juices has more than trebled. Fruit juice is twice as expensive per glass as cheap wine, which limits its sale in the poorer classes, but in the middle class this gives it a prestige appeal. Sales of many French aperitifs are lower than twenty years ago, except for *anis* drinks which have been making a come-back, helped by the dynamic publicity of the Ricard/Pernod firm. The biggest advances have been made by beer, whose consumption is up 70 per cent since 1959, and by the smart drinks – champagne and Scotch whisky. Sales of the latter have quadrupled in ten years: it is now the commonest aperitif in the middle classes, and workers are beginning to drink it too.

The sum of these trends suggest that the French, though they may not be drinking much less than before, are at least turning from fire-waters to less destructive drinks. The average quality of wines drunk is improving. No one, or hardly anyone, demands that the French become teetotal – this has never been the aim of the anti-alcoholism campaigns. No one denies that the great wines of France are among her foremost gifts to civilization. But there is a world of difference between half-a-bottle of claret enjoyed over a good meal and the Breton hospital wards overflowing with cirrhosis cases and mental defectives. Yet the problem of alcoholism will take a long time to solve. Whereas in the 1960s and early '70s the young were drinking less than their elders, since the mid-'70s there have been signs that a new generation of youth – mainly students and the unemployed – are turning back to heavier consumption of cheap wine, as a solace in their anxieties. 'If you want to get stoned, at least it's less damaging than taking drugs,' is a common remark. In the next chapter we shall look at the youth of France today, and the education system they have to endure.

CATHOLICS: THE CHURCH DECLINES,
BUT RELIGION REVIVES

Nothing reflects more vividly the post-war shift in values than the transformation of Catholicism in France. This has been as striking as anywhere in Europe. In a word, the authority of the Church as an institution is crumbling, yet a new-style liberated spirit of religion is very much alive, and takes the most diverse forms. On the one hand, regular attendance at Mass is down to 14 per cent of the population, the priesthood is alarmingly short of new recruits, the parish priest's traditional influence has been waning, and most people in practice are quite pagan. But, among those who do believe, there has been a re-examining and sharpening of faith, and a major shift of emphasis away from old-style pious liturgy and towards social action and private prayer. The Church, from being a central pillar of society, has come more to resemble a loose network of semi-autonomous groups, militants in the midst of a largely irreligious nation, and priests and laity alike are splintered into highly varied tendencies. While some priests flirt with Marxism, others return to the purest dogmas of integrism, insisting on the Mass in Latin. While some preach and even practise sexual freedom, others fiercely denounce the abortion reforms. And lay Catholics have been forming their own groups, for prayer, fellowship and social service, where the priest as spiritual leader seems an irrelevance. In the face of these diverse threats to its authority and its unity, the bewildered French Episcopate makes sporadic attempts to re-assert itself, but with no great success. The bishops themselves are divided: torn between an obedience to Rome and their sympathy, in many cases, for the new movements which are far removed from the teaching of Pope John-Paul II.

The first major change took place in the early post-war years when the Church at all levels – from bishops to laity – began to shift Leftwards and to concern itself with social issues. In the context of the pre-1944 history of the Church in France, this was a startling new departure. Although since 1905 the State has been secular and the Church disestablished, until far more recently its hierarchy identified itself closely with the ruling upper-bourgeois class and protected its interests by defending the social *status quo*. In rural areas priest and gentry were natural allies. The Church was ultra-clerical, allowing little scope for lay action, and expecting its priests to be obeyed; and it inspired bitter anti-clericalism. The Church also was anti-temporal, concerned exclusively with spiritual, not social, welfare. Yet it did dabble in politics. Many bishops collaborated under the Occupation, or at least lifted no finger to help the Resistance. So the Catholic element in the Resistance passed into the hands of lay leaders.

However, even in the 1930s the Church was not monolithic in its Right-wing stance. Forces were at work which formed the Christian trade union, CTFC (forerunner of today's CFDT: see p. 111), and started young workers' movements, the Jeunesse Ouvrière Chrétienne and the Jeunesse Agricole Chrétienne. Then in 1943 a parish priest, Abbé Godin, published an epoch-making book, *France, pays de mission*, which for the first time openly faced up to the truth that France was no longer a Christian but a pagan country, and the Church must alter its ways radically to meet this situation. Soon a new *Mission de France* was active, whose priests took an oath to 'devote their lives to the re-christianization of the working class'. In 1944 many bishops and priests emerged discredited from the Occupation: old-style clericalism received the heaviest blow to its prestige since Dreyfus, and the way was open for the rise in influence of other bishops, the liberals. In this new climate, the *Mission de France* embarked on that dramatic Christian experiment: the worker-priests. About a hundred priests took factory jobs, sharing the workers' lives and dress. The aim was partly to preach Christian example, partly to discover what the alienated working class was really like, and so bridge the gulf of ignorance separating it from the bourgeois Church. And so disturbed were the priests by this experience that some fell under Marxist influence and began to militate in the CGT. The Vatican (under Pius XII) grew worried, and in 1954 it suspended the worker-priest experiment, despite pleas from some French bishops to let it continue.

The worker-priests were no more than a small commando unit within a much wider neo-Catholic movement which gathered strength after the Liberation and was to play a big part in the reshaping of post-war France. Much of the impulse came from the laity. Many Catholics, especially younger ones, felt that it was time for the Church to broaden its role and to share in building a better world; and with their ardent faith they set about this task. Look closely at any of the grass-roots movements of post-war social reform, and in nearly every case you will find that some nucleus of Catholic militants played a central role: the farming revolution led by the JAC was the obvious example (see pp. 208–21), but there were many others too, in business, industry and civic life, and even in the campaign for birth-control. These neo-Catholics, as they were called, were influenced by Teilhard de Chardin and his optimistic world-loving, and even more by Emmanuel Mounier, founder of the review *Esprit* and one of the boldest early advocates of the need for the Church and all Christians to engage in improving the world. The neo-Catholics, you might say, were the spiritual leaven in the material modernization of France.

This new militant social Christian action took many forms. Michel Debatisse in farming, and Edouard Leclerc in commerce, were two of its most successful pioneers in the 1950s. Neo-Catholics also took leading roles in the CFDT, and in the Centre des Jeunes Patrons, the liberal pressure-group within the Patronat, as well as in bodies such as the Plan. 'We animate a large part of the upper civil service,' one Catholic told me triumphantly, as if announcing the success of some bloodless *Putsch*. And according to one estimate, by 1965 over half the mayors of France were ex-JACists or ex-JOCists. In one country town a priest told me, 'Young Catholics have been trying to widen their faith by asking what God expects of them in their daily life and work. They now feel it's more important to aid the community than not to eat meat on Friday.' Right from the beginning a number of priests and bishops were eagerly involved in this new movement. Many of the older ones remained wary at first, but steadily more of them joined, within the framework of a wide new pressure-group, Action Catholique – 'We are now working,' someone said, 'to build the Kingdom of God on earth – something that the Church never used to care much about.'

Many of the more radical figures in the new movement, priests and laity alike, began to develop close collaboration with Marxists. These were the two most dynamic ideological groups in the France of the 1950s and '60s, and they had a weird respect and fascination for each other. I am not referring to the old Stalinist diehards within the Party, nor to Sartre and his circle, but to some of the thousands of other active Marxists in France, doctors, teachers, trade-unionists and the like, many of them open-minded and pragmatic, some Communist, some Socialist, some without party label. Like the neo-Catholics they were frequently notable for their energy, dedication and urge towards practical social action; and when the two of them met, they often felt more common ground with each other than either had, respectively, with old-style Catholics or with Stalinists. This kind of field collaboration had started in the Resistance. Jean-Marie Domenach, editor of *Esprit*, told me in 1965: 'Whenever at grass-roots level you find disinterested individuals actually doing voluntary social work in France, they are nearly always Catholics or Marxists. Recently we ran an enquiry into handicapped children, and we found that nearly all the people helping in this field were militants of one group or the other.' In a poor district of Paris, I found Catholic and Marxist doctors working in harmony in a campaign to combat mental disease and alcoholism. In the intellectual field too, both sides made efforts to get together and exchange ideas. Catholics and Marxists each held national study-conferences and invited the others to take part in these debates. A motive force behind these was the unorthodox Communist philosopher Roger Garaudy, admirer of Teilhard de Chardin, who tried to explore common ground between

Christians and Marxists in these debates. Sceptics doubted whether these exchanges really added up to much – 'These people are making a false synthesis of the two ideologies, based on sloppy wishful thinking,' said one critic. Perhaps in rationalist terms this was true. But if the contacts helped each side to understand the other's point of view, they had a practical usefulness.

Only one element of Action Catholique was on the Left, but it was an important one, with Dominicans playing a key role. Their best-known leader, Père Jean Cardonnel, told me: 'We are trying to deconfessionalize and declericalize the faith. Lots of unbelievers come to my Mass, because I adapt Christ's teaching to modern life, in their own language.' He would advise his listeners to read *Das Kapital* as the best commentary on Christ's teaching, 'Thou shall not serve God and Mammon'. This tendency increased after May '68. Some priests, influenced by the militant students and workers, began to form little groups describing themselves as '*les prêtres contestataires*'. Some had political aims: the '*Echanges et Dialogues*' movement born of 1968 included nearly a thousand Left-wing priests dedicated to 'the liberation of Christianity from the Church' which they regarded as still a tool of the bourgeoisie. Many had factory jobs and never wore clerical clothes. These and others felt that the traditional role of the priesthood was now out of date: a priest must be more than 'a purveyor of sacraments', he could no longer hide behind the mystic authority of his calling, but must go out and mix with ordinary people on equal terms. Many priests began to refuse to fulfil the Church's traditional role: some would not marry their parishioners in church or baptize their children unless they were sure they were sincere believers.

The Episcopate, although worried, treated these trends with a certain tolerance. The Episcopate itself, after some years of hesitation, had in the 1960s increasingly swung its weight behind the liberal Catholic movement in France and was influenced by it. Although the bishops were not as *avant-garde* as the militants, they were in advance of the older rank-and-file clergy and the older pious masses – and it was this conservative element that became alarmed at the post-'68 trends. 'Priests don't talk about God any more, they talk about the housing crisis,' complained one old lady, while many older priests feared that Christ himself was being overlooked amid all the new secular zeal for social progress, and that the flight from orthodox piety and ritual might go too far. So it is little surprise that the neo-Catholic movement has provoked a virulent Right-wing reaction to it in certain Christian circles, and this too has been worrying the hierarchy. The tradition of integrism is dying in France, but not without a last-ditch fight: a Catholic paper *Le Monde et la Vie* was still selling 200,000 copies a month in 1968, and its pages were horrifying: long eulogies of Pétain and wartime Catholic fascists, savage attacks on worker-priest ideals or any form of dialogue with non-believers. This purist minority is particularly angry at recent changes in the liturgy. Mass is now celebrated in French, not Latin, and often there is hymn-singing. In some conservative areas, the pious have marked their displeasure at all this by pointedly continuing to make their responses in Latin. These unreconciled integrists represent only a small proportion of practising Catholics; they are far fewer in number than those who can be classed as neo-Catholics. But they are vocal and well-organized.

In the summer of 1976 an international scandal broke out when France's most notorious integrist priest, seventy-year-old Monseigneur Marcel Lefebvre, former Archbishop of Dakar, openly challenged Pope Paul VI. Five years earlier Lefebvre had set up his own 'traditionalist' seminary in Switzerland, where he set about training young men on integrist lines. In 1976, against the express orders of the Pope, he ordained thirteen of them as priests. The Pope replied by suspending Lefebvre, thus forbidding him to say Mass or administer the sacraments. Lefebvre then lashed out, as he had often before, claiming that the liberal reforms since Vatican Council II were 'a huge enterprise of self-destruction ... of tradition, religious teaching, the liturgy, the priesthood'. He planned to continue saying the Mass in Latin. In August, he held a rally in Lille attended by 7,000 integrists from all over Europe, and made a speech claiming that the Church was flirting dangerously with Communism.

The Vatican was embarrassed, but it has shrunk back from excommunicating the rebel. This would have encouraged him to set up his 'parallel Church', thus creating a damaging schism. Instead, the Church turns a blind eye while Lefebvre and his followers continue to say their Mass in Latin at their church in Paris, and Lefebvre continues to ordain his own priests. The French hierarchy and clergy as a whole are firmly against him: but they do not regard him as too serious a threat, for his support, though it is hardening, is also narrowing. Only 10 per cent of Catholics support him, according to opinion polls. His has been the most violent integrist backlash so far, but it would appear to be doomed in the long term. There is wider support for another, milder movement called *'Les Silencieux de l'Eglise'*, formed in the wake of 1968 to protect what it sees as the Church's 'silent majority' against the incursion of Leftist and modernist values. Its leaders are strongly against abortion, contraception, and priests who flirt with Marxism; but they are less worried about changes in liturgy and are not openly defying Rome. They have quite a following, especially among older Catholics.

Today an uneasy calm reigns in the Church. The stormy confrontations of the post-1968 period have died down, giving way to a tolerant diversity where multiple different tendencies coexist. Each priest follows his own style, doing very much what he likes; and the hierarchy keeps a fairly low profile, allowing both priests and laity a degree of liberty. As in French society as a whole, it is a confused, fragmented situation, where the old authority has declined and no sure system has taken its place.

On the one hand, the slow decline in the influence of the Church continues, as in many other Western countries. Although a high percentage of people still pay lip-service to Christianity through social convention (some 80 per cent are still baptized, including many infants of Communist voters), most of them neglect it entirely except at the crucial moments of christening, marriage and burial. In the middle classes, weekly church-going as a family status-symbol has fallen off, though more in Paris than in small towns. Overall figures for weekly attendance at Mass are still slowly declining, as they have been for decades. The figure is now 14 per cent nationally and 10 per cent in Paris; and though in traditionalist rural areas like the Vendée, it may reach 80 per cent, in industrial centres it can drop to 4 or 5 per cent. The Church has lost touch with its popular roots much more than in stronger Catholic countries such as Italy or Ireland, and one major cause of this has been the rural exodus: 'The Breton émigré loses his religion as soon as he steps down at the Gare Montparnasse,' said one observer. Even more serious, atheism is still spreading. According to one survey, the percentage of people claiming to believe in God has fallen since 1968 from 74 to 65, and the drop is sharpest among the young. Church leaders are acutely worried.

The weakening of clericalism has at least been followed by a softening of anti-clericalism too. And so the sharpest of all the feuds that have torn France in the past hundred years is fading into history. In a few country districts it may linger on, where villages are still ranged into two camps, behind the *curé* or the teacher: but in most regions the old quarrels between *Rouges* and *Blancs* have come to seem as much a part of folklore as horse-drawn carriages or country-dancing. The young generation isn't worried any more.[3]

The churches may still be emptying, but new more informal styles of worship are now in vogue, a trend not confined to France. This disturbs the more traditional priests, but not the modern ones. A Catholic Action *curé* in a country town told me: 'I know many young Christians here who hardly ever go to Mass and care little for the sacraments, but they seek to

3 However, the old issue of State aid for Church schools has now been revived by the Socialist Government: see pp. 490–91.

practise their faith in their daily lives, through private prayer, and through social work. Religion is no longer a matter of social convention but of real conviction, and so it is now more sincere.' Another observer said, 'A young man's faith is no longer so "protected" by the environment of family and parish. It has to pass through the ordeal of contact with atheism, and if it survives, it may be more real than in the old days.'

While social action continues as in the 1960s, simultaneously many people are now turning back to the true spiritual sources of Christianity, to the fundamentals of prayer and worship. In some cases this is due to a feeling that social action for its own sake had gone too far and that Christ was in danger of being forgotten. Or else it is that in this new age of crisis and anxiety people feel a greater need for spiritual consolation. At any rate, the trend is widespread: it does not, however, take the form of a return to traditional church services. Retreats, prayer groups, lay communities are more popular. Like some other countries, France has seen the rise of the so-called 'charismatic' movement, whereby informal groups meet regularly for prayer and discussion, often in private homes. In a Paris flat, people of all kinds may get together and sit cross-legged on the floor: a middle-aged priest, a scientist, a teacher, several immigrant workers, and students. First they will celebrate Mass very informally, then pray for more than an hour, read from the Bible, make cries of joy and thanksgiving, and sing modern hymns to a guitar. It is all vaguely revivalist, very different from old-style Catholic worship. Very often no priest is present. And the prayers are spontaneous, expressed in daily language, a complete break with the ritual rosary-type prayers of Catholic tradition.

The post-1968 period has also seen the rise of a number of religious communities of a new kind, often formed by laymen who find the traditional parish context inadequate. These are not enclosed and tightly disciplined centres like the old monasteries, but informal meeting-places where laymen can come together in their leisure time, maybe under the guidance of a priest, or maybe not. One or two of these new communities have gone far in experimenting with a new liberated form of religion. This was true notably of the notorious Boquen community in Brittany, led by a homosexual priest, Abbé Bernard Besret, who encouraged a high degree of sexual liberty, for himself and others, at his monastic centre. He was finally obliged to leave, and went to the United States where his particular style of Christianity can perhaps more easily find its place. But other communities continue, more soberly. They, and the charismatic groups, represent a new desire of laity and priests alike for more self-expression, for finding their own personal ways to God and to Christ, and for asserting the right to ignore the dogmas hitherto imposed by a Church expecting obedience. This is a typical symptom of the new post-1968 desire of the French to contest established authority. And the Church hierarchy has reacted warily. Some bishops are dismayed at these new lay movements which largely escape their control and their doctrine, and which seem to be by-passing the Church in finding their own paths to God. But the hierarchy on the whole accepts the inevitable, and the wiser bishops recognize the positive elements in the new trends.

Catholic Action today still plays a considerable role in France, but less so than in the earlier post-war days. Organizations such as the JAC no longer attract young people as they used to do. However, the various Left-wing movements among priests continue vigorously, though they are rather less militant than in the immediate post-May '68 period. One important development is that there has been a big move to the Left in previously staunchly Right-wing Catholic areas such as Lorraine and Brittany. Here many priests now vote for the Socialist Party, something unimaginable only twenty years ago. The Left-wing movements among priests and laity take various forms. Today there are several Leftish Catholic organizations that stress the need for closer links between Christians and the pagan working milieu. One is the magazine *Témoignage Chrétien*, very *progressiste*, which was upbraided by the hierarchy for publishing an article by a Communist leader. Another body is *Vie Nouvelle*, inter-ideological rather than purely Christian, a sort of intellectual boy-scout movement linking Catholics, Protestants, Marxists, rationalists and others. In Montpellier one of its leaders is Père Cardonnel who told me how he enjoyed holding public debates with prominent local atheists and touring the villages on joint preaching missions with Protestant colleagues. 'Young people welcome us,' he told me, 'but many of the older bourgeois are shocked. You see, normally in Montpellier the *haute société catholique* and *haute société protestante* just don't mix.' Oecumenical links with France's 3 per cent Protestant minority are much in vogue among the neo-Catholics; there are numerous joint youth movements and church services, all over France, and the Protestants have been playing their own willing part in the *rapprochement*, especially through the influence of their famous oecumenical centre at Taizé.

Relations with Protestants may be close: but the dialogue with the Marxists is very much less active than in the 1960s. It is not hard to see the reasons. The Communist Party has changed; it has moved back into its shell, and since 1977 is no longer so interested in trying to woo Christians or bridge the gulf. Marxism has grown distinctly out of fashion among French intellectuals, so that progressive Catholics too are far less inclined to do debate with Communists or others on this subject.

A few Catholic/Marxist seminars still take place, but they are only fringe activities. However, this does not mean that priests are shifting back to the Right: far from it. Opinion surveys since the late 1970s show that over 50 per cent of priests under forty are pro-Socialist; that six times as many priests of all ages find the Socialist Party closer to their evangelical ideals than the Gaullists; that 84 per cent of priests never wear the cassock; and that 86 per cent are against compulsory celibacy for the clergy. These figures are a startling indication of how far the French priesthood has evolved in the past two decades.

Many priests are actively concerned with trying to make a real contact with the working class, and they consider this more important than ministering to their more traditional bourgeois or rural parishioners. 'Our aim,' one Leftist priest told me, 'is to go among ordinary people, take an interest in their daily problems, identify with them, win their confidence, and show that God is concerned with the human condition here and now, not just with the hereafter, and that the Church is not an alien world.' So how do the workers react to these blandishments? It is a vital question to ask, but not easy to answer. Hitherto the working class has identified Christianity so firmly with the bourgeoisie that in some industrial areas for a worker to admit to being a Christian was like claiming to vote on the Right, a kind of betrayal. And the figures for Mass bore this out: in the middle classes, church-going was up to ten times as common as among workers. It is doubtful whether these figures have since altered more than marginally. But there are some signs of a thaw in attitudes: workers now more easily admit to being Christian, or having Christian friends.

This must be due in part to the worker-priest movement, which still continues in France even though it does not have the formal blessing of the Church. Pope John-Paul II is opposed to worker-priests, and so are some French bishops. But others will accept them, and are prepared to authorize them provided they operate discreetly. The situation thus varies greatly from one diocese to another: typical of the confused state of the Church in France today. There are estimated to be nearly 1,000 worker-priests, that is, ordained priests who choose to have a regular job in addition to their spiritual duties. And their relations with the more traditional kind of priest are often strained.

In the town of Montargis, seventy miles south of Paris, I found a dramatic example of this kind of divorce between two conceptions of the priesthood. The parish church has been taken over by a team of six worker-priests. But, in the adjacent suburb of Villemandeur, the parish is run by an elderly priest of the old school, Abbé Powet, no integrist but a conservative, who sticks to the Church's classic role of ministering to the sick, catechizing the young, and celebrating Mass in the normal way. He criticizes the Montargis worker-priests for devoting so much of their time and their energies to their paid jobs that they have little left over for the true spiritual duties of a priest; they accuse him in return of being out of touch with modern needs and of contenting himself with a small circle of believers, mainly middle class, and making no effort to go out and conquer new ground in this industrial area. The bourgeoisie of Montargis are furious that their own church has fallen victim to this 'Leftish *Putsch*', as one of them called it, and they go out to Villemandeur each Sunday, where they also send their children for catechism lessons. They have no truck with the worker-priests.

Of Montargis' worker-priests, two work in factories, one is a cleaner, one is a male nurse in a hospital (and it is said, cohabits with his mistress). They form a little commune in the presbytery, where there is hardly a crucifix in sight. The head of their group is a full-time priest aged about sixty, Abbé Gallerand, who impressed me with his cheerful, youthful alertness and optimism; Abbé Powet, by contrast, seemed lonely, sad and embittered, full of gloom about the future of the Church. Abbé Gallerand sports bright-coloured jerseys, holds jazz sessions in his church, and offers a special desacramentalized wedding service for atheists. He and his team are clearly popular: but one wonders whether the Christian baby is not going out with the progressive-Leftist bathwater.

Abbé Powet typifies the dilemma facing many older priests in traditional parishes, who wonder what will happen when they are gone. Powet gave me some astonishing statistics. In his diocese (Orléans), as many priests are over eighty years old as under forty (20 in each case); 48 are in their seventies, 63 in their sixties, 117 in their fifties, 44 in their forties. It is the same drama throughout France. Many seminaries have closed for lack of recruits, and today only 100 new priests are being ordained each year, against about 1,000 in the 1960s. The total number of priests, now 36,000, is expected to fall to 20,000 by 1995. And the problem is not simply a shortage of new entrants. A great many priests have left and gone into ordinary life, either because they have lost their faith, or in a few cases because they wish to marry. There is a growing feeling among French Catholics that the Church will sooner or later waive the celibacy rule: but clearly it is not going to happen under the present Pope.

The hierarchy of the Church in France has reacted warily to the new trends. It has swung some way to the Left since the war, and recently under Giscard it came out strongly in favour of more social equality, against the death penalty, and so on. Thus on social issues it projects, sincerely, a liberal image. At the same time, partly under Vatican influence, it is now adopting a much tougher line on abortion, birth-control, pre-marital sex, and even divorce. In the eyes of many lay Catholics, and non-believers, this seems inconsistent. But the hierarchy, while obediently preaching these doctrines, makes relatively little attempt to reassert its authority over a Catholic world that in France is increasingly disparate and free to go its own diverse ways. The hierarchy keeps a low profile, and allows priests to do more or less as they wish, unless they too blatantly step out of line, for example by ostentatiously parading their mistresses. In this case, the bishops may reassert themselves, and the offending priest is banished. But such showdowns are rare. When Pope John-Paul II paid a much-publicized official visit to France in 1980 (the first by any Pope since Napoleon's day), it was widely expected that he would demand of the French bishops – always considered far too lax by Rome – that they move on to the offensive against unorthodoxy. But it does not seem to have happened. So the French hierarchy remains enfeebled and cautious. Its problem, like that of the Vatican, is that its doctrines are no longer in tune with the actual behaviour of the majority of Catholics. The Church may preach against birth-control, yet most younger Catholics practise it and do not find it inconsistent with their Christian faith. Maybe this is the dilemma of the Church throughout the West today, but in France it is especially sharp. It seems that the Church as a formal institution is likely to see a further steady decline in its power and its authority. But this may not signify any waning of real Christian belief. In this age of uncertainty, more and more people may turn to the new charismatic groups, the new little circles of Catholic social action, which include many Socialists. This fragmentation is typical of French society today. So the individual has more freedom and choice, but is bereft of the old framework of security and moral discipline.

FOREIGNERS: GERMANS ARE NOW WELCOME, ALGERIANS LESS SO

French attitudes to foreigners, and to the world at large, rest on a paradox. The French have the reputation of being a proud, nationalistic people. And yet, they are markedly less insular than in the old days, more open to outside influences, more aware of belonging to a wider community. True, France in her official foreign policy has long been a champion at the pursuit of national self-interest, alike under Giscard and de Gaulle. Yet in personal terms I doubt that the French are any more xenophobic than the average nation. Since the early 1960s there has been a waning of the old ideal of _la gloire française_, of which de Gaulle was the last, anachronistic upholder. Today the Army has crept away humbly on to the sidelines of national life, its old glory tarnished by the Algerian *débâcle*. When the bugles sound and the flags wave on the *Quatorze Juillet*, the nation may still, out of old habit, stand to attention with a tear in its eye: but these rituals are losing their meaning. Older people perhaps will feel nostalgic: but the vast majority of younger ones have little sense of this kind of patriotism. *La patrie* is one of those traditional values that have been losing ground.

Of course the French are still glad to be French and proud of their way of life, just like the British. But there is a difference between the way these two peoples view the world. In a word, the French are more *chauvinistic*, the British more *insular*. The French feel sharply competitive towards other nations, sometimes jealous of them, sometimes scornful, but at least vividly aware of their existence; the British still cannot quite believe they are real, save for some English-speaking lands that share their culture. One has only to compare the two nations' attitudes to the EEC, where the French eagerly cooperate, for their own ends, while the British remain uneasy semi-outsiders. Plenty of examples can be found, too, in daily life. International sporting or cultural events tend to be under-reported by the British media: in the French media they get fuller coverage, but with huge emphasis on the French role. All this marks a change from pre-war days when the French, too, were enclosed behind their frontiers. But today, sometimes arrogant, sometimes defensively prickly, they are always trying to score points off other nations. This assertive competitiveness can be tiresome, yet it seems to be more healthy and realistic than the British attitude. A Frenchman may remain convinced of the virtues of his own way of life, but at least he regards, say, a Swede's or an Italian's as offering some comparison: he may feel superior to other peoples, but not fundamentally *different*, so, when he wishes to, he can easily make contact. If any last strongholds remain of old-style French insularity, they are found most often among hard-core Paris intellectuals, who shy from facing up to the truth that French culture has lost its universality. But the middle class as a whole, which rarely used to venture abroad, has now become a tribe of travellers, not only as tourists, but as explorers, exporters, students, or technicians in the Third World. For all their latent chauvinism, the French do seem to think of themselves in terms of a wider community, and in conversation will often talk of 'we in the West or 'we in Europe' where an Englishman may still say 'we in Britain'.

The greatest change since the war has been in French attitudes to Germany. Here the ferment began soon after 1945, in shocked reaction against the futility of three Franco-German tragedies in eighty years; and it was encouraged by an even sharper change of mood on the German side. Today the hatchet is firmly buried: only among a proportion of French Jews and of older French people, those who suffered directly at Nazi hands, is there any residue of the old hatreds. And this generation is now dying out. Over six hundred French towns are now happily twinned with German ones, while scores of thousands of young French and Germans cross the Rhine each year in youth exchanges, and for this newer generation the old fear of *les Boches* has faded into history. I would not say that older French people always like the Germans as individuals (often they prefer the English), but they feel admiration for the German qualities, and a desire to work along with the better elements in the new Germany: a doctor in his sixties told me, 'I fought in the Resistance and was bitterly anti-Nazi, but now I'm pro-German, I feel they've changed completely. After all, the war was so long ago . . .' – a common view today. In an opinion poll published by *l'Express* in 1979, in answer to the question, 'Which country do you consider the best friend of France?', Germany came easily first with 33 per cent, well ahead of the US (22 per cent) and Britain (16 per cent). It is true that in the past decade a new kind of anti-German feeling has appeared among some younger people on the Left, orchestrated by *gauchiste* groups and by the Communist Party. But this is not related to the Nazi past, nor is it aimed at the Germans as individuals: its target is the new rich Germany as an epitome of American-style capitalism, and as a powerful rival that threatens the French economy. Happily, this new trend does not have wide influence. German students at French universities sense very little personal hostility towards them.

Relations with Germany are in many ways closer than with Britain, and this is true on a human as well as an economic level. The British may be preferred as individuals, but they remain a mystery. A girl *lycée* teacher told me, 'The British have more *finesse* and humour than the Germans, but I don't understand them in the same way. Those yachting types who come to Cherbourg where I live are so aloof, they make me uneasy.' A young Parisian said, '*L'Allemand, c'est un con, mais un bon con. Les Anglais, ils sont trop differents de nous,*' while a student in Toulouse added, 'Young Germans may sometimes be arrogant, but they're outward-going, generous, interested, eager to get to know us: the British are too reserved and self-absorbed.' So there is an odd paradox about attitudes to Britain. On the one hand, things English have a certain snob-appeal. The upper classes have long considered it *de bon ton* to import their Savile Row suits, whiskies and nursemaids from Britain, and to cultivate English milords, while since the early '60s English pop music, clothes and slang have been in vogue with teenagers. The French, monarchists at heart, have always adored British royalty. Yet this anglomania remains curiously superficial: seldom does it relate to any deeper curiosity about what British society is really like, or how it has changed, or how it might be relevant to France. Many French still cherish an admiration for British justice and democracy, for what they call *le fair-play anglais*: but even this is now tempered by a contempt for the British over their industrial failures, trade-union troubles, laziness, and waning influence in the world. And to this is now added an irritation over what is seen as British obstructionism in the EEC. De Gaulle, so many people feel, was right all along: Britain should never have been allowed to join.

French clichés and misconceived ideas about British life remain even stronger than British ones about France. There is the old Major Thompson-rolled-umbrellas-fog-and-crumpets image, which persists, and there is the newer Beatles image, but between the two there is a void. And the French show little interest in filling the void: Britain is quaint and colourful but not 'real' to them in the way that China, America, Africa are real. And yet, those French who go to stay or live in Britain and make true British friends are usually delighted: there is a small but solid core of real anglophiles, just as there are francophiles in Britain. But these anglophiles are often the ones most aware of British 'differentness', and keenest to see it preserved. Henri Dougier, a liberal journalist who has lived in London, said to me, 'I get on easily with all Europeans, but the British are the ones I like best – they're the most human, gentle and individual. Theirs is the most civilized society of all. But they're not true Europeans, and never will be. For their sakes, and for ours, I see their role as outside the EEC.' The French see Britain as such a special case that even its best features have little validity as a model to be copied or rivalled. You can try to imitate German punctuality, or American cost-accounting, but not English self-mockery or a constitution that has no written rules!

Yet there are other societies that fascinate the French as valid challenges to their own: Scandinavia, Israel, Germany, even China, and of course the United States. Up until the late 1960s or so, the French were full of complexes about America. Her economic dominance was feared, her wealth resented, her policies criticized (especially during the Vietnam war), and her naïve tourists and brash commercialism were held in contempt; yet the French went on blindly copying many of those aspects of America they affected to despise. Today, they have settled down to a much more balanced attitude. They are now less afraid of American 'colonization', and they feel more able to look Americans in the eye as something like equals, now that Europe has narrowed the gap in terms of affluence and economic influence. The buying back of Simca from Chrysler in 1978 seemed a portent of this change. At the same time, France has succumbed less than was feared fifteen years ago, and less than some of her neighbours, to the sillier aspects of so-called 'Americanization': she has preserved her national style. So individual Americans are now accepted more warmly in France, and the Yankee tourist is no longer a figure of scorn cum-envy. In this new climate, the French are still ready and eager to learn from America, both materially and socially; but they want to do so on their own terms. Like other Europeans, they are now beginning to visit the United States *en masse* as tourists, and are gratified to find a country that after all is no glossy futurist paradise but full of ordinary folk muddling through – not so very different from Europe, only tattier.

In the early post-war decades a new and genuine feeling for Europe began to replace the old French nationalism, and many a Frenchman would express his faith in the ideal of a United Europe. More recently, as in other member countries, the EEC as such has lost popularity. People on the far Left think it too capitalist; pro-Europeans lament the loss of its earlier drive and vision. And yet, with all its faults, the EEC today is accepted as part of the landscape: very few people, save on the extremes of Right and Left, call for French withdrawal or question the need for France and her neighbours to stick together. This is simply not an issue, as it is in Britain. According to an official EEC opinion survey in 1979, 56 per cent of Frenchmen thought membership 'good' for their country, 8 per cent thought it 'bad', and the rest were not sure. In Britain, the percentages were 33 'good', 34 'bad'; in Germany, 66 'good', 5 'bad'; in Italy, 78 'good', 2 'bad'; in Holland, 84 'good', 2 'bad'. So the French are not as fervently 'European' as some: not many of them today wish supranationalism to go much further. Yet you can still find a number of dedicated idealists around, such as the businessman who told me, 'If we fail to create a true federated Europe, we'll go back to the 1930s. It may take fifty years, but it's still an exciting challenge.'[4]

It is true that the past few years have seen a slight resurgence of nationalism and insularity in France; as in other countries, this seems to be the result of economic crisis, especially high unemployment, which revives old protectionist instincts and draws people back to the security of their own known milieu, another aspect of the *repli sur soi*. It has even led to a few xenophobic outbursts against European visitors to France. In Alsace, there is some resentment against German trippers for flocking

4 For young people's attitude to Europe, see p. 525.

over in hordes, arrogantly splashing their money around, and buying up many of the choicest sites for holiday homes. Even the mild and usually discreet Dutch come in for criticism too, but their sin is the opposite one: not spending enough. Some parts of the Massif Central and Provence are today heavily colonized in summer by Dutch tourists, who buy tracts of land, construct villas and camping sites there, but then bring all their own provisions on holiday with them and shun the local shops. So they add nothing, it is felt, to the local economy, and this makes them unpopular. In some places, Dutch tourists have been physically assaulted by gangs of French youths.

It would be wrong to over-estimate these trends. Happily, they do not appear to be directed against foreigners *as such*, but only against foreigners who arrive *en masse*, behave tactlessly, and pose what is seen as some kind of threat. On the whole, the political tensions within the EEC in recent years seem to have done remarkably little damage to personal and cultural links between countries, and this applies even to Franco-British relations. Despite the endless in-fighting between Whitehall and Paris since 1974, tourism between the two nations has increased, and the number of Franco-British town-twinnings has risen since 1972 from 150 to over 300. Many of these twin-towns keep up active exchanges, involving not only mayors and other dignitaries, but also schoolkids, football teams, amateur choirs, firemen, policemen, and so on – and often the atmosphere is euphoric. The total numbers involved may be relatively small, but the moral is clear: once the British and French *do* bother to try to get to know each other, and stay in each other's homes, they nearly always end up friends, and the silly prejudices fade away. Ignorance is the only enemy.

There has also been a striking change, within the past ten years, in French attitudes towards speaking other languages, notably English. As theirs was formerly the leading world language of diplomacy and culture, the French are naturally resentful at the way it has been overtaken by English; and until recently French public servants were forbidden to speak in any other language at international meetings. But now the French have more-or-less decided, 'If you can't lick 'em, join 'em.' They recognize, regretfully, that in the interests of promoting their foreign trade and their position in the world, they have no choice but to use the world's leading language of today, as everyone else is doing. A turning point came in May 1974, when Giscard on the night of his election victory made a speech for the foreign TV networks in his fluent English. Some French diehards were shocked, and de Gaulle must have turned in his grave. But it was official recognition of the fact that to speak English was now not merely allowed, it was encouraged. For some years now, foreign language classes have been compulsory in universities and at most school levels, and 83 per cent of pupils make English their first choice; at the same time, the in-service training schemes introduced into factories and offices since 1971 have brought many thousands of young executives and secretaries into the language-labs for crash-courses. As a result, the average young educated Frenchman today speaks reasonable English, as he would not have done ten years ago. I have no statistics, but the number of French with fluent English must have at least trebled in that time. Often, of course, they will still prefer to speak French when they can, especially on their own soil: but faced with a foreigner who can only mumble a few words of bad French, they will no longer pretend to know no English, as many once did.

French attitudes to the Third World are equivocal. France spends large sums on overseas aid, mainly to her former colonies in francophone Africa. And I would say that individually the French are as ready as any Western people to play their part in helping poorer countries: many thousands of teachers, doctors, technicians and others work abroad on aid schemes. But, within France itself, the mass public has recently become rather less generous towards the sizeable coloured minorities in its midst. France, like Germany, has relied heavily on immigrants to provide the manual labour for its 'economic miracle', and of the 4.1 million foreigners in France today, 1.8 million are in jobs, representing 10.5 per cent of the total workforce. Some 90 per cent of these are ordinary workers. The largest single foreign group are the Portuguese (866,000), while Italians (483,000) and Spaniards (445,000) are also numerous. These Latins are accepted easily. But, unsurprisingly, the problem lies in frictions with the coloured immigrants, nearly all of them North African, led by the Algerians (780,000), Moroccans (400,000) and Tunisians (180,000).

The French are not especially colour-conscious, probably less so than Anglo-Saxons. And until recently the North African minorities coexisted quite easily with the French. They usually lived in poor conditions, and they were certainly not encouraged to integrate socially: but they were left alone and tensions were few, even in the difficult time of the Algerian war. Today, however, as in Germany, Britain and elsewhere, rising unemployment has worsened the climate. Foreigners are accused of taking jobs from the French, and coloured foreigners, being the most conspicuous and different, bear the brunt. It is a little illogical, since many Arabs are doing the really menial and unpleasant jobs that the French, even today, refuse to take on. However, Giscard's Government reacted to the dangers of the situation. From 1974 it put a virtual ban on new immigrant labour – though no more so than other West European countries – and in 1976 it began trying to bribe foreign workers to go home by offering 10,000 francs to any ready to do so. But this scheme did not meet with great success. In 1977–80 the foreign population fell by only 112,000, under 3 per cent. Then the new Socialist Government, with sound anti-racist motives, took some steps to ease the curbs on immigration even at the risk of aggravating unemployment. In particular, it offered to regularize the position of the estimated 300,000 illegal immigrants working in France with false papers.

Many North Africans have lived in France for some decades: they have their families with them, and their children grew up in France – like the West Indians in Britain. In the days of the housing shortage they lived segregated in grim shanty-towns. Nowadays most of them are housed properly in HLM flats, but this in turn creates new social problems, for the French often dislike having them as neighbours, and complain endlessly at their cooking smells, their rowdy kids, the untidiness, the broken lifts. So the French tend, when they can, to move out from blocks where the Muslim population has risen above a certain level, with the result that some housing estates have become virtual Arab ghettos. The French in their mass have never thought highly of their former colonial subjects in North Africa – *'les bicots'* ('wogs') is the contemptuous slang term for them – and now economic crisis has refuelled this latent racist prejudice, which has led even to sporadic beatings-up of Arabs by gangs of French working-class youths. In the winter of 1980–81 the Communist Party cynically tried to exploit this growing racist feeling among 'poor whites' (its own potential voters), and there was quite a rumpus when a few PCF mayors in the Paris Red Belt began to victimize Arab and African residents. Indeed very few French town councils either Right or Left have ever done much to help their Arab minorities to integrate or feel at home. Dubedout's Grenoble is a shining exception: here the council has gone out of its way to see that Arabs are decently housed, to cater for their own cultural needs, to provide them with special education. But even here, attempts at integration have failed (see pp. 311–13). Throughout France, the Arabs have never been made socially welcome – one Algerian worker in a Paris suburb said that in twenty-six years he had never once been invited inside a French home – and now they are made to feel positively unwelcome. Yet many of the younger men and girls were born in France, and might feel equally out of place back in Algeria. They have the sense of being stranded between two cultures.

The Blacks in France, mostly from such places as Senegal and Martinique, are far fewer than the Arabs and far less unpopular. The

French find them more friendly and easy-going, with a more emancipated attitude to women. Moreover, those living in France tend to be educated and middle-class, whereas the Arabs are a proletariat. Yet even against Blacks and Asians there is some colour prejudice. Racian discrimination is illegal, and the French may pride themselves on racial tolerance: yet there are quite a number of landlords who will not let a room to a black or brown face. In Toulouse, a suave Lebanese told me, 'I am pale and can pass for French. I found a nice room, but when I told my landlord-to-be my name, he said, "Sorry, it's let after all".' But these attitudes are not unique to France: colour prejudice of this kind is worse in Germany, and possibly just as bad in Britain.

The European minorities who have settled in France – Italians, Spaniards, Poles and others – are accepted and respected far more warmly than before the war, when nearly all foreigners were eyed with some suspicion. So you might say this is a step forward: as one Frenchman put it, 'Generalized xenophobia has now narrowed down to racism – are we to call that progress?' Today the Portuguese workers, nearly always industrious and well-behaved, are especially well liked and so are most other Latins (though the French have reservations about Sicilians). Few Europeans have difficulty in integrating socially if they wish to do so. And France continues her long and honourable tradition of granting asylum to political refugees, who today number 198,000. They include survivors of the White Russian exodus of *c.* 1920, as well as Jewish and other émigrés from Eastern Europe, and the more recent waves of refugees from Latin American Right-wing dictatorships and from the Left-wing terror in Indo-China. France took 5,000 'boat people', who are now settling down well in their adopted homeland.

If there are any discriminatory feelings today against fellow whites, they are directed above all at France's 700,000 Jews, the largest Jewish community in Europe outside Russia. Anti-semitism in France has a long and sorry history; witness Dreyfus. More recently, a number of Frenchmen took advantage of the Occupation to carry out their own private pogroms, while few people did much to prevent 117,000 French Jews being deported to the Nazi gas-chambers. This has left a sour taste, even a sense of guilt, and since the war anti-semitism has died down. But it remains latent: according to opinion surveys, 10 per cent of French admit to being anti-semitic, while less than 25 per cent think Jews are people 'like anybody else'. Very recently the dread spectre has appeared again, with fringe neo-fascist groups becoming active as in some other parts of Europe. French Jews in turn have become more assertive, more concerned with retaining their Jewish identity rather than assimilating: this has been due largely to an influx of militant Sefardic Jews from North

Africa since the early 1960s. French Jews were also stung to anger, and vocally so, at Giscard's pro-Palestinian policy. So by 1980 the 'Jewish question' was again in the air, as the neo-Nazis made attacks on synagogues and Jewish leaders. All this came to a head in October 1980 when a bomb went off outside a synagogue in the rue Copernic, near the Etoile in Paris, killing four people. At first neo-Nazis were suspected, but later it appeared that an Arab group was responsible. At all events, the incident roused the French conscience. A huge public rally of people of all parties, from the PCF to the Gaullists, claimed solidarity with French Jews and urged stronger measures against violence.

The ordinary Frenchman is certainly horrified at anti-Jewish outrages of this kind. He wants Jews to be left in peace. And yet, Jews are not treated quite like other Frenchmen: sometimes they find subtle prejudices against them in their careers. This is one of the signs of the prejudice and intolerance that still lurk below the surface of French life, despite all the moves towards a more free and informal society, described in this long chapter.

Chapter 7

A MUDDLED NEW DEAL
FOR YOUTH

The sudden upswing in the birth-rate after 1945 gave France a feeling of rejuvenation. By the mid-1960s there were twice as many people under twenty-five as in 1939, although the population had risen only 27 per cent. And as this vast new teenage generation invaded the public scene, it brought with it a new cult of youth among its elders; soon, all the French were professing their faith in *la jeunesse*. 'We may have failed, but *les jeunes*, they are made of good stuff, they will do better than us,' was a comment sometimes heard from older people still ashamed of past defeats. In a country previously dominated by the prerogatives of age, this marked quite a change of heart. However, this new generation remained remarkably elusive and reticent – until the May '68 uprising suddenly lent it a new image. Some adults were encouraged by this outburst of youthful idealism, albeit anarchic; but others were alarmed. And even though the rebels who stormed the barricades were only a minority, the youth cult never quite recovered from the events of 1968.

Today's generation, in the early 1980s, is very different again from that of 1968, more reserved, less committed. It is profoundly marked by the uncertainties of the age. It clings to its elders for security, without really believing in their values. And adults in turn are no longer sure what faith they can place in youth, that mysterious world apart. But in its name a great national debate on education continues to rage. Ever since the 1950s, the highly traditional structure of French schools and universities has been constantly under reform. But nothing is yet solved.

REFORM IN THE CLASSROOM:
DOES MORE EQUALITY SPELL DECLINE?

'*Lycées*, alas, are moving towards the American high-school model where fun-and-games, talk-ins and so-called self-expression take the place of real intellectual training. I'm appalled at our decline in standards.' The speaker was not some elderly diehard but a Leftish teacher in his thirties, and there are many who think as he does, though it might equally be argued that more of the American or English spirit is just what the rigid French school system needs! At least this system has been changing in the past two decades, amid a welter of piecemeal reforms. It has become a little more egalitarian; also less authoritarian and more humane. But the French are still far from certain how to reconcile their glorious academic traditions with modern needs and modern educational theory. In the present transitional phase, all is confusion.

The classic pattern is by no means dead. 'In *Andromaque*, did Racine respect the rule of the three unities?' – a sixteen-year-old, in tieless shirt and informal jersey, stands up in class to give the perfect formal answer, just the way he's been taught; then the teacher resumes his own brilliant didactic performance, tripping his way through the subtleties of literary analysis as only a Sorbonne *agrégé* can. Outside, the sun falls on an austere and silent courtyard. It could be any classical *lycée*, across the French cultural empire from Tahiti to South Kensington.

Much of the best and worst in the French national spirit can be imputed to this concept of education as inspired academic pedagogy confined to the classroom walls: its role is to transmit knowledge and to train intellects, not – as in Britain – to develop the full individual. Traditionally, teaching has been deductive, rhetorical, preoccupied with style, and the teacher has had little human contact with his pupils outside class. The *lycées* have provided the bourgeoisie with the loftiest academic disciplining in the world; they have moulded a cultured élite where technocrats can turn to any problem with the same clarity they were taught to apply to Racine. Scientists and classicists alike in the *lycées* have received a strong dose of the same '*culture générale*', with lashings of philosophy. And even poorer children, while not so often reaching the *lycée*, have been put through sufficiently rigorous mental hoops in their junior schools for a foreigner to be frequently impressed by the French working man's articulateness and grasp of ideas.

Despite these and other qualities, the system came under growing criticism from the 1950s onward, as being too oppressive, too unrelated to modern life, and undemocratic in its application. The State *lycées* offer mainly free tuition and in theory are open to all: yet social barriers and prejudices are such that the more prestigious of them – such as Louis-le-Grand in Paris – have in practice been almost as much the preserves of a certain class as the English £3,000-a-year public schools; and even in the average *lycée* the children of workers were always much under-represented. So various reforms have been attempted. Eighty per cent of French schools are run by the State,[1] on a centralized civil service basis: this makes reform easier to decide on paper than in Britain but often harder to apply in practice, for it has to be imposed from above rather than proceed by groundswell movement. And the great irony is this: the

1 The rest are mostly in the hands of the Church (see pp. 490–91).

Left-wing militancy of most teachers is equalled only by their stubborn conservatism in face of all academic change; especially they have tended hitherto to oppose reforms imposed high-handedly by hated Right-wing Governments, even reforms whose content they approved such as those leading to greater pupil equality. So, at least until 1981, the authorities found it easier to make structural changes, involving new kinds of school or examination, than to tackle the harder but more crucial task of updating the attitudes and methods of French teaching.

In the post-war decades a few liberal reformists in the Ministry of Education did manage to push some innovations between the Scylla of State parsimony and vacillation and the Charybdis of teacher conservatism. During the 1960s the minimum leaving age was raised gradually from fourteen to sixteen: many children do still leave before they are sixteen, but only if they join an apprentice training scheme that includes some schoolwork. Some other changes were frankly utilitarian (to provide the expanding economy with more technicians) but some were humane too: to broaden access to higher education, to modernize teaching drills, and to lighten the severities of the examination system. In 1957 the Government even pushed one jump ahead of Britain in abolishing the French equivalent of the old Eleven Plus, the *lycée* entrance exam at eleven: this had been much criticized for its academicism and the precocity of abstract intelligence it expected. Today, all streaming of the under-sixteens is decided no longer by written exams but on school record and by parent-teacher consultation. Yet the competitive ethos is by no means abandoned. In junior schools there is still a heavy accent on memory learning, and class marks are still awarded monthly, usually after a test. So a child is still under pressure from his teacher, and maybe from parents too, to outshine his rivals. Probably this does encourage him to work harder: but it can also lead to tensions and intellectual snobberies, and it may inhibit the less bright child. It has even been held responsible for some of the rivalries and discords in French adult society.

De Gaulle's reformist Government was keen to tackle the problem of inequalities of opportunity. So in 1963, in a bid to democratize the *lycée* intake, it decreed the most controversial of all pre-1968 school reforms: there would now be only one kind of State school for all children, rich or poor, between eleven and fifteen. Hitherto, though all social classes attended the same primary schools, at the age of eleven the *lycées* took their own privileged stream, while the rest were relegated to junior secondary schools from where they went straight into jobs or, if they were lucky, to some technical college. Under the 1963 reform, the junior classes in *lycées* and the other junior schools were to be merged into a network of new comprehensives, the Collèges d'Enseignement

Secondaire. Selection from these for entry to the *lycées* at fifteen would be on school record, not by exam. Streaming was thus pushed back four years, and a bright working-class child would hopefully have more encouragement than before to make the jump to a *lycée*.

Several thousand of these new CES came into being over the next few years, and the working-class intake into the *lycées* gradually increased. But it was not without a struggle. Like the comprehensives in Britain, and for similar reasons, the CES ran into strong opposition: from *lycée* staff, fearing a decline in standards, and from bourgeois parents, fearing that *lycée* entrance would now be harder and less automatic for a less bright child. So the *lycées* fought to obstruct the full application of the reform, and with some success: under a compromise solution, they were allowed to retain control of their own junior classes, which had to follow the curriculum and methods of other CES but remained attached to the parent *lycée*. In the case of the more brilliant *lycées* in big towns, this did help to ensure higher standards and more continuity for the abler children: but it also maintained some social discrimination. Even today, the staff in some of the grander Paris *lycées* still show a snobbish bias against admitting workers' children. But just as often it is the latter who exclude themselves: a worker may feel, with reason, that his child with no cultured home background will be ill-at-ease in the *lycée* atmosphere. One Paris headmaster said: 'In twenty years, the proportion of pupils here from working-class homes has risen from 10 to 20 per cent, but that's still far too few, and they still have trouble in adapting.' And as only a *lycée* or private college prepares for the university entrance exam (*baccalauréat*), higher education is still something of a middle-class privilege: since 1959 the percentage of working-class students has risen from 3.8 to 9 per cent, but this is far below Britain's 30 per cent.

In May '68, *lycéens* all over France eagerly joined in the uprising led by university students. But, when the dust had settled, the Government did not immediately proceed with any drastic overhaul of secondary education, as it did in the universities. However, by the early '70s it was clear to many people that the 1963 reforms had not been adequate and that new measures were needed to bring schools closer in touch with modern life and reduce the persisting inequalities. When Giscard came to power, he proclaimed that a new deal for education was part of the blueprint for his so-called 'advanced liberal society', and he made a surprise choice of Education Minister: René Haby, a university rector with a forceful manner and strong radical views. He was told to prepare a master-plan, which was hurried through Parliament in 1975 and began to be applied in 1977. Haby's basic aim was to ensure that all children up to sixteen would follow identical courses and receive equal chances: he wanted to complete the process which the 1963 reforms had not fully achieved. But, faced with the inevitable barrage of teacher opposition, he felt obliged to use the heavy hand in applying his measures, and this simply intensified the hostility. Once again, the Ministry lacked diplomacy; but once again the Leftish reforms of a Rightish Government were contested – on principle – by the Left. So Haby's new deal, in its turn, though by no means a total failure, became bogged down in a series of delays and compromises.

Haby decided to start at the bottom, with the primary schools for the six-to-elevens. Primary teachers are less well qualified, and much less well paid, than those in secondary schools; and the calibre of recruits to this lower end of the profession had been falling steadily, with a consequent decline in the once-so-lofty teaching standards. 'Some kids arrive in their CES barely able to read or write,' complained one headmaster, 'and that's because primary teaching attracts only the dregs nowadays. And what do you expect, with the pay they get?' – according to age, the range is around 3,000 to 4,000 francs a month, about half that of an *agrégé* in a *lycée*. So Haby improved the wage-scale, and also introduced a longer and more substantial training course for primary teachers, with the purpose of improving their quality and attracting better recruits. He tried, too, to reduce the size of classes.

Haby's aim was that all children, or all but the really subnormal, should be sufficiently well grounded in their primary schools to be capable of taking part in his major innovation: mixed ability classes in all CES, now renamed simply '*collèges*'. In these, so he decreed, there would be no more streaming by intelligence, only by age-group; future Einstein would sit next to future roadsweeper. For France, it was a sharp break with tradition. One motive of this reform was egalitarian. But another was economic: the Government decided that for the economy to be provided with a manpower suitably adaptable to the new age of high technology, then everyone must have 'a minimum baggage of knowledge'. It was no longer enough merely to select and cosset the intelligent. Haby insisted also that the curriculum be made more practical, less theoretical, with an increased emphasis on the sciences; every pupil of whatever background would now be obliged to learn some manual skills, such as metalwork or sewing. Many teachers feared that these reforms would strike yet another blow at academic standards, but others welcomed them. 'It's good for a mentally precocious child to find out that he can't wield a hammer, it makes him less cocksure,' said one headmaster; 'and it's good too for an academic dullard to be able to prove in school that he does have a flair, say, for practical mechanics. Haby is helping to redress the bias against non-academic talent.'

During 1977–80 these mixed ability classes were progressively set up in the *collèges*, including those attached to *lycées*, which thus lost some of the privilege they had managed to retain after 1963. Most *collège* teachers at least paid lip-service to the democratic virtues of the new '*école unique*' system, with all pupils now following the same course: but in practice it created all sorts of problems. One supporter of the Haby reforms told me: 'In principle, it's good to mix up the ability groups. The dullards no longer fear they're being pushed into a ghetto, even if their weaknesses in class are now more apparent. And a really brilliant pupil is *not* held back nearly as much as the old-style teachers feared – he'll always have the time and the motivation to catch up later and find his true level. American experience proves this. But I admit that the reform is less well suited to the middle range of pupils: their development does suffer from having to go at the speed of the slowest.' In many schools, teachers soon had trouble in coping with mixed ability classes, which demanded more pedagogic dexterity than they possessed, or more extra effort than they were ready to give. In theory, the reforms did provide for some hours of special tuition, both for the very weak (to help them to keep up) and for the very bright (to stretch their minds and stop them getting too bored): but most schools in practice lacked the staff or the patience for much of this.

Therefore schools tacitly began to find ways of not applying the Haby reforms too literally. In other words, they retained a degree of streaming in some classes, and were under strong pressure to do so from the parents of abler children. 'At first I tried sincerely to adopt the new scheme to the letter,' said one Paris headmistress, 'but I found that it doesn't really work. So now I put the brighter kids together – and all my *profs* support me, even the most Left-wing!' So by 1981 the new system was being only half-applied. Haby himself had been dismissed by Giscard in 1978, a sacrificial victim to the teacher and parent lobbies: his successor, Christian Beullac, was instructed not to try to impose the reforms too rigidly, and to avoid provoking the lobbies in a pre-election period. Opinion was divided as to whether Haby's new deal had been well and truly sabotaged, or not. The liberal-minded rector[2] of Toulouse told me: 'These are inevitable teething-troubles. It will take ten years for teachers to adjust to the new system, which in itself is a great step

2 In France, the main role of the Ministry-appointed rector is to look after all State schools in his region: the universities are a secondary concern for him. The rector lives in high style, like a prefect, entertaining more lavishly than most English vice-chancellors.

forward.' And so today the debate goes on, a familiar one in modern education anywhere: is equality of opportunity compatible with high academic standards? – and how much do these really matter? French teachers, at all levels, are divided and confused on the subject. The Socialists have come to power with no special blueprint of their own for education: basically they approve of the Haby reforms, and are trying to improve their implementation as best they can.

Under the Haby plan, it is now the turn of the *lycée* classes (for the sixteen-to-eighteen-year-olds) to come under reform in 1981–4. Here life is still lived in the shadow of that most sacred and imperious of French institutions, the *baccalauréat*. Taken at eighteen or so, *le bac* is a far more rigorous and brain-searching exam than its English equivalent, A-level GCE, and even more essential a passport to higher education. It has been described as the national obsession of the middle classes, dividing France into two camps, *bacheliers* and non-*bacheliers*; and though the exams are controlled as strictly as possible, there have been some notorious cases of parents paying high prices to bribe examiners or secure advance copies of papers. The French word for cramming is *bachotage*; and scores of private fee-paying *boîtes-à-bachot* have sprung up to cram those who find the large *lycée* classes too impersonal. The numbers trying for the *bac* have grown steadily since the war. The minority who fail are left not only with a stigma and possibly a complex for life, but also without skills of use for a job, for the syllabus (except in the case of the *bac technique*) is non-vocational. And even the *bac* itself is a poor job qualification, unless followed up by a degree or specialized diploma. So ever since the 1950s the *bac* has been constantly under reform, or talk of reform, amid a running national debate.

Traditionally the *bac* has possessed many virtues as a mental grounding for the more gifted child, and one of these has always been its emphasis on a high level of *culture générale*, both for those who take literary or scientific options. Until reforms in 1965, the main option on the arts side contained a severe dosage of some nine hours' philosophy a week but also five hours of science; and the principal maths and science options each had nine or more hours a week of philosophy and other arts subjects. Even a science candidate in his philosophy paper might be expected to tackle, 'Can liberty be conceived when there is no reasonable choice?' No wonder the French manager or engineer is so often a man of high personal culture. But it could also be argued that the syllabus, and notably the rhetorical and deductive teaching methods, have tended to develop a turn of mind that is conformist, theoretical and often uncreative, schooled to think and verbalize with great clarity along predetermined lines. And although a brilliant pupil might be able to contribute his own originality, others could get submerged. Doubts grew as to whether this pre-*bac* pressure-feeding was the right way to train the growing hordes in the *lycées*. Some educationalists argued in favour of lightening the academic burden; others wanted earlier specialization; others defended the *status quo*, the precious *culture générale*.

In the 1960s measures and counter-measures flowed from a vacillating Ministry in a bewildering stream, alienating even those teachers sympathetic to change. The syllabus was altered four times, ostensibly with the aim of lightening it. Finally in 1965 the options were re-arranged and modernized. Economics, sociology and statistics were at last recognized as subjects worthy of a *lycéen*'s study, and they went into a new 'modern' option. In the main arts option, there was now less philosophy and more modern languages, while French literature no longer stopped at 1900 but reached to Sartre and beyond. But *culture générale* was by no means abandoned: today, pupils taking a modern or science option must still sit a philosophy paper, with such questions as, 'Is it possible to be just when those around us are not?' Nor did the 1965 reforms put an end to the debate about the syllabus. Many 'modernists' continued to argue that specialized streaming is enforced too young: a pupil must select his option as soon as he enters the *lycée* at sixteen, thus making a choice that will influence the rest of his life. So Haby's master-plan proposed a new two-tier *bac*: the first part, at the end of the *lycée* second year, would cover a wide range of basic subjects common to all pupils; the second, a year later, would allow a free choice of specialized subjects. 'My aim,' said Haby, 'is to delay specialization by two years, then make it more intensive once it starts.' But this scheme, sensible in many ways, ran into widespread resistance from teachers fearing a further threat to standards. It was shelved, and by 1981 no decision had yet been reached on how the Haby reforms would affect the *bac*. Once again, the teaching world was in confusion over the kind of changes it wanted, if any.

At present the *bac* has eight main options, five academic and eight technical, with a wide variety of subject combinations. The most prestigious used to be what is now called 'option A' (literature and philosophy): but steadily its pride of place has been usurped by 'option C' (maths, science, economics), today seen as the royal road of entry into modern élite careers via the Grandes Ecoles or ENA (see pp. 84 and 510). And this 'tyranny of mathematics', as they call it, is much deplored by teachers of the humanities: 'We no longer get the brightest pupils,' said one, 'they all opt for "C".' Many teachers, not only the older ones, today lament a decline in the level of general culture – but then it is the way of teachers to talk like this, they've been doing so for a hundred years. It is true that in literary subjects the level *has* fallen off: pupils today read less, and less is demanded of them for the *bac*. On the other hand, the teaching of modern languages has improved, while standards in science and other modern subjects have generally risen too. This is the way France has been moving, for better or for worse.

In order to make up for the shortage of middle-grade technicians in France, the Ministry has been trying to divert non-academically inclined children away from the traditional *lycées* and into technical education. This shortage may seem paradoxical in view of the high prestige of the technocrats from the Grandes Ecoles. But this prestige belongs only to an élite and ends abruptly below a certain level. Upper-bourgeois parents will be proud for their child to move via the *bac* 'C' to a Grande Ecole and a career as an engineer: but they will turn up their noses at his going instead to one of the recently developed *lycées techniques* and taking the *bac technique*, a far more practical workshop exam leading to a middle-range technical career. Many fail the prestige *bacs* or, if they pass, they then fail Grande Ecole entry and end up with a university sub-degree which is of little use (see p. 501). At one big Paris *lycée* I visited a class immersed in the final strained weeks of cramming for the *bac* 'C', and their teacher told me: 'Most of these kids will end up in clerical jobs or small commerce. Few of them have the minds for this high-quality theoretical work: they'd have done better in a technical stream, if only their silly parents had let them.' Then the school's *censeur* (disciplinary official), a woman from a modest family, told me: 'My son went happily to a *lycée technique* and from there to an electronics college, and now in his blue-collar job he's doing better than most of these kids ever will.' So the bourgeoisie is caught in its own snooty trap. But today this is slowly changing. The Government recently has made a big effort to develop technical and practical education. It has expanded the number of schools for training skilled workers; and in the post-*bac* classes of *lycées techniques* it offers a new higher technical diploma that in job terms is worth more than an academic *bac*. Slowly, a few middle-class people are beginning to accept that this may be a chance worth taking. So the snobbish bias against technical training, much stronger in France than in Germany, is just beginning to wane.

The Government has also been making big efforts to improve adult vocational training, so that those with little schooling now have a second chance to improve their qualifications, if they wish. France used to be very backward in this field. But in 1971 a step forward was made when a new law obliged all firms to spend a sum equal to 1 per cent of their wage bill on further education, in the firm's time: as a result, staff at all levels have attended courses aimed at leading to job enrichment and better promotion prospects. Since the rise of unemployment in the mid-1970s, public money has been lavished on various other new schemes, too, directed at retraining redundant staff in new skills, or helping bright lower-paid workers to make up for their lack of paper qualifications. So France is at last moving closer to countries such as the USA and West Germany, in the opportunities offered for promotion on merit from the shop-floor. A few star cases can be cited. For example, the head of an institute in Nancy told me with pride of one of his ex-pupils who left school and went down the mines at fourteen, then attended evening classes, won an engineer's diploma, entered the élitist Ecole des Mines, and is now a senior member of the French coal board's long-term planning group. This kind of breakthrough is at last becoming a little less exceptional in France.

When the *lycéens* rebelled in May '68, it was less over exams or syllabuses than against the rigid atmosphere surrounding their education. Anyone who visited an average French school before 1968 may have been struck by the rarity of informal human contact between teacher and child, and by the relative absence of any sense of warm human community where the personality could be developed. The French themselves were growing more aware of this, and of how over the years it aggravated some of the negative traits in their national character. But it was something even less amenable to legislation than the *ex cathedra* teaching methods so closely bound up with it. Attempts at change would run into various obstacles: the ingrained unconcern of many teachers for anything but their pupils' intellects; the monolithic State system, ill suited to a matter as delicate and personal as bringing up a child; and the swelling size of many schools. In any State school the smallest departure from routine, such as an extra half-holiday, could not, before 1968, be fixed without written order from Paris; and the precise duties of each member of staff were governed by a statute from the Ministry. In the large *lycées* the civil-service atmosphere reached its height, where teachers stood on rigid ceremony and were called by their formal titles – '*Oui, Monsieur le Censeur*' – by pupils and colleagues alike. Sometimes an energetic or liberal headmaster would succeed in infusing his school with some personality of its own, without actually defying the Ministry. But this became harder as the *lycées* swelled in size, to 2,000 pupils or more – 'just pedagogic factories', as someone put it, with even less humanizing influence than before the war.

Long before May '68, *lycéens* had been growing restive. Then, when the Paris students launched their revolt, *lycéens* all over France gladly followed them. Small politically minded groups formed a national action committee, highly militant. Other *lycéens*, less political, joined in either to air their grievances or just for the hell of it. Amazing scenes took place, hardly believable in this staid milieu where schoolchildren had usually been seen and not heard. Many *lycées* were 'occupied' by the pupils, like the factories by workers, and red and black flags hoisted over them. Teachers no longer dared sit at their rostra, but either fled the classroom or, the more liberal of them, sat for hours each day on the benches beside their striking pupils, discussing school, politics, sex, careers, life. 'I never knew my girls before except as minds: now I know them as people,' one young woman teacher told me. *Lycéens* suddenly discovered their latent socio-political awareness; and though many acted stupidly, some showed a remarkable maturity. Parents, invited to take part in the impromptu *lycée* debates, were often astonished to hear thoughtful and persuasive public orations from their own sons and daughters – how the babes had grown up! Other parents hit back, even violently, storming into *lycées* and trying to beat their kids up. My favourite anecdote comes from a girls' *lycée* in Paris at the moment of its 'liberation' by a crowd of male invaders from a near-by boys' *lycée*: the foyer was filled with excited youths calling the girls out on strike, and in the midst was the *directrice*, a tiny, round elderly figure, totally bewildered, clutching at the jacket of a *lycéen* leader, a wild hippy figure towering above her, and imploring him: '*Mais, non, Monsieur, je ne refuse pas le dialogue! Je ne le refuse pas!*'

The revolt did indeed open a new era of 'dialogue' between pupils and many teachers: its permanent legacy was to have led to a more human and open-minded spirit in the *lycées*. But for the first two or three years it also left an aftertaste of unrest and contention. A small minority of *lycéens* remained aggressively political after May, calling themselves Maoists, Guevarists and so on, and not hiding their aim of destroying the system. They put up posters (which they were now allowed to do) and scrawled angry graffiti everywhere, so that even the calmest *lycée* often gave the superficial appearance of anarchy. In some cases there were riots: at the distinguished Louis-le-Grand *lycée* in the Quartier Latin, ten boys were injured in 1969 when a grenade exploded in a scuffle between Left- and Right-wing factions. Such incidents, though rare in themselves, reflected a general undercurrent of disquiet in France. However, as the 1970s wore on the next *lycée* generations showed themselves far less politically minded. The posters and slogans gradually disappeared from the corridor walls. Even the tiny groups of *enragés* began to keep a low profile.

The lasting change since '68 is that there is now less rigid discipline, more discussion, and a little more contact between the formerly hermetic *lycée* and the real world outside. In July '68 de Gaulle gave the Education portfolio to the astute Edgar Faure, a former Prime Minister, and ordered him to draw on the lessons of the May revolt by providing some new deal. Faure's main effort was directed at the universities. In the schools, he put the accent on institutionalizing the new 'dialogue'; and his main reform was the setting up of democratic governing boards (*conseils d'établissement*) in all *lycées* and CES – a total break with French tradition. Each board is made up one-fifth of parents, one-fifth of senior pupils (elected from their own ranks), and the rest of teachers and other staff, plus a few Ministry officials and local dignitaries coopted from outside. The board has no powers over syllabus and exams; but it can influence the headmaster on a wide range of decisions concerning the internal running of the school, the use of its budget, teaching methods and discipline. The boards meet once or twice a term, and their success has varied greatly. Where there is a strong headmaster, the board may be little more than a cipher in his hands. In some other cases cooperation is smooth. In others there is chaos, and a few headmasters have been driven to resigning, with the complaint that their authority has been destroyed. One liberal *proviseur* of a large Paris *lycée* told me: 'My board has become politicized, it's the teachers' fault. In true French style it has split up into rival pressure-groups which argue for hours and never get anywhere. I was certainly in favour of changing the old system, but this is no improvement.' The reform was a worthy attempt to decentralize some powers away from a Ministry which previously controlled every detail of routine down to the buying of blotters. It was also a bid to give the pupils a sense of sharing in the running of their school; but this has not worked too well. The brighter pupils often think the board a waste of time; or in other cases their delegates are virtually coopted by an authoritarian headmaster and allowed little influence. It could indeed be argued that these cumbersome 'school parliaments' are not the right means of teaching civic responsibility – still such a lacuna in French education – but are simply one more example of the French penchant for institutionalism. However, they do at least mark a step away from over-centralization.

Since 1968 the climate of classroom life has changed considerably. Discipline used to be para-military: in junior schools, a class would have to line up in order at the end of each lesson before being dismissed. Many bad teachers would resort to petty tyranny, while even the better ones would rarely take much human interest in their pupils. So a *lycéen* would usually have no one at school to whom he could turn for personal advice or comfort; and if his home life was not easy, this could be a real lack. Then as a result of May '68 something snapped, as some schools swung at first from an authoritarian extreme to another of permissiveness. A not illiberal woman teacher in a Parisian girls' *lycée* told me in 1972: 'The girls talk and smoke in class, it's impossible to control them. If you put your foot down, there's a riot or a walk-out. The Head makes little effort to impose her authority – she has orders from the Ministry to avoid trouble. I don't want to sound too old-fashioned, but there's been a huge increase in "vulgarity" – girls playing the guitar in the corridors and so on. The positive aspect is that the old prison-like austerity is gone and the girls today are happier.' Finally, after a few years, a kind of balance was achieved, and today's *lycée* generation are neither as cowed and sullenly defensive as in the old days, nor as aggressive as after May '68. Teachers too, especially the new breed of young ones (themselves the products of May '68), today make far more effort to treat their pupils with warmth and human concern, in class. '*Odile, que pense-tu?*' has replaced, '*Dupont, taisez-vous!*' Teachers put less accent on the *cours magistral* and more on question-and-answer methods and group work, and the Ministry encourages this.

I would not go so far as to say that all French teachers today are as sensitively sympathetic to their pupils' needs as the enchanting young heroine of Tavernier's film *Une Semaine de vacances* (p. 571), set in a Lyon *collège* in 1980: on the other hand, few of them any longer are the martinet-like gorgons portrayed in another well-known recent movie on school life, Diane Kurys' semi-autobiographical *Diabolo menthe*, set in a girls' *lycée* in Paris back in 1963. Recently, I visited a big mixed[3] school in eastern Paris, the Lycée Paul Valéry, built in 1959: grim utilitarian premises with poor amenities, but a relaxed and cheerful atmosphere. While I was with the headmaster, a pert girl of sixteen came to ask if she could change her class because she disliked her teacher: she was most undeferential, didn't even address the Head as '*Monsieur le Proviseur*' – so unlike the old days. He told me later: 'The kids are not supposed to smoke in the building; but if we catch them, what can we do? We've virtually given up doling out punishments – you just *can't*, nowadays.' In some *collèges* or other junior schools there is sporadic hooliganism and even some delinquency, notably in poorer districts. But on the whole today's pupils are well-behaved and do not abuse their new freedom, especially in the hard-working *lycées* where the *bac* looms. However, they seldom show any enthusiasm for the school and its life: 'This place for me is like a supermarket,' said a boy at one smart Paris *lycée*; 'I come for what I need to get out of it – the *bac* – but I feel no emotional attachment.' No question of *floreat Etona*.

And whose fault is that? – not altogether the pupils'. Discipline may have eased, staff in class may be gentler; but neither teachers nor Minis-

___

3 Older *lycées* are mostly single-sex, but those built since the 1950s are nearly all mixed. Today most primary school and *collèges* are co-ed.

try since 1968 have made much effort to turn a school into more of a real community, a focus for loyalty, a fun place for children to stay around in when class is over. That is not the French tradition. A school is a facility, for the transmission of knowledge and the passing of exams, and nothing more. Most schools do have their clubs of sorts – for chess, jazz, photography, sometimes drama, and so on, but they are feeble by Anglo-Saxon standards.

Lack of funds, and of suitable premises, are part of the problem. *Lycées* are ill-equipped for club or communal activities, and overcrowding has not helped. The august Lycée Fermat in Toulouse, one of the greatest in France, has graceful old buildings: but its largest hall holds only 400 whereas numbers have swelled to 2,000, so that any ceremony such as a prize-giving or school concert, which might help to induce some community feeling, is virtually impossible. 'The school's grown so big that it's lost all atmosphere, it's just a teaching factory,' one master told me; 'the staff is so large that we hardly know each other. Two masters met by chance on a holiday abroad, and were surprised to learn they both worked at Fermat. They didn't even know each other by sight.' At the Lycée Paul Valéry, with 2,400 pupils, the Ministry's architects provided no assembly hall at all: the largest rooms are the canteens, each seating 130, so the *proviseur* cannot even convoke a full meeting of his 200 teachers.

Edgar Faure after 1968 ordained that each *lycée* should have a *'foyer socio-éducatif'*, to be run by the pupils themselves as a centre for their clubs and for recreation. But many schools were physically unable – or else unwilling – to make a room available for the new *foyer*, nor did the Ministry supply much back-up of funds, so the scheme has met with little success. The Ministry pays lip-service to the need for more out-of-class activities, but in practice puts them near the bottom of its budgetary priorities. It does not even provide proper funds for libraries, which even in the best *lycées* tend to be miserably small and ill-stocked: most new books of general interest can be acquired only through parents' donations or the children's own modest subscriptions. In fact, many teachers are quite glad there should not be too many readable foreign or modern books around to distract the pupils from their work: better Kant or Molière, who are on the syllabus, than Updike or Fowles.

If out-of-class activities such as clubs are so few, one other reason is that few teachers are prepared to stay on after hours and help organize them. A teacher does not see this as part of his job: in fact he probably belongs to a union that militantly opposes this kind of 'unpaid overtime'. Teachers work hard, to be sure, and may spend hours each evening correcting essays. But the average *professeur* regards the school as a kind of office job: he arrives, holds his series of classes, maybe with donnish brilliance, then goes home. The children's out-of-class lives are not his business. True, this attitude has recently been changing a little among younger teachers: but it is still widespread. Older teachers will often oppose the introduction of clubs or cultural activities, which they see as frivolous and a threat to academic work: in one very grand Paris *lycée*, Henri IV, the staff prevented pupils from forming an orchestra because they thought the noise would distract boarders from their 'prep'. And one youngish master at another *lycée* gave me a firmly purist view: 'We are twinned with a German *Gymnasium*, where the pupils have class-work only from eight till one: in the afternoon they stay at school, but do music, drama and so on, under the guidance of their teachers. The result, as in America, is that academic levels are much lower than in France. Our system is best. A *lycée* is not the place for *animation culturelle* – if the kids want that, let them go to the local youth centres in their spare time.'

Out-of-class activities therefore depend on the goodwill of a minority of *profs*, or on the pupils' own initiatives. But the latter are so transitory a breed, and so soon caught up with swotting for the *bac*, that their ventures tend to be ephemeral. At one *lycée* a master told me: 'Sporadic attempts have been made here to get a drama group going, or a school newspaper, or a poetry club. But they rarely survive more than a few terms. There's no one to provide continuity: the kids can't, and the teachers won't. Also, these buildings are so gloomy that the kids understandably prefer to clear off as soon as the bell goes. Real life for them is what they get from outside, from travel, television, friends, family.' This is typical of large big-city *lycées*, where nearly all pupils live at home. But a few *lycées* do have a fair number of boarders, and here there can be more club activity and sense of community. Also the picture can be livelier in smaller *lycées* in country towns, and in some *collèges* (where the academic grind is lighter and the staff on average younger). At a *lycée* in Lorraine, I found several teachers helping the pupils to stage a Molière play, to run an orchestra, and to organize cultural sight-seeing tours into Germany and Belgium.

Since 1968 the feeling has been growing that schools should do more to encourage this kind of thing. At the Lycée Fermat, a young master told me: 'With great difficulty we've now managed to start up a roneoed magazine, produced by the pupils under our supervision, as well as a drama group which has put on a play by Lorca. But all this is marginal to the life of the school. And we get no funds from Paris for it.' So the trend is limited. I am also amazed, in a France supposedly *la mère des arts*, at the lack of time devoted to music and the visual arts in the curriculum. Every *lycée* has its music room: as often as not it is locked and silent, in contrast to the musical sounds that echo round schools in Britain or Germany. No wonder that French musical life was so long in crisis: and if today it is reviving, this has not been thanks to any general effort inside schools, but to other factors (see pp. 603–14). Art, in the land of the Impressionists, the adopted land of Picasso, fares no better. The number of hours devoted to it in *lycées* has been falling, and few pupils over sixteen study any art at all: in one large Paris *lycée*, I found the art room in mid-morning totally deserted. As art and music are of minimal importance in the *bac*, they can safely be neglected. Recent reforms, it is true, have set up a new arts option, with specializations in music or the visual arts: a fine idea in theory, but still restricted in practice to a handful of *lycées*, due to lack of funds and of qualified staff. In *collèges*, a little more attention is paid to these subjects, but less than in many countries. Teachers, when criticized, lay the blame on parents' lack of interest: the latter merely want their children to pass exams, and will not press for more art and music until the Ministry gives these a larger role in the exam syllabus. It is a vicious circle, and is certainly one of the factors behind the post-war decline in French creative culture.

In another important domain, that of sport, at least there has been some improvement. Since the mid-'60s the Ministry has put a growing emphasis on an aspect of school life previously much neglected, and has even provided the funds for it, so that most newer schools do have adequate playing fields and gymnasia. All *lycées* are now supposed to have five hours' compulsory sport and physical training a week – in practice, it is usually rather less – while the *bac* itself contains an obligatory gymnastics test. The results vary from school to school. Children do not care much for 'gym', so that unless the instructor is really good they will use this class as a chance to fool about. But they eagerly take part in real sports, such as football, basketball, tennis, or even judo. The problem here is a lack of good qualified teachers. In primary schools, there was virtually no sport until recently, and at one I was told: 'An instructor comes to give classes once a week, but the kids treat it as a joke' – I was reminded of that hilarious scene in Truffaut's *Les 400 coups* where the boys slip off to play truant in the streets of Montmartre behind the back of the daftly prancing gym teacher. But since 1969 the number of classroom hours in primary schools has been reduced, and the weekly ration of 'physical exercise' increased from two hours to six. The official motive is health and fitness. Also, sport has developed so fast in popularity since the war (see p. 438) that even pedagogues and parents have now begun to accept it as not such a waste of school time after all.

In 1973 a new initiative was made by the Ministry to add extra-curricular variety to school life. Instead of all schools following the same routines, each was now to be allowed to spend 10 per cent of working hours any way it pleased, preferably on non-academic activities. But the innovation has met with only patchy success. In some cases, enterprising staff have managed to do something worthwhile: for example, at a *lycée* in Grenoble, 400 pupils and staff spent a week of term living with farmers in mountain villages. But in many schools the teachers – predictably – have opposed the new scheme, either through fear that it would affect academic standards, or out of inertia and lack of ideas, or else from opposition on principle to any plan coming from the Ministry. And as the '10 per cent' is not fully compulsory, in some schools it has been virtually abandoned, or else is carried on intermittently in those classes where the teacher is in favour. Generally, it works better in *collèges* (where there is no pre-*bac* pressure) than in *lycées*, where staff tend to be older and more hidebound. Some teachers do take their pupils to visit local factories, museums or other places of interest; or they hold classroom debates on topical subjects; or in a few cases they incite the pupils to some creative project such as mounting an exhibition. But it is the parents who have to subsidize all such ventures, as the Ministry has again failed to come up with funds: so scope is limited. And few are the *lycée* teachers ready to put their hearts into the kind of work usually accepted as a basic part of the job in Britain or America. 'It's the usual French problem,' said one headmaster: 'teachers complain about State control, but then have no idea how to use freedom when they get it. They lack any initiative, except that of protest.' And René Haby himself told me in 1979: 'You'll never get French academics to take on this extra role. The only solution would be to create a new category of school staff, *animateurs*, to take charge of out-of-class activities. And what a fracas that would cause.'

My final criticism of the French school system concerns the lack of practical training in democracy or leadership, either on American lines where a school becomes a parliament-in-embryo, or as in Britain where senior pupils are in charge of discipline. There are classroom lessons in government, but as one teacher said to me, 'We teach them how Parliament and the communes work, but give them little chance to try it all out in practice. *We* tell them about *préfets*: *you* make them into prefects. Maybe in Britain your school prefects have too much power: here, children aren't given enough.' Discipline in class has always been left to the teacher; and outside it to the *censeur*, a kind of sergeant-major, assisted by a team of *surveillants*, mostly unqualified youngsters of twenty or so earning a little pocket-money while they complete their own studies. Their role has been to keep the schoolkids out of mischief, but not to train their character.

Since 1968 the Ministry has made a few attempts to modify this system in an Anglo-Saxon direction. The *surveillants* are being phased out: instead, many schools now have *moniteurs*, who are more like moral tutors. Their job is to look after pupils' welfare as well as discipline, and to liaise with parents when a child has personal problems. It is a small belated step forward. Also the Ministry has been trying to get senior pupils to take a little more responsibility, through the new system of delegates to school councils, and in class as well. Previously the elected head of each class did little but collect exercise books for teacher: now he is expected to keep some order when a teacher is not present. But there is still no move to establish a school prefect system; indeed French teen-agers remain firmly hostile to imposing discipline on their fellows in the name of the school authority – *'Nous ne sommes pas des flics'* (we're not cops), said one. Parents, too, remain strongly opposed to this very un-French concept: many a bourgeois father would find it intolerable for his little Pierre to be bossed around at school by the son of a neighbour, perhaps considered socially inferior! Traditionally it is the family, not the school, that is supposed to train character. Parents look on school as an academic utility, which should not compete with them as a centre of loyalty; and if a school were to attempt training in leadership or civic responsibility, this would be resented as an intrusion into their own sphere. From an Anglo-Saxon point of view, this leaves a void in the child's full education. The pre-1968 school system repressed the child's character, or forced it into private rebellious paths, and to many a foreign observer it seemed that this marked the French for life. Much of the egotism in France, the lack of civic feeling, the instinctive mistrust of authority, appeared to stem from attitudes inherited at school. Today's system is less repressive, with more accent on individual self-expression; and already there are signs that this is leading to a gentler and more tolerant ethos among young people. But – I repeat – there is still little attempt in schools to help a child to feel part of a living community or to share in responsibility for it. And although schools are less hermetic than they used to be, the gulf is still wide between their life and that of the 'real' world outside.

In a bid to narrow this gulf, one or two 'open school' experiments were made in the 1970s, notably in the Arlequin district of Grenoble where the Ministry allowed the local *collège* and primary schools to integrate with the daily life of the community (see p. 309). Progressive teachers volunteered to take part in the scheme, which bears the influence of Ivan Illich and has had counterparts in other countries, for example in Edinburgh. 'Our aim,' one pioneer told me at l'Arlequin, 'is not merely to instruct the children but to stimulate their initiative – and that's novel for France.' Groups of primary pupils were encouraged to devise and illustrate new reading primers, which then even found a publisher. The children were also invited to embark on a project for cleaning up the squalid environment of l'Arlequin, by repainting walls, tearing down tatty remains of posters, and so on. But this aroused a barrage of protest, led by local Communists, who claimed this was a job for the civic authorities and no part of education: so the scheme was dropped. The free-and-easy classroom system, with parents encouraged to share in the schools' daily life, was on the whole popular locally, even though some parents feared that their offspring were suffering academically from the Illichian emphasis. But the strongest criticism came from the Grenoble branches of the Left-wing teachers' unions: they objected to a system that obliged the staff to work as a group, to spend hours on out-of-class activities, and to share their pedagogic skills with mere parents. The unions put pressure on the Ministry, which had initially backed the experiment but then began to get cold feet. By 1981 there were signs that the schools were being 'normalized' and that the venture might not survive. Such are the hazards of trying to introduce new notions of civic training into the rigid French curriculum.

After the Socialists came to power, the debate over the Haby reforms was pushed into second place as the Left revived a much older and even more vexed issue: that of State aid for Church schools. Many a Third and Fourth Republic parliament had fought and bled over this, in the days when the power of clericalism provoked such strong feelings in France. But by the 1960s the problem seemed to be fading away. Although de Gaulle's and Giscard's regimes, both pro-Catholic, increased the level of aid to Church schools, the non-Catholic Left no longer got so worked up about it. And the two school systems, Church and State, moved steadily closer together. Today a large number of teachers in Church schools are non-Christians; many Catholic families send their children to State schools, while many State *lycées* have Catholic almoners attached to their staff. A liberal *curé* in a small country town told me in 1979: 'A parent today chooses his school more for practical than confessional reasons. The only people still interested in the *école laïque* debate are little pressure-groups made up of a few older priests and a hard core of anti-clerical teachers. The general public couldn't care less.'

The Socialists have today inherited a system whereby the State pays the staff salaries, and in some cases the running costs too, of any private school that agrees to follow the State education system, as nearly all of them do. Most private schools are run by the Catholic Church, but not all; some are Protestant, Jewish and so on. Private schools were far less affected than State ones by May '68 and its unruly aftermath; also they remained relatively immune from the waves of teachers' strikes and other agitation in 1979–80. So a growing number of parents, especially middle-class ones, have been turning to them, believing that they offer a surer education and higher standards. The percentage of children in private schools has risen since 1968 from 12 to 16 per cent, and among sixteen-to-eighteen-year-olds preparing for the *bac* it is up to 23 per cent. No great sacrifice is required by parents for, thanks to the State aid, tuition fees in Church schools are rarely more than 1,000 francs a term.

All this has angered the anti-clericalists among State teachers, who allege that the diverting of public funds to help private schools has harmed the State system. Moreover, this lobby dominates the main teachers' union, the Fédération d'Education Nationale, very Left-wing, which had persuaded the Socialist Party to write into its election programme a plan to abolish aid to private schools. So Mitterrand came to power committed to setting up 'a unified, secular public education system'. In fact, neither he nor his Education Minister, Alain Savary, a moderate, regard the matter as a high priority, and they would be ready to let matters rest a while. The new Government has merely said that it will negotiate with the private schools a phasing down of the aid over a five-year period: after this, schools wishing to stay independent can do so, but will get no aid. But the Government is under pressure from the FEN militants, who in July 1981 demanded an immediate end to all aid. And the FEN has powerful allies in the National Assembly, where half the Socialist deputies are teachers or professors. One moderate pro-Catholic teacher said to me: 'This affair will be a test case of whether Mitterrand is ready and able to stand up to demagogic pressure from the rank-and-file on his Left. It is tragic that this stupid, archaic quarrel over the *école laïque* should be revived after all these years. The result could be simply to drive many pro-Socialist Catholics into opposition, and that would be sad.'

One of Savary's first actions in 1981 was to revoke many of the austerity cuts made by Beullac, which had so much angered the unions, and to appoint 11,600 extra teachers. His hope is that, by improving the State system again, he can woo many families back to it and away from private schools, thus at least partially defusing the *école laïque* issue. In a much broader sense, too, the future of French education now seems to depend on whether the Government can succeed in winning the trust and cooperation of the teaching corps, as Right-wing regimes so signally failed to do. But it is not yet certain that the teachers and their unions will now show reason and accept the needed reforms, even under a Left-wing Government of which they supposedly approve. Eighty per cent of teachers are unionized, nearly four times the level in industry; the

Communist-led unions are especially militant, and the multiple categories of teacher are habitually involved in endless petty disputes with each other, and with the Ministry, in defence of their sectional interests. Teachers have a tight hierarchy, based on the value of their diplomas; and the privileges of the élite strata are a constant source of bitterness to those lower down the scale, for the better your diploma, the more you earn, yet the less you have to work. A *professeur agrégé* (the senior qualification) need teach only fifteen hours a week, yet earns on average 50 per cent more than a *collège* teacher who is obliged to do twenty-one hours.

Another running cause of teacher discontent is that the system, though modified since 1968, is still over-centralized. Teachers, as civil servants, must go where the Ministry posts them, and this can lead to personal hardship. For example, a woman living with her child and husband near Pau, where he worked, was refused a transfer from her teaching post in the Paris region, 550 miles away; so a large part of her salary, and much time and nervous energy, was spent on weekend visits home. This kind of problem may be alleviated if Alain Savary succeeds, as he hopes, in regionalizing State education, in the context of the Socialists' devolution programme.

And so, amid endless debate, the struggle goes on to adapt the old purist education system to a new age. Modernists detect signs of progress; traditionalists bemoan a 'degradation'; each camp tries to obstruct the other. Many people, teachers and parents alike, are simply left bewildered by the spate of often contradictory reforms and tinkerings over the past twenty years, and are sceptical as to whether the Haby solution will work any better. But it is clear that no new system will ever work successfully without a more flexible and generous attitude on the part of teachers. In and out of class, they remain the key to the whole problem. They have certainly evolved since 1968, in terms of easier human contact with their pupils. But one of their handicaps is still their lack of up-to-date training: they were taught to instil academic virtues, and few of them have much knowledge of modern methods, of child psychology, or of what might be called education for civics and leisure. Aware of this, the Ministry has begun to overhaul teacher training, making it less purely academic, with a new stress on modern pedagogic techniques. This may bear some fruit. Meanwhile, there are still years of confusion ahead, with the pupils as chief victims. Slowly and erratically, French education seems to be moving towards a more liberal and egalitarian model. Is it possible to combine this with high academic standards, or must these inevitably suffer? And if so, how much does

this matter? In all countries today, this is the debate among educationalists. In one sense, I am continually impressed by French children's
resilience and their apparent ability – helped no doubt by their home
background – to survive the system to which they are subjected. Yet I am
equally sure that a different system might go some way towards healing
the maladjustments in French society and French public life. This is true
of schools: it is even more true of the universities.

UNIVERSITIES:
THE SOUR FRUITS OF AUTONOMY

'My students are apathetic, listless, worried. They're in a coma, in face of
the slow death of the university world. It's a nightmare situation for us
all.' This professor at Toulouse was expressing his pessimism more
sharply than most; yet in recent years the malaise has been widely
shared, both among teachers and students. The brave new deal offered
to the universities after May '68 has not been working out as hoped.
Under Giscard, it fell foul of the deep mutual mistrust between the State
and the academic world. Nor has it been helped by the economic crisis,
which has underlined the irrelevance of many degree courses to the
needs of the market, a shrinking market that each year multiplies the
total of young jobless graduates.

  French students are not equal. Nearly all higher education is in the
hands of the State: but within this structure a great gulf separates the
privileged few in the Grandes Ecoles, with their strictly limited entry,
from the 'student proletariat' in the swollen, amorphous universities
where anyone with the *bac* can enrol. The former are assured of fine
careers; the latter struggle on poor grants to glean their crumbs of
learning in crowded lecture-rooms, limping along in pursuit of pass
degrees of limited practical value that may end them up as bank clerks or
sales-touts, if not in the dole queue. Even within the universities there is
equally a gulf between this lonely crowd and the rarefied post-graduate
milieu. So, for some years now, France more than most countries has
been facing a crisis of her university system. These ivory towers of
learning, geared to training an academically minded few, have not
proved easily adaptable to the needs of a modern age when far more
people are demanding higher education. Should the courses be made
more vocational? Or should the university remain *'une finalité culturelle'*,
unconcerned with practical ends, as the more conservative professors
(mostly on the Left) still insist? The debate goes on. And the dilemmas of
adaptation are even more acute than in the secondary schools.

  The situation steadily worsened during the 1960s, fomenting the student grievances that finally erupted into the May '68 revolt. Overall student numbers had risen from 12,000 in 1939 to 247,000 in 1960, then 612,000 by 1968 (more than twice the British figure) and only some 5 per cent of these were in the Grandes Ecoles. Numbers at the Sorbonne were at least 160,000 by 1968. But this rapid growth was not adequately matched by the rise in funds or by needed reforms. The Government did create seven new provincial universities in the 1960s, in a bid to relieve pressure on the Sorbonne; but this did not solve the problems. A lecture hall in Paris seating 500 was often crammed with twice that number, and some students would even sit through a lecture in a course outside their subject in order to be sure of a seat for the next one. Students complained also of the impersonal *ex cathedra* style of teaching, and of the heavily theoretical and academic content of their syllabuses. This, they felt, limited career outlets, even at a time when the economy was expanding at full tilt. The Government did respond with a few new measures: it set up technological institutes at below Grande Ecole level, and it created a new short two-year diploma course in the universities, intended as an easy option for weaker students. But these steps did little to stem the growing flood into the faculties. Some voices were raised in favour of imposing selective entry, such as a *numerus clausus*: but this was politically impossible, owing to the rooted French tradition that anyone with the *bac* has the right to higher education.

Universities before 1968 suffered also from an absurd centralization and bureaucracy, just like the schools. It was often said, 'There is just one big university in France with groups of faculties scattered round the provinces, all following identical courses', and if one university outshone the others in some subject (as Lyon in medicine, or Grenoble in science) this was usually due to some pre-Napoleonic heritage, to the prowess of some local personality, or to State policy. A university was in no sense a community and had little personality of its own: its faculties, isolated from each other, were each responsible direct to the Ministry via the Paris-appointed rector who was much more a kind of *préfet* than an English-style vice-chancellor. Ministerial approval was needed for every staff appointment and for the smallest change in routine, even for the holding of a dance in a student hostel. All this added to the students' malaise. They felt there was no one to care for them as individuals. And they were given little official support for creating their own clubs or organized leisure life – always such a striking lack in French universities, by Anglo-American standards. Above all, students before 1968 resented what they saw as their professors' high-handed remoteness. Few teachers bothered to make real human contact with them: many, lecturing to the same class twice a week for a year, might get to know the names of only a handful. So students were thrown back on themselves: if they wanted to voice their discontent on some issue, instead of being able to stroll across the quad into the dean's study for a chat, possibly even over a sherry, as in Britain, they were forced into unionized protest action like metal-workers demanding more pay. It was another of France's famous barriers.

These various frustrations came to a head in the May '68 uprising which began in Nanterre, a bleak new overspill centre for Paris University in the north-west suburbs. Here early in 1968 a few 'action groups' of extremist students – mostly in sociology, psychology and philosophy – set about plotting the overthrow of capitalist society. They were led by the notorious Danny Cohn-Bendit ('Danny le Rouge'). When they broke into open revolt, they were rapidly joined by students all over France, few of whom shared their passionate revolutionary ideals, but all of whom seized eagerly on the opportunity to clamour for a basic university overhaul. It was a spontaneous outburst, and for a few brief weeks France witnessed amazing scenes. Not to mention the barricades and the burning cars, and the brutal police repression, there was also the spectacle of the 'desanctified' Sorbonne like a cathedral in the hands of joyous pagans, with red flags and Maoist slogans stuck all over the venerable statues of the gods of French culture, Molière and others. Throughout France there was the same scenario. Students and liberal-minded professors, who in the past had hardly exchanged a word, sat around in groups in sunlit courtyards discussing future plans, or created assemblies to declare their universities 'autonomous' in defiance of a helpless Ministry. After a few weeks the excitement subsided, de Gaulle restored order, everyone cleared off for the long summer holidays, and it soon became clear that Cohn-Bendit and his friends had lost *their* revolution. But the milder majority seemed at the time to be winning *theirs*, or some of it. For the revolt did succeed in shocking the Government into rethinking the universities on a new pattern; and as never before it opened the eyes of the public to the gravity of the problems. The student world seemed to have emerged at last from its reserve, discovering its own voice. And teachers and students, hitherto afraid or shy to make contact, now found the barriers between them broken by the sheer force of events.

After consulting a range of professors and student leaders, Edgar Faure rapidly prepared an ambitious Bill, and in the autumn won a 441–0 majority for it in the National Assembly. This law abolished the 23 universities as such; then, as a first stage, it invited teachers and students to form themselves as they thought best into some 700 *'unités d'enseignement et de recherche'* (UERs), each made up of a department or group of departments within a faculty. Each *unité* next elected its own council, and then the *unités* were allowed to group themselves as they wished into new universities, smaller and more numerous than the old ones, each with some autonomy over teaching and exam methods and over how to use its budget. For France, all this marked quite a change. Faure was giving the university world a chance to *reform itself*, through a democratic process starting at grass-roots level. Only the broad framework was imposed: the rest each UER and new university could work out for itself, and the personality and constitution of each could differ. It seemed a step towards the Anglo-Saxon model, and away from the centralized French system where every rule was fixed in Paris.

The 76 new universities (using of course the existing buildings) took shape in 1969–71. Larger provincial ones split into two or three. Paris, where there are now some 300,000 students, has 13: the seven central ones, carved out of what used to be known loosely as 'the Sorbonne',[4] bear the down-to-earth names of 'Paris I', 'Paris II' and so on, while the others are in the suburbs. Certainly these new, smaller entities are more manageable than the old dinosaurs. But from the very outset in 1969–70, when the UERs came to negotiate with each other for grouping into universities, the Faure reforms ran into trouble – predictably – from the teaching corps with its penchant for political and academic feuding, and the narrow sectarianism and hostility to change of all but a few professors. Vast intrigues took place as to who should line up with whom. For example, disciplines in Leftist hands such as sociology were often reluctant to join with UERs of law or languages where the professors were often more Rightish; similarly science disciplines, relatively apolitical, fought shy of 'contamination' by the Leftists. The maths department of the old Sorbonne split into two *unités*, one Left, one Right, and each joined a different new university. When huge Aix/Marseille with its 40,000 students divided into three, the split was made not on logical grounds of geography (the two towns being twenty miles apart) but on political ones. Such squabbles have led to an irrational waste of resources in some places. Worse, they have hindered the cross-fertilization and multi-disciplinary teaching that was hitherto lacking in France and was one of the aims of the Faure reforms. At Toulouse, for instance, the three universities are little more than the old faculties under a new name: law, arts and science. This is because the law professors, mostly Right-wing, refused to cohabit with their more Left-inclined colleagues in the other faculties, and vice versa. It is true that within each university, at

4 Properly speaking, 'la Sorbonne' is merely the name of the building that housed the old headquarters of Paris University. It now houses part of some of the new universities, but is not an academic entity in itself.

Toulouse and elsewhere, there has been some progress towards inter-disciplinarity: thus, in arts, a student can now combine mathematics with economics as he could not before 1968, and all science students must now study foreign languages. But the broad exchange of courses and ideas across disciplines, such as you find in the newer English universities, has hardly materialized.

In various ways the universities have tended to abuse their new semi-autonomy. So it is not easy to draw up a balance-sheet of the Faure reforms. Many people today write them off as a failure, yet they do mark some improvements on the old system. In the post-1968 spirit of *participation*, each university now elects its own governing council, where some seats are reserved for students and for non-teaching staff such as typists and cleaners. The council then chooses its president, usually a senior professor, who has some of the powers formerly held by the rector. So, although this election requires formal Ministry approval, some step has been made towards the self-governing system long taken for granted in Britain. The council can also coopt delegates from the world outside, such as local businessmen, trade-unionists or councillors, and this has done a little to bridge the notorious gulf in France between universities and the rest of the public life. Each UER, too, elects its ruling council. And a university now has more control over its day-to-day running: no longer does the holding of a student dance require permission from Paris! Yet the Ministry still keeps reserve powers and holds many strings, both academic and financial. For example, though a university can now decide how to use its working budget, it is still dependent on the Ministry for its allocation and has few resources of its own; and the Ministry still decides on, and pays for, all major new building and equipment. It also remains in charge of awarding the 'national' degrees and diplomas (e.g. *licence, maîtrise*) and sets the exams for these. True, a university can now create its own diplomas too, if it wishes, but these have low prestige. In matters academic, centralization is very far from dead.

However, a university *is* now free to decide on its own teaching and exam methods leading to the national degrees, and it can vary the syllabus so long as it satisfies the Ministry that standards are being kept up. Thus some UERs have virtually abolished lectures and interim exams and have gone over to an American-inspired system of credits and 'continuous assessment', while others have not. 'This pedagogic free-dom is one of our few lasting gains of the Faure reforms,' said one professor. Most students prefer the assessment system, based on a record of regular exercises and orals; and although it might seem to involve less intellectual slogging, in fact they are said to be working

harder than before, on average. After 1969 there was a mass appointment of new junior lecturers and *assistants*, which has brought down the
student/teacher ratio to about 15 to 1 and has made contacts easier.
Everywhere there is now less emphasis on the old impersonal *cours
magistraux* and more on group work and seminars. This is still some way
from the British tutorial system. But the major legacy of May '68 is that it
seems to have narrowed, once and for all, the old gulf between students
and teachers. 'There's a more informal spirit and more direct contact,'
said a junior lecturer in Toulouse; 'the younger or more liberal teachers
are now more accessible to the students, readier to chat with them
outside class. Sometimes we use "*tu*" with each other, unheard of in the
old days. The tyranny of the older professors has been weakened, too:
May '68 knocked them off their sacred pedestals. Some of the old dod-
derers in the Law university now have their lectures interrupted, even
booed.'

Yet the professors, those privileged mandarins, have been fighting
back to defend their vested interests. And if the Faure reforms have not
yet worked out too well, this has been less the fault of the students (far
more quiescent than a decade ago) than of the teachers and their non-
stop vendettas with the Ministry in the Giscard era. One complication is
that university politics present a through-the-looking-glass picture of
normal voting alignments: the teachers' innate conservatism is often
strongest among those on the Left (many of them Communist) who
claim loudest to be 'revolutionary'. So, even more than in the secondary
schools, they hated 'collaborating' with Giscard's capitalist regime, nor
could they ever accept that its reforms might be sincere and benevolent:
the State was always suspected of ulterior motives. Many Left-wing
teachers, plus some student delegates, chose the new university councils
as the terrain for their fight against that regime. Hence many of the
councils became highly politicized, and sensible new projects were endlessly contested and blocked. A well-known liberal journalist told me: 'I
was coopted on to one of the Paris councils, and at first I was glad of the
chance to bring in new ideas and help bridge the gulf that isolates the
academic world. But our meetings were wasted in such futile wrangling
that I got fed up and resigned.' This was a common experience, though
matters varied from one university to another: the mainly scientific ones
were usually calmer and less politics-ridden than those dealing in such
sensitive subjects as sociology and economics. Here Left-wing teachers
often led strikes and sit-ins against Government measures.

Conservative professors, of all political shades, have reacted to
Faure's new order by intensifying their corporatism. Each discipline,
each UER, devotes much of its energies to defending its own positions,

its own share of the global budget, and few professors are concerned with forming links with other disciplines. Full professors have been digging in their heels to try to preserve their influence and their privileges against the new democratic pressures from junior staff, from student delegates and others. And amid this in-fighting, there is little energy left over for the more constructive tasks of forging a new university with its own personality and a sense of common purpose. This opportunity, clearly offered by the 1969 reforms, has been gradually eroded.

Until the mid-1970s the Government took the line that this was an inevitable transition phase: the new universities needed time to sort out their teething-troubles and work through their conflicts. 'Autonomy is like adolescence,' said one official; 'its confusions don't last for ever.' Then in 1975 the universities were hived off from the Ministry of Education into the charge of a new separate junior ministry, and the following year this portfolio was given to a most formidable lady, Alice Saunier-Seïté, hitherto *recteur* of Reims, a slinky, sexy, black-eyed fifty-year-old with a taste for tight-fitting black trousers. The Press described her as 'a juicy autumnal fruit', but there was little misty or mellow about her views. A confirmed Jacobin, she decided that the universities were getting out of hand. So she began a campaign to regain greater control, using her reserve powers under the Faure Law and even getting Parliament to rescind some of its liberal provisions. The academic world was soon after her blood.

Notably, in 1979 she increased the powers of her Ministry over the appointment of teaching staff. This is a complex issue which inevitably stirs up academic passions: should a university be allowed to select its own professors (as in Britain), or not? In centralized France, the Ministry has always had the last word. But Faure, in the spirit of his reform, granted his universities and UERs the new right to draw up their own initial short-list of candidates for each vacant post, in order of preference, for the Ministry to approve. Saunier-Seïté felt – and many people, including liberals, reluctantly agreed with her – that this was leading to too much local favouritism, as professors short-listed their own buddies often on political grounds. A national selection, she felt, would give fairer chances of promotion. So she gave stronger powers to national selection boards sponsored by the Ministry, at the expense of local ones. The universities were furious. Authoritarian Alice took other measures too. In a bid to curb Left-wing influence, she reduced the right of students and junior staff to share in the election of council presidents. She began to interfere more closely in the universities' spending of their budgets. And in many of them she cut back the range of subjects they were authorized to offer for national degrees. This was an attempt to push universities towards greater specialization and to reduce duplication of resources. It was a rational step in a time of austerity. But again it infuriated academia.

'That terrible woman, she treats a university as if it were a mere *lycée*,' said a professor in Grenoble. Another in Paris added: 'She wastes our time, bombarding us with bureaucratic controls. Our so-called autonomy is now just a joke.' The teachers with their angry chorus were maybe exaggerating the real extent of the Minister's changes: what irked them above all was her high-handed manner. Like most Government reformers in education since the war, she applied her measures with a tactless lack of prior consultation – 'like a bull in a china shop', was one comment. Yet, however foolish her methods, she had been left with little choice but to step in and take some action: the universities, or many of them, had proved unequal to the challenge of autonomy. In this war of mistrust between the State and academia, the faults were shared. Yet the whole issue raised again in many minds a fundamental question: among a people as contentious and sectarian as the French, is real decentralization ever going to work?

In the later Giscard period the malaise on the campus was stronger among teachers than students, unlike in 1968. One major grievance was the shortage of funds from the Ministry for coping with the huge student numbers. After 1968 the Government had greatly increased its spending on the universities: but this trend was reversed in the austere late '70s under Raymond Barre, and budget allocations did not keep pace with inflation. In many EERs I heard the same litany of complaints: staff reductions, and freezing of funds for badly needed new equipment and premises. A geography teacher in Toulouse told me that his UER could no longer afford to fund his student's field research, or supply the library with new books. Also, staff recruitment was virtually at a standstill and some posts were being suppressed. Teachers of all grades grew angry and worried at seeing their promotion prospects threatened.

After the Socialist victory, the departure of Saunier-Seïté provoked an immense sigh of relief on every campus, even among teachers who had not voted for the Left. The universities were now brought back under the umbrella of the Ministry of Education itself, and the new Minister, Alain Savary, at once revoked some of Alice's more unpopular measures. He promised that he would try to establish a more genuine autonomy for the universities. This might need new legislation; or it could be achieved simply by ensuring that the spirit of the Faure reforms is, this time, properly observed. At all events, by the autumn of

1981 the mood in French universities was less gloomy than for some years.

The students themselves still face many problems, which will not easily be cured by a simple change of regime. After 1968 their numbers continued to rise; and, though mercifully it has levelled off in the past five years, the total in higher education today is over a million, of whom some are in the Grandes Ecoles and in technical colleges, but about 800,000 are in the universities. Here their lot is still a hard one, despite the improvements in study systems and in relations with teachers. They are still overcrowded, they face growing job anxieties, and increasingly they are forced to ask what is the value of a degree. Also, the drop-out rate remains so high that arguably many of them should not be at university at all, and this controversial problem the Faure reforms have not solved. All students supposedly take an initial two-year course leading to a diploma called the DEUG (*diplôme des études universitaires générales*); after this, they either leave or stay a third year to sit for their *licence* (equivalent of a BA), and then maybe a fourth to try for the *maîtrise* (MA) which opens gates to research or post-graduate work. But in practice more than 40 per cent of entrants drop out in the first year or so without even sitting for the DEUG; and no more BAs (*licences*) are awarded than in Britain, for twice the number of students. One reason for the high fall-out is that, although tuition fees are minimal, many students are obliged to earn their keep. About 50 per cent get help from parents; but only one in eight receives a State grant and these are niggardly, averaging a mere 5,000 to 6,000 francs a year. This helps to explain why so many poorer families still hesitate to launch their children into the *lycée* stream. Many students take jobs when they are lucky enough to find them, maybe as porters, sales-assistants, or *surveillants de lycée*: but this combined with study imposes a strain, and the weaker ones get discouraged and give up the academic race. Some 35 per cent of students have full or part-time jobs.

The system has its admirably liberal side too, allowing a wide flexibility of choice for the more enterprising student. Anyone with the *bac* can enter almost any university, even though most people in practice opt for the one nearest to their home. A student initially can enrol for several different courses at once, maybe in more than one university in the same town, and thus can test out his or her aptitudes and interests by sampling a range of lectures and seminars, before settling down to one serious course of study. But thousands of students are not 'serious': they enrol as a kind of status-symbol, or in order to be eligible for cheap meals in the subsidized canteens, or (in the case of girls from well-to-do homes) as a way of passing a dilettante year or two before marriage. These *étudiants fantômes*, as they are called, are less numerous than a few years back, but they still infuriate teachers. A professor at Montpellier told me: 'Some 150 students signed up for my class, but I've no idea how many will sit the exams. They drift casually in and out of lectures. Go down to the beaches, and you'll find them in hordes. It's a racket, and a waste of our limited resources.'

Many other students simply feel out of their depth in higher education. The *lycées*, with their deductive parrot-learning methods and close supervision, have not prepared them for using their initiative and working on their own. This problem may have eased with the development of seminars: but even today many students feel isolated, adrift and bereft of guidance. They suffer breakdowns, or give up, or go on trying and failing the same exams – and they are allowed to sit several times. In fact, while some students drop out, others – if they can afford it – go to the opposite extreme and try to delay the end of their studies as long as possible, knowing that at the end of the road may lie only the dole queue. 'We're breeding protracted adolescents,' said one professor, 'and it adds to the strain on resources.'

Some teachers have long argued that harder or more selective entry to universities – either a raising of the pass-mark for the *bac*, or a *numerus clausus* on the British or German model – is the only rational answer to the high drop-out rate and the overcrowded campuses. This, they say, would spare much wasted effort and frustrations for all concerned. But French students, though chief victims of the congestion, remain firmly opposed to a *numerus clausus*, which they claim would be undemocratic; and the majority of professors, too, still feel that entry based on the *bac* is the only one, as any other might lead to regional inequalities or the personal bias of selection boards. 'I know we get a lot of students who shouldn't be here,' said a young teacher at Rennes, 'but at least the first year's work gives someone a chance to *prove to himself* that he's not suited to the academic grind, rather than be told so in advance by some board' – a commendably liberal approach, if an expensive one.

For years '*la sélection*' has been a hot political issue in France and no minister, not even Faure, has dared impose it. However, it has finally begun to be applied piecemeal and surreptitiously in a few places. In fact of the growing surplus of doctors (see p. 447) and the high expense of their training, a kind of *numerus clausus* was imposed in medicine in 1971: the students greeted it with a long strike, but in the end accepted it. Anyone with the right kind of *bac* can still enrol in a medical school, but at the end of his first year he must face a stiff competitive exam which only about one student in six passes. The rest must transfer to another discipline, or leave. In some universities a few other UERs have since followed suit, often applying a *numerus clausus* not by selection board but on a first-come-first-served basis, as they are entitled to do. In fact, Saunier-Seïté encouraged them to reduce their numbers, by the simple incentive of cutting their funds! So *la sélection* has been creeping in by the back door, and this is quite a change. But if you have the *bac*, and you shop around, you can still be sure of a place somewhere.

The official policy is not to dissuade people from entering higher education, but rather to channel more of them away from the universities and into new technical and business colleges, whose courses are more directly geared to job needs. Set up in 1966, the *Instituts Universitaires de Technologie* were at first not much of a success, for they ran up against the strong middle-class prejudice against all technical education below the élite Grande Ecole level. But finally this is waning, as more students come to recognize that an IUT diploma can often open the door to better jobs than a mere DEUG or even a *licence*. The IUTs offer a practical two-year course just after the *bac* and today they are quite popular, filling a much-needed gap in higher technical education below the Grandes Ecoles. Similarly, a number of students are now rejecting the golden ideal of the *licence* in favour of specialized colleges for accountancy, interpreting the hotel and catering trades, and so on. This swing of the pendulum is recent, prompted by rising unemployment, and it explains the slight fall in campus numbers since about 1976.

A general arts degree, or even a science degree has never carried the same universal value in career terms as in Britain. The French are often amazed that a firm such as ICI will gladly take on an Oxford classics graduate for an executive post, or that a degree in English can lead to a managerial traineeship in commerce. 'In liberal Britain,' said one student, 'it seems you can study anything for anything – and the results show up in the amateurism of so much British industry! In France we're more specialized. It's the influence of the Grandes Ecoles.' However, the losers in this French system are the universities, those ivory towers whose study courses even at *maîtrise* level have hitherto not been geared to the needs of the world outside. Literature and language graduates have few possible career outlets except to be teachers of future students – an absurd hermetic circle – and even in physics and biology the problem is much the same. 'The science teaching,' I was told, 'is too theoretical to be much use to industrial firms, who prefer to recruit from the Grandes Ecoles or IUTs. Our graduates become teachers.' And a student of English complained, 'The teaching is too literary. We study Shakespeare, but not modern commercial English, so we'd be useless in industry or business. Nor do we feel suited for jobs like advertising or television.' Later, his professor commented to me drily: 'This problem of career outlets simply does not interest me. The duty of the university is to provide a high level of culture and to ensure that the students imbibe it.' My mouth fell open.

The economic crisis has worsened matters. Not only are jobs in industry harder than ever to obtain, but cuts in education budgets have reduced even the number of teaching posts. For the senior teaching diplomas with their rigid *numerus clausus* – the elitist *agrégation*, and the CAPES (Certificat d'Aptitude Professionelle à l'Enseignement Secondaire) – there are now ten or twenty times more applicants than places. So most graduates must look elsewhere, and vast numbers today are obliged to take jobs well below their qualifications. Those with only the DEUG or *licence* may well end up as check-out girls in a supermarket or ushers in a town hall. And graduates must fight their own battles on the labour market, for few universities have equivalents of the English appointments boards.

By the mid-'70s even those with the *maîtrise* were not always finding jobs. So some of the more go-ahead universities began to try to gear a few *maîtrise* courses more closely to career realities outside teaching, in face of protests from the kind of diehard teacher quoted above! In 1975, with graduate unemployment rising dangerously, the Government stepped in with a helping hand. It instructed each university to devise new courses for the *maîtrise* in various disciplines 'taking account of local and national job outlets'. What is more, it invited members of the industrial and business world to sit on the Ministry's boards that were to approve the new courses. The sensible aim was to seek their advice on the kind of training needed: but for France this was revolutionary, the first time the world of the Patronat had ever been asked to have a direct say in the doings of the ivory towers. There was a storm of protest from teachers and students alike, throughout France. Universities were angry at the way the reform was foisted on them without consultation – Alice Saunier-Seïté was by then in charge of its application – and they threatened to apply their own *maîtrise* courses without ministerial approval. Students then panicked in turn, fearing that these 'local' degrees, lacking national validity, would be of little value. And Left-wing teachers and students were united in their fury at the invitation to the Patronat: 'Do we want to provide cannon-fodder for industry?' asked one militant; 'we shall be brainwashed to suit the needs of the boss class!' All too typical of the perverse French Left: the same people who for years had been protesting at the lack of job outlets were now in arms against a reform to remedy just that. In 1976 strikes broke out, lasting ten weeks in some places. 'I'm not really interested in getting a job,' I was told by a student in Toulouse; 'I just want to overthrow the regime. Better starve than be used to prop up a dying capitalism!' But in the end the revolt just fizzled out. My friend overthrew nothing: I'm sure he didn't starve either. Some new *maîtrises* were duly created – in management studies, applied electronics, audio-visual media, etc. – and they began to show results. But it was not without a fight. The director of a UER in Toulouse told me: 'When we set up a *maîtrise* in applied modern languages, we had 90 per cent of the staff against us at first, all the Leftish ones. They thought the course too non-literary, too geared to business. But finally they backed down. And now our graduates *are* finding it a little easier to get jobs, for example, in export services or with international bodies. We're breaking the vicious circle of teachers-training-teachers.'

The conflict has raised the whole question of what a university is for. Professors have written angry articles in *Le Monde*, complaining that the 'purity' of their scholarship is being degraded by the workaday world, that the university is becoming a mere utilitarian tool. Yes, maybe scholarly standards *will* suffer a little under the new system. But the ghetto-mentality of many teachers is still an obstacle to progress. Too often they live in their own tight little social cliques, meeting few people except their own colleagues, obsessed by their sectarian feuds. More than in most countries, they are divorced from the rest of national life: the average professor retains a scorn for the milieux of industry, journalism or public service. An exception is Raymond Aron, who broadcasts, writes for *Le Figaro* and is a star figure: but people are often surprised when they learn that he is also a university teacher.[5]

Some professors are today at last deigning to appear on TV programmes; others are now readier to become town councillors. But they remain resentful of the reverse trend, that is, of any intruder into their own world, however distinguished he be: when one well-known *polytechnicien* retired from the upper civil service and broke precedent by giving a course of lectures at the Paris law school, the reaction of many law professors was: 'But how *can* he? He's not a *professeur ès droit!*' Everyone must abide by his *titre*, no one must poach on another's preserve. The staunchest guardians of this ethos are those who have crossed that fearsome hurdle, the *doctorat d'Etat*, essential qualification for a full professor's chair. This involves up to ten or fifteen years' work preparing an encyclopaedic document of maybe 1,000 pages on a highly specialized subject, while probably doing a teaching job at the same time. It is exhausting, but the final prize is great. A *docteur* with a professorship can do much as he likes for the rest of his life. He get a salary of maybe 150,000 francs a year for an easy sinecure and does not have to teach more than seventy-five hours a year. Many professors do continue to work hard, but others abuse their freedom. They are held less in awe than before 1968: but no reformer has yet dared diminish their privileges.

However, willy-nilly the university is now moving slowly out of its ghetto. It is developing more foreign exchanges, both at student and teacher level. It is at last readier to help industry with research (see p. 49). And it is now playing a larger role in adult education and in service training courses. One famous experiment since 1968 has been the creation of a kind of 'open university' at Vincennes in the eastern Paris suburbs (transferred in 1980 to St-Denis). Vincennes does not require even the *bac* and has attracted large numbers of part-time 'mature students' with humble jobs in offices or factories. It also invites visiting lecturers from outside academia, such as novelists, journalists, businessmen. The result has been much vivid exchange of ideas, a good deal of cheerful chaos and Leftist provocation; and much ink has been spilt as to whether Vincennes has been an inspired success or an instructive failure. Its example has had little sequel elsewhere. But it remains one of the last rallying-points of those *gauchistes* now in their thirties who look back with nostalgia on those far-off heady student days of 1968.

Today's French students are a very different breed from those who stormed the barricades in '68. Gone is the old militancy. The vast majority share the current French disillusion with ideologies; the few politically active ones are mostly Communist, plus a very few *gauchistes* split as usual into warring groups whose influence now is minimal. When they try to organize some strike or other protest, it usually fails through lack of wider support. So there has been relatively little unrest on the campuses in the past decade, apart from the flare-up over the *maîtrise* in 1976 and another in the spring of 1980 over a Government move to restrict immigrant students. As individuals, French students are hardworking, serious-minded, worried about their own futures; they are not indifferent to the world's problems, but they are sceptical and have lost faith in collective action, in the ability to improve even their own university environment, let alone society. Significantly, only 4.5 per cent even bother to join a student union: the only sizeable one is firmly in Communist hands. And a severe setback to the 1969 ideals of 'participation' is the fact that very few students vote in the new university elections or come forward as candidates – so few, in fact, that they fall short of the necessary quorum and their quotas on the self-governing councils are underused. At the Toulouse arts university in 1979 only 5 per cent of students voted, and this left them with the right to take up only three of their allotted twenty-seven seats on the central council: the three elected were all Communists. This is an extreme example of a general trend, and as one apolitical student suggested to me, 'What's the point of voting, when to help fill up the quorum simply benefits the Communists as no one else can be bothered to stand?' So the students stay quietly in the background, their noses in their textbooks, obsessed by the hunt for diplomas that may stave off unemployment. A middle-aged professor in Rennes commented: 'Compared with the old days, even the 1960s, they've got little sense of fun. I don't hear them singing any more.'

Even in their leisure lives many feel isolated, for French universities are not warm club-like communities. Unlike in Britain, the habit is that you go to your local university – except may be at advanced level – and this has increased with money getting tighter. So more than a third of all students live at home, where at least they have the comfort of family and a nucleus of existing friends. But others, whose homes are too far away, stay in rented rooms or utilitarian hostels, and here they can be very lonely; in the French manner, they seem to be too reserved to make new friends easily, or else they lack the time or money to club together to create their own communal life. No collegiate tradition exists to welcome them, and the authorities do little to stimulate it. A small minority, children of indulgent well-to-do parents, have a jolly time: you can see them dashing about in sports cars, or in the down-town discos. But for the rest, often struggling on low grants, there is little *dolce vita*.

The paucity of clubs and organized social life has always seemed – to an Anglo-Saxon – a striking feature of French universities which have no equivalent of the big English 'union' building, a focus for community. On French campuses, the occasional club centre is usually little more than two or three drab rooms with a bar, a ping-pong table, a record-player for *surboums* (dances) on Saturday nights, and a notice-board covered with appeals for digs, part-time work or free lifts to Paris. It is true that sport is popular, and proper facilities for it have at last been provided; also the students run a few simple cultural activities as *ciné* and jazz clubs. But many large universities do not even have any student drama group or orchestra; and such initiatives have been growing even rarer, now that students are so preoccupied with work, exams and job prospects. They will passively consume what is provided, for example at the Maisons de la Culture: but they no longer create their own thing. At Nancy in the mid-'60s the students set up an ambitious cultural scene, with frequent festivals, debates, concerts: but this has since withered, for no one today is prepared to take charge of it.

'Maybe it's partly a lack of time or money, but it's also a question of temperament,' the director of a welfare body said; 'the French are not club-joiners. I've tried to start discussion-groups and the like, but the students won't come. They have their own little knots of friends, and they sit around in cafés and each others' rooms, but they're too suspicious or inert to take part in anything organized. As a result they feel adrift, with no sympathetic context to fit in to – unless they live at home, or are motivated to join some religious or political group.' A few teachers do try to help, especially since 1968, by making efforts to get to know at least some students personally: a professor at Montpellier told me, 'I try to be a kind of moral tutor to a few of them I feel they need me. Sometimes my wife and I have them to dinner.' But this is still the exception, and it is not in the French tradition: 'Our job,' said another professor, 'is to teach our students, not offer them *apéritifs*. That would be favouritism, very *mal vu*.' Other teachers complain that when they do try to make contact, the students in turn are evasive, refusing to be drawn into anything personal. Also the sheer weight of numbers makes real contact difficult. A student with problems can turn to the university's welfare service; but he is not individually assigned a 'moral tutor' to keep a friendly eye on him, as in Britain. And it is usually only at *maîtrise* or post-graduate level, where numbers are much smaller, that personal links develop.

The building of campuses has not helped. Until the early 1960s nearly all universities were down-town: here the students thronged the cafés, deriving some warmth from the town and adding to its liveliness in return. But, with the growth in numbers, most departments have now been transferred to big new campuses in the outskirts. Some of these are quite attractive, and they have eased working conditions: but the students are now more isolated than ever, especially those who live in the campus hostels. The sad case of Grenoble is instructive. Here in the mid-'60s the university welfare authorities made an imaginative attempt, very unusual for France, to tackle the human problems of the new student ghettos. They persuaded a few younger teachers to go out and live on the campus among them. They also found funds for building a socio-cultural centre, equipped with a theatre for films and plays, a record library, music room and so on. The students were encouraged to run their own community life, under the friendly guidance of the resident teachers – and they responded. After six weeks they had founded a drama club, and arranged their own debating society with visitors coming to talk about such relevant topics as birth-control. The evening I called, the music room was packed with a cosmopolitan crowd listening to a Turkish student at the piano and a Canadian guitarist. Everyone seemed happy. But then came May '68, which left the Grenoble campus more politicized than most. Led by the Leftists the students decided to put an end to officialdom's well-meaning attempts to 'direct' – as they put it – their leisure life. So the teachers departed. And though today the political mood is calmer, the scheme has not been relaunched, perhaps more through mutual inertia than anything else: the socio-cultural centre is empty much of the time, used only for the occasional dance or film-show. The campus itself *looks* quite idyllic, on a spacious site with well-kept lawns, trees, even outdoor sculptures, against a mountain backdrop; there is a swimming-pool, and plenty of sport. But this ghetto is totally cut off from the life of the town (see p. 160) and its own social life is almost nil; at night it is silent, at the weekends deserted. The students stay in their rooms, or they drift off down-town in search of amusements; yet the town too has lost its student focus, its Latin Quarter spirit. And the same is true elsewhere in France. So what is the answer? Lack of funds from the Ministry, or lack of concern by the university authorities, can in some cases be blamed for the failure to provide encouragement or amenities. Yet when the effort *is* made, it is often rejected, as at Grenoble. The students' *malaise* lies above all in their own psychology. Their *repli sur soi* has been typical of the French national mood in the period before the 1981 elections; their tacit rejection of organized university life has been one aspect of the wider French rejection of institutions. 'For us,' said one girl in Grenoble, 'this campus is just a place of transit for getting a degree. We have no urge to build it into some cherished Alma Mater.' Possibly the new regime in France will now usher in a less negative mood among students.

I have drawn a harsh picture of French universities as they were up to the spring of 1981. But at least there has been less confusion and paralysis than, say, in Italy. And now the change of Government offers the opportunity for making a new start. The Edgar Faure reforms were not bad in themselves: but they were badly executed, due as much as anything to the lack of trust between the universities and the Ministry. If the new Socialist rulers can now create that trust, there is a chance that some kind of autonomy will finally prove viable. But it will require a new degree of budgetary freedom. And there are still dangers ahead, for teachers in France remain a contentious breed, and the signs indicate that campus administration may still be prey to endless feuding between, say, Socialist and Communist cliques. In this as in other fields, autonomy still carries powerful risks in France. But the risks have to be taken.

The French are also being forced to rethink what a university is for. Can it still fulfil the Renaissance ideal of producing the well-rounded, cultivated man? Or, in this age of the masses that is also an age of specialization, should it become more vocational? There are many who believe that it can and should do both, but that its courses should distinguish more clearly than at present between these two ends, instead of blurring them. Some changes along these lines are essential, if the universities are to cease being mere poor relations to the Grandes Ecoles.

GRANDES ECOLES:
BASTIONS OF PRIVILEGE

The most distinctive trait of French higher education, and one that profoundly marks French society, is the division between the sprawling universities and the exclusive Grandes Ecoles, most of them devoted to engineering, applied science or management studies. Each has long enjoyed a good deal of freedom; each controls its numbers with its own fiercely competitive entrance exam, requiring two or three years' special study after the *bac*; and once admitted, the lucky student leads a relatively privileged existence. He has close contact with his teachers; and he is virtually assured of a worthwhile career, especially if he is an alumnus of one of the more prestigious colleges, led by the mighty Polytechnique. The Grandes Ecoles account for no more than one in twenty of the numbers in higher education, but they turn out a high proportion of France's top administrators and engineers, and on the whole they have served France well.[6] Reformers such as Edgar Faure have therefore tended to leave them alone, nor were they much affected by the virus of May '68. Yet the Grande Ecole system is constantly under criticism. Is it healthy for a modern society, this divorce between an élitist stream and the universities? And do the Ecoles really provide such a wonderful training, or are they living on their reputation and carefully cultivated mystique?

Since 'Grande Ecole' is a general and not an official term, it is hard to specify the exact number of these schools; but some 140 lay claim to the rank, with an average of a mere 400 students each. They range from ordinary provincial business schools to advanced post-graduate colleges specializing in such subjects as aerospace and telecommunications. Some Ecoles are privately-owned, some are run by local chambers of commerce, while most belong to the State but not all of these come under the Ministry of Education: Polytechnique, for instance, is responsible to the Defence Ministry.

Competition for the better schools has always been intense, and has

6 For the influence of the Grandes Ecoles, and of the Grands Corps which recruit from them, see pp. 82–92.

grown more so with the decline of the universities' prestige. An abler *lycée* pupil will tend to make a Grande Ecole his first option, but first he must face a pre-selection: that is, he must convince his teachers that he is worth a place in one of the *classes préparatoires* that exist only in certain key *lycées*, mostly in Paris, and alone prepare for the Grande Ecole exams. These special post-*bac* classes, known in slang as *hypotaupes* and *hypokhâgnes*, put their pupils through a rigorous two or three-year course; and competition is such that many of them work a crippling 70 to 80-hour week, turning into pale swots and driving themselves and their parents mad – 'Those who come out top for entry to the Polytechnique,' one professor used to tell his class, 'do not smoke, do not drink, and are virgins.' The work in these *lycée* classes is of a far higher standard than in the average university: in many ways they represent the intellectual pinnacle of French education. But for all except the most brilliant it is an unnerving obstacle-race with a large prospect of failure, as the better Grandes Ecoles have places for only about one candidate in ten. The rest try for a lesser school, or end up at a mere university. And yet, once admitted, the lucky few then find that inside the Grandes Ecoles the work is not nearly so exacting, and at *their* passing-out exams the failure rate is almost nil. So the real mind-stretching test is in the *lycée* classes – 'the cram de la crème', said a headline in (of course) the *Guardian*.

If so many *polytechniciens* and others still rise to the top posts in the land, it may be due less to the quality of the training they receive inside their Grandes Ecoles than to the schools' prestige and to their own innate brilliance, for there is no doubt that many of France's finest brains still choose this royal road to success. This is supremely true of the Ecole Polytechnique, often known as 'X' for short because of its badge of two crossed cannon. By origin this is a military college, founded by Napoleon to train engineers for the armed forces. Today it is still run as a kind of residential officer cadet school, with a serving general at its head: its pupils, *les X*, go on parade four times a year in full-dress uniform with strange curly hats. But this military spirit has been greatly diluted in recent years, especially since the school's transfer in 1976 from its old enclosed home near the Panthéon to more open and spacious premises at Palaiseau in the suburbs. Formerly, *les X* were confined to barracks most of the week; now they can come and go almost as freely as any other student, though in class they must still wear khaki boy-scout uniforms. Very few today enter a military career: most go into public service or private industry. But this diaspora has by no means weakened the power of the graduates' freemasony. Once an 'X' always an 'X': all graduates high and low call each other *camarade* whether they have met before or not, and the lowliest 'X' can write out of the blue to a famous colleague and be sure of help and sympathy.

But is the school's arrogant influence substantiated by the quality of its training? Until recently, *les X* all received the same encyclopaedic general education at a high level, with plenty of thermodynamics, astrophysics and logic, but their detailed time-table left little scope for initiative: Pétain once said of a *polytechnicien*, 'That man knows everything, but he knows nothing else.' Since 1969 the syllabus has been updated to include a large dose of economics and more foreign languages, and second-year students can now specialize and work on their own research projects. But there is still a running debate as to whether the proper role of the Polytechnique is to train good research scientists or good managers, and many people feel that it falls between these two stools. The science lobby argues that the system still does too little to encourage the kind of creative thinking required for top-level research. The counter-argument is that graduates in practice tend to move into administrative rather than boffin jobs, yet the courses are inadequately geared to modern management techniques. The school's reply is that its role is simply to provide a high-level background education in its short two-year course. Only 10 per cent of graduates then go straight into jobs: others move on to further studies, which may be a top American business school or one of the élite French *écoles d'application* of which the leaders are the Ecoles de Mines and the Ecole des Ponts et Chaussées. One such is the aeronautical college at Toulouse known as 'Sup Aéro', where 350 students come from all over France and live in elegant halls of residence. They despise the university 'proletariat' and lead a separate social life, sometimes slipping off to Paris for the weekend in an aircraft placed at their disposal. The laboratories are lavish; even the reading-room looks like the lounge of a luxury hotel. 'We've never had student unrest here,' said the director: 'what is there to protest about?'

There are many other Grandes Ecoles of all types, under- or post-graduate, each with its own old-boy network, all intense rivals in the intricate hierarchy of national influence and prestige. Among engineers, the Ecole Centrale trails second after 'X'. One special case is the famous Ecole Normale Supérieure, near the Panthéon: this concentrates on the humanities as much as on science and its primary role is to prepare university and senior *lycée* teachers via the *agrégation*. Sartre, Blum, Jaurès, Giraudoux, Pompidou were among the *normaliens* nurtured in this citadel of French scholarship. But today the Normale's influence is not what it used to be: it has suffered from the blight on the universities, also from France's post-war trend away from the classic humanities and towards commerce and technology. So the schools whose star is now rising are those dealing in business studies and *le management*, now so much *à la mode*. The leader in this field is the Ecole des Hautes Etudes Commerciales (HEC), owned by the Paris Chamber of Commerce and spaciously housed in a big wooded park near Versailles. Here 850 élite students, one-third of them girls, follow a wide-ranging modern business course that includes compulsory *stages* abroad and the learning of at least two languages. Employers fall over each other to offer jobs to HEC leavers, and *alumni* include the heads of Renault and Citroën and of some big banks. But it is not all work and no play in this residential college where the ambience – at last! – is more like that of Oxbridge or the Ivy League than of the average sad French campus. The students actually run their own drama, music and debating clubs, and stage their own gymkhanas, all subsidized by the college. Most students have cars; and though some bursaries are available on a means test, most parents pay sizeable fees. It is little surprise to learn that over half the students come from Paris and only some 10 per cent are from worker or peasant families.

HEC celebrated its centenary in 1981. On its model, scores of newer business colleges have sprung up since the war, both in Paris and the provinces, to meet the economy's new needs. They are uneven in quality, and few have won the true status of a Grande Ecole: but most of them offer the kind of vocational training that easily leads to the securing of jobs. Some are international in outlook and have developed exchange links with similar colleges abroad. The Ecole des Affaires de Paris, founded in 1974 by the Paris Chamber of Commerce, is an interesting innovation: its French students do a year in Paris, a year in Oxford, a year in Düsseldorf, including field projects and *stages* with firms in the three countries, and they emerge trilingual, with a useful multinational business background. The EAP has been muscling its way into the middle rank of Grandes Ecoles: some candidates in the *lycée* classes even opt for it in preference to the more prestigious HEC.

The Grandes Ecoles, often accused of encrusted conservatism, have recently been modernizing their courses and teaching methods, introducing more group work, practical field projects and so on. Clearly the Grande Ecole system has been, and still is, a fertile source of strength for the French economy. But its near-monopoly of the best jobs is serving to perpetuate the barriers in French society, and reformers have long argued that ways should be found of bringing the system closer to the university structure. In a few cases this has been happening, piecemeal. One or two Grandes Ecoles now share some facilities and teaching staff with the universities. And one or two new specialized universities have been created in an effort to bridge the gap: notably a new University of

Technology at Compiègne has established close working links with industry and has won the right to offer higher degree courses in engineering, thus breaking the Grandes Ecoles' monopoly in this field. But the Grandes Ecoles will fight to the last against any wider attempt to dismantle their privileges, and they want to avoid contamination by what they see as the 'university shambles'. They keep their distances. And there is little prospect of this changing, even under the new Socialist regime. So senior pupils in the *lycées* will continue to face a rigorous streaming that may dictate the rest of their lives. The system appears as a plus for economic efficiency, and a minus for true egalitarianism.

LA JEUNESSE:
RETICENCE, NOT REBELLION

What are they like, this mysterious new generation, for whom all the educational crusades are being fought? Few adults can find an easy answer. Ostensibly, young people have been following much the same paths as in other Western countries. They have their own new consumer markets for music, clothes and cars; their own world of rock groups and other singing idols; their own fringe minorities of delinquents. All, or almost all, enjoy far more freedom from parents than cloistered French youth had even twenty years ago, and far more sexual licence too. Many are conscious of the gulf between their own morality and that of their parents. Yet they are not rebels. Most of them cautiously welcome the new Socialist Government: but they are not fired with revolutionary ideals for trying to change society, like the young hotheads of 1968. Though tolerant and reflective, they seem curiously passive. And rarely do they show much sense of public initiative.

It used not to be so. In the initial post-war period, 1945–60, many of the most important changes in France were due to a new generation rising against the standards of its elders, from the young farmers of the JAC to the cinema's *nouvelle vague*. The post-1945 climate was very different from today's: more austere, but also more open and adventurous. The upheavals of wartime had broken down some of the barriers that previously kept youth in its place, and an idealistic new wave was able gradually to make inroads into the *positions acquises* of the age-hierarchy. It happened most strikingly in agriculture (see pp. 205–21), also here and there in industry, commerce and the arts. It is remarkable how youthful many of the post-war pioneers were at the outset: Leclerc was twenty-three when he began his cut-price campaign in Brittany, and Planchon founded his Villeurbanne theatre at twenty-one; a few years later, Gourvennec aged twenty-four led the North Breton farmers' revolution, while Godard, Truffaut and others made their cinema break-through in their mid-twenties. Today these and other pace-setters are established middle-aged figures, some of them in key positions: but the generations that followed them, born into an age of greater affluence but also of greater scepticism, have seldom shown the same innovating spirit.

A few much-publicized Parisian phenomena, in those early post-war years, contrived to give the world an image of French youth in revolt. First came the existentialists. After the Liberation a number of young Parisians flocked excitedly around Sartre and Camus at St-Germain-des-Prés, eager to rebel against their bourgeois background and help forge a better society (see p. 529). But this climate gradually dissipated, as many Sartrian disciples settled down to leading the prosperous careerist lives they had earlier denounced. Then in 1954 the eighteen-year-old Françoise Sagan, daughter of an industrialist, published her first novel, *Bonjour Tristesse*. Her sophisticated world of whisky and wealth was some steps away from the severe intellectual *milieu* of the true existentialists: but her heroine's cool disillusion and rejection of social morality sounded a note that seemed to borrow something, however ill-digested, from the ideas of Sartre. Two years later the young director Roger Vadim took a little-known actress to a modest Riviera fishing-port and there made *Et Dieu créa la femme* – and God-knows-who created Bardot and St-Tropez. Thousands from *une certain jeunesse*, mainly Parisian, rushed there at once. France and the world were amazed. Was this what French youth was like? Was Sagan's free-living heroine typical of French girls of eighteen? On the whole, not. But the Sagan, Bardot and St-Tropez myths remained potent well into the swinging 'sixties.

St-Tropez was then in its heyday, a phenomenon that had plenty of counterparts elsewhere, for example in Chelsea and San Francisco: but its intensity in one small, picturesque seaside location gave it a special appeal. The whole affair was hardly Vadim's fault, or Bardot's: the publicists of *Paris-Match* and other papers pounced on them while they were filming, and somehow managed to inspire a cult that answered a certain youthful need. Bardot was built into a symbol of sensualist emancipation: and the young crowds came, some innocently and some less so, to worship their goddess. I met a Dominican priest in St-Tropez who told me: 'This place is a kind of Lourdes. Young people feel a lack in their lives today, they want to be cured of their desolate yearnings, so they come here to be touched by magic and reborn. But they are disappointed: all they find is each other.' Today many of the more vicious elements in St-Tropez are foreign, not French, but the French are still there in plenty – even girls of little more than fifteen who arrive from Paris without a franc, to discover how far their charms can carry them. Any summer night you can see them by the score, wide-eyed girls with gaudy jeans and bare midriffs, hanging around the modish bars waiting for the next well-heeled pick up.

They have never been typical of French youth as a whole, any more than the Sartrians. In the 1960s, the archetype among less intellectual teenagers was the *copain* (the word means 'chum'). And in that decade it was the extraordinary pop movement of the *copains*, innocent and mildly charming but vapid, that gave a new brand-image to French youth and pushed the precocious cynicism of Sagan firmly on to the sidelines. A new generation, sipping its Coca-Colas, looked less to Bardot the sex-kitten than to Sylvie Vartan, chirpy little chum and elder sister, or to Françoise Hardy huskily leading all-the-boys-and-girls-of-her-age-hand-in-hand. It all began in 1959 when Daniel Filipacchi, a disc-jockey, launched a jazz programme called *Salut les Copains* on Europe Number One radio. Instantly it was a smash hit with teenagers, who were tired of sharing Brassens and Trenet with their elders and wanted something modern of their own, like the Americans 'had. Around the same time a boy of sixteen with fair curly hair and an ugly mouth made his hesitant début under the name of Johnny Hallyday, singing American rock'n roll tunes in French. Filipacchi took him up, and a whole generation chose Johnny as their idol and self-image. French pop was born. He was followed by scores of others, such as Adamo, Sheila, Claude François. And in 1962 Filipacchi astutely complemented his radio show with a glossy monthly also called *Salut les Copains* which reached a circulation of a million, amazingly high for France.

At first the movement was highly derivative, much more so than its Liverpool equivalent. Not only did the stars borrow American tunes: many of them found it smart to adopt Anglo-Saxon names – Hallyday was born Jean-Philippe Smet. Gradually however, the *copains* acquired a certain French style of their own, less virile and inventive, more romantic and sentimental, than either Beatledom or American folk or rock. Filipacchi and his stars were able to provide the teenage millions with an outlet of self-identification they were looking for: their own Johnny, singing ingenuously about being sixteen and its problems, was themselves and the boy next door. 'He's just like us, not like a real music-hall star', said one teenybopper, 'so we love him.' Parents at first were a little anxious, as record sales soared and Hallyday became the most-photographed male in France after de Gaulle. Their concern reached its height after the night of June 22nd, 1963, when Filipacchi staged a 'live' open-air broadcast from the Place de la Nation in Paris, and 150,000 teenagers, twisting and rocking, surged into the square and brushed aside the police. It was the first time in French history that teenagers had displayed their solidarity in public on this scale. Some observers saw it as a political event, comparing it with the mass-hysteria of the Nazi rallies. But it soon became clear that the famous *Nuit de la Nation* was really very innocent.

Parents soon came to see there was nothing to worry about. Filipacchi in fact was always shrewd enough to steer the *copains* away from rebellious paths that might have hit his trade. Their revolt was purely one of music and rhythm, not morals: the very phrase *Salut les Copains* (Hallo Chums!) gave some idea of the *Boys' Own Paper* or *True Romance* spirit of the thing. 'I suppose what we're really doing', Filipacchi's chief editor told me, 'is to prolong the age of innocence, *l'âge tendre.*' This belongs to a French romantic tradition that harks back to *Le Grand Meaulnes*: adolescents playing at love, sometimes touched by melancholy but not by cynicism or social indignation. And the endless photo-articles in *Salut les Copains* were careful to project this image of the idols, especially of Johnny and his girl-friend Sylvie Vartan who later became Monsieur and Madame Smet. Johnny, mad about motor-bikes, was in reality much as he was made to seem: the true modern folk-hero, looking just like any French youth hanging around the streets with his *vélo* on a Sunday. Sylvie, Bulgarian by birth, was more intellectual, known as *la collégienne du twist*. But with her tulip mouth and sturdy little figure, she projected the perfect image of the jolly bobby-soxer who'd become a star by mistake, and when she bounced on to the stage of the Olympia music-hall as if it were an end-of-term concert, to trill '*Ce soir, je serai la plus belle pour aller danser*', every *midinette* in the audience identified with her. Not that all the *copains* conformed quite so closely to this tame ideal: Françoise Hardy, ex-Sorbonne student, tall and languid with a sulky temperament, even brought a note of Grecoesque sorrow and self-doubt into her songs and was one of the very few *copains* to have much following among adults. But she kept roughly in line with the Filipacchi ethic, and her *mystère* did not simmer into revolt.

The *copains*' appeal was mainly to the less sophisticated middle teens of all classes: older or more alert ones preferred a more robust diet such as Bob Dylan or English pop (e.g. The Animals). On its credit side, the *copain* cult may have fostered a kind of sweet romantic comradeship, which has its sequels today among French youth. Like British pop, it helped in the struggle against delinquency; and unlike British pop it was seldom crudely hostile to real culture. Its idols had puppy charm; and, for all the commercial wire-pulling, there was something spontaneous about their appeal to youth. But the message was not a very inspiring one, and even the melodies were not exciting. Today pushing forty, Johnny, Sylvie and others still give concerts, to a varied public of all ages: but the *copain* movement as such has withered away, to be replaced by nothing very specific. The popular music today in vogue with French youth is of two very different kinds. On the one hand, young *chansonniers* such as Alain Souchon and Serge Lama with their bitter-sweet songs of nostalgia, love, and life's little cruelties: they may lack the potency of Brel or Brassens, to whose tradition they belong, but musically and lyrically they are far superior to Hallyday and co. On the other hand, there has been a recent revival of rock, with France at last producing its own ear-splitting hard rock groups such as Téléphone, drawing large mainly working-class audiences. As in the United States and elsewhere, the disco craze too made a come-back in the late '70s, with Saturday-night fever sweeping France at all social levels from industrial suburb to the Parisian *beau monde*. In the rue du Faubourg-Montmartre a young homosexual, Fabrice Emaer, took over a derelict theatre, Le Palace, and converted it into the most extravagant and sophisticated of discothèques, full of laser beams and great globes of moving, flashing lights. The vast Palace would draw up to 3,000 people a night from students and typists to countesses and film-stars, many of them in the most outré of costumes. By 1979 Le Palace had outclassed the staid world of Castel and Régine to become *the* fashionable Parisian nightspot, at least with a certain *jeunesse dorée*. It was yet another sign of the new hedonistic times. But such modes pass.

French youth today is something of an enigma, and one that many adults find disquieting. Through the '50s and '60s it remained very much under parental influence, leaving a dominant impression of docile listlessness. *Copains* were far commoner than rebels. Then May '68, giving vent to the frustrations that had lain beneath the surface, suddenly presented a very different picture. This was the golden age of faith in ideologies, when in France as in other countries a new generation – or one idealistic section of it – decided that society after all *could* be changed. Youth burst into action, bubbling with ideas, many absurd, some constructive – 'l'imagination au pouvoir' was the slogan of the day, scrawled on many a wall. But when the dust had settled, and society had not been changed very much, it soon became clear that the May crisis had not turned all French youth into revolutionaries. An enquiry carried out in 1969 by IFOP among the sixteen to twenty-four age range gave a portrait of a generation that was relatively happy and ready to accept the social order. Discontent was found to be greater among *lycéens* and students than among those in jobs, suggesting that youth's irritation might be more with the defects of the educational system than with society as a whole, except in the case of a fringe of dedicated *gauchistes* who steadily lost influence after May.

However, May was not without its permanent legacy, notably in the way it modified once and for all the relations between French youth and its elders. The old barriers of authority were broken, and this was true as much within families as in schools and colleges. During and after May, family crises broke out 'on a scale the nation has not seen since Dreyfus', as one father put it; schoolchildren disappeared from home for days on end, or hotly argued with their parents for the first time in their lives. It took some time for these wounds to heal, and for parents accustomed to strict obedience to adapt to a new and freer situation. But most parents were soon making greater efforts at last to understand their children's needs, and communication became more easy and more equal. As a result of May '68, French youth won its freedom – later, and with more dramatic suddenness, than in Anglo-Saxon countries.

But, more than thirteen years on, what use has been made of this freedom? Today's young people were many of them still in the nursery in 1968. For them, its brave ideals are past history and few of them now dream of changing the world. Growing up in a new age of uncertainty, they mirror that age with their reticence, their scepticism and passivity. Of course it is risky to generalize about a world as diverse as that of French youth: but it does seem to have some traits in common with youth elsewhere in the West, and indeed with French adulthood: a rejection of ideologies and formal organizations, a concern with private pleasures, with self-sufficiency and feathering the nest. So this is France's 'Me generation', that of the so-called *'repli sur soi'*. A friend of mine with two sisters, one aged thirty, the other twenty, said to me: 'Ten years ago, the elder one devoted herself to helping handicapped children. But today it would not occur to her younger sister to do this. Her concern is to earn a living and have fun.' It is easy to lament this apparent shift towards egotism and rejection of ideals of wider community service. Yet at the same time today's young people, or most of them, are remarkably gentle, tolerant, well-behaved, and loyal and kind to each other within their own little circle. What they seem to have lost is a sense of ambition or initiative, or the taste for work for its own sake. This trend began even before 1973: since then, economic crisis has sharpened it by adding to youth's disillusion with the outside world and anxiety about its own job prospects. Half of France's 2 million unemployed in 1982 are under twenty-five. A technical school teacher told me: 'It's tragic to see what happens to these kids who finish their studies and then for months look for a job without success. It destroys their self-confidence and faith in life, and often they end up cynical.' A common problem throughout the EEC today.

Bernard Cathelat, a clever young sociologist who has made a special study of the sixteen to twenty-fours, divides them into three broad categories. He says: 'The first group, about half the total, inhabit the territory of adults. Those in the two smaller groups are living in worlds of their own.' (1) 'The first group, whether already in jobs or still being educated, are basically conformist – about clothes, food, leisure, work, values. They want to settle into adult society as quickly as possible, and start a family. They dislike change, they value the things of the past, they are not risk-takers: they want work, but mainly for financial security. Their idealism is abstract: "I believe in God, humanity, love," they'll say, but not, "I believe in socialist self-management," and their only heroes are the great humanists of the past, Schweitzer, say, or Kennedy. At the same time, they're pragmatic materialists in their search for comfort and pleasure. This group embraces all social classes.'

(2) 'Next you have the drop-outs or quasi-drop-outs, mostly middle-class people with some education. Their aim is to keep their options open, to avoid getting caught up in the adult rat-race. They may not drop out materially, they may even take little short-term jobs and outwardly behave quite normally – but their minds are elsewhere, their psychology is escapist, a yearning for absence. If you ask them where they'd most like to be, they may say, "On a satellite circling the earth." Such people could well have stormed the barricades in '68, but today they believe in nothing: fatalistically they expect a nuclear holocaust, and many are tempted by suicide, existentialist rather than depressive. Our research puts 29 per cent of all French youth into this category. You may find this sad and decadent, but there *is* a less gloomy interpretation: many of these people in fact are *over*-adapted, students of science or arts, and it may be they are precursors of a new polarized civilization – half global technology, half local leisure – in which they could happily find a place. They are chameleons, or butterflies living for the moment – and they could easily snap out of their nihilism.'

(3) 'My third and smallest group is also *je-m'en-foutiste* ('I don't care a fuck'), but mainly from the lower classes. This is a lumpen-youth that has failed at school and now has dreary jobs or none at all, and feels frustrated partly through sheer lack of money: economic crisis has made this worse. These people feel rejected by society, they live from day-to-day, and their parrot-cry is, "*je ne sais pas quoi faire.*" Potentially they are violent, though luckily they find safety valves in motor-bikes, rock, or minor delinquency (they flirted briefly with punk, but this British import never really caught on in France). If they found decent jobs they could

well integrate into society, at least outwardly – but they might retain their present mentality which is markedly *macho*, racist and militarist. A minority of them are real delinquents.'

Juvenile lawlessness arrived later in France than in many countries and has never been widespread. In the 1960s the *blousons noirs*, gangs of leather-jacketed youths, would swipe bicycle-chains at passers-by; but finally they were severely repressed by the police. Today in the poorer suburbs some gang warfare persists, often racist in character as in Britain, with French youths attacking young blacks or Arabs (see p. 469). But most delinquency today takes the form of sporadic pilfering, or of more organized crime by groups of young professionals: they are the cause of the recent rise of mugging on the Métro and in quiet Paris streets at night. In the later 1970s the so-called *'autonomes'* briefly hit the head- lines: violent groups of young anarchists, politically motivated. They were a hangover of May '68 and some of its more extremist ideals, or you could call them a much milder counterpart of the Italian terrorists. They have since faded away.

Drugs, like delinquency, made their appearance on the youth scene later than in many countries. It was not until 1969–70 that professional pedlars began any large-scale attempts to corrupt teenagers and that 'pot' or hard drugs began to circulate in any quantities. The authorities at first turned a blind eye to the problem, but the police have since had some successes in rounding up drug-traffickers. Today the youth drug problem, though worrying, remains much more limited than in a country such as the United States or Germany. The smoking of 'pot' is slightly on the increase, but only 7 per cent of *lycéens* are said to be involved. And the number of deaths from overdoses of hard drugs, 100 to 150 a year, is only about a third of the German figure.

'I think papa is crazy to spend his life the way he does, working twelve hours a day and most weekends,' said the gifted twenty-year-old son of a top civil servant. One striking feature common to nearly all the new generation, even the more conformist, is that leisure and privacy are replacing work as the essential paths to self-fulfilment. The young will still swot hard to pass exams, but their attitude to a job or career is increasingly utilitarian. They do not reject work, but they see it simply as the means of ensuring the quality of their private lives; and few of them share the passionate work ethic which drove their elders to build the modern prosperous France. 'Our parents live for work: we work so as to live better,' said one young technician. Employers find that *cadres* under thirty try to make a clear break between their work and leisure lives, unlike their elders: they are far less ready to stay late in the office or bring work home at the weekend. Also, except for an élitist minority such as those who emerge from Polytechnique or ENA, the young today are less ambitious. 'For me,' said one student, 'to "succeed in life" is less import-ant than to succeed *with* my life.' Sometimes a young employee will pass over a chance of promotion if it means harder work or more responsi-bility; or he may prefer a job that offers security to a chancier one at a higher salary. Others prefer to dabble for a few years after ending their studies, taking a series of easy short-term jobs interspersed with periods of inactivity, and prepared to live very simply. Others again, even in today's bleak employment climate, are more choosy and exacting than their elders about the kind of work they will do: if their job bores them or their boss irks them, or if working conditions do not suit them, they may just quit. Germany too, like France, is facing this decline of the old dedicated work ethic, among its youth; and in both countries there is some concern at the possible effects of this on national economies, especially in today's tough world.

Those young people who are ambitious tend to enter an existing hierarchy – an industrial firm, say, or the civil service – and make their way up its rungs like good organization men. But they do not challenge the system from outside. Youth no longer seems to throw up its own free-lance innovating pioneers, fired with initiative and a sense of public service. Where are today's successors to the Leclercs and Planchons? Today's climate is less propitious, certainly; but above all youth lacks the same enterprise. Also, despite their qualities as individuals, young people in France have always seemed shy of forming their own group initiatives or translating their criticisms of the adult world into joint action. May '68 was the exception that proved the rule – a brief anarchic revolt. When youth does try to act in a more regular and practical way, it usually fails to make much impact. Take the case of two serious-minded brothers I met, living with their bourgeois parents in Paris. The elder, twenty-five, had a boring but lucrative job in a building firm; the younger, twenty-one, was studying psychology. Together they had founded a *'Centre pour la Diffusion des Moyens d'Expression'*, a pompous title for a real attempt to do something creative. On a modest scale, they were starting to market their own highbrow records of unusual music, to edit a roneoed intellectual magazine and run a drama group; they had also taken over a little night-bar in a side-street, as a place where people like themselves could meet and talk, away from their parents and too much pop music. It was all rather impressive, but they were pessimistic to me about their progress. One said: 'Whenever we try to get people of our age together in Montparnasse to do anything worthwhile, we meet passivity. People seem interested at first, but they expect us to do it all for them: they won't share responsibility. Or else they quarrel and form into splinter groups, often political. It's happened with our drama circle.'

They struck me with their sense of isolation; they seemed to have little feeling of unity or even contact with the scores of thousands of young Parisians who broadly shared their ideas. They said, 'Whenever you try to do anything public in France you're up against adult vested interests – whether in publishing, or journalism, or even in the pop music world which after all is an adult-run commercial operation.' Others gave me the same complaint: that youth did not seem able, or willing, to make the same breakthrough into effective public self-expression as in Britain or America. Their little roneoed magazines, with articles criticizing State or society, struck me as pathetic: paper-darts aimed at a world that took no notice. It is true that in the late '60s a few other young people, perhaps with more flair, began as in Britain to break into the commercial world, setting up their own boutiques, pop music firms or other little businesses: many had parental capital behind them. This was new and unusual for France. But in the more austere '70s such ventures found it hard to survive.

The more serious of today's youth feel a real concern for the modern world's problems, but have little faith in those proposing solutions: according to one survey, 80 per cent of young people believe in no political party. For some, ecology provides an outlet for their idealism, but only a minority are actively involved in this movement. The sense of individual isolation is such, among young people, that it makes it hard for them to identify even with community in a more general sense, outside politics. 'Society' for them is *les autres*, therefore alien – even if in fact those others are well-meaning and think much as they do – and so they cling to their own trusted circle of family and friends and reject any wider allegiance. This is very French. 'We don't feel we live in a coherent community, like you in Britain,' said one student; 'a community is a fine idea, but in France it doesn't seem to work in practice – there are too many betrayals. *Enfin, on est toujours seul.*' Feeling powerless to change society, young people resignedly accept it as it is, and largely they submit to its obligations. This is true, for example, of attitudes to the twelve-month military service, which in theory is compulsory for all young males (though in practice some 30 per cent find exemption on grounds of health, studies or family duties). According to surveys, some 60 per cent of youth would like to see this national service abolished, not surprisingly: but when their time comes, they meekly undergo it. Conscript unrest, common in the early 1970s in the wake of May '68, has now died right away.

'Young people do not rebel, they retreat,' writes the sociologist Jean Duvignaud in one of the best books[7] on modern youth; 'their great search is for a refuge against a society that they see as impersonal and unwelcoming' – and above all they turn back to the family (see p. 370). To live with one's parents until marriage has always been far commoner in France than in Britain, and as late as 1966 three in four of sixteen-to-twenty-four-year-olds were still doing so. This was due not only to convention and parental pressure, but also to the housing shortage. Then this eased as small flats or bed-sitters became more plentiful, while youth also acquired more money and May '68 brought in new ideas of independence. So more people in their late 'teens began to follow the Anglo-Saxon practice of leaving home. However, since the mid-'70s there has been a slight reverse trend, for reasons both economic and emotional. In many liberal families, a boy will shack up with his girl-friend, or a girl with her boyfriend, *in* their parents' house. This is not yet widespread. But in most families, especially in the middle classes, relations between parents and adolescent children are far easier and more intimate than in the old days. In the case of older teenagers, most parents now accept quite readily this new equal situation and the waning of their old authority. But others, with *gosses* of thirteen to sixteen, have not yet fully adapted to the new freedom of younger adolescents: it leaves them puzzled and hurt, and sometimes they blame the school-teachers who have swung from strictness to licence. One British writer living in France has commented on 'the clash between the new freedom of expression in the classroom, and the more traditional ways of bringing up the French child at home'.[8]

Today's youth may be hesitant, vaguely anxious, in some ways introverted and egotistical: yet, despite the sombre picture I may have drawn, it is not really unhappy. Within its own little milieux it is absorbed in seeking its own private pleasures and satisfactions – through sport, music and other interests, and through friendship and love. Towards each other, in their own circles, young people show a remarkable camaraderie and tolerance; the couple, wed or unwed, has assumed immense value, as much as a unit of mutual comfort and support against the world as for sexuality. Young people no longer read very much, and even the more reflective ones have few *maîtres-à-penser* (Sartre, Camus and Teilhard de Chardin have all lost much of their appeal of twenty years ago). But they go eagerly to films and concerts, they travel, and seek nourishment through contact with nature, or maybe through yoga or keep-fit fads, or religion either Christian or oriental. The new French

7 *La Planète des jeunes*, Stock, 1975.
8 Jenny Rees in the *Guardian*, June 29th, 1979.

concern with an ethos of personal fulfilment, and with hedonism, is even stronger among the young than among older people.

Youth's attitudes to 'la France' and to other countries are revealing. Bernard Cathelat's most recent survey put the question, 'Of where are you a citizen?' – and drew these replies: 35 per cent said 'of the world' and 15 per cent 'of the universe'; 19 per cent said 'of where I live' and 11 per cent 'of my region'; a mere 13 per cent said 'of France' and 2 per cent 'of Europe'. Maybe a poll of this kind should be taken with a pinch of salt: but it confirms one's general impressions of a woolly-minded global humanism linked to a growing attachment to local roots, plus a striking decline in old-style patriotism ever since the early 1960s: no longer does French youth stir to the sound of a military band on July 14th – *tout ça, c'est du folklore*. Idealism over a united Europe has also waned recently, for young people as much as their elders have grown cynical about the EEC as an institution. Yet in a more general sense they still feel 'European': they are less insular than British youth, and have no animosity towards the Germans (see p. 463). They have less sense of frontiers than the older generation – 'We go to Munich or Amsterdam as naturally as to Lyon or Bordeaux,' said one Parisian student. Many also feel solidarity and concern towards the Third World, and thousands each year express this by going to work as teachers or technicians in poorer countries, mainly in ex-French Africa: the Government runs a kind of 'Peace Corps' scheme which in some cases allows this work as an alternative to military service. But youth's ideals of social service abroad are less potent than a decade ago: one more sign of the *repli sur soi*. The poverty of the Third World, like the nuclear threat and the crisis of capitalism, is one of those giant problems that reduces the majority of French youth to a state of uneasy passivity.

It is perilous to generalize about a world so elusive and so constantly renewing itself as the youth of a nation, and there are plenty of human examples that may contradict all I have written. After the decades of hectic material change, French society today is in a phase of reappraisal, and youth takes some of its colouring from this. It has won a new freedom from parents and teachers: but the obverse of this coin is that it has lost their sure moral leadership. It cannot trust the values of an adult world that no longer offers certainties, so in the search for its own values it retreats into its shell. This seemingly negative stance disturbs many adults. 'Young people lack vitality,' they say, 'they've no more sense of public service. They seem to know what they don't want, but not to be able to formulate what they do want.' And youth in turn blames its elders: 'It's our parents' fault,' claimed a girl of twenty; '*they* created this consumer society which has anaesthetized us.' But is youth really so numbed? It seems to me more like an actor waiting in the wings. Talk to young people, and you are aware of a latent strength, a potential hitherto unharnessed: they are lucid, realistic, tolerant, alert to past follies and wary of false expectations.

So has the coming to power of the Left now given this waiting actor his cue? It is true that a majority of young people voted Left in 1981: so the election results gave many of them the hope that the new regime might now be more sympathetic to their aspirations and problems than the old one had been, and that adult society might thus become less alien. At La Bastille in Paris, and all over the provinces, young people cheered and danced and sang on the night of Mitterrand's victory. But by the end of the year a certain scepticism and passivity seemed to have returned. When questioned, many of the young generation expressed a vague disappointment that the Left Government had not done more to change their lives or create a new climate. What is more, they had now lost the comfort of being able to blame their frustrations on an unpopular Right-wing regime. 'It's a very odd feeling, not being in opposition any more,' said one student; 'how on earth do we behave?'

Chapter 8

ARTS AND INTELLECTUALS:
A CREATIVE DECLINE?

In France, more than in most Western countries, this seems to be the age
of the performing arts, rather than of individual creation; of the critic and
essayist, more than of the novelist or poet. France today is in the throes of
a new interest in music, as the opera houses and concert halls bulge at the
seams. This follows an earlier post-war revival of theatre, notably in the
provinces. For these and for other arts, audiences have grown rapidly
during the decades of rising prosperity. And yet, to balance this popular
thirst for culture, where are the new novelists, playwrights and painters?
Even the cinema is not what it was in the heyday of the *nouvelle vague*.
Even the music revival, fecund in performance, has yielded little as yet in
the way of gifted new composers.

In philosophy and literature, as in the arts, France no longer appears
as the cultural champion of the West, the unrivalled power-house of new
ideas, new expression – and the French themselves will often admit this.
The leadership has passed on – where? – maybe to New York. French
culture has lost much of its old radiant universality, as the humanism of
Sartre, Camus and Malraux yields to the arid algebra of structuralism,
which itself now seems to be leading up a blind alley.

What are the reasons for this ebbing of the tide? It could perhaps be
argued that the arts and ideas, in France or elsewhere, flourish best
either in times of settled prosperity, or under oppression and austerity,
but not in an in-between period of industrial transition and uneasy social
change, when the nation's energies are elsewhere. It may even be that
the technocratic ethos, so strong under de Gaulle and Giscard, has been
damaging to cultural creativity – or so many people believe. In 1980 one
Left-wing literary critic suggested to me: 'Since the 1950s the
bourgeoisie, the ruling élite, has opted for the economy rather than for
culture, and this trend has accelerated under Giscard. In the old days
many senior diplomats for example were also writers – Claudel, Saint-
John Perse and others. But ENA has killed all that. It stifles the creative
spirit, turning out conformist automata who are not interested in culture
except for the snob-value, say, of a visit to the Opéra.'

There were few more revealing symptoms of the France of the 1960s and 1970s than the contrast between the optimism of the average technocrat or businessman and the *malaise* among intellectuals. It was not merely that intellectuals, being mostly on the Left, disliked a capitalist regime. Their *malaise* went deeper. Many of them felt an embittered frustration at the rise of a new way of progress that brushed aside their own theories and precepts. Their dreams were drowned in the hubbub of technology. Scornful of pragmatic values, ignorant of economics and out of touch with ordinary working people, they fancied that the contemporary world had betrayed them. By 'intellectuals' I mean those writers, academics and others who have always formed a very special and recognizable caste in France, and by tradition have been respected and honoured by society, almost like the holy men of India. But in recent years they have been losing prestige, and losing their own bearings.

The coming to power of the Left soon brought signs that the intellectual climate might now improve. Giscard was something of a philistine, whose occasional TV discourse on a writer such as de Maupassant carried little conviction. But Mitterrand is a deeply cultured man. He indicated his readiness to double the State budget for the Arts, raising it to some 0.75 per cent of the national total. And in June 1981 he brought some well-known writers on to his staff at the Elysée, including Régis Debray and the historian Claude Manceron. Intellectuals all over France took heart. Their voice, they felt, would now carry more weight again, and their prestige might recover. But will this new official backing in itself prompt a new creative upsurge in the arts, literature or philosophy? That remains to be seen.

THE LEFT BANK PHILOSOPHERS: TRENDINESS AND TYRANNY

French intellectuals, as much as other Frenchmen, yearn for a charismatic leader, and in the early post-war years Jean-Paul Sartre was just that. But although he lived on until 1980, already by the late 1950s the spell that he had cast was broken; and one reason for the disarray in intellectual life over the past twenty years is that no one has arisen to fill the vacuum left by this titan. His early ideas provided a yardstick even for those who disagreed with them. And like de Gaulle, who also inspired strong devotion or opposition, he seems irreplaceable.

Like so much else in post-war France, the existentialist movement was generated during the war. It was in 1943 that Sartre brought out his key philosophical work, *L'Etre et le néant*, though he was already well known from his first novel, *La Nausée* (1938). The Occupation, with its disruption of bourgeois values, tempted many young thinkers besides

Sartre towards a similar kind of disenchanted humanism, so that on the Liberation he found an immediate and sympathetic audience. For the next few years this ugly, tousled, pipe-smoking little man would sit with groups of disciples in the St-Germain-des-Prés cafés, discussing problems of moral responsibility. They were ascetic, hard-working, often puritanical, these true existentialists (as opposed to the phoney parasitic beatniks who followed in their trail, wilfully mistaking Sartrian liberty for licence) and they had much influence in academic and Left-wing circles. It was a time of high aspiration, when it seemed that social revolution might after all be possible in France; and the early post-war years were full of intellectual fervour and creativity, amid political chaos and economic gloom; the opposite of the 1960s.

Existentialism was at first seized on hopefully as a light to live by. Before long, however, many intellectuals felt it to be leading to a moral impasse, at least in its atheistic Sartrian form. Developing the ideas of his German predecessors, Heidegger and Husserl, Sartre taught that man creates himself by his actions, for which he has freedom of choice and total responsibility; each choice is 'absurd' because there is no objective moral standard, but (and here Sartre never made himself quite clear) in the act of choosing, a man confers value on what he chooses, for all mankind. Many young French agnostics warmed to the courage and humanism of this austere philosophy, which at least seemed more hopeful than determinism. But to those who searched more closely among the paradoxes of *L'Etre et le néant* and *L'Existentialisme est un humanisme* (1945), this humanism began to look suspiciously like solipsism; and not everyone felt able to share Sartre's seemingly gloomy view of the impossibility of human relationships – 'Hell,' he wrote in *Huis clos*, 'is other people.' Existentialism had brought freedom from the bonds of convention – but to what ends?

In the 1950s the movement withered, though it was to leave an indelible mark on French thinking. Its end was hastened by external factors, such as the political failures of the Left under the Fourth Republic and the alluring rise of a new climate of prosperity. But it was destroyed also from within: by the failure of its intellectuals to pass from mental *engagement* to the effective political action that they claimed to espouse, and by the bewildering shifts and ambiguities in Sartre's own pronouncements, both philosophical and political, after about 1950. He began to assert that Marxism was the only great philosophy of the century and that existentialism was merely its handmaiden, taking charge of a field of humanist ideas that it had neglected. His hatred of Right-wing oppression seemed admirable in itself: but few people, even Marxists, could follow the logic that led him from 'absurdity of choice' to doctrinaire commitment. If man has freedom of choice, by what existentialist right could Sartre then insist that Marxism is the only 'valid' choice? He never convincingly answered this question. And, like many Marxists, he would put forward ingenious arguments for violating democratic principles, if the defence of a Left-wing cause was at stake. This behaviour led him to quarrel and break with many of his former sympathizers, notably Albert Camus.

Sartre was always harrowingly honest with himself, even when seemingly distorting historical truth, and towards the end of his life he appeared a somewhat lonely and tragic figure, despite the warm support of his life-long companion, Simone de Beauvoir. As was often said, his was the tragedy of a man with a deeply religious temperament who had killed God. And he in turn was a god that failed: it was just because his earlier intellectual magnetism had been so hypnotic that he left such disarray. In May 1968 he was quick to side publicly with the militant students and this won him their sympathy; but they did not look to him as a leader. It was *their* struggle, and he was simply on the sidelines. To modern youth, he had come to seem irrelevant: they still read his early books with interest, but as classics, as they might read Camus or Kafka. In the 1970s Sartre espoused various humanitarian causes, campaigning in the streets of Paris against abuses such as racism. This activism won him respect, even if it had little to do with his work as a philosopher or writer. In his final years he gave up supporting Communism-at-any-price and accepted that human rights were a higher consideration. He spoke out on behalf of the Soviet dissidents. And this led him to a remarkable public reconciliation with his former close friend of more than thirty years back, the liberal thinker Raymond Aron – 'It's Sartre who's changed, not me,' said Aron. In 1979, a year before Sartre died, they went together to the Elysée to plead before Giscard the cause of the 'boat people', refugees from Moscow-backed oppression. For Sartre, it was a notable gesture. When he died, there were tributes from all sides – 'I disagree with his answers,' said the young Right-wing philosopher Alain de Benoist, 'but he was just about the only man to put the right questions.'

Today existentialism has long merged into the air that a Frenchman breathes daily, like nineteenth-century rationalism. Few intellectuals any longer dub themselves 'existentialists', but all are marked by it. As a catalyst its influence has certainly been positive. It is easy to forget how stifling was the French pre-war bourgeois world, described by de Beauvoir in *Mémoires d'une jeune fille rangée*; and she and Sartre helped to open its windows a little. Nothing has been quite the same since. In modern French sociology and criticism, in the *nouveau roman* and some of the films of the *nouvelle vague*, even in cabaret songs of the Brassens type, existentialism with its sceptical voice of disenchantment has continued to show its influence. Inside the philosophical world it is still studied at universities, mainly as a tool for re-assessing the older philosophies: it weakened the sterile hold of Kant and Descartes over the Sorbonne and forced a much-needed new approach to their ideas.

For some years however existentialism left behind it a pregnant vacuum in French intellectual thought, as new writers such as Robbe-Grillet and Sollers took refuge in private worlds of fantasy and stylistic experiment. Then in the late 1960s a new trend emerged into fashion, intellectually very high-powered: structuralism. This is less a philosophy than a method, and in no sense is it a school for its exponents are most diverse. Its leaders have included Roland Barthes, literary critic, who died in 1980; Claude Lévi-Strauss, who teaches ethnology; and the influential psychoanalyst, Jacques Lacan, who died in 1981. To an extent it grew out of existentialism, with which it shares an atheistic rejection of the bourgeois view of history and morality. But whereas Sartre's philosophy saw man as the free captain of his own conscience and destiny, the structuralists regard him as the prisoner of a determined system. Sartre sprang from the humanist tradition, an old-fashioned moralist in a new guise: Lévi-Strauss and his friends use the language and methods of anthropology, psychoanalysis and linguistic philosophy. Roughly they believe that man's thoughts and actions have been determined, throughout history, by a network of structures, social and psychological, where free will plays a minimal part; and that history is like a series of geological layers, each created by the pressure of the preceding one. Lévi-Strauss has applied these ideas to the study of primitive societies; Lacan allied them to psychoanalysis; Barthes, a Marxist, used them in the field of semantics or 'seminology', the study of the set of signs or symbols which he believed to shape our thoughts and actions; Jacques Derrida and Michel Foucault apply structuralism to philosophy proper, and in *Les Mots et les choses* (1966) the latter argued: 'Man with a capital M is an invention: if we study thought as an archaeologist studies buried cities, we can see that Man was born yesterday, and that he soon may die.' This book sent tremors well outside academic circles: for months it was a bestseller, *the* smart topic of party conversation whether you had read it or (more probably) not. An educated public reacted with fascinated horror at a new philosophy which made even Sartre's ideas look humane and optimistic. Sartre had killed God: the structuralists were killing Man too!

Their movement was a symptom of the belated French discovery of anthropology and the other social sciences, which they seized on with a typical French extremism, but with imagination. Critics who were able to follow Barthes' ironic and intricate thought usually found him stimulating and mentally elegant, whether they shared his views or not. His very personal style, full of neologisms, had many imitators and was even parodied in a book published in 1978, *Le Roland-Barthes sans peine* ('Barthesian without Tears'), which showed how to turn simple remarks into his code-language ('"I" live a "desire-to-know"' – 'why?'. 'This conceptual articulation self-criticizes itself as failing to materialize' = 'it's impossible'). Barthes' seeming preciosity was also linguistic satire.

The structuralists have been frequently and violently criticized, for wilful obscurity, arrogance, aridity and much else. Richard Webster in the *Observer* (February 1st, 1981) inveighed against their 'habit of reducing human nature to pseudo-mathematical formulae'. Yet structuralism's influence has extended far outside France. In Britain, it has made more impact on academics and intellectuals than the Sartrians ever did, while in America numerous theses are written on Barthes and Lacan. But in France itself the fashion is now past its prime. Barthes is dead; the domineering Lacan was increasingly contested in the final two or three years before he too died, in September 1981. Lévi-Strauss and Foucault retain a pre-eminence in their fields, but structuralism – a much misused term – is only an element in their work. Its current reputation in France was summed up to me by one intellectual: 'In the 1960s it seemed to many of us that the new social sciences and linguistics, allied as they were to Left-wing politics through the work of Foucault and others, might at last explain the world and lead to a real change. But that hope has withered. The social sciences have failed to deliver the goods – maybe we expected too much of them. So now they have reverted to their specialized academic roles and are no longer part of an overall political ideal. And structuralism is in crisis.'

This is one facet of a general malaise today among intellectuals: 'an ideological vacuum' is the phrase often used. In the 1960s the febrile little world of the Left Bank found itself challenged by the rise outside its walls of a prosperous new society with very different ideals intent on technology and practical reform. And some *bona fide* intellectuals virtually defected to this camp, by going to work with the reformers. So there was a striking divorce between those intellectuals who broadly accepted the new modern France, and were helping to build it, and those – still the majority – who rejected it in the name of their Left-wing ideals. Each group charged the other with betrayal. The 'pragmatists' were accused of compromising with a bourgeois regime: they in turn charged the 'purists' with sticking their noses in the sand. Of course there were many famous figures who did not fit into either group, but the prototypes in the 1960s were blatant enough: the contrast between Malraux building his cultural centres and Sartre crying woe in the wilderness. Today, in the France of Mitterrand, the picture is different. Through much of the 1970s the intellectual Left was in disarray, under the impact, *inter alia*, of Solzhenitsyn's revelations and of electoral defeats at home. Now the coming to power of the Left has given many intellectuals new hope. They are heartily glad to be rid of Giscard and his technocratic creed. But the Socialist victory has not in itself dispelled overnight the 'ideological vacuum'. Intellectuals may now begin again to wield more influence in national life. They have yet to show that they can match this with new ideas and a new vision.

The traditional French intellectual is an easily recognizable species, very conscious of his status and responsibilities as *'un intellectuel'* which set him apart from other mortals, so he feels. The breed is to be found all over France, notably in academic circles: but those who seek the limelight cluster above all within their citadel, the Paris Left Bank. Many hold teaching posts, or write for Left-wing journals, or combine a living out of part-time jobs in publishing, writing novels or monographs, giving talks on the hated State radio and even – the trendy ones – taking part in highbrow TV chat-shows. Though nearly all are bourgeois by origin, they have few social contacts except maybe family ones with the despised classic bourgeoisie of, say, finance and technocracy. They prefer to cling together, meeting for drinks and business lunches in well-known Left Bank haunts such as Lipp, La Coupole or the Closerie des Lilas. It is an intense little world of rival coteries, instant fashion, endless intrigue, and today is much given to self-criticism – 'Yes,' one literary pundit told me, 'I know we're a narcissistic, hermetic society. We're constantly reviewing each others' books, so that few critics write what they really think.' This may apply to similar circles in London or New York, but less so: in Paris, the passionate and polemical French temperament, allied to sheer physical proximity, sends the intellectual temperature soaring far higher. The intellectual lives, and is expected to live, more urgently and publicly than in Britain, and his world is dominated by a few score major figures – the Lacans and Foucaults, and others – who indulge in mighty, headline-hitting, cerebral slanging-matches. These star personalities usually relish the power they wield within their tiny milieu, and by seeking through superior brain-power to impose their ideas on others they exert what is often denounced as *'le terrorisme intellectuel'* – one of today's catchphrases.

Many a visiting intellectual from placid Britain is captivated by this

Parisian climate of eager debate, the passion for ideas, the provocations, the curiosity about all that is new. Nicholas Snowman, a young musical expert who works with Pierre Boulez (see p. 606), told me of the latter's public talk-ins with Lacan, Barthes and others to explore the possible links between modern serial music and structuralism: 'We drew big audiences, as I can't imagine in London for that kind of topic. To follow the avant-garde is chic, but also a sign of real intelligence; and Parisians are truly curious to see what happens when you set one top thinker against another in a different field – like a boxing-match. Paris may generate a lot of hot air, but at least the place is alive.' Others however are more sceptical, suggesting – and I would agree – that French intellectuals tend to show rather more respect for ideas than for facts. One critic has pointed to the intellectuals' 'lack of interest in reality' and 'contempt for the authenticity of information'. Influenced maybe by the deductive, non-empirical methods instilled into them at school, they have a habit of selecting or even distorting the facts to suit their case – and especially this is so of Marxists and other Leftists. Often they give the impression that real life exists not in its own right but merely as grist to their theories. Are they afraid to peer outside the ghetto and explore actual society, lest it does not fit in with their *idées reçues*?

In its own way this is a conformist world, as much as the bourgeois milieu that it denounces. Only the most bold or brilliant spirit will dare to ignore or defy current fashions. If you cease to be seen and heard, if you go to live and work quietly in the provinces, then (unless your talent is exceptional) you cease to exist; and woe betide you if you go to a party without having perused the latest 'in' books. Intellectuals are wary of mixing with those who do not speak their language or share their basic assumptions: 'If a banker went to one of their parties, he'd be totally ignored,' said one girl. This trendy world is infatuated by novelty, so that ideas become seasonal fashions like the *haute couture* collections. Intellectuals, so hostile to modern consumer society, yet show an avid consumerist approach to their own product: as Pierre Nora, one well-known pundit with few illusions about his own milieu, has wittily written, 'Paris, obsessed by its own navel, gobbles up an ideology a week, an ontology every month.' Modes flit by so fast that it is hard to tell which have any real substance.

One such trend, which erupted noisily a few months before the March 1978 elections, was that of the so-called '*nouveau philosophes*', led by André Glucksmann and Bernard-Henri Lévy. This heterogeneous group were bracketed together by the Press, though they were no more a 'school' than the structuralists or the writers of the *nouveau roman*. Yet politically they did have something important in common. All of them were young men from the Left who, in a series of books and articles, now loudly proclaimed their loss of faith in Marx, Lenin and all their tribe. In a pre-election period, and coinciding with the Socialist–Communist rift, this intellectual outburst had some political impact: it was a portent of the young intelligentsia's growing disenchantment with Marxist or other Leftist ideals in the 1970s. For a few months the 'new philosophers' caused a furore hard to imagine in Britain, as Glucksmann's book *Les Maîtres penseurs* and Lévy's *La Barbarie à visage humain* leapt to the top of the non-fiction bestseller list, and Gilles Deleuze, a prominent Left-wing philosopher, hit back with a pamphlet denouncing the whole thing as 'a media racket mounted by the Right'. A British reporter wryly commented: 'What is happening is a piece of intellectual street theatre of a kind that the world expects from Paris and that the Left Bank has been too traumatized by post-1968 to provide.'[1]

Many of the 'new philosophers' had interestingly similar backgrounds: they were *normaliens* (see p. 512), pupils of those high-priests of the structuralist Left, Lacan and Althusser, and veterans of the May '68 barricades. Then, some years later, they read Solzhenitsyn on the Gulag, and the light dawned. Lévy is the most brilliant of the bunch. This arrogant, good-looking young man was only twenty-eight when he found fame with *La Barbarie*, a book rich in romantic pessimism: 'Life is a lost cause and happiness an outworn idea,' he pronounced. In 1979 he followed this up with an equally striking work, *Le Testament de Dieu*, an attempt to convince himself that God and His moral law might exist after all, thus giving some meaning to life. Today, their political impact achieved, the *nouveaux philosophes* are no longer so much in the limelight. They have thrown up one or two very clever writers, but philosophically they seem to have had little new to contribute beyond a variation on the old 'god-that-failed' theme dating back to Koestler and Camus. Their impact outside France has been far less than that of Sartre or the structuralists.

In 1979 Paris became obsessed with the next *dernier cri: la Nouvelle Droite*. This too was a by-product of the decline of the Left, and in this case was bred also of the economic crisis and the waning of faith in the EEC and in technocracy. Ever since the defeat of Nazism, to be an intellectual in France had meant being on the Left or possibly in the liberal centre, whereas the intellectual Right hardly dared show its face. Yet for some years it had been quietly at work behind the scenes, and in 1979 it suddenly emerged and even began to be taken seriously, so that

1 Robin Smyth in the *Observer*, July 1977.

today an intellectual is no longer laughed out of court if he claims to speak for the Right. But it is a curious animal, this New Right, and not what you might expect. The main platform for its ideas is the weekend magazine of *Le Figaro*, and its chief propagandist is Alain de Benoist, a minor aristocrat born in 1943. Since 1968 he has been running a movement called GRECE (Groupement de Recherches et d'Etudes pour la Civilisation Européenne), an acronym that deliberately reflects the doctrine of a return to an early, pure European tradition. GRECE, with some 5,000 members across France, is one element in the so-called New Right, which itself is no more than a general term for a current of thought: yet it is clear that de Benoist and his assorted fellow-thinkers are very different from the old pre-war French intellectual Right, which was usually militarist and nationalist – witness Maurras – or sometimes monarchist. De Benoist and his friends preach another creed, a vaguely mystical élitism and paganism, drawing some ideas from Nietzsche. They inveigh alike against the Left *and* the American consumer society model with its cultural 'decadence'; against modern egalitarianism *and* the Judaeo-Christian tradition. And as their prime enemies they lump together Illich, Marcuse, Freud, Marx, the Bible and *Le Monde*! Borrowing some of the latest conclusions of genetic and psychological research, they place their faith in the fundamental inequality and diversity of man, and they argue that Europe must return to the spiritual fount of its early civilizations, Hellenic, Germanic and Celtic.

This woolly ideology has an undoubted appeal, despite its sinister undertones. Its direct influence is very limited, though in a curious way it does relate to some wider trends in French society today (see p. 652). The New Right, and GRECE in particular, claim that basically their aims are cultural and that they are not seeking to influence politics. Yet unsurprisingly a storm of vituperation has descended on them from every side. They have been accused of every crime, including a latent racism and a nostalgia for the Aryan superman myths that underlay Nazism. By the end of 1980 this furore was subsiding, and François Bondy in *Encounter* commented aptly: 'The whole controversy appears to be a kind of "escapism", since it is so much easier in Paris to occupy oneself with the fireworks of intellectual polemics than with the far more complex and difficult problems of analysing the crisis of French and European society.' But then the victory of the Left in 1981 seemed to fire the New Right with a fresh sense of purpose. It began to see itself as the champion of intellectual resistance to the hated new socialization of France.

Today's best example of Parisian intellectual dandyism at its most flamboyant is the writer Jean-Edern Hallier, described by John Weight-

man as 'the most picturesque representative of radical chic in France'.[2]
Hallier comes from a wealthy Breton family and devotes a part of his
turbulent energy to promoting Breton regionalism: but he is also at the
heart of the Paris maelstrom, parading his outsize ego around the smart
salons, at once aesthete and political *provocateur*. He has a large flat in the
fashionable Place des Vosges where I called on him – fortyish, wild-eyed,
shock-headed, manically lighting then stubbing out a succession of
cigarettes, each one-quarter smoked. 'I'm a *monstre sacré*,' he assured
me affably, 'and the only living Frenchman who fulfils the role of a
great writer in the nineteenth-century sense. I'm an historic leader of
the Far Left, yet the Right too find me fascinating.' Hallier became an
active Leftist after May '68. His feelings for the Left have since cooled,
but he was virulently anti-Giscard, whom he denounced in 1979 in a
pamphlet entitled 'Open Letter to the Cold Fish'. As is clear from
his highly-coloured semi-autobiographical novels, where erotic themes
have exotic foreign settings, his literary gifts are real enough, even if
he may not be quite what the blurb of one of them suggests, 'by general
agreement, the greatest writer of his generation' (the book was produced by Hallier's own publishing firm, and no doubt he wrote
the blurb himself). The non-stop Hallier show could only take
place in Paris, and Paris amusedly takes him half-seriously, half not.
John Weightman wrote of one of his recent books: 'One could perhaps
write it off as an exceptional piece of narcissistic self-indulgence, were
it not for the pathetic bleat of the style and the fashionable mixture
of genuine social and aesthetic concern with personal mythomania.
Also, we find here, in a concentrated form, a sort of intellectual
dottiness, which is present elsewhere on the Parisian literary scene in
smaller doses, and may indeed be an essential ingredient of cultural
ferment.'

The Parisian intellectual debate is facilitated by the nature of the
publishing industry in France. Publishers habitually produce a book in a
matter of weeks – as compared with eight to twelve months in America or
Britain – and pundits thus exchange their fire in a steady stream of
rapidly written polemical *essais* (monographs) which have no British
equivalent. Another channel for the debate is provided by the monthly
or quarterly reviews, such as the *Nouvelle Revue Française*, or *Les Temps
Modernes* which Sartre used to edit. But the reviews, though still far more
numerous and influential than in Britain, have lost ground in recent
years: to the alarm of many serious people, they are being edged aside by
the more immediate if superficial outlets provided by the weekly

news-magazines and by television.[3] A virtuoso indictment of this trend came in 1979 from a leading Marxist intellectual, Régis Debray, the man who had won international fame by helping Che Guevara in Latin America.[4] His best-selling and much-discussed book, *Le Pouvoir intellectuel en France*,[5] alleged that true intellectual debate was being debased and trivialized by the lure of the new media, dominated by a new class of 'mediacrats'; and that many serious thinkers, maybe against their better judgement, were allowing themselves to be prostituted into accepting the easy fame and high fees thus provided – 'Why invest ten years of your life in writing a thesis which will make you a Ph.D. imprisoned for life in some provincial faculty, when with a mere month's work you can turn out a vitriolic pamphlet on a topical theme ("Destiny and the Gulag")which will put your name in the headlines and allow you a spirited hour on television, thus making you into a national hero?' Debray suggested that over the past hundred years the main power centre of intellectual persuasion had shifted, first from the Church to the universities (their heyday, he said, was *c.* 1880–1930), then to the big publishing houses with their reviews such as Gallimard with the NRF (*c.* 1930–68), and now to the new mass media.

His book struck a raw nerve. For months the Left Bank was loud with self-criticism, as intellectuals admitted that Debray had scored a point. But his book also sought to demonstrate, using Marxist methodology, that 'mediacracy' was a political conspiracy: the Establishment, via the State-controlled media and commercial Press interests, was using the mediacrats – editors, TV commentators, etc. – to manipulate French minds, and the intellectuals were its dupes. Here non-Marxists at least tended to part company with him. After all, the French Press and media are conspicuous more for their weakness than their strength, as we shall see later in this chapter; and Debray would seem to have much exaggerated their *political* power, however apt his castigation of their trivializing effects in intellectual and cultural terms. This latter trend is by no means confined to France: what other Western country today does not have its facile TV pundits, dispensing instant wisdom? But in Paris, where American media techniques were copied belatedly in the 1970s, the situation is rather special: this is because the impact of these new media on an intellectual world already so intense, so prone to polemics and exhibitionism, has produced a curious combustion. The media

3 The impact of these new media has been more recent than in Britain or America: see pp. 578–603.
4 In June 1981 Mitterrand brought Debray on to his staff at the Elysée, as advisor on Third World affairs – amid cries of dismay from Washington and elsewhere.
5 Editions Ramsay, Paris.

exploit the polemics as showbiz, and the mass public enjoy the spectacle, like any jousting, without necessarily caring greatly about its content. So, more than in the old days, the more assertive kind of intellectual becomes a showy star celebrity, as seldom he is in Britain or America. News-magazines and TV channels vie for what Debray calls *'le scoop idéologique'*. And authors of new books fall over each other for the privilege of appearing on the trendy TV literary programmes, which have an impact unimaginable in Britain. The Friday night *Apostrophe*, with five million viewers, is the high point of the intellectual week; and its presenter is France's mediacrat-in-chief, Bernard Pivot, who catches some of Debray's fieriest flak – 'Pivot, columnist of the Eternal, he who has transcended History because he amuses himself with *toutes les histoires.'*[6]

In world terms, the Parisian debate is an insular one. If it is concerned with foreign thinkers, past or present, it is mainly with those who can be related to French preoccupations – Solzhenitsyn, or maybe Borges, Kundera, Gramsci, Nietzsche – and such writers tend to be appropriated into a French context as if they ceased to be foreigners. The world outside is of interest less in its own right than as grist to the Parisian mill, where many intellectuals can accept foreign culture only on French terms. Invite them in a group to a party with their foreign colleagues, and they will make a few polite noises, then relapse into their own chatter. This mattered less in the old days, when French culture and thought were globally supreme and radiated their own universality. But the Parisian debate today makes relatively little impact outside France: Lévy, de Benoist, et al., or indeed modern French novelists, lack the world appeal of Gide, Camus, Sartre and other bygone giants. Yet many intellectuals find it hard to admit, or refuse to accept, this loss of the old hegemony: so it is more comforting, and mentally easier, to bury their heads in the sand. They lack the humility and the curiosity required to accept another culture's terms of reference.

Even inside France, intellectuals in recent years have made no great impact beyond their own milieu. They may imagine that *le pouvoir intellectuel* exerts vast influence nationally, but all they really do is influence each other; the rest of the nation goggles at them on TV, as a distraction, but is by no means under their sway. And with the death of Sartre there are no more 'great' writers left – save maybe for Aragon, and he is now eighty-four. So now we must wait and see whether the Socialist regime, and Mitterrand's support for intellectuals, makes any

6 A play on words, as *histoire* means both 'history' and 'petty tittle-tattle'.

difference in practice. After the past few years of self-doubt and re-appraisal, of the shedding of outworn myths, in theory the time is now ripe for an explosion of fertile new ideas. But the new political climate and Mitterrand's own good-will, however propitious, cannot them-selves create a new Sartre or Camus. Indeed, great thinking, great writing, thrive on dissent and criticism; and there are many in Paris today who fear that Socialist patronage, however well-meant, will pro-duce a new conformism harmful to the creative spirit. In 1981 one writer suggested to me: 'The French intellectual crisis goes deeper than any mere change of regime.'

HAVE BARTHES AND ROBBE-GRILLET KILLED THE FRENCH NOVEL?

The French novel today seems to have lost its universality, even more than French philosophy. In the land of Proust, Gide and Camus, what new novelists have emerged in the past twenty years to make any wide impact? One could suggest a name or two – Tournier, Le Clézio – but they do not add up to a great deal. In literature, more than the other arts, this is an age of criticism and documentary rather than of creativity; and the novel suffers, in France even more than in Britain. But the symptoms and causes of the *malaise* are very different in the two countries. You could say that the English novel has grown stale through remaining too conventional, while serious fiction in France has suffered from the terrorism of the *avant-garde* and its technical experimentation with language and form.

From the mid-'50s to the end of the '60s the scene was dominated by the writers known loosely as the 'New Novelists', led by Alain Robbe-Grillet, Michel Butor and Nathalie Sarraute. They passionately rejected plot, narrative and character portrayal. They were bourgeois writers attacking the bourgeois tradition of fiction, and this in itself set them squarely in a French anti-bourgeois tradition, stemming back to Flaubert via Sartre and Proust. Flaubert strongly criticized the bourgeoisie, though he used the narrative realism of his day. His kind of novel has since become bourgeois, that is, the middle-classes read and accept it. So more recently the 'New Novelists' turned to other weapons, those of *avant-garde* style and sensibility rather than social criticism. Their trump card was to write novels that the ordinary bourgeois reader would not understand or enjoy. As a result their sales were usually slight; but their influence on other novelists was vast, and not always for the best.

The so-called *nouveau roman* is today fading from sight. But in its heyday it caused more journalistic ink to flow than any other European literary trend of its time, and probably more than it has deserved in terms of achievement. It was never really a 'school', for its leading exponents were different from each other and frequently quarrelled. They were lumped together out of convenience, and through the smart public-relations work of their self-appointed prophet and president, Robbe-Grillet. Yet they did have some things in common. In rejecting conventional story-telling they were in the broad line traced from Proust and Joyce via Céline, Queneau, Genet and others. And the most obvious shared feature of their work was an obsession with minute physical description whether of objects or sensations. Their semi-scientific approach to literature had a clear link with structuralism, which came to the fore at much the same time.

Robbe-Grillet, now turning sixty, is the one who took up the most extreme position and formulated his theories the most sharply. Though his novels are so very dehumanized, he himself is extremely human, jolly and relaxed; talking to him one could even conclude that his whole operation might be a leg-pull at the expense of literature. 'By far my favourite author is Lewis Carroll,' he once told me. Precisely. Talking to him, or reading his books or seeing his films, one feels like Alice at the Mad Hatter's tea-party. ' "Have some wine," the March Hare said. "I don't see any wine," remarked Alice. "There isn't any," said the March Hare.' Robbe-Grillet by training is an agricultural engineer; he hates and shuns Paris literary society, and his passionate hobbies are gardening, botany, carpentry. From this picture you might think him more like an English eccentric *manqué* than a typical French writer: yet this enigmatic creature is hard to imagine at work anywhere except in France, for his literary politicking has been essentially French. From the moment that *Le Voyeur* won the Prix des Critiques in 1955 and made him famous, he set out to wage a vendetta against those who dared to write or admire any different kind of novel. This he did with *panache* but also with impish good humour, enjoying flamboyant public arguments, press conferences and manifestoes in support of his literary theories.

His foremost dogma was that literature must rid itself of what Ruskin called 'the pathetic fallacy', the tendency of novelists to describe objects emotively. Mountains must not be allowed to loom 'majestically' nor villages to 'nestle' in a valley. He has said, 'Around us, defying the onslaught of our animist adjectives, things *are there*,' and any attempt to endow the physical world with emotion is a step towards the illicit belief in God. This attitude, known as *chosisme*, was influenced by Barthes who wrote warmly of Robbe-Grillet's novels. These books are rich in *chosisme*, especially in their long painstaking descriptions of such things as the shape and measurements of a window (in *Le Voyeur*) or of a tropical plantation (*La Jalousie*) or the physiognomy of centipedes. But Robbe-Grillet, with apparent inconsistency, did not limit himself to *chosisme*. Although people, emotions and actions in the ordinary sense barely existed, he claimed that Man still held the centre of his stage and, as he told me, his detailed descriptions 'are *passionate*, an attempt to portray the world through the obsessed eyes of my heroes: if I describe a room with five chairs in it, what I am really describing is the obsession of the onlooker'. Of his scenario for Resnais' *L'Année dernière à Marienbad*, he said: 'What passes on the screen is the subjective struggle in the girl's mind, so that the spectator can never be sure of the level of reality he is observing. The amount of furniture in the room varies according to how she is feeling.'

How are we to assess the artistic worth of all this? Robbe-Grillet's strength is his sonorous and lyrical prose style, lending a dream-like fascination to many of his descriptions. But the effect, finally, is gratuitous and boring because there is no identifiable human impetus behind the images. Many critics have pointed to a basic contradiction in his work: he proclaims his theory of the pre-eminence of the observable world, yet destroys it with a 'game of mirrors' that leaves us unable to discern what is real and what is not. He first arouses our human interest and sympathy, then mockingly plants a booby-trap that snuffs it out and leaves us feeling cheated. At heart he is a scientist and iconoclast, and has seemed determined to prevent the rest of us from enjoying unscientific aesthetic pleasures of the old-fashioned sort: a curious vocation for an artist.

A less assertive 'new novelist', often linked with Robbe-Grillet in the 1960s, was Michel Butor. But in fact his earlier books were much less far removed from the traditional novel. He is a dedicated Proustian and his novels, like Proust's, are concerned with time: they even have coherent characters and plots, of a sort, though often these are turned upside-down through Butor's obsession with the relativity of time and the time–space relationship. His best-known novel, *La Modification* (1957), takes place entirely in the mind of one character on a train-journey from Paris to Rome, while *L'Emploi du temps* (1956) uses distortions of chronology to build up a nightmarish picture of Manchester where Butor once spent a year as a teacher. More recently Butor has been moving away from fiction towards experimental prose that tries to explore the new time–space relation in an age of jet travel: clocks, timetables, airports fascinate him. This mannered, obsessive writer is tending to repeat himself and is no longer taken very seriously.

Nathalie Sarraute is different again: a White Russian Jewish *émigrée* now in her late seventies. Like Robbe-Grillet she has openly condemned the moralistic novel of explicit narrative or social comment, and this has led them to be bracketed together. But her themes and subject-matter are not his. She is concerned with the living tissue of tiny, subtle sensations that she believes to make up the fabric of our lives: she admires Proust and Woolf, and uses a stream-of-consciousness technique not so very different from theirs to depict minutely a world of psychological flickerings (*tropismes*, she calls them) which for her are the real substance of human contact and sensibility. Her novels are difficult to read, and not rich in outward plot or character; but within her self-imposed range she is a psychological realist and a true poet. Other 'New Novelists' have included Robert Pinget, Claude Mauriac (son of François), and the remarkable Claude Simon, whose full-blooded evocations of his youth are a far cry from Robbe-Grillet's chilly calculations. The distinguished Marguerite Duras, now in her late sixties, has tended to be lumped in with the *nouveau roman*: her elliptical techniques of dialogue and narrative entitle her to be classed as experimental, but at heart she is less close to Robbe-Grillet than to the *engagé* Sartrian school. Witness the difference between the two Resnais films: *Hiroshima mon amour* with her script, and the never-never-land of *Marienbad*. Duras is a warm-hearted writer with a feeling for real people and predicaments, and that is something to welcome in the modern French novel. In the best of her stories – *Le Square*, *10.30 d'un soir d'été*, *Les petits chevaux de Tarquinia* – she has shown a rare sensitivity to atmosphere and place and the difficulty of communication. She has also done impressive work for the theatre and cinema.

These 'new novelists' were almost all Left-wing in their personal sympathies, but rarely did any hint of such views or of any topical social concern enter their pages. Sometimes they appeared to be chiefly preoccupied with writing novels about the problems of writing novels, especially Mauriac and Philippe Sollers. Needless to say, this inward-looking and rarefied school of literature found little success with a wider public: few of these books sold more than 4,000 copies, except for some of the *succès d'estime* of Robbe-Grillet and Butor, which reached 60,000 or so in pocket editions. By the early '70s the *nouveau roman* was expiring. Today it no longer has many imitators among young writers, and its leaders have virtually ceased producing novels; few of them – maybe Duras and Sarraute excepted – are likely to last long into posterity. Students and *lycéens* rarely turn eagerly to them as they do still to Camus, Sartre and Malraux. So what has the 'new novel' achieved? Some critics feel that it has been useful as a language laboratory or testing-ground – 'It has done for French what Joyce did for English,' said one. Maybe; except that Joyce had far greater genius than any of these new French writers. Their influence seems to have been mainly negative. For some years Robbe-Grillet and others exerted a kind of tyranny over younger novelists, making them feel unable to write in a traditional manner any more; and only now is the novel beginning to recover from this and return to humanist values.

One immediate sequel to the *nouveau roman* was the emergence in the 1960s of an arrogant and vocal coterie of young aesthetes, led by Philippe Sollers and Jean-Edern Hallier. They founded a monthly review, *Tel Quel*, which championed the Platonic ideal of formal beauty. Their style owed something to Robbe-Grillet, whom they saluted as a *maître-à-penser*, but they also claimed lineage back to Valéry and others. Their concern was for exquisiteness of language, irrespective of content; and when in 1962 *The Times Literary Supplement* made its celebrated lament for the decline of French 'clarity' into woolly abstruseness, it quoted this morsel from a prize-winning poetic passage by one *Tel Quel* writer, Michel Deguy:

> 'L'homme *est* philosophique; c'est à dire qu'il est philosophé par le passage au travers de son être de ce jaillissement dont la trace va s'appeler toute suite *philosophie*, trace oeuvre. La source se cache dans son propre flux; elle disparaît dans la fécondité de son sourdre. Penser c'est consentir à ce désir, qui nous constitue, de remémorer le sourdre indicible; c'est comme tenter de se convertir à la nuit d'où sort tout l'aube, et que les yeux, qui son faits pour les lumineux, ne peuvent voir – tentative quasi suicidaire de gagner sur cette dérobade de l'originel pour le pressentir, recul de dos au plus près du foyer de notre être qui est abîme, perte d'être.

Worthy of Pseuds' Corner in *Private Eye*, and not even verbally exquisite. The *Tel Quel* group were compared to Mallarmé and his school, with whose ingrown preciosity and disregard for coarse reality they seemed to have much in common. They were not numerous, but were typical of the kind of Left Bank obscurantism then current. And in some literary circles their dogmatic influence amounted to a kind of tyranny – 'We have created a new theology,' claimed Sollers proudly in 1971. But *Tel Quel*'s influence has since declined, and its particular brand of precious nonsense is no longer so much in vogue.

There has always been a gulf in France between the 'literary' novel and the conventional bourgeois novel with its far wider public. And while the 'New Novel' for a while stole much of the critical limelight, it did little damage to the fortunes of established writers such as Henri

Troyat, Jean Lartéguy or Gilbert Cesbron, who for decades have easily topped the bestseller lists, with sales maybe ten to fifty times those of a *nouveau roman*. Due partly to the feebleness of public libraries in France, a middle-class public is used to buying the latest fiction in some quantities, and a successful work of this kind – maybe a novel of history, adventure or family life – will readily sell well over 100,000 copies. Robert Sabatier, a respected middle-brow writer, has done very well with his sensitive studies of pre-war middle-class childhood, such as *Les Allumettes suédoises* which sold 300,000: a genre that you might call the French equivalent of L. P. Hartley.

In serious or imaginative fiction, today there is no dominant school or trend at all, nothing – maybe fortunately! – to take the place of the *nouveau roman*. A few goodish writers have emerged, of diverse kinds, but none has a talent to set the Seine on fire. Among them one could mention Georges Perec, gloomy satirist of the horrors of modern living; Patrick Modiano, who writes evocatively about life under the Occupation; Tony Duvert, whose semi-autobiographical tales of homosexual love vaguely recall Genet; and the prolific and amazing Pierre-Jean Rémy who manages to combine a career as a top civil servant (he was recently cultural counsellor in London) with an output of some two novels a year, virtuoso excursions into history, art and pornography.

After winning the Prix Goncourt in 1978, Modiano's *Rue des boutiques obscures* stayed at the top of the bestseller list for several months, selling over 300,000. It is books of this kind that generally win the coveted annual literary prizes – the Goncourt, Renaudot, Fémina, and others – which make so much difference to sales in this fashion-dominated land. If you want to show your dinner-guests that you're in the swim, then you must parade the latest Goncourt on your coffee-table within days of publication, even if you do no more than skim through it. But many critics complain that the average quality of the prize-winners has dropped considerably in the past decade or so, a sign of the decline of the novel. Quite often, too, the prizes are rigged by a few leading publishers, who virtually control the juries.

With the waning of the experimental novel, the literary trend now is back to books that tell stories and develop characters. Yet it is remarkable how few of these deal squarely with themes of contemporary France: serious writers seem to prefer to set their books in the past, or abroad, or around private subjects of love, fantasy or childhood, rather than to analyse French society today. Michel Tournier, for example, often regarded as the best living French novelist and a possible future Nobel laureate, has some affinities with Tolkien: he first won fame with *Le Roi des Aulnes*, a brilliant Gothic fantasy that took the Goncourt in 1971, and has followed this up with some vivid re-interpretations of historic myths, notably the Dioscuri and the Three Wise Men. Jean-Marie-Gustave Le Clézio, a brooding and solitary wanderer, startled the literary world in 1966 with *Le Déluge*, a cosmic allegory that tells of a young man's nightmare odyssey through the streets of a modern city, haunted by images of death and decay. Though he has not written anything so powerful since, his later books – some set in Mexico and Morocco – continue to project the same personal vision of disgust at material civilization.

In a more realistic and down-to-earth vein, Marguerite Yourcenar (who has lived in the United States since 1939) has produced a number of notable historical novels, and was rewarded in 1980 by becoming the first woman ever to be elected to the Académie Française (see p. 347). The fashionable and nostalgic concern with the past (*le mode rétro*, it is called) is seen also in the work of Modiano, and of others who write about the wartime period. Other novelists in turn deal with off-beat amorous or political adventures in exotic lands: Hallier for instance in Chile and South-East Asia, Rémy in China and London (a truly exotic location, in French eyes). Finally, it is noticeable that many of the best novels now being written in French are by foreign expatriates in France describing their homelands – Arabs, South Americans, Russians and other East Europeans.

Given the insular tendency of so much French culture, it is no bad thing that writers should concern themselves with foreign lands. At the same time it seems a pity, when France's own society has been moving through so fascinating a period of transition, that the novel has virtually abdicated its classic Balzacian role as chronicler of that society. True, there are some exceptions, such as Jean Carrière's impressive 1972 Goncourt winner, *L'Epervier de Maheux*, a stark study of rural life in the Cévennes; or Victor Pilhes' 1974 Prix Fémina winner, *L'Imprécateur*, a satire on the Paris international business world. And sharp little studies of bourgeois greed and hypocrisy continue to appear; but one has the feeling that it's all been said before, with the same *parti pris*. The French novel remains essentially bourgeois, especially when it is trying not to be: there is virtually no equivalent of the post-war English school of working-class faction (for what *that* is worth), and no new Zola. Sometimes I ingenuously ask a writer or publisher, 'France today needs her Balzac, her Flaubert, as much as ever: why is no one filling this gap?' The 'New Novelists' just laugh. Robbe-Grillet said to me, 'Balzac was a great writer in his day, but you can't write like that now. Our role is no longer to explore social values but to discover new ones.' Even those writers who disagree with this *Diktat* feel nonetheless that the legacy of structuralism and of the *nouveau roman* has been such as to inhibit them even today from writing a social novel as Balzac did. François Nourissier, a serious realistic novelist, said recently: 'The past twenty years have seen a growth of critical forms to the detriment of creative ones; a take-over of the literary heritage by pedagogues, linguists, psychoanalysts ... and this has stifled the literary spirit of adventure, the ambition and taste for imaginative writing. The quest for the "new novel", and the experimentation of the *Tel Quel* school, while legitimate, have wrought such terrorism as to cause a collective mental block among young writers.'

There may be other explanations too. Robert Escarpit, a leading critic, said to me: 'It's the fault of publishers and public, as much as of critics and writers. If anyone today wrote, say, a realistic satire on provincial life, it would fall between two stools. The highbrow critics would deride it as old hat and not what the novel is for; and bourgeois publishers and booksellers would fear that it might offend their readers.' Others have suggested that French society today is too fluid and frag-mented for a study *à la* Balzac: yet I would have thought that this very fluidity might prove fertile terrain. My own impression is that the aver-age French novelist is simply not very interested in the ordinary life of the nation, and by choice he lives detached from it, strikingly more so than British writers, most of whom dwell placidly in province or suburb, soberly reporting on the daily scene around them. But many French novelists are afflicted by what is called '*le parisianisme*': they mix only with each other, in the rarefied Parisian milieux, scorning the provinces – 'I was born in Amiens,' one told me, 'but you can't *live* there!' So their raw material is drawn mainly from their own childhood memories of family crises, or from the current intrigues and *amours* of their own little world.

It is true that nowadays an increasing number of serious novelists do live in the provinces, maybe earning their bread as teachers; and here they can often do better creative work than in Paris. But they tend to lead isolated lives, rarely integrating into the community around them. 'As a creative writer,' said one, 'I am not concerned with exploring the social tensions or crude consumerism of modern France. I would rather con-centrate on my private world, and the refinement of my style. I am not a documentarist – I leave that to the media, and to sociology.' Fair enough – provided that his talent and imagination justify this stance, which is rarely the case. So the novel survives as a fragile, anaemic creature, cut off from the mainstream of life as it never was in Flaubert's day, or even Proust's or Camus'. And it is not being helped by the latest trends in French publishing, which are polarizing the industry between big-selling paperbacks on the one hand, and luxury or specialized technical books on the other – with the serious literary work crushed in the middle.

THEATRE: THE DIRECTOR-AS-SUPERSTAR ELIMINATES THE PLAYWRIGHT

The decline of creative writing is even more apparent in the theatre. No new playwrights of any great substance have arisen in the past twenty years to take the place of the Genet/Anouilh generation; and in Paris' fifty or so theatres, nearly all the good plays on view are foreign imports (often British), or revivals of classics, or free-wheeling adaptations. So today it is commonly said that the French theatre is moribund, but this is not really true. In its own manner – a manner utterly different from London's, and not to everyone's taste – it is still lively, varied and innovative. This is due above all to the recent rise of a new kind of virtuoso director – Vitez, Chéreau, Planchon, Mnouchkine are among the big names – who becomes the real star of the play, more than the actors or the author. For better or worse, he imposes his personality on the text, often reworking it totally. This is a new theatre of gesture, lighting, movement, more than of the spoken word; and Paris is divided as to whether it marks a brilliant step forward or an artistic dead end.

As in Britain, the bourgeois commercial theatre has declined ever since the 1950s at the expense of State-subsidized repertory companies which attract younger audiences and can afford to experiment with new kinds of drama. The forty or so private *théâtres du boulevard* used to do a handsome trade by providing the bourgeoisie with their staple entertainment: a 'boulevard comedy' was a clearly-defined *genre*, a safe play that would amuse and gently provoke, without being too difficult: André Roussin's *The Little Hut*, for example. But this audience has fallen by 45 per cent since 1960; rocketing ticket prices and the rival lure of television have taken their toll, while the boulevard play itself has grown bankrupt in ideas and wit. A very few still manage to sustain long runs – *Boeing-Boeing* for instance lasted nineteen years and *La Cage aux Folles* nearly eight – thus proving that a potential audience is still there. But they are balanced by an increasing number of flops, and it seems a miracle that the boulevard theatre still manages to hobble along. Usually a play needs a star name, such as Edwige Feuillère, to have a chance of success. Personally, I find there is something fusty and dispiriting about the average Paris private theatre with its rickety seating, faded décor and surly, underpaid staff.

The small group of subsidized theatres in Paris present a picture of far greater success and enterprise, in a land where State patronage of drama dates back to 1639. Each of the national theatres is responsible to the Ministry of Culture, but its State-appointed director has a free artistic hand. And the initial French post-war theatre revival owes its greatest debt to the late and great Jean Vilar, who founded and ran the Théâtre National Populaire (TNP) at the Palais de Chaillot from 1951 to 1963. With the help of a generous subsidy and a large auditorium (2,700 seats), he was able to pursue a policy of low prices and so play to full houses; and he built up an audience very different from the boulevards' and closer to that of the ciné-clubs – students, young intellectuals, even some workers who would never dream of rubbing shoulders with the *seizième* at an Achard comedy. The TNP played some French classics but – a break with French tradition – it placed its main emphasis on foreign classics and serious modern plays, thus introducing wide new Parisian audiences to Shakespeare, Brecht, Chekhov, Osborne and others. Every summer the company would decamp with its repertoire to the Palais des Papes in Avignon, building this into one of Europe's foremost annual drama festivals. Gérard Philipe, greatest of post-war French actors, worked regularly with the TNP before his early death in 1960, and his performance in Corneille's *Le Cid* at Avignon is remembered as a supreme moment of French post-war theatre.

Vilar was succeeded at the TNP by the actor Georges Wilson; but Wilson did not do so well and audiences fell off. He and the Ministry finally parted company in 1972, and the latter then took the remarkable step of abolishing the TNP as such in Paris and transferring its title, its attributes and its subsidy to the provinces – to the great Roger Planchon (see p. 324) at Villeurbanne! So Planchon and his troupe, now in a fine new theatre, have been rewarded with the official status of France's leading modern drama company: they *are* 'le TNP', and they have the duty of mounting their own productions at home and then sending them on tour to the rest of France, to Paris, and abroad. Planchon has had with him one of France's most brilliant younger experimental directors, Patrice Chéreau, of whom more later. And the Ministry has converted the TNP's old home at the Palais de Chaillot into a kind of informal Maison de la Culture, a little like London's Round House. This project has been through a series of troubles: but in 1981 there were hopes that these would end when that other luminary of the avant-garde theatre, Antoine Vitez, agreed to take over Chaillot.

The Comédie Française, that venerable State institution dating from the seventeenth century, has had a chequered post-war career: but under its most recent director, Pierre Dux, it has proved as successfully as Stratford-on-Avon that the classics well performed *can* be great box-office. The Comédie Française considers itself the trustee of French classical drama, and of a certain stylized, rhetorical tradition of acting that I personally find tedious: it is at the opposite pole from the quiet naturalism of French cinema acting. But it has plenty of devotees. For some years the CF suffered from archaic administration: then Dux modernized it, helped by a State subsidy now running at over 50 million francs a year, and he has pulled in big audiences for a repertoire that mixes the French classics with a few modern or foreign plays. The theatre staged the French première of Ionesco's *La Soif et la faim* and (to the delight of the Left) managed to shock its traditional dinner-jacket audiences with the scene that parodies Christian conversion. More recently Terry Hands, now better known in Paris than in London, produced a successful *Midsummer Night's Dream.* In 1979–80 the theatre was packed every night, and had to turn down 150,000 requests for season tickets.

The Comédie Française also operates another leading State theatre, the Odéon, as a kind of annexe, used by various major touring companies both provincial and foreign. This is where Planchon's TNP performs when in Paris, and here the great Italian director Giorgio Strehler has successfully presented seasons of Goldoni, in Italian. Previously, in the 1960s, the Odéon was for eight years the home of the marvellous Barrault–Renaud company, invited there by Malraux. Jean-Louis Barrault there carried out a policy not unlike that of Olivier at the Old Vic; you might find Shakespeare in the repertory alongside new French plays by Duras, Billetdoux or Genet. But then came May '68; and when militant students seized the Odéon and used it as an open parliament, Barrault dramatically joined cause with them, crying, 'I am totally on your side!' For this Malraux repaid him with the sack. It was a sour ending to one of the brightest chapters in French post-war theatre. But the irrepressible Barraults soon bounced back: they took over part of a derelict railway-station, the Gare d'Orsay, turned it into an unusual circus-like open-stage theatre, and soon were drawing enthusiastic crowds of mainly young people, for their plays as well as for concerts and happenings. In the later 1970s their major successes there include *Rabelais*, *Zadig* (after Voltaire), *Harold and Maude*, and Duras' *Des Journées entières dans les arbres*, the last two both starring Madeleine Renaud (Mme Barrault), one of France's supreme actresses. But then in 1980 Giscard claimed the Gare d'Orsay for a museum, so the Barraults like some circus troupe had to move yet again, for the eighth time in thirty years, this time to a theatre off the Champs-Elysées. Now turned seventy, Barrault is as buoyant as ever. He collaborates closely with his friend Peter Brook, who runs an international drama research centre in Paris, also State-subsidized.

The variety of new theatrical enterprise in Paris takes other forms too. One important subsidized venture is run not by the State but by the Paris city council, which in 1968 took over the enormous Sarah Bernhardt, renamed it Théâtre de la Ville, and put it in the charge of Jean Mercure. Here he has built up sizeable audiences for a safe repertory of classics on the Chekhov or Giraudoux level, plus new foreign plays by, for example, Peter Nichols, and a range of concerts, ballets and recitals. Out in the provinces, the remarkable post-war crop of State-backed regional 'reps' (see p. 323) is still sturdily alive, despite inevitable financial problems in today's hard times. This decentralizing movement has encompassed also the Paris working-class suburbs, where enterprising little theatres have opened in such Communist fiefs as Nanterrre and St-Denis: Guy Rétoré with his famous Théâtre de l'Est Parisien at Ménilmontant, and Vitez himself with his Théâtre des Quartiers d'Ivry, are prominent among directors who try – with varying success – to put their Leftist ideals into action by bringing serious drama to popular Parisian audiences. Among these various suburban and provincial companies, the standards of performance are obviously very uneven: but there is no doubt that much of the best creative production in France is now taking place outside central Paris. One legacy of May '68 is that scores of little troupes have emerged, struggling along on small subsidies, many of them itinerant, performing where they can in ill-lit local halls or in Maisons de la Culture. It is all very haphazard, rarely very brilliant: but it is alive. Inside Paris, one significant vogue in the past decade has been that of the *café-théâtre*. There are now some twenty of these – tiny late-night theatres with cafés or *bistrots* attached where you watch either a kind of revue or one-man show, or a modern playlet, often foreign: I saw a fine production of Dylan Thomas' *Sous bois lacté*. The *café-théâtre*, now past its prime, is no more than a minor 'fringe', and some of its output is dismally banal: but it is all part of the variegated scene.

The theatre world today complains loudly of financial crisis, and in a sense it is justified. Official subsidies, though still generous by British standards, have not been keeping pace with rising costs; and many theatres are now having to fight harder for audiences. But, whatever the woes of the Paris 'boulevard' or the small fringe groups, a few star companies – the TNP, the Comédie Française, and others – are more popular than ever. However uneven the results, there is still plenty of sparkle left in the French theatre. In fact, the 1970s saw a revival of a kind: the French stage is now on balance as lively as Britain's – and that certainly was not so ten years ago, before London's decline. But tne two styles are very different. Classical revivals apart, Britain's forte remains the craftsmanlike production of well-written realistic new plays; France's accent is on the fireworks of experimental *mise-en-scène*. And there remains this mystery of the dearth of good new French playwrights, as compared with earlier days. Is it that the new talent is simply not there, or that the new-style directors' theatre does not encourage it?

Take a step back into time, and the new plays were brilliant: Genet, Ionesco, Beckett, Adamov, Sartre, Camus, de Montherlant, Audiberti, Anouilh – not all these were French, but they wrote in French and lived in France, and their contribution to modern European theatre has been colossal. But many of them are now dead, and of those still alive none is under seventy or still writing plays. When their work is performed in London, it arrives 'like light from a burnt-out star', as Irving Wardle wrote; and it has little relevance to the Paris theatre today, save in the form of revivals. So what good new playwrights, if any, have emerged in the past twenty years? Marguerite Duras, now in her late sixties, has made an interesting jump from fiction to drama, and some of her short plays – *La Musica*, *Suzanna Andler*, and others – are remarkable. Michel Vinaver writes clever Brechtian satires on the world of big business. And Jean-Claude Grumberg is the author of some moving and realistic dramas of Jewish life, notably *Dreyfus* and *L'Atelier*: the latter, produced at the Odéon in 1979, was much acclaimed and highly successful, indicating how starved is the French public for this kind of native French play. The *New Statesman* wrote, '*L'Atelier* is like a French version of a good Royal Court play; but there hasn't been a Royal Court in the French cultural republic.' One could cite one or two other names, but they add up to little. Young playwrights find it hard to get a break: private theatres are wary of taking the financial risk of presenting a serious play by an unknown writer, while the big national theatres make far less effort than their British counterparts to seek out new talent. So Paris fills up with revivals and imports. English plays especially – Pinter, Stoppard, etc. – are in vogue with the public. Moreover, many producers and actors consider that contemporary British and American playwrights, far better than French ones, provide them with meaty subjects and strong acting roles that relate to the real modern world. As in the case of the novel, too many new French plays are about the hang-ups of writing a play, or some equally hermetic theme.

Yet there may also be quite another explanation for the dearth. This lies in the growing dominance, during the 1970s, of a school of clever and fashionable directors who have an entirely different concept of theatre. They are simply not interested in receiving a text from an author and then faithfully staging it, like a kind of publisher. To them a live author is a potential nuisance, an impediment to their creative fancy. So they prefer either to re-interpret the plays of dead authors (who are not there to interfere!) or else to devise their own texts.

Sometimes director and cast take a theme and collectively improvise a play around it as they rehearse. The most talented pioneer of this particular trend is Ariane Mnouchkine, whose Théâtre du Soleil company performs in a former cartridge factory at Vincennes (in line with a current Paris fashion, shared by Barrault and Brook and echoed in London's Round House, for using outlandish or derelict premises rather than normal theatres – a matter of inverted snobbery, as much as of economics). Born of May '68, the Théâtre du Soleil is a young idealistic troupe, run as a workers' cooperative, each member drawing the same wage. It has echoes of Joan Littlewood's former Theatre Workshop: it too has a woman as its presiding genius; it too is militantly Leftish; it too, as in *Oh, What a Lovely War*, pastes up history into a collage of fine dramatic effect. This is what the troupe did with the French revolution, relating it to the events of 1968 in their brilliantly original *1789* and *1793*, two productions of the early 1970s which caused more stir than anything on the Paris stage for years. They have since made a long, rollicking film about the life of Molière (shown on BBC TV in 1980); and in 1979 they applied their collage technique, with equal effect, to a dramatic adaptation of Klaus Mann's novel *Mephisto*, about the early impact of Nazism on pre-1930 Germany. Mnouchkine's inventions seem to me a valid and exciting form of theatre: but they leave the poor playwright feeling a redundant species.

Antoine Vitez is another director much in vogue who takes a literary text, or maybe a political one, and works it into a kind of play – less successfully than Mnouchkine, in my view. He did this with the transcript of talks between Mao and Pompidou; he also took a novel by Aragon, *Les Clochers de Bâle*, and with six other actors turned it into an *ad hoc* playlet, with much noisy rhetoric and jumping on and off tables. Even more controversially, some of these new star directors apply their creative gifts to re-working the classics. Vitez, Chéreau and Planchon are the high-priests of this cult, which many critics now feel is being carried too far. London too has known this kind of thing: Charles Marowitz has turned Shakespeare inside-out on stage, while Derek Jarman made a punk travesty of *The Tempest* for the cinema. But Marowitz and Jarman are relatively marginal figures, whereas Vitez and his friends today dominate – tyrannize, some would say – the French theatre world as no equivalent director does in Britain. This is very much in the French tradition, where fashionable coteries for a while impose a 'terrorism of taste' in a particular sphere: Bocuse and his 'gang' in *cuisine*, or Barthes and Robbe-Grillet a few years back in literature.

Some critics find Vitez' work exhilarating, others think him tire-somely gimmicky. He has been invited to the Comédie Française, where in 1975 his version of that modern classic, *Partage du Midi*, was regarded by some as a splendid rediscovery of Claudel, and by others as a massacre. Vitez had the actors speak the lines in a Noh-like sing-song style, which stung Richard Roud to comment in the *Guardian*:[7] 'It made non-sense of Claudel's poetry, it was an unqualified disaster . . . It seems that the new French producers are unable to cope with literary texts. They do fine when they have arranged or written the work themselves, and this was certainly true of Mnouchkine's *1789*. But, faced with a text, their first reaction is to see what they can do to it. And this means, how can they distort it, or worse, how can they best display their own originality.' In 1973 the young Patrice Chéreau startled Paris with his TNP production of Marivaux's *La Dispute*: with a parade of virtuoso lighting effects and other visual inventions, he managed to spin out this subtle fifty-minute playlet to a full two-and-a-half hours. Some playgoers felt that poor Marivaux had been buried out of sight beneath the deluge of tricks – 'this dreadful, crawling horror', Bernard Levin in the *Sunday Times* called the production. But another British critic, Gary O'Connor, raved over Chéreau's 'capacity for expanding the images conveyed by words or ideas into a visual spectacle of breathtakingly epic proportions and impeccably disciplined taste. The director is always the star of the show.'[8] *De gustibus* . . .

The new directors have also set to work on Racine, and notably on Molière. It is argued that at least this has helped to liberate these authors from the dead hand of formal classic production imposed on them for so long by the Comédie Française and others: for whereas British post-war directors have managed to present Shakespeare in fresh and lively ways without departing from the spirit or text of his plays, in France hitherto the classics had remained draped in a fusty, static, centuries-old tra-dition, and to tamper with it was thought heresy. So Vitez the heretic set to work – 'The text must be given a modern force, a twentieth-century resonance,' he told me. But have not the new directors swung from one extreme to another? When in 1980 Planchon staged Racine's *Athalie* and Molière's *Dom Juan*, and Vitez put on Racine's *Bérénice*, one leading Paris critic, Pierre Marcabru, wrote scathingly in *Le Point* of 'Planchon's strip-cartoon tragedy' and 'Vitez' love of semantic fantasies and tragi-comic preciosities'. In his review headed 'The classics under torture,' Marcabru wittily analysed these directors' possible motives in chopping up, re-arranging, or even rewording the authors' texts and plot: 'Either in

7 February 9th, 1976.
8 *French Theatre Today*, Pitman, London, 1975.

mockery, or through dogmatism, they try to make the author say the opposite of what he thinks. In a director of this kind, I sense the jubilant sadistic streak of a failed would-be author who is trying to take it out on a colleague, albeit one dead for three centuries. One day, the classic repertory may become no more than a testing-ground for mime-drama, choreography and opera, a springboard for the director's day-dreams, delights and perversions. So the author, this mangy old crone, this killjoy, will finally be forced back into the silence that he had inopportunely broken. Whatever was he doing in the theatre, anyway?'

Antoine Vitez, now aged fifty, is a brilliant multilingual intellectual who in conversation expresses his ideas with dogmatic force and incisive clarity. His concept of good theatre is utterly different from that current, say, in Britain. He was a Communist Party member until early 1980 (when he resigned over Afghanistan): but, though still firmly on the Left, he is not interested in a committed Brechtian theatre dealing with moral or political problems, nor in a theatre of social realism. For him, theatre is more 'a permanent meditation on form, style and language'. He told me: 'Yes, it's true that I do not depend on new authors, but that does not mean that I reject them. The kind of new author I look for is a poet and experimentalist. I despise the plodding realism of Grumberg's *L'Atelier*. And I despise the modern British theatre, which is absurdly over-rated. The only good British director is Brook – and it's entirely symptomatic that *he* has chosen to live and work here in Paris. The average British production that arrives here, amid praise from critics and public, seems to me to belong to a dead style of theatre. It's like *light from a burnt-out star*' – he turned Irving Wardle's phrase back against itself!

Yet it may well be that the meteoric Vitez/Chéreau school will soon burn itself out and vanish, as happens so often with French cultural trends. Already the serious public shows signs of tiring of it. So maybe new authors will emerge again before too long, to take up the torch from Genet and de Montherlant. Meantime, it is hard to tell whether chicken precedes egg or not: is it the lack of good new plays that leads directors to turn to other forms of theatre? – or is it the new directors' disdainful treatment of authors that deters them from writing for the stage? Probably a little of both. I may have been harsh on Vitez, and I am not the only one. But I will admit that at least the new French theatre has virtuosity and vitality, whether or not one admires its particular style. One drama critic summed up: 'Our highly sophisticated new directors are giving us a new vision of theatre. All in all, I'd rather be excited or maddened by the latest *feu d'artifice* from Chéreau than sit through some worthy new comedy of manners *à l'anglaise*.'

CINEMA: FROM THE TRUMPETS
OF THE 'NOUVELLE VAGUE' TO THE
FLUTE-NOTES OF A NEW REALISM

Why so few good new plays or novels? One answer: over the past twenty-five years, much of the best new creative talent of this kind has preferred to express itself through cinema. The French not only pioneered cinematography, in the 1890s: since then, in my own view, they have given the world more great films than any other nation, even the United States. But today? – so often one hears the lament that even the cinema is now in decline, along with other arts, compared at least with its last golden age, that of the so-called '*nouvelle vague*' around 1960. Certainly it is true that many of these new-wave directors have now developed middle-age spread and seem past their prime. It is true too that the French cinema is again in one of its periodic financial crises, and as in many other countries it has not yet come to terms with the fearsome rivalry of television. And yet, creatively, the picture does not appear to me as bleak as it is often painted. In the past decade a new *genre* of film-making has emerged, less strikingly original or lyrical than the *nouvelle vague*, but with qualities of its own in its clear-eyed portrayal of modern French daily life, its private joys and anxieties. This is an intimate, reflective, humanist cinema, a chamber music; it rarely attempts blockbusters or 'big' public themes, and maybe that is why it has so far made little impact abroad. Within this diversified trend, a score or so of new directors of talent have appeared, but only one or two of them – notably Bertrand Tavernier – are as yet at all well known outside France. And yet this subtle, modest new cinema, very much in the French tradition, is not without promise.

The cinema has long been intellectually respectable in France, and since the war the passion for it among younger educated people has been stronger than in any other country. Thousands of new 'ciné-clubs' have sprung up across France, where people gather in a hired hall or flea-pit to watch anything from the latest Resnais to an old scratched copy of *Potemkin* and then eagerly discuss it. Paris today has scores of art-house cinemas, and at any one time this city offers the public a fantastic range of films of all sorts, old and new: a far wider choice than in London, or even New York. Not that this intellectual devotion to films is new: the cinema has never had to struggle, as in Britain, to win acceptance beside theatre or music as a major art form. In the 1920s Cocteau was turning to film as readily as to verse, as a medium for his poetry. And writers like Sartre,

Malraux and Robbe-Grillet have eagerly collaborated in film-making or even directed films. The French believe that cinema, given the right conditions, can be used just as powerfully or subtly as any other art to express a personal artistic vision, despite the pressures of a mass-entertainment industry.

This was the background from which the hundred or so young directors of the *nouvelle vague* emerged with such clamour in the late 1950s – less by accident than through an explosive necessity of self-expression. A new generation had arrived that had taught itself cinema in its teens, in the clubs and art-houses, and grew up 'speaking cinema' as its elders spoke literature. One critic suggested, 'A young creative person with something to say, who thirty years ago would have written a novel, today dreams of making a film.' But why? The difficulties of writing a humanist novel in the recent literary climate, the frustrations of working for conformist State television, these were two obvious factors that drew talent towards the independent cinema. Also the cinema combines lyricism with documentary to a higher degree than any other art, and this duality appeals to the French. As I suggested earlier, the flight from ideologies has taken the French down two distinct paths, towards the aesthetic, and towards the concrete and practical: the cinema unites the two. Location-shooting fascinates by its actuality, and the camera does not lie: but the camera is also a tool of fantasy, the perfect poetic liar.

The 1930s had been a golden age, that of the great films of Clair, Carné and Renoir. Then the early post-war years, too, were at least a luminous silver age, with such films as Becker's *Casque d'or*. But as the 1950s wore on a creeping paralysis appeared. The established older directors grew steadily bankrupt of inspiration, save for one or two rare figures like Robert Bresson. Subjects became stereotyped: *policiers*, sex dramas or costume pieces, carrying with them the stale air of the studios. Producers were scared of trusting to new talent or new themes. But meanwhile France was changing, a new mood and style of life were emerging that the cinema seemed to ignore, and a new audience began to lose patience with the artificialities offered on the screen. Television too was just making its impact. Safe-formula films started to flop unexpectedly, and scared producers wondered whether to turn to spectaculars (which few of them could afford) or try some novelty.

The new generation then proceeded to force their hand, in one of the most startling revolutions in cinema history. Scattered groups of young would-be directors were waiting their chance, sometimes even essaying their own self-financed low-budget features, and in the mid-1950s one or two unusual films began to slip into the art-houses: Agnès Varda's *La Pointe courte*, for instance. Then in 1956 a young producer, Raoul Lévy, engaged a very young journalist, Roger Vadim, to try his hand at a realistic but rarely-attempted theme, the amorality of modern pleasure-loving youth, to be set on location in St-Tropez. Today, *Et Dieu créa la femme*, slick and cynical, looks old hat: but in the prevailing climate of Fernandel comedies and studio rehashes of Colette it was startling. It was not a great film, but it broke new ground: for almost the first time in the French post-war cinema, here was youth looking at itself with a raw directness. What is more, the film won a fantastic commercial success, in France and world-wide. So this incited other producers to look for other new talent and real-life subjects. They did not need to look far. A number of directors, no longer so young, had already been working in documentary, helped by a system of State grants, and they gladly seized the chance to make their first features: thus in 1959 Alain Resnais, thirty-six, made *Hiroshima mon amour*. A second major source of talent was the very young group of critics on the magazine *Cahiers du Cinema*, led by Godard, Chabrol, Truffaut, Rohmer. Several were from moneyed backgrounds, and in their passion to get started they sank their own capital into modest features. Thus Chabrol made *Le Beau Serge* in 1958 for a mere 480,000 francs with a legacy inherited by his wife.

It was an exciting time to be in Paris. I remember in 1959 attending previews of Chabrol's first films (*Le Beau Serge* and *Les Cousins*) without having heard of him before, and enjoying the shock of a new cinema language, rather as Londoners had done in the theatre three years earlier with Osborne's *Look Back in Anger*. French cinema was back in touch with real life. Resnais and Truffaut took the leading prizes at Cannes that spring. *L'Express* invented the label '*nouvelle vague*', and journalists applied it to any new name, conveniently ignoring the wide differences between the *Cahiers* group and Resnais and his friends, or between either and lone-riders like Malle. Some of the new directors (Godard, Resnais) were genuine cinematic revolutionaries; others (Truffaut, Rohmer, etc.) were simply applying an up-to-date personal style to conventional themes and subjects. And yet the label had some validity, for in several ways the new directors differed from the earlier post-war generation. Above all, they were devoted to what is called the '*film d'auteur*', the concept of a film as a unique personal creation like a novel. This was not a new idea in France, though the new wave carried it farther than before. Many of them approached their early films just as if they were first novels: Truffaut's semi-autobiographical *Les 400 coups* was a good example. Even when they adapted from books (as Truffaut with *Jules et Jim*) they were usually careful to take little-known or banal ones which they would transform completely, rather than be inhibited by scruples of fidelity like many British films of the time.

The new directors also had in common the fact that they came straight into features at the top. Some had studied at the official French film school, but few had worked their way up through the usual slow, dispiriting channels of technical apprenticeship in big studios. What this lost them in experience it added in freshness. They arrived with anti-industry ideas on how to make films: no big stars or lavish sets, and thus less need for concessions to alleged popular taste. They were helped, too, by three other factors which they would not have found so easily in Britain. The first was the French system of aid for the cinema. Then, as today, feature films do not get outright grants but a number each year are given advances, awarded partly on a basis of quality, with the script and the director's past record taken into account. Resnais, Varda and others were thus able to take risks with commercially dubious subjects. Secondly, the trade-unions have always been more easy-going than in Britain: they have not imposed the same tough restrictions about set working-hours and large minimum crews, and this has made it easier to shoot rapidly on a low budget. Thirdly, production and distribution have been relatively haphazard in France, at least until recently: and although this has rendered the French industry more vulnerable in time of economic crisis, it greatly helped the independent producers of the new wave once they had made their breakthrough.

The *nouvelle vague* has come a long way in twenty-odd years. Today all its major directors are still at work, though some appear to have nothing new to say. Some, such as Godard, continue to make films on their own rigorous terms, outside 'the system'; others have compromised, perhaps inevitably, with a commercial cinema which they once denounced, yet they still follow the personal style of the *film d'auteur*. It is hard to generalize about so diverse a group, so let me now give a quick survey of the work of the major talents. First, the *Cahiers* group.

Claude Chabrol is the archetype of *nouvelle vague* flair-plus-perversity. He shot *Le Beau Serge* on location in his childhood village near Limoges. It told a story of alcoholism and peasant decadence in one of the poorest parts of France, and for all its naïvety and sententiousness it was clearly drawing on felt personal experience. Its raw intensity excited the critics. Next he made *Les Cousins*, about a gentle provincial student's corruption by a cynical milieu of young Parisian sophisticates. Again there was the nervously urgent camera-work, the rawness of style, the appealing sincerity of youth – and the public flocked to see the film. *Les Bonnes femmes* (1960), though dismissed by many critics, was to my mind another brilliant little film, a bitter study of Parisian schoolgirls, their naïve dreams, their cruel defeat by life. Behind Chabrol's sardonic misanthropy there seemed to lurk a despairing tenderness, a very French awareness of human isolation. There followed some years of semi-eclipse, but then Chabrol strongly re-emerged in the late 1960s as a more polished and mature, if less unconventional, film-maker. He has since turned out a succession of stylish psychological thrillers, notably *Que la bête meure*, *Les Noces rouges*, *Le Boucher* and *Violette Nozière*. He is prolific, making a film or two a year, but his work is very uneven, sometimes banal. In 1980 he boldly, but rashly, stepped outside his *genre* to film P.-J. Hélias' famous bestseller about Breton peasant life in 1910, *Le Cheval d'orgeuil*: the movie was static and hollow, missing the warmth of the novel. Several of Chabrol's thrillers have been highly praised: more than mere thrillers, they are also sharp studies of bourgeois life and hypocrisy, and this gives them their edge. But I myself still prefer his earlier, clumsier, more ingenuously personal films. He has become a little too much the craftsman-entertainer – like his idol, Hitchcock.

François Truffaut, like Chabrol, began his career in a blaze of humanism: *Les 400 coups*, the story of a boy driven to delinquency by loneliness and unhappiness, was based partly on his own childhood. Not only was this twenty-seven-year-old's debut a masterly piece of *mise-en-scène*, but the film was a model of implied social criticism without preaching sermons. But since then Truffaut has generally avoided themes that relate directly to modern French life. He says he is not interested in dealing with political and social problems and that 'the best of the permanent subjects is love'. He is no great innovator, either in techniques or ideas, and his colossal reputation rests largely on his lyrical gifts and his gentle wit and humanism, qualities seen at their best in *Jules et Jim* and *La Nuit américaine* (*Day for Night*). As Penelope Houston has put it, 'He has the gift of making film-making look wonderfully easy, like a man running down a long sunlit road with a camera in his hand.' But his more recent work has been erratic. *La Chambre verte* (1977), an austere study of a man's obsession with commemorating the dead, showed his courageous readiness to tackle non-commercial subjects from time to time, while *Le Dernier métro* (1980) was an evocative picture of life in Paris under the Occupation. But his numerous romantic comedies have tended to be slight, repetitive and self-indulgent. This humanist in the Renoir tradition seems never to have fully matured. He is still at his best when boyishly giving vent to his own feelings and pleasures: by far his finest film of the 1970s was *La Nuit américaine*, a witty and tender story about people making a film, with Truffaut cast as himself, the director. It was Truffaut's own loving serenade to the movie world, and it succeeded beautifully.

While Truffaut and Chabrol have rarely lived up to their brilliant debuts, Eric Rohmer, their contemporary, got off to a slow start but later blossomed. For my money, his *Le Genou de Claire* (1970) was *the* best French film of the 1970s. Like Truffaut, Rohmer is concerned not with social or topical problems but with private relationships: but his vision is subtler and more consistent than Truffaut's. The six films he made in 1962–71 were a series of what he called *'contes moraux'*, analysing the moral dilemmas of man–woman encounters. In *Ma nuit chez Maud*, an earnest-minded Catholic re-examines his life and principles in the light of his meetings with two very different women; in *Le Genou de Claire*, a diplomat on holiday by the lake of Annecy finds himself disturbingly attracted by two teenage girls. There is not much plot in Rohmer's films; people talk a great deal and very intelligently about their thoughts and feelings, attitudes are illumined from within, a spell is cast. It is a literary cinema, and Rohmer's best films have the texture of a good short novel: in *Le Genou de Claire* he created exquisite poetry out of minor incidents: girls by a lakeside in summer, wistful encounters between middle-age and adolescence. Rohmer's films, full of bourgeois people wrapped up in their private worlds, have often been called 'reactionary' by the Left: but those are the worlds that interest him, so he is being true to himself as an artist. His elegant films appeal to a minority, the kind of public that reads Proust. After the *contes moraux* he made two films set in the past, but not with the same success: *Die Marquise von O*, based on Kleist's nineteenth-century German novel, was somewhat frigid, while *Perceval le Gallois*, a medieval tale, was visually intriguing but over-stylized. However, Rohmer then embarked on a new series of studies of modern manners and morals, *'comédies et proverbes'*: the first, *La Femme de l'aviateur* (1980), though lightweight, was subtle and delightful.

Jean-Luc Godard could not be more different from Rohmer in his outlook, style and subject-matter: but like Rohmer he has remained true to himself in remaining outside 'the system', uncorrupted by big budgets or slick commercial subjects. It hardly needs repeating that Godard has been one of the most potent phenomena in post-war world cinema. Like many other of his fans, I regret his decline since about 1968: I do not care much for his abstruse video work of the 1970s where his impish humour seemed to have deserted him, and even his much-heralded come-back with *Sauve qui peut (la vie)* in 1980 was for me a disappointment. But the *oeuvre* of his early period, 1959–68, remains original and fascinating. He was a quintessential child of the 'sixties, also their mirror and prophet; in its quirky way, his early work was full of insights into the France of that period.

Son of a Protestant French doctor, Godard was brought up near Lausanne. His first feature, *A bout de souffle* (1959) was filmed in streets and flats with a hand-held camera for a mere 400,000 francs. Not everyone found the subject or characters especially rewarding (Belmondo's posturing beatnik, Seberg's bewildered American); but no one was in doubt that the wry, semi-improvised, *ciné-vérité* style marked a debut even more original than Chabrol's. Godard blithely broke all the cinema's textbook rules, simply by not noticing them. Over the next years his work steadily matured. By keeping to tiny budgets, he was able to choose his own terms of style and subject; and so he went on making as many as two or three films a year. It was more the way a poet or painter works, erratically and compulsively by flair or mood, than according to studio routine. He rarely prepared a scenario in advance, but wrote the script daily as the film went along, and would often change the story half-way through. Some of the films were very slight, barely more than notes for a film, and they grew steadily more individual, the prototype of *films d'auteur*. He also grew steadily more talked about – and fought over – in France. His admirers (they included Malraux) began to use the word 'genius'; his detractors (they were many) loudly called him childish and woolly-minded. For one paper, *Pierrot le fou* was 'the finest French film ever'; for another, it was 'made just for a few fanatics'.

Many people objected to the casual disregard for plot and sequence, to the flippant private jokes and the audience-teasing. Others found this endearing – as when, in *Bande à part*, after the first ten minutes a narrator's voice (Godard's) mockingly sums up the action so far 'for the benefit of late arrivals'. Many critics remarked on the fragmented, pop-art surface of Godard's films, with their sign-symbols and slogans, and he was even called 'the Rauschenberg of cinema'; some disliked this, but others felt it was just this quality in his work that made it so expressive of his time. But though he was taken up by the highbrows and exploited as a cult figure, as a person he has never been in any way modish or assertive. He is genuinely shy, meditative, even taciturn, and looks like a small-town clerk. The one time I met him, as he sat chain-smoking fat yellow cigarettes, I got the impression of a solitary, rather sad person, utterly without 'side'. And thus he has kept a kind of purity. Each new Godard film before 1968, for all the jokes and visual high spirits, struck me as an ever sharper personal statement of horror at the way he felt modern life was going. Violence and terrorism, loneliness, confusion, the dehumanizing effects of science and affluence have haunted him, and out they came Goya-like in his anarchic yet strangely topical films, with their almost prophetic grasp of psychological changes beneath the modern surface. Life, like a bright light, seemed to hurt and bewilder him. When someone asked his ex-wife, Anna Karina, why he always wore dark glasses, she said: 'It's not that his eyes are too weak. His universe is too strong.'

It was in *Alphaville* (1965) that his attitudes emerged most explicitly. This film used a tongue-in-cheek science-fiction plot to point a 1984-ish moral about the soul's destruction by computers and planners. 'I set it in the future,' he said, 'but it's really about the present.' One of the *trouvailles* behind this brilliant film was that the portrait of Alphaville, grim city of machines, was edited almost entirely from Paris location shots, filmed in modern buildings and computer centres. Lemmy Caution, secret agent and reporter for *Le Figaro-Pravda*, 'left Alphaville that night by the Boulevard Extérieur,' says the narrator – and there is Eddie Constantine driving along just that Paris street. The technocrats ruling the city are shown brain-washing their enemies *'dans les HLMs, c'est-à-dire, les Hôpitaux de la Longue Maladie'* – and the camera pans up a Sarcelles skyscraper. To a Paris audience, these typical Godard jests were both funny and frightening. *Weekend* (1968), the most ferocious and pessimistic of all his films, then prophesied a French society disintegrating into brigandry and cannibalism under the pressures of 'civilization': the motor-car, with its ritual mass-murders on French roads every weekend, was the principal villain.

In this and other films Godard remained detached from his characters, like a reporter. Indeed, he has always seen himself as a kind of documentarist – 'Each of my films is a report on the state of the nation.' However, *Pierrot le fou* (1965) stands out from this period as the most personal of his movies and, I think, the greatest. It was ten years ahead of its time. A melancholy young writer (Belmondo) escapes from Paris with the girl he adores (Karina, of course) to a desperate idyll of perfection on an island near Toulon. But their flight is counterpointed with menacing scenes of anarchic violence, gangsterish murders, bloody car accidents and reminders of Vietnam. Finally the girl betrays him, and in a climax of fierce beauty Belmondo shoots her, paints his face blue, wraps sticks of dynamite round his head, and blows himself into the clear Provençal sky where the film fades on an image of sun and space and voices whispering, *'Nous enfin réunis pour l'éternité.'* Godard described it as a film 'bound up with the violence and loneliness that lie so close to happiness today. It's very much a film about France.' It was also very much about Godard, his nostalgia for some other, purer life; and it appeared as an almost embarrassing hymn of love for Anna Karina, who in real life had just broken their marriage.

I do not claim that all his pre-1969 films were successful. Some were over-self-indulgent; but none were dull, and I would defend to the last his methods and approach to filming. Intellectually his work was often facile and muddled: but his films had their own logic, and were a sensitive picture of the world around him as he saw it. As Françoise Giroud said in her *l'Express* review of *Pierrot le fou*: 'Godard too is mad. He knows how to talk about the pain of loving. Godard's films, I like them, even the ones I don't.' But in 1968, alas, this old sad-funny-poetic Godard perished somewhere on the May barricades. That revolt, when he sided with the *gauchistes*, had a shattering effect on him. From then on, he became bound up with the Maoists' un-Godardian solemnity; he fell under the influence of a didactic young Leftist guru, J.-P. Gorin, and with him made a few leaden films preaching *gauchiste* sermons rather pompously. A serious motor-bike accident in 1971 (was there some clairvoyance in those scenes of car crashes in his earlier films?) seemed to add to this new mood and to the drain on his talent. For several years he retreated to Grenoble, where he ran a video workshop producing unwatchable documentaries. Then at last in 1980, aged fifty, he re-emerged with what he called his 'second first film', *Sauve qui peut (la vie)*: set in Lausanne, it actually had a story of a kind, and star players including Isabelle Huppert. It picked up some of his earlier themes – the difficulty of human communication, the alienating effects of capitalism, for which (as in *Vivre sa vie* and some other early films) he used female prostitution as a kind of metaphor. But this film, though interesting, individual and not too solemn, lacked the youthful fizz of his 1960s work. Perhaps Godard has burnt himself out for good, but that would not invalidate his past. And some think he is still ahead of his time, pioneering a cinema of the future that the rest of us are too blind to see.

The second most influential director of the new wave is Alain Resnais, born in 1922. Like Godard, he has been a great innovator, though in a very different manner. He is a withdrawn, elusive person, and this enigmatic quality is apparent also in his films. Although each is marked with his highly personal style, he prefers not to write his own scripts, and usually collaborates with some well-known writer: thus it is not always easy to tell how much in these strange films really belongs to Resnais. He confesses that he has no gift for narrative, and often he gives the impression of being more concerned with style than subject matter. Yet certain themes recur in nearly all his films: time and memory, the elusiveness of reality, the erosion of love and loyalties by the chaos of modern life and the passage of the years.

Resnais stunned the 1959 Cannes Festival with his first feature,

Hiroshima mon amour, regarded by some critics as one of the three land-marks of world cinema, along with *Citizen Kane* and *The Battleship Potem-kin*. The movie also annoyed some people because it began as a film about atomic war and then turned into a love-story, or rather two love-stories linked in the heroine's mind. They found this in bad taste: a minor private tragedy was being exalted above a major public one. But Resnais and his writer, Marguerite Duras, appeared to be suggesting that no public tragedy can be any more than the sum of private ones. Anyway, the film's story was of minor importance compared with its style. By marvellous editing and camera-work, by the imaginative integration of image, music and language, Resnais transmuted an aver-age script into a work of great power and subtlety. It was the mature expression of a technique he had elaborated through his earlier documentaries and was to repeat in many later films: the elegiac travelling-shots, the incantatory repetition of images and phrases that has been likened to opera, and the use of stream-of-consciousness flash-backs to convey, as in Proust, the texture and feel of memory.

Resnais trod the same path in his next film, *L'Année dernière à Marienbad*, but this time he was let down by his writer, Alain Robbe-Grillet, who produced a tricksy scenario all too characteristic of him. In a baroque luxury hotel, man meets girl and tries to persuade her that they had a love-affair the year before: the images on the screen reflect her state of mind. Whether they *did* have the affair is immaterial – the two Alains gave very different accounts of what the film is supposed to mean. In the opening sequence Resnais' mesmeric *mise-en-scène* gives promise of a masterpiece; but soon, devoid of human interest, the film lapses into chilly boredom. It showed the hazards of Resnais' reliance on writers with a strong individuality. In his next films, he returned to a more recognizable everyday world, with real characters, even if the mood was still elusive: *Muriel*, set in modern Boulogne-sur-Mer, and *La Guerre est finie*, the moving story of a Spanish Left-wing agent in France, ageing and self-doubting. Of his more recent work, the best is *Providence*, his one film in English, with a script by the late David Mercer and a fine perform-ance by Gielgud. A dying novelist looks back on his family life, distort-ing reality into nightmare. Again Resnais pulled out his familiar stops, with multiple flashbacks and shifting patterns of delusion and reality: this built up a strong atmosphere, though it somewhat lessened one's interest in the characters. Then in 1980 came *Mon oncle d'Amérique*, Resnais' least oblique and most explicit film – too much so, some would say. He and his scriptwriter Jean Gruault took three contrasting charac-ters in the France of today, wove their lives together into a melodramatic soap-opera, then wheeled on a leading real-life socio-biologist, Henri

Laborit, to pop up throughout the film with behaviourist analyses of the trio's reflexes. The result was a complex and unusual film which set some critics raving: it won the special jury prize at Cannes. But I among others found it pretentious and over-didactic: the story became a mere set of lantern-slides to illustrate the professor's boring theories. It suggested once again that Resnais, for all his stylistic and technical gifts, is too much at the mercy of his collaborators. So his films tend to be hit-or-miss.

He belongs to a group of close friends that includes Agnès Varda, one of the world's few noted woman directors. Like Resnais, she holds strong Left-wing views but rarely lets them obtrude into her films. *Cléo de 5 à 7* (1962) was a tender study of two hours in the life of a young Parisienne singer, with sensitive evocations of the city's modern daily life. Then *Le Bonheur* (1965), one of the most interesting of all the new-wave films, was an intellectual attempt, so Varda admits, to analyse the concept of happiness. She chose what she saw as a modern prototype of the happy simpleton: a young carpenter living joyously in a suburban villa with his pretty blonde wife and lovely babies. When he starts an even more joyous affair with another girl, his bliss is multiplied by two, until his wife (whom he still loves) drowns herself. But this proves to be no more than a passing cloud on the surface of his ecstatic amorality: the film ends with his domestic idyll going on just as before, save for a new blonde wife in the place of the old one. It was a shocking film in the truest sense, and was meant to be so. On the surface the style was all sweetness, with bright colours, soft smiles and Mozart clarinet music, but this made the irony all the sharper. The result was more disturbing than many a conventional exposé of violence or satire on the bourgeoisie, and some audiences were outraged. Here was a film that purported to be serenading all the solid middle-class family virtues only to stick out its tongue at them. What was Varda really getting at? In its stylized way, her film conveyed brilliantly the ruthlessness of a certain kind of mindless happiness: it was also expressing her own ambivalent attitude to a suburban milieu remote from her own intellectual world. She envied, and despised, these simple people. In its odd way, *Le Bonheur* seemed very much a critique of certain contemporary values, and it is sad that Varda has done no work of the same quality since. Her only worthwhile recent film, *L'Une chante, l'autre pas* (1977), was an endearing feminist tale of the friendship of two girls. It had some of the stylized poetic charm of *Le Bonheur*, but none of its cutting irony.

The other new-wave directors are a varied lot. Louis Malle, their contemporary, is often classed with them, but he is really a lone figure. Despite the stylistic modishness of some of his work (e.g. *Zazie dans le Métro*), he is confessedly not interested in modern French subjects and prefers to set his films in the past or abroad. He is a fine master of technique, but he lacks a defined personal approach, and his films are so diverse that it is not easy to see they were made by the same man. The one thread common to much of his work is his interest in focusing intimately on embarrassing or taboo subjects[9] – suicide (*Le Feu follet*), Indian poverty (*Calcutta*), incest (*Le Souffle au coeur*), wartime collaboration (*Lacombe Lucien*), child prostitution (*Pretty Baby*) – and this he does with tact and subtlety. His most personal film, and his best in my view, is *Le Feu follet* (1963), adapted from a 1920s novel by Drieu la Rochelle about a young alcoholic's tragic search for a meaning in life. Malle made from it a most sympathetic movie, Bresson-like in its concentration on the hero's inner suffering. But he depressed himself so much in the process that, Malle-like, he next hopped off gaily to Mexico to film Moreau and Bardot in their underpants (*Viva Maria!*). This was followed by a 'period' thriller and then, another quick-change, by his Indian documentary series. His best recent film in France has been *Lacombe Lucien*, the story of a dim-wit teenage peasant in the Massif Central who by accident came to work for the Nazis. The film had superb period detail, but as a study of collaboration it never quite came to grips with its subject. Throughout his career, Malle has veered unpredictably between the commercial and the off-beat experimental. He is now fed up with France, which he finds 'a dull and mediocre society', as he told me, and has gone off to work in America where recently he made *Pretty Baby*, an evocative study of the New Orleans whore-houses of 1916, and *Atlantic City*, which won a top prize at the 1980 Venice Festival. America is well suited to the temperament of this urbane cosmopolitan.

The new wave threw up many other talents too, such as Chris Marker, a Leftist documentarist; Jacques Rivette, who has affinities with Godard; Jean-Pierre Mocky, a delightfully anarchic satirist of bourgeois manners; and the droll clown-like Pierre Etaix, reminiscent both of Tati and the early Fellini. There was a vogue in the 1960s for making very personal films of poetic romanticism, showing a world of innocence and goodness where all villains were cardboard ones. The pioneer of this 'charm school' was Varda's husband Jacques Demy, whose first feature, *Lola* (1960), was a wistful reverie about a group of people in Nantes, their yearnings, their loves lost and found. It was an unpretentious film, made just to please himself, and it beautifully created a private imaginative world: I rate it one of the best of French post-war films. But then Demy was seemingly seduced by the commercial possibilities of his brand of make-believe: his next films, also set in the seaports of north-west

9 As the critic Philip French has noted (*Observer*, September 1979).

France, *Les Parapluies de Cherbourg* and *Les Demoiselles de Rochefort*, were far more ambitious, but more contrived, and the charm subsided into gimmickry. Demy was then briefly replaced as leader of the charm school by Claude Lelouch, who won the 1966 Cannes Grand Prix with *Un Homme et une femme*, the biggest box-office hit the new wave has ever made. This very romantic film can easily be dismissed – and has been – as a middlebrow *Sound of Music*, a banal little love-story dressed up with colour-mag trimmings and arty soft-focus photography. Yet it was more than this: it was a *film d'auteur* that communicated a real joy in film-making. And it was revealing, too, of a certain France at that point in time, a new-rich glamour-seeking world of fast cars and chic resorts. It caught a pre-1968 mood. But in Lelouch's career it has proved a flash in the pan.

So in sum what has the nouvelle vague achieved, both culturally and commercially? Several of its first films (*Les Cousins*, for example) easily recouped their slender costs. So producers jumped on the new-style low-budget bandwagon, and for a while any young hopeful with a new idea found a camera thrust in his hands. In 1959–63 more than 170 directors made a first film, a gold-rush without parallel in world cinema. But the boom did not last. Inevitably, few of the newcomers proved to have the talent of Truffaut or Resnais. Encouraged to be as 'personal' as they liked – since this was the apparent formula for success – many of them went outrageously too far. They simply made frivolous, esoteric films about themselves and their friends. So an image formed in the public's mind of a typical new-wave film, featuring the easy-going love-lives of some group of idle, well-to-do young Parisians, full of arty camera-shots and in-jokes about other films – imitations of *Les Cousins*. The mass public soon wearied of a realism that had declined into gossip, and most of the new films lost money. In fact, a few successes apart, the new wave has never been a great money-spinner inside France. Several of its finest films (including *Lola* and *Muriel*) failed because they were over the heads of a wide public, while even *Jules et Jim* recouped its costs mainly through exports. The French general public, as in other countries, prefers home-grown low comedies and Hollywood spectaculars.

Artistically, one achievement of the new wave has been to renew the great lyric traditions of French cinema, springing from Cocteau, Clair, Vigo and Renoir. Here they have been helped by some brilliant cameramen who deserve much of the credit: Sacha Vierny, Henri Decaë, Raoul Coutaro and others. The new wave has also renewed a very personal style of cinema where the director expresses his own vision of reality – in practice, more often an inner reality than a socio-political one. In fact, the *nouvelle vague* has often been criticized for neglecting modern French social issues. But is this fair? Godard, in his idiosyncratic way, has certainly tried to mirror French society as he sees it. If few of his fellow-directors have shown quite the same concern, maybe this is because their concept of 'realism' is other. It seems to me that Resnais, Varda and others, in their oblique and sometimes baffling way, *have* been trying to mirror a reality and express a mood of the times, possibly at a more subtle and disturbing level than the explicit social comment of their British contemporaries such as Reisz and Anderson. The questions they have posed are more metaphysical and spiritual, but nonetheless real. They have been less obsessed by the problems of community, but more so by solitude within community, by the chaos on the fringes of modern life, by the struggle for self-identity. It might even be argued that some of the French new-wave directors are, in a sense, poets, who in earlier times would have expressed themselves through lyric poetry, and so it could be as irrelevant to rebuke them for ignoring social themes as to complain that Keats never wrote about the Napoleonic wars.

This said, I would agree with the view that it is regrettable that the new wave – like the modern French novel and theatre – has neglected a more direct analysis of society. What are the reasons? In de Gaulle's day – though less so under Giscard – there was the danger of censorship if a film dealt too boldly with a topic involving Government policies; and this often led to a cautious self-censorship. Or producers and backers would claim that the public was not interested in workaday realism; or that a film, say, on trade unions would only lead to trouble. But sometimes such factors have simply been an alibi for the directors' own lack of interest. Many of them admit they would rather stick to what they know and care about, and it is a facet of French class rigidities that most of them are bourgeois living in Paris. They have little contact with, and seemingly little concern for, the new life of the working-class or the provinces. And so, Godard apart, they have made few films about the striking social changes of the period, far fewer than the comparable Italian or Anglo-American cinemas have given us. Truffaut's Parisian comedies skate over the surface of life there; Rohmer's characters live, however intensely, in a world of their own; Chabrol's Dordogne village in *Le Boucher* was little more than pretty wall-paper for a horror-story. It is noticeable, too, how many of the better new-wave films have been set either in the past, or abroad, or inside the director's dream-world.

Today the *nouvelle vague* is running short of wind: of its major figures' recent work, some two films in three disappoint. After their initial burst of flair and passion, why is it that so few of them have matured satisfactorily in middle age, in the manner, say, of Losey or Renoir? Is there some inherent fragility in so personal a cinema that – as with Fellini – relies more on the will-o'-the-wisp of inspiration than on solid craftsmanship and story-telling? The mystery remains. But meanwhile a 'new new wave' of a sort has appeared in the 1970s, very diverse, and even less of a 'school' than the old one. Compared with the early *nouvelle vague*, these new directors are less stylish and idiosyncratic, less innovative, and they fail to communicate the same infectious joy in film-making. In a word, they are more conventional, and individually their films tend to be slight. But theirs is still a cinema *d'auteur*, rather than a purely commercial one; and above all they are far less out-of-touch than the *nouvelle vague* with the day-to-day French life of province and suburb. With rare exceptions, they still fight shy of topical or political subjects; but in a relatively naturalistic style their better films give an honest and sensitive picture of current French preoccupations: the worry about jobs, the new role of women, the return to family as a bulwark against an anxious world, and so on. As such, this *intimiste* cinema is one more symptom of the new mood of France in the early 1980s: the *repli sur soi*, the renewal with individual values.

The most considerable figure is Bertrand Tavernier. Born in Lyon in 1941, the son of a writer, he is tall and bespectacled with a benign, serious manner, and has more the air of some quiet publisher or professor than of a star film-maker. His radical-Leftish views emerge in his films, but not too polemically, for above all he is a gentle humanist in the glorious tradition of Renoir, and without the self-indulgence of Truffaut. He also has an exceptional gift for conveying the mood of cities; and triumphantly he has restored the provincial scene to a French cinema that had grown far too 'Parisian'. All of this was evident right from his first film, *L'Horloger de Saint-Paul* (1974), set in the *vieux quartier* of his native Lyon. This adaptation of a Simenon novel told the poignant story of a local watchmaker (Philippe Noiret, superb) who is forced to reassess his life and beliefs when his son is accused of murder. It was a study in courage, melancholy, friendship, and the pain of the generation gap; and it beautifully caught the daily local life of Lyon, its gossip, its sensual pleasures – you could almost *smell* that Lyonnaise cooking on the screen! Tavernier then sharply changed subject, with two historical films: *Que la fête commence . . .* , about the contrast between poverty and courtly splendour and intrigue in the France of 1719, and *Le Juge et l'assassin*, about the impact of politics on the judicial system in a famous nineteenth-century murder trial. Neither was an entirely satisfactory film, perhaps because Tavernier did here allow his Leftish views to intrude too didactically.

His next work, *Des enfants gâtées* (1977), is one of the few recent French films to have tackled a controversial modern social issue: its subject was a tenants' committee in a Paris block of flats and their strike against their landlord. This time Tavernier avoided moralizing and produced a witty, sexy film, full of topical social comment. For him it was a personal work, as he was once involved in such a situation as a flat-dweller. Like Louis Malle he enjoys bold variations of subject (though he puts more of himself into his films than Malle does), and next he was hopping off to Glasgow, of all places, to shoot a philosophical sci-fi fantasy in English, *La Mort en direct* (*Death Watch*), with Harvey Keitel, Romy Schneider, and a budget large by French standards (£1 million). The theme of this curious film, set in the near future, was the media's insidious and tyrannous invasion of privacy: a girl with a few weeks to live agrees to having her death filmed live by television, then changes her mind but is pursued by a ruthless journalist. The moody photography of Scotland was fine, but the film proved to be a little schematic. And some of his admirers wondered whether Tavernier was not in danger of selling out to the big-star international cinema. 'Not at all,' he told me in 1979; 'I set this film in Britain because its theme, the power of TV, would make less sense in a French context. Also I was fascinated by the poetic urban desolation of Glasgow. But this non-French venture was a one-off for me. I am entirely against phoney internationalism in films: a nation must stick to its cultural roots.'

True to his word, he then returned to Lyon where in 1980 he made his finest film to date. *Une Semaine de vacances*, to my mind, *the* best French film since the mid-1970s. It is slight in plot but infinitely touching, and it lingers in the mind like a melody. In Lyon in winter a young school-teacher (delicately played by Nathalie Baye) is on the edge of a nervous breakdown. So her doctor prescribes a week off work. She spends the time mooching about, visiting her dying father, making a few new friends, and gradually she finds the courage and peace of mind to make a new start. With this simple tale Tavernier works a miracle, using the most exquisite soft photography of Lyon and the near-by countryside to counterpoint the moods and thoughts of his characters. And though the subject may sound sombre, the film's spirit is one of optimism: happiness may be fragile, death hovers, work is tough, but for those with the heart to grasp it, life is marvellously there, flowing on unceasingly, like the Rhône through the heart of the city. This is French atmospheric cinema at its Carnéesque best; more, it is a thoughtful film that subtly mirrors a real French provincial mood of the early 1980s, anxious but self-renewing. Tavernier's sympathy for his characters blazes out as warmly as in any Renoir film (are they not made a shade *too* nice?). In the school scenes, he tactfully avoids over-stating his implied criticism of the education system. And without artiness he uses snatches of poetry, memory echoes, a gentle luminous light, the wistful wintry townscapes, to forge a synthesis between the people and their city environment. 'For me, Lyon is a character in the film,' he told me, 'as Glasgow was in my previous one. I love these secretive cities that do not easily yield their inner life to the casual eye.'

Tavernier has built up a regular team of people with whom he works, including his wife Colo (a poetess), the superb cameraman Pierre William Glenn, and the actor Noiret. He believes in 'the minor heroism of daily life', and in his better films there is no conflict between his concern with moral and social dilemmas and his feeling for individuals and the raw texture of life. He is a lyricist in a quiet, unflashy way, but his films also have a narrative grasp: he sees himself, and is seen by the critics, as renewing links with the pre-war French cinema, in an up-to-date style. *Coup de Torchon*, a *film noir* set in Senegal, was widely regarded as the best French movie of 1981. So the French have a major new director at last, and not an élitist cult-figure but an entertainer too: all seven of his films have made money, and that is rare in the French cinema today.

Another notable new talent is that of Maurice Pialat, who came late to features and is now past fifty-five. Unlike Tavernier, he is a dour man, tetchy and hard to work with, and his vision of life is awesomely bleak; in a low-keyed naturalistic style, his films explore sensitively the world of the humdrum suburbs and what he sees as the mediocrity of daily living, the inadequacy of relationships. He is Zola without the politics, Bergman without the cultivated chatter. He first became well known with *Nous ne vieillerons pas ensemble* (1972), about the death-pangs of a six-year affair. Then *La Gueule ouverte* (1974) was the study of a woman dying of cancer at home, the embarrassed reactions of her family and friends, and her lonely awareness that they might be happier with her dead. For *Passe ton bac d'abord* (1979) Pialat moved to his home ground, a mining town near Lille, where he filmed a not unsympathetic portrait of a group of senior *lycéens* from upper-working-class families. But his view of the life awaiting them was typically gloomy. He showed the adult world inexorably closing in on these high-spirited youngsters, whom at the end we see settling into a rut of drab domesticity and menial jobs. He was making a topical point about the effect of unemployment on modern youth's morale, as well, it seemed, as a more general one about the dreariness of the human condition.

The same sour note persisted in *Loulou* (1980), his most highly praised film to date, starring the two leading players of the new French cinema, Isabelle Huppert and Gérard Depardieu. Here a well-off middle-class girl leaves her well-meaning husband for an earthily fulfilling liaison with a lazy delinquent layabout, and she trails around with him and his equally loutish friends. This riveting but depressing film was set vividly in a sleazy district of Paris with its tawdry bars and poky hotels. Pialat espoused low-life realism with full force, and had the courage to tackle the theme of class differences, usually as much avoided by French films as it has long been an obsession of British ones. Throughout his work, Pialat's dead-pan anti-romantic camera shows life in all its desultoriness; people are feckless, messy, uncouth, victims not only of circumstance but of their own second-rateness, incapable of nobility. He passes no judgement, and some critics even feel that he has compassion for his characters: but I myself detect more than a hint of misanthropy. His portrayal of modern French society and of the French character is at the opposite pole from *Une semaine de vacances*: but, alas, one has to admit that it, too, carries some conviction.

Claude Sautet, born in 1924, is another veteran who belatedly came to the fore in the 1970s. He is a commercial-minded director who makes realistic but not-too-inspired studies of bourgeois life, some of them verging on soap-opera. *Les Choses de la vie*, *Une histoire simple* and *Un mauvais fils* are among his better films. Jean-Claude Tacchella, also over fifty, directed *Cousin, Cousine* (1975), that delightful social satire-cum-romantic comedy which deservedly won a huge success both in France and abroad: but he has done little else of note before or since. A number of other, much younger directors have also each made one, two or more interesting films, of varying kinds, in the past decade. André Téchineé's Brechtian famila saga, *Souvenirs d'en France*, was much praised and so was *Barocco*: but he followed this with his ill-conceived *Les Soeurs Brontë*, filmed on location in Yorkshire but completely missing the mood of Haworth Rectory. Pascal Thomas (*Les Zozos, Pleure pas la bouche pleine*) has been leading a new trend in affectionate off-beat comedies of rural and provincial adolescence, and is among those directors who are taking the French cinema out of Paris and back to *la France profonde*. Nelly Kaplan, Argentine-born, is the most talented of a number of women directors who have recently won through in this male-dominated profession: she has made some witty and hard-hitting satires on sexual hypocrisy, notably *La Fiancée du Pirate* and *Néa*. A few other directors have taken more topical subjects, occasionally political or business ones: Jacques Ruffio's *Le Sucre* was about a scandal in a big sugar firm, while in 1979 Christian de Chalonge won the leading French prize for the best film of the year with *L'Argent des autres*, the story of a financial racket. And Jean-Jacques Annaud made a promising debut in 1977 with his witty satire on colonization in West Africa at the time of the 1914–18 war, *La Victoire en chantant* (*Black and White in Colour*). Among other new names worth noting are Claude Miller (*La Meilleure façon de marcher*), Jacques Doillon (*La Drôlesse*), and Alain Corneau whose bizarre thriller *Série noire* (1979) dealt with the problems of the growth of crimes of violence.

These and other directors are making civilized, unpretentious films about French life today, films with many of the traditional virtues of French cinema, its irony, its sense of atmosphere, its eye for human absurdity. My principal reservation is that individually most of these films are slight, so that one may leave the cinema thinking, 'Well, that was fine as far as it went, but was it worth the money and trouble of leaving home?' In fact, might not many of these films be more suited to television? In many respects they are not unlike the better contemporary drama made for TV in Britain, and this is easily explicable, for here the two countries are in total contrast. In Britain, TV drama is so lively and go-ahead that it has drained much of the best talent from the cinema, and this is one factor behind the near-death of the British film industry. In France, it is the other way round. As we shall see, TV's drama output in France is still on the whole so stilted and circumscribed, and offers such poor scope, that most of the top talent prefers to stay away, and this is one reason for the continued liveliness of the cinema. A serious public wishing to see good new French creative work will tend to go out to a movie rather than watch television where it will find little but routine costume pieces and old feature films.

The cinema can be, and often is, highly permissive: on TV, a bare breast or a *'merde'* or *'foutre'* are still taboo. And yet, even the cinema still seems wary of tackling the more sensitive political and social subjects of the day: for example, abortion, or the links between Government and big business, or the university chaos, or the local influence of the Communist Party. There are still discreet pressures here, leading to self-censorship; and producers still feel, rightly or wrongly, that though the public wants 'slice of life' films, it does not wish French politics to be thrust at it in the cinema. It is true that since de Gaulle's death one major taboo has been lifted, and this concerns the Resistance: the past decade has seen a spate of frank films about the Occupation, even about Vichy and collaboration, some of them good. But when it comes to contemporary life, directors prefer to stick to private themes, or to social ones as they affect the individual. There has been a wave of serious films about marriage, love-affairs, and family life. And in the present French mood a certain public responds readily: it likes to see its own soul laid bare on the screen.

These new directors are not making 'experimental' or 'art' movies on the fringe of the industry, nor are they integrated into a big-studio system in the old Hollywood manner; they are something in between, as often in France. Theirs is still a cinema *d'auteur*, of personal expression. They are not concerned with big stars, but they regularly make use of the talented new generation of French cinema players who are modest and dedicated and like to call themselves 'anti-stars' – besides Huppert and Depardieu (both a little over-used nowadays), one could mention Isabella Adjani, Nathalie Baye, Patrick Dewaere, Jacques Dutronc, Marie-France Pisier.

. The French cinema today is at least in far better shape than the British or Italian, or maybe even the German. And yet, the talent of this latest wave of directors still appears fragile. As happened with Lelouch and Tacchella in the past, it is remarkable how many new directors make an impact with one really striking film, maybe a first film, and then fade away. Either their next films are poor, or they fail to find the backing for new ventures, or both. It seems to be a crisis both of finance and of creative stamina. Relatively few of the new films make money, and their appeal is less to a mass public than to a smaller discerning one. And very few of the new directors – Tavernier is one exception – have yet become star names inside France, let alone abroad, as the *nouvelle vague* did. So it would be premature to speak of this modest revival as any great renaissance of the French cinema. But at least it is still very active. How then does it manage it, in these hard times?

'Ever since the 1930s,' says Tavernier, 'our cinema industry has lived from crisis to crisis and producers have moaned and groaned. But here we still are, we survive.' Inevitably the cinema in France today is in economic trouble, as in other countries, but it is showing more resilience than most. The belated impact of TV at first took its toll: between 1957 and 1971 one cinema in three closed, and annual attendances fell from 411 million to 177 million. But this figure has since levelled off, even risen slightly, to stand at 181 million in 1981 (the relative dullness of French TV could be a factor). In some other countries, matters have been far worse: from 1957 to 1977 the annual audience (in millions) plummeted from 915 to 108 in Britain, from 801 to 124 in Germany, from 1,180 to 165 in Japan.

On the production side, France has continued to turn out an amazing number of films. Throughout the gloom-ridden 1970s, when the British cinema was dying, France was making more full-length features than ever, well over 200 a year. Rather too many of these were 'hard-porn' or 'soft-porn' quickies, in the wake of *Emmanuelle* :[10] but the majority were 'normal' films, in 1978 totalling 160, of which only 25 were co-productions with foreign majority backing. So a young director with the right perseverance usually still *can* find some kind of backing for his untried skills: in 1978 no less than forty-seven of them made a first feature. This is healthy, artistically if not economically, for the wider the opportunities, the less the risk of some major new talent failing to achieve an outlet. Matters are helped by the continuing policy of Government aid to the industry, more generous than in most countries. Producers complain endlessly at the tax on box-office receipts, yet they are handsomely supported by a system of rebates and advance loans, amounting to some 300 million francs a year. For some 'quality' films, this may be decisive in getting a venture off the ground.

Even so, there are disquieting signs, and many a producer or director talks gloomily as if he believes his present film will be his last. The export trade, once so flourishing, is down to a mere 11 per cent of production revenue, and the reasons are clear: the *nouvelle vague* is no longer such a draw and has few successors, so the French cinema – if much less so than the novel or painting – has lost some of its world-wide appeal of former years. Only a rare smash-hit such as *La Cage aux folles* makes a lot of money abroad. And on the French domestic scene, big American successes such as *Star Wars* and *Saturday Night Fever* have been making inroads into the market for French films. Here the 'quality' films have always been at a disadvantage, for despite the cinemania of students and intellectuals, mass public taste is no loftier than in other countries. By far the biggest home-grown box-office winners are Belmondo-type gangster films and zany farces with de Funès or Les Charlots, equivalents of the *Carry on* . . . series. The top money-spinner in France since the war has been *La Grande Vaudrouille* ('the great gad-about'), a low comedy that few people abroad will even have heard of.

10   France today makes over 100 'porn' films a year, notably for the export market. The early 1970s saw an alarming growth in the number of cinemas in France showing only pornography, and in 1975 the Government finally clamped down on this under public pressure. It created a new 'X' class of films, banned to the under-eighteens either because of their sex content or their 'incitation to violence'. These films can be shown only in 'specialized' cinemas, totalling 160; they are heavily taxed, including a special V A T rating of 33 per cent; and there can be no external advertising apart from the film's title. These measures have effectively dealt with the problem: 'porn' showing is now in a ghetto, accounting for only 6 per cent of box-office. There were fears at first among serious movie-lovers that the new law might be used against erotic films of artistic worth, but this has not happened. For example, Oshima's *Empire of the Senses*, Borowczyk's *The Beast*, and even Pasolini's *The Last 120 Days of Salò*, have none of them been pushed into the 'X' category.

Compared with America, or with the British distribution system, the French industry has always been fragmented, with few large-scale cinema circuits and countless small independent producers. Although in confident times this liberal fluidity has been ideal for low-budget personal films, it leads to high costs and inefficiencies which are a burden in tougher times. So today a campaign of rationalization is under way. The three larger companies, each of which owns some cinemas and produces and distributes films, are now making dynamic efforts to increase their shares of the market and to modernize the industry: they are Parafrance, the Union Générale Cinématographique, and above all Gaumont. Their operations are still modest by American standards; and it could indeed be dangerous for the more serious or artistic film if these companies jointly were to impose the kind of monopolistic distribution structure that exists in Britain. But this is still a long way off. And Gaumont especially appears to be pursuing a genuinely enlightened policy. Its ambitious managing director, Daniel Toscan de Plantier, told me: 'We want to keep the *film d'auteur*, and help it by providing a sound financial basis, as the *nouvelle vague* never really had. The divorce between "commercial" and "art" cinema is a false one: they are complementary, and the same company can, and should, produce both. France's quality cinema is one of its cultural glories, and it is perfectly capable of making money too, world-wide, so long as it is backed by modern financial structures and a dynamic business policy. That is our aim.' Gaumont has already made a start, backing a few 'difficult' movies. It is also thanks to Gaumont, the film's producer, that Losey's wonderful *Don Giovanni* flies the banner of the French cinema.

These companies' major problem, expectedly, is to reach a satisfactory entente with television, which now accounts for 96 per cent of overall viewing of feature films. The Government here has already helped the cinema a little: the three State TV networks must not show films less than three years old; between them, the showings must not total more than some 500 films a year; and (in defiance of EEC rules) at least 50 per cent of the films must be French. But until recently these networks would pay only a pittance for each screening, maybe around 80,000 francs. Under pressure, they have increased the payments since 1975 to an average of about 400,000 francs today; but this is still poor by American standards. One French producer said: 'American films not only get a better deal from TV, they have a far wider export market too. The average US film earns a third of its money from TV, a third from exports, a third from the home market. In France, a film can expect to recoup only a tenth from TV and a tenth from exports – so no wonder we have problems.' The film companies are now pressing for better terms.

At least they are glad that the networks, following the lead of TV in Italy and elsewhere, have finally agreed to join in co-financing some cinema films, partly, it would seem, in order to safeguard their own future supplies! Recent films by Resnais, Truffaut, Tavernier and others have been co-produced by TV. So gradually these two rivals, cinema and television, are moving closer together. Inevitably, with the growth of video-cassettes, of cable TV and satellites, they will become obliged to cooperate for their mutual good, as American experience is already showing.

Europe must pull together, under French leadership, in order to fight the American challenge: that is a familiar French refrain today in matters economic, including the cinema. With Rank out of the field, and the Italians in decline, Gaumont is now setting its cap at becoming Europe's first major multinational film company; already it has co-produced Fellini, Losey, and works from Hungary, Belgium and elsewhere. Gaumont's chairman, Nicolas Seydoux, says: 'Europe may lack the means to rival the big Hollywood spectaculars, but we should fight with our own weapons, our fantastic cultural heritage and talent. We can't make *Star Wars*, but we do have Mozart!' Opera is a special case, stylized and always multinational (the team that made *Don Giovanni* came from seventeen countries). But, when it comes to films of contemporary life, is Gaumont suggesting that Europe should pool its talent to produce hybrid denationalized films with unauthentic casting? Not at all. As Seydoux is the first to admit, this is usually disastrous – the kind of film, say, about modern Germany with an Anglo-Franco-Italian cast all playing Germans and improbably talking English. By all means let nations see each others' films as much as possible: but the films must be made and shown in the authentic language of their setting, without dubbing and with casting that rings true. One shining virtue of the French cinema is that its good films, from *Sous les toits de Paris* to *Cousin, Cousine*, have always radiated a genuine Frenchness, and this has been a major reason for their popularity abroad. More successfully than the Italians, they have avoided the pitfalls of a phoney internationalism. And the 'new new wave' of French directors are following in this good Gallic tradition.

TELEVISION: AN END AT LAST
TO THE BLIGHT OF STATE MONOPOLY?

'Britain, for a telly-lover, is sheer joy!' wrote the TV critic of *Le Monde*, Claude Sarraute, after a visit to London in November 1980. 'You press a button, and you have the feeling of uncorking a champagne bottle, of being bathed in a cascade of wit, fun and imagination unknown on our side of the Channel. What light-years separate London from Paris!'

Just as the British admire and envy France for her modern industries, so the French – or those who follow these things – return the compliment in matters televisual. The output of the three State networks may not be quite as feeble as is often alleged: but it is far from inspired. The reasons? Some of them lie in that historic French conflict between Jacobinism and contentious opposition: the State, hitherto, has never dared allow this potent new medium a freedom that might be abused. So the decades of State monopoly have produced a television that is timid and self-censoring; moreover, unlike the BBC, it has never acquired the prestige or the self-confidence that are essential for creating the standards and attracting the talent required for good programmes. In de Gaulle's day, political interference was such that Ministers would ring up the obedient heads of news programmes and instruct them to include or omit some item. Giscard after 1974 liberalized a little: Government pressures became more subtle and indirect. But Giscard also introduced a new system of commercial rivalry between the networks that in terms of quality proved counter-productive. 'Today we have the worst of both worlds,' was a common lament, '– a television both State-dominated *and* commercial.' Then the Socialists came to power, committed to freeing TV and radio at last from direct State control. They rapidly set plans afoot to carry out this promise, hoping to present a new statute to Parliament in the spring of 1982. But, given the French temperament and the highly charged political climate, it was clear that the path of reform was not going to be smooth.

Television was slower to make its impact in France than in many countries. One reason was the low priority given by the State to its development: a second network started only in 1964, and a third in 1973, in each case many years later than in Britain or Germany. The conservative French public, too, was slow at first to adapt its habits to watching *la télé*: an educated family might admit to having a set only *'pour la bonne'* or *'pour les gosses'*, and would hide it in a back room. In 1959 there were still only a million sets, and no more than 3 million in 1963 compared with 12 million then in Britain. The French have since caught up: there are now 16 million sets (virtually as many as in Britain), over a third of them in colour. But although nine homes in ten have a set, the great telly-craze of the early 1970s has now passed its peak and audiences have been falling slightly. People enjoy the feature films, and a few special programmes, but in all social classes their expectations of TV's general output are low – 'what else do you expect of *la télé de l'Etat*?' has been a common reaction.

The legacy of State control dates back to the first days of broadcasting. The Office de la Radio et Télévision Française (as it was called until the 1974 reforms) began life as a mere branch of the Postal Ministry, and in the post-war years it depended directly either on the Ministry of Information or the Prime Minister's office. A few liberals made worthy efforts in Parliament to have the ORTF provided with a genuine autonomy like the BBC, but no Government dared part with so valuable a weapon. Frequently, under Fourth Republic premiers such as Guy Mollet, there was suppression of anti-Government views in broadcasts or measures against hostile staff journalists. Then the Gaullists came to power, and made matters worse: tolerance of free discussion was never their forte, and rapidly they placed their own loyalists in the key posts of the ORTF, even in the regions. The charming and otherwise liberal Gaullist who ran the Brittany station once told me: 'With only fifteen minutes of local TV news a day, do we have time to air local criticisms of official policy? We, the Government, are doing all we can to promote regional progress. The time isn't ripe to let Bretons criticize us too openly on the screen, just when we're really helping them. They're too immature.' I had rarely heard a more candid résumé of Gaullist paternalism.

De Gaulle himself was a brilliant screen performer, and he regarded TV as his fief: 'My opponents have much of the Press on their side, so I keep television,' he once said – a common official justification for control of the medium. In his day, news material was edited to show the Government in a good light, while almost any programme on a social or economic subject had to be vetted in advance by the relevant Ministry: one producer filmed an objective report on the shortage of nurses which was shown to the Ministry of Health, then banned. Kowtowing to Ministers could reach comic proportions: once the ORTF hired an aircraft to fly back a special recording of a France *v.* Ireland rugby match in Dublin because they heard that Pompidou (then Prime Minister) was a rugby fan and wanted to watch it the same night. Equally the ORTF lived in fear of the Quai d'Orsay and frequently suppressed items which it was told might not suit France's foreign interests. One amazing rule was that when an ORTF film crew went abroad it had to check in at the French embassy to collect its living expenses!

The brighter side of the coin, in de Gaulle's and Malraux's day, was that French TV at least tried to keep up a certain cultural tone. State monopoly did seem to carry one advantage: there was no need to compete with commercial TV for audiences, and so the proportion of serious or cultural programming could be kept fairly high. The ORTF bought little American pulp material; and however banal its own quizzes and variety shows, at least they were balanced by long hours devoted to the arts, history and so on: this was Malraux's influence. The approach was often conformist and uninspired, but no one could deny the cultural intent. Television was didactic in the French pedagogic manner, and took relatively little account of audience tastes. But, in television terms, the quality of these worthy programmes was generally poor, with sloppy editing and cliché-ridden scripting – odd, for a nation with such a talent for film-making. The trouble here was that most of the top ORTF executives, unlike their BBC counterparts, were not broadcasters but men brought in from the civil service or even industry: few of them had much experience or understanding of creative work, and so they failed to set high standards. A constant war raged between them and the producers, some of them talented people, all of them frustrated by a bureaucracy unsuited to a creative medium. And as TV and radio expanded, this top-heavy machine grew worse: at one point the ORTF had 12,000 administrative staff and only 250 creative staff.

Morale was low. Politically, many producers were radicals, as creative people tend to be: but they had to toe the line, or else . . . Many other employees, too, were on the Left, such as cameramen, film-editors and rank-and-file journalists. Their resentments built up. Then at last the general strike of May 1968 gave the staff its cue for a showdown with the Government, whose initial handling of the TV coverage of the Sorbonne rebellion was typical: it refused to let the ORTF screen any account of the first few days' riots, although the Press and the commercial radio stations were full of it! The staff were furious. Soon, when Gaullist power appeared to be crumbling, they staged a virtual putsch and for a few glorious days found themselves able to say what they liked on the screens. But it did not last long. The Gaullists, even in their enfeebled state, made it clear that they would not permit the TV centres to be 'occupied' like the Sorbonne or the Renault works, and they made threats of an Army takeover. Rather than risk this, the staff chose to strike, and for a month there was almost no television in France. But then in June the Government toughened its attitude and forced the strikers to yield. Its vague promises for a revision of the ORTF statute were not followed up. So the strike, a bold bid for a new deal, was a failure at least in the short run.

In a wave of reprisals, more than 60 journalists on radio and TV were dismissed; 30 others were 'exiled' to ORTF offices in the regions or abroad. Of the few relatively honest current affairs programmes, the better ones were axed. Most of the expelled staff were allowed later to return, but generally in subordinate positions: thus Léon Zitrone, a leading commentator, found himself relegated to sports reporting as repayment for his role in the strike. It was part of a new plan to purge the ORTF of many of its 'star' personalities (who might try to exploit their popularity with viewers in order to combat the regime) and to install a permanent safe mediocrity. It was a policy of depersonalizing TV programmes by easing out the clever, original people – as someone put it, 'an attempt to make TV like that other State body, the Régie Renault: all smooth production belts.'

The Government however was far from unanimous. Throughout these years, under de Gaulle and then under Pompidou, a protracted battle was going on behind the scenes at top level, between 'liberals' and 'diehards', with frequent shifts in policy. The former argued that too rigid a State control was counter-productive, a vote-loser at election times; the latter, led by Debré and Pompidou himself, replied that any relaxation was dangerous. The liberal view finally gained some ground, at least on the crucial issue of whether to allow screen time to opposition leaders. News bulletins began to give some coverage at last to the doings of anti-Government politicians; other programmes invited them for interviews or to take part in regular debates. They were there on the screen only by courtesy, and not yet by democratic right, as in Britain; but at least it was a step forward. Then in 1969 came a bigger change. The new liberal-minded Premier, Jacques Chaban-Delmas, persuaded a reluctant Pompidou to let him try an experiment. On each network, news and current affairs were hived off to form separate semi-autonomous units; and as news director for the more widely viewed First Network, Chaban chose a distinguished TV journalist known for his radical views, Pierre Desgraupes, who had played a big part in the 1968 strikes. For the next three years Desgraupes managed to inject a degree of critical comment and impartiality into his bulletins and documentaries. He was not required to submit his material in advance for higher approval; he was responsible only to the ORTF's governing board, who often held angry post-mortems but had no power to intervene save to urge his dismissal. Desgraupes, it is true, was careful not to be too provocative, knowing the tacit limits of his freedom. But his brief reign is still remembered nostalgically today as a rare golden age when French TV, or part of it, showed BBC-style objectivity-plus-frankness.

All the other programmes – variety, drama, etc. – remained as before, only worse. With Malraux gone, the accent on culture diminished and cheap American imports were allowed to flood the screens. After 1968 the Government also began to allow the ORTF to show some advertisements, as a means of shoring up its growing deficit.

This was a sensible step in itself, which had no adverse influence on programmes: but, by a sorry coincidence, it was soon followed by reports of payola-type corruption. In 1972 a senatorial enquiry produced a wealth of solid evidence that a number of TV producers had been receiving handsome bribes from commercial firms to plug their products discreetly in programmes: for example, innocent-seeming shots of Levi jeans in a travel film, or of people drinking Nicolas wines. One producer with a modest salary was said to have bought himself two country houses with his payola money. All this caused a national scandal, with newspapers and deputies suggesting that the bribery affair was the symptom of a deeper malaise: the ORTF itself was rotten. The Government, embarrassed, at first tried to play the whole matter down, contenting itself with discreet sanctions against some guilty producers. But then, with an eye on the 1973 elections, it hurriedly carried through some face-saving reforms of ORTF's structures, with the supposed aim of reducing its bureaucracy. In practice, these added up to little. The current-affairs units were re-integrated with the rest – whereupon Desgraupes resigned.

Pompidou's death in April 1974 marked a turning-point – of a kind. He was a Jacobin, whose unfortunate phrase, 'French Television is the Voice of France', was often quoted against him, and he was adamant in defending the State monopoly against the growing lobby for a rival commercial network. But Giscard had a different outlook. He accepted the need for a real change, and on coming to power he promised a new deal. He would have preferred to set up a new independent channel, maybe like ITV in Britain (his brother Olivier was a leader of the lobby for it): but he knew the fierce opposition this would have provoked, alike from his Gaullist allies and from the anti-capitalist Left. The Left-wing unions were powerfully entrenched in the ORTF at all levels; and while resenting a Right-wing Government's control of the medium, ironically enough they were equally opposed to an ending of the monopoly. This, they feared, would weaken their own power bases and endanger their members' jobs and privileges. Better, they felt, the devil that you know.

In the end Giscard compromised. His new statute, in force in January 1975, abolished the monolithic ORTF and put in its place seven smaller separate bodies. But the State was to retain ultimate control, and no private interests were introduced. Of the seven new bodies, three were television companies, one to run each network;[11] a fourth administered all State radio, including the overseas services; a fifth produced TV plays and films, and sold them to the networks; a sixth looked after

11 Télévision Française 1 (TF1), Antenne 2, France Régions 3 (FR3).

transmitters; the seventh was an audio-visual institute, dealing with archives and research. The TV networks drew their finance partly from Government grants, and partly from their own advertising revenue (except for the regional FR3). This new order then remained in force until 1981, when the Socialists set about changing it. The purpose behind Giscard's reform was to reduce the old unwieldy bureaucracy to introduce a more human scale and a more businesslike spirit, and to stimulate quality by creating a real competition between separate rival networks. These were sincere and laudable aims. But they did not work out too well, for a number of complex reasons, political, economic, and human.

Giscard did away with the Gaullist style of direct daily interference in TV. Under his regime, Ministers would no longer ring up editors to issue orders. And the new companies' governing boards included only a minority of State nominees. Yet, whatever his initial liberal intentions, Giscard soon fell for the temptation of finding other and more discreet ways of ensuring that television stayed on his side. The Government appointed each company's chairman: in practice they were all pro-Giscard, and in turn they would appoint similar-minded people to other senior posts. So if the screen generally showed the Government in a kindly light, this was less by command than because those in the key posts – including the 'star' news presenters – were sincerely promoting their own views. The Government hardly needed to interfere or censor: it could trust those in charge. Giscard did at first take the risk of appointing a maverick man-of-letters, Marcel Jullian, as head of the lively second network, Antenne 2: but his programmes became *too* lively and radical, so he was replaced by a civil servant. Elsewhere, the same old TV worthies stayed in the top posts, after a round of musical chairs in 1975: the heads of the first and third TV networks and of the radio company, amongst others, had all previously held senior jobs in the ORTF. Gaullist in de Gaulle's day, they were now ready to serve Giscard, and they would consult with his staff on such matters as choice of key personnel: rarely was a senior journalist appointed without the Elysée's approval. So boat-rockers and over-critical spirits did not win promotion. Moreover, some delicate presidential topics were taboo. When all the Press was writing about Giscard's alleged gift of diamonds from Bokassa (see p. 625), TV at first preserved a discreet silence. When two news presenters finally did dare to feature the subject, one had his programme axed and the other was shifted to another job.

Yet this paternalistic TV was more than mere State propaganda. It had learned the wisdom, in a democracy, of moving towards what the BBC calls 'balance'. That is, interviews with Ministers were now a little more critical and less obsequious, while opposition views were given a wide and regular hearing: the Left's complaints to the contrary were unjustified. An event such as the Communist Party congress won huge coverage, more or less objective; and Antenne 2 in particular staged long, lively interviews with the bumptious Georges Marchais, always good entertainment value. And yet, one serious limitation remained that this was still an institution-minded TV that would feature the official opposition, including trade-union leaders, but would seldom take its cameras out into street and factory to do its own probing reports on controversial topics: for example, asking workers, students or immigrants what *they* think. This was considered far more dangerous ground than safe studio talks with Party spokesman. And this remains a weakness today. French TV, unlike British, rarely initiates *Man Alive*-style searching enquiries into, for instance, the reasons behind strikes, or racial prejudice against immigrants, or the university malaise, officialdom's real anxieties.[12] So, except on harmless topics, French TV makes relatively little use of *vox pop* interviews. It has never achieved the same integral connection with daily life as the BBC or ITV, for it does not make the same effort to give ordinary people the feeling that they too are TV performers. It informs, and entertains, but holds its audience at a distance. It does not give the sense of keeping open house to one big national family.

At least the news bulletins, in the Giscard era, were livelier than in the plodding ORTF days and full of a new visual ingenuity. In a way, this was an improvement. But, with the networks now locked in a battle for ratings, the bulletins also became more sensational, more personalized, with 'star' newscasters trying to ape Ed Murrow in a bid to pull in the audiences. The accent was less on dispassionate reporting than on 'shows' by big-name presenter/commentators, who not only borrowed American techniques ineptly, but gave the impression of talking down to their audiences, and threw in the maddening French habit of mixing up fact and personal opinion. In British newscasting this is a cardinal sin, but the French seem to like it. Roger Gicquel, chief newscaster on the first network (TF1) in 1975–81, became a national idol: his style was to intersperse the news of some crisis with his own moralizing about it. Imagine Alastair Burnet or Jan Leeming doing that.

The rivalry over news was one aspect of a genuine new inter-network competition which brought some benefits, but not nearly as many as Giscard had hoped. In practice, one major weakness in his scheme was that the new rival companies fell into financial trouble and

12 Even a consumer defence programme was likely to be taken off the air, under Giscard, if its frankness antagonized major business interests (see p. 407).

this affected their programmes. True, the new companies were less cumbersome than the old ORTF monolith – 'This makes our life easier,' said one senior producer; 'we have a small, efficient team of top people, and I can get a decision from them in twenty-four hours which in the old days might have taken months.' But inevitably the fragmentation also increased total overheads, as each company felt the need to have its own Press service, its own studios abroad, and so on: in London, TF1 and Antenne 2 maintained rival offices, which they could ill afford, whereas the far larger BBC has just one office in Paris. So it was little surprise that overall administrative costs rose by 80 per cent in real terms since ORTF days; and three times as much money was spent on fixed overheads as on programmes. Whereas the old ORTF in its final year managed to make a 40 million franc profit, by 1978 almost all the new bodies were running up heavy deficits, and notably the film production company whose role was to supply the networks with their drama material. This made a loss of 122.7 million francs in 1975–7, and quite a crisis blew up over its alleged bad management.

Television under Giscard suffered also from an under-financing that was far from being entirely its own fault. TF1 and A2 were not allowed to draw more than 25 per cent of their incomes from advertising, while FR3 could screen none at all. So the networks were dependent largely on Government grants, derived from the licence fee (400 francs a year for a colour set, in 1981). These grants were shared out on a basis partly of merit, assessed by an independent jury, but partly also of popularity. So there ensued a non-stop tussle for high ratings; and, as in many countries, it was hard to tell how far this kind of competition led to higher quality or to trivialization. Probably a bit of both. In a country where TV is politically free, competition tends to encourage some programmes at least to be more lively and stimulating, as has happened very clearly in Britain since the advent of ITV. But France lacked this advantage; the new rivalry pushed the networks into putting more stress on easy entertainment programmes with a wide appeal. This would have mattered less if these shows had at least been well done. But the shortage of funds also led the companies to rely increasingly on cheap foreign products and on repeats. As compared with 20 per cent in Britain, by 1980 over 50 per cent of French TV material was imported, much of it American soap-opera such as *Dallas* and *Kojak*, always popular. Obliged to cut their production budgets, the networks made fewer filmed documentaries of their own, and instead relied more on studio debates, which are much cheaper. The blame for all this lay quite largely with the Government which – as in Britain with the BBC – should have increased the licence fee and then been more generous. One critic even suggested to me in 1980: 'The Government has played the same trick on television as on the universities: it has granted a pseudo-autonomy, then failed to provide enough back-up of funds to make it workable.'

It would be wrong however to suggest that all French TV output was poor in the Giscard era. Some good work by talented people reached the screen – and sometimes was even outspoken, notably when not dealing with topical French subjects. Antenne 2 in 1979 ran a remarkable series of dramatized documentaries about the Third Republic period, tackling such delicate themes as the Dreyfus affair, the rise of Fascism and Communism, even the First World War mutinies in the trenches: it was all very frank, but safely historical. One long-established and effective programme is *Les Dossiers de l'écran*, which first screens a cinema film touching on some social or moral issue (e.g. *Kramer v. Kramer*), then pursues the issue in a ninety-minute live studio discussion between assembled pundits. This can be stimulating. French TV frequently has the edge over British or American in the intellectual quality of its debates (political, literary, and so on), for the French are gifted talkers: by our crisp standards, programmes of this kind may seem over-extended, but a French public is fully used to lengthy argument – just try attending any public meeting in France! The literary chat-shows in particular, which have little equivalent on British TV, are a virtuoso battle of wits between authors of the latest serious books, yet have far more than a minority appeal.[13] In addition, TV offers a regular assorted diet of documentaries (many of them imported) on science, history, travel, etc., often accompanied by commentaries from French academics. As in Gaullist days, these tend to be a little didactic and unoriginal. And yet, for all its defects, French TV has had some positive social and educative effects, as in other countries. Its better programmes have helped to widen the horizons of the isolated peasantry and of workers, and to narrow the cultural gulf between Paris and the 'French desert'. The pity is that it could have done this so much better.

In the field of fictional drama, nearly all the best material is imported from the cinema or from abroad. Of the ten or so cinema films screened weekly on TV (see p. 577), much is routine dross: but the networks do also make an effort, and a better one than British TV, to include a fair percentage of high-quality or 'difficult' films: the great French classics, also Bergman, Visconti and their likes, even recent experimental work by directors such as Handke and Ackermann. In the case of films made specially for TV, the networks may screen *Dallas* (dubbed), yes: but FR3 for example, has also shown the BBC's ambitious new Shakespeare series

13 Notably *Apostrophe*: see p. 539.

in English, subtitled. These worthy cultural ventures partly atone for, but do not excuse, the lack of good new drama produced by French TV itself. Sometimes there is a worthwhile historical series, such as Mnouchkine's *Molière*. But serial adaptations of classic novels rarely come anywhere near the quality of the BBC's best work: in fact, one sometimes gets the impression that BBC TV is doing a better job for French literature (*Madame Bovary*, *Thérèse Raquin*, Sartre's *Les Chemins de la liberté*, to cite some recent serials) than French TV is itself! And when it comes to new TV plays on modern subjects, there is virtually nothing to compare with the work, say, of Potter or Raphael, or the BBC 'Play of the Month', while even French routine situation-comedy serials are feeble by our standards. When French TV shows a new play, very often it simply takes its cameras into a theatre to film some current boulevard hit – economical, but artistically a feeble solution.

There are various explanations for this whole situation. Actors, directors and writers get low fees from TV, often a mere tenth of what they can earn in the cinema for the same work. Compared with the cinema, union restrictions are far tighter on TV, and the risk of censorship far greater. And, at least until 1981, a director with Leftish views would not regard working for TV as any cause for pride (though of course this may now change). Small wonder that most of the better ones have hitherto preferred to stick to the large screen. Above all, French TV does little to encourage new authors, and this is the hub of the problem. One radical-minded young writer/director, on contract to TV and highly frustrated, gave me what may be a typical view: 'As compared with British TV, the people in charge of drama on the networks often have the wrong background. One was a sports journalist, another came from administration. Their low budgets are hardly their fault. But they're tired old time-servers with little concern for quality, lacking the initiative or imagination to go out and look for fresh talent. If a new author sends in a good script, it is often pushed aside – unlike in Britain – so bright people don't try to write for TV. The drama chiefs cynically think audiences have low taste, so that to change from tried formulas would set the ratings down. The result: TV drama studios are still full of the old hack cinema directors of the 1950s, men like Christian-Jacque, now over seventy but still at work, turning out routine, anodyne stuff.'

In moral matters, TV drama has hardly yet emerged from the ethos of the Hayes Code. As one critic put it, 'In a bedroom scene, in the cinema people are naked at least to the waist. On TV, they wear dressing-gowns. It's all fearfully genteel.' French TV in fact is the reflection of a society at least as hypocritical as Britain's, though in a different way. The French are highly tolerant towards all kinds of private behaviour, so long as it remains private and is not aired in public: Ministers have mistresses, of course, and no one minds, so long as the protocol of discretion is observed (see p. 358). And TV is a surviving bastion of this 'public' morality, which remains in force, however much it has been overtaken by actual permissive practice. Here British TV is now far ahead of French. For example, homosexuality is fully tolerated in France and has never been a crime: but it would be hard to imagine French TV screening the kind of programmes seen recently on BBC and ITV, where gays face the camera and openly discuss their problems. In France, the occasional discussion on homosexuality or abortion is pushed into a late-night slot and treated in impersonal terms: a respected public figure would not admit on the screen to being gay, as Peter Pears did readily on the BBC. Equally, a sexy and irreverent programme such as *That's Life* or *Not the Nine O'Clock News*, or even *The Two Ronnies*, would be unthinkable on French TV. It would draw a stream of angry letters, not only from old-style Catholics or other puritans, but even from people quite liberal in their own lives, people ready to enjoy a dirty joke between friends, or a spot of adultery, but who nonetheless feel that *publicly* the decencies must be observed. *Pas devant les enfants! Pas devant les domestiques!* So restraints of this kind on television are less a matter of official censorship than of social convention. Such attitudes have been evolving, but slowly. They may now evolve faster, under Socialism.

French TV is technologically very advanced, in its way. It makes full use of the latest electronic news-gathering techniques, and it uses split-screen and montage effects with a virtuosity verging on gimmickry. Yet, despite the qualities of the film-work, the studio continuity and presentation remain curiously slapdash and even old-fashioned. Captions may come up in the wrong place or upside-down, while the damsels known as *speakerines* seem to have strayed out of some Hollywood glamour film of the 1940s. One reason, once again, may be that the network chiefs are little concerned with setting perfectionist standards in such matters; their higher priority is simply to ensure that the screen keeps out of political trouble and fulfils its basic duties. Recruiting has always been haphazard – people drift to and fro from the Press and cinema worlds – and French TV has never bothered itself with the rigorous training of new staff in TV techniques, as the BBC does. So, though the networks may have plenty of talented cameramen and journalists, they have not been drilled specifically in this medium. It all adds to the general mediocrity. And the reactions of the great French public? They have few illusions, and they accept the inadequacies of TV with a shrug: either they watch selectively, or as a means of passing the time. When TV first made its big impact, in the 1960s, it had some disruptive social effects, and there were plenty of complaints that it was eroding the noble French art of conversation: in cafés, and in homes, people would sit in the semi-dark in front of the screen, instead of arguing. But since the later 1970s the pendulum has swung gently back. The set may still be on, but people will often lend it only half an eye or ear: it is a background, against which they carry on talking and eating. Audience levels fell by 12 per cent in 1978, while an IFOP survey in 1979 found that 44 per cent of people did not consider TV 'indispensable' to their lives. Although nine homes in ten have a set, in 1980 the average French citizen was spending longer listening to radio each day (137 minutes) than watching TV (114 minutes). And among the educated classes it is only the exceptional programme, such as *Apostrophe*, that claims many regular addicts.

Most French-made TV output originates from Paris, as you would expect in this hitherto centralized country. However, Right-wing Governments did make some efforts, modest by British standards, to develop regional programmes too, under their own aegis. In 1963 the ORTF began to use its handful of regional TV studios for brief daily news and magazine broadcasts of local interest. Then in 1973 a third channel was created, drawing a fair proportion of its material from these regional stations. Giscard's 1974 reforms took over and extended this innovation, giving the third network company, France Régions 3, a clear regional structure. It had a dual mandate: one, to network cinema films, drama and some general programmes, on a nationwide basis; two, to produce material in and for the different regions. Under Giscard, FR3 had 11 main stations and 13 ancillary ones, across France. Each main station put out a daily twenty-minute local news bulletin and a thirteen-minute documentary for its catchment area. Some of this magazine material was networked, while the stations also produced a few of their own full-length documentaries, and plays too at Lyon, Lille and Marseille, and many of these programmes were shown nationally. The regions thus were able to see each others' work, while the studios helped to give freelance work and publicity to local actors, musicians and others. Some of the documentaries were of fair quality, but they usually stuck to 'safe' subjects such as local culture and history. News bulletins, too, were even more circumspect than the national ones in Paris, with the accent on local official events rather than controversies. One typical magazine item I saw, in Nancy, consisted of deferential interviews with the region's military and police chiefs. The Left would often sneer at FR3 as '*la télé du préfet*': maybe this was a little excessive, yet certainly these stations were subject to continual local pressures, from mayors and deputies of all colours as well as from the State. If a station screened something that displeased the prefect, he soon let it know. And these stations possessed virtually no autonomy: they were controlled directly from Paris by the head of FR3, a tough civil servant, and they had no local governing boards. Thus they entirely lacked the organic links with their regions that characterize the ITV companies or BBC Scotland. They were State outposts, like prefectures. They could reflect local doings in a picturesque, even animated way: but their real contribution to local debate remained perforce limited. In a word, Giscard's regional policy over television was even more tight-handed than in other fields such as education, finance and local government: some geographical decentralization of production, but little real devolution of power.

By the spring of 1981 morale was still shaky in French television, and many people felt that Giscard's reforms had brought little improvement. Jean-Claude Averty, possibly France's most highly regarded TV producer, spoke to me bitterly: 'In America, TV is down-to-earth and doesn't pretend to be "cultural". In France it does, but isn't. We've copied the worst of the US ratings system, while keeping the worst of the French *étatiste* system.' Some others spoke to me in similar vein. Possibly they were being unfair, for Giscard's record in this field was not as black as it was often painted. Television *was* livelier than in de Gaulle's day, and on the whole more balanced and candid too. But the State monopoly was still a dreadful handicap. As Robert Mauthner wrote of Giscard's reform, in the *Financial Times* of November 15th, 1978, 'Its main short-comings have been the attempt to graft a private enterprise philosophy onto a huge public service bureaucracy.'

By 1981 it was clear that the sheer march of technology might soon render the monopoly obsolete, as the age of satellite TV loomed when a Parisian with the right kind of set would be able to twiddle a knob and pick up maybe a score of foreign networks as easily as French ones. Already, with ordinary transmitters, this had been the case for some years in frontier areas. Foreign-based TV reaches roughly one French home in five: in Alsace, 90 per cent of sets are adapted to one German channel or other; in Lorraine, up to a million people watch Télé-Luxembourg; French-speaking Swiss and Belgian TV are also viewable in some places, while BBC and ITV attract small audiences in parts of France opposite Kent and the Channel Islands. It is true that cross-frontier viewing of this kind is limited by language. But, with satellites, a commercial company could broadcast in French to all France from somewhere out in the ether, and it would be hard for any Government to prevent it.

In the case of radio, where land-based transmitters can reach so far, successive Governments have long been faced with this kind of challenge, and have found cunning ways of overcoming it. The situation here is most curious. For many years now the three State radio networks have enjoyed little more than 20 per cent of the total audience. The most popular station with French listeners is Europe One with its transmitters in the Saar, followed by Radio Luxembourg (RTL), while others tune in to Radio Monte-Carlo or the two stations in Andorra. These are all commercial, largely French-owned and backed by French advertising, and neatly dodging the State monopoly by broadcasting from just outside French soil. They are not pirates, but legally registered in their respective countries. Their forte is popular music and entertainment, plus lively news and comment notably from Europe One. The three main stations, RTL, RMC and Europe One, all need to keep large studios and offices in Paris, and the cables between them and their transmitters belong to the French Post Office: so Governments could, had they wished, have made life impossible for them. But this might have been politically unwise. Instead of doing that, they chose the more astute course of surreptitiously acquiring financial control over these *radios périphériques*.

Since 1945 a State-owned holding company, Sofirad, has held 80 per cent of the shares in RMC. Since 1959 Sofirad has acquired a hold over Europe One also, through a series of intrigues, and now controls 46.8 per cent, making it the largest shareholder, while the Matra group (closely allied to Giscard when he was President) owns another big slice. Sofirad also owns 99.9 per cent of one Andorra station, and a majority share of the other. Radio-Télé-Luxembourg has proved a harder nut to crack, for this is the only broadcasting company in that proud little country, which did not want so crucial an asset to become a mere pawn in the hands of a foreign power. When Sofirad tried to acquire a holding, the Grand Duchy said no. However, Luxembourg has since allowed a French consortium to increase its interests, and today RTL's leading shareholder is none other than Havas, the big French State-owned advertising firm. Add to this the fact that, in Giscard's day, Sofirad's chairman had previously been his Press officer, while the chairman of Havas too was a former Elysée man – and it was little surprise that in practice these 'free' stations were under almost as much surveillance as the State TV and radio networks. Their news programmes were just as wary of criticizing the Government too boldly: when one news director of Europe One went too far, he was dismissed. So Governments have had little cause to object to these stations' existence: true, they detract from the State networks' audiences, but they are also a useful source of revenue via

Sofirad and Havas. All in all, it is a cynical state of affairs. Right-wing Governments permitted business interests to make a nonsense of the legal State radio monopoly, while retaining their own *de facto* political monopoly.

For a long time the French accepted this passively, with ritual indignation on the Left, but no more. After about 1977, however, a remarkable new challenge to the monopoly emerged, at grass-roots level. Well over 100 local pirate radio stations sporadically started operation, all over France, inspired in some cases by the new free broadcasting in Italy or even by the example of Britain's offshore pirate, Radio Caroline. They have been of all kinds, these little stations, ranging from the purely commercial to the militantly Left-wing. Some have been backed by private financial interests, wanting to pressure the Government into ending the monopoly. Others have been run by the CGT or the Communist Party for propaganda purposes (e.g. the station set up by the CGT at Longwy, during the Lorraine steel crisis in 1979; see p. 59). Quite a number have been created by ecologists: for example, 'Radio Fessenheim' in Alsace has directed its fire against the local nuclear power station. Others have had no set motive beyond the public-spirited desire to prove that a need exists for local community radio, of the kind already flourishing in some other countries: such stations have generally been run by young idealistic volunteers, and they have been one more manifestation of the new French grass-roots search for new styles of local and informal *vie associative* (see pp. 313–15). Even the Socialist Party joined the *'radios libres'* crusade. As a protest against the Government's 'abuse' of the monopoly, it started 'Radio Riposte' in 1979, and Mitterrand himself put his name to it. He was charged, and was given a nominal fine.

Giscard's Government, embarrassed and angry, tried to clamp down on these variegated pirate stations, many of which were clandestine, mobile and hard to unearth. The police, where it could, seized their equipment, and some arrests were made. The Government in 1979 even passed a new law, imposing stiff penalties for illegal broadcasting. In practice this was used sparingly, for fear of provoking an outcry, but it did have some effect: many of the pirates were stamped out, or cowed into silence – yet others as quickly sprang up in their places. They have had tiny audiences, these rebels, but they were tenacious, and so the cat-and-mouse game went on.

The Socialists came to power with a pledge to sanction local radio at last. True to its word, the new Government rapidly put forward a law, passed in November 1981, which allows the licensing of a controlled number of independent local stations. Some 3,000 applications came in.

But, as the law forbids advertising, there will be no commercial interests behind the new stations: most of them will be run by town councils, local associations or other self-financing bodies. So local radio in France is likely to be on a very modest scale.

With the change of regime, is there now at last to be a genuine new deal for French television and radio? The parties of the Left had for years denounced the abuses of State control: now they are committed to practising what they have preached. And in June 1981 one Socialist leader promised: 'Our new charter for the media will not be just the umpteenth post-war reshuffle but a definitive liberalization.' Yet the Government's early actions were not totally reassuring. In the peaceful and democratic transfer of power in France that summer, TV and radio proved – curiously enough – to be the one area where knives were drawn and all did not go smoothly. In June, Pierre Mauroy promised there would be no 'witch-hunt' of network chiefs or leading TV journalists who had served Giscard too slavishly: but his Minister of Communications, Georges Fillioud, then behaved otherwise. Fillioud, a Socialist with a blunt, aggressive manner, seemed motivated by some kind of revenge for having himself been excluded from working for the radio some years back. And he proceeded (with the tacit backing of the Elysée, it was said, though not of Mauroy) to pressure all four network heads, and several news directors and presenters, into resigning. The bosses of Sofirad, Havas and their dependent radio stations were also replaced. Fillioud was abetted by Left-wingers on the staff of the various media organizations who began, gratuitously, to re-enact May '68: they set up action committees in their offices and studios, clamouring for punishment of the 'guilty ones' and the right to choose their own new directors. This was maybe understandable, in reaction to the abuses under Giscard: but it was excessive. Changes in the top posts were only to be expected, after the change of regime, but the Government's handling of the changes was crude and vindictive, and it raised some doubts as to the sincerity of its ideals of freeing the media.

However, the new appointees to the senior posts were by no means mere stooges of the new regime. Most of them were people of calibre: for example, after his fine liberal record in the Chaban–Delmas era, the redoubtable Pierre Desgraupes now came back as president of Antenne 2. Over the next few months, programmes on all three networks became just a little bolder and livelier. But there was no radical change; and for the television staff it was a strange interim period of tension and uncertainty, as they waited for the heralded new deal to come into force. In

July, the Government had set up an independent committee to suggest ideas that might help form the basis for a new statute, to be put before Parliament in the spring of 1982, and it had indicated roughly what kind of new deal it had in mind:

– The networks and radio stations would no longer be under the direct tutelage of the State, but of a new National Council for Television and Radio, independently chosen, made up of delegates from Parliament and the regional assemblies, from the trade-unions, viewers' associations and broadcasting staff. This body, and not the Government, would in future appoint the network heads. It would act as a screen, protecting the media alike from official and commercial pressures, and its brief would be to guarantee a real independence. France's planned TV satellite would go ahead, but would not increase the media's dependence on advertising. TF1 and Antenne 2 would remain structurally much the same, but would get better financing, and would no longer have to struggle for high ratings in order to qualify for higher budgets. FR3 would be properly decentralized: its regional stations would each get a high degree of autonomy, and would be protected against local political pressures. Free local radio stations would not be allowed to fall under the control of big-business interests. (Clearly the Socialists were as anxious to insulate the new media from Mammon as they were from the State.)

This sounds a promising scheme. But how well can it work out in practice, given the French temperament? In a land where people tend either to resist authority hotly or else side with it too tamely, a free and 'balanced' TV may not be easy to achieve. For the perennial problems of French broadcasting lie deep in the French character. In the old days it was many people's dream that the ORTF should have a truly autonomous statute 'like the BBC's', but what did this mean? Autonomy is not just a matter of texts. When, after May '68, some radicals began drawing up a project for a 'liberalized' ORTF, they got hold of the BBC's charter and found to their amazement that on paper it actually provided for *less* autonomy than the ORTF's statute. The BBC's board is designated by the Government, which legally has the right to instruct the BBC what or what not to broadcast. In practice, it virtually never uses this right: it is the British style of public life – *le fair-play*, so envied and inimitable – that gives the BBC and ITV their *de facto* freedom.

In France, polarization has always been such that no government hitherto has dared grant liberty to the media, lest they fall into the hands of its opponents who would be equally guilty of non-objectivity. Will Mitterrand now really have the courage of his convictions, and break this vicious circle? In the early months of 1982 there were plenty of sceptics. One pro-Giscard journalist said to me: 'Mitterrand has started out with fine liberal intentions, just as Giscard did in 1974. But by nature he's just as authoritarian as Giscard, and I doubt he'll avoid the temptation of finding ways of controlling the news programmes. Things will end up much the same.' Probably too cynical. This time, it seems that genuine autonomy is at least going to be given a trial. Whatever the risks, there is now no other sane course.

THE PRESS,
FREE BUT FRAGILE

If only France possessed a stronger and more effective Press, then the cause of full and fearless information might be better served, and the official hold over the other media might have mattered less. Newspapers are independently owned, and not subject to State tutelage; indeed, some of them have been fiercely and frequently critical of the Government. But they have endemic weaknesses of their own, both economic and editorial. One of their problems is that the French by inclination have never been great newspaper readers and are becoming even less so: sales of dailies per 1,000 inhabitants have fallen from 244 in 1914 to 214 today, compared with 287 in the United States, 388 in Britain, 572 in Sweden. Moreover, France lacks a national Press as we know it in Britain: provincial papers account for over two-thirds of the dailies' total sales of 11.2 million, while of Paris dailies only *Le Monde* has much circulation in the regions, and even this is a modest 130,000. The Paris daily Press has been steadily wilting. Its one big seller in the past, *France-Soir*, has fallen from a peak of 1.4 million to a mere 500,000 copies today, while in the mid-1970s even the stalwart *Le Figaro* came near to closure, its sales down to 300,000. Rising costs, a clumsy distribution system, union militancy, a fall in advertising revenue due to TV rivalry, these and other factors have thrown Paris newspapers into an even greater state of crisis than those of London or New York in recent years. Journalists have been dismissed by the score, papers have closed or survive only through mergers: Paris had thirty-one dailies in 1945, and today has thirteen.

This decline has been compensated, to an extent, by the rise of the weekly news magazines. Especially in hectic Paris, people are today less ready to find the time for reading a morning paper, so they want news-digest and feature material at the weekends. Sunday newspapers have never caught on as in Britain, owing partly to failures to create a distribution system for them: but *les news-magazines* have developed remarkably. Borrowing their formula from *Time* and *Der Spiegel*, they have now become far more glossy than these, with thick shiny pages full of colour ads. At a first glance, they look a little like British Sunday 'colour mags', but their content is much more newsy. By British Sunday standards their circulations are modest (*c*. 350,000 to 500,000), yet these are prosperous papers thanks to their high cover price (*c*. 9 francs) and copious advertisements. Of the three main ones, the doyen is *l'Express*, today owned by that ubiquitous Anglo-French tycoon Sir James Goldsmith: he rarely interferes editorially, but the paper broadly reflects his anti-Left views.[14] Its closest rival, *Le Point*, launched in 1972, has been the most successful newcomer to French journalism in the 1970s, and has built up a solid reputation by putting its accent on crisp analysis and reporting in a vivid, anecdotal, sometimes flippant style. Its politics, which it carefully plays down, are based on a kind of radical-Catholic liberalism, not far from what seemed to be Giscard's ethos in his first years in power. Third in this trilogy of rivals is *Le Nouvel Observateur*, pro-Socialist, more wordy and earnest than *Le Point* but as widely read, and now virtually a mouthpiece of the Government. The growth of this market has prompted the appearance of some other new weeklies too, for example, *Vendredi Samedi Dimanche*, lower-middle-brow, and *Le Figaro*'s new Saturday colour supplement, a platform for Right-wing views. Both these papers have succeeded, while the veteran *Paris-Match* too, the biggest seller, has taken on a new lease of life by shifting towards the news-magazine style and putting less stress on big photo-stories (where too often it is scooped by TV).

Why do these magazines fare so much better than the Paris dailies? One of the reasons often given for the weakness of the dailies is that till now they have been short on the kind of professional management that really understands the business. There have been no true Press barons. Many papers have been run as sidelines, none too effectively, by industrial tycoons whose main interests have been elsewhere: *Le Figaro* and *L'Aurore* both belonged to textile kings, Jean Prouvost and Marcel Boussac respectively. However, since about 1975 a far more professional figure has loomed up very large indeed, a possible saviour, though of a dubious kind. This is the controversial Robert Hersant, alleged wartime collaborator, man of the Right, man of mystery who shuns all personal limelight, never gives interviews, but powerfully pulls his strings behind the scenes. He spent some years quietly building up an empire of

14 Goldsmith is a friend of Giscard; and in May 1981 he caused a stir by sacking the paper's managing editor, Olivier Todd, for publishing a front cover hostile to Giscard during the election campaign. The editor-in-chief, the well-known writer Jean-François Revel, an anti-Socialist but disillusioned with Giscard, then resigned out of solidarity with Todd.

provincial dailies and weeklies and of successful specialized magazines such as *l'Auto-journal*. Then in 1975 he launched out by buying the ailing *Le Figaro*, and later took control of two other tottering dailies, *France-Soir* and *l'Aurore*. He has hardly saved *l'Aurore*, which today seems near death: but he has done something to revive *Le Figaro*, roughly France's equivalent of the *Daily Telegraph*. Hersant is a clever and dynamic businessman, alert to the way the world's newspaper industry is evolving, and by tough talking to the unions he has managed to introduce the new computer typesetting onto some papers. So France has a modern Press tycoon at last. But 'Citizen Hersant' is not to everyone's taste. He is ruthless in his take-over methods – he now owns more than thirty titles around France – and is not the type to let the politics of his newspapers go their own way: he is more of a Randolph Hearst than a Roy Thomson. On occasions, so it is said, he obliges his staff to twist the facts in support of his views, and some *Le Figaro* journalists have resigned in protest. So the growth of his empire has led inevitably to voices being raised, and not only on the Left, about the dangers of politically inspired Press monopolies, especially as Hersant is in clear breach of a 1944 law forbidding any one person to own several dailies. Yet Giscard's Government turned a blind eye: after all, Hersant was a personal friend of Giscard, and had proved a useful ally. The Socialist regime is now preparing to take stronger action against him.

In December 1980 another Giscard faithful acquired an even larger slice of the French media world, when the fast-growing Matra industrial group bought up the venerable publishing giant, Hachette. Thanks to this and other recent moves, Matra won control over a range of major publications, including *Paris-Match*, *Le Point* and *Elle*, as well as France's main Press distribution network and a share in Europe One radio. And Matra's dynamic chairman, Jean-Luc Lagardère, was on very friendly terms with Giscard.[15] All this happened just after the Government had begun to prosecute the pro-Socialist *Le Monde*; and it added fuel to the growing criticisms that Giscard seemed to be trying to buy over or subdue the Press in the pre-election period. But, whatever Giscard's intentions may have been, his range of manoeuvre had its limits: the Press in France may be weak, but it was not muzzled under Giscard, and nor is it today, when it is now the Right-wing papers that are anti-*le pouvoir*. True, a majority of Paris dailies and weeklies were broadly pre-Government under Giscard, and not only the Hersant ones; but this was hardly surprising under a capitalist system. Balancing them, there

15 In 1982, part of the Matra industrial group was being nationalized, and its short-lived media empire was breaking up.

has long been a small but solid body of influential Left-wing papers. The Communists have their own Press, led by the daily *l'Humanité*: its circulation has been falling and is now under 150,000, but this has been due to its own Stalinist dreariness and not to any official pressures on it. *Le Matin*, moderate Socialist, and *Libération*, independent Leftist, are two lively Paris dailies that carry some weight, despite their modest circulations. And the weekly *Canard enchaîné*, that renowned French institution, continues more robustly than ever, with sales as high as 450,000. With its lampooning style, it may at first seem a mere court jester, relatively harmless like *Private Eye*: but in fact this ultra-radical paper is deadly serious about its investigative political journalism, which it conducts far more effectively than any other French publication. Frequently it has come up with scoops on such topics as Giscard's diamonds. Governments from de Gaulle to Giscard were maddened by *Le Canard*'s revelations, and once they even tried bugging its offices: but they never managed to subdue it.

Today, under a Socialist regime of which it largely approves, *Le Canard* has relapsed into a gentler satiric style and has lost some of its old edge. Other papers too, both on Right and Left, have been reversing their roles since May 1981. It is an odd spectacle. *Le Figaro*, so long the voice of the Establishment, is now shrilly hysterical in its attacks on the new Government. *Le Quotidien de Paris*, Right-of-centre, tries commendably to preserve some objectivity. But *Le Matin* and *Le Nouvel Observateur*, hitherto so outspokenly critical of officialdom, now read in large parts as if they were written by the Elysée's Press officer. It has hardly made them livelier. And, alas, the same could be said of *Le Monde*.

Le Monde towers above the rest of the French Press, and is generally regarded both at home and abroad as one of the world's greatest newspapers. While the rest of the world changes, *Le Monde* still adheres to its austere format, with small print, no photographs (except a few ads), and lengthy articles with elaborate, almost Proustian sentences that do not make for easy reading. And yet, this evening paper has tripled its circulation since 1958 (it is now running at about 600,000) and sells more than any other Paris daily. Amazing! – it is as if *The Times* outsold the *Sun*. But then, *Le Monde* does not face the same competition as *The Times* from other quality dailies.

The paper is proud of its independence from big-business ownership: its editorial staff hold 40 per cent of its shares, and they elect its editor. In 1969 they chose Jacques Fauvet, who shifted the paper Leftwards and developed a personal hatred of Giscard, heartily reciprocated. Fauvet is due to retire in 1983: but, despite a rumpus over who should succeed him, the paper is likely to stay on its Left-wing course. In the earlier post-war decades it was liberal Left-of-centre; then under Fauvet it espoused the Joint Programme of the Left, and so for a few years was indulgent towards the Communists, to the dismay of many readers and some of its staff too. Today it warmly supports the Socialist-led Government, and treats the Communists with a wary reserve.

One of its virtues is that it allows itself to be used as a national forum: its columns are open to signed articles sometimes expressing views far removed from its own, for example by leaders of the Right or of the PCF. And yet, for all its qualities, this serious and supposedly fair-minded paper has itself come in for much criticism in recent years, and not only from the Right but from dispassionate liberals and others who accuse it of slanted and dishonest reporting, notably of events abroad. In Third World affairs it has an outsize anti-imperialist conscience, and this led it into the imprudence of greeting the Pol Pot regime's victory in Kampuchea as a triumph for democracy and turning a blind eye to the genocide. Later, it did publicly regret this. But even today its reporting on many matters is not as objective as it claims. It suffers, maybe, from the lack of any serious rival to cut it down to size. It knows too well that any educated Frenchman who wants detailed news and comment from day to day, whatever his own views, has little choice but to read *Le Monde*.

One editorial shortcoming of the French Press as a whole, including *Le Monde*, is that it has little tradition of the kind of fearless investigative reporting common in Britain and America. The Press is stronger on polemic, or on mere news digest, than on fully researched factual exposés, when some controversy is in the air; even *Le Monde*, however profusely it marshals the external evidence, is not so effective at publishing its own probes into what is going on behind the scenes. I suggest two underlying factors: (a) the well-known French concern with ideas and style, more than with facts; (b) the equally well-known French deference towards the power establishments, not only governmental. In this centralized and secretive society, most journalists rely for their news sources on their personal links with people in positions of influence – be it with Ministers or civil servants, or business tycoons, or trade-union barons, or leading Left-wing mayors and other *notables* – and they are reluctant to prejudice these sources by making embarrassing revelations. There may be honourable exceptions, such as the stories in *Le Canard*, but they are rare. Usually prudence is the watchword, so that papers publish less than they know, and not because of the libel laws, which are less strict than in Britain. Seldom do papers follow up in detail such matters as corrupt practices on town councils; or the murkier aspects of business take-overs; or the Government's electoral gerrymandering. In the long-running Manufrance crisis (see pp. 55–7), the newspapers gave blow-by-blow details of all the public developments, yet – though some reporters knew what was really happening – they failed to give candid exposés of the devious behind-the-scenes machinations by the Government, the Communists, and the judiciary. They were afraid, it seems, of making powerful enemies – 'A Watergate-style enquiry by the Press could not happen in France,' admitted one editor. One should add that the Press relies on more than 300 million francs' worth of assorted annual State aid, in the form of newsprint subsidies, tax rebates and the like. Many papers thus feel the need for some caution.

The problem is also one of journalistic tradition and resources, or lack of them. As compared with the quality Press in Britain or America (I do not speak of the popular Press), few French editors put the same insistence on factual accuracy or balanced judgements, or instil these virtues into their staff. Even on supposedly serious papers, reporting and sub-editing can be remarkably casual. Take, for example, the coverage of purely foreign stories, where French interests are not involved and thus there is no threat from the pressures I described above: here the reporting tends to be cavalier, taking refuge in easy clichés, *a priori* judgements, or irrelevant picturesque details, rather than trying to assess the real situation. For example, when they come to Britain to cover the political or social scene, few French correspondents (*Le Monde* is an exception) make much serious effort to explain to their readers how the curious British trade-union system really works, or what is the real nature of the Northern Ireland problem. They prefer to parade stereotypes: Thatcher is always '*la dame de fer*', and so on.

Régis Debray in his book *Le Pouvoir intellectuel en France* (see p. 538) points his finger not unfairly at the tendency both of dailies and weeklies to disdain detailed factual accuracy in favour of clever ideas and eloquent style: 'The higher French journalism chases two hares at once which collide and come a cropper: the brio of ideas and the substance of events; commentary and reporting; evaluation of themes and statement of facts.' He suggests this may be due to lack of money, lack of time, and lack of professional rigour. And there is another factor, too, which he might have mentioned. It seems to me that the deductive methods of teaching used in France, whereby all schoolchildren are trained first to enunciate a thesis, then to parade facts to support it, are in no small part a cause of the way French journalists' minds work and even of their mixing of news and comment. Just as they were taught at school, they use facts to prove a pre-selected point: they lack humility in the empiric pursuit of truth. It is the reverse of the inductive Anglo-Saxon tradition, which likewise spills over from our education into our journalism. And the French system, whatever its intellectual merits, is not the ally of objective enquiry.

If we turn to look at the regional Press, we find that at first sight it presents an impressive contrast with the struggling Parisian dailies, at least in terms of circulation and finances. In so centralized a country, this relative strength may seem curious: it stems in part from the Occupation, when the division of France in two, and the restrictions on transport, destroyed the pre-war provincial circulations of the Parisian Press and allowed the local papers to build up positions which they have since held and even developed. Since 1939 sales of provincial dailies have risen from 5.2 to 7.5 million, while those of Parisian ones have fallen from 6 to 3.7 million. Amazingly, the French daily paper with the highest circulation is not a Parisian one but *Ouest-France* (700,000 copies), published in Rennes, with 36 editions covering 12 departments. This is followed, in the provinces, by *Le Progrès de Lyon* (500,000), *Le Dauphiné Libéré* of Grenoble (420,000) and *La Voix du Nord* in Lille (415,000). There are 72 provincial dailies, and they have successfully resisted all efforts by Parisian ones – notably by *Le Figaro* under Hersant – to penetrate into their areas. In Caen, which is little farther from Paris than from Rennes, *Ouest-France* has four times the sales of all the Paris papers together! Moreover, the larger dailies are solid empires with fine new offices, making many Paris papers look like struggling poor relations. In most cases they have introduced the new technology sooner, and with less union opposition, than in Paris: the editor of a paper in Orléans told me, 'We moved over to computer type-setting back in 1970. The unions were wary at first, but are now enthusiastic. They get better pay, for a cleaner and more interesting job, and we've given handsome pay-offs to those we had to make redundant.'

These papers' success with their readership is certainly evidence of the strength of local attachments in France. But, alas, their editorial quality is hardly an inspiring asset for the regionalist cause. Most of them are trite and parochial. Many have built up their strength by killing off smaller rivals, thus creating a virtual monopoly in their area; and they feel that, in order to retain this, they must appeal widely and not risk alienating too many readers by flaunting bold opinions. Though many of them were vaguely critical of Giscard, with a few outspoken exceptions (the Socialist *Le Provençal* in Marseille, *La Voix du Nord* in Lille) they rarely take a strong editorial line on anything that matters: they deal in a dull, deadpan way with national news and, worst of all, most of them dismiss international and foreign affairs on a page or two of poorly edited agency news messages. Yet for most local people this is their sole source of news and political comment, apart from the hitherto State-supervised TV and radio. The papers put their emphasis on pages and pages of local news; and surveys show that this is what readers turn to first. Moreover, the multiple editions are so localized that there may be little news of the regional capital in an edition sold in another town forty miles away. The coverage is thorough, and reasonably objective, and maybe it has done something to promote the new regional awareness. But alongside the occasional article on a real public issue there are endless columns of tittle-tattle – flower-shows, Rotary dinners, local worthies' speeches reported in full, and minor accidents – what the French call *'histoires des chiens écrasés'*.

When the commercially aggressive *Dauphiné Libéré* staged a battle royal with the staid *Progrès de Lyon* in the 1960s for circulation in overlap areas, the Grenoble paper won by exploiting every kind of trivia. Then the two reached an entente and agreed to share out readership zones. This lasted until 1979, when *Le Progrès* acquired a young radical-minded and ambitious new owner, Jean-Charles Lignel. He broke the entente – landing himself in a lawsuit with *Le Dauphiné* – and declared his aim of making *Le Progrès* into one of Europe's great papers with, as he put it, 'the seriousness of *Le Monde* and the courage of the *Washington Post*'. It looked encouraging, a possible reversal of the trend towards monopoly and trivialization that had marked the regional Press since the war. Lignel made a modest start. His paper became a little less stuffy. It began to report such things as ecological rallies, or local sex scandals, which the ultra-conformist *Progrès* had hitherto ignored. But by 1981 the paper did not appear to have changed radically and was losing readers. Its own staff joked of it in private as 'Lignel's little Washington postage-stamp'. In fact, it is hard to see a staid town like Lyon accepting an American-style radical paper. Lyon, as other big French cities, has become culturally far more lively in the past thirty years, but this is not due to its Press any more than to television. It is thanks to theatre (Planchon), to gastronomy (Bocuse et al.), to cinema (Tavernier), and as much as anything to the French musical revival, of which Lyon is a pioneer.

MUSIC: A JOYOUS RENAISSANCE

The picture I have drawn so far of the current French cultural scene must seem a little sombre. But there is one very bright spot: after a long and strange silence, France is alive again with the sound of music. This revival, after a lengthy period of stagnation, has been the most cheering cultural development of the past decade: it has even surprised the French themselves, who had come to think that Malraux might have been right when he said, 'France is not a musical nation.' It has also impressed foreign critics: for example, the redoubtable Peter Heyworth devoted eight columns in the *Observer* of January 6th, 1980 to a glowing analysis of the 'remarkable surge of activity in France's musical life'. He commented: 'Music in the French provinces is on the march. *Die Meistersinger* in Toulouse! It's enough to put Bernard Levin off his cassoulet.'

The renaissance is as much at grass-roots as at élite level. On the one hand, thanks to Boulez' return from exile and the rebirth of the moribund Opéra, Paris is again one of the world's great musical capitals. But equally significant is the popular passion for music, both classical and modern, now sweeping every town in France. And not only are the French *listening* to serious music far more than ever before in this century; they have also swung back to the tradition of amateur *playing* of it. One sign is that sales of pianos have risen more than sixfold since 1966, while provincial *conservatoires* are so crammed with eager part-time pupils that many of them have had to set up waiting-lists. So this is a revolution of those who want to be more than passive consumers: a welcome trend in the Western cultural world today.

The musical explosion is comparable to that in Britain during and just after the war. Standards of performance both professional and amateur are still very variable, often mediocre, for France after her long neglect still has much leeway to make up before reaching British or German levels: but the enthusiasm is there. So why, when most of the other arts are languishing, have the French chosen this moment to rediscover music? There are many factors: one, that the State has at last woken up to the need to provide resources. But above all the musical revival seems to be an expression of the new mood of the French today, of that return to private pleasures and fulfilments which is a major theme of this book. One music critic suggested to me: 'In the post-war decades, until after 1968, the French were preoccupied with ideologies and social issues, and this climate favoured the art forms which best deal with these, such as literature and maybe theatre. But today people shun political idealism; they'd rather seek an inner world. So they turn to an art form that appeals joyously to the heart and the senses more than to the intellect or conscience. It's the turn of music.'

In the eighteenth and early nineteenth centuries France was a major musical nation: Chopin, arriving in Paris in 1831, said that he found there 'the best musicians in the world'. But the reformers of the nineteenth century proceeded to stifle this tradition. They starved music of official funds, and above all they gave it only a marginal place in the new compulsory school curriculum, so that generations of French children have since grown up with virtually no musical education. After the last war some thirty regional *conservatoires* still survived for the devotees, but these were run on stuffy, pedagogic lines and they shut their doors to any spirit of free enjoyment. A latent public interest persisted; but though concerts were well-patronized, they were few and ill-organized and suffered from the severe lack of good performers. André Malraux, as Minister of Culture in 1959–69, for some years did nothing to cure this malaise. He was not a musical man, and he once told Stravinsky that music was 'a secondary art'. His Ministry, as all musicians complained, treated this as the poor relation of the arts: music was no more than a section of the department of theatre and letters. And yet it was plainly absurd of Malraux to write off the French as 'not musical'. In this *étatiste* land, they had simply not been given the training or the means.

At last in 1966 Malraux grudgingly did something for music: he set up a new department for it under Michel Landowski, a minor composer. This was to bear fruit remarkably, for Landowski did more than anyone to prepare the groundwork for the musical revival. He drew up an ambitious master-plan to provide France with a much-needed infra-structure, and doggedly during his eight years in office he set about applying it. At first he was very short of funds, but after Malraux's departure in 1969 the Ministry vastly increased its annual budget for music: this soared from a mere 11.5 million francs in 1966 to nearly 400 million by 1979. Landowski created twelve new orchestras all over France, including the Orchestre de Paris under Charles Munch. He promoted a revival of the twelve provincial opera companies. He poured money into modernizing and expanding the *conservatoires* and helped to found scores of new ones. He persuaded the Ministry of Education to institute a musical *'bac'* in special *lycées*. And he did much besides, both for musical education and the performing of music, especially in the provinces. Conservative and classical in his own tastes, he was often criticized by the modernists such as Boulez for putting the accent on quantity more than quality: but he felt that he had no choice. French musical life was in so moribund a state that the first priority, he felt, was simply to provide massive new resources for performing, listening and studying. The raising of standards, inevitably a slow and arduous process, would follow.

While Landowski was at work amid the grassroots, helping to initiate a provincial public in the standard classics, in Paris a very different kind of musical revolution – more *avant-garde* – was being prepared. In Malraux's day, the official musical life of France was so hidebound, and so great was the prejudice of the establishment against modern music, that France's greatest composer-conductor, the serialist Pierre Boulez, was for many years spurned in his own land. French serialism had already played a big world role in modern music: but to study it you had to go abroad! Furious with Malraux's policy, Boulez declared he would no longer work in France: he spent some years living in Germany, as well as conducting leading orchestras in London and New York. But the Government then grew remorseful at having lost such a genius, and in 1972 Pompidou personally persuaded Boulez, with some difficulty, to come back and run an ambitious new research centre for modern music, to form part of the Beaubourg arts complex (see pp. 227 and 614). This Institut de Recherche et de Co-ordination Acoustique/Musique (IRCAM) was opened in 1977 and has been a success. Housed underground beside Beaubourg, its main feature is an experimental studio with mobile acoustic panels, unique in the world: by altering the position of the panels, one can change the whole tone and texture of the music. At IRCAM, musicians and scientists work side by side in evolving new approaches to music.

Boulez back in Paris is not concerned solely with research. He has conducted Berg's *Lulu* at the Opéra, as well as concerts with the Orchestre de Paris. And he has created a new chamber orchestra for modern music, the Ensemble Intercontemporain, which is very successful. So the prophet is no longer without honour in his own land: with his usual dogmatic fervour, he is now busily evangelizing Paris with his passionately held theories on modern music. In fact, for many years a small but devoted audience for modern music of various kinds has existed in France: Messaien and Xenakis live in Paris, and their concerts have long drawn eager audiences of mainly younger people. Today, thanks to them and especially to the recent work of Boulez, modern music is slowly reaching a wider public. Its devotees are still a small minority, but noticeably more numerous than in London: Boulez' chamber concerts regularly draw 1,000 people. One explanation may be the habitual French fascination with the new and *avant-garde*. But it could also be that the poverty of classical musical education in France has meant that the French are less inhibited in their approach to new concepts of music. Nicholas Snowman, an Englishman who works closely with Boulez, gave me his view of the contrast between London and Paris musical life: 'There are far more concerts in London, but look at the repertory – endless Brahms, etc. – compared with the exciting variety in Paris. London's is a conservative musical culture with high-quality performances: Paris is a city with other intellectual traditions which has now turned to music as a novelty.'

Pompidou's second *coup* in 1972 was to persuade Rolf Liebermann, the great Swiss manager, to take over the Paris Opéra. Once so glorious, the Opéra had been in decline for many years, suffering from feeble artistic direction, archaic administration and inadequate funding. It had become a European laughing-stock, and even its own public was deserting it: audiences were down to 69 per cent capacity, compared with well over 90 per cent in Hamburg, Milan or London. Oddly, de Gaulle (no doubt under Malraux' influence) never seemed too worried about this scar on France's vaunted national prestige. But Pompidou cared more for music: and when he embarked on an overall policy of trying to restore Paris's cultural pre-eminence, a key element in it was to bring the Opéra back into the front rank. No expense would be spared. The opera-house itself, the splendid Palais Garnier, was renovated at a cost of 15 million francs. Then the Government induced Liebermann, formerly in charge of the Hamburg Opera, to turn down similar offers from Berlin and the New York Metropolitan and to become artistic manager: Paris outbid its august rivals by offering Liebermann a fatter salary and a bigger subsidy. During his ensuing seven years in office, 1973–80, Liebermann pursued a policy of engaging the world's leading singers, directors and conductors, at fees often extravagant even by world opera standards – and he could do so, because he now commanded the largest budget of any opera-house in Europe. Mostly the policy paid off. Soon even many foreign critics (though not all) were admitting that the Opéra, at its best, was again the equal of La Scala, the Garden or the Met: a stunning recovery.

Some productions – for instance, Strehler directing *Figaro* under Solti's baton, or Dexter's *Forza del Destino* – were magnificent. Another great success was Patrice Chéreau's *Contes d'Hoffmann*, a wonderful poetic creation. Then in 1979, in a rare excursion by the Opéra into the modern field, Chéreau and Boulez (as conductor) mounted the first-ever production of the full version of Berg's *Lulu*, and the world's critics greeted this as a sensation and Liebermann's greatest achievement. (Chéreau and Boulez, incidentally, also marched across the Rhine to invade opera's heartland: their productions of the *Ring* at Bayreuth were acclaimed even by German Wagnerians.) But Liebermann's policy of inviting a number of directors from the worlds of theatre and cinema was not always so triumphant: René Clair's *Orphée et Eurydice* flopped, Losey's *Boris Godounov* was much criticized. Nor did the quality of the staging and décor of new Opéra productions always live up to that of the music. But at least the public returned: box-office moved up to 98 per cent capacity, with many performances sold out weeks ahead. Today, a night at the Opéra is again the height of *chic* with smart Parisians, and French Press and public alike are convinced that their opera is the best in the world. They pay little attention to the few dissident foreign voices, for example, Dale Harris in the *Guardian* of July 31st, 1979, who criticized Liebermann's policy as 'the kind of cosmopolitanism that owes everything to fashions and nothing to conviction'.

By 1981 the Opéra's annual subsidy stood at 209 million francs, twice that of Covent Garden, and accounting for 40 per cent of the Ministry's overall music budget. A seat selling for 100 to 200 francs at the box-office was costing on average a further 400 francs of taxpayers' money. And of course, as in London and elsewhere, democratic voices have sometimes asked whether it is right to spend so much public money on the élitist pleasures of a minority. The high running costs have been due in part to Liebermann's star policy, with Domingo, Te Kanawa and suchlike topping the bills, But they stem also from the Opéra's notorious administrative and union problems, which Liebermann was never given the brief to solve. The Opéra still lumbers under an archaic system of bureaucracy, whereby the spending of every franc has to be accounted for to the Ministry of Finance. And the tyranny of the Left-wing staff unions has aggravated this. They have insisted on work schedules that make flexibility of rehearsal extremely hard: for example, a musician has the right at any time to appoint a substitute who has not even attended rehearsals, and on one occasion this so infuriated the conductor, Roberto Benzi, that he threw his baton at the orchestra and walked out. The unions have also perpetuated an absurd level of over-staffing on the non-creative side: employees total 1,800, and 60 per cent of the budget goes on wages of non-artistic personnel. No wonder so high a subsidy is needed. In 1976 Jacques Chirac, then Prime Minister, forced a crisis over this, threatening that the Opéra would lose its subsidy and be forced to close unless it put its house in order. As a result the unions did make concessions, agreeing to staff cut-backs: but today the overall problems are still far from solved.

Since Liebermann's retirement in 1980, these problems have now been inherited by Bernard Lefort, a tenor, who was a successful manager of the Aix festival. For Lefort, it is no easy task to follow in the footsteps of the mighty Swiss, but so far he has made a good start. He is continuing the policy of quality productions, though on slightly less lavish a scale. His main innovation is that he intends to present the company frequently in other locations besides the Palais Garnier, both in Paris and the provinces: thus forty-two performances of *Carmen* are being staged in the vast Palais des Sports. In part this is an attempt to sidestep some of the Opéra's union difficulties; more important, it marks a bid to bring the company before a wider and more popular public. Lefort feels that this need not be incompatible with a continued dosage of new ambitious prestige productions such as *Lulu*.

Under the impulse of the *plan Landowski*, State and civic money has been poured into new musical activity all over France in the past decade, and the public has responded warmly, packing out the opera houses and concert halls. In the forefront of this resurgence are Strasbourg, Lyon and Toulouse. The proud city of Toulouse offers a remarkable case study. It has a fine musical tradition, notably for opera (*le bel canto* it is called locally), but by the 1960s this was fustily decadent. Then the revival was led by Michel Plasson, a gifted young conductor from Paris who took charge first of the city's orchestra, then also of the opera company to which it is attached. When he arrived in 1968, the members of the orchestra had an average age of sixty-five, and its concerts had thirteen regular subscribers: today the age is thirty, and the subscribers number two thousand. The opera now plays to 98 per cent capacity and keeps up a decent provincial standard. It receives some 3 million francs a year from the State, and a full 18 million from the city council: some worthies may themselves be philistines, but their pride in their city is such that they are glad to spend big sums on renewing its cultural renown. Above all, Plasson has converted a vast disused hexagonal cornmarket, seating 3,300, where he holds regular seasons of classical concerts with such visiting soloists as Igor Oistrakh and Isaac Stern. The success has been stupendous: for his Beethoven cycle, the capacity audiences of mainly young people were larger than for Giscard or even the Rolling Stones. The cornmarket is used, too, for opera, and here the discerning Peter Heyworth sat in a packed house to hear *Die Meistersinger* in the round: 'The full sound that Michel Plasson drew from his orchestra showed that even French strings can be induced to play with warmth. That a huge audience in a city whose operatic traditions have hitherto been essentially meridional stuck six hours on wooden, backless benches says much for the quality of the performance.'

Alsace too has a flourishing musical life, centred on Strasbourg, with numerous choruses and other bodies. Here the Opéra du Rhin is probably the best of the twelve full-time companies outside Paris. France today has a far livelier provincial opera scene than Britain, though it can hardly compare with Germany and its eighty-eight companies. Certainly the new vogue for opera is impressive, but standards are variable: some companies are frankly mediocre, and arguably some towns are overstraining their resources in the competition for operatic prestige (see pp. 334–6). Summer festivals too are now playing a big role in French musical life. Scores of them have sprung up in the past twenty years or so, notably in Provence, where Aix claims to be in the same league as Salzburg or Edinburgh. Many a little town is now eager for the kudos of mounting its own festival: but often they run into heavy deficit and then vanish, for there is just not enough subsidy to go round.

The public taste in serious music is remarkably catholic. As the great classics are so little taught in school, a new French generation seems suddenly to have discovered Beethoven, Brahms and others as exciting novelties, an unexpected treasure-trove of delight. People take them less for granted than, say, in Britain. Indeed, one reason for the joyous and passionate new French approach to music could well be that it is *not* associated with dull classroom hours. French taste is not chauvinistic: the great German and Russian composers are just as widely played as French ones. At the same time, the French have suddenly rediscovered Berlioz, so long ignored in his native land: Lyon, the nearest city to the great man's birthplace, has staged two major Berlioz festivals since 1979. And as well as nineteenth-century romantic music the French are showing a new enthusiasm for the medieval and the baroque. Several groups have been formed that specialize in medieval music.

Perhaps the most heartening aspect of the French music revival is the boom in amateur activity: in choral singing, and especially in the learning and playing of instruments, hitherto much neglected. The key element has been the expansion of the *conservatoires*. These are music schools, some State-run, some municipal, others independent and funded by State and/or town council; and they fulfil two main functions. A few of the major ones train future professionals, full-time; but the vast majority of the *conservatoires'* clientèle is made up of part-time pupils, some adults, mainly children, who come for the musical education they are denied in school. If you want to learn the violin, or singing, then when classwork is done you go round to your local music school, and your parents have to help pay for it, which means it is still something of a middle-class privilege. The music schools have trebled in number since 1960 – there are some 200 in the Paris region alone – and their total of pupils has risen from 250,000 to over a million: at Toulouse, the central *conservatoire's* students are up from 300 to 3,000. These schools today are the victims of their own success, for the rapid increase in their State or civic subsidies has not kept pace with rocketing demand, and many applicants are having to be turned away.

The piano is still the most widely played instrument, with flute and clarinet not far behind. Choral singing is on the increase, though it is still far less common than in Britain or Germany with their stronger traditions of amateur choirs. French young people do not burst into song as readily as the British. But many of them have now gone crazy for dance and ballet of every kind: some two million attend dance classes. And so, in short, this France of the anxious '70s and '80s has been seeking in music a new *douceur de vivre*, and the echoes can be heard on every side: medieval ballads in the floodlit courtyards of old castles; sounds of a Debussy sonata floating through the thin walls of a suburban HLM; balletomanes practising in village halls; and, in a few families, a revival of the charming Victorian habit of making music together after dinner. Music today rivals *cuisine* as the latest mode. Boulez and Béjart, as much as Bocuse, are the new pied pipers.

Among the many factors contributing to this renaissance, four are worth stressing. One, of course, the upsurge in official support since the late 1960s. Two, the role of the often-abused State radio, which in this field at least has been beneficial: two networks, France-Culture and France-Musique, equivalents of the BBC's Radio Three, have for years provided a worthy output of serious music of all kinds, and this has done much to stimulate and educate public taste. Three, music is a facet of the affluent society, for the boom years brought new money for spending on opera-going, on hi-fi, pianos and so on. Sales of records rose fifteen-fold in 1961 to 1977, and 17 per cent of these sales have been of classical music.

The fourth factor, and perhaps the most important, is psychological; and, paradoxically, it seems to be related to the new trend *against* consumerism, notably among the young. The music revival clearly has some connection with the rise of ecology, and with the revulsion against politics and ideologies. One French critic, Pierre Billard, has written.[16] 'In this age of uncertainty, technology-dominated, the return to music marks a withdrawal into intimate, individualist values, a recourse to comforting romanticism in face of the tough world outside.' Escapism, or liberation? The vogue for music is at once private and gregarious, and thus is symptomatic of both of the major new trends described in this book: the *repli sur soi*, and what the French see as the growth of *la vie associative*. The French in their homes may be turning to music as a personal spiritual balm: but in coming together so eagerly in public, to listen to it and to make it, may they not also be giving expression to their yearning for a new social warmth and community?

If France is again a musical nation, this is still relative. In average quality of performance, and even in sheer quantity of concerts, the French do not yet match the deeply musical Germans, nor even the British whose revolution occurred thirty or forty years ago. They have always produced the occasional artist of top world calibre, such as Tortellier; but their long neglect of musical education has been such

16 In *Le Point*'s cover story, January 3rd, 1977: *Musique, la France bouge.*

that they cannot yet equal their neighbours' regular output of first-rate
singers and instrumentalists. In opera, in Paris and the provinces alike,
most lead singers have to be imported, from Italy, Germany and elsewhere. And in the Franco-British musical exchanges that are now so
active, the French often are enviously aware of the British superiority of
playing. So today the authorities are making concerted efforts to improve
standards, by seeing that a future generation is properly trained. Progress
is sure, if slow. The French are still severely hampered by the shortage of
good teachers: I heard the story, at one *conservatoire*, of a flautist who knew
so little of his subject that he was learning from the same manual as his
pupils, keeping just two lessons ahead of them.

The issue of quantity versus quality lay at the heart of the public feud
between Landowski and Boulez which dominated French musical life a
few years ago. These two arrogant, prickly characters have always disliked each other: it is a clash of rival personalities, also of two very
different concepts of music. Landowski does not care for Boulez' modernism: his own taste is for nineteenth-century operas and symphonies.
Moreover, Landowski during his years in charge of French music felt it
right to put the first priority on numbers, on building as wide a new base
as possible, however uneven the quality. So he poured money into new
local orchestras and music schools, and into helping regional opera
companies including the mediocre ones (and he accepted that
Liebermann's reborn Opéra must rely mainly on imported talent).
Boulez was angry: *he* favoured a much more selective policy of quality,
including the encouragement of indigenous French creativity and com-
position: he pointed out, fairly, that France has hardly any living composers of worth (apart from himself and the aged Messaien). Then in
1974 Landowski resigned on the arrival of a new Minister, Michel Guy,
who favoured Boulez. But after 1979, with Jean-Philippe Lecat as
Minister, there was a swing back towards the Landowski approach.
Since Malraux, no fewer than seven Ministers have held this portfolio, so
the twists in official policy have been hard to follow. But the issue
between Landowski and Boulez has always seemed to me in part a false
one. Surely, the two policies are complementary. High quality is desirable: but this cannot be achieved without a broad back-up at the grass-
roots, for – just as in science, sport, art or even *cuisine* – only a widely
educated nation can throw up its share of geniuses. Germany herself has
proved this in music.

This is roughly the policy being pursued today. On the one hand,
the training of professional musicians is being stepped up. Bernard
Lefort has embarked on a new programme of training would-be opera
singers, copying the successful British post-war example. And in 1979 a

second Conservatoire National Supérieur was opened, in Lyon: hitherto, the only advanced-level music academy of its kind was the one in Paris, dating from 1795. At the same time, the Ministry is seeking to extend the musical education of children: its budget for this has risen twelve-fold since 1960. But here the villain of the piece has for many years been the Ministry of Education, which till now has virtually refused to liaise with its rival Ministry and is still hesitant to allow music any place in the intellectual curriculum (see p. 487). In primary schools and *collèges*, the subject is taught for an hour or two a week, usually just sol-fa exercises and a dash of music appreciation; in *lycées* it is an 'extra' that very few pupils take, except in the handful of schools that prepare for the music option in the *bac*. So almost all active learning of music takes place out-of-class in the local *conservatoires*, which charge fees and thus tend to be bourgeois preserves. In a land that prides itself on its free education, this is socially most unfair, and must be denying many a working-class child the chance to express a real musical talent. Today the feeling is growing that the larger *conservatoires* should specialize in pro-fessional training, while State schools should take over some of the burden of teaching music to children. But this idea still encounters fierce opposition from the teaching corps who fear (a) a decline in academic standards; (b) change of any kind, as ever; (c) that the music teachers might outshine them in popularity – as indeed they might. There is also still some hostility from utility-minded parents whose sole concern is that their children should pass the *bac*.

However, change is at last on the way. After many years of pressure from its rival, the Ministry of Education in 1979 finally introduced music as a compulsory subject in the training of primary teachers, so younger kids at least will now be taught their sol-fa properly. The Ministry also recently sanctioned a pilot scheme of 'musical workshops' in a number of schools; as a result, the total of French schools with a choir or instru-mental group rose in 1979–80 from 500 to 1,000. Big deal. Not long ago, the percentage of French secondary schools with their own orchestra was 8 in France, against 46 in Britain, 83 in the USA. But the new national passion for music now seems at last to be forcing a breach in that most entrenched of citadels, the French school system. Before too long, all French children may be allowed to receive the musical education considered normal in most other civilized countries, and that, in the long run, could lead to more Boulezes, more Tortelliers. But if music does enter the curriculum, let us hope that it does not get pushed into some formal academic mould and stifled beneath the pedagogic ethos, as might easily happen in French schools. That could spoil the exuberant and hedonistic nature of the new musical revival. It could muffle the lyrical new sounds of a nation so joyfully playing truant from its crabbed intellectualism.

In the world of the visual arts, by contrast, France is still in a state of slump, at least as far as new creative work is concerned. I have no competence myself to write of modern French painting or sculpture: but even if I had, I wonder if there would be much to say. It is a truism that Paris has long ceased to be the world's unrivalled capital of art: great painters no longer flock to live there, and New York, even London and Cologne, have become more important as markets for dealers. More serious, in the past twenty years hardly a single new French artist has arisen to make any wide impact. The French themselves are all too aware of this bleak situation, though no one can explain why it is so. The critic Jacques Michel, in *Le Monde* of September 25th, 1980, referred to 'the disarray into which our young artists are plunged, and the less young too. For decades, contemporary art has been living through a revolution of mediocrity, as steadily the old artistic values have been killed. Today there are no more "masters", no more leaders or "schools", just individual artists.' These live quietly, often in Provence, ignored by critics and public, and without much contact even with each other. There is virtually no artistic café life in Paris today.

However, what the French do still manage very well is to mount large-scale imaginative exhibitions of art, usually historical retrospectives, and these draw big and eager crowds. In particular the famous new Centre Pompidou ('Beaubourg'; see p. 276), opened in 1977, has made a speciality of panoramic surveys of the cultural links in this century between Paris and some other capitals: its 'Paris–Berlin' and 'Paris–Moscou' exhibitions, and to a lesser extent 'Paris–New York', were a success and fed the current public appetite for cultural nostalgia. So Beaubourg has done something to help revive the vitality of Paris as a forum where art is displayed and discussed, and that maybe is a step forward, even if living artists are still conspicuous by their absence. The building of Beaubourg, like the rebirth of the Opéra, was a plank in the policy embarked on by President Pompidou in the early 1970s of trying to restore the cultural prestige of Paris. He saw that the *Ville Lumière* had been losing far too much ground to New York. So he poured money into these and other new projects, such as the annual *Festival Automne*. The policy has certainly re-focused some international attention on Paris as a lively generator of the performing arts. But, except maybe in modern music, it has not done much to stimulate individual creativity.

Pompidou hoped also that more foreign artists, writers and others might again be tempted to live and work in Paris, as in the great days of

Picasso and James Joyce. And, true, there *has* been a limited migration over the past decade or so. One of the first to come was Peter Brook. More lately a number of political exiles, notably from Latin America and Indo-China, also from Eastern Europe, have chosen Paris rather than elsewhere. The great Argentinian stage director Jorge Lavelli, and the Polish film-maker Roman Polanski (after a while in Hollywood), are both now naturalized French and living in Paris; the Czech writer Milan Kundera has settled there too. Some French chauvinists have hailed all this as proof of a splendid rebirth of the old Parisian magnetism: *Le Point* even wrote, 'The idea that Paris attracts, captivates, bewitches is spreading again throughout the world. A dreamed-of, vaguely mythical destination – one embarks for Paris as for the Promised Land' – which is, frankly, a romantic nonsense. A few swallows do not make a summer; and Paris, tough, hectic, crowded (see p. 288), is still far from recovering its old glory as the world's cultural Mecca.

In the sense that there is a lot going on, Paris today *is* culturally lively, probably more so than a decade ago. At smart dinner-parties, the talk is all of the very latest operas, concerts, art shows, books, plays, films; and a fashion-conscious minority is ever anxious to show that it keeps abreast of these things. So the box-office does well, alike with this trendy bourgeoisie, and with younger, less affluent people whose interest is perhaps more genuine. But, much of the time, there seems to be a tiredness and repetitiveness today even about the desperate Parisian search for novelty. Try hard though it does, Paris is still failing to snatch back from New York the cultural leadership of the West.

Under Giscard, culture's share of the overall State budget had been falling and was down to under 0.5 per cent. Mitterrand in 1981 then promised to raise it sharply, speaking of 1 per cent as a 'reasonable minimum'. To be Minister of Culture he chose his friend Jack Lang, a brilliant, erratic maverick who had founded the Nancy experimental drama festival and is always brimming with ideas – some sane, some zany – for the popularizing of the arts. What a contrast he makes to the smoothies who filled that post under Giscard! Lang came to office with no precise programme, but full of generous talk about the need for 'new centres of creativity and animation' all over France, while his party's election manifesto spoke of 'the nation's cultural renaissance' as being 'in the forefront of Socialist ambitions'. 'It's all very exciting,' said one *animateur*; 'Lang, in his own style, could well be a new Malraux – with the same dynamic support from Mitterrand as Malraux had from de Gaulle.' Then, in July, Mitterrand, with Lang and no less than nine other Ministers in tow, paid a much-publicized visit to the Avignon Festival, to pay homage to the memory of the great Jean Vilar. 'I am not here by chance,' said the President.

In November, Lang was able to announce officially that the State budget for culture was being doubled, passing from 3 billion francs for 1981 to 6 billion for 1982. It would now represent 0.75 per cent of the overall State budget, with the likelihood of a further rise to 1 per cent for 1983. Joyously Lang told Parliament: 'The French have crossed the frontier separating darkness from light!' He promised that the extra money would be divided out among all the arts, and that the provinces rather than Paris would receive the lion's share. So the Maisons de la Culture (see pp. 325–34) may at last get a ·new lease of life. Among specific projects, Lang revealed plans for encouraging French 'pop' songs, and for extending the Louvre museum to cover the whole of the Palais du Louvre when the Economy Ministry evacuated the wing it had long occupied and moved out to new premises at La Défense.

In these austerity days, Britain and many other countries have been cutting back on official funds for the arts. But Mitterrand, himself a deeply cultured man, has chosen the opposite path – and his move has been generally welcomed in France, even by those who did not vote for him. He believes that culture has a crucial part to play in the new Socialist France that he is seeking to build, and that money for it should not be stinted. But much will now depend on how the new budget is spent. It can certainly help to promote the performing arts: but no amount of largesse can in itself ensure a revival of the French creative genius.

Chapter 9

CONCLUSION

THE NEW FRANCE UNDER SOCIALISM

The manifold changes described in this book took place mainly under the Right-of-Centre Governments of de Gaulle, Pompidou and Giscard. Then Socialists came to power with a radically different approach. This new era poses many questions for France's future. First, can the economy continue to prosper, and will modernization go ahead successfully, as it did under the preceding pro-capitalist Governments? This we examined in an earlier chapter. Next, what is this new Socialist Government really like? Is it in any danger from its Communist so-called allies? Will it really succeed in reducing the grip of the State over French life, and in inducing a more open and flexible society? If so, will some of the old French barriers give way at last to a greater community spirit and fairer sharing of privilege? These are issues for this final chapter of the book. But first let us look at the legacy of May '68, and at Giscard's strangely uneven record in power.

De Gaulle did a lot for France during his reign, 1958–69, and I am not among those who have ever regretted his return to power, nor the demise of the Fourth Republic. He solved the Algerian problem, restored French self-confidence, brought in political stability. As we have seen, his technocratic Government showed far more vigour than its weak predecessors in pushing through a number of valuable reforms in face of sectional opposition: for example, the Pisani agricultural measures and the new town-planning of Paris. But in many cases the Gaullists' high-handed approach, their failure to consult those concerned, lost them much of the cooperation that the reforms required to be fully effective. And other important projects stayed on the shelf because even de Gaulle baulked at challenging certain vested interests, for instance in land ownership. Towards the later 1960s his regime lost much of its earlier energy and idealism and veered towards classic conservatism, in closer alliance with big business; de Gaulle became ever more obsessed with national prestige, with costly and ambitious projects such as Concorde, and less with the mundane needs of social progress. For these and many other reasons, frustrations built up: yet the Left, weak and divided, offered no effective challenge. So France was in a political vacuum. The towering authority of de Gaulle held the nation together, in a sense: but while many Frenchmen found this reassuring, beneath the surface there were tensions.

This was the background to the May '68 uprising which suddenly shattered the calm. No one foresaw it; no one imagined that a revolt led by a handful of Left-wing students in Paris would spread like a bush-fire to infect the whole nation. There were various separate strands in the May movement – euphoric, revolutionary, materialist, and reformist, to put them in that approximate order of ascending importance. First, there was the element of national carnival. *'La France s'ennuie'* was the title of a much-quoted article by Pierre Viansson-Ponté in *Le Monde* a few weeks before the crisis broke, and certainly the French were growing bored with years of papa-knows-best government and were ripe for a break from routine. The barricades, the waving flags, the hitch-hiking across a strike-bound Paris, the jolly workers' picnics in the occupied factories: it is not to belittle the more serious motives behind the uprising to say that all this appealed to the theatrically minded French, especially the younger ones. Some French observers, including Raymond Aron, indeed dismissed the whole affair as little more than a euphoric irresponsible holiday – 'the Club Méditerranée run riot on a nation-wide scale', said an American writer. This had an element of truth, but was far from the whole truth.

There were also the revolutionaries: Maoists, Trotskyists, anarchists and other little groups of militants. They were in earnest: for them, this was no carnival. Although some of their leaders used provocative tactics of violence as hard to admire as those used against them by the police, and although most of them showed a naïvety of thinking and a vagueness about the kind of ideal new society they wanted, yet in most cases their sincerity and generosity were patent. 'Our society is rotten – I'm devoting my life to creating workers' communes,' said the educated young daughter of a rich Parisian. Most of the other *gauchistes*, too, were from bourgeois homes. They came from a milieu that put its stress on money values, competitive careerism and class privileges, and many of them rebelled against this and proclaimed their hostility to the boredom and greed of a consumer society. But, alas for them, this hostility was shared by few of the industrial workers whom they tried so hard to rally to their cause. Although some skilled workers and *cadres* were also up in arms against aspects of the affluent society, the rank-and-file went on strike because they wanted a larger share in that society, not because they were sated with it. This was a main cause of the revolution's failure. Had students and workers really united *en masse* for a new society, the CGT and other union leaders could not have held them back. But most workers went on strike for the usual classic reasons: better pay and conditions, linked on this occasion with vaguely formulated desires for more self-expression and more respectful treatment from employers.

The most original aspect of the uprising was that these two groups, student idealists and wage-demanding workers, were joined by large sections of the French artistic, scientific and executive intelligentsia, protesting against many of the real obstacles to the modernizing of French public life. Their revolt was against over-centralization, heavy authority and failure to delegate power, clumsy bureaucracy and rooted privilege – in nearly all the professions as well as in industrial and office life. Doctors set up 'soviets' in hospitals and proclaimed the abolition of the old hierarchies, while architects demanded of Malraux the liquidation of their 'evil' guild. Once the great national debate had started, no group wanted to be left out – even footballers occupied the HQ of their federation, hoisted the red flag and hung out a banner, '*Le football aux footballeurs*!' Maybe there was an element of carnival in all this too, and a desire to protest out of solidarity: no profession felt it could afford to stay off the bandwagon. But, significantly, nearly all the protests were similar in character: they marked a bid for a more human and tolerant system, for more democracy and flexibility. This was not a Poujadist attempt to set the clock back, like some movements in the 1950s. Quite the reverse: it was a bid to modernize old structures and practices which France's economic revolution had rendered anachronistic. The pioneers of May wanted to cure these anomalies.

How far did they succeed? It is not easy to assess the real influence of May '68, which in the next few years led to many paradoxes. It did loosen permanently some of the old barriers and rigidities and it ushered in a new freer spirit: but the other side to this coin was that it also sharpened or revived old conflicts. It repolarized French life. In the short term, there was certainly no revolution: the *gauchistes* failed. De Gaulle was able to put an end to the factory strikes early in June, by granting generous wage rises. At the same time, the fear of anarchy and Leftism provoked such a reaction among France's conservative 'silent majority' that, when a special general election was held late in June, the Gaullists secured a landslide victory. So politically the *status quo* was restored. A few reforms followed, but except in the universities they were hardly radical.

And yet, as we have seen repeatedly in this book, May '68 was nonetheless to leave a subtle and lasting impact on the climate of French life, in many spheres: throughout education, in families, in the growth of the ecology movements, in labour relations and much of working life. It was a fluctuating and uneven process. In some professions the mandarins soon reasserted their authority after May, the soviets dispersed and the brave resolutions added up to little. But in many other cases a more open and democratic spirit did emerge and has since survived, however, confusedly, in schools and colleges, in numerous firms and offices. The old authoritarianism declined, even if this then created new problems in turn, in a nation with little aptitude for group leadership or initiative. But at least there *was* now a little more human contact and discussion between the strata of the hierarchy, and Monsieur le Directeur became a little readier to listen to the views of his juniors. This was a healthy new trend, and it is likely to develop today under the Socialists, whose 1981 victory clearly had some roots in May '68.

However, the uprising did have another sequel too. So strong were the passions aroused by the crisis that they tended to reopen a number of old wounds among this contentious people. After the years of calm, it was as if a truce had been broken. The new demands and aspirations brought hidden antagonisms out into the open, so that the battle was now joined much more sharply than before between those wanting radical change and those resisting all change, a complex, many-sided struggle, with Leftists, Gaullist reformers and true diehards all at loggerheads with each other. May '68 forced the French to requestion their society; it opened their eyes as never before to all that was still wrong with it, behind the façade of rising prosperity. Maybe this was a healthy moment of truth, as a step towards solutions. But it led to fierce confrontations over what should be done. This new polarization soon put an end to much of the pragmatic collaboration that had been built up during the Gaullist years.

De Gaulle remained in power for nearly a year after May '68. During this time the results were disappointing, not only of course for the *gauchistes*, but even for liberals and radicals who felt that something *must* now happen, that the Gaullists could not just sit and do nothing to answer the grievances expressed in May. But – except in the university world – hopes steadily faded that the regime would have been shocked by the uprising into recovering its earlier reformist dynamism. De Gaulle, now showing signs of senility, withdrew into isolation, blocking most of the proposals put to him by his Ministers. Then he resigned after his defeat in the referendum of April 1969, and the election of Pompidou as President two months later marked a renewal of confidence, at least in some quarters. Pompidou quickly embarked on a seemingly more realistic policy than de Gaulle's. He devalued the franc, modified de Gaulle's extravagant prestige ventures, and above all he appointed a man of decided liberal intentions as his Prime Minister, Jacques Chaban-Delmas. Chaban in turn chose two brilliant and radical civil servants for the top posts on his staff: Simon Nora, who had worked with Mèndes-

France, and Jacques Delors, a progressive Catholic. Together they launched a Kennedyesque programme under the slogan *'la nouvelle société'*, and pledged themselves to unblock France's *'société bloquée'*. This was no mere window-dressing: they believed in what they were doing. So the hearts of progressives rose a little. And indeed in the next three years Chaban's team did have a few successes, notably in labour relations. But at the same time it steadily became clearer that Pompidou's own radicalism had the strictest limitations. Many of the more fundamental reforms that Chaban and his team wanted to carry through were either vetoed by Pompidou personally or subtly sabotaged by his more conservative Ministers.

Pompidou believed that the overriding priority for France was for her to become more wealthy and her industries more competitive: if this could be achieved, then most social problems would gradually solve themselves, for they sprang from poverty and economic backwardness. And he wanted to stage-manage this transition so gently that it would avoid provoking disorder and unrest. He was a pragmatic conservative. Thus he allowed Delors' incomes policy deals to go through, as these were clearly a way of keeping the unions quiet and encouraging productivity. But when it came to the kind of radical structural reforms that affect ingrained habits and vested interests, and thus will always arouse fierce opposition, he generally said 'no'. He sanctioned only the timidest of regional reforms; he proved no bolder than de Gaulle at dealing with land speculation; and above all he forbade the badly needed shake-up that Chaban and his team wanted to make in the work routines and hierarchic systems of the State administration. This, he felt, would have turned the *petits fonctionnaires* against him. So relations between President and Prime Minister steadily worsened. Finally, in 1972, Pompidou dismissed the excellent Chaban and replaced him with the colourless Pierre Messmer.

It would be unfair to overlook the positive aspects of Pompidou's policies. He was right in setting store by economic progress, so that there would be more wealth for the nation to share. But he was wrong in thinking that France could cure all her ills simply by getting richer. Formerly a banker, his natural associates were the big businessmen and financiers, men whom de Gaulle had disliked or ignored. After 1969 he quietly interred de Gaulle's romantic plans for worker participation, not only because they seemed unrealistic, but because they were a blow at capitalism and detested by the Patronat. He also allowed a number of shady property deals and town-planning abuses to go through virtually unchecked. As one radical suggested to me, 'De Gaulle may have been outrageous in his foreign policy and intolerably arrogant in his manner:

but at least he had high integrity, and we felt that in his day the regime had a basic morality, even to the point of puritanism. Under Pompidou, we're not so sure.'

One thing was clear: Pompidou had not learned the lessons of May. When he died in April 1974, the French then elected a more youthful President, who brought with him a bolder vision of liberal reform. He was to prove an enigmatic figure, this Valéry Giscard d'Estaing. By background more élitist and patrician than Pompidou or even de Gaulle, he has always led in private a social life of smart dinners and country *château* weekends with the rich and titled. He is an intellectual, a snob and a super-technocrat, who has spent his life aloof from the common herd. But he is also a 'modernist', with an international outlook; and even before 1974 he was pondering how France could be turned into a more open society, closer to the Anglo-Saxon model which he has long admired. Once installed at the Elysée, he proclaimed his ideal of wide-ranging humanist reforms, leading to his so-called *'société libérale avancée'*. But the results, during his seven years in office, 1974–81, were to prove uneven, to say the least. He did try sincerely to promote modern reforms and sometimes with success. But often, so it seemed, he was betrayed either by circumstances or by his own weaknesses.

He started well. Some of his early measures were matters of personal style, seeking to show that he *was* capable of the common touch. He tried to break through the stiff ceremonial habitually surrounding the President: he entered the Elysée in shirt-sleeves, phoned journalists himself in their offices, gave breakfast to his dustmen, invited himself to dinner in ordinary homes. Some of his critics scoffed at all this as PR gimmickry, or as demeaning the dignity of the French presidency by the phoney adoption of a casual American style. But the public largely approved. Maybe one or two eyebrows were raised late in 1974 at indications that some dinners were with *citoyennes* and extending well beyond dinner-time: but the discreet French were primarily concerned at the effect this might have on his work capacity. Unlike the British, they regard a public man's private life as his own business.

In his first months Giscard reduced the age of majority and franchise from twenty-one to eighteen (a generous move, seeing that the young allegedly vote Left); he made divorce easier; and he pushed through the abortion law, in face of hostility from most of his own supporters in Parliament. As we have seen, this was an example of how his reformism could be closer to the feelings of the general public than to those of his own political allies. He also set in train the Haby reforms in education; he gave what he initially aimed to be a more liberal framework to State broadcasting; and he hinted at plans for more difficult structural reforms in such areas as labour relations and local government. All in all, it was an impressive record for a first year in office. However, his reform plans were soon to fall foul of a concurrence of circumstances by no means his own fault. The first was the economic recession, which distracted attention from some of his projects, limited the funds available for them, and forced him to give priority to quite other measures, often unpopular, in the fight against inflation. With workers scared about jobs, and employers scared about profits, this was hardly the ideal climate for introducing radical co-management schemes.

The second circumstance was the growing harassment which Giscard had to face, throughout his mandate, from his Gaullist partners. He needed their backing in order to retain a majority in the National Assembly: but the coalition was never an easy one, as right-wing Gaullists constantly sought to thwart his reforms. The Gaullist leader Jacques Chirac, Prime Minister in 1974–6, was motivated by a strong personal jealousy of Giscard, as well as making no secret of his dislike of many of his liberal policies. When Chirac resigned and later became mayor of Paris, this hostility grew more open. The Gaullists sabotaged Giscard's plan for a capital gains tax and blocked a number of other measures too. So this constant rivalry put a brake on Giscard's moves towards his cherished 'liberal society'. Thirdly, he was obstructed by the rise of the Left, which damaged his hopes of achieving some kind of national consensus for his reforms. The narrowness of Mitterrand's defeat in the 1974 election (he polled 49.2 per cent, to Giscard's 50.7), far from discouraging the Left, made their leaders feel that victory next time was well within their reach. Indeed, they quite probably would have won the general election of March 1978, had not the Communists at the last moment disrupted their alliance with the Socialists. But, despite the disappointment of this breach, the Socialists continued to reject Giscard's attempts to woo them into some kind of collaboration. France remained polarized, and this hardly favoured Giscard's vision of promoting a more open society.

By the end of his seven-year term, Giscard's popularity was waning sharply, and the feeling was widespread that his reformism had failed. My own personal view is that on this score the criticisms were excessive. His own personal style of rule had become unpleasantly autocratic, I grant: but if we examine his actual record of reform, we see that under hard conditions he did in fact achieve a fair amount, if less than had been hoped. He did more than his predecessors, if less than he might have done, to reduce wage inequalities, to help the elderly and handicapped, and to usher in more social justice. In his measures to protect the environment and to check land speculation, he reduced some of the abuses that de Gaulle and Pompidou had tolerated, and he did something to answer the new French aspirations for better 'quality of life'. The Haby school reforms were a real attempt to bring more equality into education: if they partially backfired, it was by no means solely the Government's fault. The Bill devolving some power to local authorities, though timid compared with the Socialists' current plans, would certainly have marked a valid step towards decentralization. And above all, in the difficult final years when recession worsened, Giscard unswervingly backed his premier, Raymond Barre, to hold an unpopular austerity policy.

Yet it is also hard to avoid the view that Giscard lost his zeal for reforming society, as the years went by. The promises were still there, but increasingly the actions failed to match them. Is it that he was deflected by more urgent economic priorities? Or did he sadly come to the conclusion that the French, after all, were incapable of accepting the changes he was offering them, that they were too conservative, and too divided, to respond to his vision of things? And so, maybe, he lost interest. Certainly he grew fatigued and cynical, in face of the array of parties and pressure-groups so often obstructing his plans. One great handicap was that he lacked a strong political base, a party genuinely sharing his beliefs and ready to back him up. He was a lonely liberal, caught between warring armies of Right and Left: for instance, in the case of the Sudreau report on labour relations, his plans were blocked by unions and employers alike. Many moderate Socialists were sympathetic at heart to a number of his aims: but they disliked much else that he stood for (the élitist world of wealth and privilege) and for sound tactical reasons they were not prepared to support him publicly. On the other side, a large part of his own electorate was plainly opposed to his reformism. And this was the tragic irony: he had come to power aiming to change society, yet millions who had voted for him wanted precisely the opposite, a preservation of the *status quo* and their own privileges. It was a political paradox that proved his undoing.

Giscard was betrayed, too, not only by outside factors but by his own weaknesses. Those who worked closely with him would point to his secretiveness, his tendency to make arbitrary or impulsive decisions, his habit of making fulsome promises and then failing to carry them through, not out of deceit, but through imprudence. He proclaimed the virtues of open government, but his temperament led him to practise the opposite. And in his lofty role as Head of State he revealed an odd streak of insecurity, like a parvenu monarch unsure how to wear his crown. This explains a good deal about his regime. He began by trying the casual man-of-the-people style, but then found this did not come naturally to him, or was not appreciated. So steadily he swung to the opposite extreme. Betrayed by his innate snobbishness and vanity, he succumbed to the temptation of regal pomp. At the Elysée, he insisted on being served first at table even in the presence of State guests (including Mrs Thatcher). He had his son treated virtually as a crown prince. And he surrounded himself with sycophantic advisers. This monarchic style let loose a torrent of scorn – 'If he's re-elected,' said one critic, 'we're sure to see a coronation.' The behaviour was a symptom of weakness, not strength. Unsure of his ability to play the role of President, he sought refuge behind the façade of kingship.

As his reign went on, another aspect of his insecurity showed. Faced with the dual onslaught of the Gaullists and the Left, he felt the need to protect himself by putting his own trusted supporters in key posts. Especially this was so in television and radio, as we have seen, and it made nonsense of his earlier genuine liberal intentions towards these media. One observer put it another way: 'rationally, he wants to be a liberal; but his temperament is to be interfering and autocratic'. His regime became more authoritarian in style, even to the point of passing a new law that – in the interests of the fight against crime – gave added repressive powers to the police. So much for the 'liberal society'. Giscard also grew increasingly intolerant of criticism, so much so that late in 1980 he even began legal proceedings against his most consistent and respected critic, *Le Monde*, on the grounds that it had allegedly made some minor breach of national security. This brought his unpopularity to new heights, both at home and abroad. By now the regime was growing old and tired, and was even starting to show symptoms of corruption. Various scandals blew up, for which Giscard had to carry part of the blame. A respected Minister, Robert Boulin, committed suicide in distasteful circumstances. The Prince de Broglie, a Right-wing politician, was mysteriously murdered, and high Government officials were alleged to have been involved in the plot to kill him. Above all, Giscard imprudently accepted a gift of diamonds from the hated African tyrant Bokassa; then, when pressed to reveal the facts, he acted evasively. The Press made much of all this – possibly too much. It was far from certain that the average provincial elector, always cynical about politicians, felt as morally indignant about these matters as did a certain Paris milieu, or foreign opinion. Yet in other ways the French were undoubtedly growing fed up. They were bored with a regime that had quite simply been around for too long – ever since de Gaulle's return in 1958.

Giscard himself was fully aware of this. He knew the dangers to France if democratic alternation of power were delayed too long. At my own private talk with him in the Elysée, in December 1979, when I asked him what he saw as the single greatest problem facing France, he replied without hesitation: 'Sooner or later, the Socialists must share in government. In Britain, the United States, West Germany and elsewhere, you have the normal alternation of power that is vital for democratic health. But, in France, the strength of the Communists within the Left makes this much harder to achieve without great risk. So my aim is to keep the door open to the Socialists, as I have been doing, and to persuade a number of them to join me in active partnership, if I am re-elected. That way, we shall have at least a kind of *alternance*.' For some years Giscard had been wooing the Socialists, though without success. In many ways he felt closer to the more moderate Socialists, such as Rocard, than to the Gaullist Right on whom he was forced to rely; and he felt that in alliance with these Socialists he would have far more chance of carrying through his reforms. Moreover, he saw a Centre alliance of this kind as an essential means of breaking the artificial division of France into two blocs of Right and Left. Along with very many other people, he believed that this division did not correspond to public opinion: in the deep heart of the nation, as he saw it, there did exist a middle ground of consensus which was not represented politically – 'The French,' he once said, 'want to be governed from the Centre.' And many observers shared this view. One sociologist, Alain de Vulpian, gave me the results of a major enquiry made in 1979: 'We have found that most French people consider that all the political parties misunderstand their real needs. They feel that politics have become divorced from the real life of the nation, and they dislike being polarized by the political power game.'

The Socialists however rejected Giscard's advances, for a whole variety of easily explicable reasons. Theirs was a familiar and deeply rooted French reflex, especially on the Left: you must not sully your purity by being seen to consort with your enemies. More specifically, the PS was still haunted by the 'ignominy' of Fourth Republic days when the old Socialist Party under Guy Mollet, the SFIO, had lost much of its credibility on the Left through too close involvement with Right-wing Governments. Mitterrand was also under pressure from the Marxist Left of his own party, the 'CERES' group, who looked on Giscard as a wicked capitalist; and, above all, the PS did not want to risk losing votes to the PCF by laying itself open to the charge of 'collaboration with class enemies'. So the Socialists said 'no' and bided their time. Today, their tactics have been triumphantly vindicated: Giscard's ardent desire for *alternance* has been fulfilled, if not exactly on the terms he wanted! So is all for the best? That is a matter for the future to decide, and for personal opinion. There are many liberals today who fear that the change now being imposed on France is too doctrinaire to be healthy, and that better results might have come from Giscard's recipe for a reformist Centre-Left coalition. But, right or wrong, that was politically just not feasible.

My own final view on Giscard is that history may well come to judge him less harshly than he has been judged in very recent years. If he lost heart in his reformist plans, it was not because he ceased to believe in their value, but because he found them politically thwarted. I would even go further and suggest that, maybe, by the beginning of 1981, he did not very much want to be re-elected for another mandate. He knew that *alternance* had to come. He would have liked it on his own terms: but he saw how little progress he had made in dragging the Socialists towards it. So – and here I am only speculating – he may finally have been in two minds. The ambitious politician wanted to stay in power: but the realist may have felt, in his heart, 'Well, if that's how they want to play it, then let them get on with it.' At least, in his electoral campaign he did not act like a man hell-bent on victory. It was a healf-hearted, ill-judged affair. I am sure that on the evening of May 10th he did feel a personal sense of humiliation and rejection – who would not? But, if ever he comes to write his memoirs frankly, he may possibly reveal that on that fateful night, when the votes were counted, his deepest feeling was that the French had historically made the best choice. For good or ill, and with all the risks, it was time in France for a real change. And the only change on offer was Socialism.

'Enfin, l'aventure!' was the banner headline in one Left-wing paper just after the Socialists' victory. So what kind of adventure is it that France is now embarked upon? The new Government at least got off to a promising start. In May and June, President Mitterrand rapidly made a number of gestures to indicate that he intended to rule in a more open and democratic style than his predecessors, with more attention to popular feeling. He cancelled the much-contested plans for the nuclear station at Plogoff and the new Army firing range at Larzac. He dropped the lawsuit against *Le Monde*, relaxed police measures against immigrants, and announced a doubling of the State budget for the arts. All this, in addition to the range of longer-term structural reforms described in this book. One important package of reforms is aimed at eliminating some of the more repressive aspects of the French judiciary and police systems, areas where France has frequently been criticized in the past, and with reason. The police forces are being reorganized, with a new emphasis on crime prevention and less on bullying interrogations. In 1981 the much-hated State Security Court was promptly disbanded, and a recent Giscardian law giving the police added powers for dealing with suspects was repealed. The death penalty too was abolished, thus belatedly bringing France into line with the rest of Western Europe.

In Ministries and other public bodies, the new style was quickly apparent: relaxed, chummy, casual. Aides walked into the Elysée in blue jeans. In place of stiff protocol, this was now a Government of rolled-up sleeves and open doors, with an air of cheerful improvisation and everyone talking at once. I quickly sensed this new style when in June I called on the Press officer of the Minister of the Sea (a newly created portfolio). When we started discussing the fisheries dispute with Britain, he said, 'Your questions are interesting, you'd better put them to the Minister himself.' So without prior appointment I was wheeled straight in to meet Louis Le Pensec, a tall, jovial Breton who talked to me warmly in indifferent English. 'This very morning,' he said, 'I had a letter from Peter Walker' (Britain's Minister in charge of fisheries) – 'look, here it is.' And he actually gave me Walker's letter to read. Admittedly, it was just a courtesy note, with nothing secret. Even so, I could not imagine being greeted like that by a Minister under Giscard or de Gaulle. There, I felt, is Socialist open government for you.

In the civil service, the transition to the new regime went fairly smoothly. A number of senior officials either resigned of their own choice or were gently asked to leave – those who strongly disliked the new Government or had blatantly allied themselves politically with the previous one. But this kind of purge was largely confined to television (as we have seen), to the upper ranks of the police, and to certain prefects and university rectors. There was no generalized witch-hunt. In such Ministries as Defence, Foreign Relations, and the Economy, where the new Ministers were 'moderates', the staff generally expressed a readiness to serve under them and scarcely an offical changed his post, save of course in the *cabinets ministériels*. France has never had any equivalent of the American 'spoil system': when a Minister changes post, even within the same government, he takes his personal staff with him (the *cabinet*), but apart from this the top permanent officials stay in their places, including ambassadors and the like. Since the Third Republic this has been the system, at least in peace-time (the Vichy and Liberation periods were of course exceptions), and broadly it is surviving today, even under so radical a change of Government. The French civil service has a strong tradition of continuity and of service to the State irrespective of politics: this helped France to keep going during the unstable years of the Fourth Republic. Today, very many senior civil servants have Socialist sympathies; others, maybe more sceptical, nonetheless feel it to be their duty (and their career interest?) to stay on and serve. 'I'm worried about some aspects of the Socialists' economic policies,' one leading planner confided to me; 'but, if I stay on here, at least I may be able to use some influence to prevent them from acting too stupidly.'

In the summer of 1981 many *hauts fonctionnaires* who had loyally served the Barre Government were in an oddly divided state of mind. Intellectually they were worried about the new regime: but emotionally they warmed to its sympathetic human side, and willy-nilly they found themselves infected by the national mood of excitement at the start of a new era. The French, after all, love drama and novelty. That summer, France – or a large part of it – was quietly *en fête*. In many schools and universities, as the term ended, teachers and students uncorked the champagne and toasted the future together. '*C'est un mai '68 institution-nalisé*', was one comment – true, in a way, save that there were no angry demos, no wild slogans, and only a few sporadic acts of vengeance or victimization. This was the quietest of revolutions, if you can call it that. In the Paris *beaux quartiers*, and in many a *château* and smart villa, there was gloom and foreboding, and even a few attempts to smuggle money or valuables out of the country. But *les petits gens* were cheerful and expectant. In public offices, the clerks, secretaries and *huissiers* were more relaxed and friendly. Even the police were suddenly nicer.

Many middle-of-the-road Frenchmen, who in May had finally voted for Giscard out of prudence, now found themselves carried along by the wave of pro-Socialist sentiment. They came to feel that maybe the change was no bad thing after all; the Socialists should at least be given their chance. Indeed, throughout the first half of 1981 the steady swing of public opinion in favour of the Socialists was extraordinary. All through 1980, from January to December, the opinion polls had given Giscard a huge lead of 60 to 40 over Mitterrand: Giscard looked unbeatable. Then from January 1981 the polls steadily narrowed, until by April the two main candidates were, on average, level-pegging. Even so, as late as mid-April the general feeling in France remained that prudence and fear of change would carry the day, as so often they had before, and that Giscard would narrowly scrape through. But, this time, things were different. In the final round on May 10th, Mitterrand polled 51.7 per cent to Giscard's 48.2. Then the swing continued in the parliamentary elections in June, when the combined Left scored 55.7 per cent – its highest vote ever – against the combined Right's 43.1. Nor did matters stop there: during July and August several opinion surveys indicated that the new Government was now popular with over 60 per cent of the electorate. Some observers were more than a little cynical about this. 'Suddenly, everyone is a Socialist,' said one, 'just as, after the Liberation in 1944, suddenly everyone was a Gaullist or Résistant. Personally, I don't relish this tendency of the French to jump on the bandwagon, to want to be on the side of the victors, to suck up to authority. But Mitterrand's "state of grace" will wear off, you'll see. The Socialists' honeymoon with the

French people can't last for ever – not with the economy in its present shape.' Nonetheless, in the summer of 1981 the Socialists had come near to achieving the kind of national consensus that had eluded Giscard. For the first time since the heyday of Gaullism in the early 1960s, one single party had a degree of mass support from all classes and groups. According to the surveys, as many as 38 per cent of professional and executive people had voted for the Socialists (against 50 per cent for the Right), while almost twice as many workers had voted PS (44 per cent) as PCF (24). There was a broad feeling that Socialism *à la française* might be able to bring France the change it needed. But what kind of Socialism was it to be? What manner of Socialist was Mitterrand himself?

François Mitterrand has always been something of an enigma to the French, and he remains so even today. There are two very different sides to his personality. On the one hand, there is the veteran politician, tough, imperious, cunning, ambitious; but the 'other' Mitterrand is a withdrawn and sensitive intellectual, poetic, almost mystic, a lover of old trees and old books, a solitary dreamer. This duality may be a source of strength, for very possibly his private world gives him the stamina needed to face the strains of his demanding public life. But his long political career has been curiously inconsistent, and this has led many Frenchmen to feel that he is not a man to be trusted. In the 1950s, as a young Minister in several Fourth Republic Governments, he was often associated with Right-wing policies and acquired the reputation of being a wheeler-dealer, none too scrupulous. He came late to Socialism, for it was only in 1971 that he took over the then moribund Socialist Party, and during the next few years used his immense authority and skill to build it up gradually to its present strength. But whatever the doubts about his earlier fluctuations, it is certain that today he is a genuine believer in Socialism, though of a brand that is not easy to define. When I met him at the time of the 1978 elections, he said to me, 'No, I am not a Marxist. I admire Marx historically, but I do not agree with the dogma that has grown out of his ideas. So you could say I am closer to the Social Democrats.' But he has since made it clear that his model is not at all the mild West German or Swedish model of social democracy, nor indeed the pale-pink brand of Socialism practised in Britain under Wilson or Callaghan. Mitterrand and his colleagues envisage something more radical, which they claim to be a unique French invention, specially suited to France, and not based on any imported model. And Mitterrand, an ambitious man with more than a touch of vanity, wants to leave his mark on history as the ruler who succeeded in forging France once-for-all into a successful Socialist nation. At least he has the time: there will be no more national elections until the spring of 1986.

The stated aim is to go beyond a point of no return: to make a decisive change in the balance of French society, and of the economy, of a kind that the Right will not be able to reverse if they return to power at a later date. This is being done by reducing the influence of capitalism over the economy (hence the nationalizations) and by creating greater equality (hence the wealth tax, the labour reforms, and other measures). But there is no sudden revolution: all is proceeding by gradual, inexorable stages. *'La force tranquille'*, Mitterrand's election slogan, remains the watchword. However, the process raises some doubts, as we have seen. If the aim is to create a more egalitarian society and to reduce elitism, will industrial and fiscal measures be enough, so long as the system of the Grandes Ecoles and the Grands Corps remains intact? Will Mitterrand dare to attack these bastions of privilege? And what of the apparent contradiction between, on the one hand, the policy of increasing State control over the economy and, on the other, the programme of de-centralization in such areas as local government and the media? Both are broadly inspired by ideals of democracy and greater social justice: but are they compatible? Many Frenchmen who are warmly impressed by the Socialists' cultural, social, legal and regional reforms are nonetheless sceptical about their economic programme. Will the nationalizations really be of any help to the economy? Can reflation succeed in France, where it has failed elsewhere? Above all, while France is still in recession, with high inflation and a huge trade deficit, can she really afford the Socialists' generous but costly new deal for wage-earners? The Government is trying to do two very different things at once: to take urgent practical steps to cope with a crisis where two million are out of work: and also to make longer-term structural changes in the economy, with motives as much political as economic. Marxists and other dogmatists on the Left believe that these two priorities go hand-in-hand and that the latter will in itself aid the former, by reducing private profits and increasing public investment. But pragmatists such as Delors are not so sure. These are some of the ambiguities that underlie Government policy.

By the first months of 1982 the excitement of the summer had died down. France was now in a strange interim period which Mauroy himself on January 31st called *'une sorte de no man's land'* (sic): the major structural reforms were lumbering through Parliament, or queuing up to do so, but as they had hardly yet taken effect they were not yet impinging on daily life. Save that the rich were now tightening their belts, and the poor had a little more spending money, people's lives had altered little, and a visitor to France would have seen no outward sign that a new era had just begun. After the first elating novelty of change, the French were now settling back into a mood of vague disquiet over the economy, aware that this Government could no more work miracles than the previous one. The Patronat were especially worried. And many middle-class people, *cadres* and others, who had voted Socialist through disillusion with Giscard, were now beginning to wonder whether they had done wisely: their fear now was that the middle classes might be squeezed into decline, as had happened in Britain. This helps to explain the sharp drop in support for the Socialists in four by-elections in January, when they lost all of these seats, which they had expected to hold or win. And yet, all the opinion polls indicated that the personal popularity of both Mitterrand and Mauroy was still holding up well: some 60 per cent of those questioned expressed 'confidence' in them, far higher than the percentages for Giscard and Barre a year or so previously. Analysis of the polls revealed that although public doubts were growing over the Government's prospects of reflating its way out of the recession, nonetheless its leaders were still admired and trusted in wider terms, and its basic reforms were still popular (in one poll, nationalization of the banks was approved by 55 per cent, devolution by 58 per cent, the wealth tax by 76 per cent). Pierre Mauroy was especially popular. His breezy, open-minded, conciliatory approach was a welcome contrast to Barre's, as in the winter of 1981–2 he trekked repeatedly round the provinces, drawing together round the same table people of every persuasion from CGT stalwarts to angry industrialists, in a bid to work out realistic compromises. He and Mitterrand were set on a course of moderation-cum-radicalism: that is, they were determined not to yield on their reform programme, but they wanted in the process to work out a positive *modus vivendi* with the business world and the bourgeoisie. It was not an easy balancing act.

That winter I was often asked by friends in Britain whether France had changed radically and profoundly as a result of the elections, or only superficially. And I had to reply that it was still too soon to tell. As Mauroy himself declared, the decisive year would be 1982, when the main reforms would enter into force: 'I think the essential changes should be completed by early 1983,' he said. So by then it should begin to become clear whether the Socialist impact would really create a new and different France. Will the new labour laws finally give the unions a dominant role and alter the balance of power with the Patronat? If so, will this lead to a constructive new partnership, or to a damaging war of attrition? Much will depend on how the CGT chooses to act. Will the redistribution of wealth lead in turn to real changes in French class structures? – will the bourgeoisie be forced to retreat, or will it somehow find ways of holding on to its special interests and its privileges, as so often in the past? Will the French respond creatively to the challenges of devolution? And will a liberalized television service prove successful in practice? These were just a few of the vital questions still awaiting an answer at the start of 1982. My own very tentative guess, as I write these words, is that Socialist reform may well shift the balance in France, but stopping far short of anything like revolution, and that this traditionalist nation will find ways of absorbing the changes, as so often it has in the past. France will still be France, especially under so tradition-loving a figure as Mitterrand. The reforms will yield a more egalitarian society, and maybe a rather more open and democratic one. But they may not do much for the economy. And Socialism, alas, seems unlikely to put an end to the contentiousness of the French spirit.

Indeed, after the initial summer honeymoon, one of the less happy features of the Socialists' first months in power was a recrudescence of the kind of angry polarization that had marked the aftermath of May 1968. The moderate Socialist leaders had hoped to carry through their reforms with a degree of national consensus and in a relatively non-partisan spirit, as de Gaulle had done. But they were soon foiled, alike by elements of the Right and the Patronat, and by militant Left-wingers within their own party ranks, as well as by the Communists. In Parliament, fury and invective scaled heights of passion as Chirac and his allies paraded as defenders of the Republic against 'Marxist sabotage'. Maybe such rhetorical battles were only to be expected, and fairly harmless. But in the rest of France, too, the mood of change soon became fraught with political conflict, as people were forced to stand up and be counted – for the new regime, or against it. In the farming world, for instance, hitherto fairly cohesive, the members of the main union, the FNSEA, were quick to take sides, either for the new Minister, Edith Cresson (a minority), or against her (the majority). And when a rent law was drawn up, giving new statutory powers to tenants' associations, landlords rapidly complained that these would become politically motivated Left-wing pressure-groups. Usually in such matters the fault was on both sides. But there is no doubt that many militant rank-and-file Socialists and Communists were exploiting the Left's victory as an opportunity for vindictive assault on France's former bourgeois rulers. And this was not the spirit in which Mitterrand and Mauroy had intended to launch their brave new deal.

So this is the central dilemma today. In 1981 the French in their majority voted for change, but not necessarily for too radical a change. And the Socialist Party itself, like the electorate, is divided on how far change should go. Some Socialists, joined of course by the Communists, would like to impose on France a far more drastic change than the average Frenchman would accept, or than Mitterrand has a mandate for.

And so the ambiguities in Government policy could eventually lead to a clash between the various elements of a Socialist party made up of disparate tendencies. Within the Government itself, the moderate section of the party, led by men such as Mauroy, Delors, Cheysson, holds most of the key posts. But the party also has a Marxist wing, weakly represented in the Government but influential among the rank-and-file. And the large majority of the 270 Socialist deputies in the National Assembly are to the Left of the Government itself. Already by the autumn of 1981 there was clamour from many of the more Left-wing Socialists that the Government was too mild, was not moving fast enough. At the party's congress in Valence in October, one senior deputy warned that the Right was preparing 'economic counter-revolution', and urged the Government to make a purge of the upper civil service and in public industry: 'It is not enough to declare that heads will roll. You must say which heads will roll, and do so quickly.' So far, Mauroy's Government has stood firm against this kind of virulent pressure from below. But if the economic situation worsens, and if the reflationary measures fail to hold down unemployment, then a confrontation could develop within the party, between those such as Delors who might want to return to greater austerity, and the Marxists who would urge more drastic steps in the other direction, including a dose of protectionism. The success of Mitterrand's Socialist venture would then depend on his ability, and readiness, to withstand the militant Left of his own party. He would be obliged to arbitrate, using his presidential authority. It is a role he would have little difficulty in fulfilling, for his own autocratic temperament fits easily into the Fifth Republic tradition of strong presidential rule.

Mitterrand's strategy is having also to take account of the Communist Party (PCF), that eternal bugbear of the French public scene. Here, happily for him, his problems have become less acute since taking office, for one of the most striking aspects of the presidential election was the sudden drop in the Communist vote. The PCF normally polls about 20 per cent: but in the first round, on April 26th, its leader Georges Marchais scored only 15.4 per cent. This greatly reduced the Communist 'scare' which for so many years had helped deny victory to the Left. Many middle-of-road electors now saw that Mitterrand, as President, would not after all be so much at the mercy of the Communists, and so they were readier to vote for him. This was one of the reasons for Giscard's defeat, as it was for the massive swing to the Socialists in the general election in June. Here the Communist vote picked up slightly, to 16.2 per cent. But under the French electoral system, which is far removed from proportional representation, the PCF lost half of its 86 deputies in the outgoing assembly and was left very weakly placed compared with the Socialists.

Even so, although he had no need to, Mitterrand chose to appoint four Communists as Ministers. And he did so for three main reasons. First, as he said publicly, Communist voters had helped him to defeat Giscard on the second round, so he owed them some debt. Secondly, and more important, he wanted to buy the Communists' goodwill and acquiescence, especially that of their powerful union, the CGT (as Lyndon B. Johnson once said, when he allowed his sworn enemy Edgar J. Hoover to remain head of the FBI, 'I'd rather have that guy inside my train, pissing out of the window, than outside the train, pissing in on me'). Thirdly, Mitterrand hoped that the Communists, by sharing in the practical tasks of government, might finally become tamed, and integrated into French society. His long-term ambition remained for the PCF either to wither away or else to become fully democratic and liberalized. And he saw more chance of achieving this by welcoming the Party into power with him than by spurning it. He was, of course, taking risks. And Americans and others were annoyed and worried, not surprisingly. But the Socialists were quick to point out that the Communists were given only relatively minor posts – Transport, Health, Professional Training, and Civil Service Administration – where they would pose no threat to national security. The Communist Ministers adopted a low profile and set to work loyally and conscientiously in their new jobs. All proved excellent members of the Government team, notably the Transport Minister, Charles Fiterman, who is number two in the Party hierarchy. Fiterman and his colleagues did place one or two other Communists in senior jobs – the new head of Paris public transport, for instance – but such cases were few. The permanent civil servants under their command, nearly all non-Communist, were confident that they would be able to prevent their new bosses from infiltrating these Ministries on any scale with their own loyalists, as is usual Communist practice.

The position of the PCF today remains equivocal. For some years its overriding objective has been to retain its own identity and avoid being overwhelmed by the Socialist Party which has gradually become so much the stronger of the two. To achieve this aim, and to hold on to its own voters, it has felt the need to retain a staunchly Leftward stance and to manoeuvre so that the Socialists appear to be flirting with the Centre. Hence its split with them in the autumn of 1977, followed by its vigorous smear campaign against them right up until May 1981. But this turned out to be counter-productive. Many thousands of Communist voters disliked this sectarian feuding, which they saw was harming the chances of the Left's taking power: so they switched to Mitterrand. The PCF leadership, alarmed by the drop in its vote, was then divided on what course to adopt next. A hard-line Stalinist minority was in favour of continuing to hold aloof from the Socialists. But the relatively more flexible majority, led by Marchais, decided there was now no alternative to cooperation with the new Government, at least outwardly. So they accepted the offer of Ministries. But it is a partnership where each side remains wary of the other, and where discord can easily surface – as it did, in December 1981, when the PCF horrified the Socialists by supporting Jaruzelski's crackdown on Solidarity in Poland.

Mitterrand could expel the Communist Ministers any time, if he chose, though it would be to risk a CGT backlash. The Communists, for their part, could well withdraw from the Government if and when it suits their strategy; and by the end of 1981 many observers were predicting that they would probably do so within a year or two, possibly soon after the regional and municipal elections of March 1983. Under this scenario, a worsening economic situation will reduce the Socialists' popularity, and the PCF will then want to quit before it has to share in the odium. It will then have its hands free to resume its attacks on the Socialists, thus hoping to win back its lost electorate. So the Communists as much as ever are playing a double game. And their great reserve weapon remains the CGT. This in the first months after May 1981 remained docile, by order: but it could at any time be mobilized into protests, rallies and strikes against the Government.

The PCF, still so Stalinist in many of its methods and structures, remains a puzzling anomaly within France's democratic society. Today it is not nearly as subservient to the Soviet Union as is sometimes supposed abroad: yet, despite sporadic bouts of liberalization, it has not been able or willing to shake off the model of Soviet-style Communism. It is still governed by 'democratic centralism', whereby decisions are taken in secret by a small oligarchy, on whom the rank-and-file has little direct influence. It is something of a State-within-the-State, subtly separate from the rest of French life, even though its members as individuals tend to be friendly and accessible people, often idealistic, often playing an active part in the life of colleges and factories, town councils and the arts. But the Party as such, especially at the top level, retains something of a ghetto mentality, and even seems to be most at ease when safe within its ghetto. In view of this oddly archaic behaviour, it is perhaps unsurprising that the PCF's vote has been dropping slowly but steadily in the past thirty-five years, ever since its post-war peak of 25 per cent. Perhaps what is *more* surprising is that so many decent and reasonable French people – intellectuals as well as workers, tradesmen and farmers as well as students – continue to vote for it, when they have the alternative of an open and highly democratic Socialist Party. True, its vote has now slumped to 16 per cent, but that is still a sizeable minority.

There are diverse reasons why so many people go on voting Communist. One, in the case of workers and junior employees, is the traditional power and effectiveness of the CGT in battling for better pay and conditions (see p. 109): the CGT today may be losing support (just like the PCF itself), but it still commands a wide loyalty and many of its members identify it – rightly – with the Party. Two, the Party has a sound record of local administration in the many towns that it has controlled for some years: this brings it popularity, and leads many local electors to feel that it could do just as good a job nationally. Three, the Party distinguished itself in the Resistance, fighting patriotically against the Germans, and this is not forgotten by older voters. Four, the PCF has always been a repository for protest votes, especially when times are hard. Five, it benefits from the old romantic revolutionary tradition in France, which impels many intellectuals, students and others to feel it a point of honour to vote as far to the Left as possible (carefully ignoring the Party's ingrained conservatism): these are mainly middle-class people, possibly plagued with guilt at their bourgeois origins, and filled with a yearning for solidarity with the working class, however little they have in common with it.

These sentiments are today on the wane. Since 1977 the hard line of the Marchais leadership has been loudly and openly criticized by a growing number of dissident Communist intellectuals. Some have left the Party in disillusion; others stay on, seeking to use their influence to modify it. These intellectuals are delighted that the Party has now entered the Government and therefore dropped its anti-Socialist vendetta, for the time being: but most of them doubt whether there has been any real change of heart, and they still criticize 'Marchais and his clique' as much as ever for their secretiveness and intolerance of dissent and open discussion. So where does the Party go from here? Today, as a great many Socialists and others see it, there are two possible avenues of hope. One, that if the new Socialist France is a success, then the Communists – or many of them – will be proud of their part in creating it, and thus will gradually be wooed out of their old defensive paranoia and will integrate normally into society and be ready to take the risk of liberalizing. This prospect is perhaps a little utopian. It would require strong pressure from the rank-and-file, as well as a change of faces at the top of the Party, where most of the Politburo are tired, blinkered mediocrities. The alternative prospect is that the Socialists will be so popular and successful in ruling the country that gradually more and more Communist voters will switch over to them and the PCF will fade away: this is the hope of Mitterrand, and of others who feel that there is not room in France for two major parties of the Left. Of course it could be that the reverse will happen: that the PCF, by sharing in power, will gain new respectability and popular support, but without changing its Stalinist make-up. The future will soon tell. If the PCF *does* continue on its present path of decline – as seems quite likely – then France will stand to benefit. For the Party has long been one of the main obstacles to attempts to bring a new spirit of trust and consensus to this divided society.

TOWARDS A
MORE TRUSTFUL SOCIETY?

De Gaulle, who adored *la France*, but never thought so highly of the French, said of them in 1966, 'They can't cope without the State, yet they detest it. They don't behave like adults.' Possibly he would still say the same today, when this proud modern France is still agonizing over one of its oldest and most intractable problems: the power of the State, and the mistrust between State and citizen. Today, at last, a Government has arrived with the courage, so it seems, to promote some radical reforms, to shove the French in at the deep end, as it were, and force them to swim, 'like adults'. There are plenty of risks involved.

The issue is a complex one. The ubiquitous role of the State has its roots deep in royalist history and was reinforced by Napoleon. And of course one can argue, as Jacobins do, that strong State authority still carries advantages for France. The post-war economy has benefited from the intelligent lead of the planners and technocrats, while State servants have long imposed a needed cohesion on this disparate and quarrelsome nation. But what the French call *étatisme* – the pervasive role of the State – has another, less acceptable face. And today a growing number of people have come to see it as a waning asset, an obstacle to mature democracy and the quest for the 'open society'. For the State has frequently abused its power. In Giscard's time, more than ever the crucial decisions were taken in secret by a few key Ministers and officials whose dossiers were not open to scrutiny even by Parliament; more than ever, the levers of power were controlled by the privileged castes of the Grands Corps and the top Grandes Ecoles. Travel around France, and you would find a wide resentment that 'they' – the technocrats, the authorities – were out of touch with the needs and views of ordinary people, who lacked a say in their destiny except at election times. After 1968, some progress was made in education, and in a few factories and other firms: but not in relations between State administration and the public. I heard the typical story of a young *châtelain* in the Dordogne who formed a private association for improving the environment: he won wide local support, but he was thwarted by the prefect and other local State officials who did not wish his scheme to poach on their own preserves. One would often hear tales of this kind, or litanies of resentment against the clever *énarques* and *polytechniciens* who would go round the provinces taking their arrogant decisions, with scant knowledge of local conditions. When a new public housing estate was planned near Marseille, the local architects gave designs to the prefect showing the main windows facing north, to keep the flats cool from the heat of the Midi sun. But the bureaucrats in northerly Paris assumed this was an error and tried to insist that the windows face south. While the dossier passed to and fro, six months were wasted.

Jacobins might well quote examples to support an opposite case. Are there not many instances where the technocrats have proved *more* vigorous, liberal and far-sighted than local bodies might be? In Languedoc, the State planners have been more alert to modern needs than the vinegrowers; the Education Ministry's reformers have been more progressive than the teachers; Malraux in his day had a nobler vision of civic culture than the mayor of Caen. And if progress were left to the groundswell of local opinion and initiative, the *esprit de clocher* might win the day – or so the centralists argue. But this is a vicious circle. So long as *étatisme* remains so strong, it is bound to breed apathy and stunt local initiative, or else drive it into systematic opposition. This has often been the case in education. When in 1972 a Government commission began to work out some radical proposals for *lycée* reform, the main teachers' union (Left-wing) stated in advance that as a matter of principle it would reject them all, good or bad. It was a sad cutting-off-your-nose-to-spite-your-own-face approach, alas all too common. And, as usual in such cases, the fault was on both sides.

As de Gaulle observed, State/citizen relations rest on a paradox. The French grouse constantly at State interference, yet they howl just as loudly if the State fails to provide. They rely on it too much. They are seldom prepared, even when they could, to take the initiative for grouping together to solve their own problems. This at least has been the traditional pattern: a psychological flaw, bred of centuries of centralism. Alain Peyrefitte made the point forcibly in his famous best-seller *Le Mal français* :[1] 'How to break the vicious circle in which France is locked? – a population at once passive and undisciplined, thus justifying *dirigisme*,

1 Plon, 1976. Peyrefitte, rather like Giscard, was a man with lovely liberal views who, in power as Minister of Justice, then behaved anything but liberally. He fell victim himself to the syndrome he had analysed so lucidly.

and a bureaucracy which discourages initiatives, suffocates activity and manages to make citizens even more passive, to the point where, exasperated, they move in one bound from lethargy to insurrection, while the State passes from pressure to oppression.' And the man who wrote that was no Left-winger, but a Gaullist Minister under Giscard!

Happily, in recent years there have been some signs that the classic pattern is changing, under the influence maybe of May '68 and other factors. The so-called *vie associative* is developing, as we have seen. Citizens are at last becoming readier to seek their own remedies, instead of treating the State as a small child treats its nanny, screaming defiance while clinging to her apron-strings for comfort. However, for this new spirit to blossom effectively, and for the vicious circle to be finally broken, the State too must play its part, with a readiness to decentralize and to lighten and humanize bureaucracy. Today the Socialists have arrived with all kinds of noble plans for devolution, in local government and elsewhere too. Can they really succeed in carrying these plans through, where previous Governments have flinched or failed? Giscard, in 1974, came to power with plenty of promises and an apparent awareness of the problems. The State, he said, in its dealings with the public, must learn 'to accept face-to-face discussion, to respect the citizen as its equal, and to resolve issues rather than just drawing up texts'. Brave words. And over the next few years he did actually make some improvements, if fewer than promised. He encouraged State planners to be a little more tactful, and to take more care to consult local opinion in advance over major projects: this worked in some cases, but not in others, for it was not easy to break rooted habits. Giscard created the post of 'mediator', a kind of Ombudsman to act as a channel for grievances against bureaucratic injustices, and this brought a few results. He also introduced laws putting an end to the principle of administrative secrecy: in theory, citizens now had the right of free access to dossiers of the State administration, which in turn was now obliged to give the reasons for its decisions.

However, the bureaucrats soon found ways of subtly obstructing the proper application of these measures. It is the civil servants in the key Paris Ministries who are, and always have been, the most potent enemies of decentralization. Not only do they want to keep their own power intact, but they genuinely believe in centralism. And attempts at a lightening of the State machine have repeatedly run foul of their implacable hostility. Moreover, Giscard's own attitude was equivocal, to say the least. He may have believed rationally in a more open style of government; yet he too was one of the State mandarins, by background, and he believed also in the efficiency of the central machine. Stanley

Hoffmann, the American expert on France, summed him up astutely, if maybe too severely: 'On the one hand, he's a modernist, with an Anglo-American style of discourse; yet he also thinks like a man brought up in the Ministry of Finance, for whom France is governed by four or five people who come, if possible, from that Ministry. The idea that change consists essentially in creating institutions lively enough themselves to generate change is one that completely escapes him. French society has changed fantastically, but is still up against this problem of authority.'[2]

The Jacobins argue that centralism remains essential, among a people as contentious as the French: 'Give them more autonomy,' said one *énarque*, 'and they abuse it by splitting into factions. Look at the university reforms, ruined by feuding between rival teacher groups.' But today the vast majority of Frenchmen feel that this is a defeatist and short-sighted argument. If France is to evolve towards a more open and flexible society, then the only solution is for *étatisme* to wane, in education, in civic affairs and much else, even if the initial effect is a transition period of some confusion. But France, basically a very stable country, should be able to digest this. The French today want an end to the old State/citizen feud, and an end to the heavy interfering diktats of Paris. They want more say over their own affairs. The Socialists are sensitive to this mood, and they share these ideals. So today they are offering a new deal, which Mauroy has dubbed 'a new citizenship'. This will oblige individuals, local groups and local bodies to take more responsibility. And this in turn will require the development of a keener and more active civic spirit, something for which the French, aware of their deficiency, have long envied the British and Americans. For mistrust in France is not only between citizen and State. Just as much, it can be between different citizens, or groups of citizens. So the Socialist new deal presents the French with a stern challenge. If they fail to rise to it, if they do not manage to modify the old flaws in their temperament, then the brave new deal could well founder.

French society has evolved remarkably since the war, and not solely in its prosperity and life-styles. Attitudes and human relations have been changing too. This book has attempted to trace the pattern: the greater freedom for women and young people, the rise of social informality, the more free-and-easy climate in education and sometimes in working life, the sporadic signs of a new cooperative spirit of self-help, for example, in consumer defence and among farmers. Together with this has come a decline, too, in the ferocity of some of France's ancient sectarian feuds.

2 *Le Point*, July 26th, 1976.

Catholics and anti-clericals are no longer at each others' throats. Peasants, now integrated into the nation, have lost much of their suspicion of townsfolk. Social mobility has increased; people's horizons are wider.

All this might have led, you would suppose, to a waning of the old French traits built around mutual mistrust, and to the rise of a less divided and therefore more civic-minded society. And so in some ways it has. Why, then, do so many of France's most respected pundits, by no means all on the Left, still wring their hands in frustration at what they see as the stubborn persistence of the national failings that create the 'société bloquée'? Peyrefitte in 1976 devoted 1,000 pages to lamenting *le mal français*. Michel Crozier, leading sociologist, had in the 1960s been one of those who dared hope that economic change might help to unblock society: yet in 1979 he was writing gloomily of France as still 'a stratified society which, very largely, has progressed negatively, towards a greater rigidity – a society whose citizens are passionately attached to the distinctions and privileges which separate them'.[3] Is this true? Are these and other experts maybe exaggerating? Are they not excessively aware of French failings which are merely part of the wider human condition? – other nations too, including Britain, have their own full share of vested interests, class divisions, clumsy bureaucrats. Crozier, Peyrefitte and others show a touching admiration for what they see as the Anglo-Saxon model, an open society based on trust and consensus: but their idealism does seem a trifle naïve.

It is a confusing situation, for society appears to have evolved in certain respects but not in others. Personal attitudes and life-styles may have changed, but not the more formal or official structures that dominate public life. These are still blocked by three main obstructions. First, *étatisme*. Secondly, the survival of a large number of out-of-date laws, regulations and routine practices: here there has been some reform, but not enough to meet the changing needs of society. Thirdly, the persistence of Crozier's 'stratified society', with its strong vested interests right across the board. These include the closed-shops operated by chemists, taxi-drivers and the like, which have resisted reform; and, more important, the privileges and hierarchies which run through all public life and are at their strongest in the State administration, in education, and in some larger firms. Society is still too corporatist and compartmentalized, with each body protecting itself from its rivals. Thus teachers still have little contact with the world outside their own milieu. And in many organizations the hierarchies are still rigid: one big *lycée*, for example, has one dining-room for the *professeurs agrégés*, another for middle-rank teachers, a third for junior ones. It may be true in a way that, as Crozier

3 *On ne change pas la société par décret*, Grasset, 1979, p. 49.

says, the French cling to this system: yet with another side of themselves they today increasingly contest it. Especially since May '68, change towards greater flexibility is now on the way – but not fast enough. And the French today are impatient.

Over the centuries they built up a framework where each class, each group, each interest had its own position and privileges, many of them defined by written rules and laws, or at least by accepted custom. In a nation prone to violence and disorder, this was found to be the best way of avoiding conflict or the oppression of one group by another. And it brought a degree of harmony and stability, although the defensive rigidity made change and progress more difficult. The role of the State was to guarantee and defend the interests of each group, even if this meant the propping up of obsolescence. Throughout public life high importance was laid on juridical texts and defined prerogatives, so that everyone knew what was expected of him: the Code Napoléon, for instance, laid down rules even for the details of family life. It was a system that gave the individual a certain security; and, paradoxically, it left him with a good deal of freedom, so long as he kept to the basic rules. Society had found how to steer French creative individualism away from anarchy, without having to draw the reins too tight.

But the system was based also on the mutual mistrust of one group of individuals for another. A Frenchman grew up to look on his neighbour as potentially a selfish and hostile rival who might try to do him down, and laws and privileges existed to protect him against this. Those he could really rely on were limited to his family. Though he would also join vigorously in association with fellow-members of his own trade or social group, this was more for mutual self-defence than out of real sentiment or civic duty. There were few organic loyalty-groupings between the unit of the family and that of the State. And even the Frenchman's attitude to the State was ambivalent. Its agents, the public authorities, were to be evaded or hoodwinked. The rational fear of the hostility of other sections of society was extended, rather less rationally, to the assumption that the public administration, too, was some malignant rival force, operating on behalf of *les autres*. And these attitudes were enhanced, from a child's early years, by an education system that offered him little practical training in leadership or responsibility.

This climate of mistrust, between citizens, or between the State and citizens, may have been waning a little under modern conditions. But it is still quite potent. It is one of the factors that has made community development so hard on the *grandes ensembles*. In France, a stranger still tends to be treated warily as a potential enemy until proved a friend (just as the law sees you as guilty until proved innocent). So it is constantly necessary to chat people up in order to overcome their instinctive initial suspicion – a tedious process. Let me give an example of this *méfiance* between strangers. In Britain or America, if an acquaintance has recently changed his address and you do not know the new one, you ring up, and very probably the new tenant or owner will give you his phone number and whereabouts. In France, the new resident is more likely to say, 'I'm sorry, I don't know his new number.' This is because a Frenchman will be wary of giving such details to his successor who probably he does not know, and who therefore is not to be entrusted with such personal details. Fortunately, this spirit of suspicion is now less evident among younger people. And it is much less marked in smaller towns than in Paris.

The mistrust extends also to petty officialdom's relations with the public. A *petit fonctionnaire* will not often give public honesty or good faith the benefit of the doubt; and an individual will seldom believe that a public servant is on his side and trying to help him. The mask of anonymous authority stands between them; only when, by rare effort or good luck, they make informal human contact are matters improved. A Frenchman once told me with admiration of an incident at Dover on his first visit to Britain. He needed to telephone Paris urgently, but had no small change and his train for London was about to leave. 'That's all right,' said the GPO operator; 'I'll put you straight through, and later, when you've got change, just put 90 pence in any phone box.' He told me: 'It would never happen in France, where officials will seldom help you out in difficulty if it means a departure from routine.' The French have long been aware of the harm caused by attitudes of this kind. Back in 1960, a commission set up by de Gaulle recommended that public bodies should make some effort to personalize their employees' relations with the public, for instance, by putting name-cards on desks and guichets as in the United States. Since then, a number of public offices have begun to comply. Uniformed young *hôtesses* with quick smiles have been replacing the old shuffling *huissiers*. The telephone service in particular, as we have seen, has made a real effort to improve its relations with the public, and operators are now far more polite and helpful. This new trend varies from service to service; but certainly the mistrust in France between the public and officialdom has eased in the past ten years.

This campaign to humanize and simplify the administration does however run up against the obstacle of French bureaucracy itself. It is a problem by no means unique to France: many other nations, especially Latin ones, are plagued by heavy bureaucracy, often worse than in France. But in France the heavily centralized bureaucracy has tended to intensify under modern conditions, as life becomes ever more complex and more written regulations are churned out to deal with new situations. The bureaucrats, without intending it, are victims of the monster they have spawned, and even the most dynamic of technocrats can suffer from this. One senior *polytechnicien* told me: 'We feel more and more helpless in face of a machine that becomes ever harder to control. I've just spent two weeks puzzling over the new rules for part-time unemployment, and I fail to understand them – so how can I expect my junior *cadres* to do so?' The Government has been aware of all this, and Giscard did make some efforts to lighten bureaucracy. In 1977–80 his Government enacted nearly 400 measures of simplification, with some results. Thus, for instance, a simplification of the complex French fiscal system has led to a reduction by half of the number of separate categories of tax exemption. Divorce has been speeded up and made easier. And the same applies to procedures for granting building permits: the average time needed to obtain a permit is now down to twelve weeks, compared with thirty-five in Britain (in the US it is a mere five).

However, reform attempts of this kind often come up against the hostility of the *petits fonctionnaires* themselves. In a number of Ministries or public offices, bold technocratic initiative has foundered on the inability or refusal of junior staff to adapt to the changes. In a nation deeply addicted to habit, this is partly a failure of the older or duller ones to comprehend new routines. They hold up reforms either through bloody-mindedness, or idleness, or incompetence. Or the reason can be mistrust. In any office, every post or grade has its clearly defined duties and rights; and every individual fears that *he* will be the one to suffer from changes, so he digs his heels in. What then is the solution? One partial remedy could be to improve the quality of civil service training at below-ENA level: for while ENA turns out its carefully-nurtured élite, too little is done to train the middle and lower ranks. Another answer could be to raise the salaries of junior officials, reduce their numbers, and introduce more computerization and other modern methods, an operation whose investment might soon be recovered in higher 'productivity'. Albin Chalandon, Minister of Equipment in 1969–72, did manage to enforce some modernization of routines in the highly traditional Ponts et Chaussées agency, despite strong opposition from its *cadres*. But this was one of the very few cases where Pompidou or Giscard sanctioned this kind of shake-up: it always meets such resistance, even from those likely to benefit, that Governments have tended to consider it politically more trouble than it is worth. Today there is little chance of progress, for the Socialists are actually increasing the number of State servants, and for policy reasons would oppose measures that might lead to cuts in jobs.

In this book I have not attempted to describe the arch-complex French legal system, nor the current attempts to reform it: these are matters for a specialist. However, in a more general sense, the attachment to legalism has always been one of the strongest and most pervasive aspects of French life, as anyone knows who has lived in France. It is not simply that the laws and regulations themselves are ubiquitous and often abstruse: the French are also conditioned to thinking in terms of them, even when it may not be necessary. For example, there is a law of 1901 which sanctions privately formed clubs and associations as being *de l'utilité publique* (non-profit-making), and if he wants to start up, say, a sports club or a youth centre, a Frenchman will not feel easy until it has been regularized under this law. *Etatisme*, once again. Today, the French still feel a need for this framework, yet also a desire to break out of it. Their lives are spent devising ingenious rules and then finding equally cunning ways of evading them. Thus they are able to cut corners and circumvent some of the bureaucratic absurdities, and this is known as *le système D*, a long-standing and cardinal feature of French life. That is, everyone including officials accepts that red tape can be tacitly ignored from time to time, especially when it is done between pals or over a friendly *verre*. An English friend of mine with a summer villa in the Midi applied for electricity to be installed: he was told this would take years of delay and form-filling – 'But,' added the village mayor with a shrug, 'there's some old wiring stacked in the vaults of the *mairie*, and the local electrician might fix you up if you ask, but keep it quiet.' *Le système D* brings human proportion into inhuman official procedures – but it may not be the way to run a modern nation in an age of high technology.

In business terms, the French will not regard a deal as valid unless it has been drawn up in meticulous legal detail. They have little understanding of the British 'gentleman's agreement', since each party to a deal fears, as one manager put it, 'that the other will slyly introduce a fatal comma'. But, having codified their elaborate agreement, their attitude to it then is very ambivalent. They will continually refer back to these written texts: but they will also feel the need to keep on questioning or reinterpreting them, or finding ways of getting round them. The British are content with a much simpler set of rules, which they then stick to without worrying: it is all the difference between a nation with a strict written constitution and one with none at all. So in France there are always two sets of rules, the written ones and the real ones. It is a system that is workable in practice, and is not nearly as dishonest as it sounds. However, this byzantine legalism is now increasingly contested by a younger generation. In recent years the old legalistic spirit has been gently in decline, as the new pragmatic values have gained ground. The lawyer, whose prestige in France used to be paramount, has been losing position to the planner and technocrat; and it is significant that ENA today puts the emphasis on economics rather than law, whereas older generations of public executives received an essentially law-based training.[4] A new generation, especially the élites adopting American techniques, is moving to a new approach: but it is not easy, for the *actual* texts and regulations that govern French life have not been sufficiently altered. Many a transaction can still involve a maddening amount of paperwork. Even a simple matter like collecting expenses for a French TV assignment once drove me into one of those brief fits of violent francophobia which afflict every francophile. I had to fill in several long forms with such details as my mother's maiden name and my father's place of birth, then I was obliged to stand in queues at cash-desks and go across Paris to another office, and only when a tolerant official deftly fiddled the rigid rules for me was I able to collect the money at all.

One basic problem is the French concept of authority as something absolute, monarchic and anonymous, and this colours relations within organizations. Michel Crozier has suggested that one of the most characteristic of French traits is the fear of informal relations between subordinates and superiors: work routines and chains of command are therefore codified and formalized, in order to avoid favouritism and conflict. And so it becomes difficult for anyone in a junior position to act officially on his own initiative, for this means breaking the codes. Crozier points out that the desire to avoid awkward face-to-face confrontations is a common facet of French society, noticeable in all work relations. This hierarchic pattern of society, he feels, may have served France in the past, but in a period like the present it can lead to waste and strain, making it difficult to introduce modern methods, or to put younger people of initiative where they are needed, at intermediary level.

A major aspect of this situation is that there is much less delegation of power than in Britain or America. There is less sense of team responsibility: the head of an office or department will tend to concentrate the key work in his own hands rather than sharing the load. This extends even to relations between a boss and his secretary, for French bosses tend to make inadequate use of their secretaries: they merely off-load typing chores on to them, rather than treating them confidentially and letting them have some responsibility. There are even French executives who insist on opening their own mail and will not let their secretary see it.

4 The new 1981 National Assembly has only 28 lawyers among the deputies, compared with 33 in the outgoing one, while 134 deputies are from economic and technical jobs.

Once I sent an important express letter to a French editor and got no reply: a week later, calling at his office, I found him away on holiday and all his mail lying unopened on his desk, including my letter. He had given his secretary orders not to touch it. This kind of practice helps to explain why the French secretary is generally less helpful to outsiders than, say, an English one. If you write to the boss and he is away, she will probably not acknowledge your letter. If you ring up and he is not there, she may well not know his movements. And she will probably be unable to fix an appointment for you, even if you tell her that you know he wants to see you. She behaves, in short, as if her *raison d'être* was to protect him from you. But, if she is sourly unhelpful, it is more likely to be her boss's fault than her own: he has simply not given her a chance. Here once again it is true that the pattern is now changing, in many modern firms and with younger executives who have picked up American habits. But the French still have some leeway to make up.

The reluctance to delegate is one more aspect of the French centralist tradition, which operates just as much within a firm or other small unit as on the wider level of the nation. And it has some unfortunate effects. It tends to create a gulf, more noticeable than in most countries, between the dynamic few at the top and the frustrated or time-serving many at more junior levels. Often I have been struck by the brilliance of the young team on a Minister's personal staff (*cabinet*) and the gap between them and the bored bureaucrats at lower echelons who tend to mismanage or even obstruct the Minister's measures. And the same can be true in private firms. In Britain, one has the impression that the load of effort and initiative is more evenly shared: the pioneers are usually less talented, ambitious and energetic than in France, but the contrast between them and the rest is less evident too. In recent years, and especially since 1968, this whole French hierarchic system has been under heavy criticism. The French recognize it as no longer valid and they try to replace it with something else, in some cases, the group. But, as Crozier observed to me, the decline since 1968 in the prestige of established authority has led in some institutions to a kind of power vacuum: people fail to work properly because there is no one to lead them, and they have no training in organizing their own group leadership. It is a characteristic French problem, and we have seen it happening in the new university structure. Such are the traumas of a society trying to break with old habits.

'French society has evolved a lot, it is true,' writes Crozier.[5] 'In many domains, it is full of exciting activity. But all the individual initiatives, all the innovations, stay halted at a certain level.' Any observer of the

5 op cit., pp. 44–5.

French scene is constantly amazed by the contrast between the clumsy official apparatus, on the one hand, and on the other the dynamism, ingenuity and energy of certain individuals. Sometimes, if they are in public service, it seems that the very weight of the system provides them with a challenge which stimulates their dynamism. But more often these pioneers are in the private sector. This book has been full of examples of élites and leaders of a new kind who have emerged since the war, outside the framework of party politics. Unlike the old-style leaders, they are concerned with helping the community as a whole, rather than with defending this or that vested interest against the rest. They include men and women of all shades of belief, working in industry, education, social services or public affairs. A few have been in State service, such as Pisani; or they have pioneered in the commercial field, like Leclerc or Gourvennec, or in labour relations, like Bougenaux and Carayon, or in civic affairs like Dubedout, or in social or cultural projects. Dotted around France there are several thousand of such dedicated and dynamic initiators. These are the heroes of my book, and much progress in France has depended on them. But here we touch upon a weakness. Progress is *too* dependent on the rare individual leader. The French in their vast majority still expect to be led: they are not adept at shared group effort. And if the leader goes, then often the project collapses. Or else new ventures fall victim to the French habit of splitting into warring factions. Or they fall foul of 'the system' with all its rigidities and rooted resistances to change. For these and other reasons, pioneering is an uphill task in France.

However, one of the more encouraging signs of recent years is that private citizens – given the right lead – *are* now becoming a little readier to initiate their own projects, outside the framework of the State or other formal institutions. This is a break with tradition, for hitherto welfare work, for example, has always been regarded as the responsibility either of the State, or the Church, or of public civic bodies. But now the climate has been changing. The French in the past ten years or so have been growing disenchanted with the old institutions which had dominated their lives for so long. Hence the decline in the prestige alike of the Army and the Church, the universities, the unions, all the political parties (except, since 1981, the Socialists), and of course the State Administration. This disaffection could be harmful if carried too far, for it might leave a vacuum in public life. But it has a very positive side too. The French may be retreating into privacy: but they are also at last beginning to move towards the Anglo-American model of voluntary citizen-led ventures, even on a national scale. The birth-control movement of the 1960s was an early example of this, as were the post-war trends towards group activity in farming, in place of the old suspicious individualism. Now there are other portents too. At last in the 1970s an independent consumer protection movement has gathered steam, and is doing well. And one smaller example: since the mid-'70s the sociologist Evelyne Sullerot has succeeded in setting up her own national organization for helping women to re-adapt to professional life after their years of child-rearing. This kind of operation is normally left to the State in France, or not done at all: but Madame Sullerot sidestepped official channels, and won a good response from the public. A venture of this kind, perfectly normal in Britain or America, in France is something of a novelty. It is still rare, but the trend is growing.

Yet for every initiative that succeeds, there are several others that fail. And the cause, as often as not, is the French tendency to contest and split into factions. People will embark on some venture in good faith, for the good of the community: then either they will fall out for personal reasons or, more often, they will drag in politics, as we have seen in the new suburbs, where many a disinterested non-partisan effort is spoilt by some faction, usually of the far Left, that seeks either to gain control of the movement or else for political reasons does not want it to succeed. This is an aspect of what the French themselves call their *'manichéisme'*: the tendency to debate practical issues in political terms rather than impartially on their merits, the refusal to accept the good faith of an opponent. This penchant for polarization was actually made worse by May '68: one of the more negative aspects of that uprising. After the years of muzzled Gaullist calm, May '68 repoliticized France, but not always very constructively. A whole body of youthful opinion on the far Left rejected French established society more forcibly than before; and any Leftist who collaborated with that society in trying to improve it was regarded as a cowardly traitor – *'un récupéré'*, whom bourgeois society had managed to rehabilitate for its own ends.

After the early 1970s this style of *gauchisme* died down. But the new power struggle of the major parties of the Left then gave polarization a fresh lease of life, setting up countless little conflicts on a local level, not only between Left and Right but between rival Left-wing groups. The PCF, as we have seen, threw its weight in here, destructively politicizing matters non-political. In one Paris suburb, a team of mainly pro-Socialist doctors embarked on a laudable project for a cooperative health centre that would certainly have helped the community: but the Communist-led town council, jealous, succeeded in sabotaging the scheme. They did not want their Socialist rivals to succeed in running it and take the credit for it. In other towns, for example Toulouse, *gauchistes* seized control of the environmental defence associations and distorted them into becoming mere political pressure-groups against the Right-wing council. In all such situations, non-partisan people of good will have either been squeezed out, or else have been forced to take sides, thus losing much of their effectiveness. In France, it has not been easy to do civic action disinterestedly, without being pushed in one direction or another. Anne Gaillard (see p. 407) told me that when she ran her consumer defence programme on the radio, 'The Right, notably big business interests, accused me of being a subversive Leftist, while the Left accused me of being on the Right as I failed to take a systematically anti-capitalist line. In fact, I was simply trying to help the consumer. I had no political axe to grind – but neither side would believe me.' So in France it has often been hard to achieve common ground, when opposing groups or parties *a priori* will not collaborate. Often, when some scheme is proposed or problem discussed, there is quite a degree of consensus on what practically needs to be done: but for doctrinal or tactical reasons the parties involved refuse to collaborate. It can be rather depressing.

So this is the challenge now facing the Socialists, as they seek to remodel French society. Today they possess more power, and more public support, than any previous Government of the Left in France. Can they succeed in utilizing this – as many of them certainly wish – to help subdue that old fractious spirit and usher in a greater consensus? Can radicals and progressives, instead of feuding, unite and work together, now that at last they have a Government of their own colour? It is by no means certain, for the coming to power of the Left has far from killed the old sectarian politicizing, as I indicated earlier. But at least the Socialists' wide-ranging decentralization plans seem to be full of good intentions. They want to drag the citizen free from nanny at last, and thus give a real new stimulus to local initiative and responsibility. Can they succeed? Is it pious to hope that they can build up a greater sense of team-work, in line with their own ideals of co-management, or are the French fated to remain dependent on rare, charismatic leaders? Is there not also the danger – and already there are signs of it – that local associations, instead of finding their own feet, will now sit down and clamour more than ever for a dole-out of funds from this sympathetic welfare-minded Government? ('Ah, now that *our* friends are in power, we'll get all the money we need!' was the passive reaction of many local bodies in the summer of 1981.) All these are vital questions for the years ahead. The Government can set a lead, but it is for the public to respond, to rise to the challenge of the devolution it has so long demanded. At least the climate is now propitious. There is a chirpy new feeling in the air than an old stalemate has been broken, that a change of regime might even open the way to an era of greater trust and cooperation in society.

'This is not May '68,' said one Socialist, 'it's much more like 1944, the Liberation.' The sceptics smile. But let them wait.

When I wrote the first edition of my earlier book, in 1967, France was in the full flush of material modernization. I saw this as a necessary transformation, if France was to survive and flourish. But, like many other francophiles, I was also worried that some of the things we hold most precious about France might be lost in the process. 'What,' I asked, 'is to be the future of this Gallic civilization that has shed its light over Europe for so many centuries? What of the real French virtues, will these be able to adapt and survive? What will happen to the French tradition of quality, in a mass-consumer age?' On every side I saw a blind copycatting of American styles and habits, often banal – the *franglais* craze, the barbecues and hot-dogs, the pop stars with rock'n'roll names. And I found Frenchmen, too, were anxious: 'Are we becoming Americans?' was the theme of many a newspaper article.

Today, that risk seems to have been averted. The French have *not* become Americans (nor indeed Japanese, which was also suggested). Much of what appeared in the 1960s to be hectic Americanization was really just an inevitable part of the process of modernizing: when a Western nation does this, it cannot help copying the Americans to some extent, since they got there first. On a material level, the French have now modernized their country quite successfully, or most of it; and they have managed to adjust to new life-styles without losing their essential Frenchness. In fact, Frenchness keeps reappearing all over the place in new, modern guises. Take *le drugstore*: the French have borrowed an American term, and an American formula of late-closing multi-purpose *boutiques*, and have turned it into a new conception whose zippiness, half vulgar and half chic, owes much more to Paris than to any Main Street chemist's. And so, if you travel round France today, you find a country that is very modern, but in its own way; a blend of the new and the traditional, the native and the imported. Of course a motorway or a skyscraper is much the same in any land (and the French have little to boast about in contemporary architecture). Yet they can add stylishly innovative touches of their own – such as those brown signboards along the *autoroutes*, signalling the scenic and cultural points of interest. Better than the ugly publicity hoardings along the Italian *autostrade*! Or consider the new Pompidou Centre in Paris: admittedly, the architects were non-French, but the concept and the functioning of this great arts centre are typical of the continued Parisian ability to innovate imaginatively. Inevitably the new France has lost some of its old quaint picturesqueness – what modern country has not? – yet the French today show a flair for giving a phoenix-like rebirth to the picturesque, in shining new dress. A bizarre but not inept example is the saga of the *pissotière* (known officially as the *vespasienne*, for it was invented in ancient Rome by the emperor Vespasian). For a century these rough-and-ready outdoor male toilets have adorned the squares and pavements of Paris and other towns, most of them mere iron shacks. Conservationists find them oh-so-quaintly French, mild stench and all: modernists have made repeated attempts to get them removed, as unworthy of the new France. Finally in 1980 mayor Chirac put his foot down: Paris's 300 surviving *pissotières* are to go. And in their place are coming ultra-hygienic modern unisex contraptions, known as *sanisettes*. The client pays one franc admission, with the bonus of a brief concert of specially composed water music. Then, when nature's duty is done, automated machines flush and brush the place clean and a green light summons the next visitor. A genuine French invention.

The new France, then, can re-invent the lavatory: but it has shown rather less success at re-inventing the novel, the play or the great painting. For some years now, Parisian creative culture has remained at a low ebb, and this is disturbing to those who believe in France as '*la mère des arts*'. Intellectual life is dazzle and frenzy more than substance; the theatre turns to brilliant gimmicks; and France still awaits the arrival of outstanding new talent among novelists, playwrights, painters, even film-makers. But is this *malaise* any deeper in France than elsewhere in Western Europe? The French cultural staleness is part of the staleness of the West in this age of technology and mass media, and maybe it appears especially severe in France in contrast to her past brilliance. This is an epoch that favours individual creative power less than it does the disseminating of culture to new audiences, and here France is full of an impressive activity, notably in the world of music. The French have by no means lost their interest in the arts: it even shows signs of reviving, now that the craze for modernism has worn off.

Social and private life have evolved quite radically, towards more informality, more freedom for the individual. The stifling rigidities of bourgeois family life, described in the novels of Mauriac or the memoirs of de Beauvoir, have been losing their grip. And this has brought some changes in the French personality, mostly for the better. But many of the old French traits still persist, the good and the bad. The French are still argumentative, hedonistic, highly competitive, full of energy, also egotistical and in some ways still conservative. They are still as aware as ever of their own French individuality; old-style patriotism may have declined, and the E E C may be an accepted reality, but they do not intend to merge their identity into some vague Europeanism. In fact, today they are turning back eagerly to their own French traditions, after the heady love-affair with modernism. Hence the revival of interest in *cuisine*, the return to nature and the search for rural roots, the renewal of regional languages and folk cultures, and the passionate new interest in history, especially local history. A book such as *Montaillou*, Le Roy Ladurie's scholarly account of medieval life in a Cathar village, has sold well over a million copies.

For this new nostalgia to go too far could be harmful. It might even draw France back towards the decadent pre-war mood. Clearly it is one aspect of the *'repli sur soi'* that has been a constant theme of this book: a complex trend, not easy to analyse, that could prove either negative or constructive. In today's anxious world, the French have been turning in search of security, of personal fulfilments, of what can loosely be termed 'quality of life'. This could lead them as individuals to become more passive and self-absorbed, more withdrawn, more anti-social in a civic sense, and there are some signs of it. Or, under the right conditions, the new mood could be the basis of the 'new kind of progress' prefigured by Bernard Cathelat and referred to in my introductory chapter. The French today are at a turning-point. They are questioning the ethos that inspired them to modernize their country so brilliantly in the post-war decades. And with part of themselves they are tempted towards a society possibly closer to the British model (though without the specific British weaknesses), a gentler society, less hectically ambitious, with more accent on leisure, quality of environment, local self-help, and the warmth of local community. Personal fulfilments, centred around the family or private pleasures and ideals, are of course enriching and essential, but so is the community, and the two must find a balance. So the issue is whether the French can harness their abundant energies to work together for new social goals; or whether individually they will relapse into the shuttered, mistrustful isolation that is one strong facet of their nature. That would make France a duller and sadder place.

Not long ago it was prophesied that the French might become 'the Japanese of Europe', fanatically efficient, working away like robots within their big new ultra-modern firms. That now seems unlikely. The French have not turned their backs on thirty years of modern progress, but they want now to marry it with something else. 'People in this country,' said a middle-aged commuter in a village near Paris, 'have just realized that, after all, life is not as long as one may think and work is not the centre of everything. And maybe we are discovering again what *joie de vivre* means.' *Joie de vivre?* – the French invented it, or that was our old image of them. But then in the boom years they seemed too busy for it, working so hard, making all that money. *Joie de vivre* got buried under the new skyscrapers and hypermarkets. But now the hard work ethic may be on the wane. And if so, there may be a price to pay, in terms of standard of living. That is sure to cause trouble, for the French will want to have their cake and eat it. But they are still a highly resilient, resourceful and practical people, and I have some faith that they will find a balance between work and leisure. Today they may be anxious, like others, about jobs, inflation, the future. And yet, travelling around France, I do not have the impression of an unhappy society.

After the years of material effort, it is time now for a shift of emphasis, for more stress on social progress, on greater equality and openness. So the French may well have made the right choice in trying the experiment of Mitterrand's style of Socialism. Perhaps more than any other nation in Europe, they bring a vast heritage of wisdom, taste and humanism to the difficult task of preserving the best of the past in order to marry it with the future. And they have those vital qualities, energy, flair and enthusiasm. About the future of Western civilization as a whole I am not entirely optimistic. But, so long as the West survives, then France seems as well placed as almost any nation to be in the forefront of that survival.

ACKNOWLEDGEMENTS

Many hundreds of people, high and low, gave up their time to help me with my field research, and in many cases were generously hospitable. Alas, they are too numerous for me to mention them all by name. But first I wish to thank a number of personal friends who were particularly kind and helpful: in Paris, Bob Mauthner, Alice Hodgson, Claude and Christine Benoît, Robert and Judith Cottave, Jean and Vivienne Ivry, Henri Dougier, Brigitte Marger and Paul Mondoloni; in the provinces, Yves and Hélène Gonssard (Grenoble), Pierre-Yves and Cathérine Péchoux (Toulouse), the Pilpré family (Rennes and Brest), Edouard Leclerc and his family (Brittany, Paris and the Gironde).

Amongst many others, my special thanks go also to:

Politics and general: François Mitterrand and other leading Socialists, including Pierre Mauroy, Michel Rocard, Jacques Delors, Edgard Pisani, Laurent Fabius, Jean-Pierre Cot, Pierre Joxe; Valéry Giscard d'Estaing and his staff at the Elysée, notably François de Combret and Jean Sérisé; Jacques Chirac and his staff at the Paris Hôtel de Ville, notably Denis Beaudouin; Thierry Pfister, Gilbert Veyret, Bruno Delaye; René Andrieu, Lucien Sève, Jean-Michel Catala, Guy Hermier; Maurice Goldring, François Hincker, Jean Rony, Jérôme Favard; Philippe Robrieux, Annie Kriegel, Branko Lazitch, Jean Elleinstein; Alain Peyrefitte, Michel Crozier, René Rémond, Bernard Cathelat, Gérard Vincent, Alain de Vulpian, Samuel Pisar, Simon and Leone Nora, George Walden, David Wright; Jean-Louis Gergorin, Henri Vignal, Pierre Saulière.

Economy: René Monory, André Giraud, Michel Albert, Bernard Cazes, Hubert Prévot; Michel Camdessus, Jean-Yves Haberer, Michel Freyche, Pierre Achard, Christian Stoffaës; Ghislain and Muriel de Beaufort, Jean-Pierre and Nicole Marchand, Daniel Hua; Roger Fauroux, Antoine Riboud, Alain Chevalier, Yvon Gattaz, Léon Gingembre; Robert Pelletier, Philippe Combin, and their colleagues at the CNPF; Bernard Delapalme, Jean-Marie Riche, Gilles Guérithault, Yves Guihannec, Olivier Romieux, Maurice Bood, Richard Evans; the late Robert Boulin, Edmond Maire, Michel Rolant, Jean-Louis Moynot, Geoffrey Apter, Martine Aubry, Henri Appel, J.-M. and Jacqueline Belorgey, Paul and Marie-Louise Bougenaux, Alan Hatfull, the staff of Liaisons Sociales.

Regions: André Chadeau and his staff at D A T A R, especially Jacques Waline, Philippe Girbal and Michel Lecavelier; Jérôme Monod; Marc Bécam, Pierre Richard, Félix Damette, Joseph Martray. (See also under provinces, below.)

Agriculture and rural life: Pierre Mehaignerie, Michel Debatisse, Monsieur Pichon and his colleagues at the CNJA; Hugh Arbuthnot, John Sidgwick, Danièle Léger and Bertrand Hervieu.

Urban life and environment: Jean Lacaze, Pierre-Yves Ligen, Georges Mesmin, Monsieur Romain; Claude Germon, Raymond Lamontagne, William Amsallem, Monsieur Combes and his staff at Cergy-Pontoise, Monsieur and Madame Mills; Philippe Tiry, Dorothy Koechlin-Schwartz, Marianne Seydoux, Philippe Saint Marc.

Social and private life: Monique Pelletier, Edith Cresson, Dr Pierre Simon, Benoîte Groult, Marie-Thérèse Guichard; Denis and Marguerite Defforey, Etienne and Dominique Thil, André Essel, Anne Gaillard, Jacques Abihssira, Michel Leclerc; Henri Gault; Gilbert Trigano, Patricia Mortaigne, 'Tonton Jean' and Annie Viviani, and their friends at the Club Méditerranée; Alain Woodrow, Bernard and Françoise Willerval; Gilles Anouil, Barbara and Laurent Wollak.

Education and youth: René Haby, Maurice Niveau, Philippe Moret, Anne Corbett, Alain Herzlich, Robert Brechon, the staff of the Lycée Picasso at Fontenay-sous-Bois, the staff of the Collège Curie at Villiers-sur-Marne; Monica Charlot, François Bourricaud; Christian Vulliez; Hugues de Wavrin.

Arts and intellectuals: François Nourissier, Pierre Nora, Jean-Edern Hallier, Nathalie Sarraute, Alain Clerval, Jean-Pierre Angremy, Christine Brooke-Rose, Bernard Cassen, Georges Liébert, Richard Auty and his colleagues at the British Council; Antoine Vitez, Ariane Mnouchkine, Guy Dumur; Louis Malle, Bertrand Tavernier, Daniel Toscan de Plantier, Claude Degand, Robert Benayoun; Jean-Claude Averty, Jean-Marie Elkabbach, Alain Duhamel, Jean-Louis Guillaud, Jacques Thibau, Michèle Cotta, Marc Lecarpentier, Marc Gilbert, Claude Sarraute and J.-F. Revel; Olivier Chevrillon, Georges Suffert, Jean Schmitt and their colleagues at *Le Point*; Juliet Collings, Franz-Olivier Giesbert; Marcel Landowski, Michel Guy, Nicholas Snowman, Denis Jeambar.

In the provinces:

Brittany: Morley and Shula Troman, René Pichavant, Xavier Grall, Monsieur Peron; Alexis Gourvennec and his staff at St-Pol and Roscoff; Edmond Hervé (mayor of Rennes, now Minister of Energy), Michel Phlipponneau, Louis Le Pensec, Roland Le Prohon, Per Denez, Chérif Khasnadar, Charles Lecotteley, Claude Champaud, Albert Coquil, Jean-Pierre Le Verge, Flavert de Coat Parquet, Louis Arzel.

Lorraine: Bernard Bajolet and his family; Dr Paul Sadoul and his family; Serge Bonnet; Jack Lang (now Minister of Culture); Claude Coulais, Jean-Albert Cartier, Rector St-Sernin, Roland Mével, Jean-Charles Bourdier, Jean-Claude Ralite.

Grenoble: Hubert Dubedout and his colleagues at the *mairie*, notably Jean Verlhac, Bernard Gilman, René Rizzardo, Louis Ratel; Pierre Frappat, Bishop Gabriel Matagrin, Jean-Louis Quermonne, Claude Domenach, Jean-Hervé Donnard, Rector Hughes Taÿ; Georges Lavaudant, Maurice Jendeau, André and Chantal Veyrat, Rolande and Raymond Millot. *Lyon:* Paul Bocuse, Régis Neyret, Pierre Merindol, Jean Chemain, André Soulier, Richard White. *St-Etienne:* François Gadot-Clet, René Mestries, Maurice Gotton, Michel Olagnier, Monique Garnier.

Provence and Languedoc: Fernard Carayon and his staff at Aéro-spatiale, Marignane; Claude and Marianne Bonfils; in Montpellier, Raymond Dugrand, Jean Joubert, Jacques Detours, François Delmas; Jean-Claude Servan-Schreiber; Emmanuel Maffre-Baugé; Baron P. de Ginestous, Anna and Richard Scott.

Massif Central and Cevennes: in Lozère, Jacques Blanc, François and Jeannine Braget, Jean and Mireille Laquerbe, Monsieur Sastourné, Frère Gibelin, Bernard and Françoise Martin, Alain and Marie-Antöinette Boutet, Maurice Crignon, Dr Monod; in Aveyron, Michel Poux, Raymond Lacombe, Raymond Grimal, André Cazals, the Sauzays; Jean-Marie Crochet and his family; Thierry de Margerie, Monsieur Vigier; Roy Hart theatre group.

South-West and West: in Toulouse, Michel Valdiguié, John and Jenny Prince, Paul Ourliac, André Brouat, Rector Claude Chalin, Fernand Lagarde; in La Rochelle, Michel Crépeau (mayor, now Minister for the Environment), Robert Kalbach, Bernard Mounié, Dr Paul Sabatier, Alain and Anne Parent; Louis Lauga, Olivier Sérard, Paul Barriere, Hélène and François Levieux.

Claude and Emmanuelle Matthews, Michel and Nelly Dury, Jacques Denis-Le-Sève, Dr Szigeti, Max Nublat (all in Montargis); Bertrand and Hélène Harmel (near Reims); Pierre Garcette, Jules Clauwaert, Roger David (Lille area); Philippe and Marie-Christine Daudy (near Orléans); Guy Bertout (Nantes).

Finally, in London, my thanks go to my publishers, Secker & Warburg and Penguin Books, to Miss W. Marshall for her expert typing, and to my patient wife Jenny.

BIBLIOGRAPHY

GENERAL AND POLITICAL

Michel Crozier, *The Bureaucratic Phenomenon*, Tavistock Press, 1964.

Michel Crozier, *La Société bloquée*, Le Seuil, 1970.

Michel Crozier, *On ne change pas la société par décret*, Grasset, 1979.

Jacques Delors, *Changer*, Stock, 1975.

J.-B. Duroselle, François Goguel, Stanley Hoffmann, Charles Kindleberger, Jesse Pitts, Laurence Wylie, *France: Change and Tradition*, Harvard University Press and Gollancz, 1963

'Epistémon', *Ces Idées qui ont ébranlé la France*, Fayard, 1968.

Franz-Olivier Giesbert, *François Mitterrand ou la tentation d'histoire*, Le Seuil, 1977.

Valéry Giscard d'Estaing, *Démocratie française*, Fayard, 1976.

André Harris and Alain de Sédouy, *Voyage à l'intérieur du Parti communiste*, Le Seuil, 1974.

R. W. Johnson, *The Long March of the French Left*, Macmillan, 1981.

Herbert Lüthy, *The State of France*, Martin Secker & Warburg, 1953.

Henri Mendras (editor), *La Sagesse et le désordre, France 1980*, Gallimard, 1980.

Alain Peyrefitte, *Le Mal français*, Plon, 1976.

Thierry Pfister, *Les Socialistes*, Albin Michel, 1977.

Jean-François Revel, *La Tentation totalitaire*, Robert Laffont, 1976.

Anthony Sampson, *The New Europeans*, Hodder & Stoughton, 1968.

Patrick Seale and Maureen McConville, *French Revolution 1968*, Heinemann and Penguin, 1968.

Alain Touraine, *Le Mouvement de mai ou le communisme utopique*, Le Seuil, 1968.

Pierre Viansson-Ponté, *Histoire de la République Gaullienne*, 2 vols: Fayard, 1970–71.

Pierre Viansson-Ponté, *Lettre ouverte aux hommes politiques*, Albin Michel, 1975.

Gérard Vincent, *Les Français, 1946–1975*, Masson, 1977.

Vincent Wright (editor), *Conflict and Consensus in France*, Frank Cass, 1979.

ECONOMY AND INDUSTRY

Michel Drancourt, *La France du grand large*, Robert Laffont, 1981.

François Gadot-Clet, *Une Certaine idée de Manufrance*, Denoël, 1979.

Jacques-A. Kosciusko-Morizet, *La 'Mafia' polytechnicienne*, Le Seuil, 1973.

Jean-Jacques Servan-Schreiber, *The American Challenge*, Hamish Hamilton, 1968; Penguin, 1969.

Christian Stoffaës, *La Grande menace industrielle*, Calmann-Lévy, 1978.

Jean-Claude Thoenig, *L'Ere des technocrates*, Editions d'Organisation, 1973.

Ministère de l'Industrie, *The Energy Policy of France*, 1980.

REGIONS

Christian Beringuier, André Boudou, Guy Jalabert, *Toulouse – Midi-Pyrénées*, Stock, 1972.

Pierre Durand, *Industrie et régions*, La Documentation Française, 1974.

Pierre Frappat, *Grenoble, le mythe blessé*, Alain Moreau, 1979.

J.-F. Gravier, *Paris et le désert français en 1972*, Flammarion, 1972.

Jérôme Monod, *Transformation d'un pays*, Fayard, 1974.

Michel Phlipponneau, *Debout Bretagne*, Presses Universitaires de Bretagne, 1970.

Autrement (review), *Bretagnes, les chevaux d'espoir*, 1979.

AGRICULTURE AND RURAL LIFE

Michel Debatisse, *La Révolution silencieuse*, Calmann-Lévy, 1963.

Danièle Léger and Bertrand Hervieu, *Le Retour à la nature*, Le Seuil, 1979.

Henri Mendras, *Sociologie de la campagne française*, Presses Universitaires de France, 1965.

François de Virieu, *La Fin d'une agriculture*, Calmann-Lévy, 1967.

Gordon Wright, *Rural Revolution in France*, Oxford University Press, 1964.

Autrement (review), *Avec nos sabots*, 1978.

URBAN LIFE AND ENVIRONMENT

Didier Béraud and Jeanne Girard, *Une Aventure culturelle à Grenoble, 1965–75*, Fondation pour le Développement Culturel, 1979.

Marc Bernard, *Sarcellopolis*, Flammarion, 1964.

Michel Phlipponneau, *Changer la vie, changer la ville, Rennes 1977*, Editions Breiz, 1976.

Philippe Saint Marc, *Socialisation de la nature*, Stock, 1972.

SOCIAL AND PRIVATE LIFE

Simone de Beauvoir, *The Second Sex*, Cape, 1953; Penguin, 1974.

Pascal Bruckner and Alain Finkielkraut, *Au Coin de la rue, l'aventure*, Le Seuil, 1979.

Bernard Cathelat, *Les Styles de vie des Français, 1978–98*, Stanké, 1977.

Etiemble, *Parlez-vous Franglais?*, Gallimard, 1964.

Ménie Grégoire, *Le Métier de femme*, Plon, 1965.

Gabriel Matagrin (bishop), *Préparer aujourd'hui l'Eglise de demain*, Cerf, 1976.

Edgar Morin, *Plodémet*, Allen Lane, The Penguin Press, 1971.

Dr Pierre Simon, *Rapport sur le comportement sexuel des Français*, Julliard, Charron, 1972.

Alain Woodrow, *L'Eglise déchirée*, Ramsay, 1978.

Laurence Wylie, *Village in the Vaucluse*, Harrap, 1961.

YOUTH AND EDUCATION

Robert Brechon, *La Fin des lycées*, Grasset, 1970.

Jean Duvignaud, *La Planète des jeunes*, Stock, 1975.

André Rouède, *Le Lycée impossible*, Le Seuil, 1967.

ARTS AND INTELLECTUALS

Roland Barthes, *Critique et vérité*, Le Seuil, 1966.

Régis Debray, *Le Pouvoir intellectuel en France*, Ramsay, 1979; *Teachers, Writers, Celebrities*, NLB and Verso Editions, 1981.

Michel Foucault, *Les Mots et les choses*, Gallimard, 1966; *The Order of Things*, Tavistock Publications, 1970.

André Glucksmann, *Les Maîtres penseurs*, 1977.

Jean-Edern Hallier, *Chaque matin qui se lève est une leçon de courage*, Hallier, 1978.

Bernard-Henri Lévy, *La Barbarie à visage humain*, 1977.

Garry O'Connor, *French Theatre Today*, Pitman, 1975.

Jean-François Revel, *La Cabale des dévots*, Julliard, 1962.

Georges Suffert, *Les Intellectuels en chaise longue*, Plon, 1974.

I should like to acknowledge my debt to *Le Monde* and *Le Point* and their staff correspondents. Without the help of their regular coverage of French problems, I should have found this book difficult to write. I am indebted also to the Editor of *New Society* for permission to draw on an article I wrote in that paper on the Grands Corps, and to the BBC for permission to draw on my radio profiles of François Mitterrand, Jacques Chirac and Paul Bocuse.

INDEX

Principal page references are in **bold type**. Book, play and film titles are not indexed: see under name of author or director. Some general themes are indexed – e.g. 'unemployment' – but not where the location of the subject is evident from the Contents list on pages 7–9 (e.g. labour relations, feminism).

Académie Française, 347, 354, 546
Adjani, Isabelle, 575
advertising, 390–91, 407, 582–3
Aérospatiale, **70–73**, **98–100**, 117, 118, 166
Aillaud, Emile, 271
Airbus, 45, 70, **72–3**, 100, 167
aircraft industry, **70–74**, **98–100**, 163
Air France, 33, 71, 72, 177, 415
Air Inter, 180
Aix-en-Provence festival, 609
alcoholism, **448–51**
Algeria: immigrant workers in France, 311, **468–9**; oil and gas, 77–8; return of French settlers from (1962), 15, 152, 162
Alsace, 131, 198, 591, 593, 609
Alsthom-Atlantique firm, 114
Althusser, Louis, 535
America, attitudes to, 465–6; economic rivalry with, **45–8**, 66–7, 69, 71–2, 74–5, 436, 578
American influences, 17, 27, 34, 42, 401, 411, 420, 425, 586, 652
American Motors, 69
Amiens, 325, 328–9
Amoco Cadiz, 143, 340
Angers, 322
Annaud, Jean-Jacques, 573
Annecy, 330
Aquitaine, 128, 188, 338–9
Aragon, Louis, 539, 553
Ariane rockets, 75
aristocracy, **377–8**
armaments industry, 44
Armand, Louis, 83, 179
Army, the, 165, 342–3, 463
Aron, Raymond, 505, 530, 618
art, 614
Attali, Jacques, 86
Auclair, Marcelle, 390
Aurore, l', 597–8
Auto-Journal, l', 70
automobile industry, 37, 60, **62–70**
Auvergne, 241
Averty, Jean-Claude, 591

Aveyron, 176, 212, 214–16, 218, 220, 234–5, 238–9, 242, 342
Avignon festival, 549, 616

baccalauréat, 136, 152, **478–9**, 605
Ballerin, Jean, 100
Balzac, H. de, 91, 546–7
banking, 33, **119–20**, **169–70**, 178
Banque de France, 32, 169
Banque Nationale de Paris, 119, 169, 178
Bardot, Brigitte, 515, 567
Barrault, Jean-Louis, 550, 553
Barre, Raymond, 90, 291; as Prime Minister, 29, 33, **39–41**, 53–4, 57–62, 116, 119, 121, 122, 159, 165, 500, 624
Barthes, Roland, 329, 531–2, 534, 541, 553
Bas, Pierre, 391
Baudis, Pierre, 165, 318
Baye, Nathalie, 571, 575
Bazergue, Louis, 164–5, 196
BBC, 414, 579, 584–5, 587–9, 595
Beaubourg centre, *see* Paris
Beauvoir, Simone de, 351, 530, 653
Beckett, Samuel, 324
Belières, M., 215
Benoist, Alain de, 530, 536, 539
Benzi, Roberto, 608
Berliet lorries, 104, 170
Berlioz, Hector, 610
Besançon, 105–6, 299
Besret, Abbé B., 458
betting (horses), 395
Beullac, Christian, 477
Béziers, 181
Bidermann firm, 46
Billard, Pierre, 611
birth-rate, **14–15**, 106, 352, 363, 367
Blanc, Jacques, 245, 256
Blitz, Gérard, 426–7, 433, 437
Bocuse, Paul, 169, 409, **412–18**, 423, 553, 603
Boix-Vives, Laurent, 43, 50
Bokassa's diamonds, 584, 625
Bonaparte, *see* Napoleon
Bondy, François, 536

Bon Marché, le, 400
Bordeaux, 130, 163, 165, **172**, 194, 196, 228
Borel, Jacques, 422
Bougenaux, Paul, **101–2**, 115, 649
bouilleurs de cru, 450
Boulez, Pierre, 277, 534, 604–5, **606**, 607, 612
Boulin, Robert, 625
Bourdier, Charles, 59
Bourges, 326
Bourse, la, 119, 120
Boussac, Marcel, 54, 597
Boutet, A. and A.-M., 253–5
Braget, F. and J., 242, 246–7, 252–3, 255–6
Brest, 137, 140, 142, 196, 322, 330–31, 399
Brittany, 123, 124, **131–43**, 185, 340, 341, 344–6, 397–400, 459, 580; agriculture, 138, 140, 210–11, 212, 217, 218, 223, 225, 227, 234; alcoholism, 450; Celtic links, 131, 137–9; cultural revival, 131–2, **133–4**, 330; industry, 128, 140, 142, 175; language, 132, 134–7; nationalism, 132–3, 198, 203
Brittany Ferries, 138–9
Broglie, Prince de, 625
Brook, Peter, 550, 553, 555, 615
BSN-Gervais-Danone, 46, 227
Buchwald, Art, 283
Bull, Machines, 47, 74
Burgundy, 203, 374
Butor, Michel, 540, 542–3

Caen, 130, 175, **326**, 602
café life, 307, 396, 449
café-théâtres, 551
Cahiers du Cinéma, 558–9
Caisse des Dépôts, 33
Camus, Albert, 515, 524, 530
Canacos, Henri, 320
Canard Enchaîné, 599
Candilis, Georges, 146, 147
Cannes film festival, 558, 564, 566
Cap d'Agde, 147, 150
Caravelles, 48, 71, 73
Carayon, Fernand, **98–100**, 102–3, 105, 115, 649
Cardonnel, Père Jean, 455, 459
car ownership, 281–2, 442–3
Carrefour, 399, 401–4, 408
Carrière, Jean, 546
Cartier, J.-A., 335–6
Caterpillar, 46, 155
Cathars, 144, 148–9
Cathelat, Bernard, **21**, 388, **520**, 525, 654
Catholicism, 20, 242, 314–15, **451–62**; neo-Catholic movement (Action Catholique), 16, 97, 208, 453–5, 457, 459; charismatic movement, 458; integrism, 455–6; relations with Marxists, 453–5, 459–60; and education, 490–91; attitudes

to sex, birth-control, abortion, 354–6, 362, 367, 462
Cazes, Roger, 238
centralization, 25, 125–7, 148–53, **165–71**, 187–90, 492, 494, 495
Centre des Jeunes Patrons, 97, 453
Centre National des Jeunes Agriculteurs, 209–10, 212, 214, 252
Centre National pour la Recherche Scientifique, 49
Cergy-Pontoise, 263, 303, **304–5**, 308, 315, 319
Cesbron, Gilbert, 545
Cévennes, 239, 242, **247–56**
Ceyrac, François, 97, 103, 120
Chaban-Delmas, Jacques, 41, 86, 158, 165, **172**, 191, 194, 582, **620–21**
Chabrol, Claude, 558, **559–60**, 569
Chalandon, Albin, 181, 645
Chalonge, Christian de, 573
Champaud, Claude, 137, 143
Channel Tunnel, 83, 176, 183
Chasseur Français, Le, 55–6
Chauvière, J. and A.-M., 251
chauvinism, 462–70
Chavanne, Georges, 100, 102
chemists' cartel, 408–9
Chéreau, Patrice, 548–9, 553–5, 607
Chevènement, J.-P., 22, 49, 91
Cheysson, Claude, 22, 91, 634
Chirac, Jacques, 86, 633; as Prime Minister (1974–6), 38–9, 84, 174, 233, 239, 349, 608, 623; as Mayor of Paris, 261, 267–78 *passim*, **279–81**, 282, 653
Chrysler, 44, 63, 66–7, 69, 466
Church, *see* Catholicism
CII-Honeywell-Bull, 74, 117, 163
CIT-Alcatel, 48
Citroën, 44, 47, 62–3, **65–8**, 70, 96, 127, **141**, 173, 442
class barriers, **213–14, 376–81**, 432, 473–5
Claudel, Paul, 554
Clermont-Ferrand, 212, 241
Club Méditerranée, 27, 240, 372, **426–37**, 618
coal industry, 58, **76**, 176
Cohn-Bendit, Danny, 495
Collange, Christiane, 351
Collèges d'Enseignement Secondaire (CES), 474–6, 483
co-management, 93, 94, **104–5**, 114–15
Comédie Française, 549–50, 554
comités d'entreprise, 94–5, 112, 114–15
Commissariat à l'Energie Atomique, 51
Commissariat Général au Plan, *see* Plan
Common Agricultural Policy, *see* EEC
Common Market, *see* EEC
communes, **188–96**, 199, 302, 304–5

Communists and Parti Communiste Français, 19, 55–7, 81, 88, 150, 234, 349, 355, 364, 366–7, 380, 457, 459, 469, 506–7, 585, 598, 623, 626, 630, **634–8**; in Government (1981+), 22, 199, 203, 448, **635**; in civic affairs, 59, 149, 157–8, 204, **319–22**, 334, 335, 490, 650; in labour relations (*see also* C G T), 94, 109–10
Compagnie Française des Pétroles, 44, 77
Compagnie Générale d'Electricité, 44, 117
Compiègne University, 514
computer industry, 47, 74
Concorde, 52, **70–73**
Confederation of British Industries, 383
Confédération Française Démocratique du Travail (CFDT), 82, 94, 104, 109, **111**, 112, 114, 452–3
Confédération Générale des Cadres (C G C), 94, 98, 100
Confédération Générale du Travail (C G T), 56, 59, 81, 93–104 *passim*, **109–11**, 112, 114, 115, 138–9, 453, 593, 618, 632
Conseil d'Etat, 85, **86**, 92
conseils généraux, 188–9, 193, 198, 200, 203
consumer protection, **405–9**
cooperatives, 105–6, 138, 226–7
Corfù, 430–31
Corneau, Alain, 574
Corsica, 123, 198, 203, 205
Cossé-Brissac, Comte de, 213, 377
Côte d'Azur, 146, 178, 338, 437, 438
Coulais, Claude, 335–6
Cours des Comptes, 85, 86
Courtine, Robert, 410
Cousteau, Jacques, 341
Coutaro, Raoul, 568
Crédit Agricole, 119, 139, 219, 297
Crédit Lyonnais, 87, 119, 167, 169, 272
Crépeau, Michel, **295–8**, 316, 321, 334
Cresson, Edith, 236, 349–50, 633
Creusot-Loire firm, 244
Crochet, Jean-Marie, 212
Crozier, Michel, 191–2, 202, 205, 425, 642, 647, 648

Damette, Félix, 203
Dassault aircraft company, 44, 48, **73–4**, 117, 172
Dauphiné Libéré, 602–3
death penalty, abolition of, 23, 627
Debatisse, Michel, **209–10**, 211, 213, 223, 233–7, 247, 453
Debray, Régis, **538–9**, 601
Debré, Michel, 86, 202, 210, 366, 582
Decaë, Henri, 568
Decazeville, 176
decentralization, 23, 25, 92, **125–31**, **173–8**, 187–8, 197–8, **199–205**, 483, **495–9**

Defferre, Gaston, 171, 191, 198, 200
Defforey, Denis, 404
Deguy, Michel, 544
Délégation à l'Aménagement du Territoire et à l'Action Régionale (DATAR), **128**, 137, 140, 150, 161, 169, 170, **173**, **175–8**, 180, 203, 273, 339
Deleuze, Gilles, 535
Delmas, François, 299
Delors, Jacques, 22, 41, 62, 114, 117, 120–21, 621, 631, 634
Delouvrier, Paul, 262, 264–5
demography, *see* birth-rate
Demy, Jacques, 295, 567
Denez, Per, 131, 133, 135–7
Depardieu, Gérard, 573
Derrida, Jacques, 531
Desgraupes, Pierre, 582–3, 594
Dewaere, Patrick, 575
dirigisme, *see* State control
divorce, 357
doctors, 363, 365, 366–8, **445–8**
Doillon, Jacques, 574
Domenach, Jean-Marie, 454
Dougier, Henri, 465
Dreyfus, Pierre, 64, 66, 117
drugs, among young, 521
drugstores, 27, 420, 652
Dubedout, Henri, **156–61**, 190, 298–9, 301, 308, 313, 317, 332, 649
Ducellier firm, 47
Dugrand, Raymond, 299
Duras, Marguerite, 543, 550, 552, 565
Dutourd, Jean, 397
Dutronc, Jacques, 575
Duvert, Tony, 545
Duvignaud, Jean, 524
Dux, Pierre, 549–50

Eaton, 113
Ecole Centrale, 512
Ecole des Affaires de Paris, 513
Ecole des Hautes Etudes Commerciales (HEC), 84, 263, **513**
Ecole des Mines, 84, 87, 481, 512
Ecole Nationale d'Administration (ENA), 43, **84–92**, 350, 479, 527, 645, 647
Ecole Normale Supérieure, 92, 512
Ecole Polytechnique, 84–91, 263, 350, **510–12**
ecology movement, 13, **340–46**; *see* also environment
Economy, Ministry of, *see* Finance Ministry
Education, 309–10, **472–514**, 601; artistic and musical, 486–7, **613**; adult and vocational, 381, 468, 480–81; technical, 480–81, 503; for farmers, 214; school holidays, 393, 441; and the Church,

Education – *cont.*
490–91; and class divisions, 380–81; *see also* universities
Electricité de France, 77, 87, 344–5
Elf-Aquitaine, 44, 77, 118, 272
Elle, 357, 359, 390, 598
Emaër, Fabrice, 518
Encounter, 536
energy policy, **76–82**
English language, 43, **467–8;** *see also franglais*
environment, 27, 216, 258, **295–300, 336–46**
Escarpit, Robert, 547
Esprit, 453, 454
Essel, André, 405
Etaix, Pierre, 567
Etiemble, 390
Europe, attitudes towards, 37–8, 466, 525, 653
European Coal and Steel Community, 37
European Economic Community (EEC), 17, 29, 31, 32, **36–8**, 39, 45, 46, 51, 62, 87, 93, 128, 137–9, 163, 176, 266, 463, 465–7; Common Agricultural Policy (CAP), 207, **221–4**, 228, 229–32, 233, 237
European Monetary System, 40, 120
Europe One radio, 516, 592, 598
Evry, 263, 304
existentialism, 16, **528–31**
exports, 28, 32, 37–8, **45**, 50, 63, 66, 68–9, 73, 99, 138, 227–8, 576
Express, l', 390, 464, 558, 564, 597

Fabius, Laurent, 91
Fabre, Pierre, 50
family, influence of, 24, **368–70**, 524
family allowances, 14–15, 370, 444
fashion, 389–90
Faure, Edgar, his education reforms, 483, 485, **495–9**, 509, 510
Fauroux, Roger, 43, 48, 53, 87
Fauvet, Jacques, 599–600
Fédération Nationale des Achats des Cadres (FNAC), 276, 405–6
Fédération Nationale des Syndicats des Exploitants Agricoles (FNSEA), **209**, 211, 228, 233, 236, 633
Ferodo, 47
Fiat, 47, 66–8, 98, 272
Fifth Republic, the, 29, 83, 325
Figaro, Le, 536, 596–9, 602
Filipacchi, Daniel, 516–17
Fillioud, Georges, 594
Finance, Ministry of (renamed Ministry of Economy in 1981), 33, 39, 53, 86, 88, 89, 159, 167, 170, 178, 189, 202, 398, 608, 641
Financial Times, 591
Finistère, 138, 140, 143, 225, 234, 344
fishing industry, 142

Fiterman, Charles, 635
food, 387, **409–23**; processing industry, 226–7
Force Ouvrière, 94, 98, 100, 101, 111–12, 115
Ford Motors, 46, 60, 66, 172
foreign investment, **46–8**
forestry, 244–5
formality, waning of, **371–3**, 434
Forte, Sir Charles, 101–2
Fortune, 44
Fos, 57, 61, 171, 176, 337
Foucault, Michel, 531–2
Fournier, Marcel, 402
Fourth Republic, the, 16, 31, 36, 84, 208, 229, 270, 529, 580, 617, 628, 630
Framatome, 80, 170
France, liner, 52
France-Soir, 596
François-Poncet, Jean, 84
franglais, 26–7, **390–92**
Frappat, Pierre, 161, 308, 313,
French, Philip, 567
Fréville, Henri, 142, 194, 317
friendship, **370–71**
furniture, 389

Gaillard, Anne, 407–8, 651
Galleries Lafayette, 400
Gallerand, Abbé, 461
Galley, Robert, 293, 298, 299
Garaudy, Roger, 454
gas, natural, 77
Gattaz, Yvon, 97
Gaulle, Charles de: wartime and Liberation role, 34, 348; as President, **16–17**, 19, 36, 47, 65, 66, 83, 115, 140, 158, 465, 569, 579, 617, 619–21; reforms as President, 18, 31–2, 95–6, 197, 262, 267, 337, 474, 482; nationalism and prestige-hunting, 52, **75**, 80, 462, 607; personality, ideas, 378, 638
Gaulle, Yvonne de, 349, 362
Gaullists, 156, 204, 392; in power (1958–74), 127, 194, 196, 260, 450, 580–81, 617, 619; under Giscard, 41, 198, 202, 366, 623
Gault, Henri, 410, 412, 416–18, 422
Gaumont, 577–8
Gaz de France, 342
Germany; attitudes to, **463–4**, 466; economic rivalry with, 37, 48, 173, 176, 222
Genet, Jean, 434, 550, 552, 555
Germon, Claude, 306–7
Gibelin, Frère, 244
Gicquel, Roger, 585
Gilman, Bernard, 332–3
Gingembre, Léon, 51, 401
Giraud, André, 49–50, 55, 87
Giroud, Françoise, 349, 351, 564

Giscard d'Estaing, Valéry: record as President, 19, 21, 83–4, 91, **622–7**, 629; measures and reforms as President: economic and labour, 38–41, 46–7, **52**, 54, 60, 76, 80–82, 104, 115–16, 206, 343; regional and environmental, 128, 133, 139, 174, 178, 188, 194, **198–9**, 239, 258, 267, 270, 271, 275, 276, 282, **338–40**; social, 291, 293–4, 349, 366, 376, 381, **385**, 445, 448–9, 475, 640, 645; cultural, 467, 579, **583–6**, 590, **598–9**, 615; relations with Gaullists, 281, 623; relations with Left, 56, 533, 537, 626–7; as Finance Minister, 32; personality and life-style, 358, 528
Glenmor, 134, 143
Glucksmann, André, 534–5
Godard, Jean-Luc, 357, 558–9, **561–4**, 569
Godin, Abbé, 453
Goldsmith, Sir James, 597
Gomez, Mme, 350
Goncourt, Prix, 545
Gorin, J.-P., 564
Gourvennec, Alexis, **137–9**, **210–11**, 225, 234, 514, 649
Grall, Xavier, 133, 134
Grande Motte, La, **147–8**
Grandes Ecoles, 34, 42–3, 78, **84–92**, 380–81, 480, 493–4, 501, 503, **510–14**, 631; decentralization of, 130, 140, 163
Grands Corps, 84–92, 631, 638
Gravier, J.-F., 127, 174, 337
Great Britain: attitudes towards, **464–5**, 601; influences of, 420–21; relations with, 71–2, 137–8, 142, 147, 222–4, 467
Green Giant, 227
Grenoble, 130, **153–61**, 175, 469, 488, 564, 602 3; cultural life, 324, 327–8, 331, **332–4**, 335; civic and suburban life, 156–9, 194, 298, 301, **308–13** (l'Arlequin), 317, 319, 321, 398, 445; schools, 489–90; universities, 154–5, 159–60, 508–9
Grimal, Raymond, 234–6
Groult, Benoîte, 356
Groupement de Recherches et d'Etudes pour la Civilisation Européenne (GRECE), 536
Gruault, Jean, 565
Grumberg, Jean-Claude, 552, 555
Guardian, 554, 608
Guérard, Michel, 414, 417, 423
Guérin, Jean-Pierre, 407–8
Guérithault, Gilles, 70
Guichard, Olivier, 83
Guy, Michel, 612

habitations à loyer modéré (HLMs), 290–94, 295–6, 301, 303, 308–9, 312, 321
Haby, René, 381, **475–9**, 488, 624

Haerberlin brothers, 416
Halimi, Gisèle, 366
Hall, Peter (urbanist), 261
Hallier, Jean-Edern, 134, **536–7**, 544, 546
Hallyday, Johnny, 516–18
handicapped, the, 445
Hardy, Françoise, 516–17
Harris, Dale, 608
Harvard Business School, 42, 88, 91
Haussmann, Baron, 125, 261, 266, 282
Havas, 592, 594
Havre, Le, 204, 320
health service, 445–8
Hélias, Per-Jakez, 134, 560
Héreil, Georges, 70–71
Hersant, Robert, 597–8, 602
Heyworth, Peter, 604, 609
Hoffman, Stanley, 641
holidays, 23, 392–3, **423–41**
hospitality, 12, 168, **373–5**
Houston, Penelope, 560
Humanité, l', 596
Huppert, Isabelle, 564, 573
hypermarkets, *see* supermarkets

IBM, 45, 46, 74, 145, 271
Ile d'Abeau, 304
Ile-de-France, 261, 264
immigrants, 307, 311, **468–70**
inequalities of wealth etc., 18, 23, 82–3, 376, **383–6**; *see also* class barriers
inflation, 31–2, 38–40, 120
Inspecteurs des Finances, 43, **84–92**, 375
Institut de Recherche et de Co-ordination Acoustique/Musique (IRCAM), 606
Institut Français d'Opinion Publique, 354, 441, 518, 590
Institut National de la Consommation, 406
Institut National des Sciences Economiques et de l'Administration (INSEAD), 42
International Herald Tribune, 270, 297
Italy, economic rivalry with, 229–31
ITT France, 117

Jeunesse Agricole Chrétienne (JAC), 16, **208–9**, 215, 216, 453, 459
Jews, 464, **470–71**
Joint Français, firm, 143
Joubert, Jean, 342
Jullian, Marcel, 584

Kalbach, Robert, 321
Kaplan, Nelly, 573
Kindleberger, Prof. Charles P., 30
Kléber guide, 416
Krasucki, Henri, 109
Kundera, Milan, 539, 615
Kurys, Diane, 484

Laborit, Henri, 566
Lacan, Jacques, 531–2, 534–5
Lacombe, Raymond, 220, 225, 235, 241
Lacq, gas of, 77
Lafont, Robert, 151
Lagardère, Jean-Luc, 598
Lalonde, Brice, 341, 346
Lama, Serge, 518
Lamassoure, Alain, 317
Lambert, Bernard, 213
Landerneau cooperative, 227
Landowski, Michel, **605**, 609, 612
Lang, Jack, 335–6, **615–16**
Languedoc, 128, **143–53**, 162, 164, 198, 229–32, 339
Laniel, Joseph, 398
Laquerbe, Jean, 244
Lartéguy, Jean, 545
Larzac, **342–3**, 627
Lavaudant, Georges, 324, 334
Lavelli, Jorge, 615
Lecanuet, Jean, 191, 299
Lecat, Jean-Philippe, 612
Leclerc, Edouard, 102, 330, **397–400**, 401–5, 408, 453, 514, 649
Le Clézio, J.-M.-G., 540, 546
Le Corbusier, 129, 301
Lefebvre, Mgr Marcel, 456
Lefort, Bernard, 608, 612
legalism, 646–7
Léger, Danièle, and Hervieu, Bertrand, 250, 254, 256
Lelouch, Claude, 568, 575
Le Pensec, Louis, 628
Le Roy Ladurie, Emmanuel, 148, 654
Leroy-Somer, 100
Lescure, Patrick, 252
Lespine, Ginette, 248–9, 256–7
Le Verge, Jean-Pierre, 212
Levin, Bernard, 391, 554, 604
Lévi-Strauss, Claude, 531–2
Lévy, Bernard-Henri, 534–5, 539
Lévy, Raoul, 558
Libby's, 226
Libération, 599
Liebermann, Rolph, **606–8**
Liénard, Olivier, 254
Ligen, Pierre-Yves, 270
Lignel, Jean-Charles, 603
Lille, 22, 130, 172–3, 194, 196, 303, 456
Limoges, 180
Lip firm, 105–6, 113
Lipp, brasserie, 238, 533
living, standards of, 379, **381–8**
Longwy, **57–61**, 115
Lorient, 134, 137, 142
Lorraine, 54, **57–62**, 114, 176, 459, 591
Losey, Joseph, 577, 607

Lotti, Bernard, 330–31
Lozère, 216, **241–8**, 256–7
lunch-break, the, 394–5
lycées, 136, **472–88**, 501, 511, 605, 639
Lyon, 103, 104, 130, 159, **167–71**, 177, 179, 182, 196, 303, 354, 383, 413–15; cultural life, 324, 329, 335, 570–72, **603**, 610, 613

Maffre-Baugé, Emmanuel, 149, **150–51**, 232
Maire, Edmond, 109, 111
Maisons de la Culture, 130, 141, 158, 160, 297, **324–9**, 331–4, 551
Majorette firm, 103
Malle, Louis, 558, 566–7, 571
Malraux, André, 268, 278–9, **325–30**, 533, 550, 562, 580–81, **603**, 605, 607, 612, 615, 639
Mantelet, Jean, 43
Manufrance, **55–7**, 601
Marcabru, Pierre, 554
Marchais, Georges, 585, **634**, **636**
Margaux, Château, 47
Marie-Claire, 390, 419
Marignane, 98–100, 112
Marivaux, 554
Marker, Chris, 567
marriage, 356
Marseille, 51, 126, 130, **171**, 180, 183, 193, 303, 496
Marshall Aid, 31
Martin, B. and F., 252
Mary, Jean-Albert, 100–101
Massachusetts Institute of Technology, 91
Massif Central, 76, 128, 174, 207, **239–41**, 245
Massy, 302–3, **306–7**, 318–19
Matin, Le, 599
Matra, 44, 75, 117, 592, 598
Mauriac, Claude, 543
Mauroy, Pierre, 22, 41, 105, 114, 117, 120, 173, 187, 191, 194, 200, 202, 594, **632**, **634**, 641
Mauthner, Robert, 591
May 1968 crisis, 18, 64, 93, **95–6**, 133, 249, 326, 340, 348, 407, 455, 472, 475, **481–2**, 483–4, **495**, 498, 508, 510, **518–19**, 530, 550, 551, 564, 581, **618–20**, 650
Mayoux, Jacques, 178
Mehaignerie, Pierre, 236
Méline, Jules, 208, 210
Mende, 180, 243, 246, 248
Mendès-France, Pierre, 157, 449–50
Mercure, Jean, 551
Merlin, Guy, 338
Merlin-Gerin company, 155
Messiaen, Olivier, 606, 612
Messmer, Pierre, 621
Metz, 59, 130

Meynardier family, 247
Michel, Jacques, 614
Michelin tyre firm, 44, 46, 65–7, 115; guide, 416, 421
Midi-Pyrénées, 128, 164, 203
Millau, Christian, 412, 416, 422–3
Miller, Claude, 574
mistrust, 643–4
Mitterrand, François: as President, 14, **22**, 46–7, 81, 83, 92, 340, 346, 350, 386, 528, 539–40, 655; reforms as President, 116, 117–18, 120–21, 123, 200, 491, 595–6, 615–16, 627, **630–4**; May 1981 victory, **21**, 629–30; as Socialist Party leader, 593, 623, 626; personality, ideas, 27, 349, 378, **630**
Mnouchkine, Ariane, 548, **553**, 554, 588
Mocky, Jean-Pierre, 567
MODEF, 234, 236
Modiano, Patrick, 545–6
Mollet, Guy, 580, 626
Monde, Le, 157, 176, 324, 416, 536, 578, 596, 598, **599–600**, 614, 618, 625, 627
Monde et la Vie, Le, 455
Monnet, Gabriel, 326
Monnet, Jean, 16, 30, **34–6**, 57, 111, 127
Monoprix, 400, 402
Montargis, 460–61
Mont Blanc tunnel, 182
Montpellier, 144, 145, 149–52, 299, 316, 459
Morlaix, 210–11
Motorola, 46, 163, 421
motorways, *see* roads
Moulinex, 43
Mounier, Emmanuel, 453
Mouvement Français pour le Planning Familial, 361–2, 364
Munch, Charles, 605
music, 332–6, 396, 487, **603–14**; pop, **516–18**

Naegelen, Marcel, 132
Nairn, Ian, 301
Nancy, 130, **335–6**, 507, 590, 615
Nanterre university, 495
Nantes, 130, 139, 172, 177, 567
Napoleon Bonaparte, 84, 164, 197, 511
Napoleonic laws, 14, 24, 124, 189, 208, 368, 643
National Assembly, 22, 172, 200, 205, 349, 491, 495, 623, 634, 647
nationalization, **32–3**, 58, 64–5, 632; by Socialists (1981–2), 23, 29, 41, 49, 73, 75, **117–20**
Néel, Prof. Louis, 155, 160
Neuwirth, Lucien, 363
New Statesman, 552
Neyrpic, firm, 155
Nice, 171, 177, 292–3

Nicoud, Gérard, 404
Nîmes, 148, 152
Nora, Pierre, 534
Nora, Simon, 90, 294–5, 620
Nord, 54, 57, 61
Normandy, 51, 203, 214
Nourissier, François, 547
nouveau roman, le, **540–45**
nouveaux philosophes, **534–5**
Nouvelle Droite, la, **535–6**
Nouvelle Revue Française, 537–8
Nouvel Observateur, le, 597, 599
nuclear energy, 44, 76, **80–82**, 155, **343–6**
nudism, 147, 432, 437

Observer, 301, 532, 535, 537, 567, 604
Occitan movement, 144, **150–52**, 343
Occupation, the, 14–16, 30, 125, 209, 260, 380, 452, 470, 528, 574, 602
O'Connor, Gary, 554
Office de la Radio et Télévision Française, *see* television
oil industry, 33, 76–8
old age, 369, 384, 444
Olympic Games, 156, 309, 439
Opéra, the, 604, **607–8**
Organization for Economic Cooperation and Development (OECD), 31, 106, 120, 382, 385
Orgeval, 314
Ornano, Michel d', 267
Ortoli, François-Xavier, 87
Ouest-France, 602

Palace, le, 518
Parayre, Jean-Claude, 67, 69, 88
Paribas, bank, 119
Parigot, Guy, 324, 329, 330
Paris, 11, 12, 17, 26, 91, 101, **259–88**, 337, 355, 359, 393, 394–5, 419–21, 440, 457, 496, 516–18, 526, 573; population, 125–6, 262, 265, 273; centralization on, 123, **125–6**, 165–6, 167–71; new exodus from, 126–7, 130, 173–8, 323–4; problems of living in, 126, 328, 259–60, 288, 373–5; mayor and municipal council, 266–7, 280–81 (*see also* Chirac); new skyscrapers, 268–72; housing, 273–4, 291, 292; suburbs and new towns, 261–6, **301–8**, 320–22; Schéma Directeur, 262–5; transport and parking, 281–6; intellectual and cultural life, 134, **533–40**, 548–55, 606–8, 614–15; Press, 596–9, 602; Beaubourg (Pompidou) Centre, 261, **276–8**, 606, 614, 652; Bois de Boulogne, 279; Champs-Elysées, 270, 287; La Défense, 264, 269, **270–72**; Les Halles, 226, 266–7, **274–6**, 278, 285; Halle aux Vins, 274; Ile-St-Louis, 286, 419; Marais,

Paris – *cont.*
277, 278–9, 286; Métro, 112, 271, 275, 285–6; Montmartre, 288, 354; Montparnasse, 268, 269; St-Germain-des-Prés, 278, 287, 419, 515, 529
Paris-Match, 515, 597–8
Parti Communiste Français (PCF), *see* Communists
Pasteur, Louis, 48
Patronat Français, Conseil National du (CNPF), 37, 41, 46, 53, 54, 93–115 *passim*, 120–22, 454, 504, 632
Paysans Travailleurs, 234, 236
Péchiney-Ugine-Kuhlmann, 44, 117, 155, 167, 170
Pelletier, Monique, 350–52
pensions, *see* old age
Perec, Georges, 545
Pétain, Philippe, *see* Vichy regime
pet animals, 389
Petites et Moyennes Entreprises, 51, 401
Peugeot-Citroën, 44, 46, 60, 63, 67–9, 88; Peugeot, 44, 62–3, 65–8, 70, 100, 108, 442; *see also* Citroën, Talbot
Peyrefitte, Alain, 639 and n., 642
Philipe, Gérard, 549
Pialat, Maurice, 572–3
pieds noirs, *see* Algeria, settlers
Pierre-Brossolette, Claude, 87
Pilhès, Victor, 546
Pinget, Robert, 543
Pisani, Edgard, 83, 211, 214, 219, 237, 617, 649
Pisier, Marie-France, 575
pissotières (vespasiennes), 653
Pivot, Bernard, 539
Plan, the, 16, 22, 30–31, 34–6, 37, 45, 88, 121, 203, 208, 210
Planchon, Roger, 169, 324, 514, 548–9, 553–4, 603
Plasson, Michel, 609
Plaza-Athénée hotel, 46, 101–2, 115
Plogoff, 143, 344–6, 627
Point, Fernand, 413
Point, Le, 315, 390, 554, 597–8, 611, 615, 641
Poland, martial law in, 111, 636
Polanski, Roman, 615
police, 627
Pompidou, Georges: as President (1969–74), 32, 38, 80, 83, 84, 115, 177, 188, 198, 269, 272, 275–7, 337, 582–3, 606–7, 614–15, 620–22; as Prime Minister, 580
Poniatowski, Michel, 84
Ponts et Chaussées, 87, 92, 191, 201, 251, 264, 512, 645
Pope John Paul II, 367, 460, 462
pornography, 576
Port-Barcarès, 147

Port-Camargue, 147
postal services, 186
Pougnet, H. and N., 243–4
Poujade, Pierre, 51, 397, 404; Poujadism, 401
Poux, Michel, 237–8
Powet, Abbé, 460–61
Pradel, Louis, 168–9
prefects, 23, 85, 86, 92, 123, 159, 164–5, 187–90, 196, 197–8, 200–201, 295
Prévot, Hubert, 111
price-controls, 52–3, 57
Printemps, Le, 400
Privezac, 216
Progrès de Lyon, Le, 602–3
Protestants, 242, 247, 298, 320, 459
Provençal, Le, 602
Provence, 198, 609

Quimper, 139
Quotidien de Paris, Le, 599

racism, *see* immigrants
radio, 592–3; local and pirate, 593
Radio Luxembourg, 592
Radio Monte Carlo, 592
railways, *see* Société Nationale des Chemins de Fer Français
Ralite, Jack, 448
Ralston-Purina firm, 226
Rance tidal dam, 77, 140
Raymond, André, 196
Reims, 204, 327
remembrement, 215–16
Rémond, Prof. René, 20
Remy, Pierre-Jean, 545–6
Renaud, Madeleine, 550
Renault, Régie, 33, 44, 45, 46, 60, 62–70, 100, 117, 118, 170, 173, 380, 442, 582; Louis Renault, 63
Rennes, 124, 127, 131, 139, 140, 141–2, 143, 190, 194, 299, 317; cultural life, 324, 327, 329, 331
repli sur soi, 20, 313, 466, 519, 525, 611, 654
Républicain Lorrain, le, 59
résidences secondaires, 394
Resnais, Alain, 542–3, 558–9, 564–6, 569
restaurants, 409–23
Retoré, Guy, 551
Revel, Jean-François, 597
Rhine-Rhône canal, 176, 183
Rhône-Poulenc, 44, 48, 117, 167, 170
Ricard, Paul, 43
Rivette, Jacques, 567
roads: motorways, 180–82, 263–4, 265, 282, 652; road accidents, 442–3
Robbe-Grillet, Alain, 531, 540–42, 543–4, 546, 553, 565

Rocard, Michel, 22, 86, 88, 91, 117, 121
Rochelle, La, 258, **295–8**, 316, 321, 334
Rodez, 237–8, 300
Rohmer, Eric, 558, **561**, 569
Roissy (Ch. de Gaulle) airport, 264, 286
Rolant, Michel, 104
Roscoff, 138
Rossignol firm, 43, 50
Rothschild bank, 119
Roudy, Yvette, 352, 368
Rouen, 190, 299, 303
Rouquette, Yves, 151
Roussel-Uclaf firm, 117
Royer, Jean, 404
Roy Hart Theatre, 250
Rueff, Jacques, 83
Ruffio, Jacques, 573
Rungis market, 226, 274
rural exodus, 15, 17, 31, 126, 162, **206**, 213, 217–18, 220, 238–9, 243

Sabatier, Robert, 545
Sacilor, 57, 62, 117
Sagan, Françoise, 515–16
St-Chély-d'Apcher, 243–4
St-Etienne, 55–6, 180, 204, 328, 335
St-Exupéry, Antoine de, 74, 163
St-Gobain-Pont-à-Mousson, 43, 44, 45, 48, 53, 74, 87, 108, 117
St-Malo, 138–9
St-Nazaire, 113–14, 172
St-Tropez, **515**
Salut les Copains, 516–17
Sarcelles, 301–3, 306, 319, **320–22**
Sarraute, Claude, 578
Sarraute, Nathalie, 540, 542–3
Sartre, Jean-Paul, 287, 515, 524, **528–31**, 533, 537, 539
Sauna, Raymond, 336
Saunier-Seïté, Alice, **499–500**, 503, 504
Sautet, Claude, 573
Sauvy, Alfred, 15
Savary, Alain, 491, 500
Schuman, Robert, 37
scientific research, **48–50**
Second World War, *see* Occupation, Vichy
Segard, Norbert, 184, 186
Séguy, Georges, 109
Senderens, Alain, 413
Sète, 144, 149, 230
sex, **354–60**
Seydoux, Nicolas, 578
Simca, 66–7, 466
Simon, Claude, 543
Simon, Dr Pierre, 355, 360, 362, 366–8
Siparex, 170
SMIC (legal minimum wage), 384
Smyth, Robin, 535

SNIAS, *see* Aérospatiale
Snowman, Nicholas, 534, 606
Socialists: in opposition (pre-1981), 81, 88, 363, 366–7, 593, 623–4, **626**, 635; in government (1981+), 11, 21, 29, 41, 46, 62, **81–2**, 91–2, 104, 342, 349, 533, 617, **627–35**, 645, 651; reforms (1981+), **22–3**; economic and social, 26, 49, 105, 107, **116–22**, 221, 236–7, 293, **385–6**, 442, 424, 441, 469; regional, 136, 143, 171, 187–8, 194, **199–205**, 265; cultural, 319, 329, 579, **593–6**; educational, 490–92, 500, 509; Socialists in civic affairs, 149, 156–8, 164, 194, 196, 199, 299, 302, 306, 308, 316–22; and religion, 459–60
Social Security, **443–7**
Société Centrale Immobilière de la Caisse des Dépôts (SCIC), 320–21
Société Générale bank, 119, 177
Société Nationale des Chemins de Fer Français (SNCF), 87, **179–80**, 182–3, 285–6
Sociétés d'Aménagement Foncier et d'Establissement Rural (SAFERs), 219, 221, 246, 255
Sociétés d'Intérêt Collectif Agricole (SICAs), 225, 235
Sofirad, 592, 594
solar energy, **78–9**
Sollers, Philippe, 531, 543–4
Sony, 88
Sorbonne, la, 125, 494–6, 501
Souchon, Alain, 518
Soulié, Maître André, 171
space programme, 75
Spain; competition with, 128, 146, 150, 228, 232; refugees from, 162
sport, **438–9**, 487
State control, 13, 25, **32–4**, 39, 52–3, 116, 119, 121–2, 175, **579–87**, 59, **638–41**, 649
steel industry, 33, 40, 53, **57–62**
Stendhal, 154
Stivell, Alain, 134
Strasbourg, 130, 171, 173, 17, 335–6, 609
Strehler, Giorgio, 550, 607
structuralism, **531–2**
students, *see* universit
Sudreau, Pierre, 83, 1
Suez bank, 119
Sullerot, Evelyne, 6
Sunday Times, 554
super- and hyper
système D, 646

Tabarly, Eric,
Tacchella, Je

Talbot cars, 67
Tancarville, bridge, 182
Tarbes, 330
Tati, Jacques, 141, 186, 264, 389
Tavernier, Bertrand, 484, **570–72**, 575, 603
taxation, 116, **384–6**
Téchiné, André, 573
technocrats, 16, 25, **82–92**, 149, 341–2, 527, 638–9
Teilhard de Chardin, Pierre, 453, 524
telephones and telecommunications, 75, 140, **183–6**, 243
television, 307, 407, 538–9, **578–96**, 647; in provinces, 136, **590–91**; and cinema, 574, 575, 577–8, 588; local cable TV, 319
Tel Quel, 544
Témoignage Chrétien, 459
Temps Modernes, les, 537
Terrin firm, 171
theatre, 431, **548–55**; in provinces, **323–4**, 326, 330, 332–4, 551
Théâtre de France (Odéon), 550, 552
Théâtre du Soleil, 553
Théâtre de la Ville, 551
Théâtre National Populaire (TNP), 324, **549**, 550, 554
Thiers, 51–2
Third World, relations with, 40, 46, 55, 68, 1⌁ 525

unemployment, 19, 29, 40–41, 54, 61–2, **106–8**, 116, 120, 142, 159, 176, 468, 519, 572
UNESCO, 368
Union Démocratique Bretonne, 132
Union Fédérale des Consommateurs, 406–7
United States, *see* America
universities, **493–510**; growth of provincial ones, 130, 163, 172; links with industry, 49, 155, 159–60, 163
Usinor, 57, 62, 117

Vadim, Roger, 515, 558
Valbonne scientific park, 177–8
value added tax (VAT), 193, 384, 402, 403
Varda, Agnès, 370, 558–9, **566**, 569
Vartan, Sylvie, 516–18
Veil, Simone, 349, 351, 352, 366, 447
Vendée, 338, 457
Vendredi Samedi Dimanche, 597
Vergé, Roger, 414
Verlhac, Jean, 317
Viansson-Ponté, Pierre, 618
Vichy regime, 15–16, 30, 125, 208, 574, 628
vie associative, la, **313–23**, 407, 611, 640
Vie Nouvelle, 459
Vierny, Sacha, 568
Vilar, Jean, 324, 549, 616
Villeurbanne, 324, 549
Vinaver, Michel, 552
Vincennes University, 506
vinegrowers, *see* wine industry
Vitez, Antoine, 548–9, 551, **553–5**
Voix du Nord, la, 602
Volkswagen, 66
Vulpian, Alain de, 626

Wardle, Irving, 552, 555
watch industry, 52
Webster, Richard, 532
Weightman, John, 536–7
Weill-Halle, Marie-Andrée, 361, 364
⌁illot, Agache, firm, 55
⌁n, Georges, 549
⌁dustry, 144–5, 150, **228–32**, 406,